I TATTI STUDIES IN
ITALIAN RENAISSANCE HISTORY

Published in collaboration with I Tatti
The Harvard University Center for Italian Renaissance Studies
Florence, Italy

GENERAL EDITOR
Nicholas Terpstra

THE DYNAMICS OF LEARNING IN EARLY MODERN ITALY

Arts and Medicine at the University of Bologna

DAVID A. LINES

Harvard University Press

Cambridge, Massachusetts

London, England

2023

Printed in the United States of America

First printing

Library of Congress Cataloging-in-Publication Data

Names: Lines, David A., author.
Title: The dynamics of learning in early modern Italy : arts and medicine at the University of Bologna / David A. Lines.
Other titles: I Tatti studies in Italian Renaissance history.
Description: Cambridge, Massachusetts : Harvard University Press, 2023. | Series: I Tatti studies in Italian renaissance history | Includes bibliographical references and index.
Identifiers: LCCN 2022008487 | ISBN 9780674278424 (cloth)
Subjects: LCSH: Università di Bologna—History. | Learning and scholarship—Italy—Bologna—History. | Arts—Study and teaching—Italy—Bologna—History. | Medicine—Study and teaching—Italy—Bologna—History. | Bologna (Italy)—History.
Classification: LCC LF3273 .L56 2022 | DDC 378.454/1—dc23/eng/20220622
LC record available at https://lccn.loc.gov/2022008487

To Grace, with love and heartfelt gratitude

CONTENTS

FIGURES AND TABLES

. . . in quo tamen non si qua laude dignus sim, sed quid ad communem omnium fructum attulerim, aequo animo omnes iudicent volo.

I wish all to judge with equanimity, not whether I am worthy of any praise, but whether I have produced something for everyone's common use.

—Gaspare Tagliacozzi, dedicatory letter, *De curtorum chirurgia*

Introduction

A Habitation of Learning and Wisdom

At the age of nineteen, the Portuguese youngster Jerónimo Osório (1506–1580) of Fonseca, who had already begun his studies in Salamanca, continued them in Paris, where he dedicated himself to logic and natural philosophy and developed friendships with Peter Faber and Ignatius of Loyola (later to become the founder of the Society of Jesus). After a period back in Portugal, he left for Bologna, where he spent several years and, before the age of thirty, started writing his notable work of political thought, *De nobilitate civili et Christiana* (*Civic and Christian Nobility*). What had attracted him to Bologna, however, was the study of theology and of eloquence. His nephew relates that he studied Plato, learned Hebrew, and immersed himself in the early Christian writings, including especially (Pseudo-) Dionysius the Aeropagite and the Greek Church Fathers (Basil the Great, Gregory Nazianzus, and John Chrysostom) as well as Latin theologians such as Augustine, Jerome, and Thomas Aquinas. While in Bologna, however, he also refined his talent for rhetoric and gave himself wholeheartedly to improving his familiarity with Cicero and the Greek orator Demosthenes. As Osório himself relates, he frequented Romolo Amaseo (who taught rhetoric, poetry, and humanities), admired Achille Bocchi (a professor of law), and studied with Ludovico Boccadiferro (who lectured on natural philosophy). He became fast friends with two students, Antonius Augustinus Caesaraugustanus and Johannes Metellus Sequanus, who subsequently both figured as interlocutors in his dialogues *De gloria.* Reflecting on his decision to study in Bologna, he concluded that he had done well to follow the judgment of many others, that "no Italian city could be compared with Bologna for the glory of its letters." The humanity of its people, the provisions for study, and the expertise of its professors (not only in Greek and Latin, but also in philosophy and law) made it an ideal place to study. He observed, "No one should therefore be surprised that, moved by and well informed about the fame of the place, young people converge on Bologna from everywhere with a desire to cultivate their intellects through such famous subjects. For it seems clear that a most excellent habitation of learning and wisdom (*eruditionis et sapientiae domicilium*) has been erected in that city."[1]

Osório's words and experience illustrate a number of significant aspects of Bologna in the 1530s. It was, he tells us, a popular destination for students from all over Europe. Indeed, it was Italy's preeminent town for letters (an implicit put-down of Padua). The *De gloria* suggests that this "habitation of learning and wisdom" was especially strong in the humanities, philosophy, and law. This fits well with the work, whose dialogues are set in Bologna, feature two law students, grapple with a philosophical topic, and are written in Ciceronian Latin.[2] But it is equally notable that Osório's initial motive for studying in Bologna was its fame for theology. Clearly, this was an area in which he acquired expertise, given that in 1536–1537 the king of Portugal (John III) called him to teach Scriptures in Coimbra. (He later went on to serve as a bishop.) It is unclear, however, where exactly he studied the subject. The university did not yet offer regular theological teaching, although it did host a faculty of theology (see §2.1). Presumably, therefore, Osório took courses in one or more of the schools of the religious orders while also hearing the lectures of university professors such as Amaseo and Boccadiferro. This point is important, because the university had multiple connections with other centers of learning in the city (see Chapter 3). In any case, Osório's student travels embraced three of the four most illustrious university cities of his time: Bologna, Paris, Oxford, and Salamanca. The lifelong friendships he made there are a reminder of the strong bonds that students forged with each other, both personally and, as we will see, more formally.

The town that won over Osório's affections was one in which civic identity and the university, or *studium,* were strongly intertwined. Osório himself did not make a strong distinction between the university and the rest of the town, perhaps because he was thinking of Bologna's culture of learning collectively. More than a century after Osório studied there, one of the most famous maps of Bologna, by the Dutch cartographer Joan Blaeu, highlighted Bologna's learned character (Figure I.1). This map, prepared with the collaboration of local Bolognese figures, prominently declares *Bononia docet* ("Bologna teaches") and calls Bologna a *mater studiorum*—a suitably ambiguous expression that could mean either "mother of studies" or "mother of universities." In a reference to the bodies overseeing both the city and the university, the map displays the seals of the papal and civic branches of government. The motto *libertas* alludes in part to the city's freedom to manage its university, a symbol of civic pride. Like most earlier and contemporary representations of Bologna, this map tellingly presents the city from the perspective of the traveler, possibly a student, coming from the north. South is therefore at the top, hinting at the journey's continuation beyond the hills to Florence and Rome. The perspectival focus on Piazza Maggiore (bordered by the Basilica of San Petronio and the Palazzo Maggiore, housing the Senate and the papal legate) extends to the nearby Archiginnasio building. This was the magnificent seat of the university completed in 1563. It is not by accident that it is located near the center of political power and near other institutions of learning (for an enlarged view, see Figure 2.1). The map also identifies some of the other features of the city that are still visible today: its two leaning towers, its numerous churches and convents, and—leading east—the Portico di San Luca (one of the great symbols of Bologna's devotion to the Virgin, an important element for Chapter 8).

As I explain below, historians have voiced serious doubts about whether, by Blaeu's time, Bologna was still a *mater studiorum* in any significant way. They point to a number of institutional, religious, and political factors that supposedly indicate a decline in the University of Bologna by the sixteenth or, at the latest, the seventeenth century (but in certain fields, such as law, far earlier). Such considerations have led to

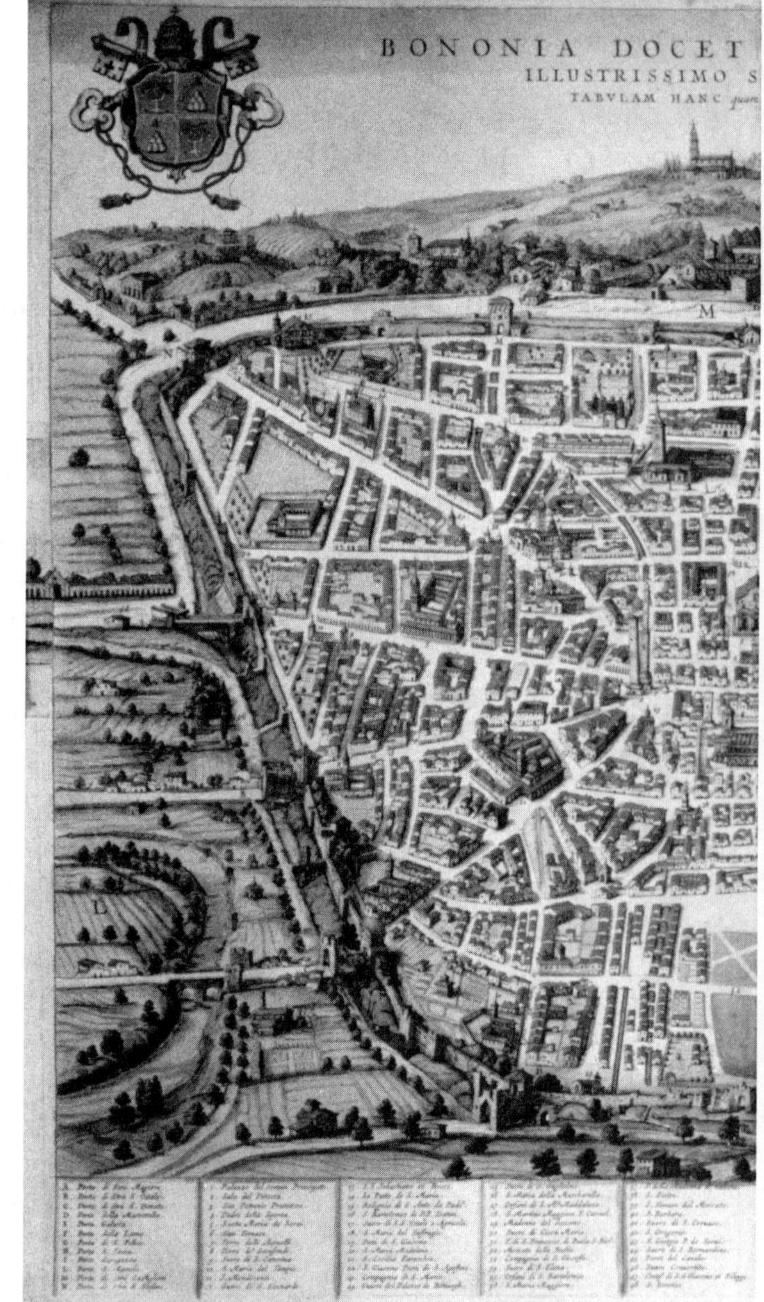
BONONIA DOCET
ILLUSTRISSIMO S
TABVLAM HANC quam

Fig I.1. Map of Bologna by Joan Blaeu, 1663.

Joan Blaeu, *Bononia docet mater studiorum,* from *Theatrum civitatum et admirandorum Italiae,* 2 vols. (Amsterdam: Joan Blaeu, 1663), vol. I: Bodleian Library J. Maps 267 [47]. Photo:

describing the curriculum in very different terms from Osório's enthusiastic judgment: as inert and ossified or, worse yet, irrelevant. According to a rather dated (but stubbornly enduring) historiography, the centers of intellectual dynamism in the early modern world lay, in any case, outside of the universities.

In this study, I focus on Bologna's teaching of arts and medicine (roughly between 1400 and 1750) and argue that this picture stands in need of thorough revision. Although the University of Bologna (like the city itself) faced a number of significant challenges, in my view its curriculum and teaching practices did not remain static over time. Rather, they underwent some remarkable developments in the early modern period. Those changes were both institutional and cultural (as I discuss in Part I) and more specifically pedagogical (Part II). The latter concerned in part the centuries-old practice of explaining a set text line by line in one's lectures. By around 1700 one notes a more systematic approach to teaching and a freer appeal to nonstandard and contemporary authorities. Also important was the creative use of a standard pedagogical exercise, the *quaestio* (question), which was repurposed in order to promote the discussion of new topics of interest. Four specific developments are especially noteworthy: university professors' increasing familiarity with Greek, and with classical antiquity more generally (Chapter 5); a turn toward professionalization and specialization in various disciplines, including the sciences (Chapter 6); a vigorous debate on the value of medical theory versus practice (Chapter 7); and a religious turn involving both the rising importance of theology and an increasing spirit of religious devotion across the disciplines (Chapter 8). I conclude that, even in a "traditional" university such as Bologna, disciplines and fields of knowledge underwent a significant reorganization, not only in their internal configuration, but in their relationships with one another and in the more general approach to learning. It is easier to appreciate this position if we step back and consider how Bologna's university (along with others) developed from its beginnings.

The University in Time

The earliest universities, or *studia,* arose out of the cultural and commercial renewal of the twelfth century, with its concomitant wave of urbanization.[3] This renewal stimulated a demand for a new, highly educated professional class, including notaries, secretaries, and experts in fields such as theology, law, and medicine. Schools for the study of such subjects developed informally at first, around individual teachers. They took on a more formal existence as students coming from afar banded together in an association or corporation called *universitas* on the model of other medieval corporations or guilds. The modern term *university* has no etymological association with "universal knowledge," but is instead a contraction of what was once known as the guild or corporation of students (*universitas scholarium*). Traces of the original expression can still be seen in the official names of most Italian universities today (e.g., Università degli Studi di Bologna).

Bologna and Paris were the first and most important medieval universities, so much so that historians view them as providing the two main models of instruction and organization in a *studium* in the medieval period. From the point of view of studies, the main difference was that Paris offered its arts curriculum as the foundation for the three higher faculties of theology, law, and medicine (though theology was the strongest of these). Bologna instead started as a center for the study of law and developed, in parallel, a joint faculty of arts and medicine, with initially no place for theology. A further important distinction concerned student power: in Bologna students hired and fired their professors (at least in its early years), whereas in Paris the masters or teachers had more control. Each model had its own followers and sphere of influence: Paris in northern and central Europe (e.g., Oxford, Salamanca, Cracow, Vienna, and Erfurt), and Bologna especially in the Italian Peninsula (e.g., Padua, Siena, Pavia, Naples, and Rome). One should not, however, overemphasize these differences—universities across Europe shared a common curriculum at least until the seventeenth century, and all featured textbooks and teaching in Latin. This made it easy for students like Osório to spend time at different universities and in different lands, at least until the movement of confessionalization turned higher education into something more regional and even local.[4]

The first universities had no foundation charters: they emerged from previous teaching establishments and were eventually recognized as degree-granting institutions. In the case of Bologna, a well-developed historiography has shown that several lay and ecclesiastical schools were already active in the second half of the eleventh century. Students gathered around particular masters to study liberal arts, notary art, theology, law, and letter writing (*ars dictaminis*).[5] Similar schools existed in Pavia and Ravenna, but it was in Bologna that teachers such as Irnerius, Pepo, and Gratian (who were responsible for fundamental developments in civil and canon law) placed the law on firmer footing in the first half of the twelfth century. Details are sketchy, but all seem to have been involved in the private teaching of law, rather than in a formally recognized institution of learning.[6]

From the middle of the twelfth century onward the university's development becomes clearer.[7] Around 1155–1158, Emperor Frederick I issued the *Habita* decree. This enabled law and arts students who traveled to places of learning (*studia*) outside of their local jurisdiction to avail themselves of special courts rather than the usual ones within a city's justice system.[8] The *Habita* did not explicitly address students in Bologna, but for various reasons scholars have tended to associate it with developments there. However that may be, the *Habita* was not a foundation charter, and later events do not point to any particular interest of Frederick I in the affairs of the Bolognese *studium*.[9] Instead it was the papacy that strengthened its ties with it.[10] Pope Alexander III (1159–1181) promoted the teaching of Roman and canon law, thus consolidating Bologna's position in these fields. Papal legates in Bologna addressed the students' difficulties in finding rented lodgings.[11] Pope Honorius III countered the hostile actions of Frederick II, who in 1225 / 1226 tried to dissolve the Bolognese *studium* while promoting the university he had founded in Naples.[12]

It was probably this threat of imminent closure that gave rise to one of the most notorious fabrications in Bolognese history—the "Theodosian Privilege."[13] This charter, claiming to date to AD 423 and to be written in the hand of the Roman emperor Theodosius II (401–450), names Bologna as a privileged place in the Empire where all students of philosophy, poetry, law, liberal arts, and other subjects can study freely under imperial protection. This initiative was supposedly confirmed by Pope Celestine I (422–432) and by a church council. The document on which this narrative rested held a prominent place in the handwritten copies of the city's and the university's privileges until at least the eighteenth century.[14] Producing it undermined the legality of the actions of Frederick II, since it showed that he was presuming to overturn a pre-

Fig I.2. The Theodosian Privilege in 1619.

Thesis engraving (270 × 345 mm) on paper, Oliviero Gatti, 1619, XIX.15.40. British Museum, London. Photo: Warburg Institute.

vious imperial decree. It also granted an important role to papal authority, which was seeking to block Frederick II's aims. Despite doubts about its authenticity raised by various scholars (notably Carlo Sigonio in the sixteenth century), this privilege formed an important part of Bologna's identity: it presented the city as an extremely ancient seat of learning, whose status both Empire and Church had recognized.[15] But it also had a particular function within internal politics, serving as a guarantee to the doctors of the *studium* of their privileges against an increasingly powerful senatorial class.[16] The prefaces to the teaching rolls mention the privilege regularly (see Appendix). The seventeenth-century engraving in Figure I.2 shows St. Petronius (bishop of Bologna and one of the city's patron saints, † c. 450) kneeling before the pope and the emperor, who pass on to him a scroll containing the privilege. But long after that this fiction still took in visitors, including the celebrated French astronomer Joseph-Jerôme Lalande (1732–1807), whose detailed diary of his visit to Italy in 1765–1766 makes explicit reference to the role of Emperor Theodosius in founding the University of Bologna.[17]

For centuries the university was contested by local and more remote brokers of political and religious power—especially the city's government and the papacy (which became the city's sovereign in 1278). After the early thirteenth century, imperial involvement in the University of Bologna waned, despite the continuing importance of imperial politics for Bologna.[18] The commune or city-state tried to occupy the power vacuum and to contain the *studium*.[19] In 1189 it required masters to swear an oath of stability (i.e., that they would not leave the city and go teach elsewhere). Through early thirteenth-century statutes, it tried to keep in check the development of student associations (*universitates*): students obtained recognition as citizens (*cives*) only in 1250.[20] The students' strongest ally turned out to be the papacy. In 1211 Innocent III sided with the students, and Bologna switched its allegiance from the emperor to the papacy. Between 1215 and 1220 Honorius III defended the students from various initiatives of the communal authorities that were unfavorable to them. In particular, he made the *podestà* repeal the laws that restricted scholars' freedom of movement.[21] He appointed the cathedral's archdeacon to the function of university chancellor in 1219. (This was an unusual arrangement; in Italy it was typically the bishop or archbishop who held this position.)[22] Subsequent years saw a legal tug-of-war between the commune and the papacy. In 1253 Innocent IV approved a set of statutes of the *universitas scholarium* (the first currently known for Bologna).[23] By 1288 the commune included various provisions for students within the city statutes.[24] In 1291 the papacy granted Bologna's graduates the all-important privilege to teach anywhere in Christendom (*licentia ubique docendi*). It thereby formally recognized the university's status as a *studium generale*.[25] (Historians of universities see this kind of license as essential for distinguishing universities from other places learning.) For its part, the commune continued to intervene in the life of the university and extend its control there by, for instance, limiting the power of student rectors. Most notably, it took it upon itself to fund the *studium* and appoint its professors, who in the meantime were also banding together into associations (*collegia doctorum;* see §1.2).[26] In 1316 it entered into conflict with the student *universitates* (not for the last time) because of questions concerning their right to carry arms. In 1321 it executed a Spanish student who had kidnapped the daughter of an influential Bolognese figure. These events gave rise to a student exodus to Siena and other cities, leading to the establishment of other universities.[27] (A similar exodus in 1222 had led to the foundation of the *studium* in Padua.)

Bologna must have formalized the relationship between masters and students early on. This was central to having a *studium,* guaranteeing the rights of teachers and especially of foreign (i.e., non-Bolognese) students in the city. When exactly this happened is a matter of ongoing scholarly debate. In the opinion of some historians, however, the protections of the imperial *Habita* decree soon lost their force in light of the struggles between Bologna and other communes and the Empire. Given that the Bolognese commune attempted to restrict their freedom of movement, students banded together in territorial units (Nations, or *Nationes*) in order to seek protection and regain control through, among other things, the election of student rectors. This new form of association, which Pope Clement III in 1189 called "a common gathering of teachers and students" ("communis audientia magistrorum atque scholariorum"), was—according to scholars such as Carlo Dolcini and Guido Rossi—the real starting point of Bologna's *studium.*[28] This therefore took shape around a century after the conventional date of 1088, selected wholly arbitrarily by Giosuè Carducci and his colleagues at Bologna in their eagerness to celebrate the university's eight-hundredth anniversary in 1888.[29] Unfortunately, the year 1088 features prominently in the University of Bologna's official seal, thus endorsing a baseless historiographical myth.

From the late fourteenth century onward, the most notable institutional developments in the *studium* concern its governance. The commune tried to tighten its oversight of the university (to the detriment of student power) by creating the committee of the Riformatori dello Studio in 1381. A second committee, the Assunti dello Studio, appeared alongside it (but with different functions) in the first half of the sixteenth century. The Senate was behind this move, which was part of a general strategy to concentrate power in its own hands against various republican factions. In the second half of the sixteenth century, the office of student rector disappeared: in his place came less powerful priors and councillors. Eventually the papal representative took this title himself.[30]

These changes were closely connected with a shifting political landscape. Between 1376 and 1506 Bologna saw the increased influence of the aristocracy, which found its most powerful expression in the supreme civic body (over time, variously denominated the Anziani, the Sedici, the Quaranta, the Riformatori dello Stato di Libertà, the Reggimento, or the Senate).[31] Especially significant during this period was the rise (1401–1466) and then the consolidation (1466–1506) of the Bentivoglio, who reached the height of their power through Giovanni II (1466–1488) and his family, although in fact they served the interests of the oligarchs.[32] After a few decades of de facto autonomy, in 1506 the mercenaries of Pope Julius II stormed Bologna and returned it to its sovereign. (Desiderius Erasmus, who witnessed the event, wrote a satirical dialogue—*Julius exclusus*—about the conquering pope.)

Thereafter, until 1796, Bologna had a "mixed" form of government (*governo misto*), an expression that reflected the (notional) sharing of power between equals already seen in Joan Blaeu's map. In this arrangement, which had its roots in the 1447 agreement (*capitoli*) of Pope Nicholas V with the city, Bologna's government and laws depended on joint decision making by the papal representative and the Senate.[33] Historians have disagreed both about the observance of this arrangement in practice and about the political and cultural significance of this period of mixed government. A particular bone of contention has been how much autonomy Bologna (or at least some of its classes and institutions) really enjoyed (see below). What is certain is that constitutional stability did not put an end to factionalism, the resurgence of famine and disease, the effects of the "Italian wars," or a series of economic crises, all of which buffeted Bologna and its territories in these and later centuries.[34] Apart from the Napoleonic period, Bologna remained closely tied to the papacy until (due to the movement of national unification) the cardinal legate abandoned it in 1859 and the Papal State collapsed in 1870.

The early centuries of the *studium* saw the dominance of law. Professors of both canon (church) law and especially civil (Roman) law held quasi-regal status and could command exorbitant salaries, and the most famous at least had striking mausolea built for them. (Some of these monumental tombs, which are elevated on columns, survive outside of religious complexes such as San Domenico and San Francesco, whereas others are in churches or have been transferred to the Museo Civico Medievale.) Bolognese professors such as Bartolus of Sassoferrato (1313–1357) were known for their learned commentary tradition on the *Corpus iuris civilis.* They attracted numerous students from abroad, many of them from German-speaking lands, but also some of the best-known names in Italian cultural history, including Francis Petrarch and Coluccio Salutati and several future popes. In later times the jurists continued to be highly sought after and included (as Osório's account confirms) famous professors such as Achille Bocchi. But in the sixteenth century they suffered a blow with the rise of a different, French approach to law called the *mos gallicus.* Thereafter, for complex reasons, the flow of students started to ebb. By the end of the sixteenth century, law no longer commanded the lion's share of the university budget, and the teaching rolls point to a reduced number of professors compared to arts and medicine. Many scholars believe that Bolognese law had its heyday in the "golden" thirteenth century and thereafter entered a protracted phase of decline (something hard to corroborate at present in the absence of a systematic analysis of lectures and other sources). Certainly the doctoral colleges of the jurists continued to be active and highly organized throughout the early modern period.[35]

The Problem of Decline

The events outlined above, and particularly the forced return of Bologna to the Papal State after 1506, left a strong impression on historians working in the second half of the nineteenth century and the first few decades of the twentieth. Anticlerical sentiment and strong notions of liberty and independence led to a focus either on Bologna in the (idealized) medieval period or on independent republics such as Florence and Venice. In anglophone scholarship too, later developments, such as the (Grand-)Duchy of Tuscany, became part of what Eric Cochrane memorably called "the forgotten centuries" (1527–1800).[36] As explained below, Bologna's renewed subjection to the papacy was widely seen as an era of decline on multiple fronts: political of course, but also social, economic, and cultural.

The past thirty or so years have witnessed a welcome resurgence of interest in the city. Although it came rather later than similar works for other cities, a richly illustrated eight-volume history of Bologna appeared in the late 1980s.[37] A new, four-volume *Storia di Bologna* (2005–2013) now reflects the strength of recent research and provides up-to-date bibliographies on many topics. Mario Fanti and several other Italian scholars continue to produce valuable work on widely varied aspects of Bolognese culture. The first English-language handbook on the city in medieval and Renaissance times came out in 2018, building on the 2013 publication of a collection of essays on Anglo-American scholarship on Bologna.[38] North American scholars especially have been questioning the "decline" narrative for areas as diverse as politics, society, medical culture, literature, art, and architecture, arguing that early modern Bologna displayed considerable vitality in these and other fields.[39] Particularly gratifying has been the inclusion of Bologna within comparative or larger studies of early modern Italian history.

So far, however, studies of the university have not benefited from this trend as much as they might. The main reason for this state of affairs is hardly a lack of documentation, which—despite some unevenness—is extremely rich throughout the period (see below). Rather, it is an adherence to the historiographical model of decline. In fact, historians have disagreed about the timing and exact nature of such a fall (as noted above, some even place it already after the thirteenth century), much less the reasons that may have occasioned it.[40] Several have argued that the humanities were an exception to this general trend, at least in the second half of the fifteenth century, when professors such as Francesco Dal Pozzo, Filippo Beroaldo the Elder, and Antonio Codro Urceo graced the *studium*.[41] Nonetheless, there is an overall consensus that a real drop of some kind occurred (whether in prestige, quality of teaching, or attraction of international students)—something that presumably justifies shifting one's attention elsewhere.

Narratives of decline are both potent and problematic. Their potency lies most obviously in their ability to direct research away from cases of perceived failure to others of supposed success and vitality. For the period 1500–1800, these interpretations have led to focusing on universities in central and northern Europe rather than Italy or Spain, both in the standard handbook on the history of universities and in other accounts.[42] Alternatively, periods of crisis seem more congenial to the interests of institutional, political, and economic historians, whose insights into the development of early modern Bologna at times also have bearing on the university.[43] Yet "decline" is also decidedly problematic as a historiographical framework.[44] In what follows, therefore, I address five specific points underpinning this narrative that have particularly discouraged the study of Bologna's university as a cultural and intellectual center in the early modern period.

The first place to start is the students (see §1.1). I have already referred to the office of the student rector, which went unfilled after the end of the sixteenth century. There were several reasons behind this development, including the considerable expense that the position entailed. But it certainly signaled a loss of student privileges and was followed by (although perhaps not responsible for) a drop in the numbers of international students coming to Bologna. In fact, charting the flows of student numbers with any precision is devilishly tricky, but some historians have seen both the effective retirement of the student rector and this decline in numbers as the beginning of the end for the *studium*—as a proxy for the university's attractiveness and the quality of its teaching. Readers belonging to excellent departments that nonetheless recruit poorly will know that matters are not so straightforward. For early modern Bologna, numerous European-wide initiatives, such as the requirement to study locally or the Church's insistence on an oath of allegiance to the Catholic Church (*professio fidei*) for degree candidates, must have had a considerable impact on numbers, although Gian Paolo Brizzi's studies have suggested that the drop in enrollments was not nearly as steep or precipitous as previously thought.[45] I also argue that competition from other *studia* within the Papal State and the Italian Peninsula more broadly is an important consideration. In other words, even if we could measure student numbers more precisely, they would still be just one factor among many and would not necessarily speak to the quality of teaching in the *studium*. More relevant is probably Bologna's tendency, starting in the seventeenth century, to recruit its teachers from among its local alumni. But for many years this did not mean that there were no professors of note.

The immobility of the curriculum is another supposed signal of decline. According to this narrative, not only did Bologna's curriculum continue, for centuries on end, to require that teaching be based on traditional (and by now outdated) authors such as Aristotle, Galen, and Ptolemy, but the survival of features such as the distinction between theoretical and practical medicine testifies that the university program was unable to renew itself. The conclusion is therefore that the Bolognese university—like many others—fostered a conservative (indeed, stultifying) approach to learning. The main problem with this viewpoint is its evidentiary basis (see below and Chapter 2). While it is true, for instance, that the teaching rolls present medicine as basing itself for centuries on the writings of Galen and Hippocrates, the lectures and lecture plans tell a very different story. Likewise, critics of the universities (including some humanists and early modern philosophers such as Francis Bacon) are not impartial witnesses, and their pronouncements should therefore be assessed more critically. A further problem is that the viewpoint of curricular immobility overlooks the instances of changing relationships between subjects. As I argue in this book, one of the most noteworthy developments in Bologna is the rise of theology as a dominant subject in the seventeenth century (Chapter 8).

On the strength of the previous assumption, some historians have dismissed the role of universities as sites for new literary or scientific discussions in the early modern period, while instead foregrounding that of academies and scientific societies. This viewpoint has proved resistant to a significant body of scholarship over the past half century that has underlined the continuing vitality of the universities; Charles Schmitt and Brendan Dooley, for instance, have pointed to the close relationship between universities and scientific developments.[46] In the case of Bologna, it has led to ignoring much of the university's philosophical and scientific production in the sixteenth and seventeenth centuries. It is telling, for instance, that the university lectures of Ulisse Aldrovandi (unlike his other writings) have so far attracted no scholarly attention. Far more research has gone instead to the Istituto delle Scienze (founded in 1711–1714) and its antecedents, on all of which Marta Cavazza especially has done highly valuable work.[47] More might be done on the mutual influences between the academies or the Istituto and the university (see §3.2). Given that professors such as Melchiorre Zoppi were often leading members (or even founders) of academies, this is a topic deserving further exploration.

The last two arguments supporting the "decline" thesis involve Bologna's relationship with Rome, both as a political and a religious entity. In line with studies on the nature of early modern absolutism, the older histories tended to describe the relationship between Rome and the periphery of the Papal State in terms of power imposed from above. Bologna figured therefore as a subject city that had been entirely deprived of its former liberty and lay supine under the yoke of its sovereign. As I note below, this narrative led several historians of the university not only to lament this development, but to conclude that the *studium* declined as its liberties vanished. This argument is weak for several reasons. First of all, other major university towns (Pavia, Padua, Pisa, and Siena) also found themselves governed by their respective capitals—indeed, most of these were the capital's official university—yet historians have not necessarily found a causal relationship between centralization and cultural decline. Therefore, why should this be the case for Bologna? Furthermore, especially since the seminal work of Bandino Giacomo Zenobi, the relationship between center and periphery in the Papal State has been rethought. Historians now give far more credit to the mechanisms by which the sovereign sought consensus with at least the most influential section(s) of the communities governed (in the case of Bologna, the Senate). In the end, therefore, there was room for negotiation and, to a limited extent, resistance (or, at least, dissent and protest).[48] In this book I will discuss several instances in which both the colleges of doctors and the Assunti dello Studio vigorously opposed instructions and power grabbing from the center, either through the city's resident ambassador in Rome or through other powerful connections. The doctoral colleges also found themselves, more than once, crossing swords with the Senate or even Rome, in standoffs that could last for years. One must also acknowledge, however, that papal control of the *studium* tightened over time. Although in some instances that helped the *studium* avoid self-sabotage, in others it led to considerable confusion about jurisdiction over the university and who should take action (§1.3).

Other interpreters link the university's decline instead (or as well) to the conservatism of the Catholic Church, which in their view attempted to suppress freedom of thought in the *studium* through a vigorous campaign against heterodoxy. For obvious reasons, this perspective is sharply critical of the activities of the Inquisition and the Holy Office, including the Index of Prohibited Books.[49] But it also treats with suspicion the activity of the Jesuits, who in Bologna had a strong influence on the university (although they did not manage to infiltrate it and take it over) until the order's dissolution in 1773.[50] Largely the product of late nineteenth-century historians whose anticlericalism is both vehement and apparent, this view rarely finds expression today, but in subtle ways it still colors various approaches and conclusions. It has led to counternarratives by historians such as Paul Grendler and Ugo Baldini, who have perhaps been slightly overzealous in their efforts to present the Catholic Reformation in a more benign light.[51] As explained in Chapter 8, other scholars such as Gigliola Fragnito, Guido dall'Olio, and Luca Bianchi have been more willing to acknowledge that the activities of the Inquisition had a tangible effect in terms of prosecutions and the availability of books, while Hannah Marcus has taken a more moderate stance.[52] I argue that the severity of the Inquisition in Bologna, which largely depended on who was in charge, had some real consequences for the *studium*, as shown by the scarcity of some books in the late seventeenth century (§4.3). But lectures also suggest that the ideas of northern European thinkers were not nearly as hard to access as one might imagine.

While, given the reasons above, the thesis of decline needs revisiting, I am not suggesting that the University of Bologna was at the forefront of innovation or scientific research in Europe or even just in Italy, although the Istituto delle Scienze did for a time provide a model for other Italian scientific academies to follow. Clearly, the *studium* faced numerous and substantial challenges. On the home front, observers noted the impunity with which some students disturbed lectures and disrespected their teachers. Some accounts describe the professors as far too numerous, or ill-prepared, or having a sense of entitlement and giving more attention to private lectures than public ones. The frequent reforms of the university proclaimed during this time show that the authorities felt that something had to be done yet were powerless to secure lasting change: new legislation and threats of punishment were obviously insufficient (§1.3). From at least 1550 onward, the university saw itself as lurching from one crisis to the next, partly involving increasing competition from other papal, Italian, and European universities. For all of these challenges, Bologna nonetheless developed ways of rethinking its educational offerings, particularly thanks to the efforts of individual professors. Despite the vigilance of the Inquisition, it also informed its students about new perspectives in philosophy, astronomy, and medicine from across Europe.

Historiography

The account offered in this book builds on a large (if uneven) body of scholarship on the university.[53]

Studies of the *studium* as a whole date to the 1930s and 1940s. Guido Zaccagnini's *Storia dello Studio di Bologna durante il Rinascimento* (1930) is chronologically focused (second half of the fourteenth century to the first years of the seventeenth) and makes liberal use of documents in the Archivio di Stato di Bologna, particularly for the colleges of doctors, but also the Senate (*Libri partitorum;* see below). Although this work belongs to the genre of what one might call "anecdotal history," Zaccagnini provides full references to (and often quotations from) the sources in the course of his highly amusing vignettes of professors and students. His judgments on the achievements of individual professors, however, can be bizarre and capricious and are not usually based on records of their teaching. And Zaccagnini is excessively critical of the effects of the Catholic Reformation.[54] Like others, he sees the seventeenth century solely in terms of decline (*decadenza*)—but the main basis for this conclusion is not so much any real or imagined cultural shift within the university, but instead the impression that the "unlimited" power of the papacy and the cardinal legates had taken away from the Bolognese any real say over the *studium.*[55]

In 1940 Albano Sorbelli and Luigi Simeoni published their *Storia della Università di Bologna,* whose two volumes deal with the medieval period and 1500–1888, respectively.[56] Although they contain useful information on the institutional aspects of the *studium,* Simeoni's volume in particular suffers from the "decline" narrative noted above (again with particular reference to the *studium*'s progressive lack of autonomy). It also hinges on an outdated model of history that praises progress and berates "traditionalists." Furthermore, Simeoni offers no convincing evidence for his claim that, in the period covered, "the power of true teaching faded away."[57]

Carlo Calcaterra's *Alma Mater Studiorum: L'università di Bologna nella storia della cultura e della civiltà* (published in 1948) has quite a different character. This cultural and intellectual history of the *studium* covers the entire time span from its origins to the Second World War in a single volume. Although here again the seventeenth century receives somewhat of a beating (it appears as a period of "crisis"), Calcaterra generally appreciates the culture of the university well. The book is readable but offers very few references to the secondary literature, and strongly depends on cameos of individual professors. Like the histories of Sorbelli and Simeoni, it gives little attention to unpublished sources.

In addition to these monographs, one should mention classic, more general surveys of universities such as Heinrich Denifle's *Die Enstehung der Universitäten des Mittelalters bis 1400* (1885) and Hastings Rashdall's *Universities of Europe in the Middle Ages* (1895), both of which offer lengthy treatments of the University of Bologna, with particular attention to institutional structures, students, and statutes. Manlio Bellomo's *Saggio sull'università nell'età del diritto comune* (1979) focuses on the twelfth and thirteenth centuries, but offers a wide-ranging narrative that includes, among others, aspects of teaching and book provision, also beyond Bologna. Over the years, the annual *Studi e memorie per la storia dell'Università di Bologna* (*SMSUB*, 1909–1983) published much valuable material. More recently, extended treatments of the Bolognese *studium* in the early modern period include the essays by Gian Paolo Brizzi and myself, in addition to various sections of Grendler's important book (discussed below) on the Italian universities.[58]

The field owes much to the productivity of medieval and legal historians, who have published numerous documents relating to the university.[59] They have also analyzed a series of important topics, including the *studium*'s origins, its institutional aspects, its relationship with the church, contemporary developments in the town's religious *studia*, student power, and much besides. These scholars have been especially interested in Bologna as a center for the development of civil and canon law in the university's early centuries, paying attention to the series of statutes and deliberations that emanated from various bodies associated with the university.[60] For the early modern period they have also studied the German Nation and the colleges of doctors.[61] But the great work of Albano Sorbelli and Celestino Piana in publishing the *libri secreti* of the College of Law remains incomplete.[62]

Studies of arts and medicine have tended to take different directions. When compared with law especially, publications on the normative aspects of arts and medicine have been rarer. (In the following I include theology because it appeared on the rolls of arts and medicine and, as I argue in this book, came to have an influential presence there.) Francesco Ehrle published the 1364 and 1440 statutes for the faculty of theology, and Carlo Malagola the fifteenth-century statutes of arts and medicine.[63] But no one has studied the later statutes or given close attention to the colleges of doctors. It is unclear whether the forms of student government that developed for arts and medicine after the demise of the office of rector are entirely comparable with those for law. Claudia Salterini's inventory of the archive of the Riformatori dello Studio has greatly facilitated its study and has obvious implications for arts and medicine, but the archival series Assunteria di Studio still lacks a comparable repertory, and the committee's workings remain rather murky.

Attention to students has followed three main lines of research, all strongly influenced by social history. One is represented by Giuseppe Bronzino's list of degrees and graduates, which has now found a correspondent in Maria Teresa Guerrini's much more developed prosopographical study of law graduates.[64] Bronzino depended especially on the *libri secreti* for arts and medicine, which remains an understudied source apart from very specific information on individual students (and future professors) such as Gaspare Tagliacozzi.[65] His results (and other sources, testifying, for instance, to theology degrees after 1500) have informed the ASFE (Amore scientiae facti sunt exules) database, which lists doctorates in Bologna and elsewhere in Italy for all subjects.[66] Currently there is a broad European project afoot to analyze student movement and degrees across Europe by using digital tools and combining various databases.[67] The work of Gian Paolo Brizzi has addressed student numbers (matriculation lists), colleges, and culture more broadly.[68] Among other projects (including ASFE), he founded and directed the Museo Europeo degli Studenti in Palazzo Poggi and was the moving force behind the publication of the student coats of arms (*stemmi*) in the Archiginnasio.[69] Yet other studies have focused on the dynamics of student violence in Bologna. Here, the work of Ilaria Maggiulli and Christopher Carlsmith (who has also given attention to institutions such as the Collegio Montalto) has been especially valuable. Their studies provide insights into the evolving aristocratization of the student body and students' behavior more broadly.[70]

In the case of professors of arts and medicine, relevant publications have provided career outlines and biobibliographical sketches for teachers of humanities, medicine, astronomy, and natural and moral philosophy.[71] (There is no modern listing for theology.) Many of these repertories have depended on archival materials in addition to the rolls published by Dallari and the biographical information in Mazzetti (not always reliable) and Fantuzzi.[72] All of these publications, however, have differing aims, coverage, and chronological parameters. That of Bònoli and Piliarvu on teachers of astronomy is the most extensive, reaching from the twelfth to the twentieth century. (Most of them stop between 1550 and 1600.) Not all of them provide specific pointers to lectures.

Generally speaking, the professors who have received extended study are the most famous ones, such as Filippo Beroaldo, Codro Urceo, Pietro Pomponazzi, Carlo Sigonio, Ulisse Aldrovandi, Gaspare Tagliacozzi, Marcello Malpighi, and Laura Bassi (the first woman professor, in the eighteenth century). Despite their usefulness, to some extent such studies necessarily suffer from the question of how representative the figures in question actually are. An effective alternative approach has been to place these professors within broader contexts. In the case of Aldrovandi, this has produced helpful results in terms of his scientific knowledge (Giuseppe Olmi), networks (Paula Findlen), book exchanges or acquisitions (Caroline Duroselle-Melish and Ian Maclean), and requests to read prohibited books (Hannah Marcus).[73] There has been limited work on professors more broadly from the perspective of social history, although Anuschka De Coster has provided valuable studies on their mobility.[74]

Outside of law, the fields that have received most attention for Bologna have been rhetoric, medicine, and mathematics (in that order). Still largely unexplored are philosophy (a major focus of this book) and theology, as well as the study of Greek. I have treated all of these areas together in the hope of unearthing more general patterns and developments, as discussed in Part II. I have also aimed to move the discussion beyond the established finding that Bologna was an important center for the humanities in the Renaissance.

Nancy Siraisi's work on medicine merits a particular mention here, due not only to its recognized excellence but to the way in which it has informed this book. In her scholarship, Siraisi modeled a careful analysis of works connected with teaching, both in manuscript and in print. She also tied these teaching materials, whenever possible, to local or broader debates, offering a rich picture of developments in medicine throughout the peninsula and proof of the continuing vitality of universities.[75] Siraisi gave extensive attention to the medical curriculum, detailing how lectures correct the misleading picture offered by the 1405 statutes. This book confirms that the statutes are a dangerous guide for reconstructing the practices of teaching and study. The reason lies especially in the evolution of such practices over the early modern period.

I have adapted Siraisi's approach in various ways. I have extended my analysis beyond 1600, where most of Siraisi's studies ended. The decision to reach up to 1750, shortly after the revised curricular arrangements of 1737 (studied by Franca Baldelli), has allowed me to consider developments over the *longue durée* and take in the seventeenth century, which most scholars have sorely neglected.[76] (A notable exception is Brendan Dooley, who has published numerous excellent studies on seventeenth-century lectures on philosophy and science, particularly for Padua.)[77] Secondly, following the example of Robert Black, I have given more prominence to archival sources and to the ties between witnesses to classroom teaching and institutional considerations.[78] I am convinced that the two belong together and deserve to be considered jointly. Finally, although it also took in Bologna and other centers of learned medicine, much of Siraisi's research on the fifteenth and sixteenth centuries focused on Padua, which had been the topic of her dissertation.[79] This had the (probably unintended) effect of reinforcing a common stereotype of Padua as Italy's preeminent university for medicine, if not indeed its preeminent university *tout court.* In this book I show that for a long time Bologna remained a strong contender for this title, and I hope this will help rectify some of the historiographical imbalance.

Other important antecedents to this study have taken different approaches and adopted different methodologies. Despite its disparate topics and very wide chronological lens, the 1956 special issue of *SMSUB,* which inaugurated the annual's new series, contained helpful articles on important aspects of the curriculum. Hardly any of them, however, addressed either philosophy or theology. Much better balanced was the three-volume collection *Sapere e/è potere* (1990), which is exemplary in treating all the disciplines in the *studium* and relating them to both intellectual debates and social practices. The editors were less successful, however, in securing contributions that studied unpublished lectures. The necessity of doing so was the focus of an important article (1997) by Dino Buzzetti, Roberto Lambertini, and Andrea Tabarroni. Building on the scholarship of Alfonso Maierù, they emphasized the importance of studying actual texts (commentaries, lectures, student notes, and so forth) for understanding teaching in the fourteenth and fifteenth centuries.[80] Many other scholars, including myself, have made this a key aspect of their research.

The most comprehensive treatment to date of the Italian university curriculum is part two of Paul Grendler's monumental *The Universities of the Italian Renaissance* (2002). The considerable merits of this work are well known, and the discussion Grendler provides of the individual disciplines constituted an extremely useful comparator for my research. My objective in Part II of this book has been to identify common developments rather than discuss discrete disciplines, as Grendler did; but Grendler's treatment is a constant point of reference, and the reader will find it useful to refer to his outlines. Grendler's discussions of Bologna are strongly informed by the archival series ASB, Assunteria di Studio. As will become clear, I have dug deeply into other series in Bologna's rich archives that fill out the picture. Both Grendler and I start our analyses around 1400, largely because the evidence of teaching becomes clearer then through rolls, statutes, and lectures.

These continuities notwithstanding, our emphases, approaches, and conclusions differ. Grendler's decision to end in 1600 gives rise to a narrative of decline thereafter (see his chapter 14), which I cannot endorse. I have also offered a more circumscribed interpretation of the role of humanism. While completely sharing Grendler's view that the humanities were a salient aspect of Bologna's university curriculum and that humanism influenced other disciplines (Chapter 5 below), I hold that other developments were equally, if not more, important (Chapters 6–8). Some of these include the use of well-worn scholastic exercises to reform the linear teaching of texts and introduce more easily the perspectives of noncanonical thinkers. But my discussion of theory and practice should also underline the variety of positions that university professors took on long-standing topics of interest. Perhaps the most unexpected conclusion is the rise of theology (Chapter 8) in Bologna between the sixteenth and the eighteenth centuries (something that Grendler glosses as either a trompe l'oeil or a specific strategy of the university authorities to contain the competition of the Jesuits).[81] Finally, my limitation to a smaller canvas enabled me to use lectures and lecture plans as a corrective to the evidence supplied by the statutes and teaching rolls, something that would have been impossible in a study of Grendler's scale.

Sources and Methodology

For this book I have made a combined use of three classes of documents.[82] The first includes statutory and regulatory materials (statutes, rolls, edicts, and so forth) testifying to what the students, the Senate, and the papal legate (among others) thought ought to happen in the *studium,* including in the curriculum. Another consists of administrative deliberations (e.g., within the committees overseeing the university, or the Senate) and written exchanges (such as those between the Senate and its ambassador in Rome). Finally, I have depended heavily on lectures and student notes (preferring, whenever possible, handwritten to published lectures, since the latter often underwent extensive revision). The first two classes of sources have been especially important for the first part of the book, whereas the last one has been of particular help for the second.

Descriptions of the Bolognese curriculum have usually relied on the 1405 student statutes of arts and medicine published by Carlo Malagola.[83] As a source, however, they are problematic for two main reasons. First, it is well known that statutes were not necessarily observed. Indeed, the fact that many statutes continued to be reiterated suggests that it was not easy to enforce them. Second, at least some statutes tend to encapsulate a situation that was outdated by the time of their publication; as a result, statutes issued in 1405 probably tell us more about how teaching was meant to take place during previous decades than about how it was delivered afterward. It is therefore unsafe to base one's view of the Bolognese curriculum solely on this source, especially if one is trying to understand developments over an extended period. The existence of later statutes (for 1561, 1583, and 1609) is not particularly helpful, since they do not provide detailed information about the curriculum and in any case would still be problematic to use (see §1.1.1).

Teaching rolls (*rotuli*), on the other hand, are potentially more useful.[84] Prepared by the committee of the Riformatori dello Studio, they provide specific and almost continuous information for each year between 1438 and 1800. For each academic year, they advertise which teachers are assigned to each subject and eventually indicate further details, such as what texts they are supposed to teach and at which hour of the day. These rolls also feature lengthy prefaces, which with few exceptions remain unpublished and unstudied. This is a serious disadvantage, for they offer a precious source of information, comparable to that of the statutes but updated on a yearly basis.[85] These prefaces deserve a comprehensive analysis. Here I have been able to use them only sporadically, although I do offer a transcription and translation of one of these in the Appendix.

The rolls produced before 1768 consist of large parchment sheets (measuring on average 870 × 630 mm) designed for public display and divided into three main sections: the decoration, the preface, and the prospectus of teachers and their teachings.[86] Figure I.3 provides an early sixteenth-century example of one such roll for arts and medicine. (There is a separate series of rolls for the jurists.) All three components underwent changes over the years, but the 1516 roll depicts St. Petronius in a central position in his traditional posture of holding the city. Next to him are the crests of the pope and the papal legate, while at the outer edges are the recognizable symbols of the city of Bologna. From 1631–1632 to 1795–1796 the rolls often also depicted the crests of the Riformatori dello Studio, but many of the surviving eighteenth-century documents no longer preserve these decorated sections, which may have been removed because of their interest to collectors. The prefaces (always introduced by the phrase *In nomine Sancte et individue Trinitatis*) continued to be a prominent feature of the rolls, although their layout varied somewhat. Likewise, the list of teachers and teachings continued to occupy the bottom portion of the rolls, but eventually specified more clearly the distribution of teachings over the course of each day. From 1526–1527 they started indicating (at least for some subjects) what textbooks professors had been assigned.

Regulatory materials also include the decisions of the Senate and the *bandi* or edicts of the papal legate, vice-legate, or governor.[87] The *studium* and its personnel figure repeatedly in documentation of the Senate, which records numerous requests by professors (for pay raises, for instance) and the results of deliberations, as well as instructions issued by the Senate (often jointly with the legate). Whereas some of these

Fig I.3. Teaching roll for arts and medicine, 1516–1517.

Archivo di Stato di Bologna, Riformatori dello Studio, b. 11, roll 70.

documents relate specifically to individual professors, others have wider implications for the *studium* and point to more general decisions. But no study of the university has referred to them systematically.

As mentioned above, these regulatory sources must be cross-referenced with documents offering a closer view of what was happening on the ground. In this case, two archival series are especially relevant. Of fundamental importance are the deliberations of the Assunti dello Studio, one of the two committees that managed the University of Bologna on the Senate's behalf (§1.3.1).[88] These documents offer insights into some of the controversies that affected the *studium,* many of which were closely related to its teaching program. But they also contain materials on a number of controversies in the *studium,* as well as the important *Requisiti dei lettori* documents, which I have not been able to use for this book. Another helpful *fondo* is the Archivio dello Studio. Here one finds substantial information on both the colleges of doctors (statutes and secret meetings, including deliberations on degree candidates) and the student *universitates.*[89] This series is relevant because many senior professors belonged to the College of Arts and Medicine, whose *Acta* and *Libri secreti* offer a mine of interesting information (see above). The *fondo*'s subseries *Università degli scolari: Artisti*—particularly the *Registri degli atti dell'Università* (nos. 378–97)—has useful day-to-day information on student life and learning (including some reforms) from 1540 to 1784.

Numerous letters survive between Bolognese civic authorities (especially relevant are those from the Senate and the Assunti dello Studio) and their ambassador in the papal court, who had a particularly prominent function and delicate task starting in the sixteenth century.[90] This correspondence offers an unusually frank account of how the Senate and its committee went about resolving the political aspects posed by developments in the *studium.* It often speaks to an adversarial relationship between the political class and the university community.

Finally, one must consider the sources most closely connected to the practice of teaching in the University of Bologna. The most direct and helpful materials are the various lectures and student notebooks related to professors teaching in Bologna. (Though plentiful, academic prolusions are often highly rhetorical, vague, and thus less relevant.)[91] For the fifteenth and sixteenth centuries in particular, these survive in fairly plentiful numbers, although they are not evenly distributed across subjects. These manuscript materials are preserved mostly in Bologna's Biblioteca Universitaria, although some appear also in the holdings of the Biblioteca Comunale (or, exceptionally, in the Archivio di Stato) or other libraries, also outside of Italy. (For examples of lectures and student notes, see Figures 6.1 and 5.2, respectively.)

Each of the sources just mentioned poses its own set of methodological challenges. Scholars have recognized this in particular for student notes, which have usually survived in an ordered state. In this case, they are typically fair copies (also called "second-order notes") of much messier (or "first-order") notes taken directly at lectures.[92] When we have such first-order notes, they are probably the closest we can come to what actually took place in the classroom, although there too errors and omissions are possible. It is unclear to what extent fair copies may have effected changes of wording and contents—not least because the production of second-order notes usually involved the destruction of the first-order ones, thus making comparisons impossible. As for lectures, scholars agree that manuscript copies are more trustworthy than printed editions (which students, professors, or editors might heavily modify before presenting them to a broader public). These sources are typically helpful for reconstructing how teaching proceeded in terms of pace, range, and questions. The *lemmata* given often aid research into the exact text or translation used. Here too, however, one needs to be wary of thinking that the words on the page necessarily correspond to what was actually said in the classroom. In some cases, what seem to be lectures are shortish and may actually simply be an *aide mémoire*. In others, a professor or amanuensis has provided a fair-copy (and possibly edited) version of a disordered lecture.

In 1641 the *Ordinationi* of the cardinal legate Giulio Sacchetti required Bolognese professors to submit quarterly or yearly plans for their teaching, outlining the material they would be covering and the sections of the relevant textbooks that they would be addressing each term (see Figure 6.2).[93] The resulting documentation survives only for selected periods.[94] One could argue that these materials are less useful than lectures or student notes, since professors may have been considering what the Assunti would think of their outlines. While some of these syllabi are short and perfunctory, however, others are much longer and more detailed, enabling insights into how professors planned to approach various subjects in the classroom, whether or not they wished to introduce material from contemporary discussions, how many lectures they were due to give, how the course would be organized, and what textbooks or authorities they would use. Furthermore, some professors submitted very detailed plans year after year, which opens the door for a study of long-term developments. I have used these materials extensively to plug gaps in the evidence from lectures. Although I have benefited from Guido Vernazza's discussion of several of these materials, at times his treatment assumes that the longevity of a particular textbook signals curricular stasis—a point that needs to be treated critically.[95]

Less relevant for my study are the theses that students had to defend in public disputations in order to obtain their doctorate or student lectureships.[96] These are not informative about classroom practice, although they may offer a sense of what was of interest to students and their publics and how this changed over time. These materials have survived in fair numbers starting with the fifteenth century. (Extant disputations by professors date to the seventeenth and eighteenth centuries.)[97] Other scholars may wish to exploit them more systematically.

Outside of Bologna, the two most relevant collections are in Vatican City and Austin, Texas. The Vatican Apostolic Archive (AAV) holds some significant series of documents. The *fondo* AAV, Segreteria di Stato, Legazione di Bologna contains the letters (*expeditiones*) between the papal legate of Bologna (who often resided in Rome) and his representative in the city (or, alternatively, between the cardinal nephew and the papal representative).[98] Although the series is not complete (it skips from 1450 to 1550 and has several subsequent gaps; the documentation is more continuous from the seventeenth century to the end of the eighteenth), it contains information on a wide range of issues concerning Bologna, including the university. Many of the university-related documents concern the situation of individual professors.[99] Others address more general issues, including attempts to prevent students from attending the lectures of foreign teachers, complaints from university administrative staff, and student disorder and violence, particularly in the various colleges. Similar topics are present in the more general correspondence contained in the archive's Fondo Confalonieri, Fondo Borghese, Carte Borghese, and occasionally in the Archivio Boncompagni-Ludovisi.[100] One should also bear in mind that some of Bologna's (arch)bishops (such as

Gabriele Paleotti) had close ties with the university or in any case received instructions from Rome concerning the enforcement of the Tridentine decrees relevant to universities. The AAV is again an excellent starting point for this material, although not much of it has so far been properly catalogued or examined.[101] The Biblioteca Apostolica Vaticana holds some copies of Bolognese lectures (particularly those of Lodovico Boccadiferro; see §8.2.1), but also an important series of *relazioni*. These documents include reports for the Holy See prepared by papal representatives in Bologna and at times contain highly relevant information about the *studium*. Few scholars have used them to shed light on the Bolognese university.[102]

The most significant collection of Bolognese-related materials outside of Italy is at the Harry Ransom Center in Austin, Texas. In particular, its Ranuzzi Manuscripts collection (which was originally part of the famous library of Thomas Phillips) is of exceptional value for its Bolognese materials dating from the sixteenth, seventeenth, and eighteenth centuries. Not yet fully catalogued, the collection contains several relevant lectures and student notebooks, mostly unknown to scholars (see §3.1.2, §6.2.2, and §8.2.1).[103] Particularly important are those related to private teaching—still a little-studied feature of the Bolognese curriculum—although there are plenty of public lectures as well. But the Ranuzzi Manuscripts also contain various significant documents (some originals, others later copies) connected with the social, political, and administrative life of Bologna. These provide informative details on various aspects of the university, including student violence, colleges, rectors, and the powers (also over the university) accorded by the papacy to its representative in Bologna in the seventeenth century. In the future, scholars will need to make fuller use of this remarkable collection.

The holdings of Bolognese archives and libraries are so rich—and the guides describing them are often so sketchy—that I have used only a small fraction of them for this study. Plenty more remains to be explored, both there and elsewhere. Over the next few years I hope to publish some of the most significant documents collected for this study.[104] But other scholars will still have abundant material to discover. I can think of few Italian cities that make the task so pleasant.

Perhaps Bologna's *studium*, like the Italian universities more generally, will obtain the place it deserves among early modern universities.

Recent years have seen a flowering of research in this field, from the multivolume history of the University of Oxford to those of Salamanca, Leiden, and many other institutions, including those in German-speaking territories.[105] In Italy, studies of Padua have continued apace, as testified by the work of Piero del Negro and Francesco Piovan as well as the journal *Quaderni per la storia dell'Università di Padova.* Other significant results have appeared as well, partly thanks to the impetus of the Centro interuniversitario per la storia delle università italiane (CISUI, founded 1990), which has sponsored a major new history of the Italian universities and continues to influence the field through its book series "Studi" and its associated journal *Annali di storia delle università italiane* (1997–). The latter for many years dedicated special issues to specific Italian universities (though not, oddly, to Bologna). There has also been excellent new work on the University of Rome and several other centers, including Perugia.[106] The most eye-catching among recent publications has been the history of the University of Pavia, in four tomes (2012–2017, nearly 2,900 pages). In addition to the work's quality and new findings, the number and range of collaborators that Dario Mantovani was able to recruit is remarkable. Equally notable has been the ongoing effort to publish Pavia's documents.[107] The series "Fonti e studi per la storia dell'Università di Pavia" reflects an attention to the edition of sources that several other universities seem to have lost. Other scholars have chosen to study the early modern universities in a more thematic or comparative way, something that has been leading to some very promising results.[108] In a field that is currently so vibrant, I hope that a book on the intellectual features and contributions of the University of Bologna not only will be welcome but will also spark interest and further research.

Part I

The Institutional and Cultural Context

1

The Academic Community and Its Overseers

Medieval and early modern universities can be hard to picture from the standpoint of the twenty-first century, when universities instantly evoke associations with research, national ministries of education, and ties to business or philanthropic donations (not to mention sports facilities and conference centers). Nostalgic hankerings for "better times" can also interfere with one's perspective. This chapter focuses on two aspects that will help orient the reader's understanding of the University of Bologna and its culture of learning: the nature of the ties binding together both students and teachers, and the reconfiguration of structures of power and influence in the long period leading up to the eighteenth century. In the interests of brevity, I have not provided a detailed and comprehensive account of all organizational aspects of the university (including the functions of beadles and other officers). Instead, I have concentrated on the main actors within the academic community and its complex web of relationships. I see the evolving nature of these relationships as central to the dynamics of learning in Bologna. Thus, this chapter examines both students and professors and their interrelationships (§1.1 and §1.2) along with the civic, ecclesiastical, and papal authorities that made claims on Bologna's university and its curriculum (§1.3).[1] It concludes with some reflections on the shifting balance of power within the *studium,* and on how this affected the activities of teaching and learning in the faculty of arts and medicine. An important point is that many significant changes to the *studium*'s character started to take shape in the second half of the sixteenth century.[2]

1.1 Students

1.1.1 Student Governance, Power, and Privilege

Already from medieval times, students arriving in Bologna from afar had banded together in corporations or *universitates,* formed on the model of contemporary guilds, which provided mutual support and legal protection in a place where they initially (as foreigners) enjoyed no rights.[3] In Bologna these student corporations (*universitates scholarium*) took the shape of two *universitates* for the Legists (one each for students on either side of the Alps, thus referred to as *universitas citramontana* and *universitas ultramontana*) and one for the Artists. Each corporation was subdivided into areas of origin, or *nationes.* Particularly important among these was the German Nation (*Natio Alemanna*), many of whose members studied law.[4] Members of the Nations had to swear to observe the statutes governing their particular Nation, as Figure 1.1 illustrates in a rare representation of students making such an oath within the German Nation. The *universitates* and Nations did not include local students, who fell under the protection and jurisdiction of the commune.

Statutes of the *universitates* and Nations outlined student governance and guaranteed a number of privileges.[5] For arts and medicine, the earliest surviving statutes date from 1405, followed by some revised or added rubrics in 1442.[6] These documents have been at the center of scholarly attention for several decades, partly because of their remarkable length and detail and partly because other contemporary ones have not survived.[7] Also well known are the various rubrics in the commune's statutes from 1454 (and earlier years).[8] These address issues such as student housing and the students' right to buy grain freely and to be treated as Bolognese citizens.[9] Later student statutes, which have attracted far less

Fig 1.1. Students of the German Nation swearing to observe the statutes.

Bologna, Museo Europeo degli Studenti, ms. CS5431 (Statuta, Natio Germanica, 1497–1516), f. 2r. Photo © Alma Mater Studiorum Università di Bologna—Biblioteca Universitaria di Bologna.

attention, date from 1561, 1583, and 1609.[10] An additional set of relevant documents is the flood of *ordinazioni* and *reformazioni* that poured out of the office of the papal legate. Starting in 1586 under Enrico Gaetani, edicts concerning the university appeared every few years or decades (although generally with few changes) until the eighteenth century.[11] Although these documents do not focus on students specifically, they offer a helpful window onto the demise of student power and of the office of the rector in particular.

The Student Rector

Discussions of student power owe much to a long-standing distinction in the scholarly literature between the structural patterns of Bologna and Paris.[12] These have considered the former a "student university":

students were in charge of significant aspects of the *studium,* including the hiring and firing of professors, the regulation of their salaries, and the subjects to be taught. Paris instead was a "university of masters," in which student power was overshadowed by the authority of the professors, who held ultimate control. Tellingly, in Paris the rector was not a student, but a professor. Whatever the merits of this differentiation for the earlier period, by the fifteenth century at the latest change was definitely afoot in Bologna.

The 1405 statutes still support the notion of Bologna as a center of student power. They indicate that by far the most important position in the university was that of the student rector, regarded as the chief officer of the *studium.*[13] They suggest that the rector heard and decided both civil and criminal cases that might arise within the *studium,* whether the litigants were students, professors, or other staff (rubs. 21–30).[14] He could also levy significant fines for a number of various offenses or infractions. All the doctors teaching in the *studium* were to swear to him that they would observe the statutes (rub. 34).[15] The rector was thus a figure of authority who was expected to remedy any disorders that might arise within the *studium.* As such, he had to fulfill several eligibility criteria: for instance, he was to be of at least twenty-five years of age, to have matriculated in medicine, and to have studied the subject for at least two years (rub. 2).[16] Like other members of the *universitas,* he could only be a foreigner (i.e., someone who hailed from outside Bologna and its territories). The rector was elected annually (by four Nations, which took turns each year in casting their votes), although a vice-rector might be elected instead (rubs. 10–11).[17] At the same time, the Nations also elected nine student councillors (who served terms of three months each). At the end of a rector's term of office, four student syndics determined whether or not he had upheld the statutes (rub. 13).[18]

Over the course of the fifteenth and sixteenth centuries, however, serving as a rector became increasingly challenging. Because of its prominence, the rector's position was also expensive to maintain. He rubbed shoulders with the highest authorities in the city and began to appear at the head of the rolls of professors in the *studium,* charged also with the teaching of medicine on feast days (*diebus festivis*).[19] In recognition of the considerable expenses he incurred (including for horses, gifts, and clothing) in order to maintain the dignity of his office, he started to receive a modest allowance of some L. 100 per year.[20] Over time, however, fewer and fewer students wished to occupy a position that had become such a financial burden, and the authorities seem not to have responded to calls to fund the position properly.[21] The last sixteenth-century listing of a rector for the Artists in the teaching rolls came in 1557–1558, while the Legists had their last rector (appointed jointly with the Artists) in 1579–1580.[22] A final gasp came early in the seventeenth century, with the election (not recorded by the rolls) of Giovanni Domenico Spinola da Genova in 1604.[23] Other attempts to appoint a student rector encountered the opposition of either the legate or the civic authorities.[24] Technically, annual elections were still to take place, and the revised statutes still offered various instructions on the office of the rector.[25] The teaching rolls continued to reserve spaces for potential occupiers. But by the seventeenth century the office was well and truly dead, not just in Bologna but throughout Italy.[26] The beneficiary seems to have been the cardinal legate (see §1.3.3). Today, the office of *rettore* in Italian universities is held by a professor, who is the institution's president.

Other student officers appeared in the statutes, presumably to fill the void left by the rector's demise. In particular, the 1561 statutes outline the office of the prior, to be elected monthly from among the councillors, whose number has been raised to twenty-one.[27] The 1609 statutes give further attention to this new office. But the priors (charged with occupying the rector's position when it was vacant) evidently held little power: not only was each of them in office for only a month, but they could not even call a meeting of the *universitas* without the legate's consent. There was a longer term of office for the arts councillors, who served for a year each and whose number grew to thirty-seven in 1612.[28] The main mark that most of these student officers left on the *studium* was material, consisting in having their coats of arms painted on the Archiginnasio's walls and ceilings. Many of these still survive and are part of the appeal of visiting the structure today (see Figure 2.3).[29]

The fate of the rector's office was the culmination of a centuries-long decline in student influence and autonomy within the *studium*.[30] Already by the end of the thirteenth century, the commune had started assuming the responsibility of hiring and paying professors. This lent it increasing influence on the affairs of the *studium* and had clear advantages, such as the limitation of student power. Episodes of student violence gave the authorities an excuse to further affirm the need to provide a steadying hand.[31] But did the absence of a rector actually matter for Bologna's culture of learning?

Disorderly Students

The evidence on this point is clear. Although scholars have not given the matter much attention, documents from the late sixteenth century onward blame the lack of a student rector for numerous problems of discipline and attentiveness.[32] A flavor of this comes from the observations on the *studium* that Gabriele Paleotti (then bishop of Bologna) sent on 30 January 1577 to Giambattista Castagna, the incoming governor and papal representative of the city.[33] When he came to the behavior of students, Paleotti not only underlined their violence, tendency to vandalize the classrooms, and readiness to lampoon doctors and professors, but also made it clear that both lectures and university exercises were suffering:

> The students lack a rector or any other good leader, so they become more licentious and insolent by the day.
>
> When they are so minded, they put a stop to all lessons and are sometimes very discourteous to particular professors, purposely disrupting their lectures. . . .
>
> The manner in which Bolognese students argue their conclusions is both indecorous and unworthy of the honor of the *studium*.
>
> In the circular disputations, they take quick offense at any obscenity, lack of respect, or unworthy behavior; thus, an occasion that should be of great dignity has now fallen into disrepute.[34]

Significantly, the first of Paleotti's proposed remedies is therefore: "Ensure that a rector be appointed, a man of authority; when this takes place, he should be given a salary increase, and he should carry out his duties."[35] Paleotti's advice either went unheeded or was too hard to implement. The third quarter of the sixteenth century witnessed a rise in violence and transgression of social norms, as well as more sustained attempts by the authorities to regulate student behavior and encourage religious observance.[36]

As Bolognese students began losing even the vestiges of their autonomy, they also became more bellicose and disrespectful. The intervention of the police (*sbirri*) in 1560 to confiscate the weapons of a student who had insulted but eluded them the previous day gave rise to tumultuous riots, which ended badly when a brick thrown by one of the *sbirri* fell on and killed a Flemish student. In protest, the students left Bologna and made for Ferrara; it was only with great difficulty that the city authorities, having intercepted them on their way, persuaded them that the culprit had been punished, and their privileges would be respected if they returned.[37] The chronicles of the time are full of similar accounts, pointing to the readiness of an increasingly aristocratic body of students to take up arms against each other on the heels of a perceived offense or insult, as when, for instance, two groups of students encountered each other on the pavement and neither was ready to yield passage.[38] Such incidents led to numerous contemporary depictions of students as closer to being soldiers than scholars.[39]

Students also became increasingly insolent toward both their teachers and college staff, particularly when they were of lower social rank. On several occasions the Senate formally forbade them from banging on their desks or otherwise disrupting public lectures.[40] Such behavior, which was common across Italy at the time, may have been a means to help the student voice re-emerge from the silence to which it had been relegated. But it was not likely to help recruit the best teachers or promote good learning.

In the absence of a rector, the authorities' actions to address this climate of unruliness were ham-fisted and actually exacerbated the problem. Just one year after the Archiginnasio's inauguration in 1563, the appearance of poems (*pasquinate*) lampooning other university members and the papal representative gave rise to an investigation of Torquato Tasso (who was studying in Bologna), starting with the questioning of various witnesses. While proclaiming his innocence, Tasso thought it prudent to withdraw to Modena.[41] In 1581 the harsh measures introduced by the papal legate Pier Donato Cesi to tackle crime led to anonymous postings against him. Cesi demanded a trial in order to bring the culprits to justice.[42] These events and innumerable later proclamations by the Senate and the papal legate show that local authorities in Bologna tried to impose order by using the full force of the law, threatening (but usually not actually levying) hefty fines and punishments. This policy was utterly unsuccessful, in part because it was almost impossible to enforce.

Among the most important reasons for this difficulty were the students' privileges and forms of protection. The 1405 statutes—approved, one should not forget, by the students themselves—affirm various student privileges, such as the obligation for the archdeacon and the college of doctors to confer two doctorates for free (*gratis et sine solutione aliqua*) each year, one on a poor student in arts and another on one in medicine (rub. 21). Rubric 22 extends to students of arts and medicine an exemption from custom taxes on clothing and food, in an echo of similar privileges already accorded to the Jurists in 1417.[43] Furthermore, the statutes consider professors and anyone else connected with the *studium* to be subject to the student *universitas* (rub. 18). The 1561 statutes reiterate various privileges, while those for 1583 spend twenty chapters summarizing historic rights. Among them is the possibility for students nearing graduation to hold a paid junior lectureship (*lectura universitatis*) and to be exonerated from paying the usual (and expensive) graduation fees (§2.2.1).[44] Although it is not always clear to what extent the authorities observed these privileges, students had various means to voice their discontent. A favorite ploy was to decamp to another town in order to put financial pressure on Bologna, whose economy relied heavily on students. Over time, such moves had resulted in the establishment of rival institutions in several Italian cities, including Padua, Ferrara, Vercelli, Florence, Pisa, and Siena.[45] As a result, the Bolognese model could spread throughout central and northern Italy.[46] Students periodically deserted Bologna in the early modern period as well: in 1562, for instance, the German Nation decamped for some eleven years until it was satisfied, by the provision of new statutes, that its rights would be respected.[47] The documentation for the seventeenth and eighteenth centuries suggests that, even without a rector, students continued to appeal to their hard-won privileges whenever a reform threatened them. They also gained new ones—for instance, to bear arms and attend private lessons instead of public ones.[48] Conversely, the priors and councillors lacked the clout to discipline student behavior, so it was hard to control litigiousness and disrespect toward authorities.

Finally, the lack of a rector had implications for the delivery of teaching. It was not just that, according to the 1405 statutes (rub. 34), professors had to swear that they would observe the statutes. In fact, rectors could exercise a certain measure of supervision and control. Ordinary professors each had their own beadle, but this figure (who was approved by the rector) served as much a monitoring as an assisting function. For instance, part of his job was to verify that the professor in question was obeying the statutes and teaching the required *puncta* or examination passages (rubs. 63, 82, 84, 85).[49] Each year, the rector also appointed four students of arts and medicine whose function was to report any professors for infractions such as failing to show up on time to their lectures or not taking part in disputations (rub. 68).[50] Instances of students trying to exercise their muscle in this area reach to at least 1594, when they ordered the professor of humanities, Girolamo Bisaccioni, to desist from his teaching.[51] Their lack of success in this instance shows that, as the office of the rector disappeared, so did a strong incentive to deliver responsible teaching (see §1.2).

1.1.2 The Changing Student Body

In addition to becoming less influential, respectful, or attentive at public lectures, students in early modern Bologna were changing in other ways. Particularly relevant are developments such as aristocratization, the admission of women, fluctuating student numbers, regionalization, and study choice.

Social and Gender Composition

In terms of their social makeup, the student *universitates* became progressively aristocratic in early modern Europe.[52] In various nation states, such as the Netherlands, government offices came to be almost exclusively the preserve of nobles, for whom university training was as much a means of socialization for the elites as it was an opportunity to gain knowledge and skills.[53] It was no different in Italy, where the high costs of studying at university and obtaining a degree deterred the great majority of prospective students, but not young aristocrats. Institutions catering to scions of the nobility sprang up in Bologna as elsewhere, creating a competition of sorts with the *studium* (§3.3.3). The phenomenon also created significant problems within the university because the lack of discipline and deference had its roots partly in differences of social class and had a deleterious effect on the culture of learning.

Furthermore, although universities remained almost exclusively male bastions, they started to show signs of opening up to women. In 1608 the Spaniard Juliana Morell gained a doctorate in law at the University of Avignon. In 1678 a degree in philosophy went to Elena Lucrezia Cornaro Piscopia at the University of Padua.[54] In 1732 Laura Bassi in Bologna obtained a degree in philosophy.[55] The difference was that, in this case, the university graduate also became a professor (§2.3.3). Clearly, these are cases of exceptions proving the rule, and one should not become too fixated on them, not least because the publicity they received served the interests of those in power. Yet they point to some developments that were highly significant in later years.

Student Numbers and Regionalization

Whereas these points are uncontroversial, historians are deeply divided on the questions of student numbers and regionalization. Did the number of students drop in early modern Bologna and, if so, to what extent? How and when did Bologna lose its ability to attract foreign students? And what conclusions, if any, should one reach?

As Gian Paolo Brizzi has pointed out, it is a historiographical commonplace that, from around 1500 until around 1900, the Bolognese *studium* experienced an almost inexorable decline, both in terms of quality and of student population, leading to a university with a regional rather than an international outlook.[56] But conclusions are difficult due to problems of evidence and interpretation.[57] In fact, it is impossible to establish exactly how many students attended Bologna's *studium* and how much these numbers fluctuated over time. The reason is that matriculation lists for Bologna (unlike, say, for universities in England and central Europe or even some Italian ones) have mostly gone lost.[58] But even when they survive (as they do, discontinuously, for the Artists in the period 1593–1769 or, more continuously, for the Legists between 1553 and 1613),[59] they do not furnish a complete picture: matriculation was expensive, and therefore many students probably avoided the official route if at all possible. Other kinds of association (e.g., membership in a particular social class or Nation) in time came to be considered more meaningful than the protection offered by the student corporation. In any case, matriculation was not a requirement for attending lectures (although it was for graduating), and some categories of students were exempt or even forbidden from matriculating. These included students studying in the city's colleges, the clergy—an especially sizable category in the seventeenth and eighteenth centuries—and Bolognese citizens. A further complication is that some people matriculated with no intention of studying. Prince Ludwig of Anhalt, for instance, stopped in Bologna around 1599 and matriculated simply to avoid the attention of customs officials while transiting through the Papal State.[60] (Students were exempt from most customs charges.)

For a more complete source of information, one can turn to records of student doctorates.[61] In addition to the paper repertories, researchers can now avail themselves of the recently released database ASFE (Amore Scientiae Facti Sunt Exules), which incorporates and extends their data.[62] But one must be cautious about equating doctorates with actual student numbers: since it was expensive to graduate in Bologna, many students opted to hold their exams and graduation in a less glorious but also more affordable seat of learning, such as nearby Ferrara—a path certainly followed by Nicolaus Copernicus, among many others—or even Cesena, also known as "the university of the two hams" ("l'università dei due prosciutti") for its readiness to grant low-cost degree certificates. Also, the vast majority of students left university without obtaining a degree, which was necessary for only a very limited number of professions.[63] Famous examples include the poets Ludovico Ariosto and Torquato Tasso. Nonetheless, Brizzi suggests that student numbers in Bologna probably declined much more slowly than is commonly thought. Using the number of degrees as a guide, he suggests that there were three main phases: one of sharp growth (1500–1580); a second of relative stability (1580–1660), although affected by events such as the famine of 1630; and a last one (1660–1796) of decline—a phenomenon that was especially marked and precipitous after 1690.[64] Yet the methodological problems referred to above remain, making this framework less than secure.

As to regionalization, this may have occurred only gradually: 35 percent of degrees went to foreign students (i.e., those coming from beyond the Alps) in the sixteenth century, while the proportions for the following two centuries are 21 percent and 18 percent, respectively. Among the graduates from foreign lands, the bulk (48 percent) hailed from the Empire, while the rest came from Spain (25 percent) and from a number of small principalities bordering the Alps but also extending beyond them to Poland, Hungary, and Switzerland.[65] A notable element of this analysis is that, at least for the greater part of the sixteenth century, Bologna was still a major international destination for students.

Going beyond Brizzi's statistical analysis, one might look at different sources. For instance, observers in the seventeenth century and later often noted the decline in student numbers. This was a constant source of worry for the *studium*'s authorities, who endlessly debated how to put a stop to it. The report or *relazione* (c. 1611) of the papal legate Maffeo Barberini (later Pope Urban VIIII) photographs the contraction of student numbers in Bologna, placing them at around six hundred, of whom at most fifty or so were Bolognese.[66] (He makes no distinction between Artists and Legists.) In 1689 the archdeacon Antonio Felice Marsili, brother of the more famous Luigi Ferdinando, claimed that the number of matriculated students that year barely reached seventy (i.e., less than half the number of professors).[67] Marsili's account may not be trustworthy, given its polemical contexts; in any case, his specification of "matriculated" students is significant. But it receives some corroboration from an anonymous memorandum written in response to the archdeacon's *Memorie* by an alumnus of the university. He recalled in his (undated) piece that forty years earlier there had been hundreds of students, whereas that number had now dwindled considerably.[68] Despite the lack of hard numbers, these accounts suggest that numbers in the seventeenth century were in the mid-hundreds or less rather than, say, in the thousands. Unfortunately, the accounts I have seen of visitors to Bologna do not comment on university student numbers.[69] Secondly, the 1560s and 1570s must have already been a turning point in Bologna's difficulties to recruit internationally. Immediately after the German Nation's abandonment of Bologna in 1562–1573, rulers in Flanders and Milan imposed limitations on the freedom of their residents to study elsewhere, causing strong concern among the *studium*'s authorities.[70] And uncertainty about how the requirement for degree candidates to swear loyalty to the Catholic Church (*professio fidei,* 1564) would be applied doubtless kept some Protestant students away or drove them to other universities, such as Padua, where they were more welcome (see §8.1 and the Epilogue). Finally, in 1577 a wave of protectionism led the College of Arts and Medicine to forbid students from attending the lectures of foreign doctors. Due to pressure from Rome and the Senate, it quickly repealed the measure, but the damage was done.[71] The college had shown more regard for local professors than for the *studium*'s international reputation and appeal to students, who came from afar precisely to hear the most famous doctors, regardless of their origins. Missteps of this kind likely affected recruitment.

Despite all of these challenges, for the better part of the sixteenth century Bologna retained a strong international appeal, and numerous testimonies from the seventeenth and eighteenth centuries (including on the walls of the Archiginnasio and in *alba amicorum*) show that it continued to attract visitors and students, many of them on their Grand Tour, although perhaps in lower numbers than previously.[72] Certainly, developments in Bologna need to be seen in the context of what was happening elsewhere. Many universities throughout Europe experienced a decline in student numbers in the seventeenth and especially the eighteenth century.[73] (France seems to be an exception.) Especially relevant, however, is that European-wide trends were starting to favor a turn toward regional, rather than international, student mobility.[74] Already from the second half of the sixteenth century, German, Dutch, Polish, French, Flemish, Spanish, and English students increasingly attended universities close to them (both geographically and confessionally). As a result, the international student population in Bologna shrank, and the *studium* had to recruit from a much smaller, less diversified, and (one must assume) less ambitious and motivated pool of students. The colleges for nobles (see §3.3.3), which apparently continued to recruit well internationally, may have picked up some of the slack.[75] But this did not help the university, whose student population changed considerably during the early modern period, becoming more ecclesiastical and leading to different kinds of careers. The clearest example of this trend comes from the matriculation list for the German Nation, which registers 2,636 names (not always students) from 1573 to 1602, but thereafter registers no entries until 1707. For the following twenty years, only 139 names appear; these individuals came mainly from Italian-speaking regions of the Empire.[76]

As for what lay behind Bologna's loss of international appeal, one wonders about the validity of some conventional explanations. Scholars have probably been too quick to contrast the tolerance of Padua and Siena with the burdensome requirement of the *professio fidei* in the universities of the Papal State.[77] Although this oath of loyalty to the Catholic Church was doubtless off-putting to Protestants, it would not necessarily have prevented them from studying in Bologna. Rather more of

Table 1.1 Table of doctorates in Bologna by half-century, excluding complex combinations

	1500–1550	1551–1600	1601–1650	1651–1700	1701–1750	1751–1800
Overall number of degrees	1,956	3,870	3,719	2,148	1,176	1,134
Law degrees *in utroque iure*	888 (45%)	2,454 (63%)	2,656 (71%)	1,294 (60%)	572 (49%)	400 (35%)
Theology degrees	108 (5.5%)	252 (6.5%)	268 (7%)	128 (6%)	126 (11%)	150 (13%)
Degrees in arts and medicine	656 (33.5%)	965 (25%)	751 (20%)	716 (33%)	403 (34%)	476 (42%)

Degrees in arts and medicine calculated by adding together degrees in *artes, medicina, philosophia et medicina,* and *philosophia.*

Data source: ASFE database, http://asfe.unibo.it/it, accessed 28 July 2017.

a problem may have been Bologna's increasingly Catholic orientation and the Inquisition's suspicion of Protestants (see Chapter 8). An even more pertinent question is whether a perceived stasis in Bologna's curriculum was responsible for its straitened circumstances. Scholars have often assumed (not unlike university managers today) that a decline in numbers must reflect a waning cultural liveliness. As outlined above, however, there were multiple factors at work. Part II of this book shows that Bologna's intellectual climate continued to be vibrant and dynamic well into the early modern period.

Degrees and Their Appeal

Over the years, the choice of degrees pursued by students at Bologna changed. Willem Frijhoff has argued that across Europe, the predominance of the arts in the fifteenth century gave way to growth in theology, law, and medicine in the sixteenth, sixteenth / seventeenth, and eighteenth centuries, respectively.[78] Frijhoff's analysis gives little attention to Italy, but it is worth noting how different the patterns for Bologna are from his conclusions. The data in ASFE suggest that Bolognese degrees in medicine actually declined in the eighteenth century, while the majority of degrees continued to be in philosophy (i.e., arts) and medicine jointly.[79] Furthermore, while law contracted severely, both arts and medicine and theology expanded over the period (see Table 1.1). The teaching rolls of the seventeenth and eighteenth centuries confirm this shift, as law professors become a progressively small proportion of the academic staff (see §1.2).

1.2 Professors and Colleges of Doctors

As just outlined, the biggest draw of the Bolognese *studium* was the caliber and renown of its professors (often known as *lectores, magistri,* or *doctores*). In a world free of institutional rankings, what counted was not which university had conferred one's degree, but the degree itself (particularly if recognized throughout Christendom) and at whose feet one had sat. Bolognese authorities and students made this clear in their grand and intensely personal way of commemorating their professors. From an early date, they erected striking funerary monuments for the most famous professors, such as Rolandino de' Passeggeri (c. 1215–1300) and Giovanni da Legnano (c. 1320–1383). These mausolea were often placed in prominent positions—for instance, outside the churches of San Domenico and San Francesco—where they still remind passersby of the high status accorded to professors at the time.[80] After the inauguration of the Archiginnasio, students honored their professors through inscriptions or plaques on its walls.[81] Unlike the mausolea, almost all of which commemorate professors of law, many of the memorials decorating the Archiginnasio extol the merits of professors of arts and medicine, such as Agostino Galesi and Gaspare Tagliacozzi. This should not be surprising, for in the period covered by this study, arts and medicine reached new prominence and (as already noted) even came to overshadow law in some ways. The reasons for this development are tied to the cultural transformation of the university (discussed in Part II), but also to the strategies and patterns of teacher recruitment outlined here.

Although the practice of erecting prominent tombs for professors declined over the course of the fifteenth century, signs of their esteem remain. An especially notable such monument survives for a professor of arts and medicine in San Giacomo Maggiore, the church of the Augustinian Hermits in Via Zamboni. The tomb of Nicolò Fava, who died in 1439, stands well preserved in the church's apse (see Figure 1.2). Below the reclining figure of the professor is a typical representation of a classroom scene, with the teacher seated in the middle (book in hand) and

Fig 1.2. Tomb of Nicolò Fava (†1439).
Bologna, apse of San Giacomo Maggiore. Photo © David Lines.

students on either side. At the top of the monument is a statue of the Virgin Mary with Child, flanked by St. Nicholas (Nicolò's patron saint) to the right and St. Anthony to the left as well as two figures in the act of praying to them.[82] This monument makes a pair with the even more tasteful tomb (just a few feet away) of Anton Galeazzo Bentivoglio, a Bolognese political figure who taught civil law at least in 1418–1419 and 1419–1420 and was interred in San Giacomo in 1443. Again, the tomb reflects the style of monuments to professors. It may be the work of Jacopo della Quercia, and Ricci speculates that it may have been meant originally for a professor of arts and medicine, Giacomo de' Vari.[83]

1.2.1 Status, Numbers, and Mobility

Bologna's professors had several features in common. Like professors elsewhere in Italy, they were generally laymen, especially so in the fifteenth and sixteenth centuries, when the earlier practice of hiring members of the religious orders to teach subjects such as philosophy became increasingly rare (although members of the mendicant orders were in charge of teaching theology and allied subjects).[84] Usually they received time-limited contracts of three to five years, which could be renewed at the pleasure of the city authorities. There were no research contracts: a professor's main function was to attract and teach students. The absence of a pension system meant that professors usually taught until illness or death prevented them from fulfilling their duties. Nonetheless, professors enjoyed a high social standing and could become quite wealthy. The mausolea referred to above show that they were considered worthy of regal treatment. Representations of their dress make it clear that they were in the highest echelons of Bolognese society. This was still the case in the early sixteenth century, as testified by one of the few funerary monuments to survive from the period, that of the jurist Pietro Canonici (†1502) in the Museo Civico Medievale. One seventeenth-century account even placed professors ahead of senators and noblemen.[85]

Although professors had a high social standing, they were not necessarily trusted to meet their obligations. Numerous official proclamations betray, through the disproportionate punishments they threaten, a lack of confidence in the professors' readiness to follow the statutes or to fulfill the terms of their appointments. Thus, systems were in place to monitor their activities. In addition to the special beadles and student "spies" mentioned above, an important official was the *punctator,* who fined professors for infractions such as unexcused absences or not completing their announced lectures.[86] Observers also verified that professors had recruited a certain minimum number of students for their public lectures, as specified by the rolls (see the Appendix).

To appreciate the professors' position in the *studium,* one needs to understand how they were funded and how variable their salaries and numbers were. From the 1430s the professors' salaries came out of the Gabella Grossa, a tax imposed on all kinds of goods that were brought into, out of, or were transitioning through Bologna's territories.[87] The arrangement was not unusual: in Rome, for instance, academic salaries came from the tax on wine.[88] Yet it had the disadvantage of not being a predictable or constant source of income. Furthermore, the Gabella was not necessarily meant to fund only the professors' salaries: as the responsibilities of the committee administering it expanded, the tax also had to cover the salaries of various customs officers (*doganieri*) and the expenses to maintain Bologna's port and canals.[89]

The best sources regarding payments to teachers are the Riformatori's *Quartironi degli stipendi.*[90] These documents (extant for the years 1465–1796) register both a professor's yearly salary and the individual quarterly payments. They highlight some remarkable aspects of the *studium.* One constant point is the large disparities in salaries. For example, excluding teachers of grammar and arithmetic in the schools, the holders of the *lecturae universitatis,* and regulars teaching theology and allied subjects, in 1574–1575 the lowest-paid professors earned L. 100, whereas a prominent professor of philosophy (Federico Pendasio) earned over L. 3,428, a figure that rose to L. 5,000 by the end of the century.[91] This made for a much larger gap than in the early fifteenth century: in 1407–1408 minimum salaries hovered around L. 50 and the highest one (for the medical doctor Daniello da Santa Sofia) reached L. 1,280.[92] By the end of the seventeenth century, the earlier variance had become smaller: most professors earned between L. 200 and L. 300 annually, and the highest-paid professor (one Domenico Gualandi, who taught the *Codex*) received a mere L. 1,550. At L. 850, Giovanni Girolamo Sbaraglia (professor of *medicina theorica*) was the highest-paid teacher in arts and medicine.[93]

The reasons for this reduction lay partly in the fate of the special chairs reserved for foreigners. In the sixteenth century there were four *cattedre di eminente scienza,* the special chairs in civil law, humanities, philosophy, and medicine designated for those who were not Bolognese citizens.[94] One of these chairs was, in fact, occupied by Pendasio, who had been lured away from Padua and earned considerably more even than the Bolognese native (and academic star) Ulisse Aldrovandi, who in 1599–1600 was being paid L. 2,875, as opposed to Pendasio's L. 5,000. Over the course of the seventeenth century, the Bolognese authorities found it increasingly hard to recruit eminent foreign scholars to these chairs, and by its end they went unfilled. The rolls cease mentioning occupiers of these posts after 1645 (philosophy), 1653 (medicine), 1655 (law), and 1693 (humanities).[95] Furthermore, especially in the second half of the seventeenth century, the city authorities were making a special effort to contain expenses within the Gabella's budget by, among other things, imposing a hiring freeze for several years.[96] They were doubtless aware that foreigners were not the only ones responsible for generating high costs. Indeed, in earlier times it was not uncommon for a Bolognese citizen of particular fame to top the list of best-paid teachers: in 1509–1510, for instance, Alessandro Achillini was paid L. 900 for his teaching of natural philosophy and medicine.[97] Just a few years earlier (1504–1505), Filippo Beroaldo the Elder received L. 600 for his lectures on rhetoric and poetry, a figure matched only by the professors of medicine Achillini and Leonello Vittori, naturalized citizens.[98]

A professor's official salary might be only one of several streams of income.[99] Professors of medicine, for instance, could (like those of law) earn considerably more money through private practice. Girolamo Manfredi, whose teaching career in the second half of the fifteenth century encompassed both astrology and medicine, could count on additional revenue from his printing enterprises and property investments.[100] Even a professor of philosophy like Aldrovandi could expect fees from graduations and private teaching to boost his earnings.[101] Nonetheless, professors' frequent petitions for raises and the intense negotiations around salaries by prospective hires indicate that the size of one's salary mattered, and not just as a proxy for appreciation and status. For several professors of arts and medicine, it was probably their main source of income, to be supplemented perhaps by private teaching and renting rooms to students.

Salary levels for academics depended on a number of factors, including seniority and the ability to attract students, and the minutes of the Senate's meetings make frequent references to requests for pay raises on these grounds. It was therefore important to enjoy the favor of those in power, since it was the Senate that approved salary increments.[102] Other factors included the nature and prestige of one's subject, whether or not it was required for the degree, and whether or not one held a special chair. "Ordinary" teachings fetched more than "extraordinary" ones;[103] subjects taught only during the holidays were paid less handsomely than regular ones; and some subjects, such as theology and astronomy, tended to be remunerated poorly compared with others, such as philosophy and medicine. In fact, though, there were hierarchies also within specific subjects, such as philosophy and medicine: natural philosophy held pride of place over logic and moral philosophy, and practical medicine eventually came to be better paid than theoretical medicine.[104]

One reason for the fairly low salaries in theology was doubtless the occupiers' affiliation with a religious order.

In the seventeenth century, this model came under sustained pressure due to two main factors: Bolognese graduates' increasing sense of entitlement to academic posts and a concomitant mushrooming in the number of teachers (see §2.3). Accordingly, the authorities took steps to curb the growing numbers and simultaneously keep costs under control. Their actions gave rise to a heated row with the professors, lasting at least from 1689 to 1694. In the end the authorities had to scale back their intended intervention.[105] But they did manage to trim the number of professors on the rolls to just over a hundred between 1688 and the end of the century.[106] The rolls for 1750 list twenty-eight doctors for law and eighty-six (including nine *emeriti* in anatomy) for arts and medicine.[107]

The issue of the number of professors and their salaries was longstanding. In 1448 Pope Nicholas V gave precise instructions about salaries for professors in various subjects.[108] In 1450 he issued a privilege outlining how many professors the *studium* should have for its various subjects.[109] There is little sign that these instructions (though often referred to) were followed very scrupulously in later years, especially because that would have imposed a straightjacket on the *studium* and, through its rather low ceiling on salaries, prevented it from recruiting outside professors. Nonetheless, the question of how many teachers were needed was one that exercised both the authorities that approved salary payments and individual professors concerned about their effect on the quality of teaching (§2.3).

A thorny question remains that of mobility. Prosopographical studies have focused on students, so presently it is impossible to say with certainty what proportion of Bolognese professors were mobile and how many instead were original Bolognese citizens during the early modern period. Charles Schmitt, whose views were strongly informed by the situation in Padua, claimed that mobility among sixteenth-century teachers of philosophy in Italy was so great that it was impossible to form local philosophical traditions.[110] The evidence for Bologna, however, suggests that—already in the fifteenth century—senior professorships (at least in law) tended to be reserved for Bolognese citizens who were members of the college of doctors, and therefore had been citizens for at least three generations. And, whereas the civic authorities and the papal legate could strongly encourage the hiring of foreign professors, the doctoral colleges were significantly cooler toward this possibility, and in several cases actively opposed it.[111] In arts and medicine, the situation was rather more fluid: the teaching rolls indicate a fair amount of movement, with several professors coming from other universities (especially Padua) to Bologna, even though their stays might not always be lengthy.[112] The initiative of reserving chairs for eminent foreigners seems to have enjoyed some success, especially in the sixteenth century, before petering out, as explained above, in the seventeenth.[113]

There were multiple factors behind this turn of events. A lack of enthusiasm was not one of them, to judge by the frequency and intensity of the attempts by the Assunti di Studio to recruit eminent teachers from abroad, including Justus Lipsius, the famous Flemish scholar (§5.1). More relevant factors included the requirement of the *professio fidei,* which limited the pool of scholars available; initiatives of various states to found local universities and keep their learned men local; and an erosion of the financial and other incentives that had made it easier to recruit from outside Bologna. The consequences were serious, particularly as Bologna increasingly hired its own graduates and therefore reduced its ability to attract students from afar. Bologna's colleges of doctors were also partly responsible for the new state of affairs.

1.2.2 Colleges of Doctors

Professors were especially influential when acting as part of a college of doctors (*collegium doctorum*). These colleges had the status of permanent committees, with restricted numbers, and were composed of senior Bolognese university professors along with (in some cases) professionals. Each was headed by a prior (elected every few months), who among other responsibilities kept minutes of the meetings, which he wrote in the college's secret book (*libro secreto*). The Colleges of Civil Law, Canon Law, and Arts and Medicine (plus Theology) oversaw candidates' private examination for the doctorate.[114] The College of Arts and Medicine also regulated professional activities in town, ensuring that only local guild members, for instance, provided medical treatment in Bologna and its territories.[115] Because the colleges of doctors included the most respected academics and professionals in Bologna, they were often in dialogue with the highest authorities about matters concerning both the *studium* and the city. Members of the colleges dressed differently from the other professors.[116] Finally, from 1509 the colleges of doctors exercised a strong influence on the financial administration of the *studium* (see below).

Privileges

A few features of the doctoral colleges deserve comment.[117] First of all, given the requirement of Bolognese citizenship, their perspective could be painfully parochial and self-interested.[118] A case in point is the initiative (mentioned above) by the College of Arts and Medicine in January 1577 to forbid students from attending the lectures of foreign doctors. The College doubtless wished to deprive foreign professors of their minimum requisite number of students and therefore win more teaching positions for the Bolognese.[119] The Assunti di Studio, who immediately saw the dangers of such a move for the reputation of the *studium,* appealed to Gregory XIII and by February had the satisfaction of seeing the college's initiative quashed.[120] This was a rather rare defeat for a doctoral college, and in subsequent decades the doctors ensured that they tightened their grip on the *studium,* often to the detriment of the authority of the Senate and others. Already in 1601 the Bolognese ambassador in Rome was doubtful about the revised statutes of the College of Arts, which seemed to suggest that the Senate was not really in charge of the *studium.*[121] Controversies leading up to the eighteenth century indicate that the colleges were suspicious of the Senate's claims on the *studium,* particularly over decisions concerning salaries. In the course of a heated debate in 1689–1694 they even raised this matter with the papacy.[122] Thus, when their privileges were in question, the colleges could engage in a long-term war of attrition to affirm their rights. No target was too formidable: between 1744 and 1765, for instance, the legal colleges opposed Rome's initiative to block graduates of universities other than its own from holding various jobs in the city.[123]

The point about privileges is important, given that the colleges, like the student *universitates,* were eager to press them. They updated their statutes periodically and made sure to present them to Rome for confirmation. Many details about the extent to which the civic and papal authorities respected the prerogatives of the College of Arts and Medicine remain murky.[124] It is clear, however, that the colleges were keen to develop close ties with those in positions of power in order to protect and further their privileges. In 1714 the College of Arts and Medicine conferred an honorary doctorate on Prospero Lambertini (the future Pope Benedict XIV; see below) and made him a member of the college. By so doing the college was tying him to its side as a controversy developed about its members' eligibility to practice medicine in Rome.[125] The colleges were also rightly proud of the 1530 concessions of Charles V, who had come to Bologna to be crowned emperor and had honored them with the title of counts palatine. Among other honors, they received the privilege of conferring degrees acting as individuals rather than as members of the college.[126]

Governing the Gabella Grossa

One of the doctoral colleges' most important functions was managing the revenues destined to support the *studium*. Up to the fourteenth century, professors' salaries came out of Bologna's general accounts.[127] This arrangement was less than ideal because it meant that professors' salaries might be paid late or not at all, depending on other urgent expenses facing Bologna. In 1433 the papal legate Marco Condulmer and the city authorities reached an agreement (confirmed by a bull of Pope Eugene IV in 1437) that the professors' salaries should be taken from the Gabella Grossa—the customs tax, which at that time constituted a substantial portion of the city's income.[128] Nonetheless, the earlier problems persisted, to judge from the frequent protests by the colleges of doctors. The administration of the Gabella remained in the hands of the city authorities (specifically, the Difensori dell'Avere) for all of the fifteenth century, although the bulk of this revenue stream went to the *studium*.

Matters changed significantly in 1509, when a brief of Pope Julius II entrusted the administration of the Gabella to the doctoral colleges.[129] In this new arrangement, which remained in place until the end of the eighteenth century, the Congregazione della Gabella Grossa became its overseer. This body was formally dependent on the papal legate (who had to approve its accounts) rather than the Senate, and its members were either exclusively (1509–1603) or mainly (1603 onward) members of the college of doctors. At the start, six syndics (*sindaci*)—elected annually by the doctoral colleges of Civil Law, Canon Law, and Arts and Medicine—administered the Congregazione. Every two months, one of these syndics became prior of the Congregazione, a position that gave him authority over payments and exclusive access to the Gabella's archive. In 1515 six further doctors joined the Congregazione as *sopranumerarii* (and therefore not entitled to be priors).

The Senate opposed these arrangements, which removed a significant portion of Bologna's revenue from its control, and made repeated attempts to access the Congregazione's accounts and demanded that part of its funds flow back to the city.[130] The notional separation of the Gabella Grossa from the city's accounts was awkward because, although the Congregazione was in charge of the funds, it was actually the Senate that had to approve the quarterly disbursements of salary payments (*quartironi*) to the doctors and other staff. All of this made for strong tensions between the Senate (which saw its financial independence from the papacy as a strong symbol of the city's *libertas*) and the Congregazione. In 1603 a brief of Pope Clement VIII added seven senators to the Congregazione's membership in an attempt to settle mutual accusations and recriminations.[131] Because the Congregazione operated on the principle of a two-thirds majority, this meant that the Senate's representatives could in effect veto unwelcome initiatives. The papacy thereby took a soft and conciliatory line toward Bologna's civic authorities. Even so, tensions remained (and even mounted) in the seventeenth and eighteenth centuries. It did not help that, when the doctoral colleges thought their privileges were under threat, they took their case directly to the pope.[132]

In the sixteenth and seventeenth centuries the Gabella continued to derive most of its revenues (some 85 to 95 percent) from customs taxes, or more accurately from the annual fee paid to the Congregazione by the customs officer (*daziere*) to whom the whole business had been subcontracted. (The balance came from rent on properties owned by the Congregazione and from other minor sources.) Records show that this fee generated an increasing amount of revenue in the Cinquecento, from L. 31,000 in 1554 to the century's high-water mark of just over L. 79,000 in 1589.[133] Thereafter it tumbled to around L. 56,000 in 1596–1602, rising eventually (although nonlinearly) to L. 70,765 in 1669.[134] The last thirty years of the seventeenth century, however, saw a sharp contraction, reaching the lowest point in 1699 at L. 30,232, with only a very partial recovery thereafter. The economic changes behind this development are too complex to be outlined here.[135] What is most relevant is the *studium*'s increasingly limited budget. The number of *lettori* therefore fell from 130 in 1675 to seventy-four in 1689, following long negotiations with the Senate.[136]

Historians have regularly seen the doctoral colleges as the chief factor behind the universities' cultural decline in Italy.[137] It is certainly true that their resistance to change (particularly when it affected their privileges) did not favor attempts to reform the *studium*. Nonetheless, they were hardly the only members of the *studium* to defend their privileges with vigor. And, as I argue in Part II, they were not necessarily slaves to the traditional curriculum. In any case, their corporatism may have made professors in early modern Bologna increasingly conscious of their status as a specific professional class, as is evident from their relations with students, colleagues, and the public powers that appointed them and paid their salaries.[138] An oddity of their relationship with local power structures is that professors lacked the power to appoint members to their own guild, as was typical of most other corporations.[139] In any case, the following section shows that, from the middle of the sixteenth century onward, the increasing strength especially of the Senate and the papal legate came to limit the influence of the College of Arts and Medicine.

1.3 Civic, Ecclesiastical, and Papal Oversight

A live question during the early modern period was who had ultimate control of the Bolognese *studium*. In addition to students and doctors, the civic authorities, local ecclesiastical figures, and the papal sovereign and his representative all claimed jurisdiction in various ways, with consequences for the processes of teaching and learning.

1.3.1 The Senate and Its Committees

The Senate (also known in the fifteenth century as the Sedici Riformatori dello Stato di Libertà and in later centuries as the Reggimento) was Bologna's main legislative and executive body, with ultimate oversight over all aspects of the city and its territory.[140] Drawn from the nobility, the Senate wielded immense power and was, after 1506, the principal interlocutor with the papacy and its local representative on all kinds of issues, including crime, banditry, the economy, food shortages, religious observance, and the health of the city's cultural institutions.[141] It also saw it as its duty to defend and promote the city's fame as a center of learning; the minutes of its meetings and its correspondence with the Bolognese ambassador in Rome therefore make frequent references to the *studium*. However, rather than governing the university directly, the commune did so through its appointed committees. The most relevant here are the Riformatori dello Studio and the Assunteria dello Studio.

The older of the two committees was the Riformatori, originally (at its foundation in 1381) a committee of eight individuals whose membership changed yearly.[142] The Riformatori not only redacted and published the teaching rolls (which were posted publicly at the start of each academic year; see Figure I.3), but kept records about payments to each professor (the *Quartironi* mentioned above), noting any fines, such as those for unexcused absences.[143] The committee maintained an archive of documents relating to the *studium*. It provides a remarkably detailed view of its activities.[144]

Probably around the 1540s the Senate placed alongside the Riformatori another committee (called the Assunti or Conservatori dello Studio) to negotiate the hiring of professors and oversee various aspects of the *studium*. This committee also changed yearly. Unlike the Riformatori, its four members came from the Senate; often they had little direct experience of the *studium* and sometimes were even hostile to it. The Senate doubtless hoped that the Assunti dello Studio would offer a counterweight to some other associations closely linked to the *studium* and help extend its own authority in the city, as it was attempting to do through other (much better known) *assunterie* and through membership in confraternities and charitable institutions.[145]

Significantly, the city authorities never gave the Riformatori or the Assunti ultimate control over the *studium*. Although they exercised day-to-day administrative oversight of it, their deliberative power was strongly circumscribed. The Riformatori, for instance, could not simply move a professor's teaching from one hour or lesson to another without the Senate's consent. And the Assunti, who were heavily involved in the recruitment of professors (and negotiation of their salaries), had no final say over the conditions of an offer. It was the Senate that decided the terms of specific hires, any changes to teaching arrangements, and whether or not to remit fines for absences from teaching. It also continued to discuss individual raises, although after 1567 that was supposedly a matter for the doctors who managed the Gabella.[146]

There was good reason for the Senate's direct involvement in the life of the *studium*. Beyond the obvious economic and cultural reasons that made it important for the university to flourish, there was the *studium*'s political resonance. Because doctors who did not come from the noble classes were excluded from a progressively aristocratic government, the university gave them a channel for affirming and exercising their privileges. The local printing of the Theodosian Privilege in 1491 with the commentary of the famous jurist Lodovico Bolognini is a sign—according to Angela De Benedictis—of the doctors' readiness to affirm their influence in the city. But this was something that often clashed with the interests of the Senate, which therefore saw its oversight of the *studium* as a way of containing the colleges of doctors.[147] As noted in the Introduction, the city and the *studium* were strongly interlinked through Bologna's reputation as a *mater studiorum*. But members of the university and the Senate both liked to think that, through their involvement, they could also share somewhat in the *libertas* that it represented.

The officers, committees, and associations mentioned above had competing and overlapping areas of competence, so much so that their respective jurisdictions over Bologna's *studium* are hard to pin down, even though some of them are outlined in the statutes. To complicate matters, how the Bolognese *studium* organized its teaching was not simply an internal affair, to be settled by members of the university and the Senate. It also involved ecclesiastical and papal control.

1.3.2 Ecclesiastical Control

The easier of the two to manage was local ecclesiastical control, in the form of the archdeacon and of the (arch)bishop. The archdeacon (who was nominated by the pontiff and served as the university's chancellor) had been given a role in the *studium* from an early date in order to guarantee the quality of the degrees conferred.[148] Much like chancellors in British universities today and presidents in American ones, he conferred degrees but did not ascertain the candidates' suitability.[149] He was not always present in person and might delegate certain functions (such as the laudatory oration) to others.[150] In earlier times he had occasionally been a professor or even a member of the college of doctors, but in the early modern period his authority was overshadowed (not to say nullified) by that of the doctoral colleges. He played no significant role in the *studium*'s local oversight. When, in the late seventeenth century, the archdeacon Antonio Felice Marsili complained about the erosion of his prerogatives of office, his points may have been technically true, but the passage of time made such protestations pointless.[151]

For his part, Bologna's bishop (from 1582, archbishop) had no official connection with the *studium.* In most other Italian universities the bishop functioned as the *studium*'s chancellor.[152] But this was not the case in Bologna, although on occasion he was named *conservator* of the privileges of the *studium.*[153] Given his eminence of office, a bishop could wield considerable cultural influence, as Niccolò Albergati did in fifteenth century.[154] But from the sixteenth century onward only two (arch)bishops took any evident interest in the *studium*'s affairs. Both of them were local men. The first was Gabriele Paleotti (1522–1597), whose influence derived in part from the important role he played within the Council of Trent (he wrote several of the decrees in the last few sessions) and his close contacts with and offices in Rome, where he belonged to the Congregation of the Council. Indeed, for many years he resided in Rome although at the same time he headed the Bolognese diocese. Paleotti was very involved in the Bolognese cultural and religious scene and had close ties with many of the doctors in the *studium,* both as an alumnus and as a past professor of law; he counted as his friends eminent teachers such as Ulisse Aldrovandi and Carlo Sigonio. He sanctioned or possibly helped establish a religious group (the Congregazione della Perseveranza) that promoted piety and good morals among both students and professors (§8.1). The second archbishop (1731–1754) was Prospero Lambertini, who maintained this office during the first years of his pontificate as Benedict XIV (r. 1740–1758). Lambertini not only was keen to support the *studium* in various ways, but also promoted the cultural life of his native city more generally—for instance, by showering the Istituto delle Scienze with scientific instruments and books (§8.3).

The Congregation of the Council in Rome also exercised a form of religious control. This Congregation was set up in the wake of the Council of Trent in order to clarify and enforce its decrees.[155] It kept an extensive correspondence with interested parties from all over the world (but especially with religious orders), clarifying the application of the

Council's decrees to their particular situations. The Congregation's remit extended to the universities of the Papal State (see §1.4).[156] The relevant archive has not yet been properly inventoried, so it is unclear to what extent this was a major preoccupation.[157] But it is likely that Rome appealed to the Council's decrees especially when they helped advance its temporal control over Bologna and other territories.[158]

1.3.3 Papal Control

Over the course of the centuries, several popes took a strong interest in Bologna's *studium*. The Holy See significantly influenced the development of the *studium* at critical junctures before 1400.[159] Thereafter, four moments are especially important. Between 1416 and 1420, Martin V issued a number of bulls in favor of the doctors and students in Bologna, ensuring a reversal of the crisis experienced by the *studium* in the first fifteen or so years of the century (largely due to the reign of John XXIII). Martin also shored up the reputation of the Collegio Gregoriano, established in the previous century by Gregory XI.[160] Furthermore, as already noted (§1.2.1), in 1448 and 1450 Nicholas V issued two particularly important bulls relating to the Bolognese *studium*. (The first of these, *Inter curas multiplices,* dealt with salaries, whereas the second, *Inter varias,* concerned the number of professors and what they should teach). For the sixteenth century, the most notable example is Gregory XIII (r. 1572–1585), whose personal experience of the *studium* (where he had studied) sometimes led to a rather *dirigiste* approach, although at the same time he strongly favored his own educational institutions in Rome.[161] Finally, in the eighteenth century Benedict XIV took a decided interest in all of Bologna's cultural institutions, including the *studium* (see above).

In many cases, popes' involvement in the *studium* went well beyond formalities such as the confirmation of its statutes. Popes proposed and approved candidates for teaching positions, tried to enforce teaching contracts, put forward names for the colleges of doctors, tried to resolve conflicts internal to the university, and attempted to influence its offices, such as that of the rector.[162] Although such initiatives could meet with considerable local resistance, they were part of a broader strategy of affirming papal power over local contexts.[163] This did not necessarily involve reducing the potency of local spiritual and civic institutions, however: the papacy was adept at allying itself with one section of power holders in a city against others, in a classic strategy of "divide and conquer." In particular, the papacy tried to keep members of the Senate onside, not least by making precarious (and therefore subject to its own continued support) the position of patrician families within the governing body.[164]

The pontiff exercised both his spiritual and temporal sovereignty on Bologna through his representative (a governor, legate, or vicelegate).[165] This figure in effect governed the city on the sovereign's behalf, with increasing independence from Bologna's civic authorities, even though theoretically (according to the arrangements of "mixed government") any political decision required the Senate's consent.[166] This progressive dominance is clear from the legate's powers *in temporalibus et spiritualibus,* whose extent only grew in the early modern period, and which often included authority over the university.[167] Furthermore, as outlined above, especially from the sixteenth century onward the legate had the power to approve or not the accounts of the Congregazione della Gabella. It is true that there were often more pressing challenges to address (including banditry, civil strife, and food shortages).[168] Yet the legates' correspondence with the papal nephew does often highlight the problems of the university, as does the series of proclamations issued by the legates on the *studium.*[169] Furthermore, while the 1454 municipal statutes conferred the position of *conservator* of the *studium* to the Bolognese *podestà,* by the end of the sixteenth century the papal legate is often named as the *protector* of the student universities.[170] Around 1741 the cardinal legate assumed the title of rector.[171]

Two figures eloquently exemplify the role of the legate in the life of the *studium.* First, Cardinal Basilius Bessarion (legate from 1450 to 1455), must have been responsible for implementing the 1448 bull of Nicholas V relative to the *studium* and for the promulgation of his second bull (1450), outlining how many professors were necessary in the *studium* and what they should teach (§1.2.1). He also intervened on numerous occasions in the payments of professors.[172] In 1452, for instance, he allocated an exceptional payment of L. 1,000 to Gaspare Ringhiera, professor of civil law.[173] His tenure also saw the promulgation of new communal statutes in 1454 (including rubrics on the *studium,* as noted above) and a flourishing of letters.[174] Bessarion's secretary was the humanist Niccolò Perotti, who also taught rhetoric and poetry in the *studium* from 1451 to

1453.[175] The documentation is fuller for Pier Donato Cesi, who was vice-legate (and then governor) in Bologna in 1560–1565 and legate in 1580–1583.[176] Cesi had a complex relationship with the *studium* and its members. He was proactive in extending his program of architectural renewal to the university buildings, an initiative that had led to the inauguration of the Archiginnasio by October 1563 (see §2.1). Some, including Gian Paolo Brizzi, have ascribed a strong political valence to this intervention, noting that it was a means for the pontiff and his representatives to exercise stronger control over the institution.[177] In any case, Cesi proved a divisive figure: the costs of building the Archiginnasio were charged to the Gabella Grossa, thus suspending pay raises and constraining the growth of the *studium* for several years.[178] He approved a reform of the student statutes in 1561 (see §1.1.1), but his harshness (especially against students from Protestant lands) deeply worried the Bolognese authorities and led to violence, protest, and a long student exodus.[179] He was doubtless behind a deliberation of the Senate (29 August 1561) that established that there should be one hundred ordinary lectures in every academic year—a point often recalled by later documents, but that probably did nothing to endear him to professors (see §2.3). As legate, Cesi exercised his rights by conferring a doctorate in arts and medicine on one Ottaviano Ottaviani of Assisi.[180] It is unclear whether, by so doing, he was issuing a warning to the college of doctors or simply doing a favor to someone from his family's region.

The extent to which papal legates influenced teaching remains unclear. Certainly, their self-perceived role in the regulation of teaching activities is evident from their numerous proclamations on general and more specific practices in the university.[181] But they do not seem to have prohibited professors from teaching specific topics or books, although some (such as Maffeo Barberini) toyed with the idea.[182] In fact, their role seems to have been highly variable depending on personal ambition and the presence of any simmering tensions involving the university. On several occasions, legates showed themselves to be culturally progressive. It is tempting to link the lectureship in Greek that started in 1455 (and was assigned to Lianoro de' Lianori) to Bessarion's legateship.[183] Cesi promoted the hiring of some famous professors such as Carlo Sigonio. The introduction of teachings in Hebrew, Arabic, and Chaldean (as well as in theology and metaphysics *in via Scoti* and *in via Thomae*) was ordered by the legate Giulio Sacchetti in 1639.[184] In the early eighteenth century, the papal legate—unlike the Senate and the doctoral colleges—welcomed Luigi Ferdinando Marsili's farsighted cultural initiatives and facilitated the creation of the Istituto delle Scienze (§3.2.4).

Over the early modern period, a messy overlap of jurisdictions could lead to significant tensions, with consequences for the university. The legate, for instance, could step on the toes of both the Senate and the (arch)bishop, whereas the doctoral colleges could antagonize the papacy and the Senate.[185] Two significant episodes within the life of the *studium* illustrate this instability.

In April 1583 Gabriele Paleotti received a letter from Filippo Boncompagni (the cardinal nephew to Pope Gregory XIII), passing on a request by the Congregation of the Council for a report on the Bolognese *studium.* The Congregation was seeking information on a number of points, including the *studium*'s statutes and the observance of Trent's decrees concerning university teaching.[186] The letter resulted in a major diplomatic incident because the Senate saw itself as the only legitimate overseer of the university and therefore as the only one to whom such a request should be directed. After a series of negotiations, Boncompagni sent a separate request to the Senate, and it was agreed that both the archbishop and the Senate should compile and send a report to Rome. These dossiers, delivered in October of the same year, involved canvassing the colleges of doctors and representatives of the students, as well as seeking counsel from the Bolognese ambassador in Rome, who was in close contact with the pope. The documents testify to the Senate's distrust of Rome's interference with the *studium* and to a temporarily more prominent role given by Rome to the archbishop.[187] They also show how ready the pope was to intervene in the life of the *studium.* In sum, the events of 1583 involved nearly all of the major actors of the *studium* and point to real ambiguities as to who could claim ultimate oversight. The only major official absent in the saga is the papal legate Cesi, perhaps because he was on his way out (he resigned from office in September 1583) and because the strength of Gregory XIII's ties with Bologna stood in the way of a full exercise of his powers as legate.[188] But other legates after him more than made up for his invisible part in this situation.

Another episode of note relates to the second half of the seventeenth century: from 1660 onward, the Assunti tried to find a solution to the problem of the exuberant number of professors on the rolls, but found their way blocked by the colleges of doctors, who insisted on the rights of Bolognese graduates to be offered lectureships. In conversations with the pope they had even raised the prospect of recalling the Senate's authority to appoint professors.[189] Nonetheless, the ambassador's interviews—first with Pope Alexander VII and then with his successor Clement IX—gave the Senate some assurance that the papacy would be favorable to reform: as a result, it issued a decree in 1668 (renewed in 1676), in essence establishing a two-year probation period for new appointees.[190] Both the tenor of the decree and delays in salary payments led the professors to protest. The legate championed their cause and in 1678 emphasized his mandate to deal with the professors. Both parties (the Senate and the professors) lobbied hard in Rome for their own position. The question dragged on for several years and became mixed up with a controversy that had arisen in the meantime with the Archdeacon Marsili (who had proposed unwelcome changes to the university; see §2.3.3). The students threatened to abandon Bologna because the various disagreements had led to a suspension in awarding degrees and in hiring professors. They suggested that they might raise their concerns with the pontiff directly. The new pope, Innocent XII, accused the Senate of mismanagement of the Gabella, but in the end recognized its right to appoint professors; as a result, in December 1694 the Senate withdrew its 1668 decree.[191] The original problem remained unsolved, despite new limits on the salaries and numbers of professors. Furthermore, instability dogged the *studium* for years to come: since the question of respective privileges had not been addressed, the colleges of doctors, the students, the Senate, and the legate would spend considerable energy guarding their respective claims and privileges and appealing to Rome if they were not altogether satisfied. This perfectly suited the papal sovereigns, who saw such disquiet as an opportunity to extend their sphere of influence in Bologna. As a result, political considerations dictated that the balance of power with regard to the *studium* should remain inherently unstable.[192]

The outcome of the situation was an institutional impasse in which no single interest group was able to impose itself. As noted above, in 1603 Pope Clement VIII decided to remove the management of the Gabella Grossa from the sole hands of the colleges of doctors. The ensuing years led to strong tensions between the colleges and the Senate, neither of which managed to exert absolute control on the Gabella.[193] As a result, very little changed. In the eighteenth century, when Lambertini was both pope and archbishop of the city, he nonetheless had to bow to the papal legate (who derived his own authority from him as pontiff!) in various matters concerning the city. The impasse over questions of supremacy thus bedeviled the *studium,* and many of its members and overseers pulled in opposite directions.[194] It was not a situation that favored long-term planning, decisive action, or consideration of what would be helpful to the university as a whole. Nevertheless, as Chapter 2 illustrates, institutional logjam did not necessarily result in curricular immobility. In fact, across the early modern period substantial changes took place in the realm of teaching and learning.

2

Teaching and Learning

Around 1564, Ulisse Aldrovandi (1522–1605)—one of Bologna's most famous doctors of arts and medicine—wrote one of the several memoranda he penned during his lifetime on teaching practices in the *studium* and how he thought these should change.[1] These *Avvertimenti e considerazioni sopra i Rotoli delli dottori artisti bolognesi* (*Points and Reflections on the Rolls of Bolognese Doctors of Arts*), probably addressed to the overseers of the university, give an insight, not only into Aldrovandi's self-interest in seeking a teaching slot all to himself (he suggests that his specialist teaching of fossils, plants, and animals will benefit "everyone in the *studium*"), but also into the university's shifting timetable of classes and its new configuration of learning. Several subjects had made their appearance only recently. These included, at the very least, his own course of medical botany (or "simples"). Moral philosophy, which had long been a feature of university teaching as a feast-day subject, had resurfaced in 1562 after a long hiatus and had become more regular. Other changes included designations for mathematics and anatomy independent from astronomy and surgery, respectively. Furthermore, theology and, later on, Sacred Scriptures appeared consistently in the rolls (see Table 2.3). For the university curriculum, it was a heady period of change.

This chapter outlines the curricular features of arts and medicine at the University of Bologna. Because of the changes just referred to (as well as many others), one needs to start with—but then set aside—the student statutes of 1405 (see §1.1.1), which have been the foundation of practically all treatments of Bologna's curriculum of arts and medicine. For, despite the continuity of various requirements, structures, practices, and even official textbooks throughout the early modern period, much more was changing than one might think. Although the 1405 statutes are rich in detail and remain an important reference point, it is unclear how current they were when they were published or to what extent they were observed in practice. The fact that they are unique in fifteenth-century Italy for the information they provide means that historians have relied on them too strongly. Fortunately, several other sources—such as teaching rolls, lectures, and lecture plans—provide helpful insights into how teaching in arts and medicine evolved.[2] Here I will use all of these in combination. After discussing the particular structural features of the Bolognese *studium* (§2.1), this chapter outlines the curriculum c. 1400 and some features of its development in subsequent centuries (§2.2). It concludes by exploring how reform initiatives attempted to address a series of challenges within the *studium* and to what extent they were successful in doing so (§2.3). I hope it will become clear that—although many aspects stand in need of further research, particularly for the seventeenth and eighteenth centuries—one should not think of the Bolognese system of teaching and learning as being very close to, or faithful to, that described in the 1405 statutes.

2.1 Structures, Features, and Places of Study

Bologna's main organizational structures require a brief explanation, since they make for a marked contrast with northern European universities such as Paris and Oxford.[3] There the arts faculty was foundational for all students, who learned the seven liberal arts and philosophy before proceeding to the study of civil law, canon law, theology, or medicine. (Not all of these higher subjects, of course, were available at all universities.) In Paris the strongest of the faculties was theology, but arts was a close second. Theologians exercised considerable influence on arts teaching. (This was partly because many students on their way to earning a higher degree in theology supported themselves by teaching philosophy.)[4] Indeed, Paris was the scene of several condemnations of arts teaching in the thirteenth century (1210, 1270, and 1277): on these occasions, either the bishop or the papal legate held that certain textbooks or teachings conflicted with the tenets of faith.[5] Furthermore, although arts had emerged quite early as a separate faculty, the vast majority of students were clerics in both Paris and Oxford—so much so that Oxford's university has been described as an "ecclesiastical institution."[6] A second important feature of the Parisian model was that it offered a graduated curriculum. Not only was there a marked progression from arts to other subjects, but within arts there was an agreed-upon ladder of studies: certain subjects needed to be studied and examined before one could proceed to others. As a result, the statutes were very specific about what should be learned at each degree stage (bachelor's, license, and master's).[7] This system of graduated learning continued to be highly influential in the early modern period. Most notably, it was adopted by Ignatius of Loyola and his followers (who had experienced it directly as students) as a model for the Jesuit colleges that sprang up across Europe, Asia, and the Americas after the foundation of the Society of Jesus in 1540.[8]

On many of these points, Bologna's structures were quite different. First of all, the northern European faculties did not have a precise counterpart in Bologna, where originally there were no faculty statutes. Indeed, for Bologna it is more helpful to think of programs of study rather than faculties.[9] Secondly, Bologna had only two such programs in the strict sense—one of civil and canon law and another of arts and medicine. These were parallel structures and represented (at least notionally) equal but different areas of teaching and learning. Significantly, there were separate teaching rolls for each of these areas. But civil (and also canon) law in fact commanded particular respect in Bologna and from early on played a dominant role. Medicine and (later on) the arts developed and received recognition more slowly. Crucially, arts and medicine formed a single program of study; the statutes for the college of medicine included arts already from their earliest surviving version (1378).[10] This made for a continuous course of study leading from grammar and rhetoric through philosophy and astrology to medicine. There were, however, no intermediate points of assessment or examination: the statutes of the college of arts and medicine (like those of law) envisioned only the terminal degree (*doctoratus*), so in effect there was no means of ensuring that a student followed a particular, graduated *iter* of studies as in Paris. Before being examined for the degree, a student needed only to show that he was matriculated, of good morals, had studied for the requisite number of years, and was considered ready by his academic sponsor (*promotor*).[11] (Later on, a declaration of religious loyalty or *professio fidei* also became a requirement.) The degrees conferred were in arts, medicine, or (quite often) both, although there are also occasional examples of degrees in more specific subjects.[12]

Another key difference is that Bologna had a lay orientation: its main purpose was to produce professionals in law and medicine, so for a long time there was no regular teaching of theology (§8.1). Nor was there a tradition in Bologna of theology students teaching arts subjects. Rather, arts teaching was in the hands of degree-holders in arts and/or medicine. The culmination of the arts curriculum was, if anything, medicine, not theology. This explains the rather secular orientation of both philosophical teaching (logic, natural philosophy, moral philosophy; note the marginal role of metaphysics) and astrology.[13] As a result, theology initially had less prominence than other subjects in the Bolognese *studium*.[14] Indeed, whereas both law and arts and medicine had their own teaching rolls, theological subjects (including *sacra scriptura* and metaphysics) appeared on the rolls for arts and medicine.[15] This was a practical expedient due to the lack of independent rolls for theology in Italian universities. Although Bologna did have, from 1364, a "faculty of theology," once again this indicated a disciplinary field along with an examining board for awarding degrees in the subject.[16] It was not a faculty in a strong sense. For a long time, theology teaching took place exclusively in the town's religious *studia,* where Dominicans, Franciscans, and Augustinian Hermits were among the most active.[17]

There is the danger, however, of underestimating the role theology played in the Bolognese curriculum, as a long scholarly tradition has done. First, several professors there had more than a passing interest in theology (one example among many is the famed professor of medicine Alessandro Achillini), and religious considerations could strongly color the teaching of subjects such as humanities and philosophy (see

Chapter 8). Furthermore, theology's importance rose during the second half of the sixteenth century. In time, theological subjects came to be taught in the *studium* itself and gained large numbers of teachers and, presumably, students (see §2.2.2 and §8.1). One could even say that they eventually dwarfed the other subjects. In other Italian universities (for instance, in Padua), theology's place was strong throughout the period.[18]

Apart from minor subjects, arts and medicine in Bologna therefore included five main areas of teaching and study: rhetoric and *humanae litterae,* including not only Latin but languages such as Greek and sometimes Arabic; astrology and mathematics; philosophy (with its main branches of logic, moral philosophy, and natural philosophy); medicine; and (starting at least in 1566) metaphysics, theology, and Holy Scriptures.[19] Curricular structures had thus expanded significantly from the early medieval programs of the *trivium* (grammar, logic, and rhetoric) and *quadrivium* (arithmetic, geometry, music, and astronomy). Some of these subjects were tackled in pre-university education, while others were left behind. Music did not have a place, although the 1450 bull of Nicholas V auspicated its presence: in 1451–1452 a *lectura musicae* appears on the rolls, but the name of the post holder is erased, and the subject never reappears.[20] Other areas now considered integral to university teaching—such as chemistry and engineering—became part of the curriculum only much later (see §2.3).

For teachers, the five fields just mentioned represented separate career tracks. In several northern or central European universities, a professor might indifferently teach subjects such as rhetoric, mathematics, and natural philosophy. In Italy the barriers between the various areas of teaching were invisible but pronounced, and with the passing of time specialization made them more evident.[21] From a student perspective, however, matters were more seamless: as long as a master agreed to teach a student (and as long as the latter paid), there was no impediment to taking whatever classes one liked. There was a limitation only in terms of expected previous knowledge in some cases (since medicine, for instance, assumed a grounding in natural philosophy). Law students were often keen to hear arts lectures, particularly by renowned professors in the humanities such as Filippo Beroaldo, or to attend anatomical demonstrations.

There is less evidence as to how long students' courses of studies lasted. A full course of study in philosophy probably took three years, and one in medicine took four, to judge from the way in which teaching was organized. But a lot depended on what one had studied before going to university, and there was considerable pressure across Europe in the sixteenth and seventeenth centuries to abbreviate the length of degree courses. The evidence for Bologna is scant because students did not necessarily matriculate, and in any case those records are neither continuous nor reliable.[22] Furthermore, historians are agreed that the vast majority of students did not attend university with the aim of graduating.[23]

Despite the fluidity of the curriculum, in terms of status (and therefore of funding and staffing) not all subjects were equal. Three subjects dominated Bologna's teaching of arts and medicine in the fifteenth and sixteenth centuries: medicine, natural philosophy, and rhetoric between them accounted for some 87 percent of the faculty's salaries and for the bulk of the teaching staff. At this point in time, natural philosophy could sometimes even come close to challenging medicine in terms of the salaries it could offer and its number of staff, whereas rhetoric and the humanities were almost always distant contenders.[24] This situation changed between 1600 and 1750. Medicine remained the most important discipline, but philosophy started losing ground, especially to theology and mathematics (see §6.1.2 and §8.1). Significantly, the proportion of theology degrees nearly doubled during the period (see Chapter 1, Table 1.1).

Another distinctive feature of Bologna concerned the location of teaching. Unlike in Paris and especially Oxford and Cambridge, where students increasingly received instruction in their own colleges, in Bologna classes initially took place in hired rooms scattered throughout the town. By the end of the thirteenth century, there were well-defined neighborhoods for students of law (who tended to have their classes in the area immediately to the south of the basilica of San Petronio, in the quarter of Porta Procula) vis-à-vis those of arts and medicine (located immediately to the west of San Petronio, in the quarter of Porta Nova, roughly between San Francesco and Piazza Maggiore; see Figure 2.1).[25] Students of canon law seem to have met originally in convents.[26]

In the mid-fifteenth century the buildings behind and to the southeast of the basilica of San Petronio (i.e., along the portico presently facing Piazza Galvani) became home to several classrooms.[27] In 1561 the papal

LEGEND:

1 Palazzo dell'Archiginnasio
2 Basilica of San Petronio
3 Piazza Maggiore and Palazzo Maggiore
4 Convent of San Salvatore (district of Porta Nuova)
5 Convent of San Francesco
6 Convent of San Domenico
7 Collegio Montalto
8 Nuns of Corpus Domini
9 Collegio di Spagna
10 Santa Lucia (Jesuits)
11 S. Giovanni in Monte
12 S. Stefano
13 Santa Maria dei Servi (Servites)
14 San Giacomo Maggiore (Augustinian Hermits)
15 Ruins of Palazzo Bentivoglio
16 Palazzo Poggi (later, Istituto delle Scienze)
17 Cathedral of San Pietro

Fig 2.1. Map of Bologna by Joan Blaeu, 1663 (detail).

Joan Blaeu, *Bononia docet mater studiorum,* from *Theatrum civitatum et admirandorum Italiae,* 2 vols. (Amsterdam: Joan Blaeu, 1663), vol. I: Bodleian Library J. Maps 267 [47]. Photo: © Bodleian Libraries, University of Oxford, CC-BY-NC 4.0.

vice-legate, Pier Donato Cesi, drew up plans to restructure these teaching spaces (on the design of the architect Terribilia) and bring together all of the *studium*'s teachings. The result was the magnificent Archiginnasio building, inaugurated in 1563.[28] As Figure 2.2 testifies, the new seat of the university (the first building on the right, provided with a *loggiato*) was close to the basilica and also directly faced a building where booksellers and bookbinders sold their wares.

Fig 2.2. The loggiato of the Palazzo dell'Archiginnasio, along with the Piazza del Paviglione (now Piazza Galvani) and Basilica of San Petronio.

Etching (138 × 180 mm) on paper, Pio Panfili, before 1789. BCAB, Cartella Gozzadini, 3, n. 135, f. 2.

Often remarked upon by visitors for its beauty, the Archiginnasio was an eloquent testimony to continuing structural distinctions. The internal courtyard (Figure 2.3) gives an initial impression of unity. There one finds the small church of S. Maria dei Bulgari (used for professors' funerals) and two adjacent rooms where professors would wait to be escorted by the beadles to their classrooms when the bell rang. In order to reach the classrooms on the floor above, however, one would have to take either the left-hand staircase leading up to the Artists' classrooms or the one on the opposite side, leading to the Jurists'. Such differentiations continued on the floor above; the classrooms were contiguous, but spaces for Artists and Jurists were separate. Each faculty had eight classrooms, including two especially large ones (Figure 2.4). At one end was the *salone* of the Jurists (nowadays known as the Sala dello Stabat Mater because this work, by Gioachino Rossini, was first performed there in 1842).[29] At the other end was the *Aula Magna* of the Artists, now serving as the first reference room of the municipal library (Figure 2.5). These classrooms all ran along the side of the palazzo facing the piazza (now Piazza Galvani). Many of these rooms now hold the library's books.

As mentioned in §1.2, student representatives commissioned thousands of inscriptions, coats of arms, and monuments to professors, which still adorn the Archiginnasio's internal walls and ceilings (see Figure 2.3) and make it a well-deserved tourist destination.[30] The building served as the main site of the university until 1803, when it moved to the present administration building (Palazzo Poggi in Via Zamboni, 33). The municipal library, which took possession in 1838, still occupies the Archiginnasio building.[31]

2.2 Teaching

2.2.1 Methods and Approaches

Professors in the early modern period inherited from their predecessors a well-developed approach to teaching that was fairly consistent throughout Europe. At its heart, across all the faculties, lay the lecture and the *quaestio,* accompanied by exercises such as repetitions and disputations. Because these forms of teaching are well known, here I present them only in outline, privileging instead the changes they underwent in the period, particularly for arts and medicine.[32]

In all fields, the fundamental form of teaching was the lecture. As Figure 2.6 illustrates, the professor would enter the classroom accompanied by the beadle at the sounding of the bell, mount the rostrum or *cathedra,* and explain to his students, seated on the floor or on benches, the material contained in the book he had before him. This procedure, consisting of a line-by-line (and sometimes word-for-word) explanation of a particular set text, might not manage to cover all of the work in question. Yet it introduced students to a particular subject area via a relevant work, provided a model of how to engage with texts, and offered the opportunity to solve difficulties and refer to other viewpoints as one went along. A question that continues to be debated by scholars is whether and how often professors dictated their classroom lectures. Given the frequency of prohibitions on the matter, dictation was almost certainly widely practiced, but did not necessarily mean that a professor

Fig 2.3. The internal courtyard of the Palazzo dell'Archiginnasio.

Watercolor and pen drawing (230×295 mm) on paper, Contardo Tomaselli and Onofrio Zanotti, 1849. BCAB, GDS, *Disegni di autori vari,* cart. 12, n. 105.

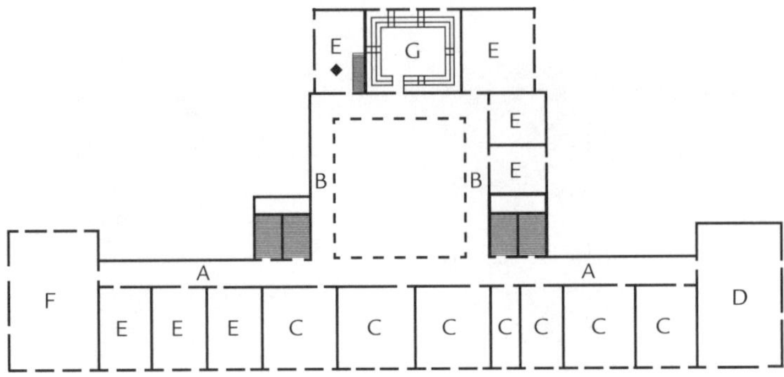

Piazza (presently Piazza Galvani)

A. Hallway leading to the classrooms, from the *aula magna* of the Legists to that of the Artists.
B. Entrance courtyard.
C. Classrooms for law.
D. The *aula magna* of the Legists (currently Stabat Mater).
E. Classrooms for arts and medicine.
F. The *aula magna* of the Artists.
G. Anatomical theater (seventeenth century).
◆ Anatomical theater of the sixteenth century.

Fig 2.4. Plan of the classrooms and anatomical theater of the Archiginnasio, *piano nobile* (second floor).

Reformatted from Francesco Cavazza, *Le scuole dell antico studio Bolognese* (Milan: Ulrico Hoepli, 1896), p. 253.

Fig 2.5. Palazzo dell'Archiginnasio: *Aula magna* of the Artists.

Photo © David Lines.

Fig 2.6. Depiction of a medieval university classroom (Bologna?).

Laurentius de Voltolina, miniature on parchment, c. 1380, in Henricus de Alemannia, *Liber ethicorum*. Kupferstichkabinett. Berlin / Wikimedia Commons.

would read out from a script (§2.3.1). In any case, as confirmed by numerous representations (including the tombs of professors; see Figure 1.2), students would often follow along in their own copies of the text, whose margins they might fill with their notes, although sometimes they wrote lectures down in a separate notebook.[33]

Types of Lectures

Like other Italian universities, Bologna had three main types of lectures.[34] "Ordinary" lectures covered material required for the degree and were typically taught by the most senior (and best paid) professors. "Extraordinary" lectures were given by more junior professors and were probably optional, although they often covered what was taught in ordinary lectures in the same or other years.[35] There was no particular time of day set apart for "ordinary" and "extraordinary" teachings, which were designated as taking place either in the morning or in the afternoon (*de mane* or *de sero*).

Initially in Bologna it was the morning lectures that signaled the most important professors, but starting in the sixteenth century the real mark of distinction was holding one of the afternoon or evening lectures, which typically claimed the higher salaries. It was perfectly normal for several professors to teach the same subject, such as logic or medicine *de mane,* at the same hour. (An exception was made for foreign scholars occupying a special chair or *cattedra di eminente scienza;* see §1.2.1.) There was not, however, a system of explicit competition between professors as in Padua, where a professor teaching logic *in primo loco* would vie for students with those appointed *in secundo loco* and *in tertio loco* during the same hour.[36] For minor subjects, there was also a third designation of "extraordinary feast-day" lectures, sometimes simply described as taking place *diebus festivis.* These were again optional. These lectures only took place on holidays, the regular days free of teaching (Sundays and Thursdays), or during vacation periods. They attracted very modest salaries. For reasons that are not entirely clear, Bologna abolished these feast-day teachings in 1570, with effect from 1572–1573.[37] By that point, some of these subjects (such as moral philosophy) had become ordinary.[38]

Bologna also had two further kinds of lectures. Poor but deserving foreign students who had just graduated or were about to do so and had performed well in a public disputation might fill one of the five *lecturae universitatis* (in medicine, philosophy, astronomy, rhetoric, or logic). These feast-day lectures received only token payments, but the post holders were exempt from paying graduation fees.[39] We know practically nothing about what or how they taught. Finally, starting in 1583, Bologna developed a new category of "supraordinary" lectures (for medicine only), whose precise topics were left to the appointees. These lectures commanded more handsome salaries than the ordinary ones. They went to particularly eminent figures, such as Girolamo Cardano or Girolamo Mercuriale.[40]

Supporting and reinforcing the lectures was a *repetitor,* a teaching assistant who daily rehearsed with students (who paid him) the lecture and questions they had heard earlier from the professor.[41] The 1405 statutes envisage such an activity for grammar (rub. 94), logic (rub. 37), philosophy (rub. 38), and medicine (rub. 40).[42] Details are most abundant for medicine: the *repetitor* is to repeat lessons in the mornings and *in nonis* until Easter, and to examine students in the afternoons or evenings (*de sero*). Evidence for the activity of a *repetitor* in early modern Bologna is thin, however, despite the mention of repetitions in rhetoric in 1496.[43]

Questions and Disputations

Teaching involved not only reading and explaining a text, but also a series of questions (*quaestiones*) on it. These could—more or less formally—punctuate a lecture or a series of lectures. It was not uncommon in medieval lectures for *dubitationes* or *quaestiones* either to be raised in the course of a lecture or to be considered independently, giving rise to commentaries proceeding exclusively *per quaestiones.* For Bologna, both the statutes and the surviving lectures and student notes indicate that professors and students were required to consider and resolve questions.[44] In addition to doing so during class time, they did so on more formal occasions.[45] The 1405 statutes, for instance, indicate the obligation for all junior teachers (i.e., those teaching *extraordinarie*) to hold disputations every week during a day free of classes (again, Sundays or Thursdays) according to a specified order.[46] These public disputations were to take place up to Lent and were to be recorded carefully: the script was to be delivered within fifteen days to the university stationer.[47] Both students and doctors in medicine, philosophy, logic, grammar, and astrology had to take part.[48] Other disputations were those *de quolibet,* which were held annually in each discipline (but twice a year in medicine), starting with the most senior professors.[49] The instructions concerning the disputations in medicine suggest that these could be quite elaborate, involving six questions posed by doctors and four by students.[50] The determination was the culmination of such exercises: a professor would offer his solution to the problems raised through an (ideally, impressive) display of logic and authorities, showing which of the proposed theses should be embraced and why. Disputations were considered so useful that the statutes obliged friars who taught in the *studium* to hold two regular disputations and one quodlibetal one each year (rub. 60). They also mention *palestrae,* exercises to be held between Lent and Palm Sunday. These may again have been a form of disputation, but unfortunately the statutes refer to them only once and do not specify their nature.[51]

Another exercise was that of the circles or *circoli.* Not mentioned explicitly in the 1405 statutes, the *circoli* apparently derived from a 1474 requirement that professors should follow their lectures by forming a circle in the piazza or elsewhere in order to confer (*conferire*) and debate with one another.[52] In the sixteenth and seventeenth centuries this exercise became a cause of grave concern, both because the participants posed unexpected or even inappropriate questions and because they could give rise to strong personal attacks.[53] A decree of the Senate on 24 November 1568 emphasized the need for these disputations to take place every morning and evening of ordinary teaching days and the requirement for all doctors to be present and, over time, to dispute with each other.[54] The renewal of this practice was such an event that a city chronicle noted it.[55]

Other sources too provide strong evidence for the importance of public disputations. In the prefaces to the teaching rolls, by 1581, the instruction about holding the *circoli* had taken the place of an earlier requirement to hold disputations and repetitions.[56] On several occasions the Assunti suggested that the disputations be brought back to their former glory, including by holding them in the *schola magna,* one of the most splendid spaces of the Archiginnasio.[57] But in the 1640s the authorities bowed to the inevitable, suggesting that the doctors hold the *circoli* in their own homes.[58]

Disputations were so popular with students that the statutes limited how many questions a student could respond to each year.[59] These occasions not only provided an opportunity to develop quick thinking and to shine in front of one's peers, but prepared students for future challenges. These included the rigors of the degree examination, which involved explaining and debating specific *puncta* (passages) from the prescribed texts before the college of doctors.[60] By the middle of the sixteenth century, degree candidates also started holding public disputations in which they defended theses on a wide range of subjects.[61] As noted above (§2.2.1), student candidates for one of the *lecturae universitatis* needed to prove their mettle through public disputations (in Italian, *conclusioni*).[62] A public disputation also became a requirement for applicants for various positions, including extraordinary lectureships in the seventeenth and eighteenth centuries.[63]

Some students in Bologna were especially keen to engage in these exercises.[64] A telling example is Daniel Carmenius, originally from Belluno, who came up for his degree in arts and medicine in 1621.[65] At the beginning of February, Carmenius asked the prior of the college of doctors for permission to present his conclusions in philosophy and medicine. Once the authorization for printing them was granted, the extraction of the four student respondents took place. The disputation occurred a few days later, and on 11 February Carmenius obtained his degree. Carmenius then secured a teaching position in Bologna (we find him teaching logic already the following year).[66] But Carmenius wished take part in further disputations. Indeed, in March he insisted on his right to do so even though he was no longer a student and had already received a lectureship. He presented 209 conclusions in philosophy and medicine to five respondents and paid the notary a fee of over L. 4.[67] The trend continued in later years, as testified by the theses to be disputed in 1707 by Ludovico Pielli, who had already received his degree the previous year.

Historians have often failed to appreciate the cultural value of such questions and disputations. They have treated them as signs of the sterility of the scholastic method, which supposedly focused on inconsequential and abstract topics and approached them by appealing to a set of infallible authorities. In fact, this image—derived from hostile commentators such as Francis Petrarch and Francis Bacon—is highly misleading. Questions were a flexible teaching tool and were a perfect means for introducing new ideas, findings, and scholarship into the teaching context (see §6.2). In the seventeenth and eighteenth centuries they served as a major tool for keeping students in Bologna up to speed with developments and discussions elsewhere in Europe.

2.2.2 Subjects and Textbooks

The Situation around 1400

The 1405 statutes present a clear program of teaching for logic, philosophy, astrology, and medicine, indicating what textbooks should be used for the various subjects and the progression of teaching.[68] As mentioned earlier, several features of the statutes invite caution, particularly in terms of the correspondence between their stipulations and actual practice. Yet a rapid overview of the rubrics on specific fields of study will help appreciate the curriculum's content and how it changed in later years.

For logic, the statutes mandate three cycles of lectures based on the system of *puncta*. Each *punctum* was equivalent to fourteen teaching days, with a cycle consisting of nine *puncta* (i.e., around twenty-five teaching weeks).[69] The cycles covered respectively: (1) the first six treatises (on modals, predicables, categories, syllogisms, topics, and suppositions) of Peter of Spain's *Tractatus* (otherwise known as his *Summulae logicales*), followed by the *Fallacies* commonly attributed to Thomas Aquinas; (2) the *ars vetus* (namely, Porphyry's *Isagoge,* then Aristotle's *Categories* and *On Interpretation*) as well as the *Topics* and the *Sophistical Refutations* from the *logica nova;* and, completing the *logica nova,* (3) the *Posterior* and *Prior Analytics.* These books could be read in both ordinary and extraordinary lectures, and minute instructions specify which portions of each work should be covered or omitted.[70] The backbone of the logic curriculum was clearly Aristotle's *Organon,* supplemented by Porphyry's popular manual (third century AD) and by two thirteenth-century works.[71]

The philosophy curriculum had three main parts, corresponding to one year each and taught through works by (or attributed to) Aristotle.[72] The first year included (presumably ordinarily) the *Physics* and the first book of *On Generation and Corruption* (whose second book was to be covered extraordinarily, like *De somno et vigilia* and *De physionomia*). The second year covered *On the Heavens, Meteorology,* and *On Sensation,* with extraordinary lectures for *De substantia orbis* (possibly corresponding to *De mundo*), *De memoria et reminiscentia, De inspiratione, De respiratione,* and *De morte et vita.* The third-year requirements were *On the Soul* and *Metaphysics* (especially the Prooemium as well as Books I, II, V–X, and XII), while extraordinary lectures addressed Book IV of the *Metaphysics* plus *De longitudine et brevitate vitae* and *De causa motus animalium.* Extraordinary lectures started with the Easter holidays.[73]

Here two main points are worth noting. One is the absence of works of moral philosophy (particularly Aristotle's *Nicomachean Ethics* and *Politics*), although elsewhere the statutes contain instructions about how much teachers of such works should be paid (rub. 38). The most likely explanation for this anomaly lies in the low status of moral philosophy, which at the time was taught solely as a feast-day subject in Italy—very differently from the practice in central and northern Europe.[74] Furthermore, although the statutes mandate the teaching of metaphysics, the subject was actually taught irregularly (and often just on feast days) in the fifteenth century, most likely in association with theology (§8.1).

Astrology—which encompassed the whole science of the stars and planets (from planetary motion to astrological medicine) and was sometimes referred to as astronomy (see §6.1.2)—was to be taught over four years, probably in parallel with teachings in medicine.[75] First, attention went to the *Algorismus,* a work on fractions and integers (possibly the textbook by John of Holywood, also known as Sacrobosco, †1244?), followed by the first book of Euclid's *Elements of Geometry* (focusing on plane geometry), read through the commentary of Campanus of Novara (†1296). Then came the *Alfonsine Tables* accompanied by the *Canons,* in all likelihood by John of Saxony (fl. 1327–1355),[76] and the *Theory of the Planets* (*Theorica planetarum*), a thirteenth-century work (now attributed to Gerard of Cremona) providing a simplified digest of Ptolemaic astronomy.[77] The second year continued this examination of Ptolemaic astronomy through the study of John of Holywood's *Sphere,* written around 1220. Then followed the second book of Euclid's *Elements,* the rules (*Canones*) written c. 1220 by Jean de Linières for using the *Alfonsine Tables,* and Messahala's *Treatise on the Astrolabe.* (The latter was a Latin translation of a work by an Egyptian Jew active in Baghdad, 762–c. 815.) In the third year, the first text to be read was the *Introduction to the Art of Astrology* by Alcabitius (fl. tenth century in Aleppo, Syria). Next came Pseudo-Ptolemy's *Centiloquium* (a work of judiciary astrology), accompanied by the commentary of Haly Rodohan (c. 998–1061) from Cairo. The third book of Euclid's *Geometry* and a treatise on the quadrant (unspecified, but possibly the one by Campanus of Novara) rounded out this year. The final year was to focus on all of Ptolemy's *Quadripartitus* (or *Tetrabiblos*), followed by a treatise (*On Unseen Urine*) that strayed into medical diagnostics.[78] The last requirement was the third part (*dictio*) of Ptolemy's *Almagest,* a foundational work in medieval and later astronomy.

Despite this rich listing of texts, some of these works probably played little or no role in the actual teaching of astrology.[79] And one should note that "astrology" had both a practical, predictive component and a more theoretical one, often overlapping strongly with astronomy, geometry, mathematics, and even medicine.[80] In later years the designation "astronomy" replaced "astrology" (see §6.1.2).

Medicine's statutory program of teaching is the most elaborate and difficult to summarize.[81] The statutes outline a four-year course of study, divided into *theorica* and *practica.* (Note that these do not correspond to modern distinctions between theoretical and operative medicine; see Chapter 7.) The former investigated the medical principles behind, for

Table 2.1 Teachings of *medicina theorica* in the second year, according to the 1405 statutes

Morning lectures (I)	Morning lectures (II)	Afternoon lectures (I)	Afternoon lectures (II)
Galen, *Tegni* Hippocrates, *Prognostica, De morbis acutis* Avicenna, *De viribus cordis*	Galen, *De accidenti et morbo, De crisi, De diebus criticis, De febribus ad Glauconem* (I), *De tabe, De utilitate respirationis*	Avicenna, *Canon* (I)	Galen, *De differentiis febrium* Avicenna, *Canon* (IV.2) *De mala complexione* *De simplicibus medicinis* Galen, *De diebus criticis*

Note: omissions not indicated. All items in the second column are by (or attributed to) Galen.

instance, diseases and included the study of four main authors: Hippocrates (*Prognostica, De morbis acutis, Aphorismata, De natura hominis*), Galen (fifteen works, in whole or part, some of them spurious), Avicenna (parts of the *Canon*), and Averroes (*Colliget*).[82] *Theorica* received both morning and afternoon lectures, each of which usually had a "first" and a "second" lecture (the latter was in all likelihood "extraordinary"). So, for instance, the program for the second year specified a sequence that included works by Galen, Hippocrates, and Avicenna (see Table 2.1). Averroes's *Colliget* was read (selectively) in the morning of the third year and the afternoon of the fourth.

Practica, again over four years, considered more closely how to treat diseases and focused mainly on selections from Avicenna's *Canon,* III.[83] The statutes envisage teaching *fen* 1–3 in the first year and thereafter progressing to *fen* 9–12 (second year), *fen* 13–16 (third year), and *fen* 18–21 (final year). Nancy Siraisi notes that these lectures covered "anatomical, pathological, or therapeutic factual detail" for the various parts of the body, starting with the head and reaching to the extremities.[84] *Practica* also included Avicenna's *Canon,* IV.1, from an early date (as testified by commentaries) and I.4 from at least 1589 (but likely earlier).[85]

The 1405 statutes list surgery separately.[86] In this case, the same lectures are repeated every year, in the afternoon. These include a first lecture covering Bruno da Longoburgo's *Chirurgia* and Galen's *Chirurgia,* as well as Avicenna's *Chirurgia* (i.e., *Canon,* IV.3–6) and Rasis's *Ad Almansorem,* VII.[87]

All branches of medicine had obvious and strong connections with anatomical demonstrations. The 1405 statutes make explicit provisions for these demonstrations, on cadavers of both men and women, specifying the maximum number of students who could view them (twenty in the case of a male body, thirty of a female), how far along a student had to be (usually in the third year of medical study), and how many demonstrations a student could attend.[88] Given that such public dissections—which for a long time required mounting and dismounting a purpose-built anatomical theater—were few, access was limited. Over time the event took on the character of a major festivity (see §7.2.1).

As with moral philosophy, the 1405 statutes do not directly address the teaching of grammar and rhetoric in rub. 78, but they do refer to the *Rhetoric* (presumably Pseudo-Aristotle's *Rhetorica ad Alexandrum*) as one of the texts that professors could read extraordinarily in return for a student fee.[89] A set of statutes of the College of Arts and Medicine, probably datable to the beginning of the fifteenth century, provides further details, specifying the main texts for the examination passages (*puncta*) to be given to degree candidates in various fields. For grammar, the main texts mentioned are the lesser and the greater Priscian (corresponding to Books XVII–XVIII and I–XVI, respectively, of the *Commentariorum grammaticorum libri XVIII* by Priscian, fl. fifth century AD in Constantinople). For rhetoric, the *puncta* are taken from the *Rhetorica ad Herennium* (also known as the *rhetorica nova* and now considered a pseudo-Ciceronian work) and from Cicero's *De inventione* (also called *rhetorica vetus*), both works from the first century BC that received a great deal of attention in the medieval curriculum.[90]

More secure details of what was envisioned emerge from the almost contemporary teaching of Bartolomeo del Regno, who in 1383 immediately succeeded the famous teacher Pietro da Moglio and taught in Bologna until at least 1408. Bartolomeo taught the great authors (*magni auctores*), which by the time of Pietro's death included Virgil, Statius, Lucan, Ovid, Horace, Persius, Juvenal, Terence, Valerius Maximus, and Seneca (*Tragedies*). To them Bartolomeo added Livy, Plautus, and the philosophical works of Cicero.[91]

The statutes make no reference to theology, whose teaching at that time usually took place in the schools of the religious orders and in the fifteenth century hardly ever appears on the rolls. As noted above, however, this does not signify theology's absence in the curriculum, particularly as it developed in later years.

Features of the Curriculum

As mentioned above, many questions persist about the 1405 statutes, including how seriously members of the *studium* took them and how long, if at all, the stipulations were followed.[92] Particularly problematic is Paul Grendler's claim that "the remarkably detailed Bolognese statutes of 1405 were in force through the fifteenth and sixteenth centuries, even though university rolls did not list the full range of texts to be taught."[93] Nevertheless, the statutes do point to some important features of the curriculum, and, when confirmed by what we know about ideals and practice elsewhere, repay consideration.[94]

First of all, in all subjects, teaching rested on specified works (usually ancient ones), supplemented as necessary by more recent handbooks or treatises. The book was therefore central to teaching—it is no coincidence that depictions of classroom scenes almost always show professors and students reading or holding a book (Figure 2.6). The concern for the accuracy of text copies emerges in the statutes' stipulation that the exemplars of manuscripts held by the beadles (and borrowed by students for copying) should be free from errors.[95] Ironically, however, the curriculum—heavily based, as already seen, on Greek and Arab works—was absolutely dependent on Latin translations. The translations of Aristotle by Boethius (c. 477–524), for instance, played a central role in the teaching of logic throughout the Middle Ages and into the Renaissance.[96] Fresh translations of other works of Aristotle from the Greek in the twelfth and thirteenth centuries, along with translations of Greek and Arab commentaries on them (most notably, Averroes), swiftly established themselves as the foundation of arts teaching throughout Europe. It was much the same in the case of medicine and astrology, where Latin translations and compendia from the twelfth and thirteenth centuries reworked and made accessible textbooks by Greek and Arab authors.[97]

Several aspects of this text-heavy teaching are particularly notable for later developments. First, although these translations had a long shelf life (not least because the commentaries associated with them made specific reference to their wording), over time fresh renderings appeared and came into use. These new translations were often more elegant and based on better manuscripts. An example is Francesco Filelfo's new translation of the *Rhetorica ad Alexandrum,* which he completed in Bologna in 1428 (see §5.1). In other cases, particularly in the humanities, Roman authors such as Cicero and Livy came to play a stronger role in the curriculum (see above). Equally relevant is that, both in medieval and later times, commentaries were often as prominent in teaching as the official textbooks. In philosophy teaching, the commentaries of Averroes, the Neoplatonic interpreters (Ammonius, Simplicius, Themistius, and others), and the great scholastic writers of the thirteenth and fourteenth centuries (Albertus Magnus, Thomas Aquinas, Giles of Rome, Walter Burley, John Buridan, and others) were central to lectures, which often engaged with them all. But none was more prominent than Averroes (Ibn Rushd, 1126–1198), the Arab scholar who had written numerous works of various length on Aristotle and whose numeration of passages (*textus*) was the standard way of referencing specific places in the text.[98] Similarly, in medicine Avicenna (Ibn Sina, 980–1037) could be as important as Galen (129–c. 216), although both of these actually stood as commentators to the much older writings of Hippocrates (see Chapter 7). This situation only intensified from the fifteenth century onward, as new commentaries appeared or older commentaries came to light.

The centrality of standard writings for the curriculum should not lead one to think that the authors on whom lectures were based became unquestionable authorities. The lecture format, with its openness to *dubia* and its relationship to more formal questions and disputations, by its very nature led instructors to ask whether Ptolemy, Aristotle, Galen, or anyone else had spoken correctly on a certain matter. The result could be a highly personal interpretation that included clear (and valued) elements of disagreement. Furthermore, the use of questions allowed the incorporation of many different viewpoints, often ones that contradicted the authors one was supposed to teach. Eventually it even became possible to offer lectures on a particular author or text that were only notionally tied to them, as works designated for teaching became ever more clearly stand-ins for specific subjects rather than passages to be interpreted (see §6.2.3). This, of course, made it increasingly easy to mold entire subject areas according to one's own philosophical, medical, or religious outlook.

The statutes' remarkably detailed instructions, not only about what portions of each work should be read, but also about how teaching should progress (one often reads in rubric 78 "quo lecto, legatur . . ." or "deinde legat") also require comment. The impression given is of an extremely well-structured—though almost certainly idealized—sequence of teaching, doubtless driven both by pedagogical considerations and by the logical connections between various works and subfields of learning. But this gives rise to a number of questions: What was the exact relationship between extraordinary and ordinary lectures? Were all the works listed actually taught, and in what order? Did teaching also include other works? How did the curriculum change over time? And, of course, if professors did not treat their texts as authorities, how did they approach them?

Evidence and Later Developments

None of these questions can be answered on the basis of the statutory evidence, but various other classes of sources can come to the rescue. Here I will provide only a rapid overview of some of the possibilities offered by studying local book production, teaching rolls, and lectures. I address other points more at length elsewhere in this book.

For the incunable period (up to 1500), local printings testify to specific interests. One of these was in British logic, including the writings of William of Ockham, William of Heytesbury, John Duns Scotus, Francis of Mayrone, and Paul of Venice.[99] This enthusiasm was common to other Italian *studia,* but seems to have been particularly intense and long-lasting in Bologna.[100] In other fields, the Latin grammar by Niccolò Perotti was printed and sold locally, doubtless as a text for instruction.[101] Furthermore, at the end of the fifteenth century Filippo Beroaldo the Elder worked hand-in-glove with the local printing industry to supply his students with material for his courses on rhetoric. His in-depth commentaries on new authors such as Propertius, Suetonius, and Apuleius, in addition to more established ones such as Cicero, stemmed from his university teaching of the humanities (particularly rhetoric). From his collection of printed orations, we know that Beroaldo also lectured on Silius Italicus and Sallust, while not ignoring standard authors such as

Virgil, Lucan, Horace, Persius, Juvenal, and Livy (see §5.1). Further study of book production in Bologna across the early modern period may provide additional details on which books were coming to market with a view to university teaching.[102] One also needs to keep in mind that not all books meant for Bolognese students and professors were necessarily printed locally.

The teaching rolls provide supplementary evidence of teaching.[103] Published every October by the Riformatori dello Studio, these large sheets informed students who was teaching which subject in the coming academic year. These *rotuli* furnish insights into at least three features of teaching, in addition to (not always reliable) information as to professors' presence in the *studium* and how they progressed from one teaching to the next. One important aspect is their specification of the main textbooks in various subjects. In 1526–1527 the rolls start indicating which books are to be read in philosophy classes.[104] Aristotle's *Physics, On the Heavens,* and *On the Soul* appear as the works taught in ordinary or extraordinary philosophy, thus complementing the indications of the 1405 statutes. Instructions for rhetoric and poetry, however, are vague, both for these and for later years: lecturers are assigned one lesson in oratory and another in poetry, but the authors and textbooks are not specified. Presumably these teachers had a great deal of freedom in choosing the texts on which they would lecture. For medicine (but not for anatomy, metaphysics, theology, mathematics, humanities, or Greek) the rolls start providing more detailed information only from 1586–1587, allowing us to see who was meant to teach which works of Galen, Hippocrates, and Avicenna.[105] Rolls also eventually provide useful information for other subjects. By 1589 they suggest that logic is based on the first book of Aristotle's *Posterior Analytics* in alternation with the second book.[106] At least in 1591, metaphysics addresses Aristotle's *Metaphysics* I; moral philosophy, Aristotle's *Nicomachean Ethics* V (*de iustitia et iure*); mathematics centers on Euclid in the morning and on Holywood (Sacrobosco) in the afternoon; scholastic theology covers the second book of Peter Lombard's *Sentences.*[107]

In other cases, the rolls correct the picture provided by the statutes. At times the differences are striking. Thus, the rolls confirm other archival evidence suggesting the development, between 1545 and 1573, of a six-year cycle of philosophy teaching rather than the three-year cycle

Table 2.2 Six-year cycle of philosophy teaching, 1545–1573

	Ordinary	Extraordinary
Year 1	*Physics*	*Generation and Corruption*
Year 2	*On the Heavens*	*Meteors*
Year 3	*On the Soul*	*Parva naturalia*
Year 4	*Generation and Corruption*	*Physics*
Year 5	*Meteors*	*On the Heavens*
Year 6	*Parva naturalia* from the start	*On the Soul* from the start

indicated in the statutes (Table 2.2). They also point to a later, sixteenth-century expansion in the teaching of ordinary philosophy.[108] In the case of medicine, they show that the four-year medical program described in the statutes was actually being delivered over three years by around 1585 (and probably earlier).[109] Likewise, surgery has changed into a three-year course instead of being repeated annually, as specified by the statutes (Table 2.3). But the rolls also point to new teachings or designations introduced over time. Table 2.4 lists them synthetically.

All of these points suggest that the curriculum described in the 1405 statutes was either an idealized sketch or a short-lived blueprint. The statutes therefore need be considered alongside a fuller range of documentary sources for the *studium,* including the rolls.

Not even the rolls, however, are always reliable. In most instances they list only one (presumably just the first) work on which a professors would lecture. Occasionally, as in the case of the famed philosophy teacher Ludovico Boccadiferro, we know that they were teaching different ones altogether. In these and other cases, the most direct evidence comes from manuscript lectures and student notes, although these sources too can be methodologically problematic.

For the seventeenth and eighteenth centuries, for which fewer lecture notes survive, helpful information comes from the teaching plans that doctors were required to submit following the new statutes published in 1641. The three surviving relevant archival units cover (albeit discontinuously) the period up to 1740. They provide a sense, not only of the subjects and textbooks that professors planned to cover, but of the intended pace of teaching, questions to be raised, and authorities to be

Table 2.3 Three-year cycle in medicine, c. 1585

	Ordinary *medicina theorica*	Extraordinary *medicina theorica*
Year 1	Avicenna, *Canon,* I	Galen, *Ars parva*
Year 2	Galen, *Ars parva*	Hippocrates, *Aphorisms*
Year 3	Hippocrates, *Aphorisms*	Avicenna, *Canon,* I.1
	Ordinary *medicina practica*	Extraordinary *medicina practica*
Year 1	Avicenna, *Canon,* IV.1	(Rasis) *De morbis particularibus*
Year 2	(Rasis, *De morbis*?) [unspecified]	(Galen) *On Fevers*
Year 3	(Galen), *On Fevers*	Avicenna, *Canon,* IV.1 (= *De febribus*)
	Surgery	
Year 1	*De vulneribus*	
Year 2	*De ulceribus*	
Year 3	*De tumoribus praeter naturam*	

Data sources: ASB, Riformatori dello Studio, b. 21, ff. 2r–4v (*Universae lectiones hic describuntur quas legunt annuatim Artistae in almo nostro Bononiensi Gymnasio* [*1585–1586*]); and Dallari, II, 245–53.

used. As an example, the surviving syllabi for 1642–1643 cover nearly every subject of arts and medicine listed in that year's teaching roll.[110] They confirm the indication of that year's teaching roll that all three professors of *theorica ordinaria* lectured on the *Aphorisms* of Hippocrates.[111] The readers of *theorica extraordinaria* read the first *fen* of Avicenna's *Canon.*[112] The plans of the two teachers of *practica supraordinaria* consider different works: Domenico Nobili lectures on Hippocrates's *Libri epidemiorum,* whereas Giovan Battista Malisardi reads a treatise (presumably by Girolamo Mercuriale) entitled *De vitiis articulorum exceptis vitiis articulorum a lue venerea pendentibus* on the basis of Hippocrates, Aurelianus, Galen, Avicenna, and other authors.[113] No plans survive for the teachers of *practica ordinaria,* who according to the rolls were to teach (Galen's?) *De febribus,* but there are three syllabi for *practica extraordinaria.* All of them focus on Avicenna's

Table 2.4 First permanent appearances of various subjects and first post-holders

1455	Greek Letters (Lianoro de' Lianori)
1464	Hebrew Letters (Vincenzo da Bologna); refounded in 1642
1506	Metaphysics (Filippo da Bagnocavallo, O.F.M. and Angelo da Arezzo, O.Serv.)
1534	Simples (Luca Ghini; becomes autonomous in 1537)
1538	*Litterae humanitatis* (Romolo Amaseo)
1562	Ordinary Moral Philosophy (Claudio Betti), previously only on feast days
1564	Mathematics (Ludovico Ferrari), separate listing
1566	Theology (Cirillo da Bologna, O.Serv.)
1570	Anatomy (Giulio Cesare Aranzi) independently from surgery
1579	Sacred Scriptures (Ludovicus Pelestrellus Lusitanus, O.E.S.A.)
1637	Cases of Conscience (Iacobus Pistorius)
1695	Moral Theology (Ioseph Maria Agudius, O.P.)
	Hydrometria (Domenico Guglielmini)
1708	Algebra (Vittorio Francesco Stancari)
1717	Canons (Thomas Caneti, O.P.), Church History (Ioseph Philippus Cagnoli), Dogmatic Theology (unspecified), and Church Councils (Ioannes Baptista Carlinus)
1732	Practical Surgery (Pier Paolo Molinelli)
1737	Chemistry (Iacopo Bartolomeo Beccari), Mechanics (unspecified), Analytic Geometry (Gabriele Manfredi), *Universa Philosophia* (Laura Bassi)

Data source: Dallari, passim.

Canon, I.4, except for that of Achille Muratori, who uses a printed announcement to advertise an anatomical demonstration to take place in 1643.[114] The two teachers of simples, the brothers Bartolomeo and Giacinto Ambrosino, announce their plans to teach purgative substances and the names, divisions, and other matters concerning plants, respectively.[115]

Finally, although the rolls do reflect the introduction of particular subjects across the early modern period, they cannot testify to abortive initiatives. Two of these were the much-discussed introduction of a Plato lectureship in 1588 and that of a chair in the Tuscan language around 1623. Since the latter is noted elsewhere (§5.2.2), here I will focus on the Plato lectureship.

By now it should be clear that the arts curriculum (and philosophy in particular) was structured around fundamental texts by (or attributed to) Aristotle. As Chapter 6 indicates, this does not mean that lecturers on Aristotle necessarily agreed with him. In fact, in the course of their teaching they often presented or referred to different points of view (both ancient and modern). This became particularly straightforward in the case of Plato and the Neoplatonic philosophers after Marsilio Ficino's influential Latin translations of the complete corpus of Plato and his commentators in the late fifteenth century.[116] (During the Middle Ages, Plato's works were known only imperfectly and mainly indirectly, except for three dialogues.) Other translations of the Neoplatonic philosophers' commentaries (which often attempted to reconcile Aristotelian and Platonic positions) followed in the sixteenth century. Although Plato's dialogues are notoriously unsystematic and therefore present a challenge for teaching, various attempts were made during the sixteenth century to introduce lectureships of Plato into the universities.[117] On the whole, these were sporadic and short-lived, even in places such as Florence–Pisa, where one might expect greater success and enthusiasm. Usually they were feast-day lectures, indicating that they were not considered integral to the curriculum. In Bologna, discussions and rumors about a potential lectureship arose in 1588. As first noted by Emilio Costa, Cardinals Agostino Valier and Federico Borromeo in Rome mooted the lectureship, which however did not receive a favorable reception by the Bolognese city authorities. The main candidates, we are told, were Jacopo Mazzoni (teaching in Pisa) and Flaminio Papazzoni, a Bolognese teaching in Pavia who wished to return to his native city (as in fact he did in 1589, but not as a teacher of Plato).[118] The information about this initiative comes from the correspondence between the Assunteria di Studio and Bologna's ambassador in Rome, Camillo Paleotti.[119] But newer letters that I have found among the Senate's correspondence show that these were not the only individuals in the running. On 16 July 1588 Cardinal Montalto wrote to recommend a certain Giulio Tassoni for this position.[120] On 10 December 1588 a *memoriale* by Cardinal Borromeo (sent to the Standard-bearer of Justice by Paleotti) includes a petition by Vincenzo Mondini applying for the same post.[121] Apart from the intrinsic interest of such a new lectureship, even though it was not approved, these documents highlight the need to explore a wide range or relevant archival *fondi,* and in particular those connected with the correspondence of the Senate and its various committees and officers. The rolls tell only a part of the story.

2.3 Challenges and Reform Initiatives

So far I have argued that developments in the curriculum of arts and medicine become especially clear once one turns away from the 1405 statutes to other sources. In this section I will show that the introduction of new subjects, cycles of teaching, or approaches needs to be appreciated within the context of ongoing—and sometimes rather heated—debates about university reform. Members of the *studium,* overseers, and observers often commented on (and proffered solutions to) the challenges facing the *studium.* The civic, ecclesiastical, and papal authorities were also keen at times to implement reforms. Some of the perceived problems or *abusi* included the rise of private teaching, the reduction in the number of public lectures, and the variable quality of lecturers. A reform of the *studium* in 1737 addressed these and curricular issues.[122]

2.3.1 Private Teaching

One of the points raised around 1586 was that the university's public lecture halls were often empty and that the practice of having students dispute against one another in the mornings of ordinary lectures had evaporated. According to many observers, this state of affairs was due to the rise of private teaching. Writing in the mid-1580s, one influential professor of law, Ferrante Vezza, admitted that private "academies" (i.e., private lessons) helped motivate students and made them ready to speak in public. But he argued that disputations attached to ordinary (and therefore public) lessons achieved the same aim. Furthermore, Vezza strongly objected to what he said was current practice—allowing private lectures during term, albeit on the days free from ordinary teaching (Sundays and Thursdays).[123] According to his account, students (and perhaps also teachers) dedicated so much effort to preparing for the private lectures that they neglected the public ones. Vezza therefore proposed limiting private teaching to vacation periods only, except in the cases of logic and the *Institutes.*[124]

Vezza also discussed two other aspects of teaching: public disputations (*conclusioni*) and vacation periods. In the first case, he noted that the *conclusioni* required of candidates wishing to obtain a lectureship often fell on teaching days; he therefore recommended issuing a decree that they be held only during the holidays. But he also suggested making these exercises optional. The reason given is telling: "Forcing them to do it [i.e., hold *conclusioni*] is unhelpful, for this is the only thing they learn (so to speak) by heart and with a great deal of effort. The exercise itself makes them think they know something, so they then become doctors while they are still children (*putti*). If they undertake the *conclusioni* voluntarily, they will only do so when they are ready, as used to happen."[125] Furthermore, Vezza observed that foreign students coming to Bologna from Padua were confused about the exact dates of the vacation periods. He therefore recommended putting together a prospectus (*tavola*) with this information and posting it on the door of the university (i.e., the Archiginnasio).[126]

Vezza's observations are almost certainly a commentary on the *Ordinationi* on the *studium* that the new papal legate, Enrico Gaetani, was keen to promulgate. The final document, approved by the Senate on 20 September 1586 and published on 25 September, reflects several of his own proposals.[127] Although they do not fully accept his suggestion about making the *conclusioni* optional, the *Ordinationi* do indicate that they should be confined to the vacation periods, as indeed should be the case for private teaching (although they ban all private lectures in termtime, including for logic and the *Institutes*). Besides strongly endorsing the idea of a publicly displayed calendar, they also list other points needing remedy in the *studium.* One of these is the professors' penchant to be accompanied by groups of their students when they leave their homes to deliver their public lectures in the Archiginnasio. This practice, often referred to in the documents as *corteggio,* was a signal of professors' fame and had the inconvenient (but doubtless intended) effect of ensuring that their students did not attend the lectures of any competitors. By depriving them of students, professors in effect put their rivals' position in peril, since the rolls specified that public lectures in arts and medicine needed to attract a minimum of four listeners.[128] Other provisions, while referring obliquely to the possibility that students' antics may wreak havoc with teaching, direct professors to start their lectures on time, teach for the full appointed hour, and not cancel classes unless allowed to do so by the legate and the Senate.

Although the colleges of doctors got swiftly to work to moderate several of these provisions (not least because Gaetani's *Ordinationi* threatened draconian fines and punishments for violations), many of the issues raised remained live points of debate in later years.[129] On private teaching, for instance, the 1593 *Reformationi dello studio* issued by the vice-legate Ottavio Bandini allowed term-time private lectures on logic and the *Institutes,* but still limited any others to vacation periods.[130] When the vice-legate Marsilio Landriani issued similar provisions on 29 October 1602, students protested so loudly that by 14 November they had secured the addition of a codicil. This actually expanded the scope for private lectures, which were now allowed for all subjects during usual teaching days (*dies legibiles*) as long as they did not cover the same material as the ordinary lectures.[131]

Later documents testify to continuing concern about private lectures. In all likelihood these had become widespread in the second half of the seventeenth century.[132] Nonetheless, observers continued to disapprove of private teaching—not so much because of any timetable clashes with public lectures, but because it negatively affected official teaching. An anonymous memorandum that considers the 1639 *Ordinationi* by Giulio Sacchetti (printed in 1641) is a case in point.[133] The author notes that Sacchetti's instructions had forbidden the "new" practice of dictating during ordinary lectures except during the holidays.[134] A series of problems had ensued. In particular, students would show up at public lectures unprepared and unable to follow the lectures sufficiently to take them down (perhaps because of the pace of teaching). Bored and discouraged, they became unruly. They expected that the private lectures would compensate for their lack of attention at the public ones. It was a dangerous, vicious cycle that lowered the quality of teaching.[135]

The scale of the phenomenon of dictation in Bologna is not altogether clear.[136] The slightly revised instructions of 1713 again try to contain dictation within the context of private teaching.[137] Nonetheless, it is likely that (at least until the 1630s), dictation was a less severe problem in Bologna than in Padua, where it became such a major headache in the early modern period.[138]

2.3.2 The Academic Calendar

Another issue that generated considerable comment was the number of ordinary lectures taking place yearly. This was a point closely connected to that of the academic calendar. According to the 1405 statutes, the academic year was to start immediately after the feast of Saint Luke

(18 October) and finish at the end of August, allowing for various breaks: nearly two weeks over Christmas, plus vacations for Carnival, Easter, and so forth.[139] In fact, as student notes testify, most lectures actually started at the beginning of November, after All Saints' Day. And ordinary lectures could get under way at any point up to the beginning of January. In theory, these parameters provided for around thirty-eight weeks of lectures, but numerous religious festivities and other occasions (e.g., graduations and funerals) punctuating the academic year made for a rather more modest number—perhaps thirty-four weeks at most.[140] In later years, the end of the academic year was brought forward, first to 14 August and then to 19 July.[141] By 1586 the prefaces to the rolls ordered that lectures should start as soon as possible after the formal opening of the *studium* in October.[142] This move may have been meant to compensate for the earlier end of classes.

An associated point of discussion concerned how many ordinary lectures there should be in any given academic year. The most influential instruction on this matter came in 1561, when the Senate (probably under pressure from the papal legate) decreed that there should be at least one hundred days of ordinary lectures per year, to take place between the first regular day after All Saints' Day up to 7 July.[143] A handwritten calendar (*tavola*) for 1578–1579, however, lists only eighty-two *dies legibiles* between 4 November and 13 July.[144] And comments by Aldrovandi on the issue in 1583 express his pessimism about raising the number of lectures to between eighty and eighty-five.[145] In any case, Aldrovandi too, like Vezza, supported the idea of publishing an academic calendar.[146] A surviving archival series shows that such a calendar came out regularly starting in 1586.[147]

The syllabi from 1642–1643 discussed in §2.2 suggest that this initiative did indeed contribute to arresting the decline in the number of lectures. In that year Domenico Cesario, for instance, promised an impressive ninety-five lectures on the first book of Tacitus's *Annals*. Ercole Betti came close with ninety-four lectures on Hippocrates.[148] In some cases, the listings of lectures bear precise dates; these indicate that (for this academic year) teaching took place between 5 November and 20 December, 8 and 28 January, 19 February and 28 March, and (at least in some cases) 13 April and 23 June. The prospectuses for the eighteenth century suggest a roughly similar situation (see Figure 6.2).[149]

Raising the number of ordinary lectures was probably part of a strategy to contain the expansion of private teaching discussed in §2.3.1. If that was the case, it failed. The analysis by Maria Teresa Guerrini suggests that private teaching continued to flourish. Monuments erected to professors in the Archiginnasio may have stopped mentioning their activity of private teaching after 1676, but an important archival series of *Requisiti dei lettori,* providing information on single professors, points to many cases in which it continued. In this way, the practice in Bologna reflected what was happening throughout the Italian Peninsula in early modern times, including at Pavia, Rome, and Naples.[150]

2.3.3 Regulating the Lecturers

Finally, recurring discussions of reform concerned two interconnected issues: the excessive number of teachings and professors, and the relative decline in the quality of academic staff. The question of how many professors the *studium* actually needed and could afford was supposedly settled by the 1450 bull of Pope Nicholas V (§1.3.3). But in the course of the early modern period it became much more acute, particularly because recent graduates came to see themselves as entitled to a university post. This led to problems in public teaching, such as the excessive brevity of lessons, many of which supposedly did not even reach half an hour.[151] At many Italian universities, it also gave rise—as Brendan Dooley has observed—to a "dual university system" consisting of a small number of engaged and possibly innovative professors, among a much larger number of post holders who regarded their university appointment more or less as a sinecure (or, alternatively, as a temporary arrangement before finding other work).[152] It is unclear whether Bologna followed Padua in keeping so many staff on hand so that students could be coached to pass the examinations, whose requirements remained linked to the older canonical texts.[153] Both Aldrovandi in the sixteenth century and Archdeacon Antonio Felice Marsili in the seventeenth put forward bold proposals to reform the university in a meritocratic sense, rewarding the best professors.[154] But even progressive professors found such ideas hard to stomach. Marcello Malpighi, for instance, opposed Marsili's proposals, arguing that it was better to have many (but modestly paid) lecturers rather than a few well-paid ones (see §7.3.1). Although such moves provoked discontent, the financial pressures on the *studium* in the second half of the seventeenth century led to hiring freezes and to containing the number of teachers on the rolls to around a hundred (see §1.2).

Invisible boundaries likewise delimited the place of women lecturers. As noted in §1.1.2, women students were a rarity in premodern universities, but that was even more the case for women graduates and professors. A notable exception is Laura Bassi (1711–1778), who received private tutoring from one of the *studium*'s professors of medicine, Gaetano Tacconi, and in 1732 both received her degree in philosophy and, in October, began teaching (see Figure 2.7). But although Figure 2.7 depicts an inaugural event in the presence of the city authorities and the more general public (the Standardbearer of Justice faces Bassi at the other end of the hall), such occasions of public teaching were quite rare. In fact, Bassi's teaching—which figures both on university rolls and on the lists for the Istituto delle Scienze—took place more regularly in her home. There, together with her husband Giuseppe Veratti (also a professor), Bassi set up a laboratory, where the pair conducted experiments and taught students. This was an activity that Bassi managed to combine with her conjugal responsibilities and the upbringing of five children. But her interests hardly remained confined to the home, and indeed she kept up a correspondence with several scientific figures throughout Europe, including her cousin Lazzaro Spallanzani. Visitors to Bologna such as the Frenchman Charles de Brosses (in Italy from 1739 to 1740) made a point of reporting on Bassi's home laboratory and lectures, at least some of which were open to outsiders and forced him to dust off his Latin.[155] But Brosses was even more impressed with Maria Gaetana Agnesi (1718–1799), the daughter and child prodigy of a wealthy merchant (not, as often stated, a professor in Bologna), whom he had met in Milan. There her father Pietro had put her and his other children under the tutelage of excellent teachers, and she particularly developed her gift for mathematics, eventually expressed in her massive two-volume vernacular textbook on algebra and differential calculus (*Instituzioni analitiche ad uso della gioventù italiane,* 1748, translated in whole or in part into at least English and French). Thanks to this work, Agnesi received invitations not only to become a member of Bologna's Accademia delle Scienze, but also (on the initiative of Benedict XIV) to take up a professorship at

Fig 2.7. Laura Bassi's first public lecture.

Miniature (400×518 mm) on parchment, unsigned, November/December 1732. ASB, Insignia degli Anziani, vol. XIII, f. 98r.

the university there. Although the Senate nominated her to such a post in September 1750 and her name appears on the official teaching rolls until her death, in fact she turned this opportunity down and remained in Milan.[156]

One should not make too much of the special education and preferment that both Bassi and Agnesi received. Agnesi's father was clearly mainly interested in his family's social advancement. Prospero Lambertini (as both Bologna's archbishop and pope) promoted and stage-managed the careers of Bassi and Agnesi in order to raise the visibility of the *studium* and foster a certain brand of Catholicism. These women's achievements did start to open the doors to women's participation in university and learned life in Bologna. But the exceptional nature of such developments is clear: a more regular inclusion of women did not start until a good century later and did not blossom until the nineteenth.[157] As long as the spheres of men and women remained strongly demarcated, a public teaching role for women remained difficult.

2.3.4 The Reform of 1737

In terms of the curriculum, this chapter has shown that Aldrovandi and others furnish a picture of shifting arrangements already in the sixteenth and early seventeenth centuries. A document from 1694 indicates that by then even the Senate appreciated that the previous five areas of teaching had become six—namely philosophy, medicine, humanities, theology, mathematics, and the new subject of hydrometry (river hydraulics).[158] In 1737, after a series of discussions informed by developments within the Istituto delle Scienze (§3.2), but actually building on debates from previous decades, various sectors of the teaching of arts and medicine underwent reform, either in name or in substance.[159] This reform, which was connected to the larger patterns of political, socioeconomic, and cultural renewal in the period and was part of a wave of changes also affecting other universities (such as Turin, Pavia, and Ferrara), aimed to bring about a profound restructuring and modernization of teaching in the *studium*.[160] The rolls now subdivided the teaching of arts and medicine into forty-five headings (outlined, except for the elementary teaching of writing, grammar, and arithmetic, in Table 2.5). Not all of these positions were filled, however, and particularly in the case of Oriental languages it was hard to recruit qualified teachers.[161] The only field that escaped unscathed from the 1737 upheaval was the humanities, where changes were not deemed necessary—perhaps because in this subject area teachers were explicitly free to choose the works on which they would lecture.

The 1737 reform in various ways mixed old and new. The humanities, for instance, remained relatively small. In medicine, previous arrangements continued in terms of *theorica* and *practica* and the names of the main authors (Hippocrates, Galen, and Avicenna). Changes included the addition of a specific teaching on bone fractures (*De ossium fracturis et luxationibus*) for surgery and on age- and gender-related maladies (*De morbis aetatum et sexuum*) for *practica ordinaria.* When compared to the fifteenth century, the major departures came in three areas. Mathematics became a much more articulated subject: it distinguished analytic from synthetic geometry (i.e., calculus from plane geometry) and included algebra, mechanics, and hydrometry, while also preserving the older teaching of astronomy.[162] These developments built on Bologna's increasing reputation as a center for infinitesimal calculus already at the start of the eighteenth

Table 2.5 Subjects and teachings in 1737–1738, following their reform

Ancient languages	Mathematics	Philosophy	Medicine	Theology
Lingua graeca	**Analytic geometry**	Logic (x2)	Surgery* (x2)	Moral theology (x2)
Particulae graecae	Synthetic geometry	**General physics**	Surgical operations	Sacred Scriptures
Particulae hebraicae arabicae et caldeae	Astronomy	**Particular physics**	Anatomy (x4)	Metaphysics
	Mechanics	**Chemistry**	Public anatomy	Scholastic theology (x2)
Humanae litterae	Hydraulics	**Universal philosophy**	Simples	Dogmatic theology
	Astronomy notebook	Moral philosophy (x2)	*Theorica*†	Church history
			Practica††	Councils

Data source: Dallari, III.2, 5–8.

* includes a new teaching *de ossium fracturis et luxationibus*.

† distinguished in ordinary, extraordinary, and supraordinary.

†† distinguished in ordinary, extraordinary, and supraordinary. Also includes a teaching *de morbis aetatum et sexuum*.

Bold denotes new chairs or designations.

century (see §6.1.2). As for philosophy, Aristotle ceased to be the subject's official focus. Although his works continued (not unlike today) to be important for logic and moral philosophy, these subjects now tended to be taught more topically. Natural philosophy featured general physics (which considered common properties of bodies such as gravitation) and particular physics (which dealt with specific aspects such as light, heat, electricity, and the balance of fluids).[163] It also included chemistry and *universa philosophia*—a subject entrusted to Laura Bassi, who probably taught it freely or *ad beneplacitum* as in previous years.[164] Finally, theology became very prominent. Despite the poor showing of the study of Scriptures, scholastic theology was staffed by nine lecturers, who made it possible to cover the four books of Lombard's *Sentences* in a single year. Moral theology (which incorporated the earlier teaching on cases of conscience) expanded, reaching seven lecturers in 1755.[165] An innovative aspect compared to other *studia* was the introduction of canons and church history.[166]

The mid-eighteenth-century rolls confirm these observations. Theology now has nearly as many lecturers as medicine (twenty-two versus twenty-three), if one includes within theology lectures on Hebrew, delivered by a Dominican friar. At some distance come philosophy and science (fifteen lecturers), whereas mathematics has six (plus someone to compile the astronomical tables), and the humanities five.[167] What is notable, other than the preponderance of theology and related subjects, is the high number of professors designated as *pater* or *canonicus* in nontheological areas: three (out of five) in logic, one in physics, two in moral philosophy, and one in mechanics. (In 1745 Benedict XIV installed twenty-four Accademici Pensionari Benedettini in the Accademia delle Scienze, but these were not necessarily monks.)[168] The university now presents an ecclesiastical character. Doubtless due in part to its changing student body, it is very distant from the more secular orientation of the fifteenth and sixteenth centuries (see Chapter 8).[169]

One should, however, be cautious of making a fetish out of a specific date. By 1737 both philosophy and medicine had already largely abandoned their previous textbooks (see Chapters 6 and 7). Lecturers showed themselves ready to redesign their engagement with their materials by giving a more systematic twist to their teaching. Like their predecessors, professors of the seventeenth and eighteenth centuries made fairly regular reference to recent or contemporary scholarship and discoveries, although their public espousal of new positions could be limited by religious prohibitions (see Chapter 8). One could therefore just as easily locate a significant break with past teaching practices within the first two or three decades of the eighteenth century.

One of the reasons for the reinventions that took place within the curriculum was that the university interacted constantly with other cultural and educational establishments in the city. Chapter 3 explores this point in detail, highlighting the ties and tensions between the university and student colleges and academies, learned and scientific circles, and the Jesuits.

3

The University in Context

Scholars working on medieval Bologna have shown that the *studium* and its members had an intense and productive relationship with the city that hosted them.[1] On this front, studies on the later period have been less abundant but have already started to show that the two were intimately bound together.[2] As noted in Chapter 1, for many professors the university was just one of their sources of activity and income. They also welcomed students into their homes, ran private practices of law and medicine, and tried to influence those in power. In addition, most had families to look after and investments to take care of. They might even occupy political office. This chapter shows that both students and professors were also deeply rooted in other local contexts that were at a remove from (but also had strong links with) official university structures. Student *universitates* met in local churches, which professors regularly remembered in their wills. Professors also offered guidance to student academies, while literary and scientific academies—such as the Gelati or the Accademia del Coro Anatomico—brought university members together with local learned circles. Para-university structures such as student colleges often had university professors among their overseers or hired them to teach. Finally, the *studium* had deep ties (and not only a relationship of rivalry) with certain religious orders, such as the Jesuits, and the schools they ran. One of their initiatives, the Congregazione della Perseveranza, served as a means for university members to deepen their spirit of devotion.[3]

In other words, the university belonged to a complex and interconnected ecosystem of learning institutions, all with strong links to the *studium*. These included residential colleges and student academies, learned and scientific academies, and the local institutions of religious orders. Evidently, the university's teaching activity took place within a rich cultural climate, to which it made a substantial contribution.

3.1 Residential Colleges and Student Academies

Bologna was a famed university town that, at least until the end of the sixteenth century, attracted a large student population, including students from abroad (§1.1). But where did these students live? To what social classes did they belong? Why were some young men attracted to educational residential colleges rather than to the *studium*? And what associations did they form in order to ensure their academic success?

3.1.1 Residential Colleges

It was common practice in Bologna (as elsewhere in Italy) for students to board together in a professor's house or rent lodgings independently wherever they were available.[4] Over time, however, the number of students and the pressures of the housing market meant that finding lodgings became ever harder for students: this is, indeed, one of the major complaints raised in university documents in and after the sixteenth century. As time passed, finding adequate rooms continued to be an unresolved issue.[5] Residential colleges seemed to many families and students to offer a satisfactory solution.

In Bologna, colleges had a rather different function than in universities such as Paris and Oxford, where colleges were large and numerous and teaching became increasingly decentralized.[6] Bologna's colleges were initially few and were mainly designed to provide for poor students from foreign lands or other cities.[7] They served almost exclusively as places of residence—although, as the examples of the Spanish College and the Collegio Gregoriano show, there were also early cases of colleges of instruction.

Residential colleges in Bologna experienced two main phases: one from the foundation of the Collegio Avignonese in 1257 to that of the Collegio Ancarano in 1414 (eight colleges in total), and another from 1528 to 1689 (thirteen colleges, six in the sixteenth century, including the Poeti, Ungaro-Illirico, Montalto, and Jacobs, the latter for Flemish students).[8] Particularly in the medieval period, these were fairly small foundations (often for some twenty or fewer students, although the Collegio Bresciano took up to fifty) meant for the poor, whom they thus encouraged to study. The statutes of such colleges, often drawn up by the testators who founded them, were thereafter safeguarded by their overseers, who initially tried to maintain their original purpose. In the early modern period, however, these colleges gradually acquired a very different social function: they catered instead to members of either noble or upper-class families, explicitly excluding those whose families engaged in any kind of manual labor. In other words, these colleges served to mold a ruling class, along the same lines as the non-university colleges for nobles discussed below.[9]

In the initial phase these colleges functioned more as residence halls than as places of teaching.[10] But those founded in the early modern period often allowed a greater degree of private teaching within them, exercised either by specially appointed teachers or by members of the *studium,* whose part-time teaching in the colleges could be a profitable sideline. Because these colleges were generally small and closed to outside students, they were not a real threat to the *studium.*[11] The fact that they often were presided over by local community figures or clerics from their homeland may give the impression they were quite separate from the university. Nonetheless, they had strong ties with the *studium:* not only were their charges university students, and their founders, on many occasions, professors, but activities of teaching and administration often fell to local university lecturers. One case among many is that of Agostino Galesi, a much-appreciated professor of logic in the *studium,* who also taught in the Collegio Montalto.[12] Each college also gave a prominent role to a student rector, chosen by his peers in the college, thus replicating the university structures.

The Collegio Ancarano encapsulates the evolution in the colleges' functions. This college was established by the testament of a famous law professor, Pietro Farnese d'Ancarano (†1415), for eight "poor and humble" (*pauperes et docili*) students of law in Bologna and a few members of his household. The college opened its doors by 1442 at the latest and was to be run by the rector and *consiliari* of the *universitas* of the Jurists. Increasingly, the municipal and ecclesiastical authorities took an interest in the college, but after 1506 the Farnese family came to treat it as its own private institution. Indeed, Cardinal Alessandro Farnese (later Pope Paul III) was named the college's *protector ac gubernator* and appointed its teachers; toward the end of the century, his successor (Ranuccio I Farnese, ruler of the Duchy of Parma and Piacenza, 1569–1622) referred to himself as the college's lord and patron (*dominus ac patronus*). The Ancarano aimed to prepare promising young men for prominent positions in, for instance, the Church. Among its students were important cultural figures such as Alessandro Farnese Jr., Odoardo Farnese, Guido Ascanio Sforza, and Camillo and Gabriele Paleotti. Members of the Paleotti and Zambeccari families, among others, served as its governors after 1589, but the college also received input from local university professors such as Ulisse Aldrovandi.[13] The college admitted some 392 students between 1595 and 1732. After that date, due to the extinction of the Farnese line, the Collegio Ancarano passed to Duke Charles I, who later became king of Naples and Sicily. A reform in 1763 recognized degrees from the Collegio Ancarano (where the main studies included philosophy and law) as equivalent to those of the universities of Naples and Messina, but a number of problems in later years led to the college's closure in 1781.[14]

Also important were two colleges, founded in the fourteenth century, that offered teaching to students: the Spanish College and the Collegio Gregoriano. The Collegio di San Clemente, more commonly known as the Collegio di Spagna, opened its doors in 1369; unlike the others, it is still functioning today. This college, founded by the testament of Cardinal Egidio Albornoz (1364), was established to support and house thirty Spanish students (eighteen in canon law, eight in theology, four in medicine), who would study in Bologna and then return to Spain as members of the ruling class. To help them in their studies, the college built up (and still owns today) a considerable collection of books (see §4.2.2). The students of the college were not, however, always a model of studiousness and moral behavior: indeed, the leadership of a student rector was to little effect and gave rise to lax discipline for fear of reprisals from other students. Because of the college's special relationship with the Spanish crown, and protection from a Spanish cardinal in Rome, the municipal authorities exercised no supervision over it, although it was subject to annual visitations by the local (arch)bishop.[15] Attempts during the second half of the sixteenth century to reform the institution, which had become a byword for violence and moral laxity, were unsuccessful. Its students, who used the privileges granted them by the college's statutes to shield themselves from any change, strenuously opposed outside intervention.[16] Even though the college was clearly independent from the *studium,* it shared many of the *studium*'s challenges during the same years: the number of students had dwindled, disputations rarely took place, few students attended class, Latin was not regularly spoken, personal enmities were a constant distraction, statutes stood in need of modernization, and students thought little of the authority of the (arch)bishop or of his representative.[17] Sometimes there were difficulties between its own officials and those of the *studium,* particularly when it came to rectors.[18]

As for the Collegio Gregoriano, founded by Pope Gregory XI in 1371 shortly after he took office, this college catered to law students and already hosted some thirty of them the following year. (Pope Gregory [Pierre Roger de Beaufort] had studied in Bologna, hence his interest in assisting students in the city.) It was meant to attract twenty poor students from the founder's home region (the diocese of Limoges and Tulle) and ten others from the papal dominions in Italy.[19] The college had a remarkable library, which already early on rivaled that of the Collegio di Spagna (see §4.2.2). Various problems, however, led this college to close its doors in 1474.

Residential colleges in Bologna provided a support system for students coming either from afar (e.g., Spain, Flanders, Croatia, Hungary) or nearer to home; as Brizzi observes, they may have helped delay the trend toward the *studium*'s regionalization.[20] Yet many of the foundations established after 1570 were explicitly directed at sons of Bolognese citizens.[21] They clearly did not serve a real need from the point of view of providing housing, so it is more likely that they provided a means for the socialization of an elite, along the lines of the Bolognese colleges for foreign students. Attestations of the trend toward social elevation are the numerous episodes of violence between students of various colleges in early modern Bologna, particularly because most of these seem to have arisen from disputes over honor and precedence.[22] But the importance of a noble clientele is a general feature of student colleges in early modern Bologna, including especially the colleges of instruction discussed below (§3.3.3). In its aristocratization, Bologna took part in a phenomenon replicated across Europe. The Staten College in Leiden, for example, was a residential university college aimed at the youth from high social classes across Holland and Zeeland who would come to constitute the country's political and ecclesiastical elite. Students were taught by university professors but originally took their lessons in the college. Fairly soon they went to hear the professors' university lectures instead. Communal life was meant to prepare them for high office.[23]

3.1.2 Student Academies

Residential colleges tended to promote a common identity for students with particular geographic roots, but there were other forms of association in Bologna that did not necessarily function as silos for students in this way. An important example is that of student academies. So far little researched for Bologna, these academies brought together students who, though studying in the same faculty, often belonged to different colleges and nationalities.

Accademia degli Oziosi

In Italy, student academies had arisen already in the sixteenth century. The best-documented ones to date are the academies formed by students in Rome.[24] For Bologna, the earliest identifiable circle is the Accademia degli Oziosi (more often referred to in the documents by its Latin name, Academia Otiosorum). Founded in 1563 by the young Bolognese nobleman Camillo Vizzani (1542–1566), this academy seems to have catered mainly to arts students, especially of philosophy and theology.[25] These students had a close association with Baldassar Gambarini, who was professor of logic and philosophy in Bologna from 1556 to the end of 1564, before continuing his career in Perugia and Pavia.[26] The intimacy between Gambarini and members of the Accademia degli Oziosi is evident in a manuscript containing several *recollectae* of his lectures, in letters written after Gambarini's departure, and in a printed work, the *De rerum principiis institutio*. All of these show that the Oziosi were a student *sodalitas* based on friendship, shared interests, and a common master. Gambarini must have been much more than just a figurehead. The academy's date of cessation is unknown, although one hears of it for the last time in 1567, a year after its founder's death.[27]

Gambarini delivered his lectures on logic and natural philosophy in Bologna between 1558 and 1563.[28] They were partly recorded by Camillo Vizzani, who (according to early testimony) wrote the statutes of the academy as well as several philosophical works of his own.[29] Closely linked to Camillo is his intimate friend Costanzo Varoli (1543–1575), who also left his traces in the notes of Gambarini's lectures and was a prominent member of the group (see below). Among other things, these lectures furnish unusual evidence of a teacher willing to copy out his lectures for the benefit of one of the students who had been unable to attend several classes.[30]

The close ties between Gambarini and various members of this academy are also evident in extant letters from 1566, pointing to a longstanding relationship of friendship with and among members of the group, and in various contemporary publications. In the first of these letters, Gambarini congratulates Camillo on his new home in Rome, in the knowledge that he is very welcome there. In the second, sent to Pompeo, he consoles him on his brother's early death.[31] Also valuable is the *De rerum principiis institutio* (1567), a reissue of the very rare *Theoremata universalia,* which was published earlier in the same year.[32] This work stems from a collective effort of the Oziosi and provides a valuable insight into the positions debated in logic, moral philosophy, natural philosophy, metaphysics, and theology by various members of the academy. Both works are notable, as are the *Conclusiones* by the academy member Costanzo Varoli, for their references to contemporary teachers of arts and medicine (including Gambarini) and to theological issues.[33] Especially numerous are the references to another professor, Antonio Maria Fava.[34] This was someone under whom Gambarini had studied and who, upon Gambarini's departure from Bologna, apparently took over as the academy's adviser and guide.[35] (Camillo Vizzani had by then left for Rome and Spain and would die shortly afterward.)[36]

Although the academy's statutes do not survive, the *De rerum principiis institutio* provides some evidence about its composition. Particularly clear is the group's structure and membership (Table 3.1). Gambarini and Fava

Table 3.1 The composition of the Accademia degli Oziosi

Ordo nascentis Ociosorum Academiae	
Illustrissimus Scipio Gonzaga	*Protector*
Excellentissimus Balthasar Gambarinus	*Pater*
Excellentissimus Antonius Franciscus Fabius	*Conservator*
Exc.s Lazarus Centurionus†	Iulius Luchinus
Camillus Vizanius†	Camillus Bertus
Exc.s Hieronymus Aius	Exc.s Iacobus Benalius
Rev. Magister Riginaldus Folianus	Christophorus Tassius
Caesar Elefantucius	Sebastianus Pontanus
Caesar Tridapaleus	Lelius Arigonus
Rev. Zacharias Andrianus	Ioannes Arigonus
Exc.s Constantius Varolius	Exc.s Georgius Scotus
Exc.s Camillus Cocchius	Hieronymus Gualterius
Exc.s Celsus Vittorius	Horatius Bartolotus
Exc.s Mauritius Cicarellus	Michael Lancius Hispanus
Exc.s Petrus Leo Golfus	Paulus Borascus
Achilles Benalius	Eugenius Calcina
Stephanus Santinus	†Camillus Scarlatinus
	Parisanus de Parisanis
ACCESSORES	Rev. F. Ricardus Baronus
Exc.s Ioannes Paulus Muzzolus	Scevola Cirionus
Exc.s Antonius Maria Venustus	Gaspar Tagliacoccius

Data source: De rerum principiis institutio (1567), page not numbered.

figure as the academy's *pater* and *conservator,* respectively, while Cardinal Scipione Gonzaga is the academy's *protector.* Fourteen names follow, presumably of the members of the academy, four of whom were deceased by the time of the work's printing in 1567. A list of twenty *accessores* indicates that others held something like associate membership in the academy.

Both this prospectus and other materials in Costanzo Varoli's 1565 *Conclusiones* show that the Oziosi were modeling themselves after contemporary academies, as the Impazienti would do in later years: they had a motto ("minus cum magis" or "less with more"), an emblem or *impresa* (an overturned bucket), and patronage from the powerful (Figure 3.1). The printed works mentioned above make it clear that the Oziosi appointed a

Fig 3.1. Impresa of the Academy of the Oziosi.

From colophon of Costanzo Varoli, *Conclusiones, quaesitis divinis, naturalibus, moralibus et dialecticis respondentes*... (Bologna: Giovanni Rossi, 1565). BUB, A.V.Tab. 1.F.1 428/1. Photo © Alma Mater Studiorum Università di Bologna—Biblioteca Universitaria di Bologna.

princeps, who changed at least every year (in 1567 it was Cristoforo Tassi).[37] One should not, however, confuse the Oziosi with an academy such as that of the Gelati (see §3.2.3). Rather than being a literary circle, this was a student group with a clear focus on disputations and theses. Their publications often mentioned and summarize the teaching of professors active in those years. Thus, the writings of the Oziosi provide a precious window onto questions being debated in Bologna in the 1560s, and onto the positions of various professors.

The list of members shown in Table 3.1 is also highly suggestive of an academy centered around students of arts and medicine. Not all of them graduated—indeed, there is no record of a degree for Camillo Vizzani or for most of those in the academy's inner circle.[38] By 1567, however, nearly all of those whose student career is identifiable had received their degree, usually in arts or in arts and medicine. A telling example is Varoli, one of the Oziosi's most important members. Varoli was a study companion of Camillo, who was one year his senior. Together they heard and recorded Gambarini's lectures on the *Physics* in 1561–1562, but it is likely that they took other classes together as well.[39] In 1565 Varoli published his *Conclusiones,* as indicated above. These were in all likelihood a form of exercise, explicitly prepared within the context of the Oziosi and the circle of Antonio Francesco Fava. Varoli would not present himself for the degree in arts and medicine until April 1566.[40] Given his caustic comments about his doctoral examination, it is unclear whether his exercises with the Oziosi had helped him.[41] In any case, he did not see his studies as having ended with his degree: indeed, he left Bologna almost immediately for Padua, where companions such as Giovanni Paolo Muzzolo had already gone, in order to perfect his knowledge of medicine and hear professors such as Federico Pendasio.[42] Around the time of his graduation, Varoli wrote to Camillo, providing some detailed information about the goings on in the Accademia degli Oziosi. He was particularly proud of Cardinal Scipione Gonzaga's acceptance of the position of *protector* of the Academy. Indeed, he transcribed the cardinal's letter to the Oziosi for his friend's benefit.[43] Varoli, who remained a close friend of Camillo, volunteered to deliver the funeral oration at his death in September 1566.[44]

The occasion of Camillo's funeral provides further testimony to the close connections between the Oziosi and the *studium.* The detailed account by Camillo's retainer, Lorenzo Poggiuoli, notes that the funeral procession stopped in front of *le scuole* (i.e., the Archiginnasio).[45] The procession included the academy's beadle; behind him came nine members of the academy and various noble students, including those of the Polish Nation.[46] The links between the Oziosi and the *studium* could hardly be clearer, although several aspects (such as the reasons for the involvement of the Polish Nation) would repay further research.

Accademia degli Impazienti

A later example of a student academy is the Accademia degli Impazienti, which again modeled itself after some traditional academies (through the use of pseudonyms, government by a prince, and so forth), but brought together students from across various colleges.[47] This academy, which started in 1689 and gave itself statutes in 1692, lasted until at least 1716. Its members were mainly law students who gathered in the houses of Bolognese notables such as the jurist Ippolito Maria Conventi, the *conservatore* Pietro Antonio Azzoguidi, and Count Alberto Fava. In many ways, the Impazienti were an association meant to help students who were preparing themselves in law (inter alia, members discussed theses and held *exercitationes*). But it is also significant from a social point of view: its members (initially drawn from the Collegio Poeti, Collegio Comelli, and Collegio Dosi, and later numbering also those from the Collegio Sinibaldi and Collegio Jacobs) may have represented a mix of nationalities and residential institutions but were selected according to strict social considerations. How selective it was can be seen from the small numbers of members added each year (on average, around four). This is an illustration of how the elites increasingly chose to become a closed social group, even within the context of what was essentially a student club.

Accademia degli Indivisi

Almost exactly contemporary with the Impazienti was another academy, that of the Indivisi (Undivided Ones). Founded in 1686, this was a more literary student society, dedicated (at least initially) to the study of Latin and again with a professor at its head: it was founded by Vincenzo Carlo Tommasini, had as its head Giovanni Battista Carlini (a professor of theology), and met in the home of Achille Fabbri (Palazzo Bargellini Panzacchi, now Pallavicini; currently Via Santo Stefano, 45).[48] At present, little else is known about this group and its activities. Again, however, it testifies that an academy could take many different forms.

3.2 Other Academies and the Istituto delle Scienze

Better known than the student academies just discussed are the literary and scientific academies and institutions that graced Bologna's cultural landscape from the sixteenth to the eighteenth century, such as the Accademia dei Gelati and the Istituto delle Scienze. These not only formed an important aspect of the larger context in which the university operated, but—as in other university towns such as Pavia—often had strong and sometimes official ties with the *studium*.[49] Indeed, in many academies, prominent members (and even founders) included university professors, whether locally or farther afield. Since Michele Maylender's pioneering work, more recent studies have been providing a new appreciation for the diversity of academies and their cultural and intellectual role.[50] The traditional view that sees academies as polar opposites of universities during the period and attributes cultural vitality only to them stands in need of thorough reconsideration.[51]

The following pages focus on the groupings with closest ties with members of the Bolognese *studium* and most relevant to the University of Bologna's cultural and intellectual milieu. They therefore do not discuss early circles such as the Accademia degli Accesi (founded c. 1500) and Giovanni Filoteo Achillini's Viridario (c. 1511).[52] Instead, they pay attention to the academies associated with Achille Bocchi, Claudio Betti, and the Gelati, before discussing the scientific circles that led to the formation of the Istituto delle Scienze in 1711.

3.2.1 Accademia Bocchiana

The Accademia Bocchiana was most closely associated with its founder, Achille Bocchi, who was a professor in Bologna, first of Greek and then of rhetoric and poetry (consistently referred to as *studia humanitatis* from 1538) between 1508 and his death in 1562.[53] Bocchi was, however, much more than a university professor: he was also a prominent cultural figure. On several occasions, the duties of political office or missions on behalf of the city interrupted his teaching. According to Rotondò, after his able service to the city with the papal legate Guido Ascanio Sforza in 1526, he was allowed to teach at home and receive his usual salary, as long as he continued his work on the *History of Bologna,* which the Senate had commissioned him to write. That project was never completed, and Bocchi is better known today for his influential work *Symbolical Questions* (*Symbolicarum quaestionum de universo genere quas serio ludebat libri quinque*), published in Bologna "in aedibus novae Academiae Bocchianae" in 1555. This work established Bocchi's importance as a writer within the emblem book tradition, and it is on this aspect that most scholarly work has focused.[54]

Few details survive about the group that from around 1543 gathered around Bocchi in his home, in an academy called by his name (and nowadays often referred to as the Accademia Hermathena because Hermes and Athena were meant to be its conjoined guiding lights).[55] But its participants included several of Bocchi's university colleagues, such as Romolo Amaseo, Francesco Robortello, Ludovico Boccadiferro, Ulisse Aldrovandi, and Antonio Bernardi Mirandolano.[56] Presumably it also attracted several local luminaries, although the studies conducted so far have not uncovered much secure documentation about this aspect. It is clear, however, that it had friends in high places: the Bocchiana's protector was Pope Paul III. After his death in 1549, the group's new patron became the cardinal nephew Alessandro Farnese (who must not have been very involved, given Italy's precarious political situation at the time).[57] The Accademia was so strongly centered on the personality of its founder that Bocchi's death soon led to its demise.

Bocchi's academy focused on legal matters, poetry, and possibly architecture. Unusually, Latin was the main language for its activities, and Bocchi apparently held lectures at least on Cicero's *De legibus* there in 1556.[58] The topic perfectly suited Bocchi's legal expertise and humanist orientation, but he saw the very intimate (*familiarissime*) disputations of his academy as contrasting with the austerity of his public teaching.[59] From this point of view, this academy may mark an interesting counterpart to the Oziosi, who, as we have seen, retained many of the textbooks and learning exercises typical of the university, but provided a more friendly and even family-like environment. Some doubt remains as to whether the academy had its own printer; only the first edition of the *Symbolicae quaestiones* lists the Nova Academia Bocchiana as having that function.[60]

3.2.2 Accademia dei Velati

Whereas the Accademia Bocchiana is well known, if somewhat shadowy, another contemporary academy, the Accademia dei Velati ("the Veiled Ones") has been forgotten. This circle (not to be confused with the Gelati) had a clear connection with at least one important professor of the *studium*.[61] Indeed, Claudio Betti, a master logician in Bologna who taught Aristotelian philosophy from 1545 until his death in January 1589, penned at least two works associated with the Velati.[62] They are preserved for us in a single manuscript (BUB, ms. 2388).[63] The works are both dedicated to Filippo Maria Campeggi, the bishop of Feltre, who may have been closely associated with the academy, perhaps as its *protector*.[64] The first is a public exposition in the Accademia dei Velati (March 1557) of a sonnet ("Giunta o vicina è l'ora, umana vita") by the contemporary poet Annibale Caro (1507–1566).[65] This work mainly consists of an outline (f. 75v) of and a commentary (ff. 76r–149r) on the sonnet in which Betti addresses, in the vernacular, issues associated with death, including the immortality of the soul, reminiscence, angels, divine providence, predestination, free will, and fortune. These topics are in keeping with the religious tone of Caro's sonnet, whose subject Betti in fact describes as "la morte cristiana" (Christian death). The second, much briefer work is a speech entitled *Discorso intorno la fortuna* apparently commissioned to Betti by the prince and the members of the academy.[66] The *Discorso* has a more strictly philosophical perspective and offers not only a definition of fortune, but also an analysis of the relationship between fortune and prudence, recalling in part contemporary discussions of *fortuna* versus *virtù*. Both compositions, offered publicly on Sundays (when there were no university lectures), show a side of Betti's intellectual activity in Bologna that was different from his Latin lectures on moral philosophy.[67]

Among other points, these writings connected with the Velati indicate that an engagement with philosophical issues in Italian was not limited to well-studied circles such as the Accademia degli Infiammati in Padua or the Accademia Fiorentina. The latter, which was still active in the 1550s, was particularly dedicated to exploring philosophical topics through works of poetry (especially Dante and Petrarch), as Betti's lectures for the Velati do.[68] One wonders, therefore, whether there were connections between the two. It is worth remembering that Benedetto Varchi and Alessandro Piccolomini had sojourned in Bologna in the early 1540s, as they heard the lectures of Ludovico Boccadiferro.[69] Given the prominent role that both Varchi and Piccolomini had played in the Accademia degli Infiammati (and Varchi's influential future role in the Accademia Fiorentina), it would not be surprising for them to have at least inspired a group such as the Velati.

3.2.3 Accademia dei Gelati

In any case, it is also clear that university professors could be heavily involved in the life of the Bolognese academies. Confirmation of this fact comes from the most famous Bolognese literary academy, that of the Gelati ("the Frozen Ones"). Founded in 1588, the Gelati quickly became one of the most prominent academies in Bologna.[70] It survived until around 1799, significantly outlasting other contemporary circles, which typically were active for only a brief period. Known for its literary activities and theatrical productions, the Gelati counted among its founding members at least two prominent professors: Melchiorre Zoppi (who taught philosophy first in Macerata and then, between 1581 and his death in 1634, in Bologna) and Camillo Gessi (who taught law there, 1594–1604 and 1607–1635).[71] Zoppi in particular, whose home served as a gathering place early in the life of the Gelati, had a considerable interest in theater (especially tragedy).[72] Apparently he saw no inconsistency between his role in the academy (where he was known as "il Caliginoso" or "the Dark One") and his appointment as professor of moral and natural philosophy for many years. In this early period, the academy enjoyed the protection of Cardinal Scipione Gonzaga (†1593), whom we have already met as the *protector* of the Oziosi.[73] The Gelati's ties with the *studium* become especially clear later on, when the academy recalled that it had obtained a privilege from Pope Urban VIII to present one student every year to the College of Law for a free doctorate.[74] (In fact, the privilege also extended to doctoral candidates in philosophy and medicine.)[75] Less relevant are the stipulations, in the *Leggi* of 1670, that only knights and gentlemen (or those of eminent scholarly attainment) could be admitted to the academy, although the point is of course common to other academies of the period.[76]

From both a linguistic and a thematic point of view, the activities and interests of the Gelati were quite varied. Members could present works or discourses either in Latin or in the vernacular (although, when women were present, they were expected to be brief and to preface their discourses with an explanation in the vernacular).[77] Judging from a collection of their writings in 1671, the Gelati discussed historical, philosophical, and scientific themes, and not just the tired points about the psychology of love that marked their discussions toward the end of the century.[78] They were not alone in this orientation toward more scholarly topics, which also characterized other academies from the last two or three decades of the seventeenth century, notably the well-documented Accademia degli Accesi (founded in 1686).[79] The period also saw the rise of new literary academies, in particular the Colonia Rena, a local manifestation of Rome's Accademia d'Arcadia founded in 1690.[80]

3.2.4 The Istituto delle Scienze and Its Background

Alongside the literary and learned academies mentioned above, early modern Bologna also boasted several scientific circles, in which university professors again played a prominent role. Around 1650 the physician Bartolomeo Massari founded the Accademia del Coro Anatomico; in 1665 the mathematician Geminiano Montanari started the Accademia della Traccia on the model of the Accademia del Cimento in Florence; in 1687 the archdeacon of Bologna and chancellor of the university, Anton Felice Marsili, established the Accademia Filosofico-Esperimentale simultaneously with the Accademia Ecclesiastica, devoted to church history; and in 1690 the future mathematician Eustachio Manfredi, then only sixteen, was one of the founders of the Accademia degli Inquieti.[81]

The Inquieti met in the home of the physician and university professor Giacomo Sandri between 1694 and 1704. The circle then underwent a significant reform: on the example of the Académie des Sciences in Paris, it centered its attention on disciplines marked by experimentation and calculation—anatomy, medicine, natural history, chemistry, physics, mathematics, and astronomy.[82] Around 1705 the Inquieti moved to the home of Count Luigi Ferdinando Marsili, a former general in the imperial army who, partly through his earlier studies with Marcello Malpighi, had developed scientific interests and started publishing in fields such as natural history, geology, and cartography. In turn, Marsili drew into his orbit several students and professors (including Giambattista Morgagni, Manfredi and Vittorio Francesco Stancari).[83] In these years he developed a cultural project that included an astronomical observatory, built in 1703 on the rooftop of the family palazzo in Via San Mamolo. He also started a museum of natural history. Marsili's family, however, did not embrace these private initiatives. Indeed, the head of the family was particularly disgruntled about the constant visits by the general's friends and even began court proceedings against him. Such opposition led Marsili to seek public support and funding. In 1709 he also proposed drastic changes to the university curriculum (including the curtailment of law and the strengthening of scientific subjects).[84] Although Marsili's plan was controversial and was never fully accepted, it did lead to the establishment of an institute that was complementary to (though formally independent of) the university, and in which experimental disciplines could be taught publicly.[85]

The Istituto, which was founded in 1711 and opened its doors in 1714, gathered within it both the Accademia degli Inquieti (under the new designation Accademia delle Scienze) and the Accademia Clementina delle Belle Arti (which focused on fine art).[86] It had its own location in Palazzo Poggi (now the administration building of the university in Via Zamboni, 33) and was dedicated to the practical and productive arts and sciences. (Marsili thought of it as a place in which teaching would be imparted "more by sight than by hearing.") Nonetheless, the Istituto had very close ties with the university: its first president, Lelio Trionfetti, was a professor in the *studium,* as were the librarian, the mathematician, the astronomer, the experimental physicist, the natural historian, and the chemist. The agreed-upon arrangement (somewhat at variance with the original plan) was that the university would deliver theoretical knowledge, while the Istituto would supply experimentation and practical know-how.[87] This aim was reflected in the palazzo's architectural spaces and structures, which included—in addition to the library and a magnificently frescoed meeting room for each academy—three rooms for physics, one for architecture and military art (including models of fortifications), three for natural history (for fossils and land animals, water creatures, and seeds, respectively), one for figure drawing, others with casts of ancient statues or sketches of ancient buildings, and finally a space for the machines built by the Istituto's own machinist. Later additions included an imposing observatory, a chemical laboratory, and a space dedicated to a new discipline—geography and *nautica* (maritime science).[88] A strong supporter of the Istituto was Cardinal Prospero Lambertini (later Pope Benedict XIV), who among other things donated to it the collection of medical instruments given him by Louis XV, king of France. Such moves led to significant developments in medicine, anatomy, and obstetrics, as well as to the acquisition of additional instruments in other fields.[89] The Istituto also came to incorporate the books and scientific collections donated to the city by Aldrovandi, Ferdinando Cospi, and others, leading to the establishment of a combined library in 1757.[90] (Many of the museum's holdings are still on display in Bologna's Museo di Palazzo Poggi, while its library formed the core of what is now the Biblioteca Universitaria in the same building.) Like other scientific societies, the Istituto also had a strong

Fig 3.2. Visit of Prince Frederick Christian of Poland to the Istituto delle Scienze.
Miniature (405 × 526 mm) on parchment, Antonio Alessandro Scarselli, November/December 1739. Archivio di Stato di Bologna, Insignia degli Anziani, vol. XIII, f. 140r.

publishing program, particularly geared toward the dissemination of the findings and papers read in its Accademia delle Scienze, although in its initial phases especially it was careful not to raise the ire of the censors of the Inquisition.[91]

This broad range of interests and activities appears most vividly in Figure 3.2, a watercolor representing the visit of the prince of Poland, Frederick Christian, to the Istituto in 1739. The right foreground testifies to an interest in the application of science to fortifications and war machines; the objects on the left and at center refer to astronomical pursuits, geometry, and even experiments on living animals. Meanwhile, to the rear one can see the library, a session of life drawing, and the museum of natural history, including bodies and skeletons for the study of anatomy.

The Istituto and the university were close in many large and small ways. Although we do not know exactly how many university students also followed lectures and experiments in the Istituto, at least one college (the Collegio Ancarano) required its charges to attend the Istituto's scientific and experimental gatherings.[92] The teachers in the Istituto were drawn, from the start, from the ordinary professors of the *studium*. Indeed, it was nearly always a requirement to be a university professor in order to obtain a teaching post within the Istituto.[93] Particularly after the reform of 1737, there was a strong correspondence between the teachings offered in both institutions. And the fact that lectures at the Istituto could take place only on Thursdays, when there were no lectures in the *studium*, meant that students could in principle easily attend classes in both settings. Yet it also meant that Bologna soon lost its leading place in the technical disciplines to other Italian cities that devoted much more teaching time to practical subjects.[94] A partial remedy was to give more prominence to private (though official) teaching, according to the direct testimony of Laura Bassi, who with her husband Giuseppe Veratti taught in their home, apparently to great acclaim.[95] The Istituto did not start offering more continuous teaching until around 1776. By that time it had lost its previous position as an innovator in the Italian landscape and had become more of a laggard.[96]

3.3 Friend or Foe? Higher Education outside of the *Studium*

University teaching in Bologna also intersected with a third large area—the schools and cultural initiatives of the religious orders. Particularly relevant are the schools or *studia* of the mendicant orders, the Jesuit college, and the colleges of instruction, in which the Jesuits played an especially active role. Although these institutions were mostly complementary to the university, at times there was also a sense of competition and rivalry. Furthermore, Bologna increasingly came to appreciate that it was vying for students and staff with other papal universities and with institutions across Europe.

3.3.1 Schools of the Mendicants (and Others)

From the thirteenth century, Bologna was home to *studia generalia* for the major mendicant orders (among others, Franciscans, Dominicans, and Augustinian Hermits).[97] These *studia* served as province-wide educational centers in arts and theology for especially promising youngsters. The hope was that these young men would commit early on to a specific order, follow its full educational pathway, and thereafter move to positions of teaching or leadership. The extent to which the teaching of these *studia* was open to interested laymen is a matter of controversy among scholars, as shown by ongoing disagreements among Dantists as to whether the Florentine poet took advantage of instruction in religious *studia,* and if so, where.[98] This debate has no straightforward answer, but in at least three areas the interaction of the Bolognese university with churches or religious orders is quite clear.

First is the issue of space. There is no doubt that local churches served as gathering places for both university doctors and students. The cathedral church of San Pietro, for instance, was where the colleges of doctors held their meetings and examined degree candidates in most subjects, at least until 1587, when Archbishop Gabriele Paleotti made available some spaces in the nearby Palazzo Arcivescovile for these functions. Numerous students and doctors of arts and medicine gravitated around the church of San Salvatore (of the Canons Regular of St. Augustine), as testified by private altars, documentary evidence, and the holding there of degree examinations in medicine and surgery.[99] It was in San Salvatore that Ulisse Aldrovandi established the first botanical garden in Bologna.[100] But especially prominent in the student statutes are the churches of the mendicant orders. Student *universitates* met in the churches of San Domenico (Jurists) and San Francesco (Artists).[101] The various Nations gathered and held their elections in these various churches. (The English students were especially attracted to San Salvatore.)[102] Their regular presence offered the orders an opportunity to recruit from among their ranks—something they were eager to do.

Furthermore, university professors had close ties with local churches, and with those of the mendicants in particular. After death, many of them were interred within their walls and courtyards. (A local favorite was San Domenico, which still preserves many tombs and inscriptions; but many others were used as well: see Figure 1.2 for the tomb of Nicolò Fava in San Giacomo Maggiore.)[103] As noted in Chapter 1 (§1.2), especially famous doctors were honored by prominent and striking arks placed outside of the church buildings—an unusual feature of the medieval Bolognese *studium.* But in fact, connections went well beyond this: many university doctors remembered these churches in their wills: money and property bought masses and prayers for their souls, while books enriched the only institutional libraries of the city.[104] The humanist and Hellenist Antonio Codro Urceo, for instance, had close ties with the monastery of San Salvatore (where he died and was buried) and gifted its library with his Greek codex of the works of Basil the Great.[105]

But contacts could flow in the opposite direction as well. Unlike in Paris and elsewhere, regulars (members of religious orders) were welcome to teach in Bologna's university. There they often taught logic, natural philosophy, moral philosophy, and of course metaphysics. Especially in the period between 1419 and 1461, some thirteen lecturers from the religious orders were hired to teach natural philosophy and related subjects.[106] Some of these were well-known figures such as the Dominican Gaspare Sighicelli (or Guaspar de Sancto Johanne in Persiceto), who taught logic, natural philosophy, and moral philosophy between 1419 and 1448; another was the Augustinian Hermit Andrea Biglia (or Andrea de Billis de Mediolano), who taught moral and natural philosophy from 1424 to 1428.[107] Many others were minor personalities who taught for fairly short periods (one to three years). In 1458–1459, the rolls list four regulars for natural philosophy: two Servites, one member of the order of St. Augustine, and one Augustinian Hermit.[108] From 1461 until at least 1600, regulars are absent in the teaching rolls, for unclear reasons. The number of regulars teaching moral philosophy is also fairly modest (eleven out of some ninety-one instructors up to 1622), but better distributed over time. A high-water mark is the start of the sixteenth century, when three Franciscans and one Servite teach moral philosophy, often in conjunction with metaphysics.[109] As noted elsewhere (§2.1 and §8.1), this pattern changed with the introduction of more regular teaching of subjects such as theology and Scriptures in the second half of the sixteenth century and later. From then on, members of the religious orders (and clerics in general) gained considerable prominence on the teaching rolls (see Table 8.1).

3.3.2 The Jesuits

The Society of Jesus (est. 1540) came to regard as one of its main missions that of offering its educational program to laymen as well as to members of its order. Hundreds of colleges sprang up across Europe, Asia, and the Americas, taking as their model the Collegio Romano (1551).[110] The contours of the Jesuit curriculum were somewhat in flux until the final *Ratio studiorum* of 1599.[111] Nonetheless, already in earlier years it consisted of three main phases that had potential overlaps with university teaching. The humanities occupied the first five years, and on its heels came (where possible) three years of philosophy and mathematics, followed by the crowning course in theology. The tuition offered by the Jesuits was both of very high standard and free of charge.[112] The Jesuits were renowned for their thorough training and for their pedagogical skills. The fact that they offered their expertise for free placed them in an excellent position to compete with the education offered by communal schools (at the lower end of humanities teaching), but also universities. The high regard they commanded also meant that they could link their educational training with a program of moral and religious reform.[113] Finally, the Jesuits brought to Italy something quite foreign to the Italian university system: a carefully graduated curriculum. From their time in the Parisian colleges (particularly those of Montaigu and Ste. Barbe), Ignatius of Loyola and his early followers had appreciated a system that led students from elementary to higher subjects along a well-defined path of graduated learning. This *modus parisiensis,* which soon officially became part of the Jesuit approach, was sorely lacking in the Italian universities, where students were free to sample various subjects and did not take examinations until they applied for a degree (see §2.1).[114] All of these factors, in addition to the Jesuits' quite deliberate targeting of young aristocrats—whom they sought to mold both morally and culturally after a long classicist tradition—made for a situation of potential conflict when they established colleges in university towns.[115] This was especially the case when they tried (as they often did) to take over local university institutions.[116] In Bologna they made no such moves, perhaps stung by their experience in Padua, which banned them from the city in 1591.[117] But their stay in Bologna was lengthy—ending only with the suppression of the order in 1773—and influential. Although much of the historiography on the Jesuits has tended to emphasize the obstacles and defeats that their curricular approach encountered in Italy, one should not underestimate the impact of their spiritual and moral aims in contexts such as Bologna (see Chapter 8).

The Jesuits settled in Bologna in 1546, started teaching in 1551, and shortly thereafter founded the college of Santa Lucia.[118] Their leader was Francesco Palmio, who until his death in 1585 was indefatigable in promoting the Society of Jesus in Bologna. Palmio paid special attention to creating close ties with its leading citizens, including the head of the diocese, Paleotti.[119] Descriptions of the Jesuit college in this early period are already quite detailed. In 1554 a letter of Francesco Scipione (one of the teachers in the college) to Juan de Polanco in Rome reports on the various classes for Greek and Latin in particular and the works that were being read.[120] In later years the Jesuits wrote that their method of instruction was being well received: a letter of Ludovico Gagliardi from 1561 suggests that around a hundred students were attending the Jesuits' classes, and that the Jesuits' teaching was receiving excellent publicity from notable professors in the *studium*. In fact, Francesco Robortello, a famous professor of Greek and Latin letters, had put his son under their tutelage.[121]

The pedagogical operations of the Jesuit college clearly evolved in later years and have received scholarly attention.[122] Documents from the seventeenth and eighteenth centuries indicate that Santa Lucia came to offer a quite varied program of studies, ranging from the very elementary to the fairly advanced. Seeing the need for basic instruction in reading, writing, and arithmetic, the Jesuits offered four years of propaedeutic study, divided in two stages of two years each, indicated as *scuoletta minore* and *scuoletta maggiore,* respectively. These included the basics of Latin grammar, reading of authors such as Cicero, and catechetical instruction. In 1681 they started a second *scuoletta,* specifically for sons of nobles. After this first stage came two years of grammar study. This involved the study of Latin literature at a higher level: pupils continued to give attention to Cicero (particularly the *Familiar Epistles* and *On Duties*), but also to other Roman authors such as Ovid, Seneca, Martial, and Virgil, and to the catechism. The two following years covered the humanities and rhetoric, respectively. In this stage, pupils studied the rules of eloquence in great detail and were trained to become expert rhetoricians, following especially the style of Cicero. The reading material expanded, however, to include historians (Caesar, Sallust, Livy, Curtius Rufus) and poets (Virgil, Horace). Pupils learned to write letters, oration, poems, and dialogues. They could also study Greek. Jesuit teachers also gave a great deal of attention to the pupils' religious life and edification. In addition to these subjects, pupils of noble origin especially could avail themselves of what we would call today an extracurricular program of study. The sons of nobles learned foreign languages (especially Italian and French), while at the same time gaining a basic knowledge of history and geography. They also learned about proper deportment, had training in music and dance, practiced fencing and other similar arts, and took part in theatrical productions. There were also private lessons in canon and civil law, offered by one of the professors in the *studium* at the students' expense. The lessons on the *Feuds* seem to have been especially relevant to these young aristocrats.

What did not develop in Santa Lucia until quite late was the study of philosophy. As mentioned above, in the Jesuit colleges the classes of humanities and rhetoric usually led directly to those of philosophy, where one would study logic, natural philosophy, moral philosophy, and metaphysics. In parallel, there was also instruction in mathematics. In Santa Lucia, for a long period this progression was not possible. Unlike the colleges in Parma, Modena, Siena, and Ravenna (in addition to many others, including the Collegio Romano), the curriculum offered in Bologna was circumscribed. Behind this restriction lay the vigorous objections of the doctors of the *studium,* recorded particularly for 1591 and 1615. In fairness, they ought also to have objected to the Jesuits' teaching of humanities and rhetoric, but the professors of philosophy were usually much more vocal than their colleagues in the humanities—perhaps because the demand for rhetorical teaching was high enough that competition from the Jesuits did not much matter. In any case, when political and military upheavals caused the Jesuit college of Parma to transfer to Bologna from 1636 to 1644, its teaching of philosophy and theology moved as well.[123] The Jesuit documents indicate that, from 1638, philosophy was being taught in the Jesuit college in addition to theology (introduced in 1635).[124] Students at the college of St. Francis Xavier (see §3.3.3) must have seen this as an opportunity to take philosophy courses with the Jesuits; they petitioned the papal legate Giulio Sacchetti on the matter, and at the end of 1638 Sacchetti acquiesced.[125]

The Assunteria dello Studio, however, voiced strong concerns about the situation. It had already been growing restless since news had arrived in 1635 of the imminent transfer of the college in Parma.[126] The Assunti feared that the Jesuits would open their doors to external students, as they had elsewhere, and draw them away from the university. Together with the college of doctors of theology (which was also apparently worried about competition), the Assunti tried to convince the legate to keep the Jesuits at bay. Giulio Sacchetti, however, was not persuaded, so they made another attempt with his successor, Cardinal Stefano Durazzo (legate, June 1640–November 1642). This time they were more fortunate. In July 1641 Durazzo issued a set of instructions (prepared by his immediate predecessor) forbidding anyone in the city from teaching higher subjects unless he appeared on the university teaching rolls. The only exception made was for the regulars and their students. (The Jesuits were not explicitly named.)[127] But the legate's instructions were less water-tight than the Assunti had hoped for, so the university decided to request a formal papal bull on the matter. After intense negotiations, on 10 November 1641 Pope Urban VIII issued the *Uberes fructus,* which named the Jesuits explicitly and repeatedly. The bull prohibited them (under pain of excommunication) from offering higher subjects that were taught in the university. However, as Grendler rightly notes, it was always unlikely that the papacy would excommunicate members of its most loyal order, and the compromise in this case was probably that the bull would be issued but not enforced.[128] In a way, the threat to the university became much less direct as the college returned to Parma in 1644. The fact that only one teacher per year is listed for higher subjects in Bologna's college suggests that demand was not high. Mathematics and experimental physics do seem to have gained ground there in the eighteenth century, though, thanks especially to the presence of eminent teachers such as Vincenzo Riccati.[129]

3.3.3 Colleges of Instruction (Colleges for Nobles)

Around the middle of the sixteenth century a different type of college arose in Bologna.[130] Rather than residential colleges or those geared to the religious orders, these were colleges of instruction with a different clientele. They were funded by their boarders, offered a varied teaching program, and served as the means of formation of an educated elite, very much like the Collegio Ancarano. The first of these institutions, often also called academies, was the Collegio degli Ardenti (later renamed Accademia del Porto Naviglio) in 1555. After the Ardenti, whose doors opened in 1558 and shut in 1732, came other colleges, many of which owed their origins to the Jesuits' enterprise. These included the Collegio dei Nobili of Santa Prisca and St. Francis Xavier, both of them discussed below. The Jesuits also established San Luigi (Gonzaga) for students not of noble birth, while thwarting the competition represented by another college for nobles, San Tommaso d'Aquino.[131]

The links between these colleges and the university (or even student colleges) were weak at best. The case of the Ardenti is telling.[132] It shows that these colleges were not meant primarily for university students; instructors were typically private teachers rather than university professors; teachings could go from the basics of grammar and rhetoric to music, dance, fencing, and horse riding; admission was selective, and in time noble birth became an absolute prerequisite; and student self-governance was not a feature. Most of the colleges of instruction became dedicated to the formation of the perfect gentleman—intellectually, morally, socially, and even physically—through an expanded educational offering.[133] This made quite a contrast with the goal of the universities to provide an intellectual education and training.[134] The differences were such that hardly any of these noblemen (many of whom came from abroad and were engaged in the precursor to the *grand tour*) bothered to acquire a degree.[135] This was perhaps because (at least from 1703) residents could study higher subjects such as law, theology, philosophy, and mathematics in the college. As a consequence, students were allowed to stay beyond the earlier maximum age of sixteen or seventeen.

The Collegio dei Nobili (founded 1588?, closed 1666–1668), entitled first to Santa Prisca and, after around 1630, to Santa Caterina, was initially a residence for noblemen who came to Bologna and studied in the next-door Jesuit college of Santa Lucia.[136] It was therefore not, in origin, a teaching college, but it gradually distanced itself from the Jesuits (who had had no small role in establishing it). In time, a committee of Bolognese citizens came to manage it. The teaching that began to take place there later on nonetheless followed the Jesuits' *Ratio studiorum,* except that it abandoned Latin for the vernacular. It faced down competition from a new college formed by the enterprising don Ludovico Micheli of San Marco, who had even managed in the printed statutes of his college (1621) to appropriate the name "Collegio dei Nobili." (The city authorities quickly foiled this early instance of trademark infringement upon request of the Collegio di Santa Prisca).[137] An early seventeenth-century diary by a German nobleman, Baron Veit Künigl Jr., provides some insight into this college. Künigl arrived in Bologna in 1607, matriculated in the German Nation, but studied (1607–1609) in the Bolognese college of the Jesuits, while also pursuing studies in Italian language, music, and dance under various private teachers.[138]

This course of studies was in perfect keeping with the Jesuits' intention to form members of the elites.

In 1634, after realizing that they had lost control of the Collegio dei Nobili, the Jesuits opened another one, dedicated to St. Francis Xavier (a Jesuit who had been instrumental in establishing the Jesuit presence in sixteenth-century Bologna).[139] Although this too was a college for nobles, it was more of a residential college; teaching continued to take place in Santa Lucia. The St. Francis Xavier college operated until the suppression of the Jesuit order in Bologna in 1773. Judging from its numbers (at its peak, in the first decade of the eighteenth century, it enrolled some 241 noblemen), this college was a considerable success, although similar Jesuit colleges for nobles elsewhere, such as in Parma and Siena, had even higher enrollments.[140]

Three points deserve comment. One is that, as Brizzi has noted, these new colleges of instruction came to be more popular than the university's residential colleges. In the period 1663–1665, for instance, the ten university colleges still in operation had a total of only thirty-nine students (versus the eighty-five foreseen by their statutes), whereas the college of St. Francis Xavier on its own counted sixty-two residents.[141] It seems therefore that a particularly attractive feature about these colleges (at least to authorities, including parents) was the possibility they offered to exercise control over the entire student experience, in a way that was impossible in the colleges that served only as places of residence (and that, as seen above, had often fallen prey to moral laxity).[142] Secondly, the colleges had rather closer ties with the ecclesiastical hierarchy than with the university, since local clergymen were often responsible for redacting their statutes. The supervisory roles of clergymen were also important.[143] Finally, the numerous prohibitions issued by the authorities did not deter the colleges from teaching subjects that were also part of the university curriculum.[144] The college of San Luigi, for instance, came to offer a range of higher subjects, including civil and canon law.[145] Although they do not seem to have taught medicine, which remained the preserve of the university, the colleges of instruction not only competed with the university by providing instruction in many of the same subjects, but extended their provision to swordsmanship, dancing, and other socially useful skills. But by far the clearest (and, to the *studium* authorities, the most worrying) case of competition came from the educational activities of the Jesuits in the college of Santa Lucia, as discussed above.

Not all of the colleges of instruction were religious foundations: the Collegio Sinibaldi (1681–1788), for instance, was established in 1605 by the bequest of Agostino Sinibaldi, a doctor of civil and canon law. This was a college meant for ten students from Lucca plus a rector, prefect, cook, and two other staff. Students (all of them of noble extraction) were to be aged eighteen to twenty-five and to reside no longer than five years. The college was meant to prepare them for service to their home republic. They mainly studied law, humanities, and philosophy under university professors who came to the college.[146] Unlike other establishments, the Sinibaldi did not include the practice or teaching of music, singing, or dancing.[147] Indeed, in many ways it seems to have followed a very rigid set of rules. This did not, however, prevent embarrassing problems of social order, as the college's residents treated its staff (including the college's governors) with insolence and contempt. The rector of the Sinibaldi complained strongly about this situation in 1768, noting that the residents "continually threaten to kick and hit [the servants]" and that "they openly flaunt the rules of the constitutions; when they are warned with all sweetness and calm, either they do not listen, or they answer disrespectfully."[148] But this was only one aspect of the numerous infractions discussed in the documentation. Despite the staff's efforts, it was unable to shield its charges from external corrupting influences. Likewise, it could not prevent gambling, disrespect for teachers, and an all-pervasive litigiousness within the walls of the college, some of it fueled by social hauteur.[149] The residents' mood must not have been improved by the college's shoestring budget and the reluctance of its overseers in Lucca to replace the worn-out curtains, tablecloths, linen, bedcovers, or furniture.[150]

This chapter has pointed to the lively cultural landscape in which the Bolognese *studium* operated.[151] Students and professors could get involved in formalized student groups such as the Oziosi (in which professors might play a guiding role) and literary and scientific academies such as the Gelati (in which professors could mingle informally with learned and prominent locals). They also found themselves literally surrounded by para- and extra-university colleges. These ranged widely in character and age—from secular to religious, from the *studia* of the Franciscans and Dominicans to the seminary established by Paleotti, and from ancient ones like the Spanish College to recent establishments like the Sinibaldi. Some of these contexts (such as the Istituto delle Scienze) called for collaboration, as it made little sense to row against the prevailing cultural tides. The university could preserve its established identity as a seat and communicator of learning while allowing the Istituto to engage in experimentation. Other institutions (such as the Jesuit college) inspired wariness at the potential for competition, which threatened defeat.

Bologna seems to have been proud of its varied landscape of learning. In 1719 a query from a prospective student from the Netherlands (a certain N. Chevallier) resulted in a twelve-page printed response, doubtless conceived as a promotional tool. There the author, Gaspar Marianus de Varrano Lentius, extolled the glories and beauties of Bologna. There were embellishments, as in all promotional literature, including about women teaching law.[152] What is noteworthy, however, is that—although there is a fair amount on the *studium,* including the obligatory material about past famous professors—one also reads quite a bit about the various colleges, the Istituto delle Scienze, the Accademia delle Arti, Aldrovandi's museum (and that of Cospi), and the antiquities of the city. Indeed, at one point the author exclaims, "The whole city is a monument to studies!" before launching into a description also of its architectural features. Incidentally, he claims that teachers read for a whole hour, timed by a sand clock.[153]

We still know far too little about the effects of these various contexts on Bologna's climate of learning. What precisely enabled exchanges of knowledge between the university and non-university schools? How did the city's various religious orders, for instance, make use of (or, vice versa, contribute to) the expertise on hand in the university? What lessons, if any, did professors draw from their experience of changes taking place in the various colleges (such as the Spanish College or the Sinibaldi), which faced similar problems of student unrest and disrespect? And to what extent did academies—long considered the real engines of intellectual renovation in the period—promote genuinely distinctive approaches or ideas? Chapter 4 examines some of these contexts more closely and from a slightly different perspective. As books traveled and changed hands, they also crossed boundaries in a city that was at times highly nervous about the spread of heterodox ideas.

4

The Culture of the Book

In the early modern period, books remained central to the business of teaching and scholarship, whether in theology, law, or arts and medicine.[1] Statutes could be quite specific about texts on which teachers were to lecture.[2] Success in disputations depended partly on mastering (and memorizing) large portions of works, which could then be made to support or undermine various arguments. Examinations taken at the end of one's studies invariably contained *puncta* (passages) that the candidate was expected to explain at short notice with reference to a vast commentary literature. Furthermore, although they may not be wholly reliable, depictions of classroom situations regularly show both the master and his students with their books open in front of them (see Figures 2.6 and 2.7). Teaching itself gave rise to books, in the form of copious student notebooks or printed lectures.[3]

Books, however, were expensive, even after the advent of print. When he arrived in Bologna as a student of civil law in 1555, Basilius Amerbach wrote to his father in Basel that he spent 1 crown per month on rent, 4 crowns on food, and 15 crowns to purchase the *Corpus civile* and Bartolus.[4] How, then, did students and masters manage to get their hands on the books they needed? This chapter will show that, in addition to purchasing books outright, possibilities included borrowing, renting, or consulting books in local collections. It was not unusual to copy such shared books in longhand, whether for personal or classroom use. Once copied or acquired, books could stay within a family for many decades or even centuries. They might be passed on from father to son to grandson and be used even by later generations for their studies.[5] This practice made sense because university textbooks did not change quickly (see §2.2.2). In philosophy, for instance, it was a long-established practice to teach Aristotle's texts through the lens of the commentaries by Averroes; in medicine, Taddeo Alderotti's commentaries on Hippocrates (composed in the early fourteenth century) were still being printed in the sixteenth century.

Inevitably, the intersection between manuscripts and printed books—as well as the slow (and never fully realized) transition from one form of production to the other—is an important aspect of the picture that follows. But this chapter focuses less on the history and processes of manuscript production and of printing than on the availability, circulation, and exchange of books. This slant is determined partly by the critical literature. There have, of course, been several older and more recent studies on Bologna's book culture, including analyses of specific figures and typographical enterprises.[6] Despite their value, these works do not provide a more general understanding of the local, Italian, and international networks in which Bolognese printers, booksellers, and book buyers operated and should be seen. This is particularly true for the *longue durée*.[7] In terms of overall syntheses, scholars are still largely reliant on Sorbelli's classic study from 1923, although Rita De Tata's recent study breaks much new ground for the fifteenth and sixteenth centuries, as does Maria Gioia Tavoni's research for the eighteenth.[8] This chapter therefore explores three broad themes that were important for the early modern university: the presence of book producers and booksellers, the function of library collections, and the effects of religious control on the availability and circulation of books, particularly in the post-Tridentine climate. In all three cases, members of the university successfully navigated a situation that was not entirely to their advantage.

A related point is that Bologna was not one of Italy's great centers for producing or collecting books. Bologna differed from other places (such as Ferrara, Florence, Milan, Naples, Rome), where the patronage of powerful local rulers fostered book production.[9] The Bentivoglio family was far from having the interests and clout of the Gonzaga or the Medici, for instance. After the end of the Bentivoglio rule in 1506, Bologna remained even more clearly in a position of political (and sometimes cultural) subordination with respect to Rome, the capital of the Papal State. In fact, the situation of Bologna's *studium* was not unlike that of Padua, Pavia, and (later on) Pisa, all of which were governed by a larger, more powerful neighbor whose rulers were keen to project their power through their cultural initiatives in the main city. Thus, the libraries in Florence (Laurenziana), Rome (Vatican), and Venice (Marciana) were collections that any Italian university city would have had trouble matching.

4.1 Book Producers and Booksellers

Already in the Middle Ages the university landscape of book production had stationers (*stationarii librorum*) at its center. Stationers' shops included exemplars of the main texts and commentaries on which teaching was based. The statutes required professors to deposit with the stationers relevant texts of interest to students, both the primary texts on which their teaching was based and also the *quaestiones disputatae* they had held. The beadles were to ensure that the stationers were well stocked.[10] These texts—which, in the case of primary authors, underwent a stringent process of verification—could either be copied by scribes contracted by the stationers or rented out so that they could be copied by the end user, usually a student, within eight to ten days.[11] Rental rates were fixed by statute, and the development of the *pecia* system meant that several sheaves (*peciae*) of a particular work could be copied simultaneously, thus speeding up the process of furnishing the final copy of the text. Alternatively, the *peciae* could be rented out individually.[12] The process involved contracts—many of them still preserved—between the commissioner (i.e., the student) and the stationer.[13] Other people involved included the *cartolarii* (who supplied the writing material, usually parchment in the earlier period), miniaturists (who did the manuscript decoration, if this was required), and *ligatores* or bookbinders. An example of a manuscript copied by a student, presumably from an exemplar furnished by the stationer, is London, BL, Add. 10738—a collection of logical treatises of the English philosopher and logician William Heytsbury (d. 1372 / 1373) scribed by a student of logic in Bologna in 1408.[14]

Stationers also sold books. Students were not to sell books to each other directly, and even when they bought them from the stationer, they were not allowed to resell them for profit.[15] All considered, the system seems to have kept up well with demand, or at least not to have generated many complaints. This suggests that the beadles, who oversaw the process as a whole, were doing their job.[16]

The stationer's shop was not, of course, the town's sole provider of manuscripts. There must have been a flourishing market of copyists who responded to requests for manuscripts. Some of these manuscripts would have been produced within the religious *studia* (including San Domenico), whose program of arts subjects overlapped with that of students at the university.[17] A manuscript of the works of Aristotle probably produced in San Francesco (XIII / XIV century) and now in the Archiginnasio library is a telling example of a book that could have served either the convent's students or the university market.[18]

Some manuscripts have clear connections to the activities of study and teaching in the *studium*. They show that a book did not need to be particularly beautiful to be used by members of several generations. BUB, ms. 920, is a miscellany formed of several relevant items. This manuscript was in use for the study of logic for over a century and retains signs of its presence in the same family for three generations. (In fact it remained in the Garzoni family well beyond that, until 1716, when the family's last heir donated it to the Istituto delle Scienze.)[19] The first item is a logical compendium subscribed by Bernardo Garzoni (a medical doctor and the father of the famous professor Giovanni Garzoni, †1505), who says he wrote and finished it in June 1417 ("scripsit ac perfecit anno MCCCCXVII 4° nonas iunii"). Most likely this part of the manuscript is connected with logical lectures Garzoni attended as a student. Other items include a *Summula logica* and a treatise by William Heytsbury (the latter item's subscription indicates that it was owned by Bernardo's grandson Marco) and logical treatises by Albert of Saxony. The *Consequentiae bonae et utiles* by Rudolphus Strodaeus (Ralph Strode) bears a note of ownership by a Carmelite friar, Blasius Silvestri of Florence. Following the *Tractatus brevissimus de sensu composito et diviso* by Paul of Pergola, there is a subscription dated 8 June 1481. The original flyleaf (now lost) contained notes stating that the book belonged to a certain Marcello, as well as references to the teaching of two different instructors of logic, Nicolaus de Saviis (1481) and Antonius Francisci de Faba (1530).[20] The manuscript indicates that books of this kind could be formed from the accretion of disparate materials over time, some of them deriving also from the personal libraries of friars, and that there was a communal element to their use.

Two fifteenth-century manuscripts owe their origin instead to a commission by the doctor of arts and medicine Giovanni Marcanova of Padua. In 1456 Marcanova (who taught ordinary philosophy in Bologna from around or after 1451 until his death in 1467) commissioned a copy of the exposition by the Servite Urbanus Bononiensis of Averroes's commentary on the *Physics.*[21] The two large folio volumes, now Venice, BMarc., lat. VI 103 (2814) and 104 (2815), both indicate the date and place of the commission, the name of Marcanova, and the names of the two (otherwise unknown) scribes.[22] Marcanova must have found plenty of important material in Bologna, given that he had at least thirteen manuscripts copied there.[23] It seems likely that this commentary on Averroes was meant as an aid to the preparation of his lectures—though it was not necessarily the work that he brought to class, since he also owned several other manuscripts of the *Physics.*[24]

So both teachers and students were busy acquiring works in connection with their activities within the *studium.* Most often they relied on the supply of books available locally, whether via the stationers or—as we shall see—other collections.

A final point worth making about manuscript culture in Bologna is that it did not, of course, die out with the eventual affirmation of print.[25] Both teachers and students kept generating manuscript materials. Professors would write down their lectures (sometimes in abbreviated form) before delivering them, and many such manuscript materials survive. Examples include Ulisse Aldrovandi's philosophy lectures from the second half of the sixteenth century, some anonymous mathematical lectures from the first part of the seventeenth century, and the lectures in anatomy by Giuseppe Guidazzolo and Giacomo Sandri from around 1709.[26] Students, for their own part, took down their professors' lectures (verbatim if possible), produced a fair copy, and often shared this final product with others. All of these materials could, and often did, lead to a print publication. But because professors or others might revise a text in view of publication, it remains essential to consult the manuscripts.[27]

With the arrival of print, some of the dynamics described above changed. As scholars have recognized, one of the most important effects was—over time—on the cost of books, and therefore on their availability to masters and students.[28] It also became less important for a book to be produced locally, as long as copies could be transported fairly cheaply.[29] But the printing industry in Bologna did not exactly have an auspicious start, and its ties to the university market were not immediate. The first dated books printed in Bologna are from either 1470 or 1471, but it was not until the end of 1472 that the first law book was printed there.[30] Its printer, Andrea Portilia of Parma, apparently encountered such difficulties in hiring the right kind of help that he left the city two years later.[31] For arts and medicine, the first printed book known was the *Libellus isagogicus* by Alcabitius (a standard book for teaching astrology), printed by Johannes Vurster in 1473.[32] In fact, although this book prominently indicates as its editor Matteo Moretti, doctor of arts and medicine and professor in Bologna, it does not give a place of printing, which was most likely Modena rather than Bologna. The same seems to have been the case for the 1474 *Liber pandectarum medicinae* by Mattheus Silvaticus. Furthermore, in Modena this same Vurster printed legal books destined for the Bolognese university market (one, a *Lectura super XI Codicis* by Bartolomeo da Saliceto, in six hundred copies), thus competing with Bolognese production. (The lower cost of paper in Modena made this advantageous.) Such events point to difficulties and teething problems in Bologna's early printing industry: in the end, as Balsamo notes, Vurster's miscalculations led to his financial ruin. The printing enterprises that flourished in Bologna (as elsewhere in Italy) were the local ones strongly tied to the university—even though the printers themselves might not be Bolognese.[33]

The instability of printing in Bologna was a challenge that members of the university met by banding together in societies (however short-lived) with financial backers and local printers, often for the production of specific books or kinds of books. Students, teachers, and even beadles were all involved in these partnerships, which could require the investment of a considerable amount of capital.[34] Already in 1470 Francesco Dal Pozzo (professor of rhetoric and poetry from 1467 to 1478; also known as Puteolanus) and Annibale Malpigli (a teacher of logic and moral philosophy between 1459 and 1474) joined forces with the banker Baldassarre Azzoguidi to form a society for printing books, time-limited to two years.[35] According to the arrangements specified in the contract, Dal Pozzo agreed to oversee the scholarly side of the publications and to promote them within the university, while the other two partners underwrote the program financially.[36] The three members shared as equals in the books and profits generated.[37] In 1474 Dal Pozzo established a partnership with Taddeo Crivelli, a famous miniaturist from Ferrara, with the aim of printing maps of the globe. In the same year a partnership between Crivelli and some Bolognese citizens looked forward to printing Ptolemy's *Geography* (*Cosmographia*). Three years later the project had not yet come to fruition. This led to establishing another partnership, this time specifically with the printer Domenico de Lapi. In that year the *Geography* finally appeared. This achievement involved the collaboration of university professors such as Girolamo Manfredi, Galeotto Marzio da Narni, Cola Montano, and Filippo Beroaldo. (Pietrobono Avogaro, one of the major figures involved, does not appear on the university's teaching rolls.) Recent scholarship has tended to downplay the typographical quality of this initiative—which is often still cited as one of the great successes of Bolognese fifteenth-century printing—as well as the active role of some of the professors named.[38] But it points to the fact that university professors had a strong interest in the power of print. Printed books made it easier for their students to acquire texts and lectures for their courses.

The humanities professor Filippo Beroaldo the Elder (1453–1505) offers a telling example of the seriousness with which some masters saw their relationship with the printing press. Between the end of the fifteenth century and the start of the sixteenth, Beroaldo oversaw the printing of several works directly related to his teaching. On 22 May 1499 he established a partnership with Benedetto di Ettore Faelli; by so doing he was building on his experience in Parma, where he had published his notes on Pliny's *Natural History*.[39] This partnership saw Beroaldo as entrepreneur and financial backer of the printing of his own works, including the *Asinus aureus* (*The Golden Ass,* 1500).[40] The work was to have a print run of 1,250 copies (of which 1,200 were to be sold), and Beroaldo promised to lecture for a time only on that work, so as to guarantee a market for his publication.[41]

This involvement of professors in printing enterprises continued in later years. For example, 1572 saw the formation of the Società Tipografica Bolognese. This involved the humanities professor Carlo Sigonio together with other scholars as well as senators and wealthy businessmen. Described by Balsamo as the last attempt by university figures to preside directly over such an editorial enterprise, this initiative entailed an official partnership with the printer Giovanni Rossi.[42] Less formalized, but also emblematic of a close attention to print, were the activities of Ulisse Aldrovandi, who worked together with gifted illustrators—many of them former students of his from the Low Countries—to produce a series of volumes of natural history in the late part of the sixteenth century. (In fact, the printing of his works continued during the course of the seventeenth century, well after his death in 1605).[43] In case after case, Bologna's professors showed a deep interest in getting their works printed and into the hands of students and colleagues, and any extra revenue was doubtless welcome. In some rare instances, a professor might himself be a notable printer, as with Aldus Manutius the Younger, who taught humanities in Bologna in 1585–1586.[44]

4.2 Booksellers and Collections

Students and professors had two main options for accessing books: they could either purchase them from booksellers, or borrow them from or consult them at institutional (and sometimes private) collections. An analysis of these contexts sheds light on the extent to which teaching and learning were dependent on the availability of books.

4.2.1 Booksellers

University members needing to purchase a book could head to the university's stationer. But books could also be bought from one of the numerous *bibliopolae,* or booksellers, who congregated in Bologna's center, especially in proximity to the university.[45] More often than not, by the end of the fifteenth century these booksellers were also printers, and although they might also stock books printed by others, their shops held particularly plentiful copies of the volumes they themselves produced.[46] For fifteenth-century Bologna, remarkably detailed evidence survives for the workshops of two printer-booksellers: Sigismondo dei Libri and Francesco (or Platone) Benedetti.[47]

At the death of dei Libri in 1484, his shop (which seems to have catered mainly to university students) contained numerous juridical texts, Latin classics, works of philosophy, medicine, theology, and other subjects, in both manuscript and print.[48] Angela Nuovo has estimated that the bookshop and its storage spaces on the floors above it contained at least 2,664 book copies.[49] She points out that some titles (especially those printed on dei Libri's initiative) were present in hundreds of copies, including 422 copies of Baldo degli Ubaldi's *Lectura super VI Codicis* (1477)—a book of civil law—and at least 324 copies of Cicero's *Letters* in various formats.[50] Dei Libri's shop also contained some forty-five codices.[51]

The inventory of Benedetti's print shop dates to 1497, just a few years later.[52] Benedetti was printing books in Bologna by March 1482, and by his death in August 1496 he had published at least sixty-seven editions.[53] In March 1497 the contents of his print shop were inventoried as part of a property valuation. The resulting notarial document, partly edited by Sorbelli and recently re-edited in full by Elena Gatti, is divided in two parts for what concerns the books themselves: jurisprudence (the more expensive section, counting 109 titles) and humanities (637 titles). Under each heading, the compilers indicated the various titles connected to the two subjects, in a roughly alphabetical order. Despite the list's numerous errors (including misspellings and a high number of duplications), it offers a valuable snapshot of a printer's workshop, including a description of the number of copies of each work. According to Gatti's calculations, the total was 10,576 book copies, not including an unspecified number of books in a deposit in Pavia.[54]

The fact that several titles are listed in dozens (more rarely, even hundreds) of copies can be explained. Benedetti was the printer favored by Angelo Poliziano, thus his workshop contained, for instance, 910 copies of the Florentine scholar's *Silva cui titulus Nutricia,* which Benedetti had printed in June 1491.[55] The list also indicates that he held 1,000 copies (in all likelihood recently printed) of the *Officioli Beatae Mariae Virginis,* a work of popular devotion that was quite possibly printed by him, but of which no copy is known to survive.[56] Several books for use in teaching reading and other subjects have not survived either, even though the inventory lists numerous copies of them. These include Antonio Mancinelli's *De modo scribendi* and a Psalter for children (*da putti*).[57] Others that are extant include *Aesopus moralizatus,* present in the inventory in some 338 copies, and Filippo Beroaldo's *De felicitate,* present in twenty-two.[58] Unfortunately, we do not know how expensive these and other books (including the numerous textbooks used for law, philosophy, and medicine) were and how they were arranged in the shop.[59]

From the perspective of arts and medicine, two points are worth making. One is the disparity between the number of printed books available for various subjects. As Balsamo has noted, volumes of law and astrological *prognostica* constituted nearly a quarter each of the total Bolognese production in the second half of the fifteenth century.[60] But there were also disparities within arts and medicine, for instance in philosophy and medicine versus rhetoric: even in Sigismondo dei Libri's shop, where books would have been displayed for sale, there were many more books connected to grammar and rhetoric (Cicero, Virgil, Ovid, and so forth) than to either philosophy or medicine (represented mainly by authors such as Giacomo da Forlì and Gentile da Foligno). Likewise, in Benedetti's bookshop, of the 637 editions listed for *libri in humanitate* (a catch-all term for subjects outside of law), approximately 43 percent were classics and Latin literature, whereas philosophy and theology account for only 14.5 percent, and medicine only 4.8 percent.[61] The reasons for this disproportion are unclear and require further study. Perhaps professors of the humanities (such as Beroaldo) were quicker than others to see the value of print for their subject. Alternatively, some printers may have gravitated more toward law and humanities, while others preferred to focus on philosophy, medicine, and theology. Yet another explanation is that for certain fields there was still a sufficient number of manuscripts in circulation, so that the need for printed books would have been less urgent.

A second point of interest is the large number of logic manuals compared to other branches of philosophy. Both inventories, for instance, list numerous copies of Antonius Andreae's logic handbook *Scriptum in artem veterem Aristotelis* (represented with 165 copies in dei Libri's list and eleven copies in Benedetti's).[62] In Benedetti's inventory, logic books outnumber those of natural philosophy by at least 3 to 1. This point may simply reflect the fact that logic was foundational for all university subjects, including law, and was also important for regulars studying in the local convents. One wonders whether students in the religious *studia* bought their books from the same suppliers as university students. It is especially unfortunate that information on the cost of these books is so fragmentary, since it might provide further evidence about their potential market.

4.2.2 Book Collections and Libraries

An alternative to purchasing books was to borrow them from others. There is evidence that booksellers (at least in Florence) sometimes lent books out, but it is unclear whether this was also the case in Bologna.[63] Bologna did, however, house several institutional and private collections.[64] Although religious libraries could be (at least theoretically) hard to access, university members could avail themselves of book collections belonging to the colleges, the Nations, and especially individuals. From the seventeenth century onward, libraries such as the one that Ulisse Aldrovandi donated to the Senate enriched the city's provision of books, but restrictions on access meant that there was no public library in Bologna until the opening of the library of the Istituto delle Scienze in 1756.

Churches and Convents

Bologna's religious institutions had rich book collections. The most important documentary sources are published in Laurent's edition of the library notes of the Dominican Fabio Vigili (1498?–1553) in the early years of the sixteenth century.[65] (In addition to Vigili's selective listings, this edition includes both earlier and later inventories of the relevant collections.) Besides the Biblioteca Capitolare, three conventual libraries were especially important: those attached to San Domenico, San Salvatore, and San Francesco (for the convents themselves, see §3.3.1). Visitors to the city regularly singled out the first two of these for the richness and the extent of their collections, but San Francesco also had a respectable number of valuable manuscripts.

The chapter library, housed in the cathedral church of San Pietro (where doctoral exams took place), held a large and varied collection of books.[66] Although its holdings in the early fifteenth century were small, the 1451–1457 inventory refers to well over 329 manuscripts, including the (mainly liturgical) books in the sacristy.[67] Most of these items (255 manuscripts) were distributed over the nineteen rows of desks (*scanni*) of the reading room, although twenty-six (including several—presumably particularly valuable—works of arts and medicine) were housed in the cupboard or *armario* of the sacristy. As was common, books were arranged by topic: the first two *scanni* contained more general material, while the third held Latin classics and commentaries, such as Quintilian, Boethius (*De consolatione philosophiae*), Statius, Ovid (*De fastis*), Virgil's *Bucolics,* Seneca's letters, and Cicero's orations and treatises. The fourth row held miscellaneous works of music, astrology, and metaphysics, but also the Psalms and the commentary on them by Nicolaus of Lyra. The fifth contained books mainly related to medicine (Galen, Averroes, Avicenna, Dioscorides, Hippocrates) and Aristotle's works on animals. Books of philosophy occupied rows six to nine, progressing from logic to metaphysics via moral and natural philosophy. The remaining *scanni* were devoted to canon law, commentaries on Scripture, and theology.[68] Thus, seven of the nineteen rows of desks (or 88 volumes out of the 255 in the reading room) were closely connected to arts and medicine—approximately 35 percent of the collection, if one excludes the reference books of the first two rows. Given the nature and extent of its collection, this library must have played an important role in Bologna's cultural life in the second half of the fifteenth century. Yet it is unclear whether university members could access it. For mysterious reasons, this collection completely disappears from view after the fifteenth century. The fate of its books is unknown.

Numerous travelogues refer to the library of San Domenico as the largest and most beautiful in the city. But it had to grow into this fame. Before 1381 it counted 472 manuscripts, besides the 13 in use in the refectory and the 145 in the sacristy, for a total of 630 manuscripts.[69] The inventory describing these book holdings presents us with a snapshot of a main library room housing fifty-two rows of desks in total (twenty-six on each side, ordered by subject), with books chained to the desks.[70] The vast majority of books related to theology, to the Scriptures and their exposition, and to the writings of the Church Fathers, although there was also a not-indifferent collection of books of law, doubtless the result of bequests by university professors.[71] But there was comparably little (just over three rows of desks) for arts subjects, and when the humanist and Camaldulese monk Ambrogio Traversari visited in 1433, his report expresses palpable disappointment.[72] In later decades the library grew significantly, thanks in part to numerous bequests (including two hundred volumes by the jurist Lodovico Bolognini) and the building of a new library space.[73] By c. 1513 the main room had sixty-four rows or *scanni*. Because Vigili did not aim at comprehensiveness, the 448 items he listed (nineteen of them printed editions) cannot be used in direct comparison with the pre-1381 inventory.[74] Nonetheless, several rows do now include subjects directly related to arts and even medicine: on the right-hand side, rows 22–28 in particular contain philosophical works (logic, natural philosophy, moral philosophy, metaphysics), plus works of medicine, geometry, and astrology (rows 26–27) and even Plato's *Gorgias* and *Phaedo* (row 27). Rows 29–30 contain works of history and rhetoric (Cicero, Valerius Maximus, Seneca, letters, lives of philosophers), while row 32 is devoted to grammar.[75] In later years the library received other donations and bequests (including the books of Leandro Alberti).[76] By the time the collection was dispersed at the end of the eighteenth century, it also held a sizable number of printed books.[77]

In addition to housing a library, San Domenico was a center for copying manuscripts and illuminating books; it also ran a bindery.[78] At least in the fifteenth century, it sponsored some printing enterprises. In 1721 a donation by Luigi Ferdinando Marsili equipped it with a printing press (he later added some non-Latin types), which gave rise to the appropriately named Stamperia S. Tommaso d'Aquino.[79]

Particularly after the French Revolution and the Napoleonic wars, San Domenico's library served many different purposes, and its architecture underwent significant modifications. Restoration work in the 1970s brought back the glory of the fifteenth-century library: one can now fully appreciate the austere beauty of this structure, where figures such as Giovanni Pico della Mirandola and Girolamo Savonarola were active (Figure 4.1).

San Salvatore's collection of books was even more remarkable.[80] The convent of San Salvatore, belonging to the congregation of the Canons Regular of St. Augustine in Santa Maria di Reno, was already active by 1149.[81] The library had rather modest beginnings, as testified by the inventories of 1322 and 1429, which register twenty-eight and forty-one

Fig 4.1. Old library of the convent of San Domenico, Bologna.
Photo © David Lines.

manuscripts, respectively—most of them liturgical and religious books, including Bibles, breviaries, and the works of some Church Fathers (St. Gregory, St. Augustine, Bede).[82] In the sixteenth century the library acquired various codices (including Greek ones) and printed books.[83] Vigili's list includes only one Greek manuscript within the fifty-three items registered—not including an unspecified number of law books.[84] The books are arranged over nine rows, the first of which includes works of logic (Kilwardby), rhetoric, and humanistic subjects. The inventory of 1533 instead lists 659 items (a mixture of manuscripts and printed books), including seventy-eight Greek codices, many of them acquired thanks to the enterprise of the convent's prior Pellegrino Fabretti.[85] The collection reflects a significant variety of topics (in little discernible order), although theology, philosophy, and rhetoric are prominent. Works by Aristotle and his commentators head the register of Greek volumes, which also includes numerous works of rhetoric (including the orations of Isocrates and Demosthenes), epic, tragedy and comedy, history, and writings of the Greek Church Fathers. These Greek holdings were so noteworthy that Conrad Gesner singled them out for special praise, placing them on an equal footing with those of the Vatican Library and Cardinal Bessarion's bequest to the city of Venice.[86] The Latin section is understandably strong on ancient and medieval Scripture commentaries and works of theology, but also includes a respectable number of volumes of Plato (in the translation of Marsilio Ficino) and his commentators, followed by Aristotle and his commentators.[87] Other parts of this inventory register books of grammar and rhetoric, in addition to many classical and humanist authors (Petrarch, Angelo Poliziano, Desiderius Erasmus, Giovanni Pontano, the classical Latin poets and orators, historians, and so forth).[88] Also present are books of astronomy and astrology as well as medicine and anatomy.[89] Finally, the inventory of 1695 lists almost 340 manuscripts distributed in twelve different categories. While five of these relate to religious writings, the list also includes works of philosophy, mathematics, medicine, sacred and profane history, and poetry.[90] This would have been the collection that Jean Mabillon saw (and described at length) on the occasion of his visit in May 1686. Among the Latin manuscripts, what especially caught his eye was a codex of Lactantius's *Institutiones,* which he dated to some 1,100 years earlier.[91] After the Napoleonic period, most of these fine items ended up among the holdings of what is now the Biblioteca Universitaria.[92]

The library of San Francesco was also one of Bologna's largest.[93] Its 1421 inventory lists 649 manuscripts.[94] Some of these came from the private collection of the professor of medicine Giacomo di Nanne d'Ughetto dall'Armi in 1396.[95] In addition to many theological books and commentaries on Scripture, there is a substantial number (seventy-four manuscripts) of books concerning grammar and rhetoric, logic, ethics, natural philosophy, metaphysics, astrology, and medicine.[96] Vigili, however, notes only 117 items.[97] Those relative to arts and medicine (items 91 to 117, mainly philosophical works) were located in desk rows 8–13 on the library's left-hand side.[98] The collection was dispersed—in mysterious circumstances—during the suppression of religious orders at the end of the eighteenth century. What remains of the manuscript holdings today is very little indeed, and of minimal relevance to this study.[99] There are, however, thirty-four incunables and 152 volumes from the sixteenth century that might merit further study, although they are not part of the original library.[100]

Little is known about the availability of these book collections to outsiders and the extent to which members of the university community could consult or borrow them. Scholars are well aware of the strong ties between the various religious *studia* and members of the university, particularly as meeting places for students (§3.3.1). But did this close relationship give students or professors privileged access to their libraries? Currently this question is impossible to answer. In the case of San Domenico, the documentation is uneven but includes several instructions for books to be returned.[101] This indicates that some borrowing was taking place, but it is unclear by whom. (Presumably, well-connected professors and citizens would have received more favorable treatment than students.) Furthermore, allowing books out of a library was typically against the official regulations (and often the best interests) of the institution in question—although, to judge by the high number of extant prohibitions, the practice was fairly common. Matters came to a head at the start of the seventeenth century. The chapter of San Domenico became so concerned that it ordered that books should not leave the library even if they stayed in the convent. In 1619, when Domenico Tamburini needed one of its manuscripts in order to prepare a printed edition, a notarial act was drawn up to ensure its return. A few years later, the general of the order asked Pope Urban VIII to put a stop to the continuing depletion of its collection: his bull of 23 March 1626 prohibited the removal of books from the libraries of all houses of the Dominican order, for any reason, on pain of excommunication.[102] As for the Biblioteca Capitolare, although there are indications that some of its books were in the hands of outsiders, identifying who these were is not straightforward.[103] As suggested below, members of the university community must have found it easier to secure access to books belonging to colleges, Nations, or private individuals.

Colleges

Bologna boasted over twenty residential colleges for its university students, deriving from two waves of foundations in 1257–1414 and 1528–1689 (see §3.1.1). Many of these institutions owned books, sometimes a legacy from the founder.[104] Two of the best-documented collections are those of the Collegio di Spagna and the Collegio Gregoriano.

The largest and most valuable college library was that of the Collegio di Spagna. It had started with the donation of books by its founder, Cardinal Albornoz, who in 1365 bequeathed thirty-six manuscripts, covering law, theology, philosophy, and rhetoric, in addition to a Bible, a missal, a breviary, and a collection of saints' lives.[105] The inventory of 1453 testifies to many more manuscripts, arranged in eight rows; most of these were books of law, but the last row contained 113 codices of classical, philosophical, medical, and theological works, around half of which the Collegio di Spagna still holds.[106] The catalogue by García and Piana indicates the presence of several works that would have been useful to students of arts and medicine, as well as law. Most manuscripts date from the thirteenth to the fifteenth century. In 1511 Fabio Vigili noted only some forty-seven items, in topographical order, but he was hardly attempting to provide a full listing.[107] What is clear is that, throughout the early modern period, the students of this college would have had an excellent collection at their disposal, particularly for law but also for other subjects. One only hopes that access was rather easier than it is today, particularly for outsiders.

Initially even larger than the Collegio di Spagna's collection was that of the Collegio Gregoriano, which in 1373 already had 211 manuscripts.[108] This college, whose number of students was eventually fixed at thirty by its founder Gregory XI, included students not only in canon and civil law, but also in other subjects.[109] As a result, it held—in addition to the expected books of law—also works of theology and philosophy, Sacred Scriptures, saints' lives, and various graduals and missals.[110] These books doubtless supported the teaching that took place within the college itself. The college grew so as to be able to support up to fifty youths, but in the fifteenth century experienced several difficulties. In 1450 it merged with two other colleges (the Avignonese and Bresciano), but the combined institution had to close its doors in 1474.[111]

Nations

The libraries of the student Nations have not received much scholarly attention, but important information survives for that of the German Nation—the most powerful association of foreign students in Bologna, many of whom studied law. Inventories of its library date back to 1335.[112] They show that this collection (though initially very small and mainly containing liturgical works) grew to include various legal instruments connected with the Nation, but also works of law, medicine, and other fields. Thirty donors enriched the Nation's library in 1602.[113] An inventory of the books prepared for its incoming librarian Carlo Pasini in 1641 lists 1,267 works, distributed in the following classes: jurisprudence, theology, grammars and dictionaries, rhetoric and poetry, medicine, philosophy, history and literature, and letters.[114] For the whole early modern period, this must have been an important repository of books. According to the statutes, access was restricted to members of the German Nation, who were able to borrow a limited number of books.[115] Due to the Nation's financial difficulties, this collection was sold off and dispersed at the end of the eighteenth century; it may make for a useful comparison with a similar library in Padua.[116]

Private Collections

Despite their richness, none of the collections listed above was open to all comers or even, it seems, to all scholars. It is unlikely that religious libraries threw open their doors to local university members, something that would have created organizational headaches and heightened concerns about the return of books (which were, of course, valuable items). College libraries almost certainly restricted consultation and borrowing privileges to their own students.[117] The cases in which they granted access to the exceptional scholar passing through the city, as happened when the Florentine humanist Angelo Poliziano visited Bologna in 1491, must have been few and far between.[118] So what were local university members to do, particularly before the age of print, when acquiring books could often be financially prohibitive?[119] In Bologna they built up effective mechanisms for borrowing and exchanging books privately, thus circumventing the restrictions of institutional libraries (at least on those who were not well connected).

The practice of borrowing books had an ancient pedigree in the university context: alongside the *pecia* system mentioned above, whereby students could rent manuscripts from the university stationer, one sheaf at a time, in order to make their own copies, they could also borrow or rent books from others, including their teachers.[120] Furthermore, books were among the visible signs of shared community; as such, they might be passed on in multiple directions, such as from teacher to student (and vice versa), from student to student, or from teacher to teacher.[121] Or, indeed, as explained below, from cultural broker to student or even professor.

A system of this kind relied on access to book collections, whether large or small. But these were not lacking in Bologna. For the fifteenth century alone, scholars are aware of the book collections of several well-known (and other less well-known) personalities. In addition to those discussed below, these include professors of arts and medicine such as Giovanni Marcanova, Giovanni Garzoni, and Filippo Beroaldo the Elder.[122] Several documents also survive for private libraries from the sixteenth century.

Many of these collections are known through probate inventories or private catalogues, both of which are fraught with a series of methodological problems, including the question of how complete they actually are.[123] This point is particularly relevant to inventories such as that of Beroaldo's library, where the absence of several expected items is highly surprising.[124] In any case, lists of this kind do not often tell us much about the *circulation* of books. A different approach, followed here, is to study lists of books that were lent (or possibly rented) out. Several owners of books in Bologna kept a special register or *vacchetta* for such items. The following comments will focus on two fifteenth-century booklenders of note: Carlo Ghisilieri and Bernardo Garzoni.

Carlo Ghisilieri (c. 1400–1467?), an important political and cultural personality in Bologna, kept a record of his loans and investments in a special *vacchetta,* which proceeds chronologically from 1426 to 24 October 1467. In addition to numerous mentions of money, land, grain, and cloth, Ghisilieri also noted books that he had lent out. These last notes refer to the period 1431–1461 and register some one hundred loans in total. They show that Ghisilieri had a wide network in Bologna, and that some people benefited from both his cultural interests and his readiness to do business. Among the people mentioned are prominent figures such as Leon Battista Alberti, Giovanni Lamola, Benedetto Morandi, Tommaso Pontano, Giovanni Toscanella, Alberto Enoch Zancari, Lapo da Castiglionchio, Tommaso da Camerino, and Bornio da Sala. Here it is not possible to offer a full analysis of this document, whose section on books has attracted little attention since Frati's brief mention (and partial edition) of it in

1899.[125] But it is worthwhile commenting on the range of Ghisilieri's collection and its relevance for the teaching activity of the *studium.*

Ghisilieri's loans indicate that he owned at least forty-three manuscripts—a rather remarkable library for his time, particularly for someone who was not a scholar. Its great strength lay in the Latin classics, especially works of poetry, comedy, and rhetoric (Virgil, Horace, Ovid, Terence, Cicero) along with Sallust, Vitruvius, and some standard works of grammar (Donatus, Priscian). Of the Greeks, Ghisilieri only lent out works of Aristotle, doubtless in Latin translation (one of them, the *Ethics,* in "translatione nova," most likely that of Leonardo Bruni). He seems to have had good coverage of Aristotle's works (logic, *De anima, Ethics, Problems, Metaphysics*), except for natural philosophy. Of the Church Fathers and early Christian thinkers, the only works mentioned are St. Jerome's *Letters* and Boethius's *De Trinitate.* The only modern work in Latin is Pier Paolo Vergerio's *De pueris educandis.*

The frequency with which certain items were lent out gives some indication of the nature of Ghisilieri's collection. It had all the hallmarks of a library oriented toward the humanities. Whereas Ghisilieri lent out the works of Virgil twelve times in total, the most-borrowed author is Cicero (thirty-nine times). Ghisilieri clearly owned the range of his works (treatises, orations, letters), sometimes in multiple copies: the items appearing most often are Cicero's *Orations* and the (pseudo-) Ciceronian *Rhetoric.* Other works of Cicero that were very much in demand were the *Topics* (with Boethius's commentary), *De oratore,* and *Letters.* Ghisilieri emerges as a major supplier of books in a period in which access to institutional libraries may have been restricted (and their stock of humanistic works somewhat limited).

Some of Ghisilieri's loans have particular relevance for the university teaching of arts and medicine. One frequent borrower was Gaspare Sighicelli (also called da San Giovanni in Persiceto), a professor at the University of Bologna, where he mainly taught natural philosophy between 1419 and 1448.[126] In 1433 Sighicelli joined the friars of San Domenico, where he took a bachelor's degree in theology and later became a *magister.* On several occasions Sighicelli borrowed Aristotle's logic and St. Thomas on the *Metaphysics* (in addition to other books). This may testify his desire to circumvent the restrictions of San Domenico's library. Giovanni Toscanella also appears several times in Ghisilieri's records. A professor of rhetoric, in 1431 Toscanella borrowed four works: (Cicero's?) *Orations,* "li 4 argomenti sopra l'oratione," the new and old *Rhetoric,* and Boethius's commentary on the *Topics.*[127] Toscanella—who was nervous about the competition of a certain Thomas (doubtless Tommaso da Camerino) for his post in Bologna—probably used these books to prepare his lectures.[128] In any case, Ghisilieri did not take academic rivalries into account in his lending practices, for on 24 September of the same year he lent Tommaso da Camerino a manuscript of Cicero's *De petitione consulatus,* in addition to various household items.[129] Another of Ghisilieri's loans provides particular insight into classroom teaching: on 29 November 1455, he lent eleven quires of Aristotle's *Nicomachean Ethics* to Albertino da Cremona, who that year taught both moral philosophy and medicine.[130] From Ghisilieri's entry we can deduce, not only that Albertino did not plan to teach the whole ten books of the work, but also that he lectured on the basis of the new translation ("translatione nova")—doubtless that of Leonardo Bruni from 1416–1417, since that of Johannes Argyropoulos was not yet available.[131]

Roughly contemporary with Ghisilieri's notes is a list of books lent out by Bernardo Garzoni to several professors (and students?) in the *studium.*[132] Although the list is undated, it probably reflects Bernardo's activity in the second quarter of the fifteenth century, when he was a professor of medicine in Bologna.[133] The list shows that Bernardo was lending out several books containing fundamental works for teaching. Thus, Nicolò Fava Sr., a professor of natural philosophy and medicine, borrowed Thomas Aquinas's commentaries on Aristotle's *Physics* and *De anima,* as well as Albertus Magnus on the *Physics, De anima, De generatione et corruptione,* and Paul of Venice's commentary on the first four books of the *Physics.*[134] A certain Daniel de Neapoli borrowed a book of medicine (Giacomo da Forlì's *In primum Canone*), possibly the same volume borrowed by one Johannes de Navara (*sic*), most likely to be identified with the medical doctor Giovanni Gozzadini da Novara.[135] Another professor of arts and medicine, Baverius de Imola, borrowed Albertus Magnus's *De coelo et mundo* and Thomas's *In Averroistas,* two works that would have been helpful to his teaching of natural philosophy in the *studium* between 1432 and 1434.[136] Finally, Lucas Siculus (unknown except for his teaching of logic, 1431–1432) borrowed Galen's *Ars parva* and Cristoforo Onesti's commentary on the *Tegni.*[137] These notes therefore help confirm what subjects were being taught in the *studium* in the first half of the fifteenth century and what commentaries were considered relevant (see Chapter 6).

Strikingly, the borrowers on Bernardo's list are entirely separate from those listed by Ghisilieri. The two records therefore testify to different (and not necessarily overlapping) book circuits in Bologna at the same time. This may have been in part because some book owners like Bernardo specialized in works of philosophy and medicine, whereas others such as Ghisilieri focused more on rhetoric and the humanities, but one should be cautious about supposing that people did not have broader reading interests outside of their particular areas of teaching.

These book collections often passed from one generation to the next. Bernardo's books went first to his son Giovanni and thence to his grandson Fabrizio (also a medical doctor). The inventory of the collection donated to the Istituto delle Scienze in 1716 indicates that by then the Garzoni family library consisted of some seventy-five volumes (mostly from the fifteenth century), in which Cicero and works of history loomed especially large, in addition to Giovanni's own writings.[138] There were also several works of medicine, as well as a few manuscripts each of astronomy, logic and metaphysics, and ethics.[139] Some of these books bear indications of further loans (Giovanni lent out a Cicero manuscript three times in 1475) or became gifts to local convents.[140] Others are strongly relevant to teaching, such as Giovanni's medical lectures.[141] A logic textbook was passed on within the family.[142]

In the sixteenth century, Bolognese private libraries became larger and more varied. Men such as the Dominican Leandro Alberti, Cardinal Gabriele Paleotti, and Count Cornelio Lambertini put together respectable collections.[143] Even more relevant here are the libraries of university professors such as Ulisse Aldrovandi and Carlo Sigonio.

Aldrovandi (1522–1605), who taught natural philosophy and natural history in the *studium,* put together an impressive collection of specimens, natural objects, and books, all of which he displayed in his home and invited visitors to admire.[144] His testament, which bequeathed these collections to the city of Bologna, makes reference to some 4,000 books (3,700 printed books and 300 manuscripts). Described in detailed catalogues, which make it possible to reconstruct how the books were ordered physically and how much Aldrovandi had paid for them, this working library (what might be called, following Rodolfo Savelli, a "biblioteca professionale") was particularly strong in areas such as philosophy and medicine.[145] Yet it also included works of rhetoric, classical and modern literature, history, religion, and so forth, in keeping with Aldrovandi's publishing projects and encyclopedic interests. Like other libraries of the time, this was therefore a rich collection, but hardly one that anyone could have entered and consulted uninvited.[146] Because books were mainly organized by format, finding one required the aid of the master catalogue. (Aldrovandi and his assistants produced four versions of one during his lifetime; Figure 4.2 shows the opening page of the latest one, which was started in 1583 and thereafter added to.) Aldrovandi's helpers would have been a constant presence, ensuring that only trusted people could enter. Thus, despite the *ex libris* "Ulyssis Aldrovandi et amicorum" ("belonging to Ulisse Aldrovandi and his friends") that adorned his books, this was actually a very personal and fairly closely guarded library. In size, it was roughly comparable to that of his good friend Gabriele Paleotti (although that one was more focused on theology).[147]

A smaller but still significant contemporary library was that of Carlo Sigonio (1523?–1584), a professor of humanities and friend of Aldrovandi who arrived in Bologna in 1563 after teaching in Modena, Venice, and Padua. Sigonio was returning to his alma mater and was a weighty cultural figure, with excellent contacts especially in Venice and Rome. But he also had powerful friends locally, including Paleotti.[148] As already noted, he was a founding member of the Società Tipografica Bolognese. Aldrovandi's notebooks have an extended entry that mentions books from his library.[149]

Shortly after Sigonio's death in his country house in Ponte Basso (Modena) in the summer of 1584, an inventory of his books in Bologna was compiled by the *libraro* Innocenzo Olmi.[150] The list indicates 632 books (some in multiple volumes)[151] and typically indicates each item's author and title, format, place of printing, and valuation.[152] The list concludes with the indication that Sigonio's library contained numerous copies of his own works: 177 copies of *De regno Italiae* (1580), 196 of *De antiquo iure [populi] Romani* (1574), and twelve of *De vita Laurentii Champegii* (1581).[153] At least the first two of these titles were remainders from the Società Tipografica Bolognese. Sigonio had received them as a return on his investment when the company was dissolved in 1582.[154] Sigonio had to ask his friends

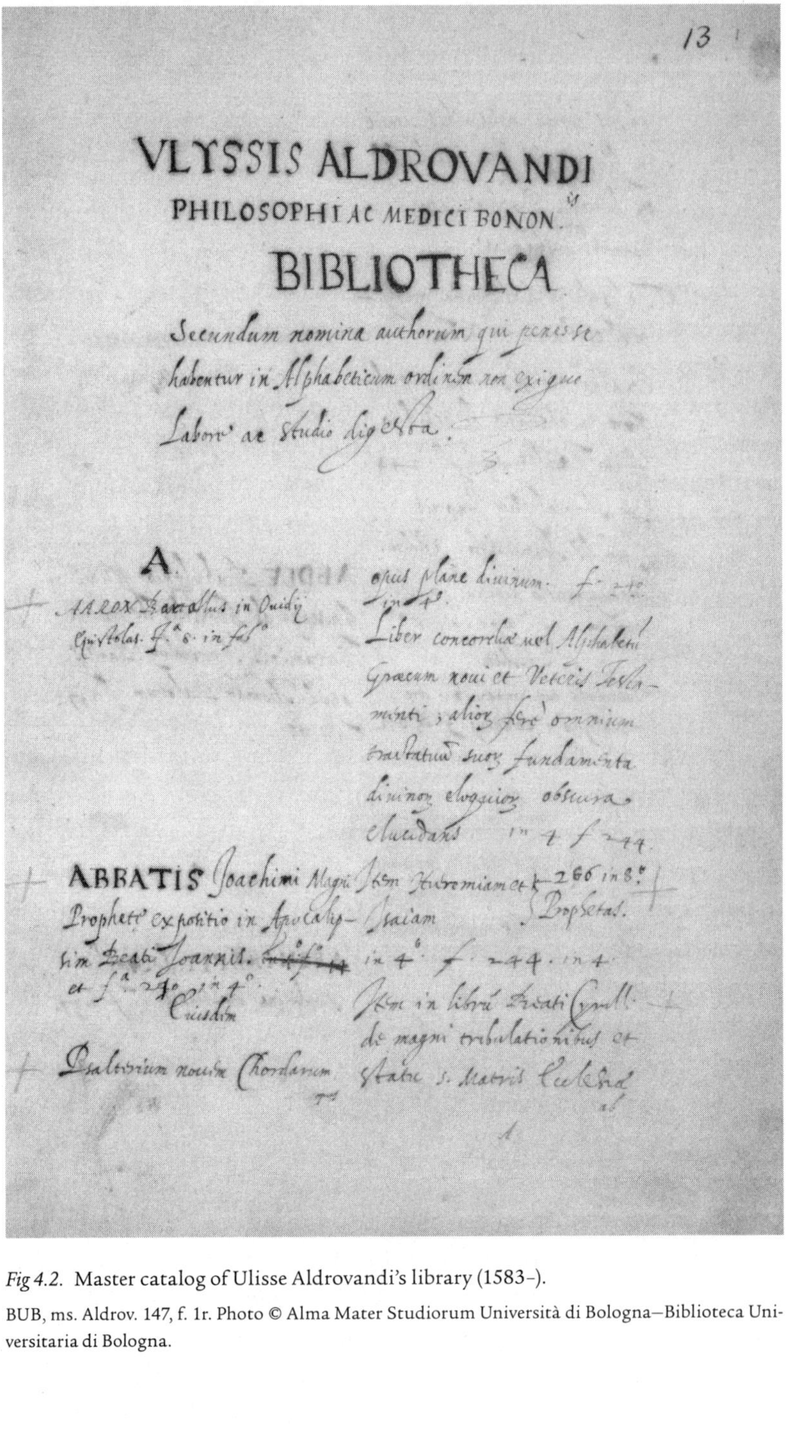

13

VLYSSIS ALDROVANDI
PHILOSOPHI AC MEDICI BONON.
BIBLIOTHECA

Secundum nomina authorum qui periisse habentur in Alphabeticum ordinem non exiguo Labore ac studio digesta.

Fig 4.2. Master catalog of Ulisse Aldrovandi's library (1583–).

to help him sell off some of these copies. It is unclear whether the probate inventory also includes the books (up to the total value of twenty-five *scudi*) that Sigonio had offered to his former student, the Jesuit Alessandro Caprara. In any case, Sigonio instructed that his other books should be sold off. They were bought in block by Giacomo Boncompagni (illegitimate son of Gregory XIII), who—acting on his father's behalf—also obliged Caprara to yield his share of the books and Sigonio's many personal papers. These seem to have made their way into the Fondo Boncompagni of the Vatican Library, where they still await a close study.[155]

Sigonio's collection of books is quite varied, in terms of both subject matter and languages. Given his commissions by the Senate to write works on the history of Italy and Bologna, it is unsurprising to see a fair number of historical works, but of course Sigonio's teaching responsibilities in rhetoric and allied areas also required relevant works, such as Cicero and Aristotle's *Rhetoric* (of which he made a fresh translation). The list also contains books of law, philosophy, and literature.[156] Works in Greek are fairly well represented and in number compare favorably with those in Latin or the vernacular. It is unclear, however, how willing the Modenese scholar was to lend his books locally. Presumably the students boarding with him had access to his books.[157]

Later Institutional Libraries

The private libraries described above often gave rise to larger institutional collections, which comprised several bequests. The classic case is Aldrovandi's library, which around 1616–1618 the Senate housed in a purpose-built space in the Palazzo Pubblico (where it grew thanks to other donations from, among others, Ferdinando Cospi). Despite the appointment of a librarian (often a university professor) and strict rules about not lending books out, over time the collection dwindled. As a result, the authorities placed ever-more stringent regulations on its access. They also locked away "dangerous" books.[158]

In the early eighteenth century, a library started to grow in Palazzo Poggi, the residence of the Istituto delle Scienze (which opened its doors in 1714; see §3.2). It incorporated the collections donated by the former general Luigi Ferdinando Marsili (the Istituto's founder) and others.[159] Marsili's library was remarkable: it included printed books in a very broad range of fields of interest to him (some of which he had secured during book-hunting expeditions to London and Amsterdam), but also manuscripts, comprising not only his own handwritten production, but 753 Oriental manuscripts (written in Arabic, Turkish, Greek, Latin, Hebrew, Persian, and Slavic languages) that he had acquired during his military campaigns against the Ottomans.[160] The appointment of a librarian (initially the mathematician Geminiano Rondelli) and further donations helped the collection's growth and organization. New catalogues aided the consultation of books. The biggest headache came in 1742 with the transfer from the Senate library of the 4,810 books donated by Aldrovandi and others. The decision to rearrange these materials by topic led to dismembering volumes containing disparate subjects and to the creation of new, thematically homogeneous ones. The person in charge of this operation was Lodovico Montefani Caprara, who oversaw the library between 1739 and 1785.[161] Caprara also catalogued the important collection of books donated to the Istituto by the generosity and interest of the Bolognese pope Benedict XIV.[162]

The library of the Istituto delle Scienze opened its doors to the public in 1756, with fairly generous opening times and a set of regulations.[163] While this development was welcome, one should also note that Bologna still lacked a university library—the Istituto's library became part of the national system of university libraries only in 1885 and came under the university's effective management even more recently, in 2017. In fact, compared to university libraries in northern and central Europe, university libraries in Bologna and other Italian cities were latecomers.[164] The collection of the German Nation mentioned above (which had counterparts in Padua at least in 1586 and 1596) did not belong to the university as a whole. The first university library in Italy was that of Padua, established around 1631; the Pisan library followed sometime later.[165] By then, college and university libraries in France, England, and other countries had been in operation for centuries.[166] Nonetheless, as this section has shown, informal networks and mechanisms of exchange enabled students and masters in Bologna to circumvent many of the local challenges to acquiring and consulting books. As we will see in the next section, the obstacles posed by the Holy Office were a rather different matter, but here too ingenuity could provide a measure of freedom.

4.3 Books and Religious Control

Printing presses, bookshops, and libraries (both private and institutional) ensured that books were in sufficient supply in Bologna, both for teaching purposes and for scholarly enterprises. The example of Aldrovandi in particular shows that, despite initiatives to limit the circulation of certain books, he was able to obtain and study a wide variety of them, published both by Italian presses and by others outside the Italian Peninsula.[167] But of course Aldrovandi was something of an exception, due to his powerful patrons and contacts as well as his position as one of Bologna's preeminent professors. To what extent did the Holy Office's measures of control on the production and circulation of certain books affect the Bolognese *studium* more generally? In particular, did the Index of Prohibited Books issued by Rome have a palpable effect on the access students and professors had to certain books?[168]

These are questions that tie into a well-known scholarly debate about the effectiveness of the Catholic Reformation, particularly in its efforts to control the reading habits of its followers.[169] Here I cannot address the more general debate, to which interpreters such as Charles Dejob and Paul Grendler have given very different answers.[170] Instead, I will strongly focus on the effects of the Catholic Church's instruments of religious control on the book culture of Bologna's *studium*—a point that has not received systematic attention.[171]

All considered, it seems that the various orders from Rome and the arrangements for approving or expurgating books had a limiting, though perhaps not stifling, effect in Bologna. Shortly after the appearance of the Roman Index of Paul IV (1559), Bologna's colleges of doctors tried to secure the continued use of certain books that were not religious in nature but were helpful for scholarship and teaching. They also suggested that licenses to read and study particular books should apply, not to individuals, but to the university's faculties as a whole. Despite Paleotti's best efforts and intense lobbying from the Bolognese ambassador, they were rebuffed on both points. The Master of the Sacred Palace confirmed that licenses would only be issued to individuals.[172] Even more serious was the flurry of different Indices issued from Rome, sometimes at cross-purposes, and the frustrating slowness of the process of correction, expurgation, and approval of works.[173] The commissions meant to examine works locally barely existed.[174] This had real and tangible effects in a variety of fields, including canon law, where the process of correction barely progressed.[175] In natural history, the lack of corrected books (particularly by Protestants such as Theodor Zwinger and Leonhard Fuchs) technically meant that they could not be used. Professors such as Aldrovandi, Camillo Baldi, and the medical doctor Gaspare Tagliacozzi therefore tried to hurry things along by taking part in the committees expurgating these works.[176] One sees no sign of the foot-dragging displayed by the college of doctors in Padua, who repeatedly claimed that they were unable to secure copies of the books needing correction.[177]

As Gabriele Paleotti's brother Camillo put it, Rome fostered a lack of *libertas*.[178] Certainly Girolamo Cardano (who taught medicine in Bologna from 1563) felt the sharp end of the Inquisition's stick when he came to its attention for his work *De rerum varietate* in 1570. Although Cardano was eventually acquitted and released, he remained under suspicion: his nonmedical works were placed on the Index, and the Roman authorities were satisfied to see his teaching contract in Bologna end early.[179] As for Aldrovandi, he received a special license to read and even own certain prohibited books essential for his scholarship, such as Theodor Zwinger's *Theatrum humanae vitae*.[180] Although he owned several editions of the Index, including the Roman one of 1559 and the Tridentine one of 1564, he did not necessarily follow the instructions to suppress particular passages, as is testified by his copy of Gaudenzio Merula's *Memorabilium opus*.[181] Yet, starting in the 1590s, he had to be more scrupulous in applying the instructions of the Index; as a result, the names of several condemned authors (e.g, Erasmus, Conrad Gesner, Leonhard Fuchs) are obscured in his books, and passages from those and other books are covered with glued-on strips of paper.[182] Egnazio Danti was successful in his request (considered by the Congregation of the Holy Office in June 1582) to read multiple books related to mathematics.[183] But some contemporaries such as Baldi were less fortunate; instead of obtaining a general license to read books of rhetoric and politics that were on the Index, he had to request permission for every individual item.[184] Requests would almost certainly be turned down in the case of works of astrology.[185]

The control over what people read was, of course, especially intense in the case of "heretical" books. Already on 31 March 1538, before the establishment of the Index, the inquisitor Stefano Foscarari (as usual, a

Dominican) ordered the burning of a great number of "Lutheran" books—discovered in various bookshops and private homes—in the *piazza* in front of San Petronio.[186]

The perceived danger of the circulation of heretical books was heightened by Bologna's large number of Ultramontane (and particularly German) students. In general, there seems to have been a fairly direct line of communication between Bologna and the Zwinglians in Zurich in particular.[187] But these were hardly the only ones: a circle of students in the Spanish College met to discuss evangelical subjects, as we know from trials in 1553–1554.[188] Various Italian members of the university, including Ludovico Boccadiferro and Aldrovandi, frequented circles with heterodox leanings, such as those of Achille Bocchi, Lisia Fileno, and Lelio Sozzini.[189] Benedetto Accolti (who arrived in Bologna to study law in 1541) exchanged his law books for Lutheran volumes.[190]

Due to the persistence of such heterodox circles, the Inquisition took a particular interest in people who participated in printing, selling, or smuggling prohibited books. These activities could result in severe fines or punishments.[191] In 1548, three printers were put on trial for heresy.[192] On 18 March 1559—following the publication of the Roman Index in Bologna in January—a bonfire in the cemetery next to San Domenico consumed twenty-nine large sacks and eighteen smaller ones containing prohibited books (see Figure 8.1). Just a few days later, seven booksellers were forbidden to be in commercial contact with Venice, probably because Venice resisted the call to apply the Pauline Index. As local representatives of Venetian *librai,* two booksellers had their books sequestered, forcing the Venetian *librai* to comply eventually.[193] In 1565 the German medical doctor Johannes Tolmer, who served as a private tutor for one of the local families, forcibly appeared before the Inquisitor Antonio Balducci; the fact that he owned books by Erasmus and Philipp Melanchthon (commentaries on Aristotle's logic and *Physics,* supposedly received as a gift a few years earlier from another German in Bologna) did not help his cause.[194] From this time onward, numerous decrees addressed the possession and printing of prohibited books, in an attempt to curtail their circulation.[195] Books were again at center stage in Balducci's suspicions about Aldrovandi aired in 1571: Aldrovandi had supposedly sold or tried to give away some heretical books.[196] In 1640 a bookbinder and a printer who had published some pages of a work on the Donation of Constantine (possibly an extract from Lorenzo Valla's famous proof that the document was a medieval forgery) had to submit to various acts of penitence. In 1644 a bookbinder and several booksellers were punished (and, in several cases, imprisoned or exiled) for selling prohibited books—the authorities seem to have been particularly concerned about the circulation of Ferrante Pallavicino's *Divorzio celeste*. In 1658 a printer (Alessandro Bellentani da Carpi) received an official rebuke for having promoted heretical ideas while attributing them to St. Augustine.[197]

Beyond these events, however, questions of interpretation persist, and (as previously mentioned) we lack a detailed study of how the Inquisition and the Index related to the Bolognese *studium* specifically. Nonetheless, one can make at least the following observations.

First, the intensity of the Inquisition's activities varied over time, depending on historical circumstances and who was in charge of enforcement. The Office of the Inquisition had a long history, dating to the 1230s in Bologna.[198] But its vigilance heightened (at least for a time) after the "Pomponazzi affair." In 1516 Pietro Pomponazzi's controversial treatise on the immortality of the soul led to an outcry and to sharp debates not only about what works should be printed, but also about the orientation of classroom teaching with regard to philosophical topics bordering on faith. The controversy concerned in part the observation of the papal bull *Apostolici regiminis* (issued in 1513), which gave precise instructions on how to teach passages that contradicted Christian doctrine.[199] As explained in Chapter 8, some professors followed these stipulations more closely than others. One should remember, however, that the application of the norms was variable and not always as effective as the religious authorities might have wished. Some inquisitors, such as the Dominican Leandro Alberti (†1551), appear to have been kindly or even lax.[200] Others (such as Antonio Balducci) were considerably more proactive. In any case, stopping the diffusion of heretical works appears to have been a tall order, and in 1614 the Roman Congregation of the Index complained that such books seemed to be on the increase.[201] As late as 1764 a collaborator of the Bolognese inquisitor had to admit to the Holy Office that it was impossible to offer cast-iron guarantees that booksellers in the city were not surreptitiously selling prohibited books, although he also provided assurances that everything possible was being done to stem their flow.[202] Whatever the effectiveness of the Inquisition's actions, however, the aim of limiting (if not stopping) the circulation of unapproved books cannot have helped the university's teaching program to keep up with developments in Protestant countries.

Over time the Inquisition may have targeted areas other than prohibited and heretical books. According to the data collected by Guido Dall'Olio, in the seventeenth century, accusations of writing, owning, or publishing prohibited works were not the most common infractions being reported. Much more numerous were the instances that came to the attention of the Bolognese Inquisition for magic and superstition (291 cases) or for blasphemy (134 cases) than for matters concerning forbidden books (71 cases). The documentation for the first part of the eighteenth century is rather incomplete, but—although infringements of dispositions concerning books climb to second place (34 cases concluded)—they are nearly equal to those in the category of enticement to immorality or "sollicitatio ad turpia" (33). Far more numerous than either of these are cases concerning magic and superstition (140).[203] Yet the usefulness of this data is unclear. Were fewer cases coming to the attention of the authorities because the Inquisition's surveillance had, by this time, established itself more firmly? Were fewer professors attempting to circumvent the dispositions in place (partly as a result of the "religious turn" discussed in Chapter 8)? Or had people simply become more adept at covering their tracks when they owned or read prohibited books? What seems clear from Marsili's book-hunting expedition in England and the Low Countries referred to earlier is that there were certain barriers to the importation of books, and these limited Bologna's ability to keep up to date with scientific developments outside of the Italian Peninsula. Whether these obstacles were due to official policy, the cost of shipping books, a cultural shift, or other considerations will require a specific study. Such research will, one hopes, indicate whether and how the circulation of books in early modern Bologna changed over the centuries and how it compared with the situation elsewhere.[204]

In any case, both manuscript and printed writings continued to play an important role in university culture throughout the early modern period. As this chapter has shown, Bologna's somewhat marginal position as a center for printing university textbooks did not prevent its professors and students from recognizing the value of owning books and of sharing them locally. The external networks of the most eminent professors (such as Aldrovandi) facilitated the acquisition of books from other parts of Europe. In the seventeenth and early eighteenth centuries, restricted access to books and the pressures of the Index put in place some barriers to the circulation of knowledge. But professors did not suddenly become indifferent to or ignorant about cultural and intellectual developments elsewhere. As the chapters in Part II suggest, several professors and cultural figures in Bologna (including Marcello Malpighi and L. F. Marsili) were very far from having a parochial outlook. They corresponded with scholars both in and beyond the Italian Peninsula, might be members of major academies such as the Royal Society and the Académie Française, and were well aware of what was being discussed elsewhere in (for instance) philosophy and medicine. As we examine four broad changes affecting nearly all subjects in arts and medicine, it will be good to remember that the life of the *studium* was strongly related to its members' continued appetite for books.

Part II

New Directions and Developments in University Learning

5

The Rise of the Humanities

As noted in Chapter 2, the traditional setup of universities included an arts program that—whether independent (as in Paris) or coupled with medicine (as in Bologna)—was roughly equivalent to a course of study in philosophy, its main subject. Some additional attention might be given to astrology (and mathematics) and grammar and rhetoric, but it is clear from their irregularity in early records and the low salaries they commanded that these were marginal subjects. The ancient system of the seven liberal arts (*trivium* and *quadrivium*) had long given way, around the twelfth century, to a new order of studies whose foundation was logic. Logic provided a method that was relevant to all higher subjects (medicine, law, theology), but most immediately prepared students for the other main elements of the arts curriculum—natural and moral philosophy and, at times, metaphysics. Grammar (i.e., the study of Latin language and literature) was, of course, important inasmuch as teaching took place in Latin on the basis of Latin texts or translations. But it was an introductory subject that students were to master at school, before arriving at university. As a result, the big players in Bologna's university curriculum were law and medicine—the subjects that drew students from afar, as the medical doctor Taddeo Alderotti did at the start of the fourteenth century.[1] The arts had relatively little power and gave only a very small space to literature and related subjects—so much so that the 1405 statutes barely mention them (see §2.2.2). Philosophy ruled.

Between the end of the fourteenth and the beginning of the fifteenth century, this picture began to change. Pietro da Moglio and then Bartolomeo del Regno were highly influential teachers of grammar and rhetoric who expanded the medieval repertoire of classical texts (*auctores*) to be studied. This came to include a wide range of works (Latin epic, lyric, satire, historical works, and Cicero's *On Duties*), some of which had been recently rediscovered (see §2.2.2). In the 1420s, when Leon Battista Alberti came to Bologna to study canon law, he found a favorable climate for the study of ancient literature and even learned Greek (see §5.3.1). By the end of the fifteenth century, the most famous professor in the *studium* was, astonishingly, one of Latin letters: Filippo Beroaldo the Elder drew students from all over Europe to study Roman authors with him (see §5.2). His colleague Antonio Urceo (Codro) also gained great esteem for his teaching of Greek, which consolidated the instruction offered by Andronicus Callistus and other famous Hellenists in the course of the fifteenth century (§5.3.1). Thus, the humanities (or *studia humanitatis,* as they were often called) gained an ever more prominent position within the *studium.* From their formerly lowly status, they attained a far higher and secure one. By the first half of the sixteenth century, Greek had become an established and "ordinary" teaching. Rhetoric and its allied subjects regularly represented around 20 percent of salary expenditures in arts and medicine, in contrast with the 12 to 15 percent for natural philosophy.[2] A university without prominent professors of humanities had become unthinkable. In Florence, one such professor (Angelo Poliziano) even argued that, as a "grammarian" (i.e., an expert in ancient texts and languages), he was entitled to break with convention and teach whatever he pleased—including philosophy—because his subject provided the methodology for all others.[3] As we will see, Codro made similar claims.

There is no doubt that these developments constitute a lasting legacy to modern universities. However threatened humanities scholars may feel today, a university or government department would be brave indeed to deny the importance of the humanities altogether. But how did such an extraordinary rise occur in the first place in Bologna? What were its different manifestations in the areas of Latin and Greek studies? How, if at all, did they spill over into a more general appreciation of the need to study modern languages (particularly, Tuscan) and history? And, finally, what other areas of the curriculum were touched by this new interest in the humanities?

To address these questions, one must first discuss a fundamental and controversial subject. For the rise of the humanities cannot be separated from the nature and development of Renaissance humanism, particularly because the professors hired were self-described humanists or *umanisti.*[4] Scholars have, of course, disagreed strongly on the exact origins, contours, novelty, limitations, and impact of humanism. This is not the place to rehearse (much less, settle) such a complex and long-standing debate. But it is worth briefly outlining the perspective taken in this chapter (roughly in line with that of Paul Oskar Kristeller and his followers), if only because it affects the discussion as a whole.[5]

I treat Renaissance humanism mainly as a cultural and educational (rather than philosophical) movement, many of whose adherents privileged subjects such as grammar, rhetoric, poetry, and history, although of course they might also study (and write on) philosophy, theology, and law. For the humanists, ancient Latin became a standard to emulate—despite disagreements, discussed below, about the relative merits of Golden Age versus Silver Age writers. Some of them became proficient in Greek and other ancient languages.[6] The literary canon expanded, not only in terms of authors, but also of genres: compared to the medieval consensus, genres such as poetry, oratory, dialogue, and drama came to occupy a more prominent place. The study of antiquity (not only of the classical world, but also of the wider Mediterranean and of early Christianity) was a common concern and gave rise to numerous historical writings. Initially this study was driven by a view of the ancients as models of language, style, morals, politics, and much else; many thought that recapturing their values and eloquence would improve humanity and help address the challenges of the contemporary world.[7] Over time, the aims became more focused on scholarship. Philology, for instance, developed to cope with the demands of disentangling increasingly challenging manuscript traditions and preparing reliable editions of texts.[8] Humanists did not, however, inhabit a cultural space entirely separate from the scholastics, who typically focused on more technical or scientific writings; indeed, they applied their efforts to many of the same authors, including Aristotle and Galen.[9] (Notably, Desiderius Erasmus prepared an edition of Aristotle's *Opera omnia.*) Their teaching, despite its advertised novelty, was not always as mold-breaking as it claimed to be.[10] Furthermore, *pace* a rather dated historiography, although humanism had its origins outside of the universities (with figures such as Albertino Mussato and Francis Petrarch), it soon also developed and flourished within them as well.[11] The success of this grafting process varied from place to place. As it happens, one of the most receptive institutions was the University of Bologna.

5.1 Institutional Considerations

Humanistic studies and university culture had a productive relationship in Renaissance Italy and were, in fact, strongly intertwined.[12] This was especially the case in Bologna, where new grammatical and rhetorical studies developed earlier than elsewhere. Bologna already had a flourishing school of rhetoric in the second half of the fourteenth century (it included teachers such as Pietro da Moglio, who taught Coluccio Salutati, and Bartolomeo del Regno) and could boast a much earlier (and equally famous) teaching of notary art and *ars dictandi* or *ars dictaminis* (official prose writing).[13] In the fifteenth century, it was graced by several eminent teachers of grammar, rhetoric, or Greek.[14] These included figures such as Guarino Veronese, Giovanni Toscanella, Lapo da Castiglionchio, Francesco Filelfo, and Giovanni Lamola in the first half of the century. In general these teachers did not stay long, but they laid a foundation on which later professors would build. Around the middle of the century, the lively circuits of exchanges of humanistic books (see §4.2.2), the influence of Tommaso Parentucelli (later Pope Nicholas V), and the presence of important men such as Giovanni Tortelli, Cardinal Basil Bessarion, Niccolò Perotti, and Cardinal Niccolò Albergati suggest a significant growth of the *studia humanitatis.*[15] Confirmation comes in the second half of the fifteenth century from the private teaching of the humanist medical doctor Giovanni Garzoni and the public teaching of other important professors such as Andronicus Callistus, Francesco Dal Pozzo (Puteolanus), Filippo Beroaldo the Elder, and Antonio Urceo

(Codro). As discussed below, it was especially due to Beroaldo and Codro that Bologna became a lively center for humanistic studies in the late fifteenth century. In the sixteenth century, this legacy continued through the pedagogical activity of professors such as Giovanni Battista Pio, Achille Bocchi, Romolo Amaseo, Ciriaco Strozzi, Sebastiano Corradi, Francesco Robortello, and Carlo Sigonio.

Two patterns in the Bolognese teaching of the humanities are especially relevant here. First, the designation of these subjects changes over time. Throughout the fifteenth century, the rolls often group grammar, rhetoric, and poetry together (*lectura retorice, poesie et grammatice*), although they also list a separate teaching of grammar to schoolchildren in their city neighborhoods (*grammatica pro quarteriis*) as well as an occasional, independent teaching of rhetoric.[16] Starting in the early sixteenth century, the latter (directed at university students rather than schoolchildren) is usually simply called "rhetoric and poetry." Alongside rhetoric, one finds the designation of *studia* or *litterae humanitatis* already in the fifteenth century.[17] Between 1538 and 1542, however, a reorganization takes place: leaving aside the elementary-level *grammatica pro quarteriis,* there is just one teaching that includes rhetoric, poetry, and other humanities: this is called *humanitatis studia* and receives morning, afternoon, and feast-day slots.[18] The senior member of this humanities teaching is the one lecturing in the afternoon hour. He occupies one of the four distinguished chairs or *cattedre eminenti* of the *studium,* meant to attract renowned foreign (i.e., non-Bolognese) professors.[19] Over time the morning and feast-day teachings of humanities disappear, leaving only the afternoon hour. Greek makes its first appearance in 1424.[20] It is nearly always an autonomous subject, although there are also instances (as with Codro, below) in which professors are appointed to Greek in combination with other teachings—usually rhetoric or, more rarely, moral philosophy. Until 1510, Greek teaching takes place on feast days, indicating that it is a minor and non-required subject.[21] Thereafter, *litterae graecae* becomes regular and ordinary (although for a time complementary feast-day teaching carries on), in a pattern that continues up to the eighteenth century. It would require a separate study to clarify why these changes to rhetoric and Greek took place when they did, although it seems plausible that the elevation of Greek to an ordinary subject reflected its mounting importance.

A second notable pattern concerns specialization. At the end of the fifteenth century, six out of thirty-four appointments on the roll of arts and medicine refer to grammar, rhetoric, poetry, and Greek.[22] In the second half of the sixteenth century, it is not unusual to have just three instructors of the humanities listed. By 1733 the rolls record just one teacher of Greek (in the morning) and one of *humanae litterae* in the afternoon, while the total number of professors has swollen to nearly one hundred.[23] Such a shift did not, as one might think, correspond to the subject's loss of prestige. In fact, two main factors were at play: one was, in all likelihood, the competition offered by the Jesuits, who were justly renowned for their teaching of the humanities (§3.3.2). This must have led to a slackening demand to hear such subjects in the *studium*, which in any case was attracting fewer students. Secondly, teachers of the humanities were now receiving substantially higher salaries. It was probably convenient for the *studium* to have fewer (albeit more expensive) instructors in this area, a development possibly connected to the more general trend toward specialization and professionalization discussed in Chapter 6. Still, Bologna's attractiveness as a center for the humanities must have received a blow around the end of the sixteenth century: after the death of Carlo Sigonio (1584), it became increasingly hard to attract world-class humanities teachers to Bologna. Efforts to hire the famous Flemish scholar Justus Lipsius in 1595–1597 came to nothing. One of the few foreigners attracted in the seventeenth century was the Scotsman Thomas Dempster (t. 1619–1625).[24]

Gaps in the documentation mean that this chapter cannot hope to cover the development of Bolognese humanities teaching in all of its richness.[25] Instead, it will focus on its most significant aspects, leading progressively to an understanding of how the *studia humanitatis* evolved up to the eighteenth century. Most important are Latin language and rhetoric (particularly the activity of Beroaldo the Elder) and Greek studies (in which Codro was a leading light)—summed up by the labels *latinitas* and *graecitas*. But the *studia humanitatis* strongly affected other fields as well, including not only philosophy and medicine, but also law and Oriental languages. By the end of this chapter, it should be clear that the study of Greek, classical Latin literature and style, philology, and ancient history was not only welcomed in the university, but largely developed within it.

5.2 *Latinitas*

Bologna boasted numerous famous teachers of grammar and rhetoric in the fifteenth century, including Lapo da Castiglionchio, Battista Guarino (the son of Guarino da Verona, t. 1456–1458), and Francesco Dal Pozzo.[26] But none was as well known and influential as Filippo Beroaldo the Elder (1453–1505).[27] Beroaldo came from a Bolognese noble family and studied with Dal Pozzo. In 1472–1473 and 1473–1474 he taught rhetoric and grammar in the *studium.*[28] He then spent a few years away in Parma, Milan, and Paris (where he taught for two years). When he returned to his alma mater in 1480, he embarked on a long and influential teaching career.[29] Throughout these years he was officially appointed to teach rhetoric and poetry (sometimes in the mornings, other times in the evenings, 1480–1505); in his last year his salary reached L. 600 (tied for highest for arts and medicine).[30] Beroaldo produced copious printed works, often taking advantage of his special relationship with agents in the printing trade.[31] He published translations of Petrarch and Boccaccio, works of philological erudition (*Annotationes centum,* 1488 and later), and editions of or commentaries on works; the most significant of his commentaries are on Propertius (1487), Suetonius (1493), Cicero's *Tusculan Disputations* (1496), and the *Golden Ass* of Apuleius (1500), but Beroaldo also wrote on Ovid's *Metamorphoses,* the *Symbola Pythagorae,* the comedies of Plautus, Cicero's orations, and many other works.[32] No contemporary representations of Beroaldo survive, but an edition of his commentary on Suetonius published the year after his death (Figure 5.1) shows him in the act of lecturing to his students, all of whom have in front of them a copy of the text—doubtless the one prepared by Beroaldo himself.

Several of these writings—all of them in Latin—are connected with Beroaldo's teaching activity, but the subjects of his lectures emerge more clearly from his printed prolusions to books (often taught in pairs). These include Virgil's *Georgics,* Propertius, Livy and Silius Italicus, Cicero's *Letters* and Lucan, Cicero's orations, Juvenal and Sallust, Cicero's *Tusculan Disputations* and Horace, Persius, Cicero's orations against Verres, and Apuleius's *The Golden Ass.*[33] In addition, manuscript evidence points to his teaching of Pliny the Elder's *Natural History* (1480 and c. 1500), the letters of Pliny the Younger, Latin grammar (1486), Statius's *Thebaid* (1495),

Fig 5.1. Filippo Beroaldo the Elder, commentary on Suetonius: [Caius Suetonius Tranquillus,] *Vitae Caesarum cum Philippi Beroaldi et Marci Antonii Sabellici commentariis. Cum figuris nuper additis* (Venice: Giovanni Rossi vercellese, 8 January 1506).
Detail of frontispiece with unattributed woodcut.

and Cicero's *De officiis* (1495).[34] It is unclear whether Beroaldo taught these works in his official capacity or, instead, as part of private teaching (on which a testimony by Poliziano provides an interesting insight).[35] And it is striking to observe how different some of these notes are from Beroaldo's printed production—for instance, on Statius.[36] Nonetheless, here it is relevant to consider both Beroaldo's renown as a teacher of Latin literature and his penchant for somewhat unusual models of style.

5.2.1 The Debate about Latin Style

Himself a published author of Latin poetry, Beroaldo engaged intensively (as shown by the list of lectures above) with Latin works of both poetry and prose.[37] His activity followed a strong reshaping of Latin literature. At the start of the fifteenth century, the teaching of Bartolomeo del Regno in Bologna shows that a series of Latin authors and works (some of them recovered only in the fourteenth century) informed the curriculum: Virgil, Statius, Lucan, Ovid, Horace, Persius, Juvenal, Terence, Valerius Maximus, Seneca's *Tragedies,* and also Livy, Plautus, and the philosophical works of Cicero (§2.2.2). Cicero became particularly important, due to the fourteenth-century rediscovery of works such as his *Epistles to Atticus,* the oration *Pro Archia* (in praise of poetry), and the letters to his friends (*Ad familiares*). The expanded awareness of Cicero's writings was particularly significant for rhetoric. While the *De inventione* and the (nowadays considered spurious) *Rhetorica ad Herennium* were long-standing mainstays of the educational curriculum, fifteenth-century scholars came to know his *De oratore, Orator, Pro Roscio, Pro Murena,* and *Brutus* as well as Quintilian's complete *Institutiones.* Other important finds included the works of Tacitus, Tertullian, Lucretius, Manilius, Silius Italicus, Vitruvius, and the *Letters* of Pliny the Younger, to mention just a few.[38]

Given this expanded collection of texts, an intense debate developed as to which authors offered the best stylistic model for prose writing. Differing positions developed among humanists as to whether to use an eclectic approach or one based on a single model.[39] Whereas many—already from the early fifteenth century—looked to Cicero as the perfect exemplar (an approach later heavily satirized by Erasmus in his *Ciceronianus*), several influential voices disagreed, including Poliziano in Florence. In Bologna, Beroaldo's strong interest in the works of Silver Age authors such as Apuleius and Pliny the Elder affected both his own stylistic choices and the authors he chose to teach. Thus, although Beroaldo could hardly avoid commenting on the works of standard Golden Age authors such as Cicero and Sallust, his lexical and stylistic leanings went instead to "obscure and rare words, and occasional excesses of syntax" (as D'Amico has observed) derived particularly from his close reading of Apuleius.[40]

Beroaldo was hardly alone in this attention to (and imitation of) less-known authors, in an un-Ciceronian vein that sometimes bordered on hostility. His student Giovanni Battista Pio (†1543) took this orientation even further, looking, for instance, to authors such as Varro, Festus, Lucretius (on whom he wrote the first Renaissance commentary), and Valerius Flaccus, adopting their archaizing and recherché style.[41] Pio also had an interest in Plautus, who had a devoted following in Bologna since the days of Codro and Beroaldo. He passed on this passion to his student Achille Bocchi, who defended Pio's teaching of the Roman comedian in his *Apologia in Plautum* (Bologna, 1508), while himself cultivating a moderate style.[42] And, of course, Beroaldo's colleague Codro had his own personal stylistic preferences, far removed from Cicero's eloquence.[43]

Such a devotion to alternative stylistic models was not, however, the only orientation in Bologna. In the fifteenth century, the humanist and medical doctor Giovanni Garzoni (1419–1505) expressed a more favorable attitude toward Cicero: he repeated the well-worn judgment that he was "a golden fount of eloquence," and—though his devotion was not nearly as pronounced and exclusive as has been claimed—produced a collection of *Epistolae familiares* that recalls and praises the Roman orator. Garzoni, who studied Latin letters with Guarino Veronese in Ferrara (1449) and Lorenzo Valla in Rome (possibly 1453–1457) and ran a grammar (i.e., Latin) school in Bologna, followed Valla in his strong respect for Quintilian, who, however, seems (along with Livy, Lactantius, and others) to occupy a lower rung than Cicero.[44] The one element that ties him more strongly to other Bolognese humanists is his embrace of philosophy and (as we shall see) history.

Garzoni's nuanced position makes for a strong contrast with that of Romolo Amaseo (1489–1552). Amaseo taught rhetoric, poetry, and humanities in the Bolognese *studium* almost continuously from 1512 to 1544, before moving to Rome.[45] Well versed in Greek and an elegant stylist, Amaseo lectured on authors such as Cicero and Virgil in 1539 and made Latin translations of Greek authors such as Xenophon and Pausanias.[46] He took full part in the linguistic and stylistic controversies of his time. He did not hesitate to attack his colleague Pio for his eclectic approach and style, and in his two orations *De latinae linguae usu retinendo* (1529), delivered in Bologna before the pope and emperor, he took a dismissive stance toward the vernacular, arguing that only Ciceronian Latin could express the glories of the Empire. Amaseo's dedication to Latin, as opposed to the vernacular, is also clear from his participation in the Accademia Bocchiana, founded by his colleague and former teacher Bocchi in his home by around 1542. This academy, which focused on legal matters, poetry, and possibly architecture, unusually conducted its gatherings and lectures in Latin (see §3.2).[47]

Amaseo has become a symbol, for some scholars, of a conservatism and elitism that supposedly captivated Bologna in the sixteenth century, even though his stance encountered resistance from various quarters. Calcaterra places this current within the context of that period's heated debates about the vernacular (the *questione della lingua*) and suggests four reasons for this insistence on Latin: a prejudice against the vernacular, a strict adherence to humanism, the convenience of using a language that foreign students could understand, and a false conviction that the use of Latin was an attestation of academic prowess.[48] Before assessing their relevance, one should consider a later move to establish a chair of Tuscan language in Bologna.

5.2.2 The Interest in a Chair of Tuscan Language

Although Bologna strongly promoted Greek and Latin, it did not focus on ancient languages alone. In the early seventeenth century, the Riformatori dello Studio also tried to establish a chair for the teaching of the Tuscan language.[49] The evidence for this initiative comes indirectly from a letter written on 21 March 1623 by Celso Cittadini (a famous grammarian and, since 1598, holder of the chair for Tuscan language in the *studium* of Siena) to Pandolfo Spannocchi (a professor of law in Bologna).[50] There the Sienese professor claims that he had been advised years earlier—probably around 1609—of the intention to establish a chair of Tuscan language in Bologna and had been offered the post with the considerable salary of 400 ducats. At the time, Cittadini says, personal circumstances did not allow him to accept (he was not free, or "sbrigato"), and the early death of Colombini, who was apparently in charge of the negotiations, prevented matters from coming to fruition.[51] Yet at the time of writing Cittadini was still interested and asked Spannocchi to renew the negotiations if possible.[52] A document sent by the Riformatori dello Studio to the Bolognese Senate on 18 September 1623 provides more direct evidence. The Riformatori proposed the establishment of a chair of Tuscan language that would "offer instruction in the rules and precepts of writing, which are little known to most people, and especially to those who make most use of it."[53] This teaching was, the Riformatori claimed, already being delivered in the universities of Florence, Pisa, and Siena, "where it has proved useful to all of the nobility and in particular to the Ultramontane students, who go there rather than elsewhere to learn the precepts of the language."[54] If this reasoning points to the proposed chair as a means of strengthening student recruitment (not unlike the establishment of certain degree programs in universities today), there was also, according to the Riformatori, a strong intellectual rationale for this teaching: just as no expense (they say) was spared in the past to recruit teachers of Latin eloquence, so it would be fitting today to teach the mother tongue, in which nearly all learning can be studied and in which very few (apparently also including Italians) are able to write correctly. In other words, this teaching would also be useful to the domestic market.[55]

The reference to other *studia* that were teaching the subject was clearly meant to suggest that Bologna was behind the curve on these matters. In fact, though, the claim was correct only in the case of Siena. Remarkably, Florence did not establish a chair of the Tuscan language until 1632, with the celebrated grammarian Benedetto Buonmattei, who also taught the subject for a period in Pisa before returning to Florence from 1637 until his death in 1648.[56] In Padua, at the start of the eighteenth century, Scipione Maffei made a plea to give renewed prominence to languages; he specifically advanced proposals for teaching Italian.[57] His recommendation, however, did not have the hoped-for effect, and for the whole of the eighteenth century the Paduan *studium* remained without a chair for Tuscan language or literature.[58]

Coming back to the Bolognese attempt to establish the teaching of Tuscan, it is noteworthy that the negotiations involved Cittadini, one of the best-known professors in Siena. Bologna was therefore not looking for a lowly figure or trying to introduce an innovation on the cheap. But the more interesting point may be that the two universities apparently had different markets in mind. Already from its first appointment of such a chair-holder (Diomede Borghesi) anywhere in Italy in 1588 / 1589, Siena was clearly responding to a request from the German Nation.[59] Although Bologna too welcomed German nobles who traveled to Italy to be instructed in the Italian language in addition to fencing, music, and dance (see §3.3.3), its home students were at least as important a consideration. Finally, in Bologna this initiative came neither from the ruler (as in Siena) nor from the professors, but from the Riformatori. This suggests that the ripples of the *questione della lingua* went far beyond the limits of debates between scholars, reaching into Senate-appointed committees of laymen. Furthermore, even when the self-interest of the doctoral colleges may have recommended sticking with well-established practice, the overseers of the *studium* could play an important role in at least trying to effect change. The role of the Riformatori and Assunti in proposing and bringing about reform deserves greater attention (see §1.3.1).

Thus, while Calcaterra's considerations of conservatism listed above may well be true, one should not look exclusively at the attitude of specific professors in judging the flexibility and dynamism of Bologna's university. Latin remained the primary language of university instruction throughout the period.[60] But the skills students needed were changing, particularly as the vernacular increasingly became acceptable as a language of learning and debate.[61] The university's overseers at least were aware of this and displayed remarkable pragmatism in trying to establish the teaching of Tuscan, even though in the end they were unsuccessful.

5.2.3 Latinity and History

Bologna's cultural environment also fostered a deep engagement with the historical writings of the Romans—a concern often linked with projects of local or (near-) contemporary historiography.[62] Garzoni, whom we met in §5.2.1, wrote not only saints' lives, but also a history of Bologna and accounts of the Bentivoglio, of Charles VIII's descent to Italy, of the king of Hungary, and the duke of Saxony.[63] He was deeply interested in Livy, whose text he emended and densely annotated, and in other ancient historians.[64] Garzoni's contemporary Francesco Dal Pozzo was more fascinated by the writings of Tacitus and worked on a new edition of his works; after his return to Milan in his later years, he took up a history of the city, in an attempt to burnish the image of the Sforza family.[65] Filippo Beroaldo the Younger published an edition of the "first six surviving books" of Tacitus's *Annals*.[66] In the sixteenth century, the Bolognese Senate entrusted the writing of a history of Bologna first to its native son Achille Bocchi and later on to Carlo Sigonio, who had done his first studies in Bologna and had been newly recruited from Padua. Both attempts are well known, the first for its incompleteness (Bocchi's account reached only to the year 1263) and the second for the problems it encountered with the censors in Rome.[67] But it is worth noting that both scholars dedicated themselves to Roman history and culture.

Bocchi translated into Latin Plutarch's *Life* of Cicero and in 1557 held a course (probably in the Accademia Bocchiana) on Cicero's *De legibus.*[68] Sigonio's historical studies ran deeper and wider: he prepared a detailed institutional history of ancient Rome (in part published in 1549), wrote a commentary on Livy's *History* (1556), delivered lectures on Roman history and political institutions (1557–1558), wrote on Roman law (1560), and published a *Life* of Scipio Emilianus (1569). But he also looked to Greece, publishing a history of the Athenian republic and a chronology of Athens and Sparta (1564) and lecturing—both before and after his arrival in Bologna—on Aristotle's *Rhetoric* and *Poetics.*[69] He also left behind an unpublished history of the church, as well as numerous other historical works.[70]

Later personalities and lectures also testify that professors of rhetoric and humanities in Bologna explained the historical works of the Romans in the classroom. In 1598 Roberto Titi (or Tizzi, t. 1597–1606), the fairly recent incumbent of the chair for the humanities, offered four prolusions on Caesar's *De bello gallico,* which was evidently the topic of his lectures for the new academic year.[71] Lodovico Scapinelli, a famous teacher (t. 1609–1618 and 1628–1634) who—despite his blindness—had acquired great learning, apparently attracted numerous students. He taught not only Virgil and Horace, but also Tacitus and Livy's *History of Rome.* His prolusions on Livy occupy an entire volume of a modern edition.[72] In 1642–1643 Domenico Cesario, professor of *humanae litterae,* planned to deliver ninety-five lectures on the first book of Tacitus's *Annals;* some of these were meant to provide occasional insights into possible political themes, such as simulation and dissimulation.[73] It is hard to know the extent to which Cesario's concerns were shared by other professors in Bologna—the surviving course plans for the seventeenth and eighteenth centuries hardly ever include lectures on rhetoric or the humanities. (This is possibly occasioned by the fact that their teaching was fairly unconstrained, and they were nearly always allowed to teach whatever they wished, or *ad beneplacitum.*)

Works of this kind most likely reflect a trend that should be linked with the rising tide of Tacitism across Europe, but also in Bologna itself.[74] In this connection, an important personality was Virgilio Malvezzi (1595–1654), who—though not a university professor—was a cultural figure of considerable standing in Bologna and published a number of works either on Tacitus or influenced by his approach. Among these are his *Discorsi sopra Cornelio Tacito* (1622) and historical works such as *Il Romulo* (1629) and *Tarquinio Superbo* (1632). Particularly well received was his *Davide perseguitato* (1634), a treatise on political matters in the form of a commentary on the enmity between David and King Saul, which unites Christian and Roman themes.[75]

5.3 *Graecitas*

In Bologna the teaching of Greek developed somewhat later than in Florence, which had already hired Leonzio Pilato to teach Greek in 1360–1362 and had seen the teaching of the influential Greek émigré Manuel Chrysoloras at the end of the fourteenth century.[76] The first known record of Greek teaching in the Bolognese *studium* comes with Giovanni Aurispa (1376–1459), who—despite being well rewarded—remained only one year (1424–1425) before moving briefly to Florence.[77] Nothing is known of the contents of his teaching, nor of that of his successor, the shadowy Theodorus de Candia (1425–1427), whose teaching in Bologna overlapped with that of Guarino Veronese and possibly Gasparino Barzizza.[78]

A bit more information survives in the case of the next public teacher of Greek, the famous humanist Francesco Filelfo (1398–1481).[79] A former student of Gasparino Barzizza and Paolo Veneto in Padua, Filelfo was very well connected, had spent the better part of 1420–1427 as a Venetian official in Constantinople, and while there had both studied Greek and built up a collection of precious Greek manuscripts.[80] Filelfo spent two spells in Bologna. He passed through Bologna in early 1428, after failing to secure a professorship of Greek in Venice, which was ravaged by the plague. At the personal invitation of the papal legate Louis Aleman (who offered to pay half of his salary), Filelfo accepted a highly paid appointment and stayed in Bologna from February 1428 until early April of the following year. He spent the first few months teaching Greek and rhetoric. In the 1428–1429 academic year he apparently taught at least rhetoric and moral philosophy.[81] He also started a new Latin rendering of the *Rhetorica ad Alexandrum* (then considered a genuine work of Aristotle) and made a translation of the oration *De Troia non capta* by Dio Chrysostom (a late Greek rhetorician, AD 40–115).[82] One of Filelfo's letters suggests that he was teaching Chrysostom on the basis of his own translation.[83] The pseudo-Aristotelian *Rhetoric* may also have been among his teaching texts, given that this work was one of those on which extraordinary lectures could be given; it may also fit with one of his prolusions.[84] During this first stay, Filelfo may also have taught Aristotle's *Nicomachean Ethics;* he was consulted by a colleague during this time about the best translation of the opening lines of that work.[85] It is unclear which works Filelfo taught during a later sojourn in Bologna in 1438–1439.[86] We do know that, over the course of his career, he also taught at least Sallust's *De bello Jugurthino,* Cicero's *De officiis,* Homer's *Iliad,* Juvenal's *Satires,* and of course Virgil.[87]

Scholars have doubted how effective or welcome this teaching of Greek was in Bologna in the first part of the Quattrocento. Some teachers of Greek—like Aurispa—clearly felt unappreciated.[88] Yet one should also recall that the 1420s also saw the presence of students such as Antonio Beccadelli (Panormita), Giovanni Toscanella, and Leon Battista Alberti, all of whom became familiar with Greek.[89] In any case, the Bolognese teaching of Greek becomes clearer in the second half of the fifteenth century, with Andronicus Callistus and especially Codro, although the understudied Lianoro Lianori may also have been an effective teacher.[90]

5.3.1 The Consolidation of Hellenism

Andronicus Callistus

A Greek émigré who probably came to Italy on the occasion of the Council of Ferrara-Florence (1438–1439) and was possibly in Padua from 1441 to 1444, Callistus spent several years in Bologna and may have offered both private and public teaching.[91] His presence is attested in the years 1453–1455, when he doubtless benefited from the friendship of Cardinal Bessarion, then papal legate in the city.[92] His first official appearance on the teaching rolls comes in 1458–1459 (appointed to teach *litterae graecae*). He appears again in 1462–1466, after a three-year absence in Padua, this time with the added duty to teach moral philosophy. No lectures or student notebooks are known to survive for Callistus's teaching, but from his letters it is clear that in Bologna he taught the poetry of Pindar, the letters falsely attributed to Phalaris (a tyrant of the sixth century BC), Theocritus (at least to Giorgio Merula), and Aristotle's

Physics, Politics, and *Economics,* all in Latin. He may also have taught Homer and Hesiod there. He was a deeply innovative teacher who traveled widely (after Bologna, he went to Rome, Florence, Milan, France, and London) and taught Greek to exceptional students—among them, the famed Hellenist Poliziano. Paul Botley remarks that he is "the first person known to have lectured in the West on Pindar, Theocritus, and Apollonius [of Rhodes]."[93] His influence in Bologna is likely to have been considerable but requires further investigation.

Codro

More detail emerges with Antonio Urceo Cortesi (1446–1500), better known by his chosen nickname "Codro," who studied with Battista Guarino and Luca Ripa in Ferrara and from that time derived a passion for Greek and rhetoric.[94] After a period as a public humanities teacher (*publicus literarum preceptor*) in the court of the Ordelaffi in Forlì, Codro taught in the *studium* of Bologna from 1482 until his death. His teaching encompassed subjects such as grammar, rhetoric, poetry, and (from 1485) Greek *diebus festivis.* Codro's prolusions (or, as he called them, *sermones*) were gathered by his students in 1502 and have lately received a modern edition, accompanied by notes and an Italian translation.[95] They show him teaching Priscian, Aristotle's *Categories,* Homer, Hesiod, Theocritus, the *Ad Herennium* (then misattributed to Cicero), Valerius Maximus, Lucan, Terence, and Euripides, as well as specific topics (e.g., the rhetorical mean and virtue). He also addressed long-standing questions such as whether one ought to marry.[96] Among his subjects, Homer and Aristotle's logic held a special place for Codro.[97] This was probably in line with a long-standing tradition uniting the study of grammar, dialectic, and rhetoric within the *trivium.*

Although Codro's prolusions do not always make clear the specific works (as opposed to authors) he was explaining, they do shed light on several features of his teaching. They showcase, for instance, his knowledge of Greek, which he quotes to such an extent that he begs his audience's patience. They also give some indication of Codro's approach, which is both critical and wide-ranging. An example of this is *Sermo* VI (c. 1497), Codro's prolusion to that year's teaching of Aristotle's *De interpretatione* and continued explanation of the *Iliad.* Here, among his notable moves is his inclusion of all of learning within his purview. He sees no good reason to exclude logic from his area of teaching. At the same time, he recognizes that all disciplines can err or be accused of falsehood. Elsewhere, Codro announces that he will take an approach that embraces all of philosophy and medicine as well as grammar and rhetoric.[98] Whether or not he kept his promise to lecture also on philosophy and medicine (including the works of Aristotle, Hippocrates, and so forth), his program is strongly reminiscent of that of Poliziano in Florence, again in the 1490s. Like Poliziano, Codro believed that his occupation as a *grammaticus* or philologist entitled him to comment on anything that came his way in terms of its good language, style, or correctness. An example is his displeasure with the volumes he had acquired of Aldus Manutius's famous Greek edition (1495–1498) of Aristotle's complete works. Upon receiving the volume containing the *De animalibus,* Codro lamented the poor text and sent Aldus a long list of corrections.[99] Unlike Poliziano, however, Codro's teaching seems not to have embraced the "new logic" contained in the *Prior* and *Posterior Analytics,* the *Topics,* and the *Libri elenchorum,* but to have focused instead on the "old logic" (*Praedicamenta, De interpretatione*).[100]

Although Codro became especially known for his 122 verses completing Plautus's play *Aulularia,* here it is worth underlining his role as a teacher of Greek and Greek literary works.[101] In Bologna, Codro taught Greek both privately and publicly.[102] He seems to have given particular emphasis to the practice of Latin translation. This approach is evident in two manuscript items containing translations of Isocrates, *Ad Demonicum,* as well as parts of Porphyry's *Isagoge* and Aristotle's *Praedicamenta.*[103] Scholars do not agree, however, on the attribution of these items to Codro himself rather than to one of his students.[104] A less controversial case is that of Codro's partial Latin rendition (825 verses) of Hesiod's *Works and Days,* possibly provided orally as part of his teaching of that author.[105] What is noteworthy is that, for Codro, translation is clearly an integral part of learning the Greek language. This emphasis seems closely connected with the approach of Codro's own teacher Battista Guarino, who made a point of endorsing this method in his *De ordine docendi et studendi* of 1459.[106] By using the *Ad Demonicum,* Codro was not really being innovative (there was a tradition for this going back at least to Guarino Veronese in 1407).[107] But his reliance on Porphyry and Aristotle as teaching aids for Greek seems to have been rather less common. It goes without saying that translation was also foundational to learning Latin.[108]

A second important element in Codro's teaching of Greek was the explanation of standard authors and of Homer in particular. Homer had been taught in the Latin West from the second half of the fourteenth century. He was one of the mainstays of Battista Guarino's classroom.[109] As noted above, Callistus may have lectured on him in Bologna. In any case, Codro started teaching Homer by 1485, and four of his prolusions testify to this activity: VII (1485–1486), VIII (1488–1489?), III (1490 or 1491–1492?), and I (1494–1495).[110] The first of these is especially interesting for its cautiousness in encouraging the study of Greek in Bologna, a city in which—Codro says—earlier attempts have not met with much success.[111] (It is unclear whether this is a brazen attempt at self-promotion.) Codro therefore promises to explain the Greek text in Latin, presumably to make Greek more accessible to his students.[112] He also tries to attract students by underlining the usefulness of Greek for a whole range of subjects, including Latin grammar, medicine, and law. Homer was not the only author Codro used to teach Greek: after his first year, he went on to teach Hesiod (1486–1487) and Theocritus (1487–1488) as well as Euripides (1494–1495?).[113] Still, he returned to the *Iliad* often, focusing, for instance, on Book III in 1488–1489.[114] Homer therefore remained foundational for him, and one of his great loves, again reflecting Battista's suggestions.

No direct evidence survives of Codro's teaching of Greek authors. There are, however, several student notebooks related to Codro's lectures on Latin authors, such as Quintilian, Gellius, Ovid, and Virgil's *Georgics*.[115] The undated notebook of his lectures on Quintilian (Figure 5.2) is an example of how Codro's enthusiasm for Greek easily spilled over into his Latin lectures: the student has noted in Greek the equivalent of the Latin *scopus* (aim, sixth line of text). Other notebooks make an even more regular use of Greek words. This evidence points to a fairly sophisticated audience, which was at least able to write down Greek expressions. The notebook on Quintilian is also helpful because it represents an initial, messy stage of notetaking rather than the later fair copy that usually survives. Like the rest of the contents (notes mainly drawn from the lectures of Beroaldo the Elder, Codro, and Beroaldo the Younger), it deserves more systematic study.

The growth of grammars, lexica, and other language resources must have greatly aided the development of Greek studies in Bologna.[116] Three Greek grammars had been especially influential in fifteenth-century

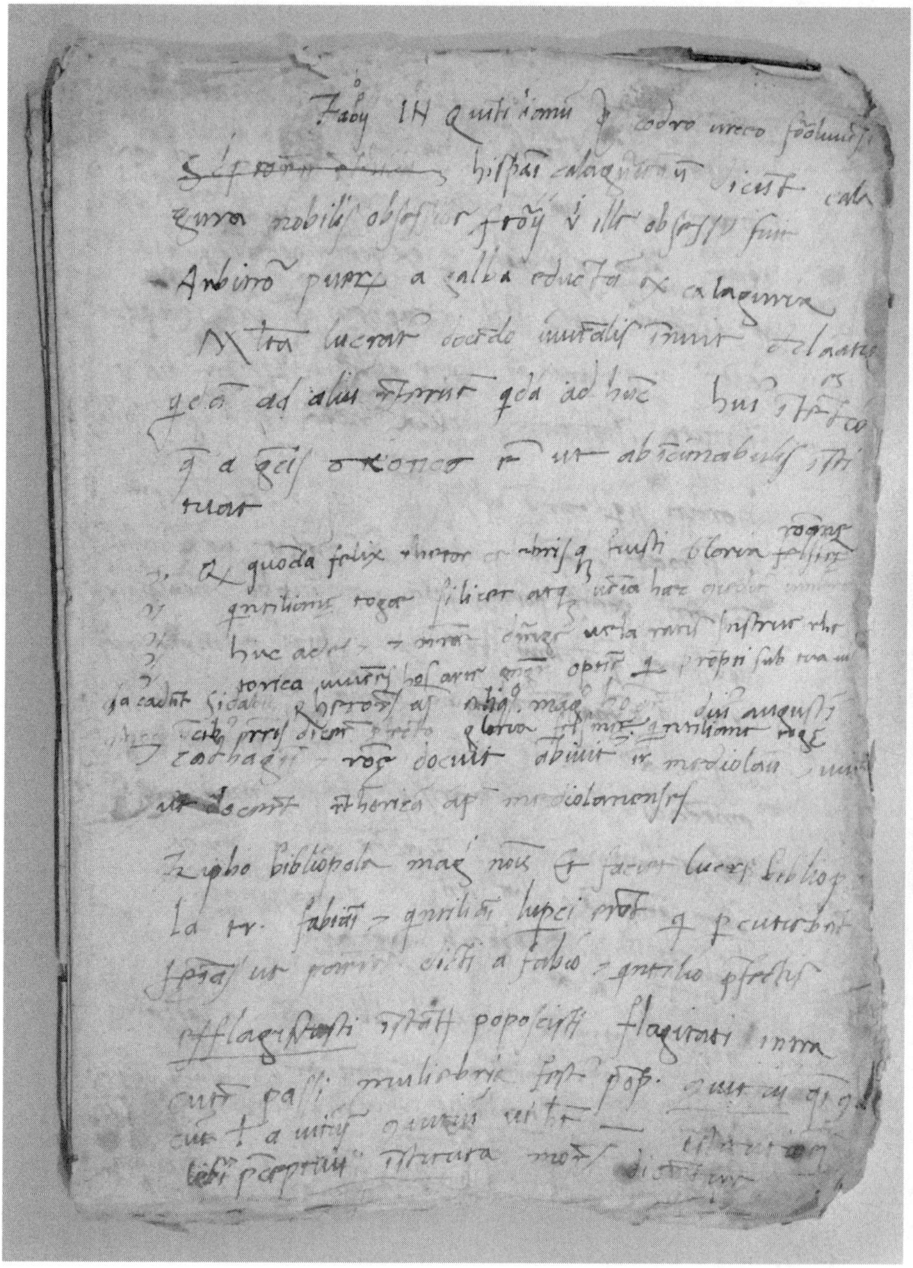

Fig 5.2. "First-order" student notes from lectures of Codro on Quintilian, late fifteenth century.

Archivio di Stato di Bologna, Studio Alidosi, b. 44, p. nn.

Italy: that of Manuel Chrysoloras, particularly in the version of the *Erotemata* prepared by Guarino Veronese and used by his son Battista; that of Theodore Gaza (owned and used by Codro's predecessor Callistus); and that of Constantine Lascaris, first printed along with a Latin translation in 1480.[117] As far as we know, none of these works (or, for that matter, any Greek text) was ever printed in Bologna in the fifteenth century.[118] This does not, however, indicate that such works were of no interest to scholars in Bologna, since the cost of paper, type, and other considerations often meant that it was more commercially advantageous to have books printed elsewhere.[119]

An unusual piece of evidence for the study of Greek in Bologna comes from three notebooks that seem to date from the end of the fifteenth century.[120] These booklets, which have not received any scholarly attention, contain grammatical outlines (mainly in Latin) for teaching Greek nouns, adjectives, and verbs. Although they await a full analysis and at present cannot be associated with any certainty to Codro's teaching, they nonetheless testify to a development of Greek grammars that was certainly gathering pace in Bologna during and after Codro's time in particular.[121] We also know of Codro's interest in Greek–Latin lexica. By April 1498 he had purchased such a book, printed by Aldus the previous year, but quickly disposed of it because he found that it added nothing to existing editions of lexica.[122] He probably had in mind those of Giovanni Crastoni, available in print since 1480 and in very common use.[123] Nicolaus Copernicus evidently learned his Greek (possibly at Codro's feet) through the 1499 edition of Crastoni printed in Modena by the Bolognese Dionisio Bertocchi.[124] But whatever the roots of Copernicus's education in Greek, Codro's acquisition of this Greek lexicon, and the mention of a similar book owned by him in a letter of April 1498, indicate his interest in such tools of the trade for teaching Greek.[125] He may also have used two very common collections of verse to teach Greek: the *Aurea verba* and Pseudo-Phocylides.[126]

5.3.2 Greek after Codro and the Study of the *Poetics*

After Codro, several professors continued to teach Greek letters as a feast-day subject.[127] But Greek also appears on the rolls as an ordinary subject in 1510 with the hire of Pietro Ipsilla da Egina.[128] Despite the seemingly momentous nature of this move to ordinary teaching of Greek, the reasons behind this shift (and the nature of Pietro's teaching) remain obscure. The only secure information is that Pietro taught Aristophanes's comedies in private.[129] We are likewise ill informed about the teaching of several other figures, such as Ciriaco Strozzi (t. 1536–1543) and Pompilio Amaseo (t. 1543–1582), the son of Romolo.[130] We do know that Amaseo was an active translator of works from the Greek; these include the *Histories* of Polybius (1543) as well as works by (among others) Diodorus Siculus and Johannes Chrysostomus. It seems doubtful, though, that these translations were related to classroom teaching, and the one printed prolusion gives no indication of the work(s) to be taught.[131]

Matters are somewhat different with Paolo Bombace (1476–1527), who in 1505 was appointed to teach rhetoric and poetry in the afternoon (*de sero*) and from the following year also taught Greek.[132] Bombace warmly welcomed Erasmus to Bologna at the end of 1506; he provided lodgings for the Dutch scholar and helped him both with his study of Greek and with his translations (e.g., of Euripides, which was printed by Aldus and by the spring of 1508 was being sold in Bologna, possibly as part of Bombace's teaching).[133] The evidence for 1507 suggests that Bombace used the *Erotemata* of Demetrius Chalcondyles for his teaching of Greek grammar and also had students translate Isocrates's oration *On Peace*. In 1510 he had one of his close associates, Scipione Forteguerri, teach Homer's *Odyssey* privately to some foreign students; when compared to the teaching of Guarino of Favera in Florence in 1493, the pace of teaching (eighty lines per class) seems rather rapid and makes one wonder whether Forteguerri's lectures were meant to supplement those of Bombace.[134] Bombace continued to teach in Bologna until 1512, when he took up a position (for one year) at the *studium* in Naples. After that he obtained a post as secretary to Cardinal Lorenzo Pucci in Rome. From there he continued to help Erasmus—for instance, with the Greek text of the first Epistle of John in the New Testament—and to correspond with other notable scholars of his time, but his teaching activity had come to an end.

Francesco Robortello

Finally, one of the most significant sixteenth-century innovations in Greek studies was the inclusion in university teaching of Aristotle's *Poetics* and *Rhetoric*. Here an important personality—though by no means the only one—was Francesco Robortello (1516–1567) of Udine, who studied in Bologna with Amaseo (presumably between the late 1520s and the mid- to late 1530s) and returned to teach there in 1557–1561.[135] One of the most prominent and controversial cultural figures of the period, Robortello first taught Greek and Latin letters publicly in Lucca (Jan. 1539–1543), where in addition to standard Latin authors (Cicero, Horace, Quintilian, and Virgil) he translated the *Hymns* of the Greek poet Callimachus. His teaching was more innovative in Pisa (1543–1549), where—as part of his appointment to *litterae humanae*—he focused on Aristotle's *Rhetoric* and *Poetics.* This assignment gave rise to Robortello's commentary on the *Poetics* and to a series of learned pieces, all of them published in Florence by Lorenzo Torrentino in 1548.[136] He then taught in the Scuola di San Marco in Venice (1549–1552), not only on the rhetorical works of Aristotle and Cicero, but also on Aristotle's moral philosophy (particularly, and unusually, his *Politics*).[137] When he moved to the chair of Greek and Latin in Padua (1552–1557), Robortello continued to teach the *Politics* and other Aristotelian works, while also publishing the fruit of his previous research in Venice, including an edition of the tragedies of Aeschylus (testimony to his lifelong interest in Greek dramaturgy). After teaching *studia humanitatis de sero* in Bologna (1557–1561), Robortello returned to Padua and taught there until shortly before his death in March 1567.

It is unclear where Robortello learned his Greek, but during his student days in Bologna he likely came across the Modenese (and former student of Romolo Amaseo) Bartolomeo Faustino, who taught Greek in Bologna from 1529 to 1533.[138] He possibly overlapped with Ciriaco Strozzi, who occupied the chair of Greek from 1535 to 1543.[139] His teacher Amaseo knew Greek well enough to publish some Latin translations of Greek historians (see §5.2.3). In any case, when he returned to Bologna in 1557, Robortello was well grounded in the language.

Robortello's commentary on the *Poetics* was a milestone publication, even though it developed within the context of several other contemporary treatments of the work by, for instance, Bartolomeo Lombardi, Vincenzo Maggi, Bernardo Segni, Pier Vettori, Alessandro Piccolomini, and Lodovico Castelvetro.[140] Although the *Poetics* was not altogether unknown in the West (it had been commented by Averroes, annotated by Poliziano, and rendered into Latin—but to little effect—by Giorgio

Valla in 1498), it was absent from the Greek *Opera omnia* edition of Aristotle published by Aldus Manutius (1495–1498) and was not part of the standard university curriculum.[141] Likewise, Aristotle's *Rhetoric*—though known in the Middle Ages and the early Renaissance—was overshadowed by the works of Cicero and Quintilian and rarely studied at school or university, though from the second half of the fifteenth century it became known especially through the Latin translation of George of Trebizond.[142] It was only in 1508 that the *Poetics*, the *Rhetoric* and the (pseudo-Aristotelian) *Rhetoric to Alexander* were printed in Greek. But the fortunes of the *Poetics* had to await a fresh (and, this time, complete) Latin translation by Alessandro Pazzi de' Medici, printed posthumously in 1536.[143] Lombardi and Maggi were probably the first to deliver lectures on these works, in the Accademia degli Infiammati in Padua (c. 1540).[144] Robortello, however, was among the very first to lecture on them at university, while in Pisa.[145] Although it is plausible that in Bologna Robortello taught the works that had made him famous, we lack direct evidence of his teaching, apart from a manuscript containing student notes of a course he held in 1557 on both Cicero's and Aristotle's *Topics*.[146] It is also unclear whether his rhetorical treatise *De artificio dicendi* is related to classroom teaching.[147]

Sebastiano Regoli

A trace of the mark Robortello left in Bologna comes, however, from one of the few Bolognese colleagues with whom he had a friendly relationship: Sebastiano Regoli (1514–1570). Regoli did his studies in Bologna, established a public school of Latin and Greek there, and, from 1541 until his death, held a series of university appointments teaching rhetoric, poetry, grammar, and *studia humanitatis*.[148] The two men became friends while Robortello held his Bolognese professorship. Regoli did not publish much and was probably more influential for his teaching than for his scholarship. We do not know whether he ever taught Aristotle's *Poetics* or *Rhetoric* (the rolls list his name only once, in 1568–1569, for a subject including Greek: *studia humanitatis latina et graeca de mane*).[149] Yet, at least the lectures he published on Virgil (in two parts, in 1563 and 1565) point to a significant engagement with these two Aristotelian works. The connection is already evident from the title of the first publication (*In primum Aeneidos Virgilii librum ex Aristotelis De arte poetica et Rhetorica praeceptis explicationes*) but requires comment.[150]

Both in his dedicatory letter to Francesco Maria II Della Rovere, the son of Guidobaldo II, duke of Urbino, and in his prefatory letter "to the students of poetics" (*artis poeticae studiosis*), Regoli clarifies his intention to show that "whatever is said by the supreme poet [Virgil] coincides perfectly with Aristotle's precepts" (7). Regoli states that he has not seen such an approach taken by others, yet it makes sense to do so: if the orations of Cicero and Demosthenes can be aligned with the precepts of rhetoric, why not do so also for poetry, by using Aristotle's precepts as a rule and plumbline (*norma et perpendiculum,* 7–8)?[151]

Regoli is keen to show that the *Aeneid* fits the instructions of the *Poetics* and the *Rhetoric* in both a general and a more specific way. For instance, the multiplicity of events narrated may suggest that the *Aeneid* lacks unity of action, but in fact—if one looks closely—one will realize that there is only one main action (the journey toward Rome) supported by a number of subordinate episodes (27–28). Or, if one thinks about the main kinds of subject praised by Aristotle (*admirabile, miserabile et horribile*), this too is something that the *Aeneid* displays (35–36). On a more concrete level, one can see how the opening of the *Aeneid* captures the goodwill (*benevolentia*) of the readers as recommended by both Aristotle and Cicero (39). This constant application of rhetorical norms to poetry may seem, from a modern perspective, to violate distinctions of genre between orations and poems, but the link for the scholar from Brisighella lies in the morally persuasive power of poetry.

Like many of his predecessors and contemporaries, Regoli sees Virgil's poem as having a strong moral function.[152] Already in the dedicatory letter, he presents the *Aeneid* as a work of moral philosophy depicting in Aeneas "the excellent man and most perfect prince" (*vir optimus et princeps perfectissimus,* 5). When, in the *accessus ad auctorem,* he pauses to consider the work's purpose, Regoli describes this as being "to present to us the image of a most patient and brave prince in adversities, and of a perfect man" (9). He then goes on to note how well Aeneas fits the image Aristotle gives of the end of man:

> Since the end of man is happiness, which is action accompanied by virtue, as Aristotle says in the first book of the *Rhetoric* and of the *Ethics,* the poet—representing his Aeneas as behaving in complete conformity to virtue—brings him to

> supreme happiness. This is the duty and end of an excellent poet. For poetics and rhetoric are subservient to politics, which like a queen reigns over the other arts. Its end is to make men happy, but it cannot achieve this, unless it has first made them good.[153]

Later on, Regoli comments on the usefulness of the *Aeneid* in terms of instilling virtue (15–16) and offers an allegorical reading of the poem, according to which Aeneas is "a praiseworthy man who flees pleasures and . . . reaches his end, i.e., happiness" (24–25).

This point is especially relevant both to the influence of Robortello and to discussions current in Regoli's time about the *Poetics* and the purpose of poetry. For Robortello was adamant that the aim of poetry is not the inculcation of virtue, but instead pleasure—a position that many contemporaries strongly debated and criticized. Although Regoli clearly disagreed with his former colleague, his comments show how pervasive the discussion of Aristotle's *Poetics* had become in teaching not just Greek works but Latin ones as well.[154]

5.4 Humanism beyond the Humanities

The interests and developing expertise in Latin and Greek discussed above did not remain confined to classes of the *studia humanitatis.* The love for antiquity promoted by the humanities provided other disciplines with a *Bildungsideal* that served to distinguish the professors following new cultural trends from the others. This process took time, but by the second quarter of the sixteenth century, professors of philosophy were starting to read texts in the original Greek. Thus, whereas Pietro Pomponazzi (t. 1511–1525) was unable to read Aristotle or Plato in the original and expressed himself in a mix of scholastic Latin and his native Mantuan dialect, in the 1530s Ludovico Boccadiferro was reading the Greek commentator Simplicius as an aid to his philosophical lectures.[155] By the time of Ulisse Aldrovandi (t. 1554–1600), matters had changed even further. Aldrovandi's first published work, on Roman statuary, written before he obtained a teaching post, emerged from his studies of classical art and architecture.[156] An avid acquirer of books, he scoured as many works of antiquity as he could find (including Dioscorides, Pliny the Elder's *Natural History*, and so forth) for precious clues that would inform his project of an encyclopedia of knowledge. His lectures on Aristotle's works make constant reference to the Greek commentators. And his style is considerably clearer than that of his predecessors, although he maintains the exegetical and other hallmarks of a scholastic approach to learning, including the use of questions and constant references to the views of medieval commentators such as Averroes. Aldrovandi's knowledge of Greek was not uncommon among professors of philosophy, although not all may have had quite such broad tastes.[157]

Possibly even more important, however, is the use to which these tools were put. For—due in part to new philological work and the humanist emphasis on history—philosophy professors found it increasingly hard to explain away the inconsistencies within a single author (e.g., Aristotle) or deny that ancient thinkers might hold diametrically opposite positions. (Many thought that Plato and Aristotle, for instance, differed only in words and not in substance.) In a move that anticipated the modern insights of Werner Jaeger, they grew more aware of the development of thought over time, even in the case of individual authors. In Padua, for instance, Francesco Piccolomini elaborated a theory reconciling the different aspects of Aristotle's philosophy on the basis of the evolution of his own thought (although he was very blind indeed to the differences between Aristotle and Plato).[158] It is likely that similar approaches took root in Bologna, but the matter has not yet been studied—indeed, at present the only sixteenth-century teacher of philosophy examined in any detail has been Pomponazzi (but see §6.2 and §8.2). In any case, although neither Aldrovandi nor Piccolomini were likely to describe themselves as humanists, the humanist emphasis on history and languages clearly strongly affected their approach.

In the case of medicine, scholars have acknowledged the importance of Hellenism, although they have disagreed about its timings.[159] While this influence may have had the unintended result of strengthening the position of Galen in the curriculum while recovering his entire written production, Nancy Siraisi has also noted that humanism led to a new appreciation of the historical diversity among medical writers of antiquity, especially in the second half of the sixteenth century.[160] Yet, for Bologna several aspects of the influence of humanism on medicine remain to be explored. For instance, it would be worthwhile studying the lectures of teachers such as Giovanni Garzoni. As seen above, Garzoni was a former student of Lorenzo Valla and, alongside his public teaching of medicine, taught the humanities privately. Of his medical lectures, the only ones known to survive are in BUB, ms. 731 (an autograph manuscript in three volumes), where the text of Avicenna is spaced in such a way that Garzoni could insert numerous interlinear and marginal glosses.[161] These have not been adequately examined, but may well be helpful in understanding how Garzoni's approach differed from that of other interpreters of Avicenna's *Canon*.[162] Developments in anatomy (in the first half of the sixteenth century; see §7.2) may also be relevant: several scholars have tied the "anatomical Renaissance" to the influence of humanism.[163] More generally, however, one expects that sixteenth-century humanistic scholarship on medical textbooks (such as Nicolò Leoniceno's new translations and editions of Galen's Greek text) re-oriented medical teaching in Bologna as elsewhere, although it took time to do so.[164] First it needed to be prepared by Latin humanism, and enough people needed to become familiar with Greek so as to create a market for publications in the original.[165]

A related and difficult question is whether university professors came to teach their texts (Aristotle, Hippocrates, Galen, or Euclid) on the basis of the Greek original. Aldrovandi's lectures on the *Physics,* for instance, make specific reference to *lemmata* of the Greek text and give the impression that students had the original text in front of them (see §6.2.3). Andrea Torelli seems to have taught Aristotle's *Politics* on the basis of the Greek text in 1642 and 1643.[166] But scholarship on the subject suggests that lecturing of this kind appeared late and was rather rare in Renaissance Italy.[167] Students seem to have found it challenging to follow even the fairly straightforward Greek of Aristotle's *Nicomachean Ethics* in the lectures given in Rome by Marc-Antoine Muret.[168] Similarly, it is unclear how often (if at all) lectures on Galen and Hippocrates addressed the Greek original. More work has been done on fresh Latin translations of the textbooks in question (particularly for philosophy and medicine). These enabled a substantially larger audience to profit from the fruits of Greek studies and philology. One should not, however, imagine that the introduction of new textbooks was necessarily quick or uncontroversial. For long periods of time, the old and the new lived uneasily side by side.

Subjects outside of arts and medicine were also affected. Students in the law faculties were free to follow lectures in arts and medicine, and we know that many of them chose to hear great teachers of the humanities such as Beroaldo.[169] The Frenchman Jean De Pins (1470?–1537), for instance, heard both Beroaldo and Codro lecture on the humanities in the several years he spent in Bologna at the end of the fifteenth century and took profit from them for his legal studies.[170] The ties between him and his teachers must have been strong, for he wrote both a biography of Beroaldo and a preface to the works of Codro.[171] Many who came from outside Italy took their newfound linguistic skills, philological expertise, and historical understanding back to their home cities and applied them to law and other disciplines there. These provided the basis for a more historically and linguistically grounded understanding of the textual tradition of the *Corpus juris civilis* and of the *Digest,* the main teaching works for civil and canon law, respectively.

They were also able to interpret those texts with stronger attention to the social and political contexts to which they made reference. This was partly because some teachers of law also started to follow humanistic methods and impart them to their students.[172] An example is Lodovico Bolognini, professor of law (taught discontinuously, 1469–1495 and 1506–1508), who was in touch with Poliziano about a passage in the *Pandects* and eagerly welcomed him on his stopover in Bologna on 5 June 1491.[173] Far more philologically able was Andrea Alciato (1492–1550), who had received a humanistic education, studied law in Pavia and Bologna, and among his various appointments taught civil law in Bologna from 1537 to 1541. It is unclear to what extent Alciato modeled his interests in philology and ancient history in his law lectures, although two of his students were among those responsible for the famous 1553 edition of the Pisan-Florentine *Pandects.*[174] As a result of this landmark achievement, some universities instituted new chairs of Pandects, whose occupants, Grendler notes, "were expected to explain the text of the *Digest* historically and philologically."[175] Rome took the lead, with Marc Antoine Muret (1567–1572); Padua followed in 1578.[176] Bologna was slower to do so: after an abortive attempt in 1588–1592, the chair was occupied continuously only from 1606.[177] Still, it is hard to arrive at conclusions about conservatism or not without examining the relevant lectures.[178] And at the moment it is unclear whether the authorities' move to place the chair of humanities on the roll of the jurists in 1584–1594 was prompted by a desire to see more crossover between jurisprudence and humanism or by other considerations.[179]

Finally, in the seventeenth and eighteenth centuries Bologna saw a rise in the teaching of Hebrew, Arabic, and other Oriental languages, although not on the scale witnessed elsewhere in Europe (particularly in Protestant lands), nor to a large enough extent to satisfy Luigi Ferdinando Marsili. In the first decades of the eighteenth century, Marsili, the guiding spirit behind the Istituto delle Scienze (§3.2), lamented Bologna's inferiority in the teaching of Oriental languages (especially Hebrew) when compared to the universities in Germany. He therefore auspicated reform.[180] His concern may have been linked mainly to contemporary discussions about the need to prepare the clergy to study the Bible and defend the Catholic faith (see §8.1). Yet this cultural atmosphere, strongly influenced by the views of Ludovico Antonio Muratori (1672–1750) and others, owed a great deal to a recognition of the need to study texts in their original languages and understand their textual transmission—in other words, to the values and approaches of Renaissance humanism.

Conclusion

This chapter has pointed to several effects that the *studia humanitatis* had on Bolognese university teaching. As we have seen, the humanities fostered a deeper knowledge of both standard and less-common Roman authors, offering models that sometimes were in keeping with (but more frequently departed from) Ciceronian style. They promoted an engagement with historical and antiquarian studies, particularly in relationship to Rome's ancient past. Especially after 1450, they increased familiarity with Greek language and literature, including works of such theoretical importance as Aristotle's *Rhetoric* and *Poetics.* As §5.4 has shown, the approach of humanism had a strong purchase in areas that lay outside of the humanities, affecting both philosophy and the higher subjects. This was true, not only at Bologna, but also at other Italian universities.[181]

Bolognese university professors who modeled this new approach in their lectures were not simply following cultural fashions and trying to ensure themselves a living. In a town where court culture was relatively weak and short-lived, they seem to have channeled their cultural energies into their official and private lectures and into the city's numerous academies. This involved taking note of new developments around them and—at other times—being at their forefront, in a context in which humanism and university culture were no contradiction at all.

One should, however, sound a note of caution. There is a tendency in much Renaissance scholarship to ignore Kristeller's sound advice about the multiple strands of Renaissance culture and to lend humanism a primary or even exclusive role within the cultural dynamics of the period, whether in the university or in other contexts.[182] There is no doubt that the intense engagement with the world and values of antiquity exercised a powerful influence on many who taught and studied at Bologna's university, as this chapter has outlined. Yet other developments were underfoot as well. The following chapters consider just three of the most important ones. They show that patterns of specialization were taking shape and that professors returned to the *quaestio* format in the name of scientific innovation (Chapter 6). Intense debates arose about the fundamental nature of university disciplines such as medicine (Chapter 7). Religious considerations too came to the fore, not only in a more prominent role for theology, but throughout the curriculum (Chapter 8). A proper evaluation of how change took place at the University of Bologna requires all of these aspects to be considered together.

6

Specialization and Scientific Innovation

Among the most striking developments within Bologna's teaching of arts and medicine is an increasing specialization of teaching in various areas, accompanied in some cases by a stronger sense of professionalization. Hints of this development have already emerged from the teaching of the humanities discussed in Chapter 5. But in numerous other areas too it eventually became the norm to focus on one specific subject, whether logic, natural philosophy, astrology, or medicine. In this chapter I examine some of these general changes, but will then focus specifically on natural philosophy and astronomy / mathematics. We will see that specialization gave rise to subdisciplines such as natural history (in particular, botany), mechanics, and hydraulics. Equally importantly, however, specialization had implications for how various disciplines came to be taught and studied. The consequences were particularly significant for previously marginal or transitional subjects (e.g., mathematics and natural philosophy, respectively), which either increased in stature or became more differentiated. The effects went well beyond institutional considerations, however: they started to transform the nature of teaching itself, leading to a departure from the style of teaching based on line-by-line exposition of standard texts to a more systematic and textbook-like approach (see §6.2.2). Such an approach—while notionally still tied to the discussion of Aristotle, Ptolemy, and other "authorities"—offered even more flexibility to introduce new topics, approaches, and references to contemporary debates (§6.2.3). In this context, one should emphasize the continued—but differently oriented—use of questions (*quaestiones*) within teaching, something that also influenced fields such as medicine (§6.2.4).

By "specialization" I do not mean to suggest that individuals became increasingly trapped within their own disciplinary domain or blinkered as to what was taking place in other fields. Rather, I am referring to a process by which teaching came to focus in a more concentrated (and often productive) way on particular (sub-)branches of learning. Examples are the rise of *protologici* who dedicated many years of their teaching to logic alone, or that of professors of natural philosophy, who taught their subject for numerous years without progressing to teach medicine. A synchronous development that often (but not always) overlapped with this one was the gradual emergence of new subjects, as some disciplinary subfields broke off from others but then forged new alliances.

The relationship between these two phenomena is complex, and neither of these processes was in any way linear: along the way there were significant reversals and changes of course; not all subjects followed the same timings (natural philosophy and astronomy did not necessarily move synchronously in this regard); and, most importantly, by the late seventeenth century a new ordering of the disciplines was gaining acceptance, bringing the previous development of specialization into question. The result was a new model, whereby medicine, for instance, once again found a close connection with the findings and methods of physics and other scientific fields—but this time, in an order of knowledge rather different from that of the sixteenth century.

As this chapter explains, these changes had multiple roots, ranging from institutional pressures to individual choices and a shifting cultural landscape. They also gave rise to loud and even violent reactions at times. But it is significant that the developments discussed here took place as much within as outside of the university context, which was supposedly so impervious to change. Thus, specialization and the multiplication of disciplines were multilayered and, to an extent, unstable affairs. As to their ties to scientific innovation, these were in no way straightforward, despite various attempts by historians to link them together. Yet these trends had profound effects on the teaching of arts and medicine and on the configuration of the disciplines.

Finally, while this chapter will focus especially on the period between the start of the sixteenth and the start of the eighteenth century, it is worth recalling that the sources available are not altogether continuous, particularly in the case of lectures.[1] At times this makes for some uncomfortable chronological gaps, especially for the seventeenth century, which deserves further study.

6.1 Institutional Aspects

Specialization affected all areas of the curriculum. In the humanities, the fifteenth-century practice of teaching Greek and Latin letters jointly (as Francesco Filelfo and Antonio Codro Urceo did) gave way to a focus on either one or the other (see the cases of Ciriaco Strozzi or Sebastiano Regoli in Chapter 5). Likewise, moral philosophy—which was for a long time an optional feast-day teaching added to the responsibilities of professors of rhetoric, philosophy, or medicine—emerged as an independent and "ordinary" subject from 1562 onward.[2] It was much the same in the case of logic: this subject started out being poorly paid, and for most instructors of philosophy and medicine it was the first rung on the teaching ladder. After three years of teaching it, professors were generally keen to move on to other subjects such as natural philosophy and, eventually, medicine. Yet in a considerable reversal of earlier patterns, in the second half of the sixteenth century several professors started to teach this subject for long periods of time. In part the situation was due to a glut of hired teachers, caused in turn by the decreased opportunities for progression for professors of higher subjects. But there were also clear pedagogical reasons for encouraging this move. The documentation for Bologna points to discussions about hiring a long-term logician (*logico perpetuo*) in the second half of the sixteenth century, resulting in the appointment of Camillo Baldi in 1586.[3] Public inscriptions in the Archiginnasio building show how much students valued skills in teaching logic, as is clear in their monument to Agostino Galesi.[4] Other fields affected by this development included natural philosophy and astrology.

6.1.1 Natural Philosophy

As outlined in Chapter 2, the faculty of arts and medicine was not a partnership of equals: medicine played an outsize part, regularly offering the highest salaries and attracting the most experienced professors. These professors had typically spent several years teaching logic and natural philosophy (§2.1). In other words, natural philosophy was a required stepping-stone to something else, leading (in the case of professors) to the higher status and rewards of medicine. Even students saw philosophy as something to be gotten through quickly, so as to reach their aim (or their family's ambition) of living comfortably as a physician and doctor of medicine.

In the sixteenth century this picture changed. The three most important subjects continued to be medicine, natural philosophy, and rhetoric (or humanities), which together accounted for some 87 percent of the faculty's yearly salaries for most of the century. But natural philosophy's share rose considerably, at medicine's expense: by the end of the century its proportion of the staffing costs for arts and medicine had skyrocketed from a maximum of 15 percent to 32 percent, whereas medicine had shrunk from around 56 percent to 38 percent.[5] This development is related in part to the numerous appointments of eminent professors. Although there had also been well-known figures earlier on, from Pietro Pomponazzi onward one witnesses a remarkable sequence of professors of natural philosophy, including Ludovico Boccadiferro (t. 1515–1524, 1527–1545), Mainetto Mainetti (t. 1539–1543, 1547–1557), Claudio Betti (t. 1545–1589), Ulisse Aldrovandi (t. 1554–1600), Giovanni Ludovico Cartari (t. 1557–1570, 1575–1593), Federico Pendasio (t. 1571–1604), and Melchiorre Zoppi (t. 1581–1634), to mention just a few.[6] Bologna was clearly one of Italy's great centers of philosophical teaching and a worthy competitor to Padua. It attracted and inspired entire generations of students.

The teaching of natural philosophy underwent notable developments during this period. From an official point of view, as reflected in the rolls, the three-year sequence of books to be taught expanded. As reflected by the 1405 statutes, the most important textbooks were Aristotle's *Physics, On the Heavens,* and *On the Soul,* which were taught both ordinarily and extraordinarily, in a staggered three-year cycle. In the course of the sixteenth century, an official six-year cycle of teaching developed, adding to these works *On Generation and Corruption, Meteorology,* and *Parva naturalia.* Finally, from 1573 onward, although this six-work sequence was maintained, ordinary teaching received two different slots (morning and evening), while extraordinary teaching continued.[7] This multiplication of teachings had repercussions on the timetable of classes and created several obstacles for the university authorities when they wished to introduce new subjects.[8]

The rolls, which do not start mentioning the works assigned to philosophy professors until 1528, need to be used with caution because they do not always reflect changes taking place. Between 1521 and 1524, for instance, Pomponazzi revived the teaching of *De partibus animalium,* an Aristotelian work that had been neglected in earlier centuries.[9] The rolls give no indication of the works he taught. Pomponazzi's colleague Boccadiferro lectured on several works (including *De motu animalium*) that lay outside of the official sequence of books, and there is often a mismatch between the lectures we know he gave and the works assigned to him on the rolls.[10] Further research into both published and unpublished philosophy lectures will likely turn up several other such instances, particularly for the teaching of nonstandard works. Especially interesting may be feast-day and private lectures, in which a professor was even freer (one supposes) in his choice of particular works.

Specialization emerged in part due to institutional factors. A glut of graduates and teachers slowed down the earlier (and fairly quick) passage from natural philosophy to medicine. As a result, professors increasingly had to teach natural philosophy for much longer than the three years that were previously the norm. Of the thirty or so professors who taught natural philosophy for five or more years in the second half of the sixteenth century, only seven went on to teach medicine; the rest continued to teach natural philosophy, sometimes in alternation with logic or moral philosophy. Their teaching of natural philosophy lengthened, often to twenty-five or more years, in a clear contrast with previous patterns.[11]

The case of Ulisse Aldrovandi (1522–1605) suggests that specialization could also be a personal choice leading to curricular developments. Aldrovandi, who came from a prominent local family and obtained his doctorate in arts and medicine in Bologna on 23 November 1553, started teaching the following year, rising quickly from logic (1554–1555) and extraordinary philosophy (1555–1559) to ordinary philosophy. In earlier years, someone with his training would soon have obtained a chair in medicine, and Aldrovandi's reputation as a physician indicates that this would have been well within his competencies.[12] Instead, Aldrovandi taught ordinary philosophy from 1559 until his death in 1605 (although in fact he was not obliged to teach from 1600 onward). Even more notably, over time his teaching became focused on natural history. From 1561 the designation of his philosophy teaching became "fossils, plants, and animals" (*de fossilibus, plantis et animalibus*), areas of natural history that can be linked to Aldrovandi's oversight of the local botanical garden and to the growing collection of natural objects (and books) in his home.[13] In fact, Aldrovandi seems to have reveled in this subject, and eventually he became best known for his expertise in natural history. But this specialization does not indicate a narrowing of interests, almost as if medicine had ceased to attract him. His teaching of medical simples (*lectura de simplicibus medicinalibus*) in 1556–1561 was related to herbs used in medicine.[14] Furthermore, although the rolls do not list him as teaching medicine, Aldrovandi was interested in (and lectured on) Dioscorides, *De materia medica*.[15] At some point he seems to have taught Hippocrates, possibly in a private capacity.[16] And, of course, his activities as a maker of the theriac (a famous medicinal compound used against pestilence) are well known.

Aldrovandi's activity left its mark on figures both within and without the university. The successors in his chair mostly lacked his knack for combining observation with bookish learning. Yet Giacomo Zanoni (1615–1682) oversaw Bologna's botanical garden, assembled a museum, published works such as *Istoria botanica* (1675) in which artists played a major role, and kept an ongoing scientific correspondence with a very international group of learned men.[17] Another heir to Aldrovandi's method was Lelio Trionfetti (1647–1722); part of Bologna's scientific avant-garde, he directed the botanical garden, co-founded the Istituto delle Scienze, and taught (among others) Antonio Maria Valsalva (1666–1723) and Eustachio Manfredi (1674–1739). Manuscript copies of his botanical lectures especially survive (although he also wrote on fossils and other matters) and may repay further consideration.[18] Trionfetti was one of the several members of the clergy who taught scientific subjects in the *studium*. He was ordained priest in 1680.[19]

6.1.2 Astronomy and Mathematics

Astronomy and mathematics underwent an even clearer reorientation. Initially designated "astrology," astronomy was one of the five main subjects studied in the faculty of arts and medicine and included the teaching of mathematics as well as of areas bordering on medicine.[20] Bologna's 1405 statutes illustrate its main components (see §2.2.2). The four years of study were to cover:

1. The *Algorismus* (possibly the one by Johannes de Sacrobosco or Holywood) on fractions and integers; Euclid's *Elements,* Book I, with the commentary by Giovanni Campano da Novara; the *Alfonsine Tables* with *Canons*—a basic tool of Ptolemaic astronomy; and the anonymous *Theory of the Planets* (an explanation of the Ptolemaic system)
2. Sacrobosco's *De sphaera;* Euclid's *Elements,* Book II; the *Canons* on the *Alfonsine Tables* by Jean de Linières; and Messahala's *Treatise on the Astrolabe*
3. Alcabitius's *Introduction to the Art of Astrology;* Ptolemy's *Centiloquium* with the commentary of Haly Rodohan; Euclid's *Elements,* Book III; and *Treatise on the Quadrant*
4. The whole of Ptolemy's *Quadripartitus* (or *Tetrabiblos*); the (inconclusively identified) treatise *De urina non visa* (On Unseen Urine); and the third part (*dictio*) of Ptolemy's *Almagest*

The statutes need to be used with considerable caution, but even this very quick summary highlights the perceived links between astrology and both mathematics and medicine. Complex numeracy skills were required to read and produce the annual prognostications demanded of professors of astrology. (Next to a professor's name in the rolls there is often the indication: *faciat tacuinum* or *faciat iudicium et tacuinum.*)[21] Girolamo Manfredi, for instance, published numerous astrological prognostications during his tenure as professor in Bologna (see below). One link to medicine concerned the common role of horoscopes in understanding how and when to cure specific patients and their diseases. Some professors of medicine were also renowned for their expertise in and practice of judicial astrology; examples include the controversial figure Girolamo Cardano.[22]

The place of astrology in the curriculum changed over the centuries.[23] Initially it appeared as one of the minor subjects, like moral philosophy: its teaching took place on feast days, often as an addition to professors' teaching duties in medicine, natural philosophy, and even grammar. The rolls list it as an ordinary subject in Bologna in 1469 with the teaching of Manfredi, who, however, coupled this teaching with that of medicine.[24] Another contemporary teacher of note was Domenico Maria da Novara, who taught this subject exclusively from 1483 to 1504. (For both of these figures, see below.) In 1508, Ludovico Vitali's teaching of ordinary astronomy was reclassified—for unknown reasons—as a feast-day subject, which is how it appears in the rolls until 1572.[25] After that date, the designation *astronomia* disappears from the rolls altogether, with the exception of the *lecturae universitatis,* held by students.

It was not, however, that the teaching of astronomy ceased: rather, it became merged with mathematics, which started appearing with some regularity on the rolls from 1554 (as *praxis mathematicae,* taught by Pompeo Bolognetto). In 1564 this teaching started running in parallel with the newly instituted (and much better paid) chair of mathematics. The first occupier of this *cattedra eminente* was Ludovico Ferrari (t. 1564–1565).[26] This teaching of mathematics / astronomy developed into a cycle of three years (as opposed to the previous four), which covered at least Euclid's geometry, the *Theorica planetarum,* and Ptolemy's *Almagest,* respectively.[27] This arrangement seems to have continued until 1737, when astronomy reappeared on the rolls, this time alongside mathematics. Five professors taught the two subjects.[28]

The careers of various professors illustrate the extent to which astrology developed patterns of specialization similar to natural philosophy. Two contrasting figures are of particular interest for the fifteenth century. Girolamo Manfredi (t. 1455–1457, 1458–1459, 1462–1492) was a local professor who—after the customary three years of teaching logic, followed by philosophy—spent long periods teaching either medicine or astrology (or, indeed, both subjects together). Manfredi was famous for his medical knowledge and for his vernacular work *Il libro del perché* (also known as *De homine*), in which he treated and synthesized a number of medical and natural problems already discussed by the fourteenth-century physician Pietro d'Abano on the basis of the pseudo-Aristotelian *Problems.*[29] He was such a believer in the complementary nature of medical and astrological knowledge that he stated, "Although medicine is a perfect science in its own right, a physician is not perfect in his work without astrology." It was during his time that the redaction of annual prognostications started to take place in Bologna (the first surviving manuscript redactions date from 1469; the practice, which soon gave way to print publications, stretched until the end of the eighteenth century). These could be written in either Latin or Italian (or both) and included, in addition to the prologue, sections on the planet due to dominate a particular year, the list of lunar or solar eclipses, comets and other celestial wonders, illnesses, earthquakes, predictions about the weather, a list of favorable or unfavorable days for administering medicines or performing operations, and even political reflections.[30]

Whereas Manfredi's career shows the tight connection between astrology and medicine, that of Domenico Maria da Novara suggests a more specialized approach. Although we lack firsthand details about Domenico's life (1454–1504?), he seems to have received his doctorate in both arts and medicine. He taught in Ferrara, Rome, and perhaps also Perugia before starting his teaching in Bologna in 1483, where presumably he taught until his death.[31] The rolls describe Domenico exclusively as a teacher of ordinary astronomy in Bologna, and Copernicus almost certainly studied with him while he was in the city (1496–1500). The only original works by Novara to have reached us are his *Prognostications* for various years between 1484 and 1504, but in the prologues to these works he discussed astronomical and philosophical topics of great interest, such as the movement of the eighth sphere, the gradual shifting of the earth's polar axis, the reliability of the Aristotelians, and the existence or not of a world soul.[32] Particularly noteworthy is the point that the earth is not necessarily immovable. Several of these opinions (especially that from 1489 about the movement of the polar axis) may have motivated Copernicus to go hear him in Bologna. Later scientists studied them closely.[33]

In the sixteenth century, it was Novara's approach that won out, not Manfredi's. Although teachers of astronomy in Bologna continued to produce prognostications as part of their job description, they became progressively less enthused about the divinatory aspects of astrology. Over time, the ties between natural astrology and medicine also loosened. According to Fabrizio Bònoli, teachers of astronomy were also fairly uninterested in Copernicus's heliocentric theories of planetary motion embedded in the *De revolutionibus* (1543)—a work so mathematically complex that few could make sense of it.[34] Rather, they tended to address two practical problems: the reform of the calendar promoted by Pope Gregory XIII and the construction of accurate territorial maps through the use of astronomical and other data.[35]

These interests coincided for Egnazio Danti (1536–1586), a Dominican friar who came from a mathematically gifted family and enjoyed the early protection of Cosimo I in the court of Florence. Danti was a scientific figure of considerable heft, who published widely both on usual topics within mathematics and astronomy but also on mapmaking, perspective, cosmography, and many other areas. He also produced Italian translations of the works of Euclid, Heliodorus, Proclus, and others.[36]

Danti, who taught mathematics in Bologna from 1576 to 1583, had an unusual background. In Florence, Cosimo had charged him to make maps of all the known regions of the world on the basis of materials in the Palazzo Vecchio. He also started to measure the discrepancies between the Julian calendar and the actual astronomical year. (In the sixteenth century, the difference amounted to some ten days.) When Cosimo died, Danti lost his chief patron and his order transferred him to Bologna. While there, he developed various instruments (including a meridian line or *meridiana,* which no longer survives, in the basilica of San Petronio) in order to verify his theories. He also took part in topographical and corographical surveys of the Papal State. By invitation, he joined Rome's committee for the reform of the calendar. (This reform took effect in October 1583 and skipped from Thursday, 4 October to Friday, 15 October.)

Following Danti's departure, three professors in Bologna were especially significant for developments in mathematics and astronomy. Danti's replacement was Pietro Antonio Cataldi (t. 1583–1626), whose interests seem to have been more mathematical than astronomical, and who is important in the development of innovations for which the school of Bolognese mathematicians (including Scipione dal Ferro and Ludovico Ferrari) became famous.[37] A colleague of Cataldi was the Paduan Giovanni Antonio Magini (t. 1588–1617), who earned at least his arts degree in Bologna (1579)—possibly after studies with Danti—and was offered one of the chairs of mathematics over the less experienced candidate Galileo.

He gave particular emphasis in his teaching to geometry, astronomy, and astrology. He was not a supporter of Copernican theory (he rather favored Tycho Brahe, though not openly), but was an able mathematician, medical astrologer, and especially geographer and cartographer. His major work in this direction was an atlas (*Italia*), published posthumously in 1620 and containing sixty-one tables accompanied by explanations. After Magini's death, his chair was offered to Johannes Kepler, who, however, turned it down in view of his Protestant loyalties.[38] Also very important for Bologna was Gian Domenico Cassini (1625–1712), who taught astronomy and then mathematics there from 1650 to 1669 before leaving for France, where he spent the rest of his life.[39] Cassini was especially dedicated to astronomical observation and built (or had made) instruments to measure the movement of the sun and of various planets (Jupiter, Mars) and comets. His university lectures of 1666 consider the apparent movement of the fixed stars and suggest (although they do not explicitly endorse) a preference for the Copernican system.[40] In France, Cassini became a member of the Académie Royale des Sciences. He helped to conceive (and later directed) a new observatory, leading to numerous astronomical discoveries concerning planets (such as Saturn) and the moon. But Cassini was also strongly interested in mapping the earth: in his later years he contributed to realizing the *Carte de France,* a project that was taken forward, after his death, by his descendants, who presented its 182 folios to the French Assembly in 1790.[41]

In the years after Cassini's departure from Bologna, astronomy went through a fallow period there because eminent personalities could not be hired to replace him. The interests of mathematicians were increasingly geared to hydraulics and the science of numbers, which appeared on the rolls as subjects in their own right. Astronomy's fate revived, however, with Eustachio Manfredi, a figure of exceptional cultural importance in Bologna. Manfredi founded the Accademia degli Inquieti (1690), in which astronomy played a central role, and was one of the conceptual architects of the Istituto delle Scienze (which opened in 1714).[42] Furthermore, Manfredi taught mathematics in Bologna (1699–1737) and, in the last two years of his life, astronomy—a subject that the curricular reform of 1737 had reintroduced (see §2.3). Astronomy was, in fact, a lifelong passion that inspired Manfredi's numerous contacts with correspondents across Europe (including Cassini) and was the focus of many of his publications.[43] But Manfredi's interests and career again serve as a reminder that, at least since the middle of the sixteenth century, the association between astronomy / astrology and medicine had weakened, doubtless due in part to papal prohibitions against judicial astrology from 1559 onward.[44] The subject's reorientation toward mathematics, as well as geography and problems of the calendar, seems to have suited many professors, who came to consider the compilation of the prognostications a burden to be endured, but often dedicated their energies to other areas. One should note, however, that this development happened rather late in the period (toward the end of the seventeenth century), and that until then there are significant examples of continuing interest in (and practice of) astrology in the university. For the sixteenth century, one of the most famous astrologers remains Girolamo Cardano, although in Bologna he only taught medicine (see §7.1.2).

6.2 Cultural and Pedagogical Reorientations

What were the broader implications of the move toward specialization? Did the fact that professors increasingly taught only (bits and pieces of) natural philosophy for long periods of time lead to any changes in their approach to teaching the subject? And did astronomy's progressive separation from medicine have any effect on how it was repositioned within the general configuration of subjects? This section highlights developments leading to a more systematic and less authority-based approach, which found expression in numerous ways.

6.2.1 Increased Production

One important change was a rise in the production of commentaries and other works devoted to natural philosophy and astronomy. Due to a series of methodological problems, quantifying such an increase is not straightforward.[45] But an analysis of teachers of natural philosophy in Bologna shows that—while commentaries and other works also survive in good numbers for the earlier period—the sixteenth century especially witnesses a large number of philosophy professors who left behind works (such as lectures, commentaries, and treatises) on Aristotle, whether in manuscript or print.[46] In addition to obvious cases such as Pomponazzi, professors such as Boccadiferro, Betti, Aldrovandi, Cartari, Galesi, and Pendasio authored numerous works on natural philosophy.[47] This pattern fits well with the more general observation by historians of philosophy that the sixteenth and seventeenth centuries were a period of even greater engagement with Aristotle's works, as scholars tried (despite the frustrating nature of the enterprise) to reconcile his views with new perspectives and discoveries.[48] For astronomy, the contrast between the fifteenth and sixteenth centuries is even starker: in the fifteenth century, only around nine out of forty-two professors (21.4 percent) in Bologna left behind works connected with astronomy or mathematics; for the sixteenth century, every one of the eleven professors listed by Bònoli and Piliarvu did so.[49] Although these percentages are inflated by the new requirement to publish prognostications (see above), only two of the sixteenth-century professors listed published prognostications only. The others include well-known figures such Ludovico Vitali and Luca Gaurico (although the latter taught in Bologna for only one year)[50] and other giants already discussed, such as Danti, Cataldi, and Magini. So in this case as well, an increasing independence from medicine was in all likelihood linked to a higher rate of writing on one's principal, long-term subject.

6.2.2 Systematic Manuals and Approaches

As well as increasing in number, works of natural philosophy and astronomy changed in terms of genre and approach, reflecting a common development across Europe.[51] Until the end of the seventeenth century, linear commentaries associated with the university *lectio* continued to be commonplace, but—as Charles Schmitt observed—more systematic treatments increased and eventually replaced these kinds of works. These manuals or textbooks reordered texts and fields of study according to a sequence of topics or schemes chosen by the author. Tools of this kind (including the *Summa naturalium* of Albertus de Orlamunde, fl. c. 1230, often misattributed to Albertus Magnus) had already appeared in the medieval period, but from the late fifteenth century onward they really grew in use, by both humanist and scholastic writers. In the case of natural philosophy, the most successful of the sixteenth-century manuals was that of a Franciscan from Flanders, Frans Titelmans (1502–1537), who wrote for his local convent in Louvain as well as university readers. His *Compendium naturalis philosophiae* (1530) manages, in the short space of 227 folios in a pocket-size format, to cover Aristotle's *Physics, Parva naturalia, De anima,* and even parts of the *Nicomachean Ethics.*[52] It accomplishes such a feat by emphasizing just a few topics and then weaving together Aristotle's comments on them from various books. The remarkable editorial *fortuna* experienced by this compendium shows how useful contemporary (and even much later) readers found it.[53] Italian professors such as Aldrovandi found it helpful too: he listed it as one of his sources for his public lectures on the *Physics,* but also taught the work (doubtless in a private capacity) to a prince from Flanders who was visiting Bologna in 1565–1566.[54]

Titelmans's compendium offered a foretaste of the kinds of systematization that would meet with particular success in both the Protestant and the Catholic worlds of the sixteenth century and later—many of them providing a way of grafting elements from theology onto the Aristotelian tree of knowledge. Yet, later manuals sometimes incorporated or even emphasized elements from other philosophical traditions as well and recast natural philosophy by inserting findings and subjects of recent interest in areas such as geography, optics, astronomy, and physiognomy.[55] Although the latter tendency was especially strong in Protestant writers such as Clemens Timpler (1563–1624) and Bartholomaeus Keckermann (1572–1609), Catholic writers were not far behind in their interest in manuals that could reorder and systematize learning in such a way that students could learn new (but also doctrinally "safe" or even theologically edifying) perspectives (see §8.2). The Jesuits, in particular, developed an impressive series of textbooks that guided students either in the mastery of a particular field (e.g., natural philosophy) or in the whole of philosophy, ranging from dialectic to metaphysics, typically taking in moral and natural philosophy along the way.[56]

In the Italian universities, one of the most enthusiastic writers of systematic manuals was Francesco Piccolomini (1523–1607), a professor at the University of Padua who published—in addition to an extremely important reorganization of Aristotle's moral philosophy in his *Universa philosophia de moribus* (first published in 1583)—a five-volume overview of natural philosophy.[57] His *Libri ad scientiam de natura attinentes* (1596) covered not only the *Physics* but also Aristotle's teachings on the heavens, generation and corruption, meteorology, and the soul, using a thematic approach combined with Christian considerations.[58] These writings doubtless owed a great deal to Piccolomini's classroom teaching of natural philosophy. At the same time, one should not think of the increasing popularity of such manuals as something tied exclusively to the university context: Francesco's kinsman Alessandro Piccolomini (1508–1579), for instance, as well as the Frenchman Scipion Dupleix (1569–1661), each offered in his own native tongue a series of works providing overviews, syntheses, or paraphrases of Aristotle's philosophy.[59]

Treatises of this kind did not, however, immediately supplant literal commentaries, which continued to appear until (and even beyond) the middle of the seventeenth century.[60] Nonetheless, the rising trend toward systematization had a palpable effect on university teaching in two areas especially. First, systematic or thematic treatments came to inform the lecture format, which by statute was based on a linear and progressive explanation of mandated works, accompanied by questions and disputations. One could, in fact, describe the development as an increasing emphasis on questions rather than literal commentary. At the same time, it became ever easier to base university lectures on new authors and works (see especially §6.2.3). The literal commentary had always been a fairly open and flexible genre, allowing classroom discussions to take in the views of a wide range of interpreters. But systematized treatments of specific subjects (as opposed to works) gave teachers increasing freedom to promote their favored authors, whether ancient or modern.

Natural Philosophy

A telling example of this new approach is the little-known Carlo Sassi (Carolus Saxius), who, after his degree in arts and medicine (17 March 1650), taught logic and then natural philosophy in Bologna from 1654 to 1696.[61] Sassi's lectures on the *Posterior Analytics* follow Aristotle's text fairly straightforwardly, as do those on *De anima* in 1657, but matters are very different when he teaches *De anima* in 1660 or the *Physics* shortly afterward.[62] Formally, these are still lectures on Aristotle, yet they are so intent on addressing a particular set of problems in a preconceived and systematic order, that they no longer have the structure of a literal commentary. Aristotle's text has become, not so much a text to be explained, but a pretext for introducing whatever matters may be of interest to a teacher and his students.

In his later lectures on *De anima,* for instance, Sassi weaves from one *textus* (or portion of text in the commentary of Averroes) to other passages and works in a disorienting way. Thus, his consideration of the inherent difficulties of speaking of a "science of the soul" takes the reader from Book I, *textus* 4 to 9, to Crisostomo Javelli's question 7 on *De anima* (on the method of division) and from there to the *Posterior Analytics* (on the distinctions between the *via divisionis* and the *via compositionis*) and back again to *De anima,* Book I, *textus* 2 (on accidents and the soul).[63] Rather than following Aristotle's text linearly, Sassi is clearly trying to impose his own particular order on the discussion. He takes the same approach when he teaches the *Physics* in 1662–1663 and again in 1668–1669. The initial lines of the first set of lectures argue that the principles of nature are contrary to each other (*Physics* I, *textus* 42), yet not all of them are (ibid., *textus* 68); such opinions are not contrary to those of the ancient philosophers (*textus* 48); the reasons for this are clear from other passages (*textus* 41 and 35). In quick succession, Sassi then refers to other scattered portions of Aristotle's text (*textus* 62, 41, and 60) as he raises other points.[64]

Sassi's approach was evidently not unique to him, for in these same years the overseers of the university considered proscribing the use of *quaestiones* in favor of more literal expositions of Aristotle's text.[65] By the eighteenth century, however, this procedure seems to have become close to the norm. In 1713–1714 Nicolò Artemini (†1734) taught Aristotle's *De coelo et mundo* as part of the course in extraordinary philosophy.[66] Rather than offer a progressive examination of Aristotle's work, Artemini proposed to proceed entirely by questions and disputations. Thus the first disputation, articulated in four questions, deals with *de generatione mundi* (asking, for instance, whether or not the world is eternal),[67] while the second addresses *de mundi perfectione,* which allows the examination of points such as whether the universe has a soul (*an mundus sit animatus*) or how it is organized (*quodnam sit systema mundi*). Such teaching officially conforms to a centuries-old curriculum, but the use of questions allows Artemini to lead the discussion in unexpected directions, covering several topics of contemporary interest.

Likewise, the 1730–1731 lectures on the *Parva naturalia* by Domenico Maria Gusman Galeazzi (1686–1775) display only a formal connection with the Aristotelian works in question. Galeazzi, who was part of the reformist wing of the university and later taught Luigi Galvani, did not submit particularly detailed lecture plans.[68] He did, however, promise to cover *De sensu et sensibilibus* according to "what Aristotle *and other philosophers* thought" (emphasis added). This was not—it turns out—just a matter of expanding his reach beyond Aristotle. Galeazzi's treatment of Aristotle's work is much more physiological than philosophical, as his considerations quickly turn from the external senses and their causes to the internal ones. Galeazzi also skips the books on generation and the movement of animals (stating that these would require a longer discussion) and concludes with a section on breathing. He takes this as an opportunity to talk about the circulation of blood and, from there, about health and disease.[69]

Another example of a systematic, questions-based approach united with a dependence on different sources comes from the three volumes of manuscript lectures by the Camaldulensian monk Bonifacio Collina (t. 1722–1770). These lectures—which cover logic, metaphysics, and physics—bear the title *Philosophia ad recentiorum mentem* and are divided in *partes,* with subdivisions in *articuli.* These have questions and conclusions interspersed and are reminiscent of medieval scholastic treatments such as Thomas Aquinas's *Summa theologiae.*[70] The *recentiores* referred to in the title are rather less in view than one might expect, but Collina does offer favorable mentions of modern authors such as Titelmans and Benedict Pereira.[71] He also comments positively on the ideas of Plato and his followers. Around the same time, Ercole Corazzi—Collina's colleague in mathematics—makes reference to a more modern set of authors, including René Descartes (see below).

Astronomy and Mathematics

Parallel developments took place in the teaching of astronomy and mathematics. Here I will not focus on the question (already addressed by scholars) of the following that Galileo's ideas and approach enjoyed in the Bolognese *studium,* or of explicit references to Copernicanism, whether before or after its condemnation in 1616.[72] It is more relevant that lectures increasingly distance themselves from a sequential treatment of authors such as Ptolemy and Euclid and adopt a topical structure.[73]

A student of the innovative mathematician Bonaventura Cavalieri (see below), Pietro Mengoli appears on the Bolognese rolls from 1648 until his death in 1686 as a reader of arithmetic, mathematics, and mechanics.[74] The different denominations of his teaching reflect some of the changes that this field was experiencing during the period, particularly in terms of specialization and the appearance of "new" subjects. In what follows, I do not wish to give the impression that mechanics had not been taught before the establishment of that chair with Pietro Mengoli in 1650: it is just that it had usually remained part of more general lectures in natural philosophy, and especially physics. In Bologna there is, in fact, an earlier and more explicit appearance of the subject in the private lectures (1556–1565) of Baldassarre Gambarini, which are entitled *Lectiones variae mechanicae et philosophiae.*[75] In Padua, Giuseppe Moletti taught the subject in 1586–1587.[76] Other occurrences, again in Padua, were with Pietro Catena and Galileo.[77] It is unclear, however, whether these were occasional teachings or part of an established chair.

Although he may not have been at the forefront of contemporary mathematical developments, Mengoli was an important teacher in Bologna, and the first to occupy the newly founded chair of mechanics there (1650).[78] Lecture plans connected to this teaching survive for the years 1654–1655 and 1656–1657.[79] These plans are unusual compared to others, for two main reasons. First, they make little reference to authors studied, preferring to take an explicitly topical approach.[80] The ninety-six planned lectures for 1654–1655, for instance, are distributed in ten sections: these deal with physical bodies, their divisions, gravity and various solids (here lecture 18 is "iuxta methodum Archimedis"), and composite formations of three kinds—conservative, restitutive, and dissolving (with references to atoms in various lectures; to Galileo's studies of motion in lectures 50, 55, and 96; and to Giovanni Battista Baliani in lecture 56).[81] The second set of planned lectures, delivered in 1656–1657, is rather different and focuses on a single topic, *De centro gravitatis.*[82] Mengoli explicitly states that he has covered, in previous years, various methodological aspects of mechanics, but now wishes to address more specific points of the subject and over a longer period.[83] He divides mechanics into three main parts, the first two of which he treats here, while he leaves the other (unspecified) one for later years. These lecture plans are also unusual because of their printed format. This suggests that Mengoli was either expecting or hoping for a large audience, and may have been quite keen to share his new subject matter and approach, also beyond Bologna. (In fact, printed announcements of the *Series lectionum* only generally survive for anatomy.) It is not particularly notable that Mengoli mentioned Galileo's theories of motion.[84] It is especially relevant, though, that the formation of independent fields such as mechanics allowed university professors to build disciplines that could proceed according to their own particular order, presumably governed by considerations such as ease of learning.

A lecture plan for the mathematician Domenico Pasi (Passus, †1749; Figure 6.1) shows the extent to which university teaching often still relied on manuals and compendia.[85] Pasi appears on the rolls as a teacher of mathematics from 1699 to 1750 (though he taught only until 1740).[86] The subject assigned to him for 1713–1714 was Ptolemy's astronomy, and Pasi's plan indeed outlines seventy-six lectures over the course of the year, covering the first two of the *Almagest*'s thirteen books "iuxta ordinem Johannis de Regiomonte." This reference to the *Epitome* of Regiomontanus (1436–1476), first published in Venice in 1496, is laden with significance. It is unclear, though, how closely Pasi followed Regiomontanus and whether he taught his students a geocentric or heliocentric model of the universe: he promises that two of the early lectures (13–14 November) will demonstrate that "the earth lies at the center of the universe, at least according to the senses" ("eandem [terram] in medio mundi saltem quoad sensum collocari probabimus"). This was a prudent statement, given that the Catholic Church would have deemed it heretical to promote heliocentrism. But the phrase *saltem quoad sensum* (with its implicit suggestion that things may not always be as they appear) indicates a potential opening toward other perspectives. Most importantly, at the end of the month Pasi held sessions addressing various questions *pro et contra*. These would have been an excellent opportunity to debate different opinions.

Student notes confirm this orientation toward manuals and point to an increasing use of systematic treatments in teaching. Bartolomeo Aldrovandi (who later taught moral philosophy in the *studium;* see §8.2.2) provides the fullest illustration I have found of what the study of arts entailed in Bologna between the end of the seventeenth century and the first half of the eighteenth. Aldrovandi did his studies from 1691 to 1701. His copious student notebooks, which deserve a more detailed and extended examination, provide several insights worth highlighting here.[87]

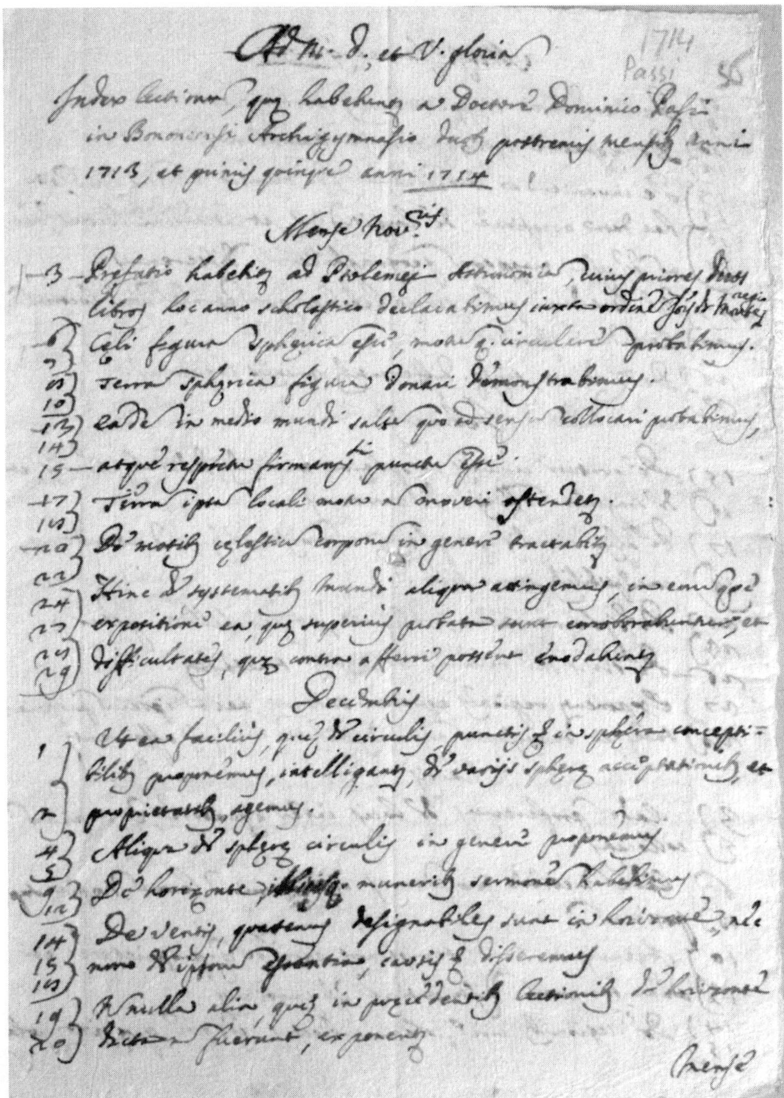

Fig 6.1. Lecture plan of Domenico Pasi on Ptolemy's astronomy, 1713–1714. Archivio di Stato di Bologna, Assunteria di Studio, Annue lezioni, b. 61, f. 56r.

The most relevant of these is that, despite the instructions in the rolls as to what works are to be taught year by year, to a large extent the education Aldrovandi receives seems to derive from manuals, treatises, or textbooks. Thus, the materials include a *Tractatus de logica* (dictated by the professor), a *Tractatus metaphysicus,* a *Tractatus De anima,* and a work

In Physicam universam that is anything but an explanation of Aristotle's text. Material entitled *Animastica* is divided into three parts, dealing with vegetative, sensitive, and intellectual beings, respectively. There is abundant space for questions and disputations, which often roam freely and display rather unexpected features. The *Disputatio De motu,* for instance, demonstrates a clear application of mathematics to issues of physics within a discussion on weight and movement (*Quaestio quarta: De passionibus motus*), even though it does not mention Galileo by name. *In Physicam universam* has a strong religious flavor, but also contains numerous diagrams, discusses issues such as *De motu gravium* (f. 60v), and refers to matters bordering on chymistry (*De chymicorum principiorum mixtione* . . . , Pars I, chap. XI). Perhaps the most striking aspect of Aldrovandi's notebooks is that, by the end of the seventeenth century, professors are clearly thinking of their teaching as covering entire fields rather than specific works by Aristotle. This development was not unique to Italy, nor did it necessarily take root that late in the Italian universities. Indeed, there is reason to believe that its beginnings date to the sixteenth century. But these sources offer insights far beyond what statutes and teaching rolls can offer.

Finally, Aldrovandi's notebooks suggest that especially in the second half of the seventeenth century the expression *tractatus* comes to be used as a synonym (and, eventually, a replacement) for *lectiones.* While the shift, which deserves a detailed study, is indicative of a more topic-oriented mode of teaching, awareness of this change could lead to uncovering many more classroom materials that lurk under this label.[88] Historians of education have typically privileged materials that, from their titles, explicitly refer to lectures or student notes.

6.2.3 Sources and Authorities

The turn toward systematic approaches discussed above not only affected the linear approach of traditional classroom teaching, but also promoted a changing attitude toward and use of sources and authorities. Through a comparison of sixteenth-century lectures with those on record for the later period, this section charts a looser attachment to particular authors and textbooks. Old and new could mix together in unusual and highly individual ways.

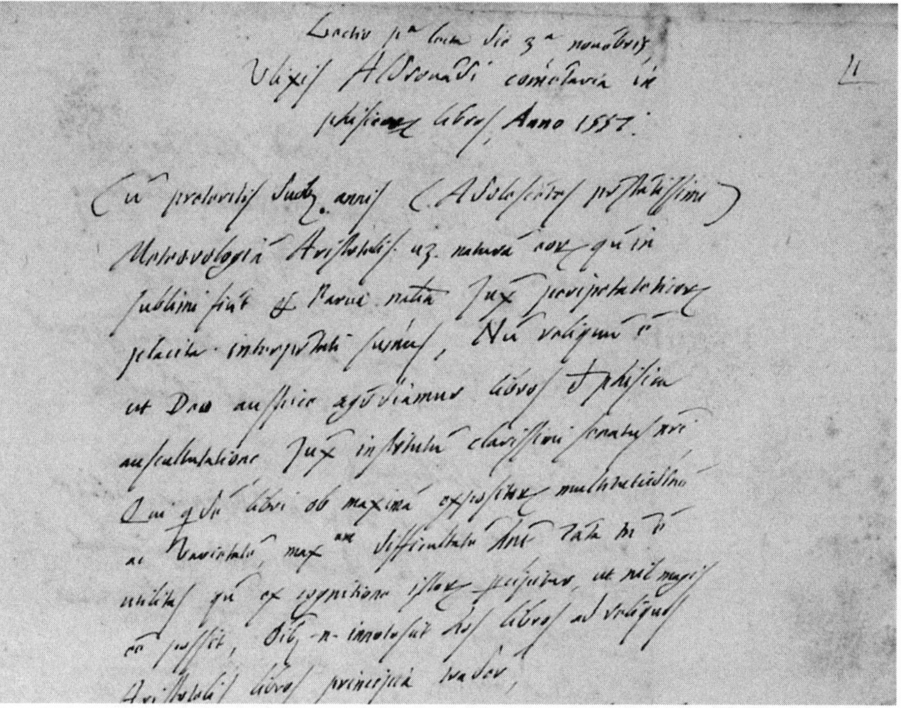

Lectio pa hora die 3a novembris
Ulixis Aldrovandi commentaria in
physicos libros, Anno 1557.

Fig 6.2. Ulisse Aldrovandi, unpublished autograph lectures on Aristotle's *Physics,* 1557. BUB, ms. Aldrovandi 60, f. 1r. Photo © Alma Mater Studiorum Universitá di Bologna—Biblioteca Universitaria di Bologna.

Natural Philosophy

Several professors of natural philosophy in the sixteenth century provide helpful insights into their sources, but perhaps the fullest and clearest example is Ulisse Aldrovandi. As outlined above, Aldrovandi had a long public teaching career in Bologna (1554–1600). In 1557 he lectured on the *Physics* as part of his appointment *ad philosophiam extraordinariam de sero.* The autograph manuscript of these lectures survives (Figure 6.2) and is just one among dozens of similar cases for philosophy teaching in early modern Bologna.

Aldrovandi prefaced his lecture notes with a document (most likely for personal use) headed "Authors I am using to comment on Aristotle's *Physics.*"[89] This lengthy list (sixty-three entries) contains at least five orders of works. First are what we would call primary sources, which consist of the Greek text of the *Physics* ("Aristotelis graece de phisico auditu")[90] as well as the *Problemata* (with the commentary of Pietro d'Abano), Plato in Ficino's Latin translation, and Pliny's *Natural History.* The list also includes Greek and Arab commentators on the *Physics* (Alexander of Aphrodisias, Simplicius, Philoponus, Themistius, Psellos, Averroes), early Latin commentators (e.g., Albertus Magnus, Thomas Aquinas, Giles of Rome, Walter Burley, Jean of Jandun), recent and contemporary authors and works (e.g., Alessandro Achillini, Paul of Venice, Agostino Nifo, Simone Porzio, Ludovico Boccadiferro, Jacques Lefèvre d'Étaples, Jacob Schegk, Sebastian Fox Morcillo), and finally works we might describe as epitomes and encyclopedias. This last item includes at least Ermolao Barbaro's *Compendium scientiae naturalis,* Titelmans's *Philosophiae naturalis compendium* (examined above, §6.2.2), and the *Margarita philosophica.* Clearly, it is one thing to note the breadth of one's reading and another to bring all of these various authors to bear on the relevant discussions. Only a full analysis of Aldrovandi's *Physics* lectures will show just how many of these sources he actually used or how he used them. But the fairly large number of sixteenth-century interpreters on Aldrovandi's list should serve as a reminder of widespread expectations: university professors not only explained to students a certain set text (in this case, Aristotle's *Physics* with Averroes's commentary), but modeled for them how to make one's way among so many conflicting interpretations. Obvious ways of bringing them in included the interpretation of difficult and contested passages and the use of *quaestiones.* Aldrovandi and his successors often used both of these. Good examples of the evolution in approach are the lectures of Claudius Scharpe, Astorre Arnoaldi, and Charles Hébert.

The 1646–1647 lecture plan of Claudius Scharpe (t. 1637–1649) outlines his intended teaching of Aristotle's *Physics,* Book I.[91] This promised a (more or less) linear examination of the text, punctuated by the discussion of several questions, which in fact seem to provide the most important framework for Scharpe's teaching. He observes, for instance, that nearly all interpreters struggle with five doubts emerging from the first chapter of the *Physics,* such as the meaning of the words *principia, causae,* and *elementa.* He therefore asks what these terms really mean. Other questions concern well-worn topics such as matter, form, and privation or whether, in order to know something perfectly, we need to know all of its causes. At the end of his outline, Scharpe offers a brief listing of his main sources, indicating especially Averroes, Thomas Aquinas, Duns Scotus, and Jacopo Zabarella.[92] This listing is clearly not accidental; Scharpe's lectures on the *Physics* for the first term of autumn 1642 cite precisely the same authors.[93] His 1645–1646 lectures on Aristotle's *Metheora* IV include a slightly expanded list, with ancient authors such as Plato, Hippocrates, and Galen next to modern ones such as Pomponazzi and Thomas Erastus.[94] The different set of sources is doubtless due to the particular features of this book, which Scharpe links with his explanation of *De ortu et interitu* (*On Generation and Corruption*) held the previous year. Scharpe does not, however, explicitly tie this book to discussions about chymistry, which was a hot topic throughout Europe in the first half of the seventeenth century thanks to the treatments by Daniel Sennert, Libert Froidmont, and others, including the Franciscans Bartolomeo Mastri and Bonaventura Belluti in Padua.[95]

Arnoaldi takes a rather different approach and chiefly models his lectures on the writings of one modern author. One of the real longtimers at the university (he is listed on the rolls from 1632 until his death in 1680), for 1643–1644 Arnoaldi presented a program of lectures on the *Physics,* Book I.[96] There he explicitly sets out to offer his teaching according to the opinions of Aristotle, Averroes, and (Francesco) Piccolomini (*in viam Aristotelis, Averrois et Piccolominei*). What is unusual here is the reference to Piccolomini, whom we have already encountered. Arnoaldi must have been a real fan, for in another (and much more detailed) course plan on *Physics* I, the ninety-five lectures outlined closely follow portions of Piccolomini's textbook, including an initial section that summarizes the opinions of the ancients.[97] Although Arnoaldi also makes reference to other interpreters—including Alessandro Achillini's commentary on the *Physics,* Alessandro Piccolomini (work unspecified, but presumably *La prima parte della filosofia naturale*), Simplicius, and (with considerable regularity) Jean of Jandun's questions—Piccolomini's presence is pervasive. Arnoaldi's plans suggest a strong influence of the "school of Padua," perhaps testifying to an orientation different from that of Scharpe, who—as seen above—favored Zabarella rather than his rival Francesco Piccolomini.[98]

The lectures of Charles Hébert (t. 1731–1752) carry the reader into a very different cultural milieu, one in which eighteenth-century science features strongly.[99] Hébert's lectures *De meteoris* of 1733–1734 again display the trend toward systematization, something facilitated by Aristotle's ordered discussion of the four elements of nature.[100] But the details of the lectures under "fire" indicate that recent scientific insights are informing the old subject matter: Hébert gives attention to the nature of light and of colors (he explicitly mentions the theories of Isaac Newton, Edme Mariotte, and others), as well as to pyrotechnics, phosphorus, and the *coronae sidireae.*[101] Likewise, he announces that his discussion of water will take in evaporation and water's division into atoms. And he shows that the topic *de mixtorum compositione* will be supported by experimentation ("pluribus experimentis investigare possimus").[102] Hébert's lectures on physics likewise display a tendency to distance themselves strongly from Aristotle and his works. His course outline for 1735–1736 focuses on sound and the faculty of hearing. There Hébert engages in some humorous wordplay, stating that his subject will be *de audito physico* (an allusion to the Latin title of the *Physics,* which commonly went by the name *De physico auditu*). He also puts forward questions such as "What is sound or a voice generally?" (*Quid sit sonus vel vox in genere?*) and "What are the principal voice organs in man and other animals?" (*Quae sint organa praecipua vocis in homine et caeteris animalibus?*). He also makes specific reference to the "machina Stankariana," to be examined in one of the lectures. This was a reference to a device developed by the Bolognese Vittorio Francesco Stancari (1678–1709), a follower of Leibniz, who from 1698 taught mathematics in the university there.[103] The machine helped measure the pitch of sounds. These aspect of Hébert's lectures hint at his particular interests in musical performance and theory, including in the violinist Antonio Montanari and his playing of Arcangelo Corelli's sonatas.[104] They therefore fit right into the Bolognese cultural sphere, which was so well known for its music in the early eighteenth century.

Astronomy and Mathematics

In the case of astronomy and mathematics, the lecture plans of Bonaventura Cavalieri repay attention for their references to quite recent scholarship. This member of the order of the Gesuati, who studied with the Benedictine Benedetto Castelli in Pisa and became a friend of Galileo, taught mathematics in Bologna from 1629 until his death in December 1647.[105] Although his particular interest was geometry, a field in which he was greatly distinguished, Cavalieri taught the courses specified by the rolls: *Theorica planetarum* in 1642–1643. His lecture plan shows him offering, like other professors, a systematic analysis rather than a commentary on the work.[106] (In this case, the principle of organization consists of six hypotheses on the order of the planets with respect to the universe.). More relevantly, the lengthy bibliography Cavalieri offers at the end of his lecture plan is notable for the presence of some fairly recent publications, such as the 1622 *Astronomia Danica* by Longomontanus (Christen Sørensen) of Denmark, a supporter of Brahe's whose work handily compared the three world systems.[107]

Cavalieri's contemporaries did not, however, necessarily share his interest in very recent writings. A clear example is Ovidio Montalbani (1601–1671), who also taught the *Theorica planetarum* but looked to much older (indeed, Hermetic) sources. Montalbani was a prominent cultural personality in Bologna and among other things served as the warden of Aldrovandi's museum and library. After taking his degree in arts and medicine (1622), he taught in the university from 1625 until 1665 (though he appears on the rolls until his death), with a special focus on mathematics from 1633 to 1651. Montalbani is often caricatured today as a conservative follower of Aristotle and as a writer of some odd and old-fashioned astrological observations, which decorated his prognostications.[108] Yet he was a learned man, who founded in his home the Accademia dei Vespertini (dedicated to the discussion of astronomy, astrology, and geometry) and was a member of various other Bolognese academies, including the Accademia dei Gelati (§3.2.3) and the Accademia degli Indomiti.[109] In his only surviving course plan, for *Theorica planetarum* (1643), Montalbani mentions many of the same authors as Cavalieri, but his methodology is less mathematical, and his allegiances are more Platonic and Hermetic.[110] He displays strong leanings for Kepler (rather differently from contemporaries such as Geminiano Montanari), a position he also takes in his vernacular work *Cometoscopia*.[111]

As might be expected, teaching in the early eighteenth century shows signs of considerable hostility toward (some of) the ancients, while also turning to Plato for support. The mathematics lectures by the Benedictine monk Ercole Corazzi (Hercules Corazzus, †1726) are a case in point. Corazzi, who taught practical geometry and mathematics in Bologna (c. 1710–1720) after a stint in Padua (and perhaps Perugia), had succeeded

Vittorio Francesco Stancari in the first Italian chair for algebra (established in 1708).[112] He was active in the Istituto delle Scienze and was famous enough to be summoned to Turin by Vittorio Amedeo II in 1720 to teach and help with the reform of the university there.[113] Corazzi's plan for mathematics (1717–1718) does not provide many details on the authors used, but expressly underlines the "uselessness of Aristotle's logic and the excellence of our own mathematics" ("inutilitas logicae Aristotelis et nostrae logisticae praestantia").[114] At the same time, Corazzi takes a strongly Platonic approach.[115] In one of his course prolusions, Corazzi contrasts his own subject (analytical mathematics) with old-fashioned geometry; thus, he mocks those who spend so much time trying to commit to memory the sayings of ancient geometricians.[116] After a call for his students to pursue *necessaria et philosophica libertas,* Corazzi emphasizes the importance of algebra and analytical mathematics for freeing the mind from matters of sensation and penetrating those that are abstract.[117] In fact, Corazzi is calling fairly openly for an acceptance of the new philosophy. Another prolusion is misleadingly entitled "De pace et perenni concordia inter Aristotelem et Cartesianam philosophiam" (On the Peace and Eternal Concord between Aristotle and Cartesian Philosophy) and was delivered in Turin (1723), where Corazzi had moved in the meantime. Here he makes no pretense that ancient writers may be worth studying: instead students should grasp the discipline from first principles, following the examples of Galileo, Descartes, Torricelli, Newton, and Leibniz.[118] Corazzi presents Aristotle (or "Vetus Philosophia") as a doddering old fool who comes to blows with a beautiful young woman ("Nova Philosophia"). Ironically, for an approach that explicitly wishes to cast the ancients overboard, in several lectures Corazzi implicitly appeals to Plato's teachings.[119]

6.2.4 A New Science?

So far I have argued that the specialization that developed in Bologna from the sixteenth century onward had notable effects such as increasing and diversifying the sources and textbooks used in natural philosophy, astronomy, and mathematics. It also changed their orientation, loosening their ties to the literal-commentary format. This development allowed them to become more systematic and even freer to give attention to contemporary discussions.[120] Signals of these changes are the enthusiastic embrace of forms such as the *quaestio* and the treatise (*tractatus*). Furthermore, new (sub-)fields of knowledge developed, including natural history (and, within that, botany) and mathematical areas such as mechanics and hydraulics. As the earlier bonds uniting both natural philosophy and astronomy to medicine weakened, all of these subjects could develop more autonomously.[121] Some prominent figures outside of the universities (such as the Jesuit Niccolò Cabeo) argued for a separation between matter theory, metaphysics, and mathematics.[122] That independence led to considerable expansion, so that—with the reform of 1737—mathematics boasted five separate teachings: *geometria analytica, geometria elementaris sintetica, mechanica, hydrometria,* and *astronomia*.

It is possible, however, to exaggerate patterns of specialization and the extent to which these various fields multiplied and became separate.[123] Montalbani, for instance, covered a variety of subjects in his long teaching career: logic, theoretical medicine, mathematics, and (in the concluding phase of his career) moral philosophy and law. Furthermore, from the second half of the seventeenth century new relationships and alliances formed, giving rise to a new science built on different foundations. One of the strong signals of this new state of affairs is Marcello Malpighi (1628–1694), whom we will meet again in Chapter 7. Malpighi's mechanical vision of nature—applied to his domain of anatomy and medicine—depended on the developments in natural philosophy and mathematics examined in this chapter as well as on the growing use of instruments in fields across science. Yet it also testified to the new ties and relationships that were forming between the disciplines and that came to unite medicine with other areas as part of an organic whole.[124]

Another clear example of how the configuration of subjects was being reorganized is the Bolognese Domenico Guglielmini (1655–1710), whose career embraced and reunited empirical science and medicine. Guglielmini obtained his degree in medicine in 1678, having studied with Geminiano Montanari (one of Bologna's most eminent astronomers) and Malpighi.[125] He came to teaching rather late, around 1690. Before then he cultivated astronomical interests (he was in frequent touch with Cassini in Paris), was the warden of the Museo Aldrovandi, and oversaw the Waters Commission for Bologna's territory. Appointed to teach mathematics, Guglielmini has a particular importance as the holder (from 1695) of the new university appointment of river hydraulics (*hydrometria*), probably the first such chair in Europe (although aspects of this subject had been taught earlier within the purview of mathematics).[126] He was the first in Bologna to teach Descartes's principles of analytic geometry.[127] Guglielmini shared Montanari's perspective (in turn probably influenced by Francis Bacon) that natural philosophy should be based on natural history, a point that features strongly in his *De salibus dissertatio* (1705).[128] He used a microscope for his research in this area, seeing chemistry as having an empirical and experimental foundation. His most important work—*Della natura de' fiumi, trattato fisico-matematico* (first printed in 1697)—unites various approaches that were part of the Galilean tradition with the medical-naturalistic approaches of Malpighi.[129] But what is especially relevant is Guglielmini's career: although he left for Padua in 1698 to teach mathematics, from 1702 he held the chair of theoretical medicine there. In fact, Guglielmini had an understanding of natural phenomena (including those concerning the body) that united everything under the umbrella of mechanics, geometry, and arithmetic. He was affected by the vision of the universal applicability of the theory of mechanicism that had such a success during his time and had been illustrated by men of science such as Giovanni Alfonso Borelli (1608–1679), Lorenzo Bellini (1643–1704), and Malpighi.[130] This was a step further from Galileo's insistence on uniting the titles of mathematician and natural philosopher at the court of the Medici.

The points above are not meant to give the impression that the university was the only or even necessarily the main place in which change took place in Bologna. In fact, one should avoid drawing sharp distinctions between the university and other contexts. At the local level, scientific discussions in Bologna were the product of a three-way conversation between university teachers, teachers in the Jesuit college (such as the strongly anti-Copernican mathematician G. B. Riccioli), and the academies that eventually gave rise to the Istituto delle Scienze.[131] As we have seen (§3.2), there was a particularly strong interaction with the Istituto and its predecessor (the Accademia delle Scienze) from the end of the seventeenth century. A strong voice in all of this was Luigi Ferdinando Marsili, whose *Parallelo dello stato moderno della Università di Bologna con l'altre di là dai monti* (1709), presented to the Senate, made some bold proposals: to institute four lectureships in the *studium* that would replace

Euclid's *Geometry* with algebra, further the study of astronomy in the Observatory, consider physical subjects with the benefit of geometric demonstration, and teach mathematics in terms of practical subjects such as mechanics, military and civilian architecture, perspective, and so forth.[132] Some scholars have argued that these proposed reforms took place only in the Istituto (later established by Marsili).[133] Yet Corazzi (as noted above) received an appointment in the *studium* shortly afterward and gave great emphasis both to algebra and to geometric demonstrations. Mechanics and hydraulics had already been introduced some time before. Furthermore, the Istituto and the *studium* were interlocking entities, and it was common for professors to belong to both. This makes it difficult to draw neat boundaries.

Nor did the discussions and changes in Bologna occur independently of much broader debates throughout the Italian Peninsula and, indeed, the Republic of Letters. Several of the leaders in scientific and mathematical developments in the second half of the seventeenth century had spent time elsewhere: Malpighi, for instance, had worked with Borelli in Pisa, while Montanari had spent most of his lifetime in his native Modena, as well as in Florence and Vienna. Many engaged in correspondence and controversies with learned men from across Europe—sometimes involving disputes with other adherents to the "new science," such as when Montanari disagreed with the atomist Donato Rossetti (1633–1686), a former student of Borelli.[134] Others cultivated ties particularly with the Royal Society in London, which was deeply influential on Bolognese scientists.[135] Figures such as Cassini and Montanari, who left Bologna for elsewhere, continued to be in contact with their Bolognese colleagues and inform them of developments in Paris and Padua, for instance. People such as Corazzi offered guidance when other universities were implementing reforms. The important astronomer Eustachio Manfredi, who taught mathematics (from 1737, astronomy), was a member of both the Académie des Sciences and the Royal Society.

But scientific innovation in Bologna was slow, contentious, and nonlinear. The city continued to require the *studium*'s professors to produce astrological prognostications long after some of its most distinguished scientists had expressed strong criticisms against the practice.[136] (Montanari was engaged, but to little effect, in a long-standing campaign against judicial astrology, while his student Guglielmini reluctantly agreed to continue preparing the annual prognostications for Bologna well after his departure in 1698.) The struggles between conservative and new factions within the city and the *studium* were bitter, and led both Montanari and Guglielmini to seek refuge in Padua, where they enjoyed higher salaries and Montanari occupied a personal chair in astronomy and the study of meteors. Montanari was also able to teach very practical subjects there, including military architecture and engineering. Opposition to Malpighi by more traditional professors degenerated into vandalism, with a (partially successful) attempt by one disgruntled colleague to burn down his countryside estate. Finally, there was the problem of obtaining certain publications. When Marsili visited London in 1721, he went armed with a list of books he wished to acquire; some of these dated as far back as the 1670s, indicating that finding these in Bologna was no easy task.[137] Evidently even the mechanisms of book exchange described in Chapter 4 had become unequal to the task of keeping up to date with scholarship across Europe. The Inquisition and the Index of Prohibited Books must have been partly responsible for this state of affairs.

Yet, it would be churlish to deny that much had changed by the first half of the eighteenth century. The Istituto delle Scienze—with its Accademia delle Scienze and Accademia delle Belle Arti—had been founded. There was an important periodical in the *De Bononiensi scientiarum et artium Instituto atque Academia Commentarii.*[138] Donations and support from Pope Benedict XIV would considerably raise the Istituto's profile, from which the university could only benefit. The teaching and experimental activities of Laura Bassi, her husband Giuseppe Veratti, and Luigi Galvani attracted international attention.[139] The Istituto would serve as a model for other such scientific organizations throughout Italy in the eighteenth century.

Conclusion

As noted above, aspects of the reorientation of teaching discussed in this chapter are not immediately apparent in the teaching rolls, which until 1737 continued to reflect many of the traditional designations for various subjects. Yet many professors were able to communicate their ideas by imagining themselves as teaching, not a specific book, but a particular area of knowledge. This led to a new systematization of subject matter, with all of its potential implications and advantages. At the same time, professors often used the technique of the *quaestio* to go beyond the boundaries of the text they were supposedly explaining. This technique—inherited from medieval commentators—made it possible to raise numerous issues with which students needed to be familiar, not least to pass their doctoral exams.[140] But it also created the freedom to discuss a wide (and increasingly contemporary) set of topics and sources. Thus, by a curious circumstance, Aristotle and Ptolemy were dethroned quietly, without a fuss, through an even more frequent use of the *quaestio* format that had so actively promoted them in the Middle Ages.

The use of the *quaestio* (so readily embraced even by students in Bologna) was not just a local phenomenon. Various Italian cultural personalities—both within and outside of the universities, such as Ludovico Antonio Muratori, Gian Vincenzo Gravina (Rome), Scipione Maffei (Padua), and Giambattista Vico (Naples)—criticized the level and content of teaching in the universities of the early eighteenth century, but not, as far as I am aware, the practice of questions and disputations.[141] I suspect that a study of other universities across Europe would find a similar intensive use of this technique within the classroom.

These findings both confirm and challenge the conclusions of Brian Lawn's 1993 study *The Rise and Decline of the Scholastic Quaestio Disputata.* On the one hand, Lawn intuited that the question format had some relationship to the development of the "Scientific Revolution" (for which, in his words, it "lay the foundations").[142] Yet he argued that this format eventually gave way, under the pressure of the experimental method, to other classroom approaches such as "the straightforward question-and-answer technique without argument [and] the classroom lecture."[143] On the other hand, the slight confusion between the use of questions in commentaries and formal exercises such as the *quaestio disputata* leads to some contestable claims.[144] For instance, Lawn dates the format's decline to the seventeenth century, although he locates its demise in the eighteenth. In my view, questions continued to be an important aspect of teaching, even if not aired in public disputations, long after the seventeenth century.

In part the continued popularity of the *quaestio* was due to its flexibility as a vehicle for discussions: it freed both teachers and students from the letter of the statutes and the tyranny of the text (at least in philosophy and medicine).[145] More specifically, questions provided a mechanism for introducing nonstandard works or ideas into teaching. Thus Plato, Democritus, Epicurus, Lucretius, and other ancients could put in an appearance, along with several contemporary authors such as Descartes and Newton (see above).[146] As Lawn noted with reference to a French manuscript (1643) containing disputations on Aristotle, it became possible to build on "a foundation of Aristotelianism," while at the same time "incorporating much early and late scholastic philosophy, Renaissance ideas, and contemporary scientific knowledge."[147]

In turn, this reorientation toward questions (which might pass today for "problem-based learning") emerged at least in part from the patterns of specialization described in this chapter—something that did not have to wait until the seventeenth or even the eighteenth and nineteenth centuries to develop.[148] Rather, already from the sixteenth century natural philosophers, mathematicians, and astronomers started to rethink their disciplines and their configuration in the broader curriculum. A new relationship with medicine emerged (Chapter 7), and a religious turn strongly characterized all fields, including science (Chapter 8). But there can be no doubt that, from an institutional and organizational point of view, university learning did not stand still.

Finally, this chapter's findings suggest an important methodological and historiographical lesson. Modern scholars have often described the premodern curriculum of arts and medicine (in Bologna and elsewhere) as ossified and unchanging, because the textbooks that stood at its foundation changed slowly if at all.[149] Conversely, they have expressed particular enthusiasm at the introduction of newer authors such as Hippocrates (see §7.1.2)—a development that not just older histories have viewed as vital for a renewal of medicine.[150] But it is easy to make too much of the importance of particular textbooks. Aristotle and Ptolemy were standard requirements of the study program for centuries on end (as were Galen, Avicenna, and Hippocrates for medicine, and as Bartolus was for law). But this does not necessarily mean that they were taught in a traditional way, or that they were accepted as authoritative mediators of truth. Nor did it exclude the discussion of other authors and works. Already medieval lectures and questions are full of references to contemporary debates.[151] In the early modern period, this tendency accelerated as teaching texts became increasingly less important. There is still a great deal to learn about how exactly this process took place and why, but we can no longer be content to claim that there was a lack of innovation in teaching methods without a systematic examination of the lectures over the *longue durée.* It is a tedious but necessary work—at times providing (as the work of Brendan Dooley suggests) precious insights into the dynamics of teaching and learning.[152]

7

From Theory to Practice

Few aspects of the medieval and early modern universities have attracted as much biting irony as their bookishness and supposed emphasis on speculation or accumulation of useless knowledge. Already the early humanist Francis Petrarch (1304–1374) satirized the Aristotelians of his time for their attention to details of the natural world such as the number of feathers in a hawk's tail, while neglecting (or so he said) human nature and humanity's purpose. He extended this criticism to moral philosophy, claiming that Aristotle in his *Ethics* "teaches what virtue is . . . but his lesson lacks the words that sting and set afire and urge toward love of virtue and hatred of vice."[1] In other words, Petrarch intimated, Aristotle's work may be helpful from a theoretical standpoint, but does not lead or urge one to ethical practice: for that, one needs rhetoric and poetry. Likewise, in the 1520s Henricus Cornelius Agrippa of Nettesheim (1486–1535) pilloried the medical systems of his day. He saw knowledge of physiology as useless for the therapeutic task at hand: in the interests of healing, therefore, one may as well jettison Hippocrates and Galen, since medical theory is an impediment rather than a help.[2] Over the centuries, numerous historians have echoed such sentiments, holding, for instance, that early modern university culture was so beholden to theory and ancient or medieval authorities, that it was unfertile ground for the development of practical subjects or of science.[3] The universities emerge as failures, not only for not having opened the way to modernity but for having blocked it.

This chapter examines the relationship of theory and practice within the context of the Bolognese *studium* and from the viewpoint of medicine. A widespread belief is that medical studies at Bologna and other early modern universities in Italy were strongly traditional, relieved only by the intermittent appearance of individuals of great fame and distinction and occasional developments of note in anatomy and surgery. Common arguments supporting such a viewpoint include the universities' perpetuation of the long-standing division between theoretical and practical medicine and the dependence of the curriculum on canonical authors such as Hippocrates, Galen, and Avicenna. From here it is but a small step to conclude that university medical learning remained quite conservative and that little changed until the end of the early modern period. Even Nancy Siraisi's superb research would seem to point in this direction, for despite the variety of views she notes in the discussion of theory and practice in Padua, ultimately new perspectives (such as those of Giambattista da Monte) did not gain a following there.[4]

There are, however, significant elements of the traditional picture that need readjusting. In this chapter I will show that, under the surface, rather more change was taking place than meets the eye. Discussions about *medicina theorica* and *medicina practica* in Bologna are a reminder that official statutes and teaching rolls should be treated with caution. In fact, Bolognese professors held a variety of views on the nature of medicine. Within surgery and anatomy, they emphasized specific links between theory and clinical practice. Figures such as Marcello Malpighi and Luigi Ferdinando Marsili testify to a curriculum that was rapidly evolving. Ultimately, it is important to recognize that theory and practice were very tightly bound in the mentality of the time, so that even subjects such as surgery remained closely associated with book learning. This chapter will investigate this nexus and its implications for our understanding of the early modern university.

In what follows, one needs to be careful not to fall into one of two traps. The first is that of adopting a Whiggish approach that applauds the "progress of science," particularly when it occurs in terms familiar to us such as experimental method and the applicability of technical and scientific discoveries. Such an outlook potentially leads to evaluating the culture of early modern universities such as Bologna from our own perspective and to looking with undue eagerness for any signs of a turn toward the "modern" university. Furthermore, one must not forget that, from the start, universities offered their students a technical and professional training primarily geared to help them secure jobs and status and—in areas such as medicine—to prepare them for practice.[5] For all of that, it is also true that university professors operated within a context that privileged certain knowledge (based on immutable principles rather than experience) and sophisticated conceptual approaches such as the examination of the "four causes."

The terms *medicina theorica* and *medicina practica* do not neatly map onto current understandings of theoretical and practical (or operative) medicine. In medieval and early modern times, medicine was fundamentally a discipline that enquired into how and why health could be maintained or restored. So *practica* did not refer to consultative or clinical practice. Rather, *theorica* and *practica* were both indispensable components of learned medicine, which studied physiology. The former referred to an understanding of the principles and causes of health and diseases; the latter, to a study of how and why suitable remedies could be applied to illnesses. *Practica* was therefore (following Avicenna) a rational science or *scientia intellectualis* in a way comparable to (though not identical with) *theorica*. As witnessed already by the Bolognese medic Taddeo Alderotti (†1295), both of these components were distinct from a physician's treatment of patients or *operatio*.[6] Likewise, surgery (the third main component of learned medicine) was not so much about cutting bodies, but about this activity's principles, which were tied to anatomical knowledge. As for anatomy, for a long time its status lay outside of learned medicine, but eventually (like medical botany or simples) it became part of the official curriculum. Professors of medicine and surgery were hardly unaware of the practical value of their subjects: most of them ran private practices outside the university and derived a large proportion of their incomes from this activity—a subject that lies outside of this chapter's exploration.[7] But university medical training was commonly understood as providing the principles and knowledge that *governed practice,* as opposed to something gained *through practice.*

Because of the potential for confusion, throughout this chapter I will refer to *theorica* and *practica* by their Latin labels and treat both them and surgery in distinction from clinical practice. What each involved, the place of anatomy, and how their relationships shifted will become clearer in the sections that follow.

7.1 *Theorica* and *Practica*

An analysis of the relationship of *theorica* and *practica* needs to consider both its institutional dimension (in terms of how the subjects were organized, taught, and remunerated) and how professors of medicine in Bologna themselves understood the nature of medicine.

7.1.1 Institutional Considerations

Bologna's 1405 statutes outline a medical curriculum embracing a very large number of texts, supposedly meant to be lectured on over a period of four years. As mentioned earlier, it is hard to know to what extent such instructions were actually followed. Bologna's teaching rolls, for instance, do not specify the medical teaching texts until the late sixteenth century, and even then they may not be wholly reliable. It seems safe, however, to assume that professors taught a rather smaller selection of texts, in keeping with a more general reorientation toward intensive (rather than extensive) reading (see §2.2.2).

Archival documents and teaching rolls for Bologna from around and after 1585 delineate a three-year course of medical study based on the texts in Table 7.1. These represent ordinary lectures.[8]

But both *theorica* and *practica* received extraordinary lectures as well. These followed a similar cycle but had a different starting point. A complete outline of lectures looked something like that of Table 7.2 (cf. Table 2.3).

Furthermore, from at least the second half of the sixteenth century Bologna had "supraordinary" chairs of medicine that gave professors the freedom to teach *ad libitum.*[9] Holders of the chair of *theoricus supraordinarius* included, among others, Girolamo Cardano, Girolamo Mercuriale, and Giovanni Costeo, but after Costeo's death in 1603 few professors

Table 7.1 Teaching patterns in *medicina theorica* and *practica,* c. 1585

	Theorica	*Practica*
Year 1	Hippocrates, *Aphorisms*	Avicenna, *Canon,* I.4
Year 2	Avicenna, *Canon,* I.1 (*prima pars*)	Rasis, *De morbis particularibus*
Year 3	Galen, *Ars parva* (= *Tegni*)	*De febribus* (= *Canon,* IV.1)

Table 7.2 Ordinary and extraordinary teachings of *theorica* and *practica,* c. 1585

Theorica ordinaria	*Theorica extraordinaria*	*Practica ordinaria*	*Practica extraordinaria*
Hippocrates, *Aphorisms*	Avicenna, *Canon,* I.1	Avicenna, *Canon,* IV.1	Avicenna, *Canon,* I.4
Avicenna, *Canon,* I.1	Galen, *Ars parva*	Avicenna, *Canon,* I.4	Rasis, *De morbis*
Galen, *Ars parva*	Hippocrates, *Aphorisms*	Rasis, *De morbis*	Avicenna, *Canon,* IV.1

filled it. The only exception seems to be the appointment of George Scharpe for 1634–1637 (see below). The rolls indicate that there was also a chair for *medicina practica supraordinaria* (again with a free choice of subject). Its first attestation is with Antonio Maria Alberghini and Giovanni Costeo in 1583–1584.[10] This teaching continues to be listed on the rolls long after the reform of 1737.

Professors' careers, salaries, and the staffing of medicine indicate that in Bologna (as in Padua) *theorica* was initially the more prestigious of the two branches.[11] In 1433–1434, for instance, ten professors appear on the rolls for medicine, plus two for surgery and binding broken bones. Of these, four teach *practica,* each receiving between L. 150 and L. 300; the others receive salaries of variable size (starting at L. 100), but the senior professor of *theorica,* Nicolò Fava, earns a very substantial L. 1,000.[12] The sixteenth century saw a leveling out of the compensation for the two branches, while the careers of professors such as Panfilo Monti (who taught *practica* from 1545 until his death in 1553, after teaching *theorica*) suggest that *practica* had become more respectable as the culmination of one's *iter* of teaching.[13] The rolls from the seventeenth and early eighteenth centuries also suggest a rather more equal distribution of professors in both of these branches. In any case, career patterns provide numerous examples of professors moving fluidly between *theorica, practica,* and surgery. By 1737 the rolls list eight professors for *theorica* and ten for *practica.* In addition (excluding the *emeriti*), there are five professors dedicated to surgery, one to surgical operations, four to anatomy, and one to medical simples.[14]

The developments outlined above fit well with the more general consensus among scholars that *practica* experienced a reputational rise, particularly in sixteenth-century Italy, as *theorica* increasingly became an introductory subject with lower prestige. Yet one should also remember that *theorica* and *practica* were complementary and inseparable aspects of medical education.[15] A better understanding of their relationship emerges from writings connected to the Bolognese teaching of medicine.

7.1.2 Perspectives on *Theorica* and *Practica*

As outlined above, in Bologna *theorica* was studied especially through three texts: the *Aphorisms* of Hippocrates, the first section or *fen* of Avicenna's *Canon,* Book I, and Galen's *Ars parva* (also referred to as *Tegni*).[16] The first and third of these works were typically part of the collection of medical texts known as *Articella,* which throughout Europe enjoyed a substantial commentary tradition.[17] For Bologna, however, the number of surviving lectures and commentaries associated with the works of Galen and Avicenna is overall rather small (particularly when compared to, say, Padua) and remarkably uneven.[18] This considerably limits the range of texts used as anchors for classic discussions of the nature of medicine.[19] Nonetheless, Bologna provides several instances testifying to the teaching of Hippocrates, so what follows will focus on discussions of *theorica* and *practica* in his *Aphorisms* (particularly aphorism one: *Ars longa*). It will simultaneously contribute to the study of his reception, which has received less attention compared to that of Galen and Avicenna.[20]

Girolamo Cardano

A good place to start is the teaching activity of Girolamo Cardano (1501–1576), whose sojourn in Bologna (1562–1570) is well documented in terms of lectures and has been the object of several studies.[21] Cardano was appointed to teach medicine in 1562, after lengthy negotiations and against the wishes of the Bolognese authorities.[22] He occupied the morning teaching of ordinary theoretical medicine (*lectura theoricae medicinae ordinaria*) together with several other professors and lectured on a standard, if introductory, text within the curriculum of *theorica:* the *Aphorisms* of Hippocrates, on which he had lectured in Pavia as well. The following year he appears on the rolls in a position on his own; this must have been an appointment to *theorica supraordinaria* in the fourth morning hour.[23] He would maintain this slot until his trial by the Inquisition in 1570. Such an eminent position placed Cardano in the company of previous illustrious occupiers of that chair—at the very least Matteo Corti and Benedetto Vittori.[24] The "supraordinary" designation enabled him to lecture on whatever he liked. This helps explain the range of texts Cardano taught after 1562—nearly all of which were by or attributed to Hippocrates and lay outside of the works usually classified as "ordinary" at Bologna: in 1563–1565 he lectured on the *Epidemics,* Books I and II; in 1565–1566, on *Prognostic* and *De septimestri partu;* in 1567–1568, on *Airs Waters Places;* in 1568–1569, on *Aliment;* and in 1569–1570, on *Regimen in Acute Diseases.*[25]

Cardano's appointment to *theorica* is somewhat ironic, given that his interests throughout his life were much more in *practica* (which had been his subject in Pavia) and that all the texts on which he lectured could, in any case, be classified more easily under that heading. Cardano had an aversion to an excessively theoretical approach to medicine, something that informed his sustained criticism of Galen. He was also distrustful of Galen's status as an authority accepted uncritically by his contemporaries.[26] Much preferring the approach of Hippocrates, Cardano saw himself as following in his footsteps and presented himself as a second or "new" Hippocrates.[27] He considered the *Aphorisms* a work that could, much better than Galen (and independently from Galen's commentary on it), function as a systematic treatise appropriate for *theorica.*[28] Indeed, Cardano planned a substantial and detailed commentary on this work and the rest of the Hippocratic corpus (in some 1,200 folios), only parts of which appeared, including an incomplete commentary on the *Aphorisms.*[29] Yet his view of the *Aphorisms* was not as a work of exclusive relevance to *theorica.* Rather, as Nancy Siraisi has noted, he saw this work as "constitut[ing] a complete and systematically ordered manual of medical practice."[30] That last word is all-important, for it refers to Cardano's impatience with everything (including philological analysis) that did not, in his view, bear fruit in and affect the exercise of medicine.[31] He therefore declares, "We should learn the medical art transmitted by the *Aphorisms* so as to make appropriate and immediate use of it."[32] On this basis, one might expect Cardano to eschew or minimize discussions of topics such as the development of fevers and the function of nutrition in those cases, opting only for very practical aspects, but that is not quite the case, presumably because he recognizes that practical medicine requires, at its base, a theoretical foundation.[33] Cardano also sees the *Aphorisms* as having a recognizable internal structure, a point addressed by later commentators.

But Hippocrates is only part of the larger story of Cardano's teaching in Bologna. In 1563 he also lectured on Avicenna's *Canon,* I.1, which was a standard text for discussing the principles of *theorica.* Cardano's Bolognese lectures as such do not survive, although his prolusions from Pavia (1546?) and Bologna, as part of a planned commentary on all of the *Canon*'s four books, do. (The work is dedicated to Pier Donato Cesi, the papal legate in Bologna at the time.)[34] Neither of the prolusions provides helpful insights into Cardano's understanding of the nature of medicine, but relevant points emerge when, in his commentary on the first *fen,* he glosses Avicenna's claim that medicine is a science ("Dico quod medicina est scientia"). Emphasizing the role of sensation, Cardano distinguishes two kinds of medicine—not *ars* and *scientia,* but instead *theorica* and *practica.* He lists six kinds of *habitus* associated with different kinds of knowledge, concluding that medicine sits between the second (*scientia* in the proper sense, being deduced from first principles) and the fourth (*scientia practica,* which derives from *scientia* and is oriented toward action). The *habitus* relevant to medicine is one "that is deduced by reason from sensible things as if they were [first] principles, and this is the *habitus* of science (yet not science in the true sense of the word); and medicine is of this kind."[35] So medicine is not quite like natural philosophy, since its principles proceed, not from eternal first principles, but from the realm of sensation; medicine also differs from moral philosophy, which is geared toward action and in which *exercitatio* is a prevalent aspect.[36] Once again, Cardano's viewpoint is that medicine should be equally balanced between theory and practice, neither of which is conceivable without the other.

Scholars have discussed Cardano's views on the nature of medicine within the context of contemporary thinking on the issue, particularly in Padua.[37] But how do these views fit within the Bolognese tradition of teaching and commentary on Hippocrates? In what follows I briefly examine this topic on the basis of the lectures of Matteo Corti, Benedetto Vittori, and especially Giovanni Zecchi, although some attention also goes to Domenico Guglielmini. They show that a particularly unusual view was that of Zecchi, who considered medicine to be primarily an art. Understandings of the nature of medicine could, however, be highly personal and differentiated.

Matteo Corti

In the case of Matteo Corti (1475–1544), a famed professor of medicine who taught *theorica* in Bologna from 1538 to 1540, the clearest indications of the nature of medicine come, not in his Bolognese lectures on Hippocrates's *Regimen acutorum,* but in those on Galen.[38] There Corti regards the teaching aspect of medicine as an *ars factiva,* but not therefore as comparable to one of the crafts. Rather, he uses "art" in a strong sense, with reference to something that is not self-evident and has a theoretical basis. He notes that medicine needs theory because it "teaches an unknown way of doing" (it is an *ars docens modum faciendi non notum*).[39] Ultimately, *theorica* and *practica* are not very distinct for Corti, who emphasizes anatomical studies as fundamental for the physician. Indeed, his most famous work is a commentary on the anatomical work (Figure 7.1) of the famed Mondino de' Liuzzi (†1326).[40]

Benedetto Vittori

The close association of *theorica* and *practica* also emerges from the little-studied writings of Benedetto Vittori of Faenza (†1561), who after his doctorate in arts and medicine in 1503 proceeded through the usual range of subjects and taught medicine in Bologna from 1511 until his death, except for a period in Padua from 1532 to 1539.[41] In addition to several commentaries on Aristotle,[42] Vittori published works related both to *practica* and to *theorica.*[43] Although the commentary on *Prognostic* offers a well-ordered discussion of the nature of medicine in general (especially in its preface), Vittori's commentary on the *Aphorisms* (1556) is more relevant to the present topic. Of particular interest is the discussion of the famous first aphorism, *Vita brevis, ars vero longa*—a classic occasion to expatiate on the methodology of medicine.[44] Vittori often discounts the views of Avicenna (much preferring those of Galen and Hippocrates) and makes helpful points about medicine's dependence on both speculative principles and experience. The theoretical dimension of medicine emerges from the fact that it needs to be learned (*addisci*). Yet he encourages putting these teachings to the test with due regard for experience. This is complicated because "judgment derived from experience is fallacious and dangerous."[45] *Theorica* and *practica* therefore work closely together, although their exact relationship is not altogether clear.

Giovanni Zecchi

But the most unusual and influential discussion of *theorica* and *practica* is by Giovanni Zecchi (1533–1601), who emphasized the practical aims of medicine and argued that all of medicine is an art of the kind that produces something (i.e., health). Zecchi taught in his alma mater from 1559 to 1595, aside from a period in the Roman *studium* from 1588 to 1593.[46] Today he is seldom remembered, but Zecchi was one of the most famous medics of his day and served as personal physician to Popes Sixtus V and Clement VIII.[47] As primary (but not supraordinary) professor of theoretical medicine in Bologna, in 1586 Zecchi published his lectures on the first section of Hippocrates's *Aphorisms,* followed by his works on *De purgatione, De sanguinis missione, De criticis diebus,* and *De morbo Gallico.*[48] The editor of this volume, dedicated to the king of Poland, Stephanus Bartorius, was one of Zecchi's students, the colorful Scipione Mercuri (1540/1550?–1615?).[49] Mercuri adds to every lecture—which appears in abbreviated form—some scholia that clarify (or, at times, soften) Zecchi's statements.

Several aspects of Zecchi's commentary are notable, particularly in view of the perspectives of the interpreters already examined. For instance, Zecchi seems rather more interested than others in points of textual tradition and in the secure attribution of the *Aphorisms* to Hippocrates.[50] Thus he indicates three aspects of Hippocrates's style that mark out his work (*summa brevitas, veritas,* and *gravitas*) and refers to the understanding of *gravitas* by the Florentine philologist Pier Vettori. At the same time, with regard to Galen's statement that Hippocrates's sayings are like the voice of God, he notes that this "is absurd according to the Catholic truth."[51] Also, Zecchi implicitly contradicts Cardano by stating that there is no particular order to the aphorisms—not that this should be held against Hippocrates, since he was a busy practitioner and wrote them down whenever he could; presumably he did not have the time to reorder them.[52]

Especially relevant to the present discussion are Zecchi's comments in lectures one and two, covering Hippocrates's aphorism *Vita brevis, ars vero longa*. Given their significance, they are worth covering in some detail. When Zecchi starts discussing Hippocrates's intention, a standard section of the usual introductory comments to a work, he describes the Greek physician's aim as that of providing the general or universal principles of medicine (*universa medicinae praecepta*). Yet—he argues—Hippocrates limited himself in three ways: first, he presents only the less-known aspects of medicine, not other well-known ones such as anatomical dissection (whose knowledge, Zecchi concedes, is entirely necessary). Furthermore, Hippocrates only discusses principles that are related to practical medicine (*medicinae pars activa*). Thus, he does not discuss humors, temperaments, and other such matters. (Given that the *Aphorisms* were part of the teaching of *theorica,* this is quite a claim.) Finally, Hippocrates limits himself to matters that can be treated concisely; this explains why he does not discuss medical simples and other subjects that would require much more elaborate treatment.[53]

Zecchi's point that the *Aphorisms* provide "universal principles" should put one on guard, for Giambattista Da Monte (a famous professor of medicine at the University of Padua, 1489–1551) had similarly spoken of a "universal medicine" in his attempt to link together *theorica* and *practica* more tightly. He had done so by arguing—not entirely originally—that all of medicine (including *practica*) should be regarded as a science.[54] Furthermore, deploring the separations between *theorica* and *practica* common at his time, Da Monte advocated—possibly under the influence of the French medic Jean Fernel (1497–1558)—the teaching and study of all of Avicenna's *Canon,* I.[55] But Zecchi's approach is fundamentally different. Indeed, he has no qualms about declaring that medicine is, in fact, an *ars*—something that he anticipates in his gloss of *ars longa* in the first aphorism: "Art is a making or factive art (*habitus factivus*) accompanied by right reason according to Aristotle, *Nicomachean Ethics,* VI.5 . . . from which we deduce . . . that, according to Hippocrates, medicine is an art, not a science."[56]

Zecchi develops this point in his second lecture on Hippocrates. Here the classic doubt "Is medicine a science or an art?" rears its head, as the third of the five questions treated. Zecchi offers a clear, if bald, response: "All of medicine should be considered a making art; none of it is science."[57] Zecchi proves his point by appealing to authority and reason. Under the first heading, he refers to the consistent usage of Hippocrates and the somewhat less consistent usage of Galen (who, however, admits that he has used the term "science" for medicine improperly). Reason leads to the same conclusion because of medicine's subject (which considers beings or *entia* whose principles are external to them) and aim (which is directed to action). Zecchi also argues that if medicine were indeed a science, it would need to fit under one of the three speculative *scientiae* (theology, metaphysics or mathematics, and natural philosophy). But evidently none of these would be fitting—in the last case, "because Aristotle separated [medicine] from natural philosophy in that well-known saying 'Where the philosopher leaves off, the physician begins.'"[58] According to Zecchi, this distinction stems not from the differences between the objects considered by philosophy and medicine, but from their aims, "for the philosopher contemplates for the sake of the truth only, whereas the physician does so in order to turn his reflections to the business at hand, that is, health."[59] Whether Zecchi's colleagues in philosophy would have accepted this point is open to question; numerous commentators had noted Aristotle's treatment of ethics and medicine as practical disciplines, partly due to their shared consideration of the changing world of the contingent. Nonetheless, what is really significant is Zecchi's next move, which is to state that because medicine is not a science, it cannot therefore be divided into *theorica* and *practica*.[60] On this basis, all of medicine has an orientation toward practice.

One might see Zecchi's solution as a counterpart (but on a very different basis) to Da Monte's attempt to unite *theorica* and *practica*. Both of those efforts were doomed to failure. Just three years after Zecchi's lectures, one of his Bolognese colleagues, Giovanni Costeo (t. 1581–1598), maintained the scientific nature of *theorica* in particular, leading to a stronger separation between the two branches of medicine, even though he then tried to couple anatomy to *theorica*.[61] The rolls continued to distinguish *theorica* and *practica* until the end of the eighteenth century. Historians have regularly interpreted this point as a signal of curricular stasis and of the traditional perspectives of the college of doctors, which was allegedly resisting change in order to protect and promote its own interests. But examples such as Da Monte and Zecchi serve as reminders that some professors at least were suggesting different approaches.

Zecchi's clear demarcation of medicine and natural philosophy and his emphasis on medicine as *ars* left their mark in contemporary discussions. Especially relevant are the views of his Paduan colleagues Oddo Oddi (whose lectures on Hippocrates were published in 1564 and those on Avicenna in 1575) and Bernardino Paterno (whose commentary on Avicenna appeared posthumously in 1596).[62] Oddi (1478–1558) revisited the classification of the arts and bracketed together both medicine and building as arts producing a result, in the vein of Zecchi's "factive art." Nonetheless, he held that natural philosophy played a role in furnishing a foundation for medicine.[63] Paterno (†1592), on the other hand, emphasized the differences between philosophy and medicine, which he wished to separate as much as possible. Given their views of medicine as one of the *artes factivae,* it would be helpful to know the extent to which these Paduan professors were acquainted with Zecchi.[64] A later Paduan professor, Santorio Santorio (1561–1636), whose commentary on Hippocrates first appeared in 1629, also argued very much along Zecchi's lines. But his view of medicine as an art seems more strongly linked to the various instruments for which he is known—the pulsilogium, the thermoscope, and the weighing chair.[65]

Whatever Zecchi's influence on contemporary and future colleagues, he clearly left his mark on his student Mercuri, who placed him in the same class as other Bolognese giants of medicine such as Ulisse Aldrovandi (whom he credited with notable contributions to the study of Hippocrates) and the famed anatomist Giulio Cesare Aranzi.[66] At least in Bologna, Zecchi continued to be read and cited as an authority more than half a century later—and indeed to be considered on a par with Girolamo Mercuriale, to judge from the 1642 course outline by Ercole Betti.[67] He also enjoyed longer and more widespread attention outside of his native city due to his medical *consultationes.*[68]

Seventeenth and Eighteenth Centuries

The distinction between *theorica* and *practica* may have lost importance over time, even though it continued to inform the teaching rolls. A competing fivefold scheme (physiology, pathology, semiotics, hygiene, and therapy), derived from antiquity and championed in the *Institutiones me-*

dicinae (1611 and later) of the German medic Daniel Sennert (1572–1637), soon started circulating in Bologna.[69] The Scotch medic George Scharpe (t. 1634–1637) continued to divide medicine into *theorica* and *practica.* Yet he not only stressed their complementarity, but tried to marry the twofold and fivefold systems by assigning the first three elements (*physiologia, pathologia,* and *semiotices*) to *theorica* and the last two (*conservativa* and *curativa*) to *practica.*[70] The 1694 *Theses iatrophysicae* of Giovanni Battista Giraldo (who had graduated in 1687 and was evidently seeking a teaching appointment) divided medicine into *conservativa* and *curativa* only.[71] Giraldo stated that it was possible to disagree with Hippocrates while still respecting him and teaching his works. Some of his doctrines, Giraldo maintained, could not be considered true.[72]

Domenico Guglielmini, who left Bologna in 1698 to teach *theorica* in Padua until his death in 1710, emphasized instead the ties between medicine and experimental science.[73] In his Paduan lectures on Hippocrates he claimed that dividing medicine into branches that considered either how to maintain or how to re-establish health could work only *in abstracto.* From that perspective, of course, medicine might be regarded as a science. But Guglielmini preferred to refer to it as an *ars.* In his view, Hippocrates's aphorism *ars longa* in fact alluded to the slow accumulation of knowledge (over several generations and even centuries) necessary to establish the bases of the discipline of medicine. But Guglielmini's emphasis on medicine as *ars* is a red herring, as shown both by his numerous references to Francis Bacon (*Verulamus*) and by the importance he attributes to reason, observation, and experience in establishing this discipline. In the end, Guglielmini is less interested in medicine's classification than in ensuring that it proceeds by the methodology of experimental science.[74] As he argues in his prolusion against the exponents of empirical medicine, there is a natural marriage between medicine, mathematics, and philosophy, such that "the occupation of healing is nothing but a continuous activity of philosophizing, which must be carried out truly and solidly. Medical practice consists entirely in applying the theoretical part of medicine for the use and benefit of the sick."[75]

One supporter of this position in Bologna was the medical doctor Francesco Antonio Oretti (t. 1697–1737). In his 1730–1731 lecture plan on Hippocrates's *Aphorisms* (in particular, *ars longa*), Oretti dwells on the fact that modern medicine consists, not just in the interpretation of the ancients, but also in investigating the secrets of nature through, among other things, auxiliary sciences such as chemistry, mathematics, and anatomy. Tellingly, he refers to recent experimentalists such as Giovanni Alfonso Borelli.[76] Again, the debate's focus has shifted from the differences between *theorica* and *practica* to the methodology of acquiring medical knowledge and medicine's alliance with the experimental sciences.

7.2 Surgery and Anatomy

Bolognese discussions about *theorica* and *practica* informed discussions not only about the nature of medicine but also surgery and anatomy. It is worthwhile to revisit in more detail the institutional context of these two subjects (but see also §2.2.2 and §7.1.1) as well as to consider how professors of surgery and anatomy in Bologna—in particular, Berengario da Carpi and Gaspare Tagliacozzi—treated *theorica* and *practica*.

7.2.1 Institutional Considerations

Perhaps most importantly, in Italy learned surgeons were not too distant in training and status from learned physicians.[77] Although the 1405 statutes list the dispositions governing the teaching of surgery separately from those for medicine, surgery was a full-fledged university subject receiving "ordinary" teaching.[78] The fines referred to in the statutes hint that professors of medicine were not assiduous in frequenting the disputations put on by professors of surgery, yet the fact that these disputations were mandated points to the learned character of surgery. So do the examinations, based on passages of required textbooks, that students of surgery needed to pass.[79] Such students also doubtless followed the rest of the medical curriculum.

Surgery professors were in charge of the anatomical demonstrations put on in the winter months to supply students and other onlookers with refined knowledge of the human body. Yet anatomy did not gain an independent chair until 1570, when the Senate finally acceded to the request made by the professor of surgery Giulio Cesare Aranzi ten years earlier.[80] Even then, it often played second fiddle to surgery and struggled to achieve independence. One should not imagine, on this basis, that Bologna did not have a long and distinguished tradition in this area. One of its most renowned teachers was Mondino de' Liuzzi (†1326),

Fig 7.1. Mondino de' Liuzzi, *Anathomia Mun[d]ini* ([Leipzig: Martin Landsberg], 1493). Frontispiece with woodcut and later coloring. Private collection.

whose *Anatomia* was the main textbook for teaching the subject for around three centuries, including outside of Italy (see Figure 7.1).[81] Anatomy also makes several appearances in the university statutes (1405 and 1561), as well as in dispositions relating to the provision of cadavers in at least 1697 and 1737.[82] Its high number of teachers, particularly compared to central European universities, is a further sign of its importance.[83] But the number of anatomy teachers was also highly variable: in the 1590s the rolls usually indicate three or four professors each for surgery and anatomy. In the second half of the seventeenth century, the rolls list many names under the heading *ad anatomen* (presumably to help with the anatomical demonstrations), but there is usually just one actual professor of anatomy.[84] After the *studium*'s reform of 1737, the rolls typically list two professors of surgery (teaching on different subjects) and three or four professors of anatomy. The latter occupied both the first and the second morning teaching hours.[85]

Like medicine and surgery, anatomy had both its theoretical and its practical sides. The difference was that they were both exercised in the university context (as opposed to medicine, for instance, where clinical practice took place outside of it). From November 1607, students and citizens could enjoy a new style of public dissection—the "funzione pubblica di Anatomia disputabile." There had always been an element of public interest in the university's dissections of cadavers, and learned medicine was also a prominent aspect of these performances. What was new, however, was the cycle of public lectures (eventually amounting to sixteen) and the disputations and responses by the attendees.[86] These events took place in the university's stable anatomical theater, built in the Archiginnasio in 1595 and then transferred to the larger classroom next door, which was fully completed in 1649.[87] The new space—which eventually housed twelve statues of famous medics (Hippocrates and Galen in addition to ten local "greats," such as Giovanni Girolamo Sbaraglia and Gaspare Tagliacozzi)—made it easier to welcome the crowds that made of this dissection an urban and academic festivity (see Figures 7.2a and 7.2b).[88]

It is not straightforward to uncover the exact contents and approaches of classroom teaching in either surgery or anatomy. Documents from the Riformatori dello Studio indicate that, around 1586, a four-year cycle of surgery lectures was to treat *De tumoribus, De ulceribus, De vulneribus,* and *De luxatis et fracturis,* respectively.[89] It is not clear, however, whether a professor was to use specific textbooks in these explanations of tumors, ulcers, wounds, and fractures, although the titles could well allude to homonymous works in the Galenic and Hippocratic traditions and, possibly, by Paul of Aegina.[90] The rolls, however, suggest that

Fig 7.2a. Final lecture of the public demonstration of anatomy in the Anatomy Theater, Palazzo dell'Archiginnasio, with Laura Bassi taking part.

Miniature (395 × 527 mm) on parchment, Bernardino Sconzani, November / December 1734. Archivio di Stato di Bologna, Insignia degli Anziani, vol. XIII, f. 105r.

Fig 7.2b. Anatomy Theater, Palazzo dell'Archiginnasio.

Photo © David Lines.

a cycle developed for only the first three of these. Similarly, information for anatomy is scarce, although a bit less so with the lecture outlines in the Serie di Annue Lezioni. It would be helpful to know whether works that became newly or better known in the sixteenth century (such as Galen's *On the Usefulness of the Parts of the Body* and *On Anatomical Procedures*) became part of the regular curriculum.[91]

7.2.2 Treatments of *Scientia* and *Ars*

The fifteenth and sixteenth centuries featured lively discussions about the nature of surgery and anatomy within the framework of *scientia* and *ars*. This was hardly a new topic, since it had immediate antecedents in the writings of important personalities such as Dino del Garbo of Florence (†1327).[92] But for the period covered by this book, the most relevant comments are those of Berengario da Carpi and Tagliacozzi. Both of these figures offer rich insights into the developing understandings and practices of anatomy and surgery.

Anatomy

Jacobo Berengario da Carpi (†1530) emphasized the theoretical and scientific aspects of anatomy, tying it closely to the realm of medical knowledge and stating that it had to be learned both from books and from experience. Berengario taught ordinary surgery in Bologna from 1502 to 1527. His 1521 commentary on the *Anatomy* of Mondino de' Liuzzi was a work of long-lasting influence.[93] This is not the place to discuss Berengario's contribution to Renaissance practices of anatomy and surgery or the value of this work's illustrations of the human body (a significant innovation) as a model for later writings.[94] These aspects have given support to a widespread view that Berengario gave considerable attention to the power and importance of observation.[95] This point is not in dispute here. But his prefatory comments are also notable for their discussion of the relationship of anatomy and *theorica*.

Already the dedicatory letter to Cardinal Giulio de' Medici suggests that Berengario will explain "the things that we have disseminated and learned *with experience as our teacher*" (*magistra experientia*, emphasis added, f. 2r) and "sensation as our constant guide" (*dux semper sensu*, f. 4r). This would seem to give his work a character of strong dependence on sensory observation, particularly when, among discordant opinions, sensation is seen as the ultimate arbiter.[96] Yet he also notes that he has chosen

Mondino as his guide (*dux*) and light (*lumen*), and that he will therefore expound Mondino's writings—although he will, when necessary, be unorthodox in settling or reconciling discordant opinions (ff. 2v, 4r). To this powerful reminder that—even in areas such as anatomy—learned medical culture was heavily dependent on books, one should add his comments prefacing his explanation of Mondino's work.

Of these, the most relevant sections are those on the usefulness, necessity, and nature of anatomy. Berengario first addresses the criticisms of those who note that a dead body is quite different from a living one and therefore hold that anatomy is neither necessary nor useful—an objection that Empiricists continued to air some two centuries later (see below). What is striking here is how often the lemma *cognoscere* appears, along with its cognates, pointing to anatomy as a form of knowledge.[97] Berengario assigns to anatomical knowledge the function of revealing the illnesses (*aegritudines*) of the internal members of the body. Furthermore, this knowledge contributes to the healing of bodies and their retention in health.[98] Indeed, for Berengario anatomy is so fundamental that he considers it the physician's alphabet and the first thing to be studied (f. 5v). This metaphor might suggest that anatomy is therefore also introductory, instrumental, and lacking in scientific value, but Berengario combats that impression in the next section, when he discusses the nature of anatomy. One could see anatomy simply as the act of cutting and exposing the hidden aspects of the body (from this perspective, it would be neither a theoretical nor a practical science, but simply an action or *operatio,* f. 6r). But it is better, Berengario says, to take it for what it is—a *scientia.* It is so in a double sense: first, because "by it both the simple and the composite members and their operations, compositions, relations, places, and the like are known [*cognoscuntur*]," and secondly because anatomy "is the science of knowing [*cognitionis*] the [body's] members and of transmitting [to others] how to perform manual operations and demonstrations of those same members."[99] Although Averroes privileged the latter sense and therefore connected anatomy with practical medicine, Berengario argues that in both cases it belongs undoubtedly to the theoretical branch, as held by Avicenna. He quickly sets aside as irrelevant the question of whether it is more of an art or a science.[100]

The theoretical nature of anatomy also figures prominently when Berengario explores what makes a good anatomist (ff. 6v–7r). Here he does underline the importance of observation (*visus et tactus*) and the need to acquire scientific knowledge (*scientia*) by examining, for instance, the fetuses of various species of animals. But—apart from the fact that this approach is hardly new, since Berengario appeals to the example of Galen—Berengario also emphasizes the role of theoretical knowledge. Indeed, he holds that "first of all and above all, [the good anatomist] must be learned in the science of medicine and its allied areas; he must delight in reading, over and over again, what Aristotle, Galen, Avicenna, and others said about both live and dead animals, and what the more recent [writers] have said."[101] This point is important because, as we learn later, the senses can be deceptive. Comparing one's own experience both with the authorities and with others who are versed in anatomy makes it possible to see things that a single individual cannot (f. 7r). Anatomy is therefore a science that one learns both from books and from sense experience.[102] Exercising it takes place within a community of learned men joined by a common tradition. This viewpoint does not prevent Berengario from disagreeing (albeit respectfully) with authority, particularly when it comes to matters such as the retiform plexus (*rete mirabile*) supposedly observed by Galen.[103] French rightly notes that, for Berengario, "Where sense and authority agree, all is well, but where it can be seen that sense cannot be made to agree with the authorities, they must be rejected."[104]

This union of learned medicine and observation receives visual expression in several works of the time, including Mondino's *Anatomia* (Figure 7.1) and Berengario's *Isagogae*.[105] These show that the explanation of an anatomical textbook would inform the actual cutting of a body. Nancy Siraisi is right to caution against deducing from such depictions that anatomy professors necessarily had others take care of the actual work of dissection.[106] But the union of theory and practice is clear even in the supposedly revolutionary work on anatomy by Andreas Vesalius (who, however, seems quite unconcerned with the relationship of anatomy to theory or practice).[107] One also notes it in various contemporary attempts to insert anatomy formally within the teaching of *theorica*.

Surgery

Like anatomy, surgery too had strong links with theoretical knowledge. These ties partly reflected the influence of the Galenic ideal of the unity of medicine in treatises such as the *Method of Healing* (which circulated mainly in Thomas Linacre's translation, first published in 1519) and the—now considered spurious—*Introduction* (translated by Guenther of Andernacht in 1528). These and other works stressed the connections between book knowledge, practice, and experience.[108] Developments throughout the sixteenth century (in France as well as Italy) suggest both a broadening of the domain of surgery and the perceived need for surgeons to be trained in the *Aphorisms* of Hippocrates and Galenic method.[109] Particularly in France, the vernacular played an important but understudied role in the movement to exalt surgery as the culmination of medicine, as the works of Ambroise Paré (1510–1590) and Jacques Dalechamps (1513–1588) indicate.[110] The barber-surgeon Paré emphasized his distance from bookish learning as he dealt with the new problem of gunshot wounds.[111] But in many other cases the connections between medicine and surgery became more prominent, and surgery remained rooted in theory while also becoming more independent.

In Italy, Hippocrates played an important role in surgery. The work of translators and commentators such as the Florentine Vidus Vidius (or Guido Guidi, 1509–1569) on Hippocrates underscored and reconstructed on the page (through 210 woodcut illustrations in an in-folio volume) Greek tools and instruments for surgical practice, thus providing models for its readers.[112] In Bologna, Giulio Cesare Aranzi (1530–1589), nephew of the famous professor of surgery Bartolomeo Maggi, prepared a less expensive work on Hippocrates's *On Wounds in the Head.* Edited from his lectures by Aranzi's student Claude Porral, this volume—printed in Lyon in 1579—tried to transmit to surgeons of his time the best ways to cure particular head wounds on the basis of ancient precedent.[113] The work's lack of illustrations should not make one blind to its "severe practicality" (as Vivian Nuttton has described it) and to the fact that its focus on Hippocrates does not result in a merely antiquarian interest.[114] A further witness to Aranzi's outlook is his *De humano foetu* (first published in Bologna in 1564). Later editions of the work also included his *Anatomicae observationes* and *De tumoribus praeter naturam.*[115]

For the purposes of this study, the most relevant practitioner and professor of surgery in sixteenth-century Bologna was Gaspare Tagliacozzi (1545–1599).[116] A student of Aranzi (from whom he learned elements of rhinoplastic technique), Tagliacozzi became famous for his contributions to plastic surgery and facial reconstructions or repairs, feeding into a broader interest of the period in these areas.[117] Here, however, Tagliacozzi deserves consideration for the way in which he moved between theory and practice. Already in 1568, two years before his graduation in medicine, he was offering care to patients at the Ospedale della Morte (an institution abutting the Archiginnasio).[118] Furthermore, like other doctors of medicine, Tagliacozzi supplemented his rather meager university salary through private practice. Already before his marriage in 1574, he had a consulting room in his mother's house. He was also much in demand as a physician, both in Bologna and in other cities.[119] All of this points to an interest in clinical practice alongside his university studies and teaching, yet one should be cautious about generalizing from it. Certainly Tagliacozzi did not decide that learned medicine was not worth pursuing: although he initially taught surgery (1570–1590), after the death of his mentor Aranzi in 1589 he added to this the teaching of anatomy and (from 1590 onward) *theorica*. He continued to teach the last two subjects together until his death, leaving the official teaching of surgery behind.[120]

Most relevant for the discussion of theory and practice is Tagliacozzi's masterpiece, *De curtorum chirurgia per insitionem* (On the surgical restoration of defects by grafting), published in 1597. The work's two main parts address the theory and the practice of surgery, respectively.[121] The first of these gives an explanation of the reasons the various parts of the face are so important, as well as an account of the safety of various surgical techniques, whereas the second provides step-by-step instructions on how to carry out various operations. Both parts of the work are illustrated (the second especially so). In the first part, Tagliacozzi complements his discussion of nose operations with a striking figure representing the geometrical and mathematical considerations involved (Figure 7.3).

Tagliacozzi does not, however, attempt to turn the area of surgery into a science. Rather, in his dedicatory letter to the Duke of Mantua Vincenzo Gonzaga he states his desire to elevate it to that of a true art. Most telling is the following statement: "I believe that I have accomplished this much, not only to have been useful in treating people but to have brought this area [of surgery] at last to the true level of an art, so that it can be transmitted in writings and any man, even one of only moderate skill, can safely and successfully operate with its rules before

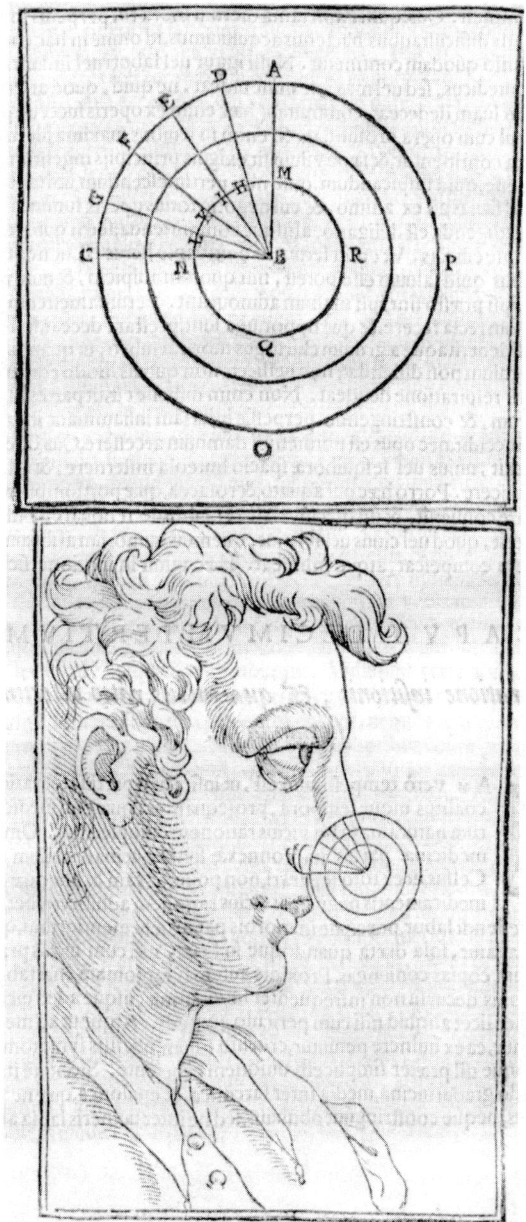

Fig 7.3. Woodcut illustration for an operation of nose surgery.

Gaspare Tagliacozzi, *De curtorum chirurgia per insitionem* (Venice: Gaspare Bindoni Jr., 1597), 57. London Wellcome Collection, CC BY 4.0.

him."[122] As Tagliacozzi explains, the status of plastic surgery as an art does not mean that it cannot operate without principles, drawn in combination from the writings of the ancients and of experience. Nor does it suggest that it cannot be communicated and taught. In these comments, he takes it for granted that *ars* now refers to a highly respectable skill, based on certain knowledge. It is for this reason that he is disparaging of the "so-called art" of a group of practitioners in Tropea (Calabria), who proceeded more "by irregular and haphazard methods than methods based on reason."[123] In the same way, the opening pages of the work argue that if there is no shame in describing medicine as an art (or, indeed, as the most excellent one), surely the same attitude needs to be taken toward surgery and the realm of *operatio*.[124]

It is unknown whether Tagliacozzi was drawing from or alluding to the work of his colleague Zecchi in advancing his view of medicine more generally (but surgery as well) as an art.[125] Nonetheless, Tagliacozzi saw the rules and the practice of surgery as closely related. There was not yet a sense that the insights of the ancients should be thrown overboard as somehow irrelevant.

7.3 Discussions of the Late Seventeenth and Early Eighteenth Centuries

In the seventeenth and early eighteenth centuries, the understanding and practice of medicine underwent momentous changes throughout Europe. William Harvey's *De motu cordis,* positing the circulation of blood, appeared in 1628; Paracelsianism continued to be influential and became a rival to Galenism; the mechanical philosophy of Descartes was quickly gaining new adherents; the new science, supported by numerous new societies and academies, proposed that observation, experimentation, and mathematics held the key to advances in knowledge; as a result, the status of the ancients, as providing the foundation for philosophical and medical systems, came under threat.[126] Many of the proponents of these new viewpoints came from outside of the Italian Peninsula. One may wonder how the representatives of learned medical culture in Bologna responded. The answer is especially clear in the cases of Marcello Malpighi (1628–1694) and Luigi Ferdinando Marsili (1658–1730), two men of exceptional importance for the development of the *studium* between the second half of the seventeenth century and the first half of the eighteenth. Because discussions of *theorica* and *practica* had by now taken a backseat, what follows focuses on the relationship between theoretical and clinical medicine, or indeed, between theoretical subjects *tout court* and their practical correspondents or applications. These were issues discussed in connection with the purpose of the university more generally.

7.3.1 Marcello Malpighi

For some scholars, Malpighi is (quite rightly) a symbol of the influence of new approaches in seventeenth-century Bologna, particularly in his emphasis on the importance of mechanistic philosophy and scientific instruments to medicine. While not discounting this aspect, here it is more relevant to note his conviction—shared with many predecessors and contemporaries—that theoretical knowledge is inseparable from clinical applications. The main point that differentiated Malpighi from colleagues in Bologna was his view of what kind of theoretical knowledge is relevant to, and useful for, practice. Also relevant is how one gains such knowledge in the first place.

Malpighi hailed from Crevalcore and did his university studies in nearby Bologna, graduating in 1653. In his student years he attended the private anatomy lectures held by his teacher Bartolomeo Massari in the Coro Anatomico academy, which met in Massari's home. Already at that time tensions were simmering between medical factions that pitted more conservative professors against experimentalists and others. It may have been the hostility of some professors that led Malpighi to spend periods away from Bologna, as a teacher in Pisa (1656–1659, when he became friends with the famed physiologist, physicist, and mathematician Giovanni Alfonso Borelli) and later Messina (1662–1666). But Bologna remained very much his home base—so much so that he continued to be listed on the rolls even during these years of absence—and Malpighi took an active part in the controversies there. He made enemies both because of his opposition to the reform plan of the Archdeacon Antonio Felice Marsili (see §2.3) and because of his spirited writings against his more conservative colleagues.

Particularly telling is Malpighi's confrontation in the late 1680s with his colleague and main Bolognese opponent, the Empiricist Giovanni Girolamo Sbaraglia (t. 1664–1710).[127] By this time Malpighi had become famous for his work on the tissue of the lungs (which conclusively proved Harvey's theory of the circulation of blood), for his anatomical discoveries with the aid of the microscope, and for his studies of plant respiration. In 1669 he had also been made a fellow of the Royal Society in London. But none of these achievements could protect him from long-standing rivalries and disagreements. The dispute with Sbaraglia—intensified by *studium* politics and family rivalries—is well known, but it is worth analyzing because of the light it sheds on different understandings of medicine.

In 1687 Sbaraglia anonymously published *De recentiorum medicorum studio: Dissertatio epistolaris ad amicum* (The studies of recent medics: A treatise in the form of a letter to a friend).[128] The work, which does not name Malpighi explicitly, argues that the three kinds of more recent anatomy (*subtilior anatomen, anatomen comparata,* and *dendranatomen*) may have their merits, but contribute little or nothing to *medicina practica* (by which he means clinical medicine). Sbaraglia states that the study of minute parts with the assistance of the microscope is an example of empty curiosity (*curiositas*) without any usefulness (*utilitas*) to the art of healing. Discoveries in animal anatomy may inform natural history, but hardly speak to the art of the clinician. Likewise, the study of plants has little relevance for actually curing the sick. An important consideration is that "philosophizing and healing are two different things" (*aliud est philosophari, aliud mederi*), a point that goes to the heart of Malpighi's method.[129]

It is easy to scoff at treatises such as Sbaraglia's, which ended up on the "wrong" side of history. But his comments are valuable for the emphasis he correctly assumed his contemporaries would place on the success of healing. Malpighi's lengthy reply (published in both Latin and Italian) treats bodies as machines whose structures need to be understood and appreciated if they are to be regulated and repaired.[130] Malpighi's approach underlined the investigation of signs, causes, and *indicationes.*[131] But his goal of healing was ultimately the same as Sbaraglia's, and one should not divorce his theoretical interests from his activity in the realm of therapeutics and clinical practice.[132] From 1691 until his death in 1694 he served as archiater (chief personal physician) to Pope Innocent XII. Furthermore, from at least the 1670s, he issued a large number of medical consultations (*consilia*).[133] These gave considerable attention to the probable causes of the symptoms communicated by a patient's physician, but then went on—often on the basis of Malpighi's anatomical studies—to list *indicationes* and remedies, including where to find the required preparations. This point reinforces the impression that, although in principle there could be strong institutional (as well as social and reputational) divisions between medical theory and clinical practice, matters on the ground could be considerably more fluid.[134] They also confirm the exalted place that the practice of medicine had gained by the early seventeenth century.

Due to the institutional tensions mentioned above, in Bologna Malpighi only taught medicine—never anatomy. Yet his legacy lived on in some of his students. An especially devoted one was Giacomo Sandri (1657–1718), who, after taking his degree in arts and medicine in 1680, went on to teach logic (1691–1694) and then surgery (and often anatomy) from 1694 to 1717. The Accademia degli Inquieti—which attracted a considerable number of medical doctors—often met in his home from 1694 to 1704.[135] Fortuitously, in Sandri's case the extant documentation includes both the outlines of his lectures in the Serie di Annue Lezioni and actual lectures, both of which are in need of careful study.[136]

The neatest part of Sandri's production is in his lecture plans, where, for instance, he provides a very detailed outline of his 1709–1710 lectures in surgery on tumors (*De tumoribus praeter naturam*).[137] There, he ties surgery together with all the *scientiae physiologicae,* and in particular with chemistry and anatomy, but also goes on to show that developing a "rational" surgery requires a knowledge of matter and motion, as well as a certain understanding of mechanics (*notitia mechanica,* f. 8r–v). As he shows later (f. 10v), an understanding of anatomy and reproductive processes is also relevant to the discussion of tumors. (This point had been a bone of contention between Malpighi and Sbaraglia.) Thus Sandri shows his support for Malpighi's interest in scientific topics that did not always seem immediately relevant to clinical applications.

7.3.2 Luigi Ferdinando Marsili

But the relationship between theory and practice was not just the object of medical discussions: it increasingly became an issue in broader conversations and proposals about the direction of the university as a whole. Most telling among these was the initiative of the naturalist (and former general) Luigi Ferdinando Marsili, who returned to Bologna in 1708 after years of travel and military operations and led a determined—if controversial—campaign to reform the university.[138] Like Sandri, Marsili had studied in the Bolognese *studium* and was strongly influenced by his teacher Malpighi, though he probably did not complete his studies. He was conversant with contemporary cultural and scientific issues—so much so that he published various treatises and eventually became highly esteemed for his scientific endeavors. (He was made a fellow of both the Royal Society and the Académie des Sciences in Paris.) In the course of his extensive travels (some of them connected with military campaigns), he made a point of acquiring books and instruments that would benefit scientific activity in Bologna (see §4.2.2). Nonetheless, his cultural orientation very much emphasized practical subjects and applications, as his proposed reform of the university indicates.

In his *Parallelo sullo stato moderno della università di Bologna con le altre di là dai monti* (Comparison between the current state of the University of Bologna and others beyond the Alps, 1709), Marsili applied his considerable international experience to what he believed to be the university's main problems. Among the various subjects, he gave particular attention to medicine and mathematics.[139] In the case of medicine, he made no comment about *theorica* and *practica,* but auspicated two main changes: a much stronger emphasis on anatomy, and the establishment of a chair of chemistry. He proposed the introduction of three winter courses for anatomy (including both the visualization of the parts of the body and experimentation on them), plus a fourth one geared (as in Montpellier) to the surgeons. These would replace the all-too-brief demonstrations (seven to ten days) given over to the public dissections. Regarding his second major proposal, concerning chemistry, Marsili claimed that the nature of fluids was known in Bologna only at a remove, through foreign books, and that experimentation was in fact essential. He therefore strongly pushed for the establishment of a chair of chemistry (ideally in combination with physics), something that he felt would be of particular importance for the discovery of new medicines. Although the *Parallelo* also mentions other subjects, such as physics, botany, secular history, Greek, and Oriental languages, Marsili's second major area of concern was mathematics, a field that in his view merited four main chairs. He distributed these in algebra (not Euclidean geometry), astronomy (cultivated through observation), physical matters demonstrated by geometry, and practical mathematics (including mechanics, military and civilian architecture, perspective, planimetry, arithmetic, geometry, and military matters, perhaps including engineering). He described this subject as "the most useful for our children."[140]

Although these proposals place a strong emphasis on observation and experimentation, one should not imagine that Marsili was suggesting that the university be converted into a technical institute: he despised neither books (indeed, he proposed to donate his library to the city) nor, apparently, the standard disputations on various subjects (even anatomy).[141] Rather, he hoped that the university would be a place in which both great learning and experimentalism could be combined. In fact, matters turned out rather differently: turned down by the city authorities, his proposal in the end found success only in the establishment of a distinct Istituto delle Scienze (opened in 1714 with the support of Pope Clement XI in the teeth of local opposition). The Istituto was complementary to the university, but already its statutes formalized a strong division between the lectures delivered in the Archiginnasio's classrooms and the experiments or exercises (*esercizi*) to take place in the Istituto's premises in Palazzo Poggi (currently in Via Zamboni 33).[142]

Some commentators have seen the resistance to Marsili's original proposal as a failure on the part of the university (or, more precisely, its professors) to embrace a modern, experimental, and practical orientation to learning. In this view, the *studium* therefore limped on as it followed its traditional emphasis on theory and outdated books, while the Istituto became a beacon of innovation and proved that change was possible only outside of Bologna's university structures. There are, however, several reasons for nuancing this interpretation. First, opposition to Marsili's original proposal was due to a complex set of circumstances, including his commandeering attitude and poor relations with the *studium* authorities. It cannot be attributed solely to the self-interest of the doctoral colleges. Second, many of the Istituto's members were also university professors. It is hard to believe that they were conservative in one context but innovative in the other. Furthermore, the Istituto itself was devoted to experimentalism, but not necessarily to *practical* learning. Indeed, Marsili had envisaged an even more practical function for the Istituto, which was supposed to issue in the application of scientific knowledge to the mechanical arts and technology in ways beneficial to the city and its territory. But this aim was never achieved.[143] Finally, the members of the Istituto themselves were not necessarily among the most enlightened, and their emphasis on "social value" sometimes led them to odd conclusions. A case in point is Geminiano Rondelli (the second holder of the chair in hydrometry, 1698–1730), whose dissertations presented to Bologna's Accademia delle Scienze in 1718 and 1720 dismissed algebra and infinitesimal analysis because of a supposed lack of benefit to society—a salutary lesson for modern research bodies and the governments funding them![144]

Two further points deserve attention. One is that we do not know enough about the content of university lectures in this period to say whether and to what extent they were theoretical or traditional. (This would be a fertile field for future research.) Nonetheless, there are indications that changes were afoot. Many of these highlighted the necessary links between university teaching and practical outcomes. The establishment of Bologna's chair in hydrometry (1695–1696), for example, derived from the very pressing and practical challenges being faced by the city at the time—a potential project was being discussed to link the local river Reno as a tributary to the much more important Po.[145] The career of Pier Paolo Molinelli, who held the first Europe-wide chair of practical surgery (*De chirurgicis operationibus*) from 1732 is also relevant. Molinelli appears initially on the university rolls, although later (1742)—due to a specific request on his part—he joined the staff of the Istituto as a teacher of surgical techniques (*medicina operatoria*).[146] The text of Molinelli's 1741 request is notable for, among other things, its clear comments on the complementary relationship between anatomical knowledge (i.e., his university teaching) and surgical practice.[147] Finally, the year 1737 saw significant events, such as the establishment of the chair of chemistry proposed by Marsili. Its first holder was Iacopo Bartolomeo Beccari, who also taught ordinary medicine. There was a shift in the nomenclature of other subjects, such as natural philosophy, whose principles were declared in lecture courses but demonstrated through experimentation (see §3.2). In all of these cases, university teaching was hardly irrelevant to practical applications. Instead it was foundational to them, in the same way as Malpighi, Sbaraglia, and others agreed that learned medicine had to provide the principles for healing patients.

Finally, one should remember that early modern universities were places of teaching rather than research. Marsili's proposal was undoubtedly ahead of its times, but—even with its concession to exercises such as disputations—it failed to take into account that universities did not understand their purpose to be the making of new discoveries. Rather, they served (as scholars including Laurence Brockliss have noted) to share with their students the most important notions and approaches—new or old—in various fields.[148] Such, at least, was the view of the conservative party in Bologna, and Archdeacon Marsili expressed this well when he elaborated his own proposals in 1689, as he sought to reward the *studium*'s best teachers.[149] European universities did not reorient themselves toward research until the nineteenth century.

Conclusion

In Bologna the relationship of theory and practice in medicine was nuanced and complex. It is true that the marriage of medical study with clinical practice did not become an explicit requirement for medical degree candidates until the nineteenth century. Yet, as we have seen with Tagliacozzi, clinical training was available in local hospitals long before then. Scholars such as Elena Brambilla have also observed that the medical degree was not so much the end of one's training as a point of passage to its practical phase—it continued in a sort of traineeship under the guidance of a more senior physician within a clinical practice.[150] University professors were very much aware that their discipline's more theoretical elements needed to give rise to effective treatments. Some, like Zecchi and Tagliacozzi, even went so far as to describe medicine as an art, although a most noble one. There were disagreements about the foundations of medicine: some placed them in *medicina theorica,* while others increasingly in experiment (Sbaraglia) or microscopic anatomy (Malpighi). But no one suggested that one should focus exclusively on either theory or practice: the two belonged together. In the same way (at least in the minds of some professors), bookish learning and experimentation were two sides of the same coin.[151]

That did not, however, mean that the university needed to provide the context for *operatio* as well as *disputatio.* Clinical settings and engineering sites (but also the Istituto's premises) lay beyond the walls of the Archiginnasio for a good reason. Professors were aware that their main function was to provide a training in the art of reasoning and of distinguishing true from false opinions. They applied this training to specific fields, enabling future medics, for instance, to become familiar with the strengths and weaknesses of past theories and approaches. By so doing, they built up a conceptual armory that would be essential when their trainees confronted real-life cases, whether in medicine or other areas. The step of learning theory, however, remained essential, otherwise what would practice draw on? Perhaps such a setup made for a compartmentalized approach to their discipline. Yet professors seem to have been perfectly capable of focusing on the theoretical elements of medicine within the teaching setting, and on the practical ones outside of it. A strong foundation in concepts, knowledge, and debate before moving to applications ensured a close and strong alliance between theory and practice.

But perhaps the most significant insight of this chapter is that university professors were not content to accept—and meekly follow—inherited notions about their disciplines. The examples of Zecchi and Tagliacozzi in particular show them questioning and reconceptualizing fundamental ideas about the nature of medicine. Recent studies have shown that medicine was being rethought in its relationship to the sciences throughout Italy.[152] The same kinds of processes were taking place in other fields, as professors regularly discussed the nature of theoretical versus practical philosophy and humanities instructors revisited the aims and foundations of their own studies. As we saw in Chapter 6, questions also intensified about the borders between certain disciplines and others (for instance, between astrology and mathematics). Here again, a traditional historiography has failed to capture the complexity, the intellectual independence, and especially the changes that were possible within the university environment, even when professors saw it as their main aim to communicate a body of knowledge. As Chapter 8 shows, these changes were not always related to developments within the disciplines but could be related to broader cultural trends.

8

The Religious Turn

As illustrated in earlier chapters, Bologna's faculty of arts and medicine traditionally included the areas of humanities, philosophy, and medicine, in addition to the study of astrology and mathematics. But one of the most notable developments in the early modern period was the establishment of theology alongside these other subjects—not only as an area of study, but as a point of reference for other disciplines. The most visible manifestation of this change was the rise in chairs for theology and related subjects. But other subjects within arts and medicine (particularly philosophy) came to reflect a religious turn: sixteenth-century discussions about the immortality of the soul, for instance, both grappled with the question of the respective spheres of philosophy and faith and evinced a deeply religious outlook. Between 1650 and 1750 religious and theological concerns became even more influential, especially in areas such as science and medicine. Equally importantly, the prevailing culture of piety and religious devotion affected professors and students as much as others in Bolognese society.

The "religious turn" referred to in this chapter's title requires some clarification. It does not allude to the exercise of power by religious figures such as (arch)bishops and papal legates in Bologna, who were often in tension with each other and the city's Senate or even at times in an adversarial relationship with the Holy See (see §1.3).[1] Nor does it primarily concern the development of local religious institutions or even larger topics within religious history such as heterodoxy, the efficacy of the Inquisition's Holy Office and the Index of Prohibited Books, or the practice of (self-)censorship (all of which I only touch on here).[2] Rather, this chapter starts from the observation that Bologna (already a religious town) became a much more ecclesiastical city in the early modern period. Presenting itself as a second Jerusalem, it attracted numerous new religious orders and confraternities, particularly between the 1540s and 1620s.[3] The proportion of priests and clerics rose to high levels in the late seventeenth century; they served not only in Bolognese churches, but also as teachers in public schools or as private tutors.[4] At the same time, devotions to St. Dominic and to female saints such as the Virgin Mary and Caterina Vigri, together with processions, public preaching, and a culture that placed high value on relics, religious music, and spiritual painting, speak to a town utterly drenched in religious sentiment.[5] How, if at all, did this climate affect the organization and delivery of university teaching, or the attitudes of professors and students? Did they consider religion as a form of social control imposed from above and therefore resist it, or did they engage with and embrace it?[6] A broader and deeper study of the topic remains a *desideratum* for early modern universities.[7] This chapter suggests that early modern Bologna provides an unusual example of university-based "learned devotion." This was not in opposition to or in tension with popular devotional practices or attitudes.[8] Instead it was the manifestation of a more general religious spirit and devotional culture that came to permeate all strata of Bolognese society, including the university.

8.1 The New Status of Theology

As suggested in §2.1, Bologna's faculty structures made it and other Italian universities considerably different from those following the model of Paris, which included a higher, separate, and sometimes domineering faculty of theology. For a long time, medicine—along with natural philosophy and rhetoric—was the dominant subject in arts and medicine. Unlike Padua, there was no consistent tradition of teaching theology in Bologna's *studium*.[9] Although a theology faculty was established in the 1360s, it did not have the same function or status as the faculties of law or arts and medicine.[10] Rather, it was a doctoral commission that depended on the teaching imparted by the various religious *studia* in the town and granted degrees. Theology rarely appeared on the teaching rolls.[11]

From the second half of the sixteenth century onward, however, this picture changed dramatically. A study of the first complete official teaching roll of arts and medicine to survive (1438–1439) versus the last one for our period (1749–1750) yields telling contrasts.[12] The number of specific teachings (bearing designations such as *philosophia naturalis extraordinaria*) balloons especially in the seventeenth and eighteenth centuries, as does the number of professors listed (see §2.3). But most striking is the growth in the number of teachings on and related to theology (*theologia moralis, lectura Sacrae scripturae, theologia scholastica, theologia dogmatica, lectura Historiae ecclesiasticae, lectura Conciliorum,* metaphysics, Hebrew, and *particulae hebraicae*).[13] The proportion of lecturers who are priests, monks, or regulars also rises sharply: eventually, they represent a third of the teachers listed in a particular year (Table 8.1). Benedict XIV's appointment of twenty-four (later, twenty-five) "Benedictines" within the Accademia delle Scienze to mark his interest in the Academy (see §2.3.4) was also an indication of mounting ecclesiastical control by the archbishop and papal legate.

This growth in the number of professors who were either priests or tied to religious orders may not seem noteworthy, given the increment in theology-related subjects. But clerics taught regular arts subjects as well as theological ones. (There was a long-standing prohibition against regulars teaching medicine.) In 1649–1650, for instance, the Franciscan Domenico Valla was one of those teaching *philosophia extraordinaria* (*De coelo*) in the afternoon; the Carmelite Giovanni Ricci lectured on mathematics. Likewise, a century later Charles Hébert, a member of the order of St. Jerome, taught physics. Others taught moral philosophy (Pater Aloysius Maria Sambucetti, Hercules Antonius Cossinus *canonicus*), mechanics (Pater D. Abundius Collina), and logic (Pater Bonifacius Collina, Pater Ioannes Baptista Grossius).[14] This development mirrors, to some extent, the considerable growth in the number of clerics and regulars in Bologna.

Table 8.1 Teaching patterns in theology, 1438–1750

	1438–1439	1549–1550	1649–1650	1749–1750
Teachings	15	18	27	44
Theology-related	–	1 (metaphysics)	5	9
Professors	31	37	55	76
Theology teachers	–	1	9	25
Regulars, etc.	3 (10%)	1 (2.7%)	10 (18%)	25 (33%)

Finally, religious considerations strongly colored the teachings and writings of lay professors teaching subjects such as philosophy (§8.2). This observation, linked to the changes referred to above, raises a number of questions: Why and how did this reorientation occur? How significant was it? To what extent did the relationship between philosophy and theology, for instance, change?

In order to answer these questions, it helps to give more detail on the historical development of theology and allied subjects in the Bolognese *studium.*[15] Theology, which had previously appeared on the rolls only irregularly, established itself more firmly starting in 1566—initially as a subject taught in the morning by just one instructor. Soon, however, it developed into a teaching offered both according to the orientation of John Duns Scotus and of Thomas Aquinas (*ad mentem Scoti* and *ad mentem Thomae*), as in Padua.[16] Its main textbook was Peter Lombard's *Sentences.* Eventually it was renamed "scholastic theology." In the early eighteenth century its teaching (split into morning and afternoon slots dedicated to different books of the *Sentences*) reached peaks of four or five instructors per teaching hour. In 1717–1718 the authorities brought this exuberance under control (limiting it to two lecturers per teaching slot) and added dogmatic theology—also called *super controversiis.*[17] In 1579 Sacred Scriptures also started appearing more often in the rolls, but it suffered from long periods of discontinuous teaching. This was partly due to the fact that it needed the support of instruction in Hebrew and other Oriental languages, which was often lacking. Toward the end of the seventeenth century, it increasingly dealt with contemporary controversies of theological or political nature and apparently attracted few students.[18] Various other theological subjects first appeared on the rolls in the seventeenth and eighteenth centuries: cases of conscience in

1637, moral theology (which eventually replaced cases of conscience) in 1695, and teachings of church history, canons, and church councils (later reduced to the first two of these) in 1717.[19] The growth of moral theology is especially remarkable: it reached seven lecturers in 1755. The subject's ascendance is connected to the pastoral concerns of Archbishop Prospero Lambertini.[20]

Metaphysics belonged to these theological subjects. It had been taught off and on in the fifteenth century (often in combination with astrology), but—according to the rolls—not as regularly as the 1405 statutes might suggest. Often it was a feast-day subject (see §2.2.2). It developed independently especially from 1506–1507 onward, but given the small number of staff teaching it, must not have attracted many students.[21] By 1585—but possibly earlier—the subject ran on a three-year cycle clearly based on Books I, VII, and XII of Aristotle's *Metaphysics.*[22] It was not, however, an integral part of the philosophy course (as it was in northern Europe and in the Jesuit colleges). According to Ulisse Aldrovandi's *Informatione del Rotulo del Studio di Bologna di Philosophi et Medici* (1573), metaphysics was more than anything a subject for novices, especially friars.[23] In 1648, when the Dominicans asked that the chair of metaphysics be assigned to one of their order rather than to someone from an "inferior one," they lumped metaphysics together with theology.[24]

But the clearest proof comes from the 1639 *Ordinationi* of the papal legate Giulio Sacchetti and the course outlines submitted by instructors of metaphysics in the seventeenth and eighteenth centuries. The *Ordinationi* bracket together the readings of theology and metaphysics; they also mandate that there always be two teachers of metaphysics (one expected to follow the teachings of Thomas, the other the teachings of Scotus) and two of theology on the rolls.[25] As for the course outlines, in 1642–1643 Giuseppe Costanzi (Canon Regular at San Salvatore) planned a series of lectures on Book VII of the *Metaphysics;* initially these seem to be interpretations of Aristotle, but it soon becomes clear that students were supposed to keep to the commentary by Thomas Aquinas, supplemented by the writings of Francisco Suárez and Dominicus de Flandria.[26] The questions outlined are not necessarily theological, but the ontological issues in view (such as the relationship of substance to accident, or whether being is the first object apprehended by our intellect) have an obvious potential application to theological matters such as the doctrine of the Eucharist.[27] By the eighteenth century, the ties between metaphysics and theology are even clearer. Benedetto Tassoni, lecturing on *Metaphysics* XII in 1707–1708, spends most of his course outline listing questions about the First Mover, including whether he is eternal, infinite, and the most beautiful and best being.[28] The lectures of the Franciscan Carolus Antonius Cantopholus for 1714–1715 deal with the relationship of form and matter in the sacraments.[29] Others indicate that the textbook for the course is not Aristotle, but Thomas.

By now it should be clear that theology came to play an outsize and growing role in the faculty of arts and medicine, particularly from 1566 onward. But who or what was responsible for introducing into the Bolognese *studium* a subject that was already taught in the local schools of the religious orders, and why did this move happen when it did? In what follows, one needs to consider the decrees of the Council of Trent alongside the local influence of both Cardinal Paleotti and the Jesuits.

The Council of Trent (1545–1563) issued decrees of a doctrinal nature as well as others relating to the piety and practice of the faithful. Two decrees have particular relevance here. The first, from Session V, notes the need not to neglect "the heavenly treasure of the sacred books" and mandates the exposition of Sacred Scriptures (also sometimes called "theology") in churches, monasteries, and public colleges. It also points specifically to the need to provide adequate teaching in this area:

> In the public colleges also, wherein a lectureship so honorable, and the most necessary of all, has not hitherto been instituted, let it be established by the piety and charity of the most religious princes and governments, for the defence and increase of the Catholic faith, and the preservation and propagation of sound doctrine; and where such lectureship, after being once instituted, has been neglected, let it be restored.[30]

But the Council also issued a more overarching and highly relevant decree concerning the universities:

> Moreover, all those to whom belong the charge, visitation, and reformation of universities and of (places of) general studies, shall diligently take care that the canons and decrees of this holy Synod be, by the said universities, wholly received;

> and that the masters, doctors, and others, in the said universities, interpret and teach those things that are of Catholic faith, in conformity therewith; and that at the beginning of each year they bind themselves by solemn oath to this procedure. And also if there be any other things that need correction and reformation in the universities aforesaid, they shall be reformed and regulated by those whom it regards, for the advancement of religion and of ecclesiastical discipline. But as regards those universities which are immediately under the protection of the Sovereign Pontiff, and are subject to his visitation, his Blessedness will take care that they be, by his delegates, wholesomely visited and reformed in the manner aforesaid, as shall seem to him most advantageous.[31]

The decrees just cited therefore (1) institute lectureships of theology or Sacred Scriptures in the "public colleges"; (2) underline the need to reform universities in line with the Council's decrees; (3) state the obligation for masters and doctors to "interpret and teach those things that are of Catholic faith"; (4) institute an annual oath in this sense that masters must take; (5) state the intention of reforming the universities; and (6) in the case of papal universities, emphasize the pontiff's sovereignty over them.

In recent years, scholars have underlined that the Council's decrees took time to implement and that the success of this process could vary locally, even significantly.[32] Some scholars have even concluded that the whole project of Tridentine reform in the 1600–1750 period was a failure, at least in Italy.[33] Without presuming to settle such a thorny issue, here I would note that, in Bologna at least, these decrees led to considerable changes in the second half of the sixteenth century, although they also generated resistance and foot-dragging from the professors and the Senate.[34] With reference to the first aim, subjects that soon joined metaphysics included—as noted above—Hebrew (1565), theology (1566), and Sacred Scriptures (1576). As to the other aims, the spring and summer of 1583 saw instructions from the papal see concerning a university reform that would bring the *studium* in line with the Council's decrees.[35] This took care of aim five and, partly, of six, although the mounting influence of papal legates on university politics in later centuries achieved this fully. The third point restates and confirms previous requirements for professors to defend Catholic positions in their teaching—something that, as illustrated below (§8.2), tended to be observed at least in spirit from the first part of the sixteenth century. In support of the fourth point, Pope Pius IV issued a separate bull (*In sacrosancta*) on 13 November 1564 requiring doctors and degree candidates to swear loyalty to the Church.[36] There is at least some evidence that the university observed this instruction, at least in the second half of the sixteenth century.[37] Grendler has illustrated the lengths to which Padua went to circumvent the bull by setting up a parallel Collegio Veneto that allowed students to graduate without observing the *professio fidei* requirement. (This enabled Padua to continue to recruit Protestant students, especially from Germany.) He also maintains that counts palatine would not have insisted on it.[38] Some historians disagree and hold that doctoral candidates had to be vetted by the doctoral colleges and submit to the *professio fidei* even in the latter case. For Bologna, the problem comes down to a lack of evidence. Despite recent interest in degrees and the mechanisms of conferring them, the *professio fidei* has not received sufficient attention.[39] It seems unlikely, though, that the authorities of the Papal State would have allowed Pius IV's bull to be flouted right under their noses.

Several of these moves received support from Gabriele Paleotti (1522–1597), one of the key cultural players in the second half of Cinquecento Bologna.[40] Paleotti was the scion of a fairly prominent (though not aristocratic) Bolognese family. He had studied in Bologna, obtaining his degree in civil and canon law in 1546. He then taught civil law in his alma mater until his appointment as a member of the Sacra Rota Romana (the supreme court of the Papal State) in 1556. Later he presided over the last phase (1562–1563) of the Council of Trent. He acquitted himself well enough to attract a number of honors on his return to Rome. He was made cardinal (1565) and became a member of what was to become the Council's Congregation, formed to oversee the implementation of its reforms. He also received the bishopric (1566) and subsequently the archbishopric (1582) of Bologna, an office he held until his death. As (arch) bishop of Bologna, Paleotti was a strong proponent of religious renewal and fought hard against Rome's attempts to ride roughshod over the authority of bishops. He was also highly intellectually curious and had close friends (particularly Ulisse Aldrovandi and Carlo Sigonio) in the university as well as among the painting workshop surrounding Annibale Caracci. He tried to soften the harshness of the papacy (particularly under Pope Pius V) and to limit the local reach both of the Inquisition and of the Index of Prohibited Books.[41]

As part of his concern for the formation of the clergy, Paleotti instituted a seminary (founded in 1567 and operative from 1568) and—both in the cathedral and in the oratory he founded—a regular teaching of cases of conscience.[42] As we will see, the latter bore fruit in the university teaching that went by that name in the seventeenth century. Paleotti was also instrumental in instituting the university chairs for theology and Sacred Scriptures, although he was not successful in providing continuous instruction in Hebrew and Greek so as to support the latter chair in particular.[43] Under his guidance, there was a considerable surge in the number of degrees taken in theology.[44]

One might ask why Paleotti sensed the need to intervene so directly and strongly in university teaching. After all, for Bologna this was a significant departure from customary action on the part of a bishop, who had no official function within the *studium* (see §1.3.2). One answer is that, as a member of the Congregation of the Council, he was expected to ensure the implementation of its decrees, including those on universities. His *Memoria per le cose dello Studio* (sent to the Senate for consideration in December 1585) emphasizes in particular the Council's mandate for a lectureship in Sacred Scriptures, underlining that it should be paid comparably to theology and be supported by the teaching of Hebrew and Greek.[45] Furthermore, Paleotti had a genuine concern for his alma mater. Already in 1577 he briefed his friend, the incoming governor of Bologna Giambattista Castagna, on a series of problems in the *studium* that required attention. These ranged from student misbehavior and insolence to the organization and delivery of teaching. For many of these points, Paleotti suggested potential remedies.[46] Several other documents also testify to the real interest he took in the university and to the fact that university professors thought it worthwhile to keep him abreast of their thinking about how to reform the *studium*.[47]

But Paleotti's interest was not merely organizational or intellectual: he also saw a need to foster piety among university students and teachers as well as among the rest of the population.[48] He was therefore a strong backer of the Congregazione della Perseveranza, a religious association for university members that seems to have enjoyed considerable success: its meetings apparently drew over eighty participants in 1575 and more than one hundred in 1580. These included prominent professors (such as the legist Giovanni Angelo Papio and the professor of philosophy Federico Pendasio in 1575) as well as students (many of them noblemen). Paleotti was strongly involved in and may even have started this society, which—founded in 1574—aimed to develop piety and good morals, aided the city in tricky areas such as finding suitable lodgings for foreign students, and had as one of its unstated aims the conversion of Protestant students.[49] In 1580, at least, Paleotti celebrated Mass for this society at the start of the academic year. He was certainly favorable to (and, at the very least, endorsed) the new statutes that the Perseveranza gave itself in 1582.[50] Scholars do not agree on the role of the Jesuits in starting the society, but shortly after its inception it was surely in their hands, as testified by the glowing reports they were sending about it to Rome and the monthly Mass the congregation attended in the Jesuit church of Santa Lucia. In 1608 the Perseveranza merged with another Jesuit society, the Congregazione dell'Assunta.[51]

As just suggested, the Jesuits played a major role in giving the *studium* a religious orientation. Their involvement in the Perseveranza was part of a canny strategy both to widen their appeal among university students (and attract them to their teaching) and to inspire all members of the university with their religious devotion. In the sixteenth century their relationship with the Bolognese *studium* was amicable, but in later years it became fraught. Initially the Jesuits offered a limited curriculum in Bologna that did not seriously overlap with what was taught in the *studium*. But they had established a full college in Bologna by 1636, when the college of Parma temporarily moved there. The university clearly felt threatened by this development and began intense deliberations about how to contain the Jesuits (§3.3.2). The decision to introduce a university teaching of cases of conscience in 1637 may have partly sought (as Paul Grendler has suggested) to meet the Jesuits on their own ground, since their college had for many years offered a very popular teaching in this area.[52] But one should also remember that several institutions in Bologna taught the subject.[53]

8.2 Philosophy

One alternative explanation for the rise of theology might be to suppose that it was meant to compensate for the perceived deficiencies in the local seminary's program of studies (a matter on which documentation is lacking) as well as in other institutions for the formation of the clergy that arose up to the middle of the eighteenth century.[54] But the Council's decree referred to above had in view chairs of theology for the benefit of university students, and seminarians could presumably have availed themselves of theological teaching taking place in Bologna's numerous convents, not to mention the college of the Jesuits. That being the case, it is worth looking more closely at the program of arts and medicine for signs of a potential reorientation toward theology or coloring by religious considerations. Especially telling are the cases of natural and moral philosophy, but mathematics and medicine are relevant as well.

8.2.1 Natural Philosophy and Discussions on the Soul

One of the features that made philosophy in Italy different from elsewhere in Europe was that it was strongly tied to medicine rather than to theology (see §2.1). This meant that natural philosophy in particular could focus on topics that laid a foundation for medical study and practice. Scholars have maintained that this gave a more secular flavor to philosophy in Italy, making philosophers more inclined to develop their subject independently of theology. One should not, however, think that this led to a complete separation of philosophical and religious concerns. In fact, at least three problems in natural philosophy strongly overlapped with issues of Christian doctrine. The first was whether the soul is immortal, something on which Aristotle never expressed himself with absolute clarity but on which the Church had developed a significant body of doctrine. Greek commentators such as Alexander of Aphrodisias (early third century AD) saw Aristotle as taking a materialist position: because the rational soul depends on sensation and the body for its functions, when the body dies, it dies too. Another source of tension concerned the unity (or better, unicity) of the intellect: Does each human have an individual reasoning faculty, and if so, how do we explain the fact that we perceive objects, sounds, and colors in the same way? Is there perhaps a universal intellect of which all humans partake—in which case, an individual afterlife becomes problematic? Here the most famous interpreter was the Arab philosopher Averroes (Ibn Rushd, d. 1198), whose commentaries on Aristotle (including *De anima*) became standard textbooks of the philosophical curriculum early on.[55] Finally, scholars debated a subset of the unicity problem—namely, whether the rational soul is, in effect, the substantial form of man or not; or, phrased more technically, whether the soul is a *forma informans* or instead a *forma assistens*. The debate involved, among others, influential thinkers such as Paul of Venice (c. 1369–1429) and Nicoletto Vernia (d. 1499).[56] In addition to these, other problems emerging from natural philosophy included the number and kinds of souls in man, whether creation (including of souls) can occur out of nothing (*ex nihilo*), whether the world is eternal, and so forth.

Several of these matters had been the subject of pronouncements by the papal legate and the bishop in late thirteenth-century Paris.[57] (Particularly well known are the condemnations of 1270 and 1277.) They had instructed professors there to counter, in their lectures, pagan philosophical ideas that were inimical to faith, or even to argue *pro fide*.[58] In Italy, however, such restrictions found little echo. Certainly there is no trace of them in Bologna's statutes of arts and medicine of 1405, although some fifteenth-century discussions about potentially sensitive philosophical issues, such as the mortality of the soul or the eternity of the world, do occasionally compare the conclusions of the philosophers with Catholic truth.[59] Likewise, it is unclear how aware teachers of philosophy in Italy were that the Council of Vienne (1311–1312) had condemned anyone who denied Christian doctrine concerning the eternity and individuality of the rational human soul.[60] But this does not mean that philosophers could necessarily teach the views of Averroes on the unicity of the intellect or of Alexander of Aphrodisias on the materiality and mortality of the soul without restrictions.[61] In 1396 the bishop of Pavia reprimanded the Alexandrist teacher Biagio Pellacani da Parma. In 1489 the bishop of Padua (Pietro Barozzi) and the inquisitor Marco da Lendinara prohibited disputations on the unicity of the intellect in the town. (Here the target was probably Nicoletto Vernia, a famous Aristotelian with Averroistic leanings.)[62]

In the sixteenth century, however, matters became rather more complicated. This is not the place to offer an extended treatment of the relationship between philosophy and theology in Italy or even just in Bologna, but several crucial developments need mentioning. The first is the Fifth Lateran Council's bull *Apostolici regiminis* (1513), which not only condemned "those affirming that the rational soul is mortal or single for diverse men," even if they did so only from the philosophical point of view, but instructed all those teaching philosophy that

> when they teach or explain to their hearers the principles or conclusions of philosophers in which it is clear that they deviate from the true faith—for instance, the mortality or unicity of the soul, or the eternity of the world, or other doctrines of this kind—they must with all their strength make manifest and, inasmuch as possible, persuasively teach them the truth of the Christian religion.[63]

At the same time, professors were to refute and resolve the contrary arguments of the philosophers. Philosophers were free, therefore, to teach controversial or dangerous texts, but while so doing they were to do everything in their power to correct any falsehoods in them and teach the Christian truth.[64] In practice, they were expected to take on the role of theologians, something that led both Niccolò Lippomano (bishop of Bergamo) and Thomas de Vio (or Cajetan, general of the Dominican order) to voice their dissent from the second part of the bull.[65]

Decrees in later years also affected what could or could not be taught. One in 1616 allowed the teaching of Copernicus's heliocentric doctrine, but only as a hypothesis. Following the condemnation of Jansenism in 1660, professors had to swear that they would not hold this position.[66] Furthermore, various publications were either delayed or stopped because of concerns by the Congregation of the Index or local authorities.[67] And, clearly, not all books (or professors) were welcome.

Pietro Pomponazzi

Historians disagree as to the actual effects of the decree of the Fifth Lateran Council on the *libertas philosophandi* that many teachers claimed.[68] The case most often cited is that of Pietro Pomponazzi (1462–1525), an eminent professor of natural philosophy who, after teaching in Padua, concluded his career in Bologna, where he taught from 1511 to 1525. In 1516, just three years after the issuing of the *Apostolici regiminis,*

Pomponazzi contravened its instructions in a very public way. In his printed work *De immortalitate animae* (*Treatise on the Immortality of the Soul*), he interpreted Aristotle according to the materialist position of Alexander of Aphrodisias, laid bare the difficulties of proving philosophically the immortality of the soul, and neglected both to refute the opinions contrary to faith and to "persuasively teach . . . the truth of the Christian religion," as the Council's decree obliged him to do. He opted instead, in a hurried (and, according to many contemporaries, insincere) conclusion, to declare that he trusted in the doctrines of the Church to resolve this philosophically "neutral" problem: like Scotus and Ockham before him (but very much unlike Thomas Aquinas), he opined that a fideistic approach was the only one possible for affirming with certainty the immortality of the intellective human soul.[69] Pomponazzi's treatise provoked a strong reaction, as philosophers and theologians rushed to prove him wrong and burnish their own credentials as faithful Catholics. But he himself never recanted his position, nor was he hauled before any civic or ecclesiastical tribunal. Some historians have therefore questioned whether the *Apostolici regiminis* had any real effect, while others have noted a more muted and circumspect tone in his later writings.[70] In order to shed some light on the issue, in what follows I examine later Bolognese lectures on *De anima*. Surprisingly, these do not ignore theology, but instead give more space to it and religious considerations more generally.

Ludovico Boccadiferro

Particularly relevant is the teaching activity of Ludovico Boccadiferro (1482–1545). A pupil of Alessandro Achillini (1463–1512), a noted professor of philosophy and medicine in Bologna, Boccadiferro was a generation younger than Pomponazzi.[71] He taught philosophy in Bologna almost continuously from 1515 until March 1545 (except for the years 1524–1527, mainly spent in Rome) and was highly influential on a remarkable generation of thinkers and writers, including Flaminio Nobili, Federico Pendasio, Alessandro Piccolomini, and Benedetto Varchi.

The few recent studies that have considered Boccadiferro have tended to see him as more careful in his pronouncements than Pomponazzi; they have also noted his references to the Fifth Lateran Council in some of his lectures, but they have not seen a particularly strong influence on him of its mandate (or, for that matter, of the pronouncements of the Florentine Council that met two years after it).[72] Luca Bianchi has suggested that the first half of the sixteenth century was relatively quiet in terms of dogmatic repression, given that the Church lacked the instruments that would later help it to more effectively control teaching and the dissemination of dangerous books. (The Holy Office was established in 1542; the Index of Prohibited Books, in 1558–1559.)[73] But another possible explanation for that quietness is that professors were already adjusting their teaching to the *Apostolici regiminis* bull and exploring a different way of treating philosophical problems.

The evidence is clearest in Boccadiferro's 1535–1536 unpublished lectures on the third book of *De anima*.[74] Here one sees a close and sustained engagement with theological problems, leading to rather surprising outcomes. In fact, although Boccadiferro explicitly states that he will address philosophical problems that border on issues of faith philosophically, he does precisely the opposite. Not only does he evaluate Aristotle's conclusions in the light of Christian doctrine, but on several occasions he refers to the Scriptures and theological matters.

A foretaste of his approach comes from a statement in Lecture XII, where a discussion about what the Divine Intellect knows (*Metaphysics*, XII) leads to reflections on what Aristotle and Averroes thought about the issue. Boccadiferro explains that, according to Averroes, the first intelligence knows only itself, whereas the other intelligences know more. In this Averroes shows himself to be a true Aristotelian, he says. Yet Aristotle erred if one considers his view according to (theological) truth ("Aristoteles erraverit secundum veritatem"). Furthermore, Boccadiferro states that even though on several occasions he will need to deal with issues relevant to theologians, he will address those points *apud peripateticos*. In other words, he will explain how the Aristotelians see them.[75] This statement suggests that Boccadiferro will follow Pomponazzi in keeping philosophy and theology strictly separate, but that is hardly the case. A clear indication is Boccadiferro's extended treatment of the first two classic questions referred to above.

In treating the problem of the immortality of the soul, Boccadiferro subordinates philosophical conclusions to Christian and theological ones by setting up a contrast between Aristotle's opinions and Christian truth. He observes that many interpreters of Aristotle (including, among others, Thomas Aquinas, Scotus, Cardinal Cajetan, and Pomponazzi) see Aristotle as holding that the rational soul (or the potential intellect) is a faculty caused by matter, and therefore subject to generation and corruption. This, he says, is "contrary to the truth of orthodox faith, for there can be no doubt that it is separate from matter, that it is generated (by God), and that it is incorruptible."[76] He adds that the main question under discussion (whether the potential intellect is separate from matter) can be considered in two ways. The first is to seek out the truth—but this would be pointless, since the truth (i.e., that the intellect is separate and immortal) is already known to us by the pronouncements of Peter Lombard and the words and resurrection of Christ, who is "the way and the truth." The second possibility is to investigate the opinion on this matter of Aristotle and the Peripatetics.[77] He then declares that this will be his focus. This move may seem innocuous and superficially similar to Pomponazzi's explicit separation of the realms of theology and philosophy. But in fact Boccadiferro has already declared for the Christian viewpoint.

The significance of this approach emerges from Boccadiferro's treatment of the second major question, on the unicity of the intellect, which perfectly reflects the instructions of the *Apostolici regiminis*. The miracle of the resurrection shows, according to Boccadiferro, that there cannot be a single intellective soul, and that there are as many souls as there are individuals; therefore Aristotle erred, as shown by the opinion of all theologians, whose view (that each rational soul is created immediately by God) is "the true opinion and truth."[78] Boccadiferro goes on to rebuke theologians such as Scotus and Antonio Trombetta, who tried to twist Aristotle's words to make him conform to Christian truth. He claims that Aristotle's approach is fundamentally different. We might as well, therefore, admit that Aristotle did not know everything and that he was mistaken, both in this matter and in others.[79] Shortly afterward, when exploring the possibility that a rational soul might change location, Boccadiferro asks a searing rhetorical question: "What did Aristotle know about the truth? This is the truth, and Aristotle erred."[80] Here, what is striking is not so much Boccadiferro's admission that Aristotle might have erred (a point often conceded in earlier philosophical discussions), but the sustained and explicit way in which he contrasts Christian truth (*veritas*) with the pronouncements of the Stagirite.[81] Furthermore, Boccadiferro makes extensive use of examples from Scripture. To prove the point that the movement of the rational soul is possible, for instance, he refers to the appearances of the angel Gabriel. He is thus following both the spirit and the letter of the *Apostolici regiminis.* By emphasizing the truth (*veritas*) of the Christian position, Boccadiferro distances himself from Pomponazzi's approach of simply stating and clarifying Aristotle's teachings, without critiquing them theologically.

One might argue that, as a thinker who had close ties with heterodox evangelical groups, Boccadiferro was probably an exception in the Bolognese context. In fact, however, several later Bolognese philosophers confirm the view that Pomponazzi's separation of philosophy and theology did not gain many followers.

Claudio Betti

A case in point is Claudio Betti, who might not follow Boccadiferro's approach either, but does not need to invoke Christianity directly because he has already accommodated Aristotle's teachings to Christian doctrine. Now altogether forgotten, though a renowned teacher in his own time, Claudio Betti (†1589) did his studies in Bologna and, after graduating in 1545, spent his lifetime teaching both moral and natural philosophy there.[82] The only printed work clearly associated with this teaching is his *De recta discurrendi ratione institutio brevissima* (first printed in 1568; repr. 1590), which serves as a reminder of his fame as a logician. But Betti lectured on the whole gamut of Aristotle's philosophy. His unpublished lectures include multiple treatments of *De anima.*[83]

Directly relevant here is Betti's *Micrologia librorum tres de anima.* This work—based very clearly on the Greek text—offers a painstaking explanation of the meaning of the terms used by Aristotle in each passage. When Betti does lift his head to consider the larger philosophical issues that have a bearing on Christian doctrine, he does not follow Boccadiferro in correcting Aristotle. This may give the impression that he is walking in Pomponazzi's footsteps, but in fact Betti does not need to contradict Aristotle because he has already made him into a Christian thinker. One finds a revealing statement to this effect in one of his questions: "When [Aristotle] says that the soul (as to the intellect) is immortal and eternal, someone might ask: 'Why then does the soul [once separated] have no recollection of the things that it knew through the intellect when it was connected to the body?'"[84] The description of the soul as "immortal and eternal" for Aristotle shows that Betti has already decided that there is no ambiguity in Aristotle's position, and that he supports a Christian view of the soul. As a result, Betti can avoid discussing the opinions of the theologians: there is nothing for them to rebut.[85]

Giovanni Ludovico Cartari

Christian allegiances are far more prominent in the treatise on the soul of Giovanni Ludovico Cartari (†1593), which is at the opposite end of the spectrum from Pomponazzi's approach.[86] Cartari's *De immortalitate animae,* printed in Bologna in 1587 after some thirty years of teaching philosophy (mainly in Bologna, where he also did his studies), sets out to defend Aristotle's reputation from those who would besmirch it.[87] The conviction that Aristotle holds the soul to be immortal is so obvious that this is not even one of the questions listed in the table of contents. From this perspective, Cartari's work is part of a widespread sixteenth-century effort to (re-)Christianize Aristotle.[88] But it also bears other clear signs of Christian influence. The opening invocation "Iesus illuminatio mea sit" is just one of these and recalls similar prayers offered at the start of lectures in the teaching of Achillini and others, around a century earlier.[89] Rather more telling and unusual is the work's concluding and extended statement of praise to God and submission to the Church. Here one again finds a reference to the importance of Catholic truth (*veritas*):

> And may these matters be settled to the praise of Almighty God and of Jesus Christ His Son. If this work contains anything that is contrary to the Catholic truth, this should be understood as referring to the sayings of others, and not to what I myself believe. For in those and all other matters, I always steadfastly submit to the determination of the Holy Catholic Church. So help me God.[90]

The fact that the work, issued with the standard Inquisition-era license ("Facultate a superioribus concessa"), is dedicated to a cardinal (Costanzo Sarnano, bishop of Vercelli) is doubtless meant as a further sign of Cartari's piety and reliability. Although there is no immediate reason to doubt the sincerity of Cartari's declaration, it would be helpful to know whether he participated in the activities promoted by Paleotti and the Jesuits, including the Congregazione della Perseveranza.[91]

Cartari's statements deserve to be read in the light of some recent events. In the period 1560–1572, the Bolognese Inquisition had been especially active, thanks to the work of the Inquisitor Fra' Antonio Balducci of Forlì and the interest of Pope Pius V (r. 1566–1572).[92] In a *reprise* of the anti-heretical actions of the 1540s (which had caught several local figures in their net, including Ulisse Aldrovandi), Balducci established the bases for an efficient enforcement of Catholic positions in Bologna; exposed, tried, and executed several individuals with Protestant or otherwise heterodox sympathies (leading to some twenty condemnations to death just in 1566–1569, in addition to condemnations to prison); and did not hesitate to investigate prominent individuals, including members of the senatorial class and university doctors.[93] Among the latter was the renowned medical doctor Girolamo Cardano, who in 1570 lost his teaching post and was imprisoned due to questions about the orthodoxy of the views expressed in his *De varietate rerum* (1559).[94] Aldrovandi also appeared before the Inquisition (as a witness) because of suspicions concerning the priest Giovanni Grisostomo, with whom he was apparently in close contact.[95] Clearly, however, there were also reservations about Aldrovandi himself.[96] Furthermore, in 1578 the Spanish canonist and theologian Francisco Peña issued an edition of Nicolas Eymerich's *Directorium inquisitorium,* which became a standard manual for inquisitors in the Catholic Reformation, also in its 1585 enlarged edition. This work included a full reproduction of various documents, including the *Apostolici regiminis.*[97] It doubtless served as a reminder to inquisitors to be vigilant regarding the activities of the university. It would hardly be surprising if, in the light of all of the above, Cartari's work was careful to avoid pronouncements that might attract attention from the Inquisition. But his approach, as indicated already, did not require following the procedure, mandated by the *Apostolici regiminis,* of countering the false statements of pagan philosophers: he had already rendered them perfectly orthodox. From this point of view, Cartari's approach has much in common with Betti's.

Delimiting Philosophy

In addition to what may be called the separatist, corrective, and Christianized approaches examined so far (represented by Pomponazzi, Boccadiferro, and Betti and Cartari, respectively), in the seventeenth century one sees another way of dealing with the tensions between philosophy and theology. This consisted in restricting what they considered, so that philosophers could avoid delving into theological issues.

An example of this orientation is Francesco Natali, a little-known professor of philosophy who spent most or all of his career in Bologna (t. 1635–1676) and died in 1677.[98] His lectures on Aristotle's *De anima* and *De coelo et mundo* show him limiting himself to "safe" territories, avoiding anything that might be controversial from a religious point of view. Whereas the plans for Natali's public lectures are somewhat generic, we are well informed about his private teaching through five manuscript volumes containing his students' notes.[99] One of the remarkable aspects of the ones on *De anima* (whose fair copy dates to 1652) is that they cover only the first two of the work's three books.[100] This restriction (already announced in the title) seems motivated by Natali's insistence that, although there are certainly aspects of the soul that pertain to the consideration of natural philosophy, others—particularly those involving the functions of intellection without the aid of *phantasmata*—are more appropriate to metaphysics.[101] Natali most likely did not cover Book III (the especially controversial part of the work) for fear of exceeding the boundaries of his discipline. This strategy would be entirely in keeping with his lectures on *De coelo et mundo,* in which Natali quickly mentions the heliocentric position (*opinio*) of Copernicus and Galileo, but then refuses to examine it more closely. Natali's justification is that it has been both condemned by the Church (as being opposed to the faith) and rejected by astrologers. Thus, he states, "it is not our concern to examine it."[102] By Natali's time, then, at least some professors were censoring themselves even in the course of their private lectures. They had given up parts of the territory of natural philosophy to other disciplines more closely tied to theology, such as metaphysics. Rather than outlining and then arguing against opinions deemed contrary to faith, they simply circumscribed the boundaries of philosophy and restricted themselves as much as possible to natural considerations.[103]

This approach is understandable within the climate created by the first decree of the Congregation of the Index against Copernicanism (5 March 1616) and Galileo's condemnation in 1633.[104] Significantly, Pope Urban VIII (Maffeo Barberini) gave specific instructions on 16 June 1633 that professors of mathematics and philosophy in Bologna and

Padua should be informed of Galileo's fate. The same year also saw the publication of Melchior Inchofer's *Tractatus syllepticus,* which explicitly recalled the provisions of the *Apostolici regiminis* and therefore the obligation to affirm the doctrines of the Christian faith in one's teaching. Closer to home, when Barberini was papal legate in Bologna (1611–1614) he instructed his theological adviser Agostino Oreggi to consider whether Aristotle's *De anima* impugned the immortality of the soul—in which case, Barberini was apparently minded to prohibit teaching of that work.[105] In fact, Barberini issued no such proclamation, whether as legate or, subsequently, as pope. Such a move would have certainly caused consternation in Bologna. But some professors—although there were certainly exceptions—thought it more prudent to leave Book III of *De anima* to the metaphysicians.[106] The implications for philosophy were rich.

Domenico Maria Gusman Galeazzi, already encountered in Chapter 6, is an example of how a delimiting approach could give a professor freedom to focus his teaching on his own scientific interests. Galeazzi's teaching plan for 1717–1718 on the *Tractatus de anima* starts with the standard distinction between vegetative, sensitive, and intellective soul. His treatment clearly embraces, for the first two, the school of interpretation that connects discussions of the soul with Aristotle's *Parva naturalia,* along with some more modern views (and elements of natural history) thrown in. He thus promises to discuss plants and the various kinds of animals in particular (not without making reference to Descartes's *automata*) and hopes, if time allows, to arrive at man as well. He is, however, careful to specify that he will not be treating the rational soul, "which will be discussed separately in metaphysics."[107] Galeazzi's orientation reflects the attention of his other course outlines to physiological matters such as breathing and the circulation of blood. Such instances support the views of Ugo Baldini and Marta Cavazza that the period 1650–1750 saw a distancing of metaphysics and natural philosophy, so that considerations of the natural world (and studies, for instance, of natural history) were able to take on a new intensity and dynamic.[108]

It is also entirely possible that this movement reflected contemporary anxieties about the dangers of falling into (and being punished for) heresy. In his painting *San Domenico e l'esperimento dei libri ortodossi* (1614–1616, Bologna, Basilica di San Domenico), the Bolognese artist Lionello

Spada (1576–1622) represents a scene in which a group of Dominicans (on the left, headed by St. Dominic himself, in the act of throwing a book onto the fire) confronts a group of heretics (who are giving special attention to their own book).[109] The painting alludes, of course, to the thirteenth-century confrontation between the Catholic Church and the Albigensians, but the warning to contemporary "heretics" is clear. In 1679 Giuseppe Maria Mitelli (1634–1718) reproduced Spada's painting as part of a series of etchings based on famous paintings in San Domenico. His effective rendition (Figure 8.1) would have served as a powerful reminder that books and learning could lead one astray. The association between St. Dominic and the resident inquisitor was an easy one, given that the Holy Office in Bologna had its headquarters in the convent of San Domenico.

A Theological Physics?

Already in the late seventeenth century, a substantially different approach was sweeping through the Bolognese *studium*. This one pulled in the opposite direction to that of drawing boundaries around one's teaching: instead, it used discussions of natural philosophy (and nearly any other topic) as an occasion to discuss God and theological issues. This was certainly the approach taken by Lelio Trionfetti (1647–1722), professor of philosophy and simples in the *studium* from 1669 until his death (although he held an honorary status from 1707).[110] An heir to Ulisse Aldrovandi's teaching activity, Trionfetti garnered praised from some contemporaries for having been the first to introduce the methods of Descartes in the public schools. But his manuscript lectures on Aristotle's *Physics* and *De coelo et mundo* (1674–1675) tell a rather different story.[111] Baldini's study of these works and the questions they contain shows that Trionfetti's innovations were, in fact, rather limited.[112] Furthermore, his approach does not favor an independent treatment of philosophy. In the second set of lectures, for instance, he asks questions about the possible existence of other worlds ("An mundus sit unum tantum") or the eternity of this one ("An mundus sit ea natura sua in eternum duraturus"). But heterodox positions understandably receive short shrift, whereas theologians (among others, Thomas, Scotus, Anselm, Hurtado, and the Jesuits) loom large in his resolution of these points, and the discussion takes a deep religious coloring.

Fig 8.1. St. Dominic burning "heretical" books.

Etching (507 × 313 mm) on paper by Giuseppe Maria Mitelli, 1679, after a painting by Lionello Spada in San Domenico. Collezioni d'Arte e di Storia della Fondazione Cassa di Risparmio in Bologna, stampe, 2039.

Others who followed this approach include Bonifacio Collina and Pietro Mengoli. Collina, a Camaldulese monk (t. 1722–1770; see §6.2.2), offered lectures on logic, metaphysics, and physics—in that order. The unpublished lectures from the early 1730s are full of references to theological matters, even when Collina is discussing logic.[113] A similar orientation emerges from mathematics lectures dating to the late seventeenth century. Here the best example is Mengoli, professor of mathematics and mechanics (see §6.2.2), who in February 1682 wrote down the lectures he was preparing to dictate to his students.[114] The subject (*arithmetica realis*) may not seem to call for a religious approach, but that is precisely what the students get. Already in the preface Mengoli considers the events narrated in Genesis 1. His comments are rich with theological implications. He emphasizes, for instance, that God created light, not darkness. In discussing the creation of the firmament, Mengoli suggests that the result may not have been what He wanted, although He allowed it. Later he discusses how the disposition of all things—including number, weight, and measure—proceeded from God and was communicated by the angels. Mengoli does not hesitate to quote Scripture in support of his observations.[115]

Mengoli's position is extremely complex and sits at the confluence of multiple intellectual currents.[116] Furthermore, despite Baroncini's studies, the development of Bolognese thought from the second half of the seventeenth century onward is still murky.[117] Nevertheless, one wonders whether and to what extent this theological outlook may be associated with the rise throughout the same period of a "pious natural philosophy." Recent studies of this *physica sacra* place its home firmly in northern Europe, especially within Protestant circles, but the situation in Bologna and other Italian (and Catholic) contexts merits further exploration.[118]

8.2.2 Moral Philosophy

In moral philosophy, teaching developed in a rather different way from natural philosophy, but one observes a similar reorientation toward theology by the eighteenth century. As in the rest of the Italian Peninsula, in Bologna moral philosophy was for a long time an optional, feast-day subject, usually added onto the responsibilities of professors in other areas, such as rhetoric, astrology, natural philosophy, and medicine.

After disappearing in 1528, it resurfaced on the rolls in 1563, this time as an "ordinary" teaching assigned to Claudio Betti as his sole subject.[119] The reasons behind this change are unclear. If, as the chronology might suggest, they are connected to the moral aims of the Catholic Reformation, the Assunti chose the wrong man. Betti's teaching of moral philosophy did not bother making any of numerous potential connections between Aristotle's *Nicomachean Ethics* and Christian moral thought. Rather, his lectures reflect his interests and expertise in logic: they outline Aristotle's arguments in the form of syllogisms, often by supplying the missing middle term, but go little further. Likewise, his successors Agostino Galesi and Camillo Baldi gave little space to religious considerations, although in his *Notanda* on the *Ethics* Galesi did include two different sets of questions at the end of each section—one philosophical and the other theological.[120]

The lecture plan of Florio Gessi (Floridus Gypsius) on *De humana felicitate* in 1642–1643 continues to offer quite a philosophical and secular treatment of ethics.[121] His proposed course is still strongly based on Aristotle and outlines discrete and fairly standard topics in the *Nicomachean Ethics,* such as the appropriate student of this subject ("De auditore scientiae moralis," lecture 8). Gessi makes a few noteworthy departures, such as when he discusses (lecture 4) the opinions of ancients such as Plotinus and Seneca on the definition of the good. He also gives attention to the views of Plato and Pythagoras (lectures 22–24). But in the end he tends to confirm Aristotle's this-worldly outlook even though the theme of happiness is one of those most amenable to combination with Christian considerations. After discussing the Stoics' thinking about the supreme good (*summum bonum*), he concludes that one should support Aristotle's views on the matter ("Aristotelis sententia de summo bono est confirmanda"). The fact that the opinions of Epicurus receive little attention is a possible signal of a Christian orientation, but in itself this omission is unremarkable and reflects a widespread aversion to Epicurean positions.[122]

Although the treatments discussed so far exhibit little or no interest in comparing Aristotle's views with Christian ones, by the early eighteenth century the course in moral philosophy inhabits an unrecognizable landscape in which theological considerations are dominant. This is most obvious with Bartolomeo Aldrovandi, who appears on the rolls for moral philosophy from 1708 to 1756.[123] Superficially, Aldrovandi's plans for 1709–1710 and 1714–1715 might seem to follow Aristotle quite closely, given that each year considers topics such as happiness, virtues, justice, or contemplation (which Aristotle's *Nicomachean Ethics* covers at length). If anything, though, these course plans illustrate a slide from moral philosophy toward moral theology. Thus, Aldrovandi's discussion of happiness in 1709–1710 is very much centered, particularly in its later stages, on heavenly beatitude in contrast with, for instance, hell.[124] These plans also display a surprising resistance to the opinions of Peripatetics in addition to the more usual criticism of Epicureans and Stoics. Instead, Aldrovandi's sympathies lie firmly with Platonism and, in particular, the ideas of St. Augustine. This would seem to be a way to model a fairly straightforward alliance between pagan and theological ideas, but it is not fundamentally new: particularly in the sixteenth century, interpreters of Aristotle's moral philosophy such as Crisostomo Javelli, Francesco Piccolomini, and his kinsman Alessandro Piccolomini had used Platonic thought as a bridge between Aristotle's views and Christianity.

8.3 Late University Initiatives and Debates

The religious turn described above went well beyond theology and philosophy. In the seventeenth and eighteenth centuries it affected most (and possibly all) areas of the curriculum of arts and medicine, as well as more general reform initiatives.

We have already discussed (see §7.2.1) the new series of public lectures on anatomy that got under way in 1607. These attracted paying observers to the dissections as well as to the lectures (Figure 7.2a). After the scientific discussions, in which both students and teachers participated, the proceedings culminated in a theological intervention on the part of a Dominican or Franciscan friar in representation of the Inquisition.[125] More research into this intervention would be welcome, in order to determine its nature, what lay behind the initiative, and whether it continued as a permanent feature throughout the period. But it testifies that even public anatomies could be a manifestation of religious spirit.

It is also relevant to consider three figures who exercised a strong influence on the *studium* in the late seventeenth and the early eighteenth centuries: the Marsili brothers and Prospero Lambertini. Two of these occupied high clerical positions, but equally (if not more) significant is the role of religious considerations in their proposals and activities.

Antonio Felice Marsili (1651–1710) was a strong proponent of Catholic renewal who, as archdeacon and therefore chancellor of the university, used his position to attempt to redirect the *studium* in various ways, but was also responsible for significant cultural initiatives reflecting his religious and scientific interests. During his studies in Bologna he was heavily influenced by his teacher Vitale Terrarossa (1623–1692), a Benedictine monk who taught in the *studium* (c. 1656–1692) and supported the study of the ancient thinker Democritus (460–370 BC) and his atomism.[126] Terrarossa could reconcile atomism with Aristotelianism and did not see either of the two as a threat to Christianity.[127] Another important influence on Marsili was the work of Giovanni Battista Ciampoli (†1643), the papal secretary who had been close to Galileo and had advocated bringing science and faith together in a new union. In this model, unlike that of Thomas Aquinas, both areas would have their own independent spheres, much as Galileo had advocated.[128] Marsili clearly found this a powerful example to follow: he had strong interests both in experimental science and in the study of church history (an area in which he provided mentorship to Ludovico Antonio Muratori), although they remained strongly compartmentalized. After his elevation to archdeacon of San Pietro (the cathedral) in 1586, Marsili revived an earlier Accademia dell'Arcidiacono but split it into two: one dealt with matters of church history and the other with science.

Marsili was also behind the controversial proposals to reform the university discussed earlier. Given his position and religious orientation, it may seem strange that his *Memorie* (which appeared anonymously in 1689) give no attention to matters of faith, religion, or theology.[129] But Marsili was doubtless being careful not to reveal his authorship and being mindful that practical suggestions would have more persuasive power with the Senate than religious points. However that may be, it is true that his proposals failed and that he was forced out, so that eventually he finished his days as bishop of Perugia.[130] The problem was not, however, his religious vision, but rather his naked attempt to claim powers over the university that had long since passed to the colleges of doctors. The fact that he even attempted such a power grab suggests that he thought the cultural position of religion in Bologna was strong enough to support changes of privilege and jurisdiction. He had not, however, reckoned with the tenacity of the colleges of doctors.

Another deeply committed Catholic with interests in reforming the university was Antonio Felice's younger brother Luigi Ferdinando (1658–1730), a well-educated military leader who played a leading role in establishing Bologna's Istituto delle Scienze (see §3.2). In Luigi Ferdinando's case the religious impetus of the proposed reforms and initiatives is considerably clearer. His 1709 memorandum to the Senate highlighted various areas in which the Bolognese university had fallen behind with respect to foreign ones.[131] In his comments on the *studii sacri,* Marsili pointed out that "modern-day heretics" in Protestant countries were far better versed in the Oriental languages, which they studied with remarkable diligence, than their Catholic counterparts. He thus auspicated a considerable strengthening of this area (and especially of the study of Hebrew) in Bologna.[132] Furthermore, the Istituto's foundation documents (1711) give a prominent place to religion. They begin with a chapter "Del culto sacro," which points to the Virgin Mary and other saints as protectors of the enterprise, requires the erection of a chapel in their honor, and even stipulates the use of the old calendar *ab incarnatione* (with 25 March as the beginning of the new year) except for astronomical observations.[133] It is also well known that Marsili founded a press named after Thomas Aquinas, which he eventually donated to the friars of San Domenico. One of its first printed works was the monumental *Theologia scholastico-dogmatica iuxta mentem d. Thomae Aquinatis* (sixteen volumes) by the university's professor of theology Vincenzo Gotti, to whom Marsili was very close.[134]

Finally, a prominent example of Bologna's religious turn lies in the activities of Prospero Lambertini, archbishop of Bologna (1731–1756), who rose to the papal see as Benedict XIV (1740–1758). In both of these capacities, which for much of his lifetime he occupied simultaneously, Lambertini strongly favored the cultural renewal of the Bolognese *studium,* including by donating to Bologna a considerable cache of books and scientific instruments. He fostered the teaching of moral theology and the establishment of academies in Bologna dedicated to church history.[135] He was also conscious of the areas in which expertise was lacking, particularly the study of Oriental languages, which was still a concern in 1755.[136] But just as significant was Lambertini's cultivation of a renewal of devotion and piety in line with Muratori's new vision.[137] In several of these ways, he recalls Paleotti's activities and dedication to promoting piety in the university and the city.

Conclusion

The religious turn discussed in this chapter is easier to describe than it is to interpret at the deeper level of causes and effects. As the following pages illustrate, this topic is particularly complex and controversial, not least because of the influence of one's own religious (or antireligious) biases. Furthermore, long-standing debates on the effects of the Catholic Reformation more broadly have made it clear how hard it is to make valid generalizations. The following comments will focus especially on the effects of the Catholic Reformation on university teachings and scientific culture. Although this discussion is somewhat selective, it may help place the developments in Bologna into a wider perspective. Along the way, it will address some of the most relevant historiographical perspectives.

Two questions about the effects of the Catholic Reformation are especially germane here and point to some very different conclusions. Charles Schmitt famously put forward the view that its initiatives led to creating new university posts in theology and ethics at the expense of scientific subjects.[138] This presumably led to a more limited scientific activity, for which scientific academies and other such institutions compensated. In Bologna, however, matters were not so straightforward, and other chapters have shown that several new scientific and medical chairs were introduced in the early modern period, as well as theological ones. Although the teaching of theology increased and became highly prominent (see Table 8.1), in Bologna it did not clearly squeeze out other subjects.

Another much-debated point is whether the Catholic Reformation was responsible for a general cultural decline, particularly in contexts where its instruments (such as the Inquisition and the Holy Office) were most powerful.[139] This question is particularly relevant to the generally acknowledged lag of Italy's seventeenth-century scientific culture with respect to Protestant countries. Some scholars have countered that Catholic reform actually freed science from the influence of metaphysics in the second half of the seventeenth century and thereby enabled it to develop independently. Others have emphasized that science and theology were not necessarily at odds with each other, as witnessed by the growth of science within the religious orders.[140] Ugo Baldini has even proposed that Italy's scientific lag in the seventeenth century is an optical illusion: it is not so much that Italy stood still, but that others raced ahead, aided by the rise of analytic geometry.[141] For Bologna, this chapter confirms that a religious outlook did not necessarily constrain the development of science or philosophy.

Behind these and many other conclusions often lie different assessments about the efficacy or ineffectiveness of the Catholic Reformation's decrees, instruments, and practices, including censorship and the Index of Prohibited Books. Luca Bianchi's work on responses to the *Apostolici regiminis* argues that the bull had a wider resonance and applicability in Italian philosophical teaching than scholars have usually acknowledged.[142] This chapter largely supports this view, although Boccadiferro's approach should inspire caution about deferring the bull's influence to the second half of the sixteenth century. For his part, Paul Grendler has attributed the rise of theology and other related subjects (especially cases of conscience) in Italian universities, not to the pressures of the Catholic Reformation, but instead to mechanisms of local competition between Jesuit colleges and universities. In his view, in Bologna university authorities attempted to contain the Jesuits by meeting them on their own ground.[143] The rise of theology is therefore, for Grendler, a trompe l'oeil. This view relies partly on the assumption that not all of the theology teachers listed on the rolls actually taught. That is a plausible argument, but would apply equally to teachers of other subjects. And one would need to explain why such a strong proportion of surviving course outlines relates to theology; indeed, from the 1730s theology subjects even predominate among these.[144] By contrast, Miriam Turrini has been much less skeptical about the importance of theology in Bologna, not only in the university but in other contexts such as the seminary and the schools of the religious orders. Her studies are so far the only ones to have taken seriously the developments in this field in the early modern period and to have examined surviving lectures in any detail. Her research suggests that, since appearing on the rolls gave one the right to teach privately, honorary positions in theology might have contributed to an even more capillary instruction in theology throughout Bologna than is usually recognized.[145]

The varied (and at times conflicting) views just listed usefully highlight the question of agency. Who was actually behind the rise in the number of teachings of theology? Was this something foisted on the *studium* by papal or religious authorities, or did lay institutions such as the Senate or the colleges of doctors have a meaningful role? Did the Jesuits play any part at all? Because studies of theology teaching at Bologna and other universities are so few, any answers can only be provisional at this point. But it is worth noting a combination of factors, some from above and others from below, related to the more general context.[146]

Historians have often emphasized the role of social and religious control in the Catholic Reformation. As mentioned in this chapter, this aspect is undoubtedly relevant. Professors in the first half of the sixteenth century already took the *Apostolici regiminis* seriously. The Inquisition was active in Bologna and brought several individuals, including professors and students, to trial. The initiatives of Archbishop Paleotti in the second half of the sixteenth century helped implement the Tridentine Council's decrees and introduce a more stable provision of theological subjects. Likewise, the multiplication of such chairs in the late seventeenth century occurred during the archdiaconate of Antonio Felice Marsili and may be, at least partly, due to his influence.[147] Papal legates too were sometimes involved: the 1641 *Ordinationi* by Stefano Durazzo (which published the 1639 provisions of his predecessor Giulio Sacchetti) established two permanent positions each in metaphysics and theology.[148]

One should not, however, exaggerate the power and influence of the religious authorities. The case of Paleotti shows that they often worked at cross purposes, in a struggle for supremacy.[149] And their initiatives were not always successful or long-lasting. Paleotti had to balance his power as (arch)bishop against the competing claims of the papacy, the papal legate, the archdeacon, and the Inquisition (not to mention the civic institutions). He was successful in establishing chairs of Sacred Scripture, but they did not last.[150] Furthermore, in 1573 Paleotti still felt the need to remind professors of arts and medicine to abandon questions forbidden by the Fifth Lateran Council.[151] Thus, sixty years after its proclamation, enforcing the *Apostolici regiminis* was still problematic. Likewise, the 1641 *Ordinationi* make specific reference to the Council of Vienne and the requirement for lectureships in Hebrew, Arabic, and Chaldean. As a consequence, the legate ordered the authorities of the *studium* to find someone as soon as possible to offer this teaching. But nothing happened. In fact, given the polyphonic nature of university control in Bologna and the lack of jurisdictional clarity within power structures (see Chapter 1), introducing change was hard. Making it stick was even harder, since it involved an arduous process to reach a broad consensus. Organs such as the Senate could throw up obstacles, such as in 1574 when it resisted Paleotti's efforts and held that one reader of theology in the *studium* was enough.[152] (Its attitude over time remains to be studied.)

It is therefore all the more important to consider how the rise of theology should be inscribed within Bologna's broader religious culture.[153] Some of this culture's features included confraternities, festivals, processions, sermons, saints' days, and the like. The transformation of the city's spaces over time reflected several of these associations and activities.[154] Furthermore, an increasingly wide array of devotional objects and religious prints found a place in the homes of rich and poor; these included printed sheets that might decorate the walls, as well as holy cards (*santini*) and domestic altars. More public objects included religious posters, displayed especially in proximity to places of worship, while booklets for teaching Christian doctrine were also, of course, highly charged religiously.[155] Religious music, for which Bologna was especially famous, would have played a significant role in both fostering and expressing devotion.

Of particular importance was the veneration of Mary, an aspect of Bolognese devotion that had deep historical roots but became especially prominent from the Quattrocento onward. It was during the fifteenth century, thanks to the Bentivoglio, that Mary was made the patron saint of Bologna. A sculpture of the Madonna was added to the façade of the Palazzo Pubblico. Every evening, torches were lit to this Virgin, a bell sounded, and passersby were expected to genuflect three times before her.[156]

But the veneration of Mary was not just a "popular" devotion. The Jesuits' Marian Congregazione dell'Assunta, for instance, continued to attract university students and professors long after the Congregazione della Perseveranza had merged with it at the start of the seventeenth century. Between 100 and 150 of these members gathered together regularly for prayers, hymns, communion, acts of devotion and penitence, and processions. Their meetings often included readings from the Scriptures or devotional works. This community, with its attention to the spiritual and religious development of individual university members, played a role in fostering good morals and in some cases led to decisions to embrace the religious life. Its influence on the spiritual direction of the university may well have been powerful.[157] Student piety and religious instruction took encouragement from the initiatives of Paleotti mentioned above and from the sessions of the Council of Trent held in Bologna between 1547 and 1548.[158]

The religious devotion of some professors emerges in unexpected places, including medical writings. In his 1551 commentary on Hippocrates's *Prognostic,* Benedetto Vittori on several occasions comments on passages of Scripture, such as Mark 5. On one occasion he refers to Jesus's healing of a woman and his instruction "Go, daughter, your faith has saved you: go in peace" (v. 34). On this basis, he argues that healing requires not only faith, but God's grace as well.[159] He also discusses issues such as whether God is the cause of illness.[160] Particularly striking is the long note appended to Vittori's commentary on Hippocrates's *Aphorisms,* where he thanks God, His son Jesus, and the Virgin Mary for helping and protecting him in the completion of his work.[161] This does not sound like a perfunctory statement added to satisfy anyone with doubts about his orthodoxy. A couple of centuries later, the public orations of the medical doctor Giuseppe Pozzi in 1732 likewise contain a sustained hymn to the greatness of God as seen in the human body. The presenter of the work comments favorably on Pozzi's exaltation of God's wisdom, love, and providence.[162] Countless plans in the Serie di Annue Lezioni start or end with invocations of God and, often, the Virgin, in expressions such as *Ad maiorem Dei gloriam.* At times these may appear (and even be) formulaic, but that is not to say that they are insincere. Finally, this chapter has shown that several Bolognese professors of the seventeenth and eighteenth centuries were familiar with the Europe-wide movement of physico-theology, which extolled the Creator in the course of discussing the natural world. For Italy, this understudied current deserves serious attention, also because of its devotional qualities.[163]

Developments in lower-level education may have been a major contributing factor to the religious tone of many Bolognese professors' works. Paleotti may not have been quite successful in permanently shaping the landscape of higher education, but he did much that left its mark at the elementary level. In this work, carried on by Paleotti's successors throughout the seventeenth century, youngsters were encouraged to embrace a devout lifestyle. They received a much firmer foundation in Christian doctrine. Schools run by Jesuits and other orders supervised an educational curriculum that was both religious and rigorous (see §3.3.1 and §3.3.2).

The religious character of education spilled over into the university program of learning, as becomes clear from the studies and educational theory of Bartolomeo Aldrovandi. Details about his life are scarce, but Aldrovandi (whom we have met as a professor in §8.2.2) seems to have started his philosophical studies in 1691. He took his arts degree on 30 October 1701 and, after an interruption of several years (during which he probably taught privately and possibly followed some courses in medicine), taught moral philosophy in the *studium,* starting in 1708.[164] The documentation on Aldrovandi's studies is unusually rich: five folders contain dozens of autograph items testifying to his education.[165] Notebooks in the first folder document his initial studies (c. 1691) in logic and metaphysics under university professors Pietro Maria Ciani and the Franciscan Luigi Sabattini, respectively.[166] The second contains notebooks relating to his studies of moral theology (*De actibus humanis*), natural philosophy, and the soul.[167] After these come notes and notebooks on geometry, trigonometry, astronomy, and mechanics (third folder). Matters of moral theology, systematic theology, and metaphysics predominate in the fourth folder. The final folder is a miscellaneous grouping of notes on medicine (apparently from a course Bartolomeo followed on the topic), lectures he gave on moral philosophy, and course plans for his teaching in 1709–1710 and other years. These materials suggest that a student of arts and medicine at the end of the seventeenth century would follow, not only the usual subjects, but also moral theology, systematic theology, and metaphysics. Thus theology did not inhabit a separate sphere of studies from the faculty of arts and medicine.[168]

Aldrovandi's surviving materials contain an undated but significant work, *Quo ordine studiis incumbendum sit* (What order one should follow in one's studies), placed within the materials on logic.[169] There the author (presumably Aldrovandi himself) outlines an ideal ladder of learning: after the initial rung of logic, one should proceed to arithmetic and geometry, followed by metaphysics; then come physics and the study of the heavens, after which one can move on to medicine. Ethics and theology complete this order of studies. Those wishing to study law can follow a curtailed program involving logic and metaphysics as the minimum preliminary steps. At the moment it is unclear whether this ladder reflected common ideals or practices in Bologna around the start of the eighteenth century. But the presence of theology and its allied subjects as relevant for both Jurists and Artists is a signal of new priorities. At long last Bologna's university had both gained a religious spirit and granted an honored place to theological subjects. These would remain important features of its physiognomy until the end of the century.

Finally, I offer two observations on the effects of the Catholic Reformation on Bologna's *studium*. Although the prohibition of various books, the requirement of taking oaths of loyalty to the Church, inquisitorial investigations, and other mechanisms of control did not stop the circulation of ideas or books in Bologna, they seem to have functioned as a constant drag, delaying them and pushing them underground when they had the potential to arouse suspicion.[170] Yet the evidence gathered so far does not support Dall'Olio's view that, by the seventeenth century, religious suppression in Bologna had reached such levels that lay people were only allowed to consider the sciences and humanities, but not religious subjects or the Scriptures.[171] If anything, what one sees is an intensified religious spirit.

Secondly, scholars have often emphasized that a freer climate was available elsewhere in Italy, where it was possible to continue to attract Protestant students either by circumventing the *professio fidei* requirement (Padua) or by turning a blind eye (Tuscany, and especially Siena).[172] But this narrative has usually depended on a poor appreciation of the role of theology in the Italian universities.[173] In the early modern period, these were no longer necessarily secular institutions as in the period up to the fifteenth century. Despite Paul Grendler's pioneering research in this area, the contours and extent of this phenomenon throughout Italy are poorly understood, particularly for the seventeenth and eighteenth centuries.[174] What is striking, however, is that Bologna does not easily fit within Schmidt-Biggemann's paradigm of a progression from theology to jurisprudence and then to philosophy in the early modern universities.[175] Rather, theology increased its influence, as also happened in Padua and, beyond Italy, at least in Salamanca.[176]

More work is needed on the mechanisms of fostering devotion and restraining heterodoxy in the universities. Scholarly judgments for the sixteenth century differ significantly. Grendler, for instance, inclines toward a mild influence of the Catholic Reformation in Italy—one that, in any case, was no harsher than the attitude taken toward Catholics in Protestant universities.[177] The situation, however, was highly differentiated, both in Italy and throughout Europe, where, in addition to confessional universities, one also found more tolerant ones.[178] Specific studies on ecclesiastical attitudes toward universities (and, conversely, on attitudes of professors and students to matters of faith) will need to gather much more evidence before any firm conclusions can be reached, but the topic is ripe for additional study.

Epilogue

This book's findings prompt some observations relating to Bologna and to university history more generally. The University of Bologna also deserves to be placed more firmly within the broader context of the Italian universities—both those of the Papal State and the University of Padua, with which Bologna had deep links.

First, it is worthwhile noting that institutional patterns do not necessarily find a perfect correspondence in curricular ones. This study has highlighted that the University of Bologna suffered a series of major, long-term challenges (both cultural and structural) between the second half of the sixteenth century and the first half of the eighteenth. These included the loss of student autonomy, attitudes of entitlement on the part of students and professors, ballooning numbers of lecturers, trends of regionalization and localism, financial pressures, jurisdictional unclarity, a declining reputation, and difficulties in acquiring certain recent publications from across Europe. Furthermore, recurring economic crises and outbreaks of the plague created situations requiring the urgent attention of the civic authorities. On the basis of these difficulties, historians have assumed that Bologna's mechanisms of teaching and learning were likewise in serious trouble in the early modern era. Here, however, one needs to tread carefully. While conceding that there were certainly difficulties in this area as well (including a variable enthusiasm for teaching and the rise of dictation and private lectures), in this study I have argued that teaching and learning retained a dynamic quality throughout the period. The four trends discussed in Chapters 5–8 testify, not to a static curriculum, insulated from the waves of broader cultural change, but rather to a number of significant developments and debates, culminating eventually in the reform of the curriculum itself. The claims that Bologna suffered immobility and crisis in the areas of teaching and learning seem hard to substantiate.

A second observation concerns the sources that historians have most regularly relied upon to arrive at conclusions on teaching patterns. As we have seen, these are deeply problematic, while others merit more attention. Studies of Italian universities in particular have made repeated use both of Bologna's 1405 statutes for arts and medicine and of the teaching rolls, which conveniently chart teaching appointments up to the Napoleonic era. Yet the 1405 statutes (whose observance is open to question) not only cover the curriculum of arts and medicine unevenly but offer an idealized and very likely outdated vision of what would actually be taught and how. Furthermore, they are unable to register the changes that took place in later centuries. Teaching rolls have their own drawbacks—not only because their all-important prefaces have not been published, but because their listings offer a false impression of curricular immobility. Historians who wish to study educational practice therefore need to privilege other sources, which can often provide clearer insights into curricular change and cultural reorientations. As this book has suggested, there is much to be gleaned from official and unofficial correspondence, memoranda by institutional bodies and individuals, and especially records of lectures. Notes by professors or students and lecture plans have their own methodological difficulties, but they have the potential to yield significant insights. This is true not just of Bologna or Italian universities but of universities more generally. Current or recent projects to study the lectures of institutions such as the University of Helmstedt or the Collegium Trilingue in Louvain, for instance, point to these sources as a rich vein of investigation that cries out for continued attention.[1] Given the growing supply of repertories that include lectures among them, this line of research will become increasingly viable, particularly if pursued in a collaborative way.

Finally, it is worthwhile framing the discussion of the Bolognese environment within the broader context, both in terms of the universities of the Papal State and other *studia* throughout the Italian Peninsula—particularly Padua. For Bologna did not stand alone. Rather, it belonged to a highly concentrated group of papal universities: there were eight of these at the end of the seventeenth century (Bologna, Ferrara, Perugia, and Rome, in addition to the smaller universities of Cesena, Fermo, Macerata, and Urbino), and Camerino was added in 1727.[2] This was not a network of friendly or collaborative institutions but instead a conglomerate of rivals. Thus, although Bologna was the second-largest city of the Papal State, it increasingly found itself vying with other *studia* for a limited pool of students, all from the same geographical area, although the competition came mainly from the other three large *studia*.

Of particular importance for Bologna was the competition with Rome. Here the dynamic was especially complex and vexing. On the one hand, in the second half of the sixteenth century a succession of pontiffs started to take a special interest in the University of Bologna, with an eye to bringing the *studium* and the city even further within its sphere of influence (§1.3.3). On the other hand, the papacy started to invest heavily in the educational institutions in Rome—not only the university, but also the various Jesuit colleges, including the famous Collegio Romano.[3] This latter strategy posed as much of a challenge to the flourishing of the Bolognese *studium* as the former one. Indeed, it became clear that a "Rome first" policy could be seriously damaging to Bologna. Pontiffs were reluctant to let famous professors teaching in Rome move to Bologna to teach there. In 1570, when the Prince of Flanders prohibited students from leaving his territories to study, the Holy See secured an exception for Rome, but not for Bologna. (Loud protests from the Bolognese reversed the situation, but not for long.)[4] Furthermore, in the early decades of the eighteenth century, a tug-of-war took place between Bologna and Rome over whether Bolognese graduates could or could not be admitted to the colleges of doctors in Rome.[5] (Rome wished to exclude them in favor of its own graduates, something that would have been devastating to the attractiveness of the Bolognese *studium*.)

The new and bolder competition from Rome came on top of a long-established rivalry with Padua, which—as noted in §8.1—was less handicapped by restrictions imposed by the Catholic Church. Padua also had other advantages, including a closer proximity to the German territories and therefore a potential to attract students from there. Overall, its reputation as a center for learning remained strong.[6] Over the centuries, Bologna and Padua enjoyed a deep relationship, reflected in part by flows of students and professors in both directions. Alessandro Achillini and Pietro Pomponazzi were just two among many professors who first taught in Padua, then finished their years in Bologna. Several professors moved in the opposite direction. Ulisse Aldrovandi was just one Bolognese who spent part of his student days in Padua.[7]

In the sixteenth century, difficulties in Bologna and the apparent flourishing of Padua led to an inferiority complex. Padua was an offshoot of Bologna (it had been founded by a disgruntled group of Bolognese students in 1222), and the two universities' programs of study were quite similar.[8] Yet Bologna started to look to Padua as a model. It was Padua that, ahead of Bologna, first united its teachings in a glorious building (the Palazzo del Bo) in 1552. In the sixteenth century, Aldrovandi's reform proposals make constant reference to his experience of teaching practices in Padua (including the use of concurrents or *concorrenti* for the same teaching and time slot). Gregory XIII at one point voiced irritation with this exaltation of Padua, stating the "Bologna should be a model for Padua and the other universities, not the other way around."[9] Yet it was hard for many contemporary observers to shake the impression that Bologna would be rid of many of its problems if only it could imitate Padua. In any case, the overseers of the *studium* were conscious of the need to compare their own situation and initiatives with what was happening elsewhere.[10]

But Padua did not remain a model for long. By the early seventeenth century it was facing many of the same challenges that were troubling Bologna. In addition to student violence and competition from other *studia* (Parma, Bologna, and other Italian universities), these included difficulties attracting students and having too many professors, whose salaries put significant strain on the university at a time of mounting financial constraints.[11] Other developments highlighted by the documentation include increasingly short periods of study, irregularities in the matriculation of students, and the reservation of more teaching posts to its own graduates. (The last of these problems seems to have arisen much later than in Bologna and to have been less acute.) But the reluctance of the Venetian authorities to have too many Paduan professors was not just down to the ideal of attracting the best teachers regardless of their origins: one important consideration was that of ensuring that the local aristocracy did not have too much control over the *studium*.[12] Padua also suffered from some practices (such as the illegal communication of examination *puncta* to candidates long before the event) that degraded its degrees and were not, it seems, common in Bologna.[13]

There are few specific studies on the flows between the two universities in the early modern period.[14] But in the case of professors discussed in this book, the direction of travel seems to have strongly favored Padua, at least from the 1670s onward, with the departure for Padua of Geminiano Montanari (1678), Domenico Guglielmini (1698), and Giambattista Morgagni (1711). This shift may be important because students were attracted by famous professors, and several of the professors just named were renowned. Yet it is also true that others, such as Giovanni Girolamo Sbaraglia, Marcello Malpighi, and Giacomo Sandri, remained tied to Bologna—in several cases, partly because the local literary and scientific academies appealed to their broad interests. The whole matter deserves further attention, along with competition from the University of Florence-Pisa, which reopened in 1543 and, under Duke Cosimo, started a strong recruitment campaign. Those whom Cosimo attracted to Florence from Bologna included the famous printer Lorenzo Torrentino, who had operated in Bologna from 1532 to 1547.[15]

In any case, by Padua's reform of 1771 the relationship between Bologna and Padua seems to have rebalanced somewhat. The Paduan reform started officially in 1761 and had been anticipated by, among others, the reflections of Giovan Francesco Pivati in 1738.[16] It highlighted several of the features that we attribute to modern universities—the preeminent place accorded to scientific and "practical" subjects (both in law and in arts and medicine), the development of laboratories, the reduction of public holidays, the introduction of seminar-style teaching, the use of more specific course plans, the adoption of textbooks, the turn to the vernacular in teaching, and the practice of yearly examinations.[17] Bologna did not experience such a significant upending of its teaching practices in the eighteenth century. But it is notable that it was Bologna's example that Giovanni Poleni appealed to when he proposed to the Riformatori of Padua in 1719 that they fund a laboratory to complement the teaching of science.[18] In 1768, Padua was still discussing the need to reform the teaching of physics by distributing it into two branches—"fisica in generale, ed in particolare."[19] Bologna had introduced this distinction some thirty years earlier (see §2.3.4).[20] One should not, therefore, be too dismissive of the initiatives that took place in Bologna, just because they are not well known at present.

It is here that historical analysis finds its greatest challenge.[21] Despite the wealth of its records, only a small part of the relevant documents for the University of Bologna has been published, particularly for the period after 1500.[22] There is currently no counterpart to the admirable collection of documents by Piero del Negro and Francesco Piovan in *L'Università di Padova nei secoli.* Statutes, prefaces to the rolls, minutes of the doctoral colleges, correspondence, and the voluminous records of the ASB series Archivio dello Studio, Assunteria di Studio, and Riformatori dello Studio (in addition, of course, to manuscript and printed lectures and student notes) are abundant and largely accessible, but remain unknown to the larger scholarly community.[23] The lack of modern editions only confirms to young historians (in a particularly vicious kind of circle) that these materials are not worthy of attention.[24] This book will, I hope, suggest otherwise and encourage further studies on the intersection of the history of knowledge, the history of the book, and institutional history.

APPENDIX:
PREFACE TO THE TEACHING ROLL FROM 1586–1587

ABBREVIATIONS

NOTES

BIBLIOGRAPHY

ACKNOWLEDGMENTS

INDEX

APPENDIX: PREFACE TO THE TEACHING ROLL FROM 1586–1587

The following is the preface to the roll for arts and medicine for 1586–1587 dated October 1586 in ASB, Riformatori, b. 12, roll 138 (for the teachings listed, see Dallari, II, 223–25). I have silently expanded most abbreviations. References to fines and so forth are expressed in terms of the local currency of *bolognini* (or *lire*), subdivided in *soldi* and then *denari*, as described in Chimienti, *Monete*.

In nomine Sanctae Trinitatis, Patris et Filii et Spiritus Sancti, ac gloriosae et Beatissimae Virginis Mariae et Beatorum Apostolorum Petri et Pauli, ac gloriosi confessoris sancti Petronii Episcopi civitatis Bononiae, cuius intercessionibus civitas ipsa reaedificata fuit ac generali omnium scientiarum studio sublimata per sacratissimum Theodosium Romanorum Imperatorem anno Dominicae nativitatis quadrigentesimovigesimotertio tempore Caelestini Pontificis Maximi tunc ibidem praesentis et auctorantis, necnon ad laudem et gloriam Sacrae Romanae Ecclesiae et Sanctissimi et beatissimi D. Domini Sixti Quinti divina providentia Pontificis Maximi necnon Magnifici ac invictissimi populi Bononie etiam praesentis status libertatis eiusdem.

Incipit Rotulus almi Studii Bononiensis Medicorum et Artistarum compositus et ordinatus pro augumento Studii per spectatos et claros viros perillustrem Senatorem ac Equitem Dominum Raffaelem Riarium, illustrem Dominem Comitem Ascanium Bentivolum, Magnificum Dominum Achillem dal Bo ac Dominum Hieronymum de Alè Bononienses cives qui anno praesenti Studium Bononiensem reformarunt et in praesenti Rotulo scribi fecerunt infrascriptos doctores et alios ad legendum deputatos cum capitulis et provisionibus et statutis infrascriptis. Ut Studium ipsum et eius clarum nomen non solum ulla in parte diminuatur, sed cum laude et gloria huius inclitae Civitatis merito augeatur, ad utilitatem etiam et commodum scholarium virtutibus et disciplinis in eo incumbentium. Quod quidem Studium, Deo favente, incipiet primo die non festivo post diem festum Sancti Lucae mensis Octobris praesentis annis. Quo die omnes doctores et alii ordinarie legentes omnino legere incipiant et continuent omnibus diebus quibus ordinarie legetur.

Serventur et adimpleantur omnia statuta, privilegia, immunitates et decreta scholaribus Studii Bononiae ac doctoribus et aliis in dicto studio legentibus concessa, et maxime privilegium Studii indultum Civitati Bononiae per sacratissimum Romanorum Imperatorem Theodosium, anno superius descripto. Si quis ex infrascriptis Rotulatis non propriis expensis vixerit nullum salarium pro sua lectura habeat, hoc tamen non intelligatur pro iis qui ad gramaticam, Poeticam vel Rethoricam deputati sunt et pro iis qui lecturas Universitatis legitime obtinuerint.

Si quis fuerit ad duas lecturas rotulatus non possit nec debeat habere salarium nisi pro una duntaxat lectura. Nullus doctor vel licentiatus seu scholaris qui in praesenti Rotulo non sit descriptus, aliquo modo publice legere possit, sub poena bononenorum (!) centum auri. Omnes doctores et alii rotulati lectura personaliter legant atque continuent diebus et horis deputatis per suas horas et unam ad minus continuam secundum Statuta Universitatis sub poena pro quolibet centenario taxae eorum salarii et solidorum XX bonon. pro quacunque lectione non integre lecta pro quolibet centenario ut supra.

Teneantur ipsi doctores et alii rotulati sine aliqua intermissione vel ommissione processum facere prout in dictis statutis continetur usque ad et per totum diem vigiliae Sanctae Margaritae Virginis de mense Iulii sub poena amissionis tertiae partis salariorum suorum. Quicunque deputatus ad lecturam Medicinae ordinariam tam de mane quam de sero et ad lecturam Philosophiae ordinariam et extraordinariam singulis diebus non habuerit continue dum leget quattuor scholares qui sint veri scholares et pro scholaribus habeantur punctetur ac si eo die non legisset. Caeteri vero habere debeant tres scholares modo et forma suprascriptis et qui eos non habuerit punctetur ut supra.

Pro honore Studii et scholarium utilitate praedicti doctores legere et concurrere teneantur secundum prout inferius sunt descripti ut non solum in tempore et hora, sed etiam in lectionibus, adeo quod quilibet procedens eandem lectionem legat, quam suus concurrens leget. Postea, finitis lectionibus, omnes concurrentes in locis deputatis circulum faciant et ibi simul conferant et disputent, sub poena soldorum XX pro qualibet vice, et circuli fieri debeant singulis diebus a principio Studii quibus ordinarie legetur tam de mane quam de sero donec et quousque quilibet doctor seu legens vel proponens vel et respondens suas vices egerit sub eadem poena.

Cum non deceat lecturas Universitatis concedi ignaris et indoctis, propterea nullus scholaris aliquam de dictis lecturis habere possit nisi per annum continuum ad minus in Studio Bononiensi studuerit in ea facultate in qua lecturam petet, et nisi prius eodem anno quo lecturam petet in ipso studio semel disputaverit publice in facultate praedicta de quibus legitima fides fieri debeat per huiusmodi lecturas petentes. Quae quidem lecturae legi congruis diebus et horis ac continuari debeant a scholaribus qui illas obtinuerint, sub eisdemmet (!) poenis impositis lectiones suas ommittentibus vel eas non integre legentibus nec tamen de numero scholarium punctare debeant. Adiicientes quod nullus aliquo pacto possit habere nisi unam lecturam tantum in Medicina ac unam solam in Artibus et e contra, de quibus quidem lecturis aut aliqua earum non possit fieri permutatio, alienatio, substitutio vel contractus alicuius formae, sed scholaris ad illam electus et non alius graduari et doctorari debeat in fine anni eius lecturae per ipsum tamen ut supra lecta, qui si doctorari nolet vel non posset morte praevenutus nullatenus substitui debeat neque possit nisi per partitum Illustri Regiminis coram Illustrissimo et Reverendissimo Domino Legato seu Vicelegato aut Gubernatore legitime obtentum.

Conducti et rotulati ad Rethoricam et Poeticam legere debeant ad minus per duas horas continuas, unam in Oratoria, aliam in Poetica arte et Reformatoribus significare debeant quos libros sint lecturi et cum eis conveniant et concordes sint de libris praedictis ut bonas et utiles lectiones auditoribus eligant. Dominus Rector Universitatis doctores aut alii legentes nullam vacationem aliqua ratione vel causa faciant aut mandent ultra vacationes a Statutis concessas nisi cum licentia et mandato Illustrissimi et Reverendissimi Domini Legati vel Vicelegati aut Gubernatoris aut Illustrium Dominorum Quadraginta sub poena D. Rectori librorum XXV bon. et doctoribus ac legentibus pro quacunque lectione dimissa soldorum XXX bonon. pro quolibet centenario et ad rationem centenarii taxae eorum salarii. Et vacationes Carnisprivii fieri non debeant priusquam per tres hebdomadas ad plus ante diem cinerum sub eadem poena. Nec propter disputationes scholarium ordinariae lectiones impediantur. Nullus disputare debeat nisi diebus festis et feriatis vel temporibus vacationum sub poena suprascripta.

Cum praecipue Universitati Medicorum huius almi studii utile sit habere singulis annis Tacuinum seu Almanach hoc est motum et aspectum omnium planetarum, qui deputati sunt ad Astronomiam Tacuinum facere teneantur in quo contineantur omnium planetarum motus singulis diebus anni et cum signis, gradibus et minutis una cum capite Draconis, insuper et aspectus omnium planetarum ad lunam similiter et capitis Draconis et aspectus omnium planetarum inter se una cum litera Dominicali et ferialibus per cursum totius anni. In fine totius Almanach describantur coniunctiones Solis et Lunae una cum Farmacis totius anni. Tacuinum autem praedictum in principio Ianuarii debeat praesentari Domino Rectori qui debeat ipsum collocari facere in Apotheca Universitatis ubi Medici congregantur, ut commune sit omnibus per totum annum qui illud videre voluerint. Elapso anno in camera actorum reponatur sub poena ipsi Domino Rectori si contrafecerit librarum X bonon. et ipsis Astrologis librarum XX bonon. de suo salario retinendarum si praedicta aut aliquod praedictorum facere ommisserint modo quo supra scriptum est.

Et ut sciri ac intelligi et plena notitia illorum haberi possit qui in suis lectionibus legendis praedicta non observabunt, teneatur Officialis ad hoc deputatus tempore congruo ire ad videndum omnes et singulares doctores et alios in Studio Bononiensi legentes, et postea singula hebdomada fideliter referre et in scriptis dare Notario et Cancellario Dominorum Reformatorum Studii quoscunque punctaverit ac invenerit non legisse, ac ea omnia ad quae tenentur ex forma statutorum Universitatis et praesentis Rotuli non fecisse sub poena dupli eius in quod ipsi doctores et legentes punctantur incurrissent. Et ipse Notarius omnia et singula sibi relata notare debeat, ut postea in distributionibus expediens unicuique rotulato salarium suum solvi possit sive integrum sive diminutum, prout ab ipsis lectum et suprascriptis capitulis satisfactum fuerit.

Et ne aliquod dubium suboriri possit casu quo aliquid inveniatur quod praesenti Rotulo obstet: observentur et adimpleantur omnia et singula suprascripta capitula pro ut in eis continentur, amotis omnibus exceptionibus et contradictionibus quae quoquomodo dici et allegari aut excogitari possent, et nihil in contrarium admittatur. Non obstantibus quibuscunque statutis et decretis, constitutionibus, reformationibus, legibus, iuribus et aliis in contrarium quomodolibet facientibus, et iis de quibus habenda esset mentio specialis vel expressa. Quibus omnibus et singulis quoad contenta in praesenti Rotulo tantum praesens capitulum derogatum sit et esse intelligatur.

Pro observatione Capitulorum praesentis Rotuli et omnium in eo contentorum Depositarius Doctorum et aliorum in Studio Bononiensi legentium nihil solvere debeat alicui Rotulato absque expressa commissione et mandato Illustrissimi et Reverendissimi Domini Legati seu Vicelegati aut Gubernatoris ac Illustrium Dominorum Quadraginta quod in scriptis more solito expeditum appareat, et hoc ut intelligere possit dictus Depositarius quibus aliquid detraheri et retineri sit de salariis suis ob lectionibus non lectis et alia ommissa contra formam praesentis Rotuli, alioquin de suo solvisse intelligatur. Ultimo praesens Rotulus praesentetur et ponatur ad locum solitum, seu ad stationem Universitatis Dominorum Scholarium Medicorum et Artistarum ibidem debito tempore mansurus ut ab omnibus videri, legi ac intelligi possit. Deinde ponatur in Archivio publico per Notarium et Cancellarium suprascriptum.

English Translation

In the name of the Holy Trinity, Father, Son, and Holy Spirit, and of the glorious and most Blessed Virgin Mary and the most Blessed Apostles Peter and Paul, and of the glorious confessor of the faith Saint Petronius, bishop of the city of Bologna, through whose intercession this city was rebuilt and elevated to a general *studium* for all the areas of knowledge by the most holy Roman Emperor Theodosius in the year of our Lord 423, at the time of Pope Celestine, who was present and confirmed [the same], and to the praise and glory of the Holy Roman Church and of the most holy and blessed Sixtus V, pope by divine providence, and [to the glory] of the magnificent and free people of Bologna and its present condition of liberty.

Here begins the roll of the *medici* and *artisti* of the venerable *studium* of Bologna, composed and ordered for the increment of the *studium* by the following worthy and famed men: the most excellent Senator and

Knight Raffaele Riario, the illustrious Count Ascanio Bentivoglio, the magnificent Achille dal Bo, and Girolamo da Alè, citizens of Bologna, who in the present year again established the Bolognese *studium* and ordered that the following doctors and others appointed to teach should be included on this roll, along with the following agreements and provisions and statutes. This is so that that *studium* itself and its reputation be not only not diminished in any way, but that it rightly be magnified, to the honor and glory of this great city, and that the students attending it in virtue and knowledge profit from it. God willing, this *studium* will have its start on the first working day after the feast of St. Luke in the month of October of this year. On that day, all the doctors and others reading ordinarily should without fail start to teach [their classes] and continue to do so on all days in which [it is the custom] to read ordinarily.

Let all statutes, privileges, protections, and decrees made to the students of the *studium* of Bologna and to the doctors and those reading in the same *studium* be observed and fulfilled, and especially the privilege to have a *studium* granted to the city of Bologna by the most holy Roman Emperor Theodosius, in the year mentioned above. If anyone of those whose names appear on the rolls is not self-supporting, he should receive no compensation for his teaching. This does not, however, apply to those who have been appointed to teach grammar, poetry, or rhetoric or to those who have been legitimately appointed to a *lectura universitatis.*

If anyone has been listed for two lectures, he can only receive the salary for one. No doctor or degree-holder or student who is not listed on the present roll is allowed to teach publicly in any way. The fine for doing so is 100 gold *bolognini.* All doctors and other registered on the roll must give their lectures themselves and continue to do so on the days and at the times appointed for their slots; they must teach at least for a full hour according to the statutes of the *universitas.* They will otherwise incur a deduction for each instance in which a lecture is not fully given of 20 *soldi* for every 100 *bolognini* of their salary.

The doctors and the others registered on the rolls must continue to teach, as specified by the statutes, continuously and integrally until the eve of the feast of St. Margaret the Virgin (in the month of July) inclusive, on pain of losing a third of their salary. Whoever is appointed to teach ordinary medicine (whether in the morning or in the afternoon) or ordinary or extraordinary philosophy must each day continuously have at least four students present. (These must be true students, and held to be such.) Otherwise he will be fined, even if he did not lecture that day. As for the others, they must have three students in the sense and form specified above; whoever does not have them is to be fined as above.

For the honor of the *studium* and the profit of the students, the doctors mentioned above are obliged to lecture concurrently with others as listed [in the roll] below. Their teaching is to be concurrent, not only in terms of time, but also in terms of the lectures given: everyone must lecture on the same material as his competitor. After the end of the lectures, every competitor should hold a *circulum* in the appointed place. There they should discuss and hold disputations, on the pain of 20 *soldi* for each omission. The *circuli* must take place every day in which there are ordinary classes, from the opening of the academic year, both in the morning and in the afternoon, until each doctor or lecturer has had his turn either to propose or to respond. In case of infractions, the same penalty as above will apply.

Because the *lecturae universitatis* should not be given out to the ignorant or the unlearned, no student is eligible for one of these lectureships unless he has studied in the Bolognese *studium* for one year at least the subject that he wishes to teach. In the year in which he applies for such a lectureship he must also already have disputed publicly in that same subject. Those applying for such lectureships need to provide legitimate assurances. These lectures need to be read on the appropriate days and at the appropriate times. Those appointed must teach without interruption and are subject to the same fines as those who omit to give their lectures or do not read them fully. They are not, however, subject to fines with regard to the number of students. We add that no one can under any circumstance hold more than one such lectureship in medicine or in arts or vice versa. Of these lectures, none of them can be exchanged or transferred or replaced or subcontracted in any way: the student appointed to any such lecture (and no one else) must graduate and receive his doctorate at the end of the year of his lectureship (filled by himself as specified above). If he decides not to graduate or death prevents him from doing so, he should not and cannot be replaced unless by an official decision (taken legitimately) of the illustrious Senate, gathered in the presence of the illustrious and most reverend legate or vice-legate or governor.

Those who have been appointed and placed on the rolls for rhetoric and poetry must lecture for at least two hours continuously: [they must give] one lecture on the art of oratory and another on that of poetry. They must indicate to the Riformatori what works they intend to teach. Let them discuss and agree with them about the said works, so that they choose good and useful topics for those who hear them. The rector of the *universitas,* the doctors, and other lecturers should not for any reason proclaim or extend any vacation beyond the vacation periods specified by the statutes unless this is with the permission and on the instruction of the most reverend legate or vice-legate or governor or the illustrious Quaranta. The fine otherwise will be of 25 *bolognini* for the rector and, for the doctors and lecturers, 30 *soldi* per 100 *bolognini* [?] of their salary for each canceled lecture, according to their rate of pay. The Lent holidays should not start any earlier than three weeks before Ash Wednesday. (The same punishment will apply.) The ordinary lectures should not be impeded on account of the student disputations. No one is to hold disputations unless on official or other holidays or during vacation periods. (The same punishment will apply.)

Given that it is especially useful for the *universitas* of medicine of this *studium* to have each year the *taccuino* or almanac presenting the movement and aspect of all planets, those who are appointed to astronomy must style the almanac containing all the movements of the planets for all days of the year together with the [relevant astrological] signs, degrees, and minutes and the head of the dragon.† Furthermore, they must specify the aspect of all the planets and of the head of the dragon in relationship to the moon, and the relationship of all the planets among themselves. They must also compile the calendar of Sundays and holidays throughout the course of the whole year. At the end of the almanac they must describe the conjunctions of the sun and moon together with the medical compounds for the various times of year. At the start of January they must present this almanac to the rector; he will ensure that it is placed in the pharmacy of the *universitas* where the *medici* gather, so that it is available to everyone who wants to view it during the course

† I.e., the Draco constellation.

of the whole year. At the end of the year it must be deposited in the archive; the rector will have to pay a fine of 10 *bolognini* if he does not observe this instruction. The astrologers will be fined 20 *bolognini* of their salary if they omit to follow any or all of the instructions specified above.

And in order that there may be full knowledge and intelligence about those who lecture but do not observe the instructions above, the official deputed to this task [i.e., the *punctator*?] must at a proper time go and observe individually all the doctors or lecturers in the Bolognese *studium*, and after a week must make a written report to the notary and secretary of the Riformatori dello Studio about those whom he has fined or has found not to be lecturing, or who have not fulfilled all their obligations according to the form of the statutes of the *universitas* and of the present roll. If he fails to do so, he will pay a fine amounting to twice what the doctors and lecturers would have received. The notary must note all matters individually so that later, when it comes to making the payments, everyone may receive either the amount due him (whether the full or the reduced amount), according to whether they have followed and fulfilled the stipulations above.

And so that no doubt may arise in case something is found that is an impediment to the [contents of] this roll: each and every instruction should be observed in full according to what is specified, without regard for any exceptions or contradictions that may be stated or alleged or invented to militate against them. These instructions are valid notwithstanding any statutes and decrees, constitutions, articles of reform, laws, rights or anything else somehow indicating the contrary, including any matters that should have been mentioned either specifically or expressly. It should be understood that the present article can be modified only in accordance with what is contained, both generally and specifically, in this roll.

In order to promote the observance of the instructions in the present roll and all matters contained in it, the *depositarius* [= financial officer] of the doctors and other lecturers in the Bolognese *studium* should not disburse any payment that would usually be recorded in writing to anyone on the roll without the express authorization and instruction of the illustrious and most reverend legate or vice-legate or governor and of the Quaranta: the said officer must know whose salary should be docked or withheld due to lectures not read and other omissions, in contravention of the present roll, otherwise he will be seen to have made payments on his own authority. Finally, the present roll must be presented and displayed in the usual place, that is, at the home of the *universitas* of the students of medicine and arts. It must remain on display for the requisite amount of time, so that all may see, read, and understand it. Thereafter the notary and secretary must deposit it in the public archive.

ABBREVIATIONS

LIBRARY AND ARCHIVE COLLECTIONS

AAB	Archivio Arcivescovile di Bologna
AAV	Archivio Apostolico Vaticano (formerly Archivio Segreto Vaticano)
Ambasciata	Senato: Ambasciata bolognese a Roma
Annue Lezioni	Assunteria di Studio, Serie di Annue Lezioni, b. 60–b. 62
ASB	Archivio di Stato di Bologna
BAV	Biblioteca Apostolica Vaticana
BCAB	Biblioteca Comunale dell'Archiginnasio di Bologna
BUB	Biblioteca Universitaria di Bologna
HRC Ranuzzi	Harry Ransom Center (University of Texas at Austin), Ranuzzi Manuscripts
Quartironi	Riformatori dello Studio, Quartironi degli Stipendi, b. 32–b. 49
Tesoreria	Tesoreria e Controllatore di Tesoreria

ONLINE CATALOGS AND DATABASES

ASFE	Amore scientiae facti sunt exules (online at asfe.it)
EDIT16	*EDIT16: Censimento nazionale delle edizioni italiane del XVI secolo* (online at edit16.iccu.sbn.it)
GW	*Gesamtkatalog der Wiegendrucke* (online at www.gesamtkatalogderwiegendrucke.de)
IGI	*Indice generale degli incunaboli delle bibliotechee d'Italia,* 6 vols. (Rome: Istituto poligrafico and Zecca dello Stato, Libreria dello Stato, 1943–1981)
ISTC	*Incunabula Short Title Catalogue* (online at www.bl.uk/catalogues/istc/)

WORKS FREQUENTLY CITED

AMDSR	*Atti e memorie della R. Deputazione di storia della Romagna.*
ASUI	*Annali di storia delle università italiane.*
Baiada / Cavazza	Enrica Baiada and Marta Cavazza, "Le discipline matematico-astronomiche tra Seicento e Settecento," in *L'Università a Bologna,* II, 153–64.
Bònoli / Piliarvu	Fabrizio Bònoli and Daniela Piliarvu, *I lettori di astronomia presso lo Studio di Bologna dal XII al XX secolo* (Bologna: CLUEB, 2001).
Bronzino	Giovanni Bronzino, *Notitia doctorum sive Catalogus doctorum qui in Collegiis Philosophiae et Medicinae Bononiae laureati fuerunt ab anno 1480 usque ad annum 1800* (Milan: A. Giuffrè, 1962).
Carboni I	Mauro Carboni, "La Gabella Grossa di Bologna: La formazione di una grande azienda fiscale," *Il Carrobbio* 16 (1990): 114–22.
Carboni II	Mauro Carboni, "La Gabella Grossa di Bologna: Crisi di una grande azienda daziaria," *Il Carrobbio* 17 (1991): 100–109.
Chines	Loredana Chines, *I lettori di retorica e le humanae litterae allo Studio di Bologna nei secoli XV e XVI* (Bologna: Il Nove, 1992).
Cristiani	Andrea Cristiani, *I lettori di Medicina allo Studio di Bologna nei secoli XV e XVI* (Bologna: Analisi, 1990).
Dallari	Umberto Dallari, *I rotuli dei lettori legisti e artisti dello Studio di Bologna dal 1384 al 1799,* 4 vols. (Bologna: Regia Tipografia dei Fratelli Merlani, 1888–1924).
DBI	*Dizionario biografico degli italiani,* 100 vols. (Rome: Istituto per l'Enciclopedia Italiana, 1960–2020).
DSB	*Dictionary of Scientific Biography,* ed. Charles Coulston Gillispie, 18 vols. (New York: Scribner, 1970–1990).
DSI	*Dizionario storico dell'Inquisizione,* ed. Adriano Prosperi, 4 vols. (Pisa: Edizioni della Normale, 2010).
ERP	*Encylopedia of Renaissance Philosophy,* ed. Marco Sgarbi (Cham: Springer, online at https://doi.org/10.1007/978-3-319-02848-4).

Fantuzzi — Giovanni Fantuzzi, *Notizie degli scrittori bolognesi,* 9 vols. (Bologna: stamperia di San Tommaso d'Aquino, 1781–1788).

Frati, *Indice* — Lodovico Frati, *Indice dei codici latini conservati nella R. Biblioteca Universitaria di Bologna* (Florence: successori di B. Seeber, 1909).

Frati, *Inventario* — Lodovico Frati, *Inventario dei manoscritti,* 8 vols., ms. catalogue of the BUB.

Lines, "Teachers" — David A. Lines, "Appendix: Teachers of Natural Philosophy in Bologna, ca. 1340–1600," in idem, "Natural Philosophy in Renaissance Italy," 278–323.

Lohr — Charles H. Lohr, *Latin Aristotle Commentaries,* 5 vols. (Florence: Olschki, 1988–2013).

Malagola, *Statuta universitatis scolarium* (1405) — *Statuti delle Università e dei Collegi* (as below), 203–307 ("Statuta nova universitatis scolarium scientie medicine et artium generalis studii civitatis Bononie" = Lines, *Selected Documents,* I, doc. 1).

Malagola, *Statuta universitatis scolarium* (1442) — *Statuti delle Università e dei Collegi* (as below), 313–21 ("Riforme agli statuti dell'Università di Medicina e d'Arti del 1405 promulgate nel 1442" = Lines, *Selected Documents,* I, doc. 2).

Malagola, *Statuti* — *Statuti delle Università e dei Collegi dello Studio bolognese,* ed. Carlo Malagola (Bologna: Nicola Zanichelli, 1888; repr., Bologna: Forni, 1966, 1988).

Malagola, *Statuti Collegio* (1378) — *Statuti delle Università e dei Collegi* (as above), 425–52 ("Statuti del Collegio di Medicina e d'Arti del 1378").

Malagola, *Statuti Collegio* (1395) — *Statuti delle Università e dei Collegi* (as above), 453–84 ("Statuti del Collegio di Medicina e d'Arti del 1395").

Malagola, *Statuti Collegio* (c. 1400?) — *Statuti delle Università e dei Collegi* (as above), 485–93 ("Frammento di Statuto [del Collegio di Medicina e d'Arti] del principio del secolo XV" = Lines, *Selected Documents,* I, doc. 3).

Malagola, *Statuti Collegio* (1410) — *Statuti delle Università e dei Collegi* (as above), 497–522 ("Constitutiones, statuta et ordinamenta collegii doctorum scientie medicine civitatis Bononie" = Lines, *Selected Documents,* I, doc. 4).

Manfrè I	G. Manfrè, "La biblioteca dell'umanista bolognese Giovanni Garzoni (1419–1505)," *Accademie e biblioteche d'Italia* 27 (1959): 249–78.
Manfrè II	G. Manfrè, "La biblioteca dell'umanista bolognese Giovanni Garzoni (1419–1505)," *Accademie e biblioteche d'Italia* 28 (1960): 17–72.
Matsen I	Herbert S. Matsen, "Students' 'Arts' Disputations at Bologna around 1500, Illustrated from the Career of Alessandro Achillini," *History of Education* 6 (1977): 169–81.
Matsen II	Herbert S. Matsen, "Students' 'Arts' Disputations at Bologna around 1500," *Renaissance Quarterly* 47.3 (Autumn 1994): 535–55.
Maylender	Michele Maylender, *Storia delle Accademie d'Italia,* 5 vols. (Bologna: L. Cappelli, 1926–1930; repr., Bologna: Forni, 1976).
Mazzetti	Serafino Mazzetti, *Repertorio dei professori dell' Università e dell'Istituto delle Scienze di Bologna* (Bologna: San Tommaso d'Aquino, 1847; repr., Bologna: Forni, 1988).
MPSI	*Monumenta Paedagogica Societatis Iesu,* ed. Ladislaus Lukács, 7 vols. (Rome: Apud Monumenta Historica Societatis Iesu, 1965–1992).
Salterini	Claudia Salterini, *L'archivio dei Riformatori dello Studio* (Bologna: Istituto per la Storia della Università, 1997).
SMSUB	*Studi e memorie per la storia dell'Università di Bologna.*
Tiraboschi	Girolamo Tiraboschi, *Biblioteca modenese o Notizie della vita e delle opere degli scrittori natii degli stati del serenissimo signor duca di Modena,* 6 vols. (Modena: Società Tipografica, 1781–1786; repr., Bologna: Forni, 1970).

NOTES

INTRODUCTION

1. This sketch is a composite of Jerónimo Osório the Younger, "Hieronymi Osorii Lusitani Vita" (pages not numbered), and his uncle Jerónimo Osório the Elder, *De gloria* (11–15; quotations at 11 and 12), in idem, *De gloria libri quinque,* in his *Opera omnia* (Lyon: Jean Pillehotte, 1609), vol. I. The longer passage reads: "Cum igitur in Italiam me excolendi ingenii gratia contulissem, et ex multorum sermone intellexissem, nullam tunc Italiae civitatem esse cum Bononia literarum gloria conferendam, eam delegi potissimum, in qua studia, perturbatione rerum mearum impedita, longo tamen intervallo revocarem. Postquam vero in ea consedi, re ipsa cognovi fuisse mihi ab omnibus quorum praedicationem sequutus fueram, egregie consultum. Est enim illa civitas et opibus florens et omnibus maximarum artium disciplinis exculta, tum gentis humanitate et rerum omnium copia ad studia litterarum satis instructa. Florebant ibi multi doctrinis Graecis et Latinis non mediocriter eruditi; multi in omni philosophiae genere excellentes; multi postremo dicendi facultate praestantes et in omni liberali doctrina summa cum laude versati. Quid dicam de utriusque iuris studio, cum illud constet, Bononienses iureconsultos omnibus, qui se huic gravissimae disciplinae dediderunt, admirabile semper acuminis et prudentiae lumen praetulisse? Non igitur mirum videri debet, si tanta loci celebritate commoti bene informati adolescentes undique Bononiam conveniant ad animum clarissimis disciplinis excolendum, cum in ea constitutum esse videatur egregium quoddam eruditionis et sapientiae domicilium." See also Sorbelli, *Bologna negli scrittori stranieri,* I, 35–41.
2. For a full study and edition, see Torrão, "D. Jerónimo Osório e o Tratado 'De Gloria.'"
3. In addition to Southern's classic *The Making of the Middle Ages,* see at least *Renaissance and Renewal.*
4. For a more detailed and nuanced account, see §2.1; Verger, "Patterns."
5. On these schools, see Fasoli, *Per la storia dell'Università,* chap. 3.

6. Dolcini, "Pepe, Irnerio, Graziano," esp. 21; idem, "Lo Studium fino al XIII secolo"; more celebrative and less reliable is Sorbelli, *Storia della Università,* 31–42.
7. For some studies of the University of Bologna before 1400, see Denifle, *Die Entstehung,* 132–218; Rashdall, *The Universities of Europe,* I, 87–268; Malagola, *Monografie storiche;* F. Cavazza, *Le scuole;* Sorbelli, *Storia della Università;* Calcaterra, *Alma mater studiorum;* Fasoli, *Per la storia dell'Università;* Cobban, *The Medieval Universities;* Bellomo, *Saggio sull'università; L'Università a Bologna; Storia illustrata di Bologna,* vol. VI; Cencetti, *Lo Studio di Bologna;* Pini, *Studio, università e città.* Recent essays, with considerable bibliography, include Dolcini, "Lo Studium fino al XIII secolo"; Mazzanti, "Lo Studium nel XIV secolo." See also Lines, "The University and the City."
8. See, among others, Fasoli, *Per la storia dell'Università,* 82–91, 117–32; Kibre, *Scholarly Privileges,* 10–17; Nardi, "Relations with Authority," 78–79; Dolcini, "Lo Studium fino al XIII secolo," 489–92. Scholars disagree on the dating and place of emanation of the decree, usually referred to as *Authentica Habita.* For a modern edition, see Koeppler, "Frederick Barbarossa," 606–7; Stelzer, "Zum Scholarenprivileg."
9. Nardi, "Relations with Authority," 79.
10. For the *studium*'s ties with both papacy and empire in this period, see De Vergottini, "Lo Studio di Bologna, l'Impero e il Papato." The work of Lorenzo Paolini has particularly underlined the role of the Church; see, e.g., his "La chiesa di Bologna e lo Studio."
11. Nardi, "Relations with Authority," 80–81. This was a constant problem also in later years. There is no basis for the widespread myth that Bologna's famous porticos developed as a means of providing housing for students; see Ceccarelli and Guidotti Magnani, *Il portico bolognese.*
12. Pini, "Federico II" (for the exact date, see esp. 69–72).
13. Pini, "Federico II," 74–78.
14. For the text of the Theodosian privilege, see Fasoli and Pighi, "Il privilegio teodosiano"; further editions in Fasoli, "La composizione del falso diploma," and eadem, "Il falso privilegio." For copies, see, for instance ASB, Archivio dello Studio, b. 216, where it appears on 137–39.
15. See Prodi, *Il cardinale Gabriele Paleotti,* II, 247–50; Fasoli, "Appunti sulla 'Historia Bononiensis'"; in general on Sigonio, see McCuaig, *Carlo Sigonio.*
16. See De Benedictis, "Luoghi del potere e Studio"; and §1.3 below.
17. Sorbelli, *Bologna negli scrittori stranieri,* IV, 322.
18. For this and the situation up to 1506, see Fasoli, "Bologna nell'età medievale"; cf. Hessel, *Storia.*
19. See Hessel, *Storia;* Greci, "Bologna nel Duecento"; Vasina, "Dal Comune verso la Signoria"; Paolini, "La Chiesa e la città."

20. In general on these processes, see Hyde, "Commune, University, and Society."
21. Nardi, "Relations with Authority," 85. The documents issued by Honorius III in favor of the student *universitates* at Bologna are edited in Rashdall, *The Universities,* II, 731, 733–34.
22. For details about this position, see §1.3. The document is edited in Rashdall, *The Universities,* II, 732.
23. Maffei, "Un trattato"; Nardi, "Relations with Authority," 91. On recent discoveries of the oldest statutes, see Sarti, "Le edizioni degli statuti," 161–63.
24. Dondarini, "Provvedimenti e aspetti normativi," 74; see also Sacco, *Statuta,* 95–106.
25. Nardi, "Relations with Authority," 90–91, 94–95; Dolcini, "Lo Studium fino al XIII secolo." On the *studium*'s relationship with the papacy, see Paolini, "La chiesa di Bologna e lo Studio"; Vasina, "Bologna nello Stato della Chiesa."
26. Nardi, "Relations with Authority," 94.
27. See the literature cited in Vasina, "Dal Comune verso la Signoria," 619.
28. Dolcini, "Lo Studium fino al XIII secolo," 489–92.
29. This is not, of course, to take anything away from the value of the initiatives and publications to which the celebrations of 1888 gave rise. Especially important projects and publications connected with the eighth centenary include the *Acta Nationis Germanicae;* Malagola's *Statuti;* Dallari; and Malagola's new edition of Sarti and Fattorini, *De claris Archigymnasii Bononiensis professoribus* (see Lines, "The University and the City," 461–62, for these and later publications).
30. See Chapter 1.
31. For what follows, see De Benedictis, "Popular Government"; eadem, "Lo 'stato popolare di libertà'"; Duranti, "*Libertas*"; Gardi, "Making of an Oligarchy"; briefer surveys in Dondarini, "Il tramonto del Comune," and De Angelis, "Istituzioni e città," esp. 63–66.
32. Robertson, *Tyranny;* cf. Ady, *The Bentivoglio of Bologna.*
33. De Benedictis, "Il governo misto"; eadem, *Repubblica per contratto;* Terpstra, *Lay Confraternities,* 172–79.
34. Gardi, "Lineamenti della storia politica"; Giacomelli, "La storia di Bologna"; Fanti, "Bologna nell'età moderna."
35. Morelli, "I collegi di diritto"; Guerrini, *Collegi dottorali;* cf. Grendler, *Universities,* 403–6.
36. Cochrane, *Florence in the Forgotten Centuries.*
37. *Storia illustrata di Bologna.*
38. *A Companion to Medieval and Renaissance Bologna; Bologna: Cultural Crossroads.*

39. Blanshei, "Introduction," 10–18.
40. Some scholars have pointed to a decline in the fourteenth century, whereas others have emphasized a lower profile, especially in the fifteenth; see Mazzanti, "Lo Studium nel XIV secolo," 968; Sorbelli, *Storia dell'Università,* 237; Zaccagnini, *Storia dello Studio,* 48; Calcaterra, *Alma mater studiorum,* 143 (but cf. Ady, *The Bentivoglio,* 210–20). It is tempting to map Bologna's economic and political troubles in the fourteenth century onto the *studium* (Mazzanti, "Lo Studium nel XIV secolo"), but one needs to remember that the fortunes of universities do not necessarily follow other kinds of upturns and downturns very precisely.
41. See esp. Padovani, "Lo Studium nel XV secolo," 1017–22, 1031–35. Also see Raimondi, "Umanesimo e Università nel Quattrocento Bolognese"; idem, *Codro e l'Umanesimo a Bologna;* Pezzarossa, "Un profilo quattrocentesco"; and Chapter 5.
42. *History of the University in Europe,* vol. II. For an excessively glum assessment of Italian universities in general during the period, see Hersche, "Die Marginalisierung der Universität," esp. 275. For Spain, historians have seen similar patterns of renaissance, decline, and resurgence across the sixteenth to the eighteenth century; see at least Navarro Brotóns, *Disciplinas, saberes y prácticas.*
43. See, among others, the studies of Gardi, Giacomelli, and De Benedictis in the Bibliography.
44. For a recent discussion of the issue of decline within the context of Renaissance Italy, see Monfasani, "The Rise and Fall of Renaissance Italy."
45. Brizzi, "Matricole ed effettivi."
46. Schmitt, "Philosophy and Science"; Dooley, "La scienza in aula"; see also Porter, "The Scientific Revolution and Universities."
47. Cavazza, *Settecento inquieto,* and her other publications in the Bibliography. For some general comments on seventeenth-century university philosophy, see Forlivesi, *La filosofia universitaria,* chap. 3.
48. Zanobi, *Le ben regolate città.* Also see (among many other studies) Terpstra, *Cultures of Charity,* 99–138; De Benedictis, *Repubblica per contratto;* Gardi, *Lo Stato in provincia.*
49. The classic treatment is Dejob, *De l'influence du Concile de Trente.*
50. Costa, "Contributo."
51. Grendler, *The Roman Inquisition; Catholic Church and Modern Science.*
52. Fragnito, *Proibito capire;* eadem, "The Central and Peripheral Organization of Censorship"; Dall'Olio, *Eretici e inquisitori;* Bianchi, *Pour une histoire;* Marcus, *Forbidden Knowledge.*
53. For studies up to 1983, see Zanella, "Bibliografia," supplemented by the various individual publications that have appeared since then, as discussed below.

54. Zaccagnini, *Storia dello Studio,* 159–63.
55. Zaccagnini, *Storia dello Studio,* 301 (depending on Costa, "Contributo").
56. Sorbelli, *Storia della Università;* Simeoni, *Storia della Università.*
57. Simeoni, *Storia della Università,* 3.
58. Brizzi, "Lo Studio di Bologna"; Lines, "The University and the City"; Grendler, *Universities,* 5–20 and passim. Also of interest are the essays in *A History of the University in Europe,* vols. I and II, but there are no discrete chapters dedicated to Bologna.
59. Among others, see *Chartularium Studii Bononiensis;* Piana, *Nuovi documenti;* Dallari.
60. Malagola, *Statuti; Acta Nationis Germanicae; Statuta Nationis Germanicae;* Sarti, "Le edizioni degli statuti."
61. *Statuta Nationis Germanicae; La matricola; Annales, 1595–1619; Annales, 1640–1674;* Guerrini, *Collegi dottorali.*
62. *Il "Liber secretus iuris caesarei,"* ed. Sorbelli; *Il "Liber secretus iuris caesarei,"* ed. Piana.
63. Ehrle, *Statuti;* Malagola, *Statuti.*
64. Bronzino; see also Guerrini, *"Qui voluerit in iure promoveri."*
65. Pierce Webster and Teach Gnudi, "Documenti inediti."
66. See http://asfe.unibo.it/it.
67. Héloïse—European Network on Digital Academic History, online at http://heloise.ish-lyon.cnrs.fr.
68. See the Bibliography.
69. *Imago universitatis.* Brizzi has also been, for many years, the director of CISUI.
70. See the Bibliography. For the broader context, see at least Angelozzi and Casanova, *La nobilità disciplinata;* and *Violence and Justice in Bologna.*
71. Chines, Cristiani, Bònoli/Piliarvu, and Lines, "Teachers."
72. For these publications, see the Abbreviations.
73. Olmi, *Ulisse Aldrovandi;* Findlen, "The Formation of a Scientific Community"; Duroselle-Melish, "A Local-Transnational Business"; Maclean, *Episodes,* 101–6; Marcus, *Forbidden Knowledge.*
74. De Coster, "La mobilità dei docenti."
75. Siraisi, *Taddeo Alderotti;* eadem, *Avicenna;* eadem, *Medieval and Early Renaissance Medicine.*
76. Baldelli, "Tentativi di regolamentazione."
77. For Dooley, see the Bibliography.
78. Black, *Education and Society;* idem, *Humanism and Education.*
79. Siraisi, *Arts and Sciences at Padua.*
80. Maierù, "L'insegnamento della logica"; Buzzetti, Lambertini, and Tabarroni, "Tradizione testuale."
81. Cf. Grendler, *Universities,* chap. 10.

82. For a slightly different perspective on the sources below, see Lines, "The University and the City," 458–61. A fundamental guide for the archival documents is Cencetti, *Gli archivi.*
83. Malagola, *Statuta universitatis scolarium* (1405), esp. 274–77, rub. 78; see below, §2.2.1.
84. For a description of this archival series (ASB, Riformatori, bb. 3–16), see Salterini, 9–29. The rolls are published in Dallari. For more information on the teaching rolls, see §2.2.2.
85. Dallari published only selected prefaces.
86. For detailed comments on the rolls, see Dallari, I, v–xvi; Cencetti, *Gli archivi,* 75ff.; Salterini, *L'archivio,* 9.
87. The decisions of the Senate appear in ASB, Comune-Governo, Riformatori dello Stato di Libertà: Libri partitorum; and ASB, Senato: Partiti. See also BCAB, ms. B.506: Baldassarre M. Carrati, *Lettori pubblici dello Studio di Bologna dalli Indici dei Partitorum del Reggimento sotto diversi paragrafi estratti fedelmente* (covering 1503–1805). For the edicts (often in the form of printed broadsheets), see *Bononia manifesta.* The decrees or *ordinazioni* relative to the *studium* often run to several pages. See Lines, "The University of the Artists."
88. ASB, Assunteria di Studio; see the description in Lines, "The University and the City," 459–60.
89. ASB, Archivio dello Studio; see Cencetti, *Gli archivi,* 109–33 (the items he lists as belonging to the Archivio Arcivescovile are now in ASB); and Lines, "The University and the City," 460.
90. ASB, Senato, Lettere del Senato, Serie I, and so forth.
91. For prolusions (some of the incorrectly dated), one must still rely on Müllner, *Reden und Briefe.* For some examples, see Chapter 5.
92. The English terminology is modeled on the distinction in German between *Mitschriften* and *Reinschriften* or *Nachschriften;* see Blair, "Student Manuscripts and the Textbook" (esp. 40). On these and other characteristics of *reportationes* and *recollectae* (including those taken under dictation or not), see, among others, Hamesse, "Reportatio et transmission de textes"; and eadem, "La Technique de la réportation." Unlike some scholars, I do not find that the term *recollectae* is specific to Bologna.
93. For the requirement of submitting plans of lectures, see Sacchetti, *Ordinationi* (1641), particularly points 23 and 24 (n.p.). This documentation may be compared with the *Vorlesungsverzeichnisse* in Helmstedt; see Bruning, *Innovation in Forschung und Lehre.*
94. ASB, Assunteria di Studio, b. 60–b. 62 (Serie di annue lezioni, c. 1642–1740). In fact, b. 60 contains scattered outlines from the 1620s, 1630s, and 1640s; b. 61 covers various years from 1706 to 1718; b. 62 includes various years between 1721 and 1740.

95. Vernazza, "La crisi barocca."
96. See ASB, Riformatori dello Studio, b. 57 (Dispute e ripetizioni di scolari per ottenere letture d'università, 1417–1526), b. 59 (Tesi e dispute di scolari e dottori, Artisti, 1510–1571).
97. ASB, Riformatori dello Studio, b. 60–b. 61 (Tesi e conclusioni dei lettori, 1601–1678, 1668–1725).
98. Several of these documents have been exploited before, including in Gardi, *Lo Stato in provincia.*
99. For instance, AAV, Segr. Stato, Legaz. Bologna, b. 178, contains a series of letters from around 1544–1545 in which cardinal Morone laments the absence of Romolo Amaseo from Bologna and the fact that the pope wants him nearby, to adorn the teaching of the *studium* in Rome.
100. Most of these series lack modern inventories, but see Venditti and Quaglieri, *Archivio Boncompagni Ludovisi.*
101. See especially AAV, Congr. Concilio, with the two subseries Libri Litter. and Positiones Sess.
102. BAV, Barb. lat., 5105, contains an informative *relazione* by the cardinal legate Maffeo Barberini between 1611 and 1614 (Lines, "A Papal Legate's *Relatione*").
103. For a preliminary inventory, see Wells, *The Ranuzzi Manuscripts.*
104. Lines, *Selected Documents.*
105. Some relevant studies that have appeared since the *History of the University in Europe,* vol. II (1996), and *Le università dell'Europa,* VI (1995), include: *The History of the University of Oxford,* vols. III–V; Otterspeer, *Groepsportret met Dame,* I; *Historia de la Universidad de Salamanca;* Freedman, *Philosophy and the Arts in Central Europe.*
106. See *Storia delle università in Italia; L'Università di Padova nei secoli (1601–1805); Almum Studium Papiense; Studieren im Rom;* Lupi, *Gli* studia *del papa; Maestri, insegnamenti e libri a Perugia;* Frova, *Scritti sullo Studium Perusinum.*
107. For instance, *Documenti,* vol. III, ed. Simona Iaria.
108. For some recent examples: *European Universities; Early Modern Universities; Les Universités européennes du XVIe au XVIIIe siècle; Les Échanges.*

1. THE ACADEMIC COMMUNITY AND ITS OVERSEERS

1. Not all of these actors have received equal attention in the historiography, which has especially favored students. On students in medieval and early modern Italy, see at least Bellomo, *Saggio sull'università,* esp. chaps. 2, 4, 8, 9, and 11; Roggero, "Professori e studenti"; and *Studenti e dottori.* For Bologna, see esp. *Studenti e università degli studenti* and *L'Università a Bologna,* II.
2. Helpful pointers in Brizzi, "Il governo dello Studio."

3. The critical literature on Bolognese students is vast. For the medieval period, see at least the articles and relative bibliography in Pini, *Studio, università e città.* For early modern Bologna, see at least the studies by Brizzi, Carlsmith, Guerrini, and Maggiulli in the Bibliography, plus the publications mentioned below.
4. On the Nations and student corporatism in Bologna, see at least Colliva, "'Nationes' ed 'Universitates,'" and Pini, "Le *nationes* studentesche," with further bibliography. Particularly important for early modern Bologna is the documentation for the German Nation in *Annales, 1595–1619; Annales, 1640–1674;* and *La matricola.*
5. See especially Kibre, *Scholarly Privileges,* 18–53.
6. For 1405: *Statuta nova universitatis scolarium scientie medicine et artium generalis studii civitatis Bononiae,* in Malagola, *Statuta universitatis scolarium* (1405). These statutes are clearly not the first ones, since they are designated as "new." For 1442, see the reformed statutes in Malagola, *Statuta universitatis scolarium* (1442).
7. One of the reasons for the exaggerated emphasis on Bologna's 1405 statutes is the loss of contemporary statutes, such as those for Pavia. See D. Mantovani, "Tracce."
8. Morelli, "'De studio scolarium,'" provides a survey and edition for the years 1335–1454. The documents concern students in all faculties. See also Sacco, *Statuta,* I, passim; Trombetti Budriesi, *Gli statuti,* 91–102.
9. See especially the rubric "De privilegiis scolaribus concessis et universitati ipsorum ac portantibus et conducentibus libros ad civitatem Bononiae" in Sacco, *Statuta,* I, 289–93; Morelli, "'De studio scolarium civitatis manutenendo,'" 159–62; Trombetti Budriesi, *Gli statuti,* 99–102.
10. For the 1561 statutes, see *Reformatio statutorum almi Gymnasii Bononiensis philosophorum et medicorum, facta anno Domini 1561, comprobata per Rev. D. Vicelegatum, Vexilliferum et Senatum Bononiensem,* in BUB, ms. 1394, 121–34; Lines, *Selected Documents,* doc. 3. These statutes were approved by Pier Donato Cesi and, unanimously, by the Senate; see ASB, Senato, Partiti, b. 7, ff. 159v–160r (28 April 1561). For the 1583 statutes, see [*Statuti riformati dati da i deputati de i scholari Artisti*] in Lines, *Selected Documents,* doc. 4. It is unclear whether these 1583 statutes obtained the necessary and customary confirmation by the authorities as was the case for the 1561 statutes. They were sent to Rome as part of a dossier of considerations on the university put together by the Archbishop Gabriele Paleotti (see §1.3.2). For some initial considerations see Lines, "Gabriele Paleotti," and idem, "Reorganizing the Curriculum." The 1609 statutes are in Giustiniani, *Philosophiae ac Medicinae . . . statuta;* see Lines, *Selected Documents,* doc. 5. These statutes, promoted by the papal legate Benedetto Giustiniani, were promulgated three years later by his successor Maffeo Barberini.

11. For a prospectus, see Lines, "The University of the Artists," esp. 145; also see Costa, "Contributo," 73–80, and Baldelli, "Tentativi di regolamentazione."
12. Classic treatments are Denifle, *Die Entstehung;* Rashdall, *Universities of Europe;* Cobban, "Medieval Student Power." See also Verger, "Patterns."
13. Malagola, "I rettori"; corrections and additions in Piana, *Nuovi documenti,* I, 11–61. Also see Malagola, *I rettori.*
14. On this point see esp. Malagola, "I rettori," 39–44.
15. Malagola, *Statuta universitatis scolarium* (1405), 247, rub. 34. For the functions of the rector and others in the fifteenth-century statutes, see Malagola, "I rettori," 15–19, 27–30, 34, and passim.
16. See also Malagola, "I rettori," 25. As Malagola observes on 32–33, the rule that a rector could not serve for more than one year was often ignored.
17. Malagola, "I rettori," 34–36.
18. On these and other officers (*consiglieri, massari*), see Malagola, *Statuti,* vi–viii.
19. The first such instance reported in the rolls is that of Magister Lucas de Parma in 1438–1439 (Dallari, I, 11). Likewise, the rector for the Jurists was appointed to teach the *Decretum* on feast days. The payment records before that, however, indicate that the rector taught either medicine or another subject, as was the case, for instance, with Stephanus de Faventia (Dallari, IV, 32), who taught metaphysics on feast days, although he had been appointed to teach astrology.
20. See Malagola, "I rettori," 50–60; Aldrovandi, "Commentario alle lettere," 19–20. A rector's pay settled at about L. 100 starting in 1438; see Lucas de Parma in ASB, Comune-Governo, Riformatori dello Stato di Libertà, Libri mandatorum, b. 392 (a. 1438–1442), f. 21r (20 January 1439). It rose during the sixteenth century. During the 1560s the payments list the rector of Arts and Medicine at L. 300, although no disbursements are actually made. See ASB, Quartironi, bb. 36 and 37, *ad annum.*
21. See the proposals by the Artists of 1583 in AAB, Miscellanee Vecchie, b. 802, olim L. 87, fasc. 33, ff. 25v–26r; and by Ulisse Aldrovandi in the same year (*Bononiensis Gymnasii Reformatio,* cap. 15 "De eligendo rectore," ff. 66v–67v).
22. For the Artists, see Dallari, II, 141, which mentions Ioannes Garcia de Brignas; but cf. Simeoni, *Storia della Università,* 16, which also lists Giovanni Bernardo Aysper (1559–1560) and Orazio Gabuzzi di Macerata (1560–1561). Whereas the first of these is correct according to the documents of the College of Arts, the second was merely prorector of the Jurists; see Malagola, *I rettori,* 59. The last rector for the Legists was Lope Varona di Villananne di Burgos; see Dallari, II, 203; Simeoni, *Storia della Università,* 16; Malagola, *I rettori,* 60; see ASB, Quartironi, b. 37 (a. 1580): listed

without name at a salary of L. 900. Thereafter the position disappears from the payments.

23. Costa, *Ulisse Aldrovandi,* 17–18, 60–68; Malagola, "I rettori," 60–63, 119–26; Simeoni, *Storia della Università,* 18.
24. In 1583 the student Jurists complained that a decree had been passed that year prohibiting them from electing a rector. Attempts in 1632, 1666, and 1681 to revive the institution were unsuccessful; see Costa, "Contributo," 6–7, 12–13, and Malagola, "I rettori," 71–72.
25. For the 1561 statutes, see Lines, *Selected Documents,* doc. 3, caps. [1]–[3]; for the 1583 statutes, see ibid., doc. 4, cap. 1.
26. This development has received considerable attention from scholars, including Sottili, "Le istituzioni universitarie," 14–18.
27. *Reformatio statutorum . . . 1561,* in Lines, *Selected Documents,* doc. 3, rubs. [4] and [7]; cf. Malagola, "I rettori," 16 (where he gives the impression that the number of councillors is thirteen). On priors and councillors, see Malagola, "I rettori," 14–19.
28. Daltri, "*Memorie* e consigliature," 32. This study also provides a good overview of the archival documentation on student *universitates* between the sixteenth and eighteenth centuries.
29. The Archiginnasio building took a direct hit from an Allied bomb raid on 29 January 1944, requiring a long and challenging work of restoration. As a result, not all of the original monuments and coats of arms survive; for photos comparing the damage and restoration work, see *Bologna trema,* 60–63.
30. Steffen, *Die studentische Autonomie;* De Benedictis, "La fine dell'autonomia studentesca"; Kibre, *Scholarly Privileges,* 42–49.
31. See, for instance, the events of October and November 1564 referred to in Brizzi, "Modi e forme," 60. But there are many more. See, for instance, *Le università e la violenza studentesca,* including Maggiulli, "'Tu ne menti,'" and Carlsmith, "Collegiate Conflict"; also idem, "Quarrels under the Portico."
32. The office of rector is mentioned only incidentally in Grendler, *Universities* (but see 158), and not at all in connection with the rise of student violence in Italian universities (500–505).
33. On Paleotti, who was bishop of Bologna from 1566 (and then archbishop from 1582, when the status of the diocese changed), see esp. Prodi, *Il cardinale Gabriele Paleotti.*
34. *Alcuni avertimenti circa lo studio di Bologna che havriano bisogno di provisione* (AAB, Miscellanee Vecchie, b. 802, olim L. 87; full text and English translation in Lines, "Reorganizing the Curriculum," 36–41).
35. Paleotti, *Alcuni avertimenti:* "Procurare che si faccia un Rettore di authorità, al quale accadendo s'accreschi la provisione, et faccia il debito suo."

36. Both of these phenomena applied to Bolognese and Italian society more generally, and not just to students; see at least Angelozzi and Casanova, *La nobiltà disciplinata,* and most recently Carroll, "Revenge and Reconciliation" (with discussion of Bologna in a comparative Italian and European context).
37. For a full account of these events see Brizzi, "Town and Gown? Bologna 1560."
38. See, for instance, Carlsmith, "*Siam Ungari!*"; more generally, Grendler, *Universities,* 500–505.
39. Maggiulli, "'Li scolari.'"
40. Among the many documents, see ASB, Senato, Provvisioni, b. 11, ff. 7v–8v (29 November 1569).
41. Gualandi, *Il processo fatto in Bologna;* Masetti Zannini, "Scolari e dottori del Cinquecento," 221–25.
42. G. F. Negri, *Annali di Bologna dall'anno 1001 sino al 1600* (BUB, ms. 1107, vol. VIII/2, f. 73r).
43. See Malagola, *Statuta universitatis scolarium* (1442), 318, note.
44. Lines, *Selected Documents,* doc. 3, Part II, cap. 11. For some graduation fees in Bologna, see Teach Gnudi and Pierce Webster, *Gaspare Tagliacozzi,* 50–53; the expense may partly explain why, in 1570, Tagliacozzi presented himself only for a degree in medicine. In 1556 Giulio Cesare Aranzi (later a famous professor of medicine) tried to cut expenses by applying to graduate as a non-native, thus paying 23 *scudi* instead of 74 ducats.
45. On the various Bolognese student migrations until the fourteenth century, see Rossi, "'Universitas scholarium' e comune." For a brief prospectus, see Rashdall, *The Universities of Europe,* I, 589. Specifically on the migration to Siena, see most recently Nardi, "La *migratio* delle scuole universitarie."
46. See, for instance, Denley, *Commune and Studio,* 249–50.
47. Brizzi, "Aspetti della presenza della Nazione germanica."
48. On the latter two points, see Lines, "The University of the Artists."
49. This provision was struck from the statutes in 1561; see Lines, *Selected Documents,* doc. 3, rub. [15].
50. Within three days they were to "denuntiare Rectori seu Sapientj et Syndico Universitatis si contingat suum doctorem aliquam penam incurrere seu non intrare tempore debito, vel non disputando, vel quocunque alio modo' (Malagola, *Statuta universitatis scolarium* [1405], 270, rub. 68).
51. Their effort did not meet with success: see Costa, "Contributo," 10–11.
52. Di Simone, "Admission," 311–24; Frijhoff, "Graduation and Careers," 386–93.
53. As in the case of the Staten College in Leiden; see §3.1.1.

54. Kristeller, "Learned Women," 195–97, 199–200, 202–3; Cavazza, "'Dottrici' e lettrici.'" More generally, Findlen, "Translating the New Science."
55. Bronzino, 233, gives the date as 12 May 1732. On the event, see also BUB, ms. 1052, f. 83r–v, which reports the event from the point of view of the College of Philosophy.
56. Brizzi, "Lo Studio di Bologna," 48.
57. For the following I rely on Brizzi's studies, particularly "Maestri e studenti," "Modi e forme," "Matricole ed effettivi," "La presenza studentesca," and "Aspetti della presenza della Nazione germanica." Cf. the different conclusions in Simeoni, *Storia della Università,* 88–89, 101–2, and Grendler, *Universities,* 513, table A.2. For some comparative estimates for early modern Italy, see di Simone, "Per una storia delle Università europee," and eadem, "Admission," 307–9. Kagan, "Universities in Italy," and idem, "Le università in Italia," remain learned reference points, but use controversial (and likely unreliable) data, as does Grendler.
58. On matriculation practices across Europe, see Paquet, *Les Matricules universitaires.*
59. See ASB, Archivio dello Studio, Università degli Artisti, bb. 373–77; Modena, Biblioteca Estense, fondo Campori, ms. 460 (Matricola dell'Università dei legisti dello Studio bolognese, 1553–1613, also known as "matricola Belvisi"). Further data can be gathered from the matriculation lists of the German Nation; see *La matricola.* See also Daltri, "*Memorie* e consigliature."
60. Sorbelli, *Bologna negli scrittori stranieri,* I, 104–5.
61. Helpful and fairly complete repertories of doctoral degrees for Bologna have been published for all subjects except theology: for arts and medicine (1480–1800), see Bronzino; for civil law (1378–1796), see *Il "Liber secretus iuris caesarei,"* ed. Sorbelli; *Il "Liber secretus iuris caesarei,"* ed. Piana; and Guerrini, "*Qui voluerit in iure promoveri . . . ,*" which also covers canon law; for theology (1364–1500 only), see Ehrle, *Statuti.*
62. See asfe.unibo.it. On the database, which registers all the student names and doctorates for Bologna and other Italian universities that have been uncovered for the period 1500–1800, see Brizzi, "ASFE"; Guerrini, "A proposito di ASFE."
63. For example, only one-third of French-speaking students coming to Italy between 1483 and 1600 seems to have obtained a degree there; see Bingen, "Les Étudiants." In the case of Bologna, the proportion of students from the Empire who actually obtained a degree in the last quarter of the sixteenth century was a mere 8.5 percent. For this and other examples, see Brizzi, "Lo Studio di Bologna," 55–56.
64. Brizzi, "Lo Studio di Bologna," 52–53; cf. Brizzi, "Matricole ed effettivi," 255, Tav. 4.

65. Brizzi, "Lo Studio di Bologna," 49–52; further data for Italy more generally in idem, "Per una geografia umana." On the factors that may have affected the presence of international students in Italy, see Roggero, "Professori e studenti" (1052–53 for Bologna). Also see *Über Mobilität von Studierenden und Gelehrten.* For students from specific lands, see Tervoort, *The Iter Italicum and the Northern Netherlands;* Woolfson, *Padua and the Tudors;* Bingen, "Les Étudiants"; and eadem, "Studenti francofoni."

66. Vatican, BAV, Barb. lat. 5105 (s. XVII), 35 folios, esp. ff. 25v–28v; see Lines, "A Papal Legate's *Relatione.*" The number fits well with the estimate in Kagan, "Le università in Italia," 284–85. One possible control on these statements is to evaluate variations in how many blank forms for matriculation the university ordered: see Carnevali, "Cheap, Everyday Print," 200–201, with data for 1609, 1613, and 1618 indicating a progressive drop in the number of forms printed from 500 to 400 to 300, respectively. This was, however, a particularly hard period for the *studium,* due to famine and other challenges.

67. A. F. Marsili, *Memorie per riparare i pregiudizi,* 4. For Marsili, see §8.3.

68. Untitled and anonymous memorandum in ASB, Archivio dello Studio, 207, carton K-23, *inc.* Io N.N. nato in Imola . . . , 25 (for the relevant passage, see 15).

69. Sorbelli, *Bologna negli scrittori stranieri.*

70. ASB, Senato, Lettere, Serie VII, b. 49 (10 November 1574).

71. See §1.2.

72. Sorbelli, *Bologna negli scrittori stranieri;* Daltri, "La decorazione parietale"; *Imago Universitatis;* Brizzi, "Una fonte per la storia studentesca."

73. See di Simone, "Admission," 302–11.

74. See de Ridder-Symoens, "Mobility."

75. See Brizzi, *Formazione,* 71–130; the same was true in Padua (del Negro, "L'età moderna," 62).

76. Brizzi, "Aspetti della presenza della Nazione germanica," 37; *La matricola.*

77. Cf. de Ridder-Symoens, "Mobility," 425: "The Italian universities in the Papal States of Bologna, Rome, Ferrara and Perugia lost their international clientele" after the 1564 requirement of the *professio fidei.* Cf. Grendler, *Universities,* 190–94.

78. Frijhoff, "Graduation and Careers," 380–81.

79. The data in ASFE shows a strong growth of degrees in medicine alone, as opposed to philosophy and medicine, in the second half of the seventeenth century (267 vs. 393; in the first half of the century it had been 120 vs. 548); this dwindles considerably in the first and second halves of the eighteenth century, where the figures are 120 vs. 205 and 70 vs. 256, respectively.

80. Many of these monuments have now been moved to the Museo Civico Medievale. On the professors' tombs, see Grandi, *I monumenti dei dottori.* On

professors' social standing, see Duranti, "Il collegio dei dottori di medicina."

81. See *Imago Universitatis.* For a vivid account of this student interest, see Maffeo Barberini's *Relatione* (c. 1611), in Lines, "A Papal Legate's *Relatione,*" 245: "per ciascun mese s'elegge un Priore, il quale ha cura di vedere tutti i bisogni dello Studio et riferirli al Legato, e alla prima neve che caschi in terra quello, che s'abbatte esser Priore, va raccogliendo dal Legato/Vice legato/Auditori civile e criminale/rettori di Collegio et dottori una certa quantità di danari, de i quali nelle scole si fabrica una memoria di bellissimo marmo a quel dottore che più piacerà al Priore della neve, che così lo chiamano."
82. For Nicolò Fava's career and teachings, see Lines, "Teachers," 287–88.
83. Dallari, IV, 41, 42; Ottavio Banti, "Bentivoglio, Antonio (Antongaleazzo)," *DBI,* VIII (1966), 603–5. Cf. Ricci, *Monumenti sepolcrali,* 23–24.
84. See §2.2.2.
85. Carlo Antonio Manzini, *Il duello schernito overo l'ofesa e la sodisfattione: Trattato morale* (Bologna: Eredi del Pisarri, 1680); see the table in Carroll, "Revenge and Reconciliation," 127. For interesting considerations, see Zannini, "I maestri."
86. See, among others, *Ordinazioni sopra del studio di Bologna lette nel magnifico reggimento in sufficiente numero sedente à di 5 luglio 1565, priore il Marescotto,* in ASB, Assunteria di Studio, b. 4, f. 55r–v. The importance of this official continued to be stressed in 1649: see Costa, "Contributo," 80.
87. Carboni I and II; Piana, *Nuove ricerche,* 199–204.
88. Chambers, "*Studium Urbis* and *gabella studii*"; Frova, "The Financing of the University of Rome."
89. Giacomelli, "Le Bolle pontificie," 279 and passim.
90. ASB, Quartironi, bb. 33–48; see Salterini, 38–76.
91. ASB, Quartironi, b. 37 (1563–1583), ff. 47–50 (a. 1575); b. 38 (1584–1612), ff. 60–62 (a. 1600).
92. ASB, Quartironi, b. 32 (1401–1410), a. 1408.
93. ASB, Quartironi, b. 42 (1685–1705), a. 1700. I would like to thank Rebecca Carnevali for providing me with reproductions of the relevant documents for this year.
94. Dallari, II, v–vi, also provides earlier instances of hiring excellent foreign doctors.
95. Details in Costa, "Contributo," 26–38.
96. Costa, "Contributo," 44–49; Carboni II, 105.
97. ASB, Quartironi, b. 34 (1498–1512), folder XII (a. 1510).
98. ASB, Quartironi, b. 34 (1498–1512), folder VIII (a. 1505). On Vittori, see Cristiani, 47, no. 349. For the salaries of various professors and how they relate to broader patterns within arts and medicine, see Lines, "Natural Philosophy and Mathematics"; and Chapter 6.

99. See Brizzi, "Maestri e studenti," 127, 130, on an extremely rare case, datable to around 1640, in which we have precise information on the income streams of a member of the college of theology in Bologna: his university salary was a mere 21 percent of his total income; the rest came from private lessons (19 percent), income from the college (13 percent), degrees conferred (7 percent), students boarding with him (21 percent), and various other sources (17 percent).
100. Duranti, *Mai sotto Saturno,* 21; see 22–25 for his general economic condition.
101. On private teaching see §2.3.1. Professors were also allowed to charge students up to 40 soldi per year each in annual fees according to the 1405 statutes (Malagola, *Statuta universitatis scolarium* [1405], 248–50, 252–53, rubs. 36, 38, 39); the sum seems to have varied depending on the length of the textbook being taught. It is unclear whether a charge of this kind was still levied in the sixteenth century and later.
102. On this point see Simeoni, *Storia della Università,* 30–31.
103. For the meaning of these designations, see §2.2.1.
104. Lines, "Natural Philosophy in Renaissance Italy"; idem, "Natural Philosophy and Mathematics."
105. Costa, "Contributo," 49–55; Giacomelli, "Le Bolle pontificie," 318–22.
106. In 1674–1675 the rolls list 83 teachers in law and 65 in arts and medicine (Dallari, III, 69–74); in 1689–1690 they list 53 in law and 51 in arts and medicine (Dallari, II, 143–47). In 1700–1701 there are 45 teachers in law and 63 in arts and medicine (Dallari, II, 191–96).
107. Dallari, III, 64–69.
108. See the bull of 23 April 1448 (*Inter curas multiplices*), ed. in Sacco, *Statuta,* II, 272–74; Trombetti Budriesi, *Gli statuti,* 81–83.
109. See the bull of 25 July 1450 (*Inter varias, multiplicesque curas*), ed. in Sacco, *Statuta,* II, 281–83; Trombetti Budriesi, *Gli statuti,* 87–90; a précis in Zaccagnini, *Storia,* 49–50.
110. Schmitt, "Aristotelianism in the Veneto." Grendler, *Universities,* 163n69, rightly criticizes him on this point, suggesting that possibly some 80 percent of professors largely stayed put.
111. See De Coster, "Foreign and Citizen Teachers"; eadem, "L'immagine dei docenti forestieri"; eadem, "La mobilità dei docenti."
112. In general, on the relations between Padua and Bologna, see *Rapporti tra le Università.* Examples of professors poached from Padua include, in the sixteenth century, Pietro Pomponazzi and Federico Pendasio (see the Epilogue). For brief lectureships in the humanities in the fifteenth century, see esp. §5.2.
113. This pattern had already begun in the fifteenth century. For some bibliography, see De Coster, "La mobilità dei docenti," 238n34.

114. See Cencetti, "Sulle origini dello Studio," 22. Most historians of the University of Bologna do not discuss the College of Theology; see, for instance, Simeoni, *Storia della Università,* 13–14. For details, see §8.1.
115. In the case of law, there were separate colleges dealing with matters concerning the *studium* and professional practice; see Trombetti Budriesi, *Gli statuti;* Brambilla, "Collegi dei dottori universitari e collegi professionali."
116. Maffeo Barberini, *Relatione* (1611), in Lines, "A Papal Legate's *Relatione,*" 245.
117. Brief but useful observations also in Duranti, *Mai sotto Saturno,* 48–50.
118. Malagola, *Statuti,* xiii–xvi; Cencetti, *Gli archivi,* 53–54; Kibre, *Scholarly Privileges,* 49–51; Siraisi, *Taddeo Alderotti,* 12–13, 19–20, 22–23.
119. For ordinary medicine and both ordinary and extraordinary philosophy, the minimum number of students at public lectures was four (three for other subjects) in the sixteenth century; see the preface to the roll for the Artists for 1577–1578 in ASB, Riformatori dello Studio, b. 12 (roll 129); and see the 1586 roll (roll 138) in the Appendix.
120. Letter of San Sisto to the Conservatori (i.e., Assunti di Studio), 20 February 1577 (ASB, Ambasciata, Registrum, b. 3, 376); letter of San Sisto (Filippo Boncompagni) to legate Giambattista Castagna, 9 February 1577 (AAV, Seg. Stato, Legaz. Bologna, 180). See also Costa, *Ulisse Aldrovandi,* 87. Castagna also supported the case of the Assunti: see the letters published in Masetti Zannini, "Docenti del clero," 189–90, 178.
121. Letters from the Bolognese ambassador in Rome to the Assunti in ASB, Assunteria di Studio, b. 76 (30 May 1601 and 16 May 1601).
122. Costa, "Contributo," esp. 47–55.
123. Guerrini, *Collegi dottorali in conflitto.*
124. The various statutes for the College of Arts and Medicine published in Malagola, *Statuti,* have received only limited attention, particularly when compared with those for the legal colleges (on which see esp. Trombetti Budriesi, *Gli statuti*). The statutes of the Bolognese colleges of doctors will need to be compared in due course with the ones newly found for Pavia; see D. Mantovani, "Il Collegio dei dottori."
125. See Guerrini, *Collegi dottorali in conflitto,* 36–39.
126. Charles V, *Privilegium Palatinatus in ampla forma pro Collegiis Artium et Medicinae* (24 February 1530), in ASB, Archivio dello Studio, b. 216, folder "Statuti del 1507," 185–200; multiple printed copies in b. 245; also published in Sacco, *Statuta,* II, 426–30, Diploma IX. A similar privilege was conferred by Pope Paul III on 18 February 1536, but revoked by Gregory XV on 25 February 1622 (Giacomelli, "Le Bolle pontificie," 275, 303). For fifteenth-century Padua, see Martellozzo Forin, "Conti palatini e lauree."
127. See ASB, Ufficio per la condotta degli stipendiari, libri delle bollette (covering 1375–1437), and ASB, Tesoreria (1364–1437), where names of pro-

fessors are listed among the names of military men and other people employed by the city.

128. For this and what follows, see Carboni I and II, and Giacomelli, "Le Bolle pontificie."
129. See also the documents further defining the juridical position of the Congregazione: in 1512, the *Transazione fra i Collegi di Legge e Medicina e i Tesorieri della Camera di Bologna, in seguito di avere i Collegi ottenuta l'amministrazione della Gabella Grossa* (ASB, Gabella Grossa, Instrumenti, b. 146); and in 1513, a brief of Leo X (ASB, Gabella Grossa, Relazioni, b. 238: Bolle e brevi riguardanti la Gabella Grossa dated 1644), both of them addressed in Carboni I, 115.
130. In 1529 they were apparently successful in making the Congregazione agree to an annual contribution of L. 400: Carboni, I, 116n14.
131. Brief of 1 February 1603 (ASB, Gabella Grossa, Relazioni, b. 238: Bolle e brevi riguardanti la Gabella Grossa, Copia del breve di Clemente VIII).
132. Carboni II, 101–3.
133. Carboni I, 119.
134. For these and other figures for the seventeenth century, see Carboni II, 104–5.
135. They are discussed in Carboni II, 106–8.
136. Carboni II, 105.
137. E.g., Costa, "Contributo"; De Benedictis, "Le università italiane," 69–71; Baldelli, "Tentativi," 10–12, 25n28; and Brizzi, "The Jesuits and Universities in Italy," 190–91: "These doctoral colleges, themselves part of the city oligarchies, showed an inability to renew the content and methods of the traditional curricula, implicitly preferring that education and research be undertaken outside the universities, in scientific or literary academies, or in Jesuit colleges."
138. Relevant comments in Zannini, "Stipendi e status sociale," esp. 13–16. Cf. Frijhoff, *Modifications des fonctions sociales de l'université.*
139. Zannini, "Stipendi e status sociale," 14.
140. The Senate was also referred to as the *Quaranta,* from its forty members, in a restructuring brought about by Pope Julius II shortly after he entered the city in 1506. Pope Sixtus V expanded its membership from forty to fifty in 1590; see Gardi, "Lineamenti della storia politica di Bologna," 24. On this institution, the fundamental work remains Guidicini, *I riformatori dello stato di libertà.*
141. In what follows, I do not analyze the interaction of the Bentivoglio family with the *studium,* a topic that has received scant attention (some comments in Ady, *The Bentivoglio of Bologna,* 162–65). For the papacy's relationship with Bologna in the second half of the fifteenth century, see at least Robertson, *Under the Mantle of St. Peter,* and Duranti, "*Libertas.*"

142. Two Riformatori were to be drawn from each quarter of the city; in later years, the size of the committee fluctuated, often counting between four and six members. In theory, at least, in addition to fulfilling age and citizenship requirements, the Riformatori were to come from different social classes ("un cavaliere, un senatore, un gentilhuomo et un mercante") and not be related to any of the professors. See Salterini, vii.
143. The Quartironi degli Stipendi are in ASB, Riformatori dello Studio, bb. 32–49. This is a very useful and neglected source for ascertaining the actual presence in Bologna of professors listed on the rolls.
144. See Salterini.
145. De Benedictis, "Governo cittadino e riforme." On the Senate's increasing authority in Bologna (but also the challenges it encountered), see also Gardi, *Lo Stato in provincia,* 102–7, 317–96; Terpstra, *Lay Confraternities,* 172–79, 186–216.
146. For the numerous deliberations concerning the *studium,* see ASB, Senato, Partiti, passim; for the relevant correspondence with the ambassador in Rome, see ASB, Assunteria di Studio, bb. 75–79; ASB, Ambasciata, Posizioni, bb. 128, 206, 210. Cf. De Benedictis, "Luoghi del potere e Studio," 208, 214.
147. De Benedictis, "Luoghi del potere e Studio." On the class and political tensions within sixteenth-century Bologna, see at least Terpstra, *Cultures of Charity,* 99–137; Colliva, "Bologna dal XIV al XVIII secolo"; Giacomelli, *Carlo Grassi.*
148. See "The University in Time" in the Introduction. On the archdeacon, see Paolini, "L'evoluzione di una funzione ecclesiastica"; idem, "La figura dell'Arcidiacono"; idem, "L'Arcidiacono della Chiesa bolognese e i collegi dei dottori"; idem, "La chiesa di Bologna e lo Studio." For a listing of archdeacons in Bologna from 1045 to 1619, see BUB, ms. 2948 (Miscellanea Tioli), vol. X, ff. 86–89 (see also Parmeggiani, "L'arcidiacono bolognese," 111).
149. For this and what follows, see the evidence (especially from the legists in the fourteenth century) in Parmeggiani, "L'arcidiacono bolognese."
150. The practice of the graduation oration seems to have passed, by the end of the fourteenth century, to the master presenting the degree candidate; see Malagola, *Statuti Collegio* (1378), 445, rub. 31, and 472, rub. 29 (1395, college of doctors); see Maierù, *University Training,* 70.
151. See §2.3; and at least Giacomelli, "Le Bolle pontificie," 319–22.
152. See at least Sottili, "Istituzioni universitarie," 8–13; Boehm, "*Cancellarius Universitatis.*"
153. Dondarini, "Provvedimenti e aspetti normativi," 75.
154. Zarri, "Chiesa, religione, società."
155. Bibliography in *DSI,* I, 385–86.

156. These included Bologna, Rome, Perugia, Macerata, and from 1598 also Ferrara. On these universities and reform initiatives in the early modern period, see Lupi, *Gli* studia *del papa*.
157. AAV, Congr. Concilio.
158. As suggested by Mazzone, "'Evellant vicia . . . aedificent virtutes,'" 725.
159. See "The University in Time" in the Introduction; see also Kibre, *Scholarly Privileges,* 31–34.
160. Zaoli, "Lo Studio bolognese e papa Martino V"; for the activities of Boniface IX, John XXIII, and Martin V, see also Pio, "Lo Studium e il papato tra XIV e XV secolo." For the library, started in 1373, see §4.2.2, and Laurent, *Fabio Vigili,*180–202.
161. Particularly on Gregory XIII, see Lines, "Papal Power."
162. Lines, "Papal Power," 678; and the Epilogue. Virulently negative comments on papal influence in Costa, *Ulisse Aldrovandi,* 50–53, and passim.
163. See at least Mazzone, "'Evellant vicia . . . aedificent virtutes.'"
164. Terpstra, *Lay Confraternities,* 172–79.
165. Unlike legates, governors were not of cardinalate rank. Legates were; they might represent the papacy directly (if they resided in Bologna) or govern through a subordinate (vice-legate) while they themselves resided elsewhere. See Gardi, "Il cardinale legato."
166. This arrangement of "mixed government" (*governo misto*) was based on Nicholas V's 1447 *capitoli* with Bologna (Sacco, *Statuta,* II, 265) and lasted throughout the early modern period, but over time the importance of these *capitoli* diminished as others were produced. The classic study is De Benedictis, *Repubblica per contratto,* but see also Colliva, "Bologna dal XIV al XVIII secolo"; Verardi Ventura, "L'ordinamento bolognese dei secoli XVI–XVII"; and Gardi, *Lo Stato in provincia.* For a brief but useful sketch, also see Dondarini, "Provvedimenti e aspetti normativi," 74–79.
167. On the legate's powers, see at least Mazzone, "'Evellant vicia . . . aedificent virtutes'"; idem, "Vita religiosa e vita civile." For some of the dynamics between center and periphery in the Papal State, see Fosi, *Papal Justice,* 191–206. As an example for the sixteenth century, the faculties conferred on the legate Enrico Caetani (undecimo kal. Septembris 1586) are fairly typical: "Ac quoscunque in utroque vel altero Iurium et Theologia ac Artibus et Medicina et aliis facultatibus existentibus duobus vel tribus in eadem facultate doctoribus seu magistris et eorum votis iuratis dummodo iidem in aliqua universitate studii generalis per triennium saltem facultati in qua gradum suscipere intendunt operam dederint, professionemque fidei iuxta articulos pridem a sede apostolica propositos, in eisdem manibus tuis emiserint ac previo examine ad doctoratus et magisterii ac alios quoscunque gradus promovendi eosque doctores ac magistros creandi ac doctoratus ac magisterii aliaque insignia eis exhibendo.

Ita quod omnibus et singulis privilegiis, gratiis, exemptionibus, prerogativis, antellationibus, indultis et honoribus quibus alii doctores et magistri in publica universitate creati utuntur, potiuntur et gaudent preterque in his casibus in quibus expresse requiritur quod in publicis gymnasiis seu universitatibus studiorum gradus huiusmodi suscipiant pariformiter et absque ulla penitus differentia utantur, potiantur et gaudeant" (ASB, Senato, Bolle e Brevi, b. 14, f. 214v). Similar powers had been given to Cardinal Alessandro Sforza in 1569 (ASB, Senato, Bolle e Brevi, b. 13, f. 205v). For further details, see Gardi, *Il cardinale Enrico Caetani;* idem, "Il cardinale legato." These powers continued in the seventeenth century: see the faculties given to Pier Luigi Carafa on 3 July 1651, which included conferring doctorates and authority over the various student colleges, including the Collegio di Spagna (HRC Ranuzzi, Ph 12882, 256–57 and 273–76). But powers over the Bolognese *studium* had been accorded to Bolognese legates at least as far back as 26 January 1374, when Pope Gregory XI gave Guglielmo di San Angelo authority to reform it (*Chartularium Studii Bononiensis,* II, 324).

168. On these problems, see von Pastor, *The History of the Popes,* XX, 513–59.
169. On the proclamations, see "Sources and Methodology" in the Introduction. For the correspondence between legates and Rome, see esp. AAV, Fondo Confalonieri, and AAV, Segr. Stato, Legaz. Bologna.
170. On the *podestà* as the university's *conservator,* see Dondarini, "Provvedimenti e aspetti normativi," 78. On the legate's position vis-à-vis the student universities, see Giustiniani, *Philosophiae ac Medicinae . . . gymnasii statuta,* cap. 9, 23–24, in ASB, Archivio dello Studio, b. 249. Comments in Malagola, "I rettori," 69–70.
171. Malagola, "I rettori," 72–74; Malagola, *I rettori,* 61.
172. See AAV, Segr. Stato, Legaz. Bologna, b. 1, passim.
173. Nasalli Rocca di Corneliano, "Il Cardinal Bessarione legato pontificio in Bologna"; Bacchelli, "La legazione bolognese." See also Duranti, *Mai sotto Saturno,* 29, 31–32, 37; L. Labowski, "Bessarione," *DBI,* IX (1967), 687–96.
174. Bacchelli, "L'insegnamento di umanità a Bologna," 150.
175. Dallari, I, 31, 34.
176. On Cesi, see Agostino Borromeo, "Cesi, Pier Donato," *DBI,* XXIV (1980), 261–66; but also Seccadenari's chronicle in BUB, ms. 769, ff. 127r–128r, and G. F. Negri, *Annali di Bologna,* in BUB, ms. 1107, vol. VIII/2, 73 for the period of his legateship, during which his harshness severely dented his popularity.
177. Brizzi, "La storia sui muri," 10–12. The insignia of the papacy were present in several places.
178. This is the import of the letter of Pius IV of 8 March 1561 (F. Cavazza, *Le scuole,* doc. LXV), which introduces a hiring freeze rather than giving the

vice-legate authority to suppress "cattedre inutili," as claimed in Simeoni, *Storia della Università,* 20.

179. On the violence that greeted Cesi's tenure, see Brizzi, "Lo Studio di Bologna," 60–61.
180. For Cesi's *facultates,* see the document of 5 July 1580 in ASB, Senato, Bolle e Brevi, b. 14, ff. 73v–79r, esp. f. 75v; cf. copy in BUB, ms. 2320, ff. 28r–32v, esp. ff. 29v–30r. For the degree he conferred on Ottaviani, see the document from 4 April 1583 in BCAB, ms. B.3182, ff. 13v–16r.
181. Costa, "Contributo," 73–78; De Benedictis, "Luoghi del potere e Studio," 214.
182. See §8.2.1.
183. Lianori was a Bolognese citizen and was certainly in touch with Bessarion at least in 1453, the year by which he obtained his doctorate in canon law. See Chines, 37.
184. Sacchetti, *Ordinationi* (1641), rubs. 45 and 46. Prepared in 1639, the *Ordinationi* were published two years later by Sacchetti's successor Stefano Durazzo. The restoration of the teaching of these languages had been strongly supported by Pope Urban VIII for reasons of faith; they returned to the rolls, but only briefly. See Costa, "Contributo," 23, and §5.4 and §8.3.
185. For an overview of shifting relationships in the *studium,* see De Benedictis, "Luoghi del potere e Studio." For specific officeholders, see Zarri, "Chiesa, religione, società" (with a focus on bishops and archbishops); Mazzone, "Vita religiosa e vita civile" (with a focus on papal legates).
186. On the decrees from the Council of Trent with reference to universities, see Chapter 8. For the details in this paragraph, see Lines, "Papal Power."
187. Due to various factors, Paleotti's role in Bologna had not been as free or effective as he would have liked (see Prodi, *Il cardinale Gabriele Paleotti,* II; Zarri, "Chiesa, religione, società," 957–65; Mazzone, "Vita religiosa e vita civile," 1028–34). In this case, he seems to have been given a more prominent role.
188. Pompeo Vizzani, *I due ultimi libri delle Historie della sua patria* (Bologna: eredi di Giovanni Rossi, 1608), 112. I wish to thank Andrea Gardi for suggesting this possibility.
189. On the complex situation and its evolution, see Costa, "Contributo," 43–55.
190. See the decrees of 29 August 1668 (ASB, Senato, Partiti, b. 25, f. 78v) and 14 December 1676 (ASB, Senato, Partiti, b. 27, f. 152v). I am grateful to Rita De Tata for reproductions of these documents.
191. Decree of 2 December 1694 (ASB, Senato, Partiti, b. 28, ff. 154r–155v). Reproductions kindly supplied by Rita De Tata.
192. I owe this observation to Gian Paolo Brizzi.

193. Giacomelli, "Le Bolle pontificie," 294–300.
194. Giacomelli, "Le Bolle pontificie," 322–23, rightly emphasizes the multiplicity of actors responsible for this sorry state of affairs.

2. TEACHING AND LEARNING

1. BUB, ms. Aldrov. 44, ff. 128r–131r, discussed in Lines, "Reorganizing the Curriculum," 9–11.
2. For an overview of these and other sources, see "Sources and Methodology" in the Introduction, and §2.2.2.
3. Here I highlight the features most relevant to the curriculum. For more general comments on the differences separating Italian universities and those in northern and central Europe, see, among others, Rashdall, *Universities;* Cobban, *Medieval Universities;* and Gieysztor, "Management and Resources." Recent historiography has tended to question the extent to which Bologna and Paris were followed as models in new foundations, and indeed to temper the supposed differences between northern and southern universities. From a curricular viewpoint, however, several points of divergence remain significant.
4. Lines, "Moral Philosophy in the Universities," 41–43.
5. See, among others, Bianchi, *Il vescovo e i filosofi;* idem, *Censure et liberté intellectuelle.*
6. Brockliss, *The University of Oxford,* e.g., 16; and Chapter 2.
7. See the discussion and bibliography in Lines, *Aristotle's* Ethics, 67–74 (for Oxford, also 75–77).
8. A useful starting point is Codina Mir, *Aux sources de la pédagogie des Jésuites.*
9. For the use of the term *facultas,* see Maierù, *University Training,* 72–82; Weijers, *Terminologie,* 52–55. Statutes in Bologna are always for either the student *universitates* or the colleges of doctors; both of these have separate provisions for the Jurists and the Artists.
10. Malagola, *Statuti,* 425–50; cf. Federici Vescovini, "Astronomia e Medicina," 123.
11. See, for instance, Malagola, *Statuti Collegio* (c. 1400?), 487, rub. 5, which indicates that a student was to have studied for at least five years in every area in which he wished to obtain a degree, although there was room for reductions due to earlier studies.
12. The statutes allowed for specific fields such as philosophy, logic, astrology, rhetoric, grammar. See Malagola, *Statuti Collegio* (c. 1400?), 488, rub. 8; Maierù, *University Training,* 57, 81–82 (a degree *de arte dictaminis* is preserved for Domenico da Arezzo: Chines, no. 76). But the degrees reported in Piana, *Nuove ricerche,* 113–74, and Bronzino provide evidence for the use

of such specific designations only rarely (for *loica et philosophia*) and not after 1426 (see Piana, *Nuove ricerche,* 116, 121, 139, 148). Documents for other universities, such as Pavia, testify to the presence of specific degrees only early on: in 1372 Giovanni Traversio obtained his degree in rhetoric, for instance. But in the first part of the fifteenth century this practice ceased there, although it remained on the statute books in Parma (Sottili, "Eine Postille," 409, 419–20). On surviving diplomas (which are rare for arts and medicine), see *Diplomi di laurea conservati nell'Archivio storico* and *Lauree.* On publications relating to occasions such as graduations in the BCAB, see http://badigit.comune.bologna.it/foglinfesta/seta.htm#collapse17. I am grateful to Rebecca Carnevali for this indication.

13. Metaphysics was taught at least from 1406, but not continuously and often in combination with other subjects; see Dallari, IV, 30 and passim.
14. The following observations are tentative, given that a detailed history of theology in Bologna has yet to be written. See the observations on the relative silence of the documents in Turrini, "L'insegnamento della teologia," 437–39.
15. Although metaphysics could also be a philosophical teaching, here I include it among those tied to theology. See §8.1.
16. See Ehrle, *Statuti* (for the revisions of the statutes in subsequent years, see clviii–cxcix); Calcaterra, *Alma mater studiorum,* 122–25. Also see Piana, "La facoltà teologica dell'Università di Bologna nel 1444–1458"; idem, "La facoltà teologica di Bologna nella prima metà del Cinquecento"; see also Gordini, "La Facoltà teologica," which, however, suffers from several inaccuracies.
17. See Turrini, "L'insegnamento della teologia," 442; Grendler, *Universities,* 357–60. For good observations on this issue, see Lambertini, "Intersezioni." More generally, see Denley, "Teologia, poteri, ordini, università."
18. Padua's university for a long period boasted two chairs for theology—one *in via Scoti* and another *in via Thomae;* there was also a chair in *sacra scriptura.* See Poppi, *Ricerche sulla teologia e la scienza;* Gaetano, "Renaissance Thomism." For Pavia, see Negruzzo, "La *Facultas Theologiae.*" The importance of theology at Italian universities is underappreciated in most of the literature, including Kristeller, "The Curriculum of the Italian Universities," and Monfasani, "Aristotelians, Platonists, and the Missing Ockhamists," 253–58. Cf. Grendler, *Universities,* chap. 10.
19. I do not include here teachings of notary, arithmetic, and *grammatica pro quarteriis.* Historians have sometimes mistaken the latter especially for a university-level subject, but it was actually delivered in communal schools, as was common practice in many other Italian cities. In the seventeenth and eighteenth centuries the payments also indicate support for the

Scuole Pie established in Bologna. On primary education in Bologna, see Fantini, *L'istruzione popolare;* Brizzi, "Istruzione e istituzioni educative."

20. Dallari, I, 32; Mischiati, "Un'inedita testimonianza"; Sottili, "Eine Postille," 413–14, with indications of Franchino Gaffurio's teaching of music in Pavia (or rather, Milan) from 1493 to 1499. For the instructions of Nicholas V, see §1.2.1. Although music was not part of the university curriculum, it was occasionally mentioned within university prolusions: Gallo, "La musica in alcune prolusioni."
21. For more on this, see Chapter 6.
22. See §1.1.2 (student numbers).
23. Frijhoff, "Graduation and Careers"; Grendler, *Universities,* 157–59, 166–80, for more information on students and student life. But the example of Ercole Gonzaga's studies at Bologna (166–67) is surely atypical. Especially interesting for comments on how students learned is Brambilla, "*Verba* e *res.*"
24. Lines, "Natural Philosophy and Mathematics."
25. For the location of these classrooms, see esp. the map in F. Cavazza, *Le scuole.*
26. F. Cavazza, *Le scuole,* 23–29.
27. See esp. Fanti, "Prima dell'Archiginnasio."
28. On the Archiginnasio, see esp. Fanti, "Prima dell'Archiginnasio"; Tuttle, "Il palazzo dell'Archiginnasio"; Foschi, "La fabbrica dell'Archiginnasio"; Ceccarelli, "*Scholarum Exaedificatio.*" See also Giacomelli, "Le Bolle pontificie," 280–82.
29. See http://www.archiginnasio.it/stabat.htm (accessed 13 December 2021).
30. See http://www.archiginnasio.it/stemmi.htm (accessed 13 December 2021).
31. See, for further details, Roncuzzi Roversi Monaco, *L'Archiginnasio;* Roversi, *L'Archiginnasio.*
32. For a brief outline, see Grendler, *Universities,* 152–57. More extended treatments in *Linguaggi, metodi, strumenti* and *Dalla lectura all'e-learning.* On disputations in medieval universities see, for the arts faculty, Weijers, *La "disputatio,"* and, for the higher faculties, eadem, *Queritur utrum.* More generally, eadem, *In Search of the Truth.* For the later tradition, see Lawn, *Rise and Decline.* On teaching more generally, the fundamental study is Grabmann, *Die Geschichte der scholastischen Methode;* see also Maierù, *University Training; Luoghi e metodi; Manuels, programmes de cours;* and *L'Enseignement des disciplines.*
33. On the practice of note-taking, see Blair, "Student Manuscripts." See Chapter 4 for how university members obtained and shared books.
34. Maierù, "Gli atti scolastici," 258–74 (idem, *University Training,* 45–58), distinguishes two main categories (ordinary and extraordinary lectures), but those offered only on holidays (*diebus festivis*) are important as well. Maierù does not find any substantial differences of approach, whereas

Dallari, II, vii, suggests that extraordinary lectures developed difficult points from the ordinary ones. But this cannot be the case in the sixteenth century, when extraordinary lectures clearly cover different works from those taught ordinarily. The actual development of these various designations requires further study.

35. Cf. Grendler, *Universities,* 144–46. Maierù, "Gli atti scolastici," 261–63 (idem, *University Training,* 47–49), emphasizes the complementary nature of extraordinary teaching with respect to ordinary teaching, but his evidence is taken mainly from law teaching and may not apply to arts and medicine.
36. Confirmed in Ulisse Aldrovandi's *Avvertimenti,* discussed at the start of this chapter.
37. See ASB, Senato, Partiti, b. 9, ff. 34r–35v, *Ordinationes Studii* (22 November 1570); the move to abolish these teaching is also discussed in the documentation relating to the professor of law Francesco Gioannetti and his teaching (Lines, "Managing Academic Insubordination"). On the meaning of "ordinary," "extraordinary," and other kinds of teaching, cf. Grendler, *Universities,* 144–46.
38. Lines, *Aristotle's* Ethics, 86–91, 290–94.
39. On these *lecturae universitatis,* see Malagola, *Statuta universitatis scolarium* (1405), 257–59, rub. 5; idem, *Statuta universitatis scolarium* (1442), 317, rubs. 14–17; 1609 statutes, chap. 17 (Lines, *Selected Documents,* I); 1641 and 1713 statutes, rub. 44 (Lines, *Selected Documents,* I). See Matsen I and II, and idem, "Selected Extant Latin Documents," 293–94. Brief summary in Weijers, *La "disputatio,"* 271–75.
40. Dallari, II, 215, for the first occurrences of *supraordinaria,* which may have been introduced in imitation of practice elsewhere, including Padua and Pisa. An early example of such a teaching in Pisa is Simone Porzio, appointed to *philosophia supraordinaria* in 1547–1548; see Florence, Biblioteca Nazionale Centrale, Corte d'Appello, ms. 3, f. 16v (payments, dated 10 December 1549); and Del Soldato, *Simone Porzio,* 11–14. For Cardano's teaching, see §7.1.2.
41. For instance, Malagola, *Statuta universitatis scolarium* (1405), 251–52, rub. 37. See esp. Maïer, *Die Vorläufer Galileis,* 255–56; Maierù, "Gli atti scolastici," 268–70, 274–77, 285 (idem, *University Training,* 55–57, 59–62, 69); Buzzetti, Lambertini, and Tabarroni, "Tradizione testuale e insegnamento," esp. 78–82, 87–88. For the thirteenth-century evidence, Weijers, *Terminologie,* 365–72. Despite a distinction between the *repetitor generalis* (for logic) and the *repetitor specialis,* we lack much information on this figure. Note that what Maierù says about the *repetitio* in law does not seem to apply to arts and medicine.
42. See Malagola, *Statuta universitatis scolarium* (1405).

43. Matsen, I, 177–78.

44. The 1405 statutes stipulate that, in logic as in philosophy, along with each lecture a teacher should pose or determine one question. See Malagola, *Statuta universitatis scolarium* (1405), 252, rub. 38: "Item quod quilibet legens predicta seu aliquid predictorum, teneatur super unaquaque lectione movere unam questionem vel motum determinare. Et sic successive dictam questionem determinare." On both the general and the quodlibetal disputations in Bologna, see Maierù, "Gli atti scolastici," 281–85 (idem, *University Training,* 65–69); Weijers, *La "disputatio,"* 195–98.

45. On the relation of questions to number of lectures in logic and medicine in fourteenth-century Bologna, see Buzzetti, Lambertini, and Tabarroni, "Tradizione testuale e insegnamento," 84.

46. Malagola, *Statuta universitatis scolarium* (1405), 260–61, rub. 54. Apparently one weekly disputation *de mane* was followed by a determination of the same disputation *in nonis* one week later, at least in the fourteenth century. There may have been different practices in arts and in medicine. See Jacquart, "La Question disputée" Crisciani, Lambertini, and Tabarroni, "Due manoscritti con questioni mediche."

47. The fact that disputations were to be officially published has led to their re-elaboration, so that surviving manuscripts do not necessarily reflect the actual events: see Buzzetti, Lambertini, and Tabarroni, "Tradizione testuale e insegnamento," 85–86; Weijers, *Queritur utrum,* 213–22.

48. Malagola, *Statuta universitatis scolarium* (1405), 261–62, rub. 55.

49. Malagola, *Statuta universitatis scolarium* (1405), 262–64, rubs 56–57. On Bolognese quodlibetal disputations in medicine, see Weijers, *Queritur utrum,* 236–39; on the frequency of *quodlibetal* versus other kinds of disputations in Bologna, see Buzzetti, Lambertini, and Tabarroni, "Tradizione testuale e insegnamento," 86. For astrology, see also Malagola, *Statuta universitatis scolarium* (1405), 264, rub. 60.

50. Malagola, *Statuta universitatis scolarium* (1405), 262–63, rub. 56.

51. *Palestrae* were to take place in the period after Lent (Malagola, *Statuta universitatis scolarium* [1405], 260–61, rub. 54: "Item statuerunt quod palestre fiant a festo Carnisprivii usque ad festum Olivarum"); the passage just quoted is the only one referring to this exercise in the Bolognese statutes. For brief comments and comparisons with Florence and Perugia, see Maierù, *University Training,* 63 (also see idem, "Gli atti scolastici," 279nn120–121); more detail in Bakker, "Les 'palestrae' de Jean de Spello," and Weijers, *La "disputatio,"* 192–94.

52. Dallari, I, viii. See Maierù, "Gli atti scolastici," 279–80 (idem, *University Training,* 64–65, 123–24); cf. Grendler, *Universities,* 156. In early modern Padua, instead, the *circoli* referred to the last fifteen minutes of a professor's lecture: the teacher was to descend from the rostrum, mingle with

the students, and answer their questions; see del Negro, "'Pura favella latina,'" 121–22.

53. Anonymous document *Alcuni avertimenti circa lo Studio di Bologna* (AAB, Miscellanee Vecchie, 802, olim L. 87; Lines, "Reorganizing the Curriculum," 17–18, 36–41, with translation), probably by Paleotti in or around 1579, listing the various causes for concern in the *studium:* under "Difetti de' dottori": "Il modo che si usa nelli circuli di proponere come all'improv[viso] le questioni causa molti'intrichi, et si potria riformare meg[lio] con più utile de scolari." Under "Difetti de' scolari": "Li scolari cominciano le loro *licentie* nelli circoli, li quali sono div[enuti] come luoghi infami, né si può dire honestamente le cose che si dicono ivi a' dottori et a' scolari, etiam nominatim, et questa petulantia si accende poi nelle scole di mano in mano." Probably the expectation was for people to submit questions beforehand in writing, as was the practice for disputations elsewhere: see Maierù, *University Training,* 63n107 and 64n111, with reference to Padua's 1465 statutes, according to which students wishing to debate questions on the lessons they had heard needed to publish in advance the thesis they planned to discuss ("Si quis autem scholaris super aliquibus lectionibus auditis conclusionem aliquam substinendam proponere vellet, eam publicari faciat in mane aut in die precedenti in scholis vel in apothecis"). For brief comments on Italian *circoli,* see also Weijers, *La "disputatio,"* 194–95; and, for medicine, Weijers, *Queritur utrum,* 240–41.
54. See ASB, Senato, Partiti, b. 8, ff. 188v–189r (24 November 1568).
55. See, for instance, Pirro Legnani Ferri, *Diario delle cose accadute in Bologna,* in BUB, ms. 896, vol. II, f. 6r, for 9 November 1568.
56. See the preface to the roll of 1581 (ASB, Riformatori dello Studio, b. 12, item 133 [seen in microfilm]), which corresponds to the 1586 roll transcribed in the Appendix: "Postea, finitis lectionibus, omnes concurrentes in locis deputatis circulum faciant et ibi simul conferant et disputent."
57. See, for 1583, the proposal by the Assunti in ASB, Assunteria di Studio, b. 1, unnumbered folder ("1566"), cap. 24 (*Circulares disputationes non turbandas et sine rixis peragendas esse*): "Cum circulares disputationes maximo semper fiant strepitu rixisque, poterit Illustrissimus Senatus lege cavere, ne quis audeat eas turbare ut hae sine scandulo et contumelia fiant. Disputaturus nempe qui proponit cathedram ascendat. Concurrens vero inferiori loco collocatus ad proposita modeste respondeat in schola magna ut olim fiebat." On 6 October 1649 new instructions of the Riformatori dello Studio together with the legate (Fabrizio Savelli) stipulated that "in luogo de' Circoli già tralasciati i dottori leggenti siano tenuti far publiche dispute in Casa agli scolari, assistendo essi medesimi al difendente almeno due volte l'anno" (ASB, Assunteria di Studio, b. 4, item 18, f. 67r–v).

58. See ASB, Assunteria di Studio, b. 2, unnumbered folder ("1645, Relazione degli Assunti di Studio per rimediar ai disordini di essa") point 6: the Assunti suggest "Che ogni lettor pubblico in luogo de' circoli già oltremodo usati e comandati dalle costituzioni del rotolo, debba tenere ogni anno almeno due accademie o dispute di quelle medesime materie, che gli è assegnata su le scuole." See also ASB, Assunteria di Studio, b. 3, item 18, point 1.
59. Malagola, *Statuta universitatis scolarium* (1405), 261–62, rub. 55.
60. Malagola, *Statuti Collegio* (c. 1400?), 486–87, rub. 6, and 488–89, rubs. 9–10; see also Maierù, "Gli atti scolastici," 271–72 (idem, *University Training,* 57–58, also 82–92, 95). The statutes in Malagola refer to a situation in the early fifteenth century in which a degree candidate was required to have disputed publicly either three general questions or two general ones and one *quodlibet.* At his examination, the candidate received from the college of doctors various *puncta* which he was to lecture on and dispute the same evening. The passages are specified only rarely in the documents; a relevant case is that of Francesco de Trestut de Villa Olivae in the diocese of Valencia, a candidate for the degree in arts and medicine who in 1480 was assigned *puncta* from *Physics* III.10 on the infinite and from Hippocrates, *Aphorism* 19; see Piana, *Nuove ricerche,* 218. In another case in 1484, a candidate in arts was assigned passages from the *Posterior Analytics* and *Physics* I; see Piana, *Nuove ricerche,* 222.
61. This is probably the purpose of the printed prospectuses (in broadsheet format) of disputations that have survived, especially for the years 1557–1571, although Salterini seems to suggest that they were disputations held in view of obtaining a teaching position; see ASB, Riformatori dello Studio, b. 59 (Salterini, 138, 156–58). These documents deserve a fuller study: Salterini is right to say that these are often by students who usually graduate sometime after the date of the public discussion and thereafter teach in the *studium,* but in several cases the disputation was not held in Bologna at all (item 13 by Fr. Ioannnes Baptista Librantius was held in Ferrara; item 20 by Fr. Petrus Franciscus Rainerus, in Perugia) and not always at a university. Furthermore, some proponents are not registered in Bronzino as having received their degree in Bologna, while others did not teach there. An open question is whether the numerous points listed in the disputations were actually covered. For comments and fuller listings, see *Bononia manifesta,* xviii–xix, 505–24, and *Bononia manifesta: Supplemento,* 63–80. For a discussion of the theses from the standpoint of "cheap print," see Carnevali, "Cheap, Everyday Print," esp. 207–10; for similar comments on Jesuit theses, see Tinti, "Le tesi a stampa nei collegi gesuitici."
62. On the various disputations (1417–1526) held to obtain these lectureships (ASB, Riformatori dello Studio, b. 57), see Salterini, 138–50. Some of these are studied in Matsen I and II.

63. ASB, Riformatori dello Studio, b. 60, contains fifteen broadsheet theses from 1626 to 1678 (Cencetti, *Gli archivi*, 85ff; Salterini, 159–60). The twenty-four conclusions preserved between 1668 and 1721 are more extensive; see ASB, Riformatori dello Studio, b. 61 (Salterini, 162–64).
64. Cf. Lawn, *Rise and Decline.*
65. For what follows, see ASB, Archivio dello Studio, Università degli scolari: Artisti, b. 387, ff. 11r, 12r. For the degree date, see also Bronzino, 128. I have been unable to locate Carmenius's disputations.
66. Dallari, II, 350. He continued to teach in Bologna until 1643 (see Dallari, ad indicem).
67. Bolognese disputations were often characterized by the large number of theses defended, something that was a feature not only of university culture (cf. Giovanni Pico della Mirandola's proposal to hold a public disputation on nine hundred theses). In 1553 Paulus Scalichius defended 1553 conclusions in connection with his degree in theology: see Rossi Monti, "Paulus Scalichius," 355–56, 370–74. For a late sixteenth-century case by a teacher of logic, see Grendler, *Universities*, 154–56.
68. For the curricular points that follow, see Malagola, *Statuta universitatis scolarium* (1405), 274–77, rub. 78 (rev. eds. in Maierù, *University Training*, 113–16, and in Lines, *Selected Documents*, doc. 1); cf. Lines, *Aristotle's* Ethics, 87; Bianchi, "I contenuti," 125; Duranti, *Mai sotto Saturno*, 32–38; and, for Pavia, Azzolini et al., "La Facoltà di Arti e Medicina," 517–21, and Mazzarello and Cani, "Insegnare la Medicina."
69. For the length of a *punctum*, see Weijers, *Terminologie*, 302–6; Maierù, *University Training*, 47.
70. For logic, see the edition of rub. 37 of the 1405 statutes in Maierù, *University Training*, 113–16, as well as Maierù's sketch, 94–98.
71. See also Bianchi, "I contenuti," 127–28; and esp. *L'insegnamento della logica a Bologna.* Porphyry's manual, originally written in Greek, circulated throughout the Middle Ages in Boethius's translation (as did many of Aristotle's works on logic). For a useful, though somewhat dated, exploration of medieval logic, see the essays in *The Cambridge History of Later Medieval Philosophy.* For an up-to-date treatment of Boethius's activity as an interpreter of logical works, see at least Ebbesen, "The Aristotelian Commentator"; Casey, "Boethius' Works on Logic in the Middle Ages."
72. For an indication of which works are now considered doubtful or spurious, see the table of contents for *The Complete Works of Aristotle.* I give in English the titles of Aristotle's most familiar works; in order to avoid confusion, I list the minor works (several of which are component parts of the *Parva naturalia*) as listed by the statutes, but with the standard spelling.
73. Malagola, *Statuta universitatis scolarium* (1405), 274, rub. 78: "Et quod semper lectura extraordinaria incipiatur legi in festivitatibus paschatis

resurrectionis." Some interpreters (e.g., Maierù, *University Training,* 52; idem, "Gli atti scolastici," 267) have applied this stipulation to all extraordinary subjects, but it is unclear whether it is true of subjects outside of philosophy.

74. Lines, *Aristotle's* Ethics, 65–108.
75. For a prospectus, see Grendler, *Universities,* 410–11. I have combined Grendler's explanations with those of Federici Vescovini, "I programmi," 211–15, and eadem, "Astronomia e medicina," 134–41 (see these works for descriptions and further bibliography). Also see Duranti, *Mai sotto Saturno,* 35–36, 40–42; Caroti, *L'astrologia in Italia;* and most recently Rutkin, *Sapientia Astrologica,* 388–91, on the 1405 statutes. Cf. the description of the curriculum in Pavia in Azzolini et al., "La Facoltà di Arti e Medicina," 562–68. I am grateful to Dario Tessicini for comments and further bibliography on this discipline.
76. See Poulle, *Les Tables Alphonsines.*
77. Pedersen, "The Origins of the 'Theorica Planetarum.'"
78. Possibly by William of England; see French, "Astrology in Medical Practice," 43–46.
79. Federici Vescovini, "I programmi," 213n, comments on the absence of *De urina non visa* from most Italian libraries.
80. Federici Vescovini, "Astronomia e medicina," 125–27, 142–48; see also §6.1.2.
81. For details, see Malagola, *Statuta universitatis scolarium* (1405), 274–77, rub. 78; the clearest summary is Park, *Doctors and Medicine,* 245–48 (cf. Grendler, *Universities,* 318–23). See also Siraisi, *Taddeo Alderotti,* 118–46; eadem, "The Faculty of Medicine"; and, for other comparative perspectives, Azzolini et al., "La Facoltà di Arti e Medicina," 546–62 (on Pavia); Pedersen, "Tradition and Innovation," 452–55; Brockliss, "Curricula," 609–15; *El aprendizaje de la medicina;* McVaugh, *The Rational Surgery;* Duranti, *Mai sotto Saturno,* 34–35. On the development of medicine in Italy before the fifteenth century, see Crisciani, "Curricula e contenuti dell'insegnamento," esp. 183–91; Siraisi, *Taddeo Alderotti,* 96–117; Duranti, "La scuola medica" (with bibliography); and the numerous studies by Tiziana Pesenti, such as *Marsilio Santasofia tra corti e Università.*
82. On the prominence of Galen, see Murano, "Opere di Galeno nella facoltà di medicina di Bologna," 137–66. For Avicenna in Italy generally, see Siraisi, *Avicenna,* 55–58; Chandelier, *Avicenne.* For Hippocrates, see Chapter 7.
83. Park, *Doctors and Medicine,* 247–48, lists only selections from Book III of the *Canon;* see Siraisi, *Avicenna,* 55–56, for possible use also of selections from Book IV. Note that although Park indicates that lectures in *practica* are all held in the evening, this is not actually stipulated in the statutes;

the teaching rolls indicate that it was taught both *de mane* and *de sero* (see, for instance, Dallari, I, 15, for 1440–1441). Grendler, *Universities,* 323, refers to a special chair that was established in the last quarter of the century to deal specifically with *Canon,* III; but this did not last after 1500.

84. Siraisi, *Avicenna,* 54; for detail on the material covered, see 54–55.
85. Siraisi, *Avicenna,* 55n.
86. Malagola, *Statuta universitatis scolarium* (1405), 247–48 (rub. 35); Siraisi, *Taddeo Alderotti,* 108–9; Park, *Doctors and Medicine,* 63–66, 248. For a fuller discussion of surgery, see §7.2.
87. Bruno da Longoburgo is also known as Bruno da Longobucco. Hailing from Calabria, Bruno received at least part of his medical formation in Bologna before going to Padua, where he taught and completed the *Chirurgia magna.* He died there around 1286. See Focà, *Maestro Bruno da Longobucco.* For further details on the *Chirurgia,* see Pesenti, "Arti e medicina," 174–76.
88. Malagola, *Statuta universitatis scolarium* (1405), 289–90, rub. 96.
89. Malagola, *Statuta universitatis scolarium* (1405), 252, rub. 38.
90. Malagola, *Statuti Collegio* (c. 1400?), 488, rub. 9; for summary information on these works, see Grendler, *Universities,* 199–202; Bianchi, "I contenuti," 126–27.
91. Student lecture notes (*recollectae*) testify to Bartolomeo's teaching of Cicero's *De officiis* in 1403. See Modena, Biblioteca Estense, ms. V 8 19 (lat. 300); see Gargan, "La lettura dei classici," 468n2; Quaquarelli, "Umanesimo e lettura dei classici," 100; Chines, no. 28.
92. The point is made forcefully in the publications of Dino Buzzetti, Roberto Lambertini, and Andrea Tabarroni, who had envisioned a project (later abandoned) to study all aspects of Bolognese teaching in arts and medicine during the fourteenth and fifteenth centuries, including payments of teachers, literary production, *acta scholastica, quaestiones,* degrees, the production and circulation of manuscripts, book collections, and so forth. For details see esp. Buzzetti, "La Faculté des arts"; Buzzetti, Lambertini, and Tabarroni, "Tradizione testuale e insegnamento." For further considerations on the problematic nature of university statutes, see the essays in *Statuti universitari;* and, for England, Feingold, *The Mathematicians' Apprenticeship,* 23–44 and passim.
93. Grendler, *Universities,* 323.
94. For a general (but not always reliable) sketch, see Brockliss, "Curricula"; more focused on Italy is Bianchi, "I contenuti," which should be used along with more specific studies such as, for Pavia, Ferraresi, "Il curriculum delle Arti," and Mazzarello and Cani, "Insegnare la Medicina."
95. On the *pecia* and Bolognese book culture, see §4.1.
96. For translations of Aristotle and what works became available in Latin from the eleventh century onward, see Dod, "Aristoteles Latinus."

97. On the processes and stages of translation of medical works, see Jacquart, "Principales étapes." As an example for astrology, Ptolemy's *Tetrabiblos* was read in the translation (c. 1138) by Plato of Tivoli.
98. For especially stimulating comments on the influence of Averroes in the Renaissance, see Hasse, *Success and Suppression.*
99. Bühler, *University and the Press,* 90 (36.A.9, 36.A.13) and 91 (36.A.27) for Ockham; 93 (36.B.8) for Heytesbury; 72 (13.A.1) and 78 (19.A.41) for Scotus; 72 (13.A.6) for Francis of Mayrone; and 93 (36.B.12) for Paul of Venice.
100. See Bianchi, "Fra Ermolao Barbaro e Ludovico Boccadiferro," also with reference to Schmitt's contention that the influence of these works ceased thereafter.
101. For the editions, see Bühler, *University and the Press,* 59, 60, 72. On the twenty-two copies in a stationer's shop, see Fava, "Un grande libraio-editore"; Poli, "Contributi sopra Sigismondo de' Libri."
102. Now see De Tata, *Il commercio librario;* see also Chapter 4.
103. For background details on this archival series, see "Sources and Methodology" in the Introduction.
104. Dallari, II, 48–50. The books for law had been specified in the rolls for a long time previous.
105. Dallari, II, 223–25. See Chapter 7.
106. Dallari, II, 234, 237.
107. Dallari, II, 242.
108. Lines, "Natural Philosophy and Mathematics," 144, table V.
109. ASB, Riformatori dello Studio, b. 21, ff. 2r–4v (*Universae lectiones hic describuntur quas legunt annuatim Artistae in almo nostro Bononiensi Gymnasio* [*1585–1586*]); and Dallari, II, 241. The introduction of a three-year cycle probably dates to a few decades earlier (Lines, "Reorganizing the Curriculum," 8–16); if so, this would support the theory of a three-year cycle in Padua in the 1540s: see Nutton, "Fracastoro's Theory of Contagion," 209–10.
110. For the roll, see Dallari, II, 433–35.
111. For Agostino Odofredi, see ASB, Annue Lezioni, b. 60, ff. 316, 323 (Piccinno, *Fonti,* 20, item 4); for Giacomo Jacchini, see ASB, Annue Lezioni, b. 60, f. 392r (Piccinno, *Fonti,* 24, item 9); and for Ercole Betti, see ASB, Annue Lezioni, b. 60, ff. 499, 510r (Piccinno, *Fonti,* 29, item 21).
112. For Marco Antonio Fabri, see ASB, Annue Lezioni, b. 60, f. 423 (Piccinno, *Fonti,* 26, item 14); for Francesco Severini, see ASB, Annue Lezioni, b. 60, ff. 596r, 600r (Piccinno, *Fonti,* 33, item 25).
113. For Nobili, see ASB, Annue Lezioni, b. 60, f. 324r (Piccinno, *Fonti,* 21, item 5). For Malisardi, see see ASB, Annue Lezioni, b. 60, ff. 361, 368 (Piccinno, *Fonti,* 23, item 8). The fourth book of Girolamo Mercuriale's *De cognoscendis et curandis humani corporis affectibus* (Venice: Giunti, 1617), deriving from

his teaching in Padua, is entitled *De vitiis articulorum et lue venerea.* Note that Mercuriale also taught in Bologna (1587–1593).

114. For Carlo Riario, see ASB, Annue Lezioni, b. 60, f. 511 (Piccinno, *Fonti,* 31, item 22); for Francesco Cesi, see ASB, Annue Lezioni, b. 60, f. 454 (Piccinno, *Fonti,* 28, item 19); and for Muratori, see ASB, Annue Lezioni, b. 60, f. 342r (Piccinno, *Fonti,* 22, item 6).

115. ASB, Annue Lezioni, b. 60, ff. 617r (Bartolomeo Ambrosini) and 618r (Giacinto Ambrosini); for both, see Piccinno, *Fonti,* 34, item 26. It is unclear whether Bartolomeo's teaching "de simplicibus purgantibus" is connected at all with a work such as that of Gabriele Falloppio, *De simplicibus medicamentis purgantibus* (Venice: ad insigne stellae Iordani Ziletti, 1565) or, perhaps more likely, simply refers to purgative compounds.

116. Hankins, *Plato in the Italian Renaissance.*

117. Grendler, *Universities,* 297–309 for an overview.

118. Costa, *Ulisse Aldrovandi e lo Studio bolognese,* 90; Grendler, *Universities,* 307.

119. ASB, Assunteria di Studio, b. 79.

120. ASB, Senato, Lettere del Senato, Serie VII, b. 61, pages not numbered.

121. ASB, Senato, Lettere del Senato, Serie XVI, b. 1.

122. For a discussion of many other interesting problems or proposals in the sixteenth century, including by Ulisse Aldrovandi, see Lines, "Reorganizing the Curriculum." For other issues, see Baldelli, "Lo Studio bolognese tra Sei e Settecento," 261–69; eadem, "Tentativi di regolamentazione"; and esp. M. Cavazza, "Riforma dell'Università," centered on changes in the late seventeenth century.

123. The practice in law may have been different from that in arts and medicine. As noted above in the case of Gambarini, private lectures could take place both during *dies legibiles* and during vacation periods.

124. *Parere del Vezza come si doveria reformare il Studio,* in ASB, Assunteria di Studio, b. 1, unnumbered folder ("1585, 1586"), pages not numbered: "Ancora che l'uso delle Accademie paia che sia utile perché fa li scolari facili e pronti nel dire, facendoli animosi, ma in verità facendosi come oggi si fanno mentre che si leggono le lettioni publiche ancora che si facciano li dì non leggibili hanno causato grandissimo danno alli studii et alle lettioni publiche et alli scolari istessi perché, per voler una Gioba [= Giovedì] o una festa far una lettione nelle accademie, ponevan tutto il suo studio in quella, [e] lassiavano di studiar la lettione publica. Così le lettioni publiche restano poco studiate, et per ogni poca cosa si rompe il legger publico, il che già non era così quando non erano queste accademie, ma le lettioni erano studiate con molta diligentia, dal che nasceva honor al studio, fatica et honore alli dottori perché bisognava che fossero diligenti nella lettione, perché vi erano scolari che argomentavano ogni mattina et molto valentemente et era bisogno che il dottore stesse molto bene in

ordine perché li scolari a gara si sforzavano di argomentare. Questo argomentare così publicamente al suo dottore facea il scolare pronto nel dire, sotile in argomentare. Hora perché si attende a queste accademie non v'è chi argomenti più, così li dottori se la passano con manco fatica. Pertanto io non vorria che si levassero in tutto le accademie, ma che non si potessero in modo alcuno fare in nessun dì mentre si leggano le lettioni ordinarie ma solamente alle vacantie come di Natale, di Carnevale, di Pasqua, delle Purgationi et altre vacanze, et commandar alli dottori che in casa loro non possan adunarsi accademie se non come di sopra." Next to this recommendation is written: *Piace.* For Vezza, see also Lines, "Reorganizing the Curriculum," 21–22.

125. *Parere del Vezza:* "facendolo, necessariamente non si procede come è dovere, ma imparano come si dice a mente, con molto essercitio, solo questo. Il che facendo, credono saper poi, et putti s'addottorano. Quando lo faranno volontariamente, non lo faranno se non bene provetti, come era già solito farsi."

126. *Parere del Vezza:* "Perché molti abusi delle vacantie di Padoa si sono messe in uso in questo Studio, sì perché li scolari forestieri non sanno gli ordini nostri come altre cause quale è bene tacerle, saria bene fare una tavola dove fossero scritte quando in ciascheduna terzaria si hanno a principiare le vacanze, come a Natale o S. Thomaso et non prima, a Carnevale, a S. Antonio et così dello altro, quale fosse affisa alla porta de l'università."

127. Gaetani, *Ordinationi* (1586), in ASB, Assunteria di Studio, b. 1, folder "1585, 1586" (for their approval, see ASB, Senato, Partiti, b. 11, ff. 131v–136r). See Lines, "The University of the Artists," 145–46.

128. See the Appendix.

129. For a synthetic discussion of the instructions on the *studium* issued by the papal legates between 1586 and 1712, see Lines, "The University of the Artists."

130. Bandini, *Reformationi dello studio* (1593), in ASB, Assunteria di Studio, b. 1, folder "1593, Reformazioni dello Studio." Another sign that the tide was turning is the monument erected in the Archiginnatio to Orazio Giovagnoni, named as a teacher of the *Institutes* both publicly and privately (Guerrini, "Tra docenza pubblica e insegnamento privato," 186).

131. Landriani, *Ordinationi* (1602), in ASB, Assunteria di Studio, b. 3, ff. 57r–59v; Lines, "The University of the Artists," 146.

132. Guerrini, "Tra docenza pubblica e insegnamento privato," 186; the issue deserves to be examined in further detail.

133. ASB, Assunteria di Studio, b. 94, fasc. 31, undated, three-page ms. *Memoriale delle università degli scolari sulle lezioni private.*

134. See Sacchetti, *Ordinationi* (1641, published by Sacchetti's successor Durazzo), rub. 25: "si proibisce sotto le medesime pene et altre arbitrarie il

dettare, far scrivere o dar a scrivere le lettioni lette alle publiche Scuole, eccetto che nei tempi delle vacanze." In ASB, Assunteria di Studio, b. 2, folders "1639, Nuove costituzioni" and "1641, Ordinazioni dello Studio." A subsequent decree of the Senate rolled this back: see its deliberation dated 6 October 1649 (ASB, Assunteria di Studio, b. 4, f. 67r–v), point 2: "Che [ai] detti dottori leggenti sia concessa ancora facoltà di dettare in scritto dalla publica catedra agl'uditori." For further notes on dictation in Bologna, see Lines, "The University of the Artists," 149–50.

135. ASB, Assunteria di Studio, b. 94, fasc. 31, undated three-page manuscript, untitled, *inc.* Nel tempo che.

136. See, for instance, Pietro Mengoli, *Arithmeticae realis lectiones secundae,* whose *explicit* (in BUB, ms. 1066, vol. III) reads "Scribebam die prima Februari anni 1682 dictaturus aptis scholaribus, Petrus Mengolus." In 1691 Bartolomeo Aldrovandi noted down the logic lessons of Pietro Maria Ciani, who was clearly dictating them ("dictante Petro Maria Ziano, Philosophiae publico lectore, scribente Bartolomeo de Aldrovandis"), probably in the course of private teaching, since publicly he was to teach *De anima* in 1690–1691 and *Parva naturalia* the following year, according to the rolls (Dallari, III.1, 152, 156).

137. Casoni, *Ordinazioni* (1713), rub. 25 in ASB, Assunteria di Studio, b. 3, folder "1713, Ordinazioni": "Et per cooperare al maggior profitto de' medesimi scolari si permette alli lettori, che oltre le lezioni fatte per essi su le publiche Scuole, possano dettare alle case loro tanto quelle lezioni che havranno lette su le medesime Scuole, quanto ogn'altra che appartenga alla loro professione e che conosceranno essi di maggior vantaggio alli scolari medesimi."

138. del Negro, "'Leggere a mente'"; cf. Brambilla, "*Bricolage* didattico," who claims that jurists in Bologna were already dictating for at least one hour a day at the end of the fifteenth century, something that came to replace the *repetitiones.*

139. Malagola, *Statuta universitatis scolarium* (1405), 267, rub. 65.

140. See also the considerations in Grendler, *Universities,* 143–44.

141. See the prefaces to the rolls in Dallari, esp. I, xxii (1475–1476); in 1545 the summer holidays started on the Feast of the Assumption (15 August).

142. See the Appendix.

143. ASB, Senato, Partiti, b. 7, f. 167v, deliberation dated 29 August 1561 (also ASB, Riformatori dello Studio, b. 19, f. 97r; ASB, Assunteria di Studio, b. 5).

144. Large manuscript *calendario* in ASB, Ambasciata, b. 210.

145. Lines, "Reorganizing the Curriculum," 14–15.

146. AAB, Miscellanee Vecchie, 802, olim L. 87, fasc. 33, containing on ff. 50r–69r Ulisse Aldrovandi's *Bononiensis Gymnasii Reformatio ad Illustrissimum et*

Reverendissimum Cardinalem Palaeotum Protoarchiepiscopum Bononiensem (cap. 6).

147. The first surviving printed calendar dates from 1586 and was printed by Alessandro Benacci: ASB, Assunteria di Studio, b. 88 "Taccuino astronomico e calendario, 1586–1800," printed calendar for the academic year 1586–1587; see Carnevali, "Cheap, Everyday Print," 202, 232–36. As she rightly observes (202n197), one should not confuse these calendars with astronomical *taccuina*.
148. For Cesario, see ASB, Annue Lezioni, b. 60, ff. 443r–446v; for Betti, see ASB, Annue Lezioni, b. 60, ff. 510r, 501r–502v (Piccinno, *Fonti,* 29–30, item 21).
149. See, for instance, the syllabus for scholastic theology of the Servite Aurelio Savini, who in 1735–1736 taught during the following periods: 3 November–19 December, 9–26 January, 16 February–24 March, 11 April–18 May, and 2–23 June (86 lectures); see ASB, Annue Lezioni, b. 62, ff. 180r–181v.
150. ASB, Assunteria di Studio, Requisiti dei lettori; see Guerrini, "Tra docenza pubblica e insegnamento privato," esp. 184–86, 188–89; Grendler, *Universities,* does not address the issue of private teaching.
151. See ASB, Assunteria di Studio, b. 2, unnumbered folder ("1660"), document dated 9 March 1660.
152. Dooley, "Social Control," 232–39.
153. Dooley, "Social Control," 231–32.
154. See the anonymous (but in all likelihood by Ulisse Aldrovandi) *De Bononiensis Gymnasii reformatione animadversiones Collegii Artium et Medicinae ad illustrissimum Senatum Bononiensem* in ASB, Assunteria di Studio, b. 1, unnumbered folder ("1566"), on which see Lines, "Reorganizing the Curriculum," 15–16. The proposals of Archdeacon Marsili appeared anonymously in *Memorie per riparare i pregiudizi.* For Marsili, see §8.3, and Lines, "Reorganizing the Curriculum," 59n159.
155. See Cavazza, "Early Work on Electricity and Medicine"; eadem, "'Dottrici' e lettrici'"; eadem, *Laura Bassi;* Findlen, "Science as a Career"; eadem, "Always among Men"; eadem, "The Scientist and the Saint." For Charles de Brosses, see Sorbelli, *Bologna negli scrittori stranieri,* III, 79–81.
156. On Agnesi, see Mazzotti, "Maria Gaetana Agnesi."
157. Cavazza, *Laura Bassi;* di Simone, "Admission," 295–97.
158. Deliberation of 2 December 1694 (ASB, Senato, Partiti, b. 28, ff. 154r–155v at f. 155r–v): "5°. Che le materie da esprimersi ne' memoriali di chi domanderà come sopra la lettura siano distinte nelle seguenti classi: per li Signori Leggisti, 1. La legge civile; 2. La legge canonica; 3. La somma Rolandina. Per li Signori Artisti, 1. La filosofia, sotto la quale si comprenda la logica e tutta la filosofia naturale e morale; 2. La medicina teorica e

pratica, sotto la quale si comprenda la chirurgia, l'anatomia e li semplici medicinali; 3. Le lettere humane; 4. La teologia, sotto la quale si comprenda la scolastica, la morale e la Sacra Scrittura; 5. La matematica, sotto la quale si comprendano le meccaniche; 6. L'hidrometria."

159. For what follows, see Baldelli, "Tentativi di regolamentazione," 16–20; cf. Dallari, III.2, 5–8. For some notes on the significance of the 1737 reform for mathematics and the sciences, see Pepe, "Le discipline fisiche, matematiche e naturali," 156–58.

160. See esp. Giacomelli, *Carlo Grassi;* Baldelli, "Tentativi di regolamentazione."

161. See Chapter 8.

162. Mathematics was especially innovative in Bologna through the teaching of Gabriele Manfredi in the first part of the century; see Pepe, "Tra università e scuole militari," 171–72. For a broad and fairly technical survey, see Bortolotti, *La storia della matematica.*

163. Particular physics should be distinguished in some respects from experimental physics; see Pepe, "Le discipline fisiche, matematiche e naturali," 147–48. For the view of the Bolognese Sebastiano Canterzani in 1788, see Cavazza, "L'insegnamento delle scienze sperimentali," 161–62.

164. For the intersections between the university curriculum and that of the Istituto delle Scienze, see §3.2 and §7.3. For the meaning of *universa philosophia,* see Cavazza, "Fisica generale e fisica sperimentale."

165. See Chapter 8; and Turrini, "Le letture di casi di coscienza," 228–29. These changes are due in part to the pastoral concerns of Archbishop Prospero Lambertini (1731–1754), who in 1740 ascended the papal see as Benedict XIV.

166. Turrini, "L'insegnamento della teologia," 463.

167. Dallari, III.2, 66–69 (roll for 1749–1750). In the numbers given I have eliminated double- and triple-occurrences of the same name and included the numerous names listed as *emeriti* for anatomy. More precisely, the roll lists one staff member for *chirurgia* in the morning, two *ad operationes chirurgicas,* two for *chirurgia* in the afternoon; nine *emeriti* and three *ordinarii* for anatomy in the morning, three for *lectura anatomica* (distributed across the second and third morning hours and the second afternoon hour), and one *ad sectiones et ostensiones anatomicas;* eight for theoretical medicine and five for practical medicine (in both cases including *ordinaria, supraordinaria, extraordinaria*). Theology includes four appointments for moral theology, one for Sacred Scriptures, four for metaphysics, eleven for scholastic theology, one for dogmatic theology, one for church history, one for the Councils, and one for Hebrew. Science and philosophy have five in logic, one in universal philosophy, four in moral philosophy, four in physics, and one in chemistry. Mathematics has one each for analytic and synthetic geometry, one for mechanics, one for hydrometry, one in

astronomy, and one to compile the astrological calendar. The humanities list two for humane letters, two for Greek, and one for Hebrew.

168. Angelini, "Introduzione," 210–15, 528–35; Cavazza, "Innovazione e compromesso," 342–43; cf. Guerrini, "Université et académies à Bologne," 16. The monks were to be paid from the legacy of the Collegio Panolini, and each had to present a scientific paper annually.
169. On the need for the university's teachings to appeal in 1716 to a mixed student body of laymen and clergy, see the document quoted in Turrini, "L'insegnamento della teologia," 461–62.

3. THE UNIVERSITY IN CONTEXT

1. Pini, *Studio, università e città.*
2. Lines, "The University and the City," with bibliography; Brizzi, "Lo Studio di Bologna."
3. On the Congregazione della Perseveranza, see Chapter 8.
4. The practice has been referred to as *paedagogium;* see Brizzi, *Formazione,* 15–17.
5. Brizzi, *Formazione,* 76–77.
6. For the broad picture, see *I collegi universitari;* Brizzi, "Studenti, Università, Collegi"; idem, "Università e collegi"; Denley, "The Collegiate Movement"; Roggero, "I collegi universitari"; *Die universitären Kollegien.*
7. On the transition in their aims, see Brizzi, "Da *domus pauperum scholarium* a collegio d'educazione"; also helpful for Italian colleges more broadly (including for Bologna's Spanish College) is *Dai collegi medievali alle residenze universitarie.*
8. For this sketch, I depend on Brizzi, "I collegi per borsisti," with prospectus on 35 and with information on relevant archival sources for various colleges (Ancarano, Ferrero, Ungaro-Illirico, Poeti, Panolini, Montalto, Sinibaldi, Palantieri, Jacobs, Comelli) on 53–172. See also idem, "Maestri e studenti," 135–38; idem, "Lo Studio di Bologna," 28–36. Some of these colleges have received specialist attention in recent years. See, for instance, *Annali del Collegio Ungaro Illirico* and *Libri in collegio.*
9. Brizzi, "Maestri e studenti," 138.
10. There were some exceptions: the teaching of grammar was often allowed, and the college envisaged in the 1326 will of Guglielmo de' Corvi da Brescia made explicit provision for the teaching of metaphysics and natural and moral philosophy; see Siraisi, *Taddeo Alderotti,* 53.
11. Brizzi, "I collegi per borsisti"; more generally, Carlsmith, "Student Colleges."
12. In 1596 the college pleaded with cardinal Montalto to encourage the city authorities to give Galesi a pay raise, something Montalto promised to do (ASB, Archivio Demaniale-Collegio Montalto, 72/7293, f. 33v): "S'intende che sia

per darsi aumento di salario alli lettori in questo Studio: Et perché habbiamo il Sig. Dottore Galesio uno di essi dottori dell'Accademia nostra di logici et filosofi, quale oltre all'essere molto affettionato del Collegio, assai s'affatica di legere a' nostri Collegiali, et con grande utilità le sopra dette facultadi, talmente che, sì per questo, come anco per altre sue buone qualità siamo sforzati di raccomandarlo a V. S. Illustrissima, quale pregamo et supplicamo resti servita di favorirlo con lettere presso il Reggimento, il che connumeraremo tra l'infinite gratie fatteci da V. S. Illustrissima, che perciò a lei solo ci teniamo obligatissimi" (10 July 1596). For the involvement of other university professors, see also f. 126r (20 July 1621). Starting in 1627, students were obliged to sit an entrance exam (ff. 158v–160r). More generally on this college, see Cagni, "Il pontificio collegio 'Montalto' in Bologna." On Galesi's teaching in the *studium,* see Lines, *Aristotle's* Ethics, esp. 301–7, 525–27.

13. A letter from Aldrovandi to Alessandro Farnese Jr. (6 September 1578) informs the cardinal that his protégé Leandro Teuci (?) Bresciano has successfully passed the entrance exam in Latin, based on a letter of Cicero, and has paid 25 gold *scudi;* see BUB, ms. 4679, pages not numbered.
14. My account of the Collegio Ancarano follows Brizzi, "I collegi per borsisti," 22n36, 59–63; see 64–67 for a list and a description of archival sources for the Collegio Ancarano; the statutes are edited in idem, "Statuti di Collegio."
15. For some of these visitations in the fifteenth century and other details, see Piana, *Ricerche,* 47–60.
16. Fanti, "Tentativi di riforma."
17. See the 1587 reform proposals in Fanti, "Tentativi di riforma," 504–7.
18. Cortese, "L'Università di Bologna e il Collegio di Spagna."
19. On the Collegio Gregoriano, see Piana, *Nuove ricerche,* 385–405; idem, *Nuovi documenti,* 162–69; Brizzi, "I collegi per borsisti," 17; Galeazzi, "Il Collegio Gregoriano a Bologna."
20. Brizzi, "Maestri e studenti," 138.
21. Carlsmith, "Student Colleges," 73–74.
22. For examples and analyses of student violence in Bologna, see Carlsmith, "Student Colleges," 77–80; idem, "*Siam Ungari!*"; idem, "'Cacciò fuori un grande bastone bianco'"; idem, "Student Conflict." Also Maggiulli, "'Li scolari'"; eadem, "'Tu ne menti.'"
23. Otterspeer, "The University of Leiden," 327–28; also idem, *Groepsportret met Dame,* I, 151–63.
24. Conte, *Accademie studentesche a Roma.*
25. Camillo Vizzani was brother to the nowadays better-known Pompeo (the historian who authored an important history of Bologna) and Giasone. He was the son of another Camillo, who died in 1541. Some details in Gurreri, "'Nec longum tempus,'" 193n3. On this academy (also mentioned in Maylender, IV, 82), now see Lines, "Aristotelismo a Bologna."

26. For Gambarini's teaching in Bologna, see Lines, "Teachers," 315, no. 173. Gambarini appears on the roll for 1564–1565 (Dallari, II, 161), but only in the first set of payments for that year, dated December 1564.
27. The academy is mentioned in the dedication to Tagliacozzi's *De curtorum chirurgia* (1597) as "quondam Academi[a] nostr[a] Otiosorum"; see Teach Gnudi and Pierce Webster, *Gaspare Tagliacozzi,* 181–82. See Table 3.1, where Tagliacozzi is listed among the *accessores.*
28. HRC Ranuzzi, Ph 12622 (s. XVI); see Kristeller, *Iter,* V, 209–10; Wells, *The Ranuzzi Manuscripts,* 78. Other relevant materials (which I have not been able to see) are in Kraców, Bib. Jag., ms. 2169 (Kristeller, *Iter,* IV, 406).
29. See *In Camilli Vizanii comitis et equitis Bononiensis atque academici Ociosi funere, Antonii Mariae Venusti, Philosophi et Medici, atque Academici Ociosi, laudatio* (Bologna: Giovanni Rossi, 1567), pages not numbered. The listing of works is repeated in Fantuzzi's sketch of Camillo Vizzani; see Fantuzzi, VII, 195–96. For some of Vizzani's works, see HRC Ranuzzi, Ph 12853, folders 28–31 and passim.
30. Lines, "Aristotelismo a Bologna," 43.
31. HRC Ranuzzi, Ph 12670, ff. 78r (letter from Gambarini to Camillo, 21 May 1566, from Perugia) and 86r (letter from Gambarini to Pompeo, 27 September 1566, from Perugia).
32. The full titles of these works are *De rerum principiis institutio, publicis disputationibus florentissimae Ociosorum Academiae examinanda a Zacharia Andriano Brixiensi, ordinis Canonicorum tituli S. Georgii in Alga* (Bologna: Pellegrino Bonardo e Giovanni Antonio Fava, 1567) and *Theoremata universalia: De ordine et divisione scientiae comtemplativae et activae* (Bologna: Pellegrino Bonardo e Giovanni Antonio Fava, 1567) with colophon reading: "Theoremata haec examinabuntur in Ociosorum Academia, die XXVI mensis Februarii, annuente magnifico ac generoso Christophoro Tassio Academiae principe meritissimo."
33. Costanzo Varoli, *Conclusiones, quaesitis divinis, naturalibus, moralibus et dialecticis respondentes, ad disputandum propositae in nobiliss: Otiosorum Academia. Apud praestantiss. & inter omnes huius aetatis philosophum summum, Antonium Franciscum Fabium, Academiae vigilantissimum conservatorem. Ad illustrem et admodum Rever. D. Bartholomaei abbatem dignissimum Anselmum Dandinium* (Bologna: Giovanni Rossi, 1565), ending with a colophon showing the *impresa* of the Oziosi (*minus cum magis*).
34. On his career: Lines, "Teachers," 310, no. 154.
35. Fava's connection with the group is recalled in the text, which on several occasions makes reference to Fava as *praeceptor noster.*
36. For biographical details on Vizzani, see Lines, "Aristotelismo a Bologna," 43–44.
37. See the colophon of *Theoremata universalia* (above).

38. The names not registered in ASFE are: Lazarus Centurionus, Camillus Vizanius, Hieronymus Aius, Caesare Elefantucius, Zacharias Andrianus, Camillus Cocchius, Achilles Benalius. There is no precise match to Stephanus Santinus, although a Iohannes Stephanus Santinus received his degree in law on 9 October 1573 (Guerrini, "*Qui voluerit in iure promoveri,*" no. 2508).
39. For Gambarini's lectures on the *Physics,* see HRC Ranuzzi, Ph 12622.
40. Bronzino, 68; ASB, Archivio dello Studio, b. 217, vol. C, ff. 145v–146r.
41. Varoli's rather elliptic comments are in HRC Ranuzzi, Ph 12670, f. 79r. Cf. the entry in the *libro secreto:* ASB, Archivio dello Studio, b. 217 (Libro segreto del Collegio di Medicina ed Arti), ff. 145v–146r.
42. HRC Ranuzzi, Ph 12670, ff. 79r (letter to Camillo Vizzani, 13 April 1566) and 80r–v (letter from Padua, 26 May 1566).
43. HRC Ranuzzi, Ph 12670, f. 79v (letter from Padua, kal. Aprilis 1566). When he graduated, Varoli was *insignitus* by Fava, as was Muzzolo: see ASB, Archivio dello Studio, b. 217, f. 146v.
44. HRC Ranuzzi, Ph 12670, f. 87r (letter of Varoli to Pompeo Vizzani, 25 September 1566, in which he declares that he obtained from the Oziosi the privilege of delivering the oration for Camillo, which had initially been assigned to Venusto).
45. HRC Ranuzzi, Ph 12670, ff. 91r–93r.
46. HRC Ranuzzi, Ph 12670, ff. 91v–92r: "seguitavamo noi tutti di casa . . . , poi venivano molti amici particolari di casa . . . , poi succedeva il bidello dell'academia pur vestito dell'habito della famiglia, dietro al quale si vedevano 9 academici con le gramaglie e torcie in mano, poi ne veniva per fine una squadra de scolari tutti nobili et in spetie la natione polacca, la quale fece un grande e notabile vedere."
47. Guerrini, "L'Accademia degli Impazienti," which also discusses the academy's statutes, found in BCAB, ms. Gozzadini 261, *Leges legalis Academiae.* For this paragraph, I have drawn on Guerrini's study.
48. Bergamini, "Dai Gelati alla Renia," esp. 39–42; Guidicini, *Cose notabili,* V, 69 (with a list of eight early members of the academy other than Tommasini).
49. For interactions between academies and the university, see the case of Pavia discussed in Pissavino, "Università e Accademie."
50. Maylender. In addition to recent collective volumes in Italian (such as *Le virtuose adunanze*), English-language ones include *Italian Academies of the Sixteenth Century* and *The Italian Academies, 1525–1700,* as well as Testa, *Italian Academies and Their Networks.* See also the information on the (now concluded) research project "The Italian Academies 1530–1650: A Themed Collection Database" (PI: Jane Everson, https://www.bl.uk/catalogues/ItalianAcademies/About.aspx), which includes a rich bibliography.

51. For a broad survey of Italian academies, see Quondam, "L'Accademia"; for those in Bologna, Battistini, "Le accademie nel XVI e nel XVII secolo."
52. For some literature on these, see Gurreri, "'Nec longum tempus,'" 186 and n2; Lucioli, "Intorno all'Accademia del Viridario"; and *Notizie e insegne.* The academy of the Accesi should not to be confused with one by the same name that arose in the late seventeenth century (see §3.2.3).
53. For specific appointments, see Dallari, passim. On Bocchi, see esp. Antonio Rotondò, "Bocchi, Achille," *DBI,* XI (1969), 67–70; Puccetti, "Achille Bocchi"; Watson, *Achille Bocchi;* Chines, no. 42; Pezzarossa, "La storiografia a Bologna," esp. 224–27; Gareffi, "L'Hermathena"; Chines, "Il lettore elegante di Achille Bocchi"; Angelini, *Simboli e questioni.*
54. See, most recently, Rolet, *Dans le cercle d'Achille Bocchi.* Rolet has also published a critical edition with commentary: Achille Bocchi, *Les Questions symboliques d'Achille Bocchi (Symbolicae quaestiones, 1555),* ed. Anne Rolet, 2 vols. (Tours: Presses universitaires François Rabelais, 2015).
55. The exact starting date of the academy is disputed (it is often given as 1546), but the first solid evidence seems to be from 1543: Watson, *Achille Bocchi,* 56–61.
56. Watson, *Achille Bocchi,* 58–63, 153–54; Battistini, "Le accademie," 181–83.
57. Gavino Sambigucci, *In Hermathenam Bocchiam interpretatio . . .* (Bologna: Antonio Manuzio Jr., 1556), 14; Battistini, "Le accademie," 182.
58. Chines, no. 42.
59. Rotondò, "Bocchi, Achille."
60. Rhodes, "Due questioni." EDIT16 (CNCE 21) also lists an additional item (Paulus Abstemius, *In funere amplissimi patris Francisci Vardaei episcopi Transilvaniensis oratio*) printed "ex Academica Bochiana MDXXVI." The matter requires further study.
61. I owe my information on the Velati to a private communication from Professor Andrea Gardi, who generously shared with me his notes on BUB, ms. 2388. These rectify a long-standing error of transcription that made Betti a self-proclaimed member of the Gelati rather than the Velati (see Tiraboschi, I, 271, and Fantuzzi, II, 165), a misreading perpetuated in Giorgio Stabile, "Betti, Claudio, detto Betto Giovane," *DBI,* IX (1967), 713–14. The information on the Velati in Maylender, V, 432, is very fragmentary and possibly refers to another, later academy. The "Italian Academies" database mentions only an academy by that name starting in 1615; see http://www.bl.uk/catalogues/ItalianAcademies/.
62. For bibliography and more details on Betti's teaching, see Lines, "Teachers," 313, no. 166; and Chapter 4. Starting points are Stabile, "Betti, Claudio," and Lohr, II, 42–43.
63. The manuscript is scribed by a certain Giulio Ricci, but, as Gardi notes, Ricci's name has been erased at several points and replaced by that of a

certain Domenico Lanzoni in 1585, possibly in view of a publication of the work. I am grateful to Andrea Severi for supplying me with a reproduction of this manuscript.

64. For a brief profile, see Gian Paolo Brizzi, "Campeggi, Filippo Maria," *DBI,* XVII (1974), 441–42.
65. BUB, ms 2388, ff. 74r–149v, entitled "Del Betto, giovane filosofo ordinario su lo Studio di Bologna et academico Velato sotto il nome di Momo, espositione d'un sonetto del Caro intorno la morte christiana, da lui publicamente esposto ne la nobilissima academia de i Velati ne l'anno de la salute MDLVII, la quarta Domenica di Quaresima" (i.e., 28 March 1557). The manuscript includes (ff. 75r, 149v) two versions of Caro's sonnet, which had not yet appeared in print. See Claudio Mutini, "Caro, Annibale," *DBI,* XX (1977), 497–508.
66. BUB, ms 2388, ff. 150r–162v: "Discorso intorno la fortuna del Betto giovane, academico Velato sotto il nome di Momo, da lui fatto in publica audienza, ne la nobilissima Academia de Velati, la terza Domenica, cioè il diciottesimo giorno, di Decembre, l'anno de la salute MDLVIII, in Bologna" (i.e., 18 December 1558).
67. On Betti's teaching activity and his lectures on moral philosophy in the *studium,* see Lines, *Aristotle's* Ethics, 310–24.
68. For insights into the technique of commenting on poems and other writings in the Accademia Fiorentina (but also the Accademia degli Infiammati), see at least Andreoni, *La via della dottrina* and its bibliography.
69. For brief notes on this, see Lines, "Philosophy Teaching and Filiations of Learning."
70. For bibliography, see Battistini, "Le accademie," 186–193; Gurreri, "'Nec longum tempus,'" 194n6; Maylender, III, 81–88.
71. On Zoppi, see Lines, "Teachers," 319, no. 192; cf. Lines, *Aristotle's* Ethics, 419, no. 87. On Gessi, see Dallari, ad indicem; Gardi, "Riflessioni." As noted by Gardi, 426, Camillo's brother Berlingero taught in the university for only two years (1589–1591). But Fabio Pellini also taught in the *studium:* he lectured on medicine almost continuously from 1592 to 1638 (Dallari, ad indicem).
72. Gurreri, "'Nec longum tempus,'" 187–88; eadem, "'Haec est ultima voluntas.'"
73. Gardi, "Riflessioni," 429; Gurreri, "'Nec longum tempus,'" 188.
74. Already as papal legate in Bologna (1611–1614), Maffeo Barberini participated in this academy and offered it his protection; see Schütze, *Kardinal Maffeo Barberini,* 175–180. Some of his poems are listed in the catalogue of the academy's library (BCAB, ms. B.2037). On the breadth and cultural capaciousness of the Gelati's book collection, see Battistini, "Le accademie," 192. For the privilege, see AAV, Segr. Stato, Legaz. Bologna, b. 395:

unpaginated fascicle of five pages from the Accademia de' Gelati; they affirm that they were given a privilege by Urban VIII (which they can no longer find) entitling them to present every year one student to the College of Law for a free doctorate; they have, however, found a concession in this sense from the legate Cardinal Barberini.

75. See *Leggi dell'Accademia de Signori Gelati di Bologna* (Bologna: Manolessi, 1670), 13: "Quando l'Accademia avrà da preporre a gli eccellentissimi Collegi di Leggi, di Filosofia, e Medicina, i suggetti per dottorarsi gratis, giusta il privilegio a lei conceduto dalla santa memoria di Papa Urbano Ottavo nostro accademico, quelli che desiderano esser presentati sieno tenuti far porgere memoriale, che si leggerà in pubblica adunanza, e avutane la relazione convenevole, porrassi il partito, il quale vinto, sarà il dimandante presentato a' detti Collegi rispettivamente dall'Accademia, mediante l'attestazione in iscritto d'uno de' Segretari, o di tutti due." For the text of the approval of this privilege by the college of doctors in civil and canon law, see 18–20. For the earlier practice, see Schütze, *Kardinal Maffeo Barberini,* 180.
76. *Leggi dell'Accademia,* 11 (referred to in Gurreri, "'Nec longum tempus,'" 189).
77. *Leggi dell'Accademia,* 14.
78. *Prose de' Signori Accademici Gelati di Bologna* (Bologna: Manolessi, 1671); for a brief register of its contents, see Maylender, III, 84–85, who also refers (85–86) to a subsequent collection of writings in two volumes published in Bologna in 1753: *Orazioni di Accademici Gelati di Bologna dedicate alla Santità di N.S. Benedetto XIV.* On the later discussions, see Battistini, "Le accademie," 192–93; on the Gelati in the second half of the seventeenth century, see Bergamini, "Dai Gelati alla Renia," 12–18.
79. On the Accademia degli Accesi, see Bergamini, "Dai Gelati alla Renia," 31–38, 45–52 (for topics discussed, 36–38, 45–48).
80. The most complete study is *La Colonia Renia;* see also Battistini, "Le accademie," 196–200.
81. For a rapid sketch of these academies, see Battistini, "Le accademie," 200–205; further details in Cavazza, *Settecento inquieto,* essays 1, 2, and 5; Angelini, "Introduzione," 51–77; Bresadola, "Medicina e filosofia naturale." For the Inquieti, see also the more recent sketch in Cavazza, "Innovazione e compromesso," 321–29; for the scientific culture of the seventeenth century, eadem, "Bologna e Galileo."
82. Cavazza, "Innovazione e compromesso," 322–23.
83. Cavazza, *Settecento inquieto,* 179–201.
84. See Marsili, *Parallelo;* and discussion in §2.3 and §6.2.4.
85. On the events leading up to this move, see Cavazza, "Innovazione e compromesso," 325–29.

86. For useful overviews, see, among others, Cavazza, "L'Istituto delle Scienze: Il contesto Cittadino," and Tega, "L'Istituto delle Scienze." Older, but still useful, is Bortolotti, *La storia della matematica,* 146–61.
87. Details in *Anatomie accademiche,* vol. II.
88. On all this, see specifically Cavazza, "Innovazione e compromesso," 329–32, but the essay as a whole provides the most up-to-date overview and bibliography of the Istituto up to its closure in 1802.
89. Cavazza, "Innovazione e compromesso," 341–42.
90. On Lodovico Montefani Caprara, who as librarian was charged with ordering the books, see De Tata, "'Per Instituti aedes migraverit.'"
91. Cavazza, "Innovazione e compromesso," 334–40; for the *Commentarii,* see esp. *Anatomie accademiche.*
92. It appears that this was an innovation of the college's reform of 1763; see Cavazza, "Innovazione e compromesso," 343. Other examples are few and far between: see Guerrini, "Université et académies à Bologne," 20–21.
93. Guerrini, "Université et académies à Bologne," 16–20.
94. Cavazza, "Innovazione e compromesso," 347–49; eadem, "L'insegnamento delle scienze sperimentali."
95. Cavazza, "Innovazione e compromesso," 347. For other instances of private teaching, see Cavazza, "L'insegnamento delle scienze sperimentali," 156–57.
96. Cavazza, "Innovazione e compromesso," 350–51.
97. For further information, see esp. *Ateneo e Chiesa di Bologna;* Lines, "The University and the City," 448–49; and details in Chapter 4.
98. See, most recently, Pegoretti, "Filosofanti."
99. Loschiavo, "I canonici regolari," 73n71; also Robison, *Healers in the Making,* 87–90.
100. Loschiavo, "I canonici regolari," 84–85.
101. See, for instance, Mulchahey, "The Dominicans' Studium at Bologna."
102. Fanti, "Le chiese di Bologna," 3.
103. Many funerary monuments and inscriptions have now been moved to the Museo Civico Medievale.
104. See Chapter 4.
105. Loschiavo, "I canonici regolari," 86n8. For the library at San Salvatore, see Chapter 4.
106. Lines, "Natural Philosophy in Renaissance Italy."
107. For Sighicelli and Biglia, see Lines, "Teachers," nos. 46 and 51, respectively.
108. These were Tadeus de Garganellis (O.Serv.), Paulus de Venetiis (O.Serv.), Paraclitus de Corneto (O.Sti.Aug.), and Simplicianus Dominici (O.E.S.A.). See Lines, "Teachers," nos. 97, 100–102.
109. Names: Philippus de Bagnocavallo (O.F.M.; t. 1507–1510), Angelus Aretinus (O.Serv.; t. 1506–1508), Hieronymus Gadius de Gaggio (O.F.M.;

t. 1510–1529), and Albertus Fantinus de Bononia (O.F.M.; t. 1512–1514). See Lines, *Aristotle's* Ethics, 414–15, nos. 74–77.

110. For the Jesuit educational program, the fundamental source is *MPSI.* Helpful studies include Scaglione, *The Liberal Arts; La pedagogia della Compagnia di Gesù;* and *Les Jésuites à la Renaissance.* For the Jesuits' activity in Italy, see esp. *Storia della Compagnia di Gesù in Italia;* Baldini, *"Legem impone subactis"; La "Ratio Studiorum";* and Grendler, *The Jesuits and Italian Universities.*

111. The document is published in *MPSI,* V, 401–2.

112. The point was underlined by many observers, including Valerio Ranieri, whose *Diarii delle cose più notabili seguite nella città di Bologna* notes (BUB, ms 2137, vol. I, f. 81r): "tengono nel detto loro convento publiche scuole per ammaestrare nelle lettere et buoni costumi i gioveni et putti di questa città senza però premio o pagamento alcuno."

113. On this point, see Angelozzi, "'Insegnarli la vita christiana insieme con bone lettere.'"

114. See Codina Mir, *Aux sources,* esp. 258–68, 316–30; idem, "The 'Modus Parisiensis'"; Pascoe, "Response"; Brizzi, *Formazione,* 28–30, 90–91; idem, "I collegi religiosi," 112–16.

115. See esp. Quondam, "Il metronomo classicista."

116. On this phenomenon, see Hengst, *Jesuiten an Universitäten und Jesuitenuniversitäten; Gesuiti e università in Europa (secoli XVI–XVIII);* for Italy, Grendler, "I tentativi dei gesuiti." The instances in which the Jesuits attempted to take over local *studia* are too numerous to mention, but especially relevant, for its proximity to Bologna, is the case of Parma (see Grendler, *The Jesuits and Italian Universities,* 154–88).

117. The fundamental collection of documents is in Favaro, "Lo Studio di Padova e la Compagnia di Gesù." For further bibliography, see Brizzi, "The Jesuits and Universities in Italy," 187n2.

118. On their presence there, the most recent account is *Dall'isola alla città.* For narratives providing opposite evaluations of the Jesuits' activities in Bologna, see Costa, "Contributo"; Fabrini, *Lo studio pubblico di Bologna ed i Gesuiti;* idem, *Le congregazioni dei Gesuiti a Bologna.*

119. On Palmio, see at least Prodi, *Il cardinale Gabriele Paleotti,* ad indicem; Brizzi, *Formazione,* 86–97.

120. *MPSI,* I, 454–57 (15 November 1554); Brizzi, *Formazione,* 90–91.

121. Brizzi, *Formazione,* 91–92. Cf. the figure of 150 pupils given in Antonio Francesco Ghiselli, *Memorie antiche manoscritte* (BUB, ms. 770), XIV, 702.

122. The following is based on Brizzi, *Formazione,* 209–56, and Grendler, *The Jesuits and Italian Universities,* 286–91, 306–17. Note that the classes of Latinity offered by the Jesuits did not always flourish: see the account by Francesco Adorno (12 October 1574) in *MPSI,* IV, 552–54, indicating small numbers and an unacceptably low level.

123. For this transfer, see Grendler, *The Jesuits and Italian Universities,* 291–97.
124. Baldini, "*Legem impone subactis,*" 415–16. For a comparison of the number of courses offered by the Jesuit college in Bologna vis-à-vis those of other Jesuit colleges in the Provincia Veneta, see Brizzi, "Scuole e collegi" (esp. the tables on 507–10). For a year-by-year prospectus of the teachings of the Bolognese Jesuit college, as well as other ones of the Jesuit Provincia Veneta, see Baldini, "*Legem impone subactis,*" 427–36.
125. Brizzi, *Formazione,* 275n269.
126. For what follows, see Grendler, *The Jesuits and Italian Universities,* 293–305. For a less sympathetic view, see Zaccagnini, *Storia,* 162–63.
127. Sacchetti, *Ordinationi* (1641), discussed in Grendler, *The Jesuits and Italian Universities,* 300–303.
128. Grendler, *The Jesuits and Italian Universities,* 303–5.
129. Brizzi, *Formazione,* 232–33. On the Jesuits' Bolognese activities in mathematics and science, see Battistini, "La cultura scientifica nel collegio bolognese"; more generally, at least Baldini, "*Legem impone subactis*"; Baroncini, "L'insegnamento della filosofia naturale"; and Romano, *La Contre-Réforme mathématique.*
130. For what follows, see esp. Brizzi, *Formazione,* 71–86, esp. 73; and (more generally) idem, "*Ritterakademien* e *seminaria nobilium.*" Colleges of this kind also developed in other cities; for Pavia, see Negruzzo, "I Collegi di educazione."
131. Founded in 1645, the college of San Luigi owed to the Bolognese Carlo Zani its transformation from an earlier *paedagogium* into an actual college; see Brizzi, *Formazione,* 85–86; Boffito and Fracassetti, *Il collegio San Luigi.* The Collegio di San Tommaso was founded by Girolamo Canuti c. 1657 and was under the protection of the duke of Mantua; its first statutes were printed in 1663; it did not last long, however, as it closed its doors in 1673. See Brizzi, *Formazione,* 108, 128n123.
132. On the Ardenti, see Brizzi, *Formazione,* 79–85.
133. For a general discussion of this extracurricular instruction in the period, see Brizzi, *Formazione,* 235–56, and Grendler, "Fencing." In some cases, the extracurricular subjects seem to have been foremost in students' minds; see the letters sent home from Bologna by Christopher Kress (1541–1583), a young nobleman from Nuremberg whose Bolognese letters are preserved for 1559–1560. Kress, who resided not at a college but with his uncle, often emphasizes his dedication to studying Italian, Latin, and arts fit for noblemen (*adeliche exercitia*), including music. See especially his letters of 26 September 1559, 30 October 1559, and 24 March 1560; see Kress, "Briefe," 142 (letter 38), 145 (letter 39), 156 (letter 47); cf. Aldrovandi, "Commentario alle lettere," 24–26. Kress gives no details about his other studies.

134. Brizzi has rightly observed: "Le istituzioni educative e culturali tradizionali, le scuole publiche e private e le Università, avevano come obiettivo, quasi esclusivo, quello dell'istruzione; al contrario il collegio mirava a un'educazione globale, non solo in senso intellettuale e morale, ma capace di provvedere convenientemente a prepararli alla conversazione, alla vita mondana e finanche ad addestrarli sul piano fisico-atletico" (Brizzi, *Formazione,* 236).
135. For a recent study on the tour of some Austrians to the University of Pavia in 1576, including a rich bibliography on the *peregrinatio academica* and the *Kavalierstour,* see Spadafora, "*Instruction.*" Also see at least Brizzi, "La pratica del viaggio d'istruzione"; Guerrini, "La pratica del viaggio di istruzione"; Leibetseder, *Die Kavalierstour.* For the sojourns of travelers in Bologna, a useful source remains Sorbelli, *Bologna negli scrittori stranieri.*
136. Brizzi, *Formazione,* 97–108.
137. Brizzi, *Formazione,* 102–3.
138. See Spadafora, "*Felicem peragrat Italiam,*" esp. 49, 87–89.
139. Brizzi, *Formazione,* 109; more generally on the Jesuits and the *seminaria nobilium* in Italy, see 22–26.
140. For enrollment figures in Jesuit colleges, see Brizzi, *Formazione,* 65nn99–101.
141. Brizzi, *Formazione,* 74.
142. On this trend in Italy and across Europe more generally, see Roggero, "I collegi universitari in età moderna," 117–21, 123–25.
143. Brizzi, "Istruzione e istituzioni," 300–302.
144. Brizzi, *Formazione,* 84–85.
145. Brizzi, *Formazione,* 85–86.
146. Marchesini, "Lo studente di collegio," 284–85; additional info in Fantuzzi, III, 193; Mazzetti, *Memorie storiche,* 290; Barsanti, *Il pubblico insegnamento in Lucca,* 97.
147. Marchesini, "Lo studente di collegio," 315.
148. See Marchesini, "Lo studente di collegio," 300; more broadly, Roggero, "I collegi universitari in età moderna," 126–28.
149. Marchesini, "Lo studente di collegio," 296–307.
150. Marchesini, "Lo studente di collegio," 307–14.
151. For a slightly different and more rapid sketch, see Lines, "The University and the City," 450–54.
152. This section of the document is transcribed in Rashdall, *Universities,* II, 745.
153. Gaspar Marianus de Varrano Lentius, *Responsum viro Batavo circa ea, quae Bononiae de studiis praecipue notabilia sunt* (Bologna: successori del Benati, 1719), in ASB, Assunteria di Studio, b. 100, folder 11, pp. 7 (quotation) and 4 (sand clock). I have not been able to identify the author, who very likely had an official function within the *studium.*

4. THE CULTURE OF THE BOOK

1. Some relevant observations for Bologna in Lines, "The University and the City," 445–47; more broadly, Ferrari, "Libri e studenti"; de Ridder-Symoens, "Management and Resources," 195–204; *Dalla pecia all'e-book.*
2. For the textbooks specified by the Bolognese statutes, see §2.2.2.
3. On the process of book- and library-formation, stimulating comments in Mattone and Olivari, "Il libro universitario." On student notebooks and lectures, see "Sources and Methodology" in the Introduction.
4. For Amerbach, see Sorbelli, *Bologna negli scrittori stranieri,* I, 67–73, from *Bonifacii et Basilii Amerbachiorum epistolae mutuae, Bononia et Basilea datae,* ed. A. Teichmann (Basel: Schultze, 1888). On the transition from manuscript to print in Bologna from an economic point of view, see Bonifati, *Dal libro manoscritto al libro stampato.*
5. On books passed on from one generation to the next, see comments in §4.1 on BUB, ms. 920.
6. Some of the classics include Sorbelli, *Storia della stampa in Bologna;* Cencetti, "Alcuni documenti"; Bühler, *The University and the Press;* Balsamo, *Produzione e circolazione libraria; Alma Mater Librorum;* and Avellini, "In margine a: *Alma Mater Librorum.*"
7. Studies limited to the late sixteenth century include Duroselle-Melish, "A Local-Transnational Business." For the broader Italian context, see Maclean, *Episodes,* esp. 69–211.
8. Sorbelli, *Storia della stampa in Bologna;* De Tata, *Il commercio librario;* Tavoni, "Tipografi e produzione libraria." Partial exceptions include Donattini, "Il mondo portato a Bologna"; De Tata, "Il commercio librario." For explorations of similar issues for Perugia, see Frova, "Possedere libri," and Capaccioni, "Biblioteche e università."
9. See De Franceschi, "Le biblioteche a Bologna."
10. Curiously, the 1405 statutes for arts and medicine specify only the medical texts that were to be kept on hand in the stationer's shop, although there was also the flexibility to add others. See Malagola, *Statuta universitatis scolarium* (1405), 295, rub. 105; see also 284, rub. 90: "Item statuerunt et firmaverunt quod bidelli generales Universitatis habeant et habere debeant et tenere continuo in statione infrascriptas petias de bona littera et bene correctas, videlicet Galieni *De simplici medicina, De alimentis, De febribus ad Glauchonem, De virtutibus naturalibus, De accidenti morbo, De malicia complexionis diverse, De iuvamentis membrorum, De interioribus, De crisi, De creticis, De flobothomia, De tabe, De secretis* Galieni, *De motibus,* [*De*] *liquidis, De pulsibus* omnes, *De ingenio sanitatis* a principio usque ad quartumdecimum, *De complexionibus, De differentiis febrium, De elementis* primi, secundi, tertii, quarti et quinti Avicenne, Sarapionis *De simplicibus, Coliget* et Guilelmine; et dictas petias continuo tenere in statione et de eis petentibus

copiam facere. Habere insuper et habere debeant dicti bidelli quandam cartam, sive tabulam, in qua scripte sint omnes et singule petie quas habebunt, et tituli questionum disputatarum."

11. Malagola, *Statuta universitatis scolarium* (1405), 285, rub. 91.
12. There is a large literature on the *pecia* system, starting with the essential study by Destrez, *La Pecia;* see also Brugi, "Il catalogo dei libri degli stationarii," 31–35. For more recent bibliography, see Orlandelli, "I testi manoscritti."
13. These are preserved, for contracts of over L. 25, in ASB, Memoriali del Comune di Bologna; those between 1265 and 1270 were published in the *Chartularium Studii Bononiensis.* See Morelli, *Copisti a Bologna.*
14. The manuscript ends (f. 51) with the note: "Expliciunt regule Tisberi . . . Explete fuerunt per me Marianum Vannis de Math[eli]ca dum Bononie studebam in logicalibus anno domini 1408 die 20 mensis Aprilis quo fuit dies Veneris" (Kristeller, *Iter,* IV, 90).
15. Malagola, *Statuta universitatis scolarium* (1405), 285–87, rubs 92 and 93; on juridical codices, see Orlandelli, "Il codice scolastico bolognese"; idem, "I testi manoscritti"; Morelli, "L'editoria medievale bolognese," 51–52. The bibliography on manuscript university books in Bologna is surprisingly thin (exception made for the *pecia* system) compared to that on printed books, particularly for arts and medicine. Quaquarelli, *Il Quattrocento dei copisti,* does not focus on university books specifically.
16. See BUB, ms. 473, containing Cicero's *Tusculan Disputations;* the book indicates on the flyleaf: "Istas quaestiones tusculanas ego magister Bernardus de Garzonibus emi in studio bononiensi a quodam bidello floreno uno aureo et bononis 21° 1436 die vigesima hoctobris" (Manfrè II, 29). See Soetermeer, *Utrumque jus in peciis;* Pini, "Per una storia sociale"; Nuovo, *The Book Trade,* 266. For similar arrangements in Pavia, see Gavinelli, "Manoscritti a Pavia," 715–17.
17. For San Domenico's scriptorium, see Alce and D'Amato, *La biblioteca di S. Domenico,* 94–100; D'Amato, *I Domenicani a Bologna,* 381–83. On the educational program of the Dominicans, see Mulchahey, "*First the Bow Is Bent in Study*"; for the Franciscans, see Roest, *A History of Franciscan Education.*
18. BCAB, ms. A.127, described in Morelli, "L'editoria medievale bolognese," 63.
19. Manfrè I, 258–62.
20. "Memoratio ut ego incepi studere logice anno Domini Millesimo quadringentesimo octuagesimo primo, intravi sub Magistro Nicholao de Saviis"; this is followed by a note in a sixteenth-century hand: "Memoratio ut ego incepi studere logice anno MDXXX, mense Octobris die vero XVII sub disciplina Magistri Antonii Francisci de Faba." On this manuscript, see Frati, *Indice,* no. 519; Frati, *Inventario,* III, f. 253r; Manfrè II, 253; Piana,

Nuove ricerche, 146n1, 190n1; de Rijk, *Die mittelalterlichen Traktate,* 35, 39, and 103 where it is mistakenly indicated as ms. 519; Muñoz Garcia, "Albert of Saxony, Bibliography," 171, 171n32, 182. On Nicolaus de Saviis (or Nicolò Savi, †1499) and Antonius de Faba (Antonio Fava, †1571), see Lines, "Teachers," 295, no. 76, and 310, no. 154, respectively.

21. For Marcanova's teaching, see Dallari, passim; Lines, "Teachers," 296, no. 88 (no roll survives for 1457–1458). Marcanova may have started his actual teaching as late as 1453, according to Cogo, "Francesco Buzzacarini," 448, followed by Vitali, "Contributi," 1037. See ASB, Quartironi. The precise identity of Urbanus Bononiensis is disputed, but the work is likely to be from the early fourteenth century. The colophon of the early printed edition (Venice, 1492) gives the year of its writing as 1331; see Lohr, I.2, 198–99, with bibliography; Vitali, "Contributi," 1046.
22. The best study is Vitali, "Contributi," which indicates the scribes Iohannes de Rupe and Alardus Iohannis de Ollandia; cf. Quaquarelli, *Il Quattrocento dei copisti,* 30.
23. Sighinolfi, "La biblioteca," 190.
24. See the list in Sighinolfi, "La biblioteca," 206–19.
25. The point (made convincingly in Bühler, *The Fifteenth-Century Book,* 15–39) can be extended to the literary sphere: see Richardson, *Manuscript Culture;* Stallybrass, "Printing and the Manuscript Revolution," 111–18; *Scribal Culture in Italy.* On the transition from script to print, still useful is Hirsch, *Printing, Selling and Reading,* 1–12. See also McKitterick, *Print, Manuscript and the Search for Order.*
26. For Aldrovandi, there are numerous autograph lectures (not always by him) in BUB, mss. Aldrovandi (cf. Frati, *Catalogo dei manoscritti di Ulisse Aldrovandi*). For mathematics, see BUB, ms. 3647, caps. II, item 21. For Guidazzolo and Sandri, see BUB, ms. 1077, vol. VI.
27. Lines, "Philosophy Teaching and Filiations of Learning."
28. On the problems associated with determining the cost of books in the period, see Nuovo, *The Book Trade,* 335–46; Bonifati, *Dal libro manoscritto al libro stampato;* Nuovo and Ammannati, "Investigating Book Prices."
29. For useful comments on how the transition from manuscript to print affected the university book across the Italian Peninsula, see Mattone and Olivari, "Dal manoscritto alla stampa."
30. For the first printed books, see Bühler, *The University and the Press,* 59 (1.A.1). But see also Francesco Cieco da Firenze, *Torneamento fatto in Bologna il 4 ottobre 1470 per ordine di Giovanni Bentivoglio* (Bologna: Scipio Malpiglius, after 4 Oct. 1470; ISTC if00279300). In the case of law, see Alexander Tartagnus, *Lectura super II parte Digesti veteris cum apostillis* (Bologna: Andreas Portilia, 21 December 1472 [also: 1473]); see Bühler, *The University and the Press,* 61 (3.A.1); GW M45083; IGI 9337, 9283; ISTC it00026600.

31. Balsamo, "Primordi della stampa tipografica a Modena," 93.
32. Bühler, *The University and the Press,* 62 (4.A.1). On the *fortuna* of Alcabitius, an Arab writer from the tenth century, see Arnzen, "Vergessene Pflichtlektüre."
33. For Vurster, see Balsamo, "Primordi della stampa tipografica a Modena," 95–96; idem, "Università e editoria."
34. For the role of beadles and students, see Balsamo, "Università e editoria," 125; Quaglioni, "Dal manoscritto alla stampa." More broadly on the involvement of university members in printing enterprises, see Hirsch, *Printing, Selling and Reading,* 19–24.
35. For several of these years Malpigli is listed on the rolls but not in the payments, so he may not have taught continuously (Lines, *Aristotle's* Ethics, 409–10). This may partly explain why his functions were not comparable to those of Dal Pozzo from the point of view of promoting publications within the *studium.*
36. For examples of other contracts between professors and printers, see Sorbelli, *Corpus chartarum Italiae.*
37. Balsamo, "Imprese tipografiche in Emilia," 14–15. For the contract, see Sighinolfi, "Francesco Puteolano e le origini della stampa," 455–56. On Dal Pozzo, see also Balsamo, "Università e editoria," 123–25; Avellini, "Promozione libraria," 114–21.
38. Donattini, "Il mondo portato a Bologna," 546–52.
39. Donattini, "Il mondo portato a Bologna," 552–53.
40. Sorbelli, *La stampa,* 24; Balsamo, "Editoria a Bologna," 74–76; Balugani, "Università e stampa," 65–66.
41. Sorbelli, *La stampa,* 24.
42. Balsamo, "Editoria a Bologna"; Sorbelli, "Carlo Sigonio e la Società tipografica bolognese"; Zuffo, "La stampa in Bologna"; Balugani, "Università e stampa," 89–93.
43. Tavoni, "Stampa e fortuna delle opere di Ulisse Aldrovandi."
44. Dallari, II, 221.
45. De Tata, "Il commercio librario," 80, fig. VI. More generally on the mechanisms of selling books in Italy through stationers (*cartolai*), booksellers, and so forth, see Nuovo, *The Book Trade,* 315–46; cf. Hirsch, *Printing, Selling and Reading,* 61–77.
46. In fact, these print shops could be more than just points of sale: as we know from other cities, print shops like that of Aldus Manutius could function as gathering places for (usually unofficial) academies or discussion circles. For Bologna the evidence is unclear. In general, see Nuovo, *The Book Trade,* 411–20, and the literature cited there; De Tata, "Il commercio librario," 40–41.
47. For broader comments on Italian shop inventories up to the end of the sixteenth century, see Nuovo, *The Book Trade,* 347–87 (esp. 365–71).

48. Inventory published in Fava, "Un grande libraio-editore," 89–97; see also Pezzarossa, "'Vita mihi ducitur inter paginas,'" 120–21; Nuovo, *The Book Trade,* 121–23, 353–54. Insights into the long-standing activities of the Libri family, which was involved in the book trade from at least the beginnings of the fifteenth century, in De Tata, *Il commercio librario,* 48–64; see also the notes about manuscript purchases by Gaspare da Sala in Tugnoli Aprile, *I libri di famiglia dei da Sala.*
49. Nuovo, *The Book Trade,* 123.
50. Nuovo, *The Book Trade,* 122; Fava, "Un grande libraio-editore," 95–96.
51. Nuovo, *The Book Trade,* 353.
52. For the following, see Sorbelli, "La libreria"; idem, "Il magazzino librario"; Pezzarossa, "'Vita mihi ducitur inter paginas,'" 121; Nuovo, *The Book Trade,* 123–25. For the longer history of the Benedetti family's operations into the sixteenth century, see De Tata, *Il commercio librario,* 64–78.
53. According to Bühler, *The University and the Press,* 75–80. Sorbelli also notes ("Il magazzino librario," 98–99) that, in several cases, copies of Benedetti's book production seem not to have survived.
54. Gatti, *Francesco,* 208–9; cf. the slightly different number given in Sorbelli, "La libreria," 269.
55. Bühler, *The University and the Press,* 77 (19.A.28); Sorbelli, "La libreria," 290, no. 44.
56. Sorbelli, "La libreria," 317, no. 387; cf. Gatti, *Francesco,* 313.
57. Sorbelli, "Il magazzino librario," 98–99; for Mancinelli, see Gatti, *Francesco,* 246–47; for the Psalter, see 334, no. 530.
58. For *Aesopus moralizatus* see Gatti, *Francesco,* 281, nos. 186–88; for Beroaldo's *De felicitate,* see 271, no. 114.
59. Here I cannot address the question of whether some of the books belonged to Benedetti's private library; see Sorbelli, "Il magazzino librario"; idem, "La libreria," 273; cf. Gatti, *Francesco,* 212, 216–18, 389–91. On the methodological problems posed by book lists consisting of printed books, see Barbieri, "Elenchi librari."
60. Balsamo, "Il libro per l'università," 50.
61. Gatti, *Francesco,* 244–350, 367.
62. Fava, "Un grande libraio-editore," 97; Gatti, *Francesco,* 300 (item 297) and 346 (item 613); cf. Bühler, *The University and the Press,* 72 (13.A.7). In Benedetti's shop, more copies are found of Paolo Veneto (37) and Paolo da Pergola (23), for some reason. Were the two printers appealing to different customers?
63. For an example from Florence, see Nuovo, *The Book Trade,* 330.
64. For a rapid Europe-wide overview of libraries in this sense, see Balsamo, "Il libro per l'università nell'età moderna," 63–65. For general historiography on private libraries in Italy, see Serrai, "Biblioteche private in Italia."

On public libraries in Italy, see at least Gargan, "Biblioteche pubbliche in Italia" and *Atlante della letteratura italiana,* II.

65. Laurent, *Fabio Vigili.* Vigili's manuscripts (Vatican, BAV, Barb. lat. 3185, and Vat. lat. 7134) also include information on libraries in Florence, Ravenna, Cesena, and elsewhere; for Bologna, they report on books in San Domenico, San Francesco, San Giacomo Maggiore, San Salvatore, San Michele in Bosco, San Paolo in Monte, San Procolo, the Collegio di Spagna, and Collegio Gregoriano (see https://www.mirabileweb.it/manuscript/città-del-vaticano-biblioteca-apostolica-vaticana-manuscript/24836, accessed 25 December 2020). See also Frati, Vatielli, and Galli, "Biblioteche della Provincia di Bologna"; De Franceschi, "Le biblioteche a Bologna."
66. On the church, see *La Cattedrale di San Pietro in Bologna.*
67. Inventories survive for 1420 and 1440: see Sorbelli, *La Biblioteca Capitolare,* 72 and 166–69 (for 1420) and 72–73 and 169–73 (for 1440). For the 1451 inventory (with additions from 1457), ibid., 83–155. For a summary, see De Franceschi, "Le biblioteche a Bologna," 350–56.
68. See Sorbelli, *La Biblioteca Capitolare,* 36–37.
69. The date is given as 1386 in Alce and D'Amato, *La biblioteca di S. Domenico,* 80; a date before 1386 or 1390 had been proposed in Lucchesi, "L'antica libreria," 207–10. Zaccagnini, "Le scuole e la libreria," proposed a date at the start of the fifteenth century. The best recent study, which also identifies several of the manuscripts mentioned in the oldest catalogue, is Murano, "I libri di uno Studium generale," 289–303.
70. Lucchesi, "L'antica libreria," 227–50; Laurent, *Fabio Vigili,* 203–35.
71. Frati, "La biblioteca del convento dei Domenicani."
72. Avellini, "Note," 121–22; Pellegrini, "La biblioteca e i codici," 147–48.
73. For Bolognini's will and testament, see Frati, "Ludovico Bolognini." The document is interesting for its stipulation that Bolognini's books should be made available both to future students of the family and to poor students in Bologna. I am grateful to Rita De Tata for this information.
74. Avellini, "Note," 127n48.
75. Laurent, *Fabio Vigili,* 32–56; Vigili comments extensively on several of the items.
76. Alce and D'Amato, *La biblioteca di S. Domenico,* 103–9.
77. Registered in BCAB, mss. B.1946–1968 (see Petrella, "Nella cella di fra Leandro," 110–12). Most of the manuscripts and printed books of San Domenico went to the Biblioteca dell'Archiginnasio, but some can also be found in other libraries (including the Biblioteca Universitaria) and await a thorough analysis. (Rita De Tata kindly informs me that the 111 manuscripts chosen for what is now the BUB are listed in ASB, Assunteria d'Istituto, Diversorum, b. 23 [Catalogo dei libri scelti dalla Deputazione per l'amplificazione dell'Istituto nazionale nelle biblioteche delle Corporazioni religiose

del Dipartimento del Reno], and that some ninety of these can be identified; see also Murano, "I libri di uno Studium generale"). For a list of eighty-nine manuscript signatures (some in multiple volumes) in both libraries deriving from San Domenico and identifiable with items listed in the two inventories discussed above, see Avellini, "Note," 115n21. Useful observations on several surviving manuscripts from San Domenico are in Pellegrini, "La biblioteca e i codici." For a rapid sketch of the library in the fifteenth century, see also De Franceschi, "Le biblioteche a Bologna," 343–50 (348–49 for books concerning the humanities). For the library's fate after the Napoleonic suppressions, see Ferrari, "I fondi librari delle corporazioni religiose."

78. Some scholars have doubted the existence of a formal scriptorium: Pellegrini, "La biblioteca e i codici," 151–54; cf. Alce and D'Amato, *La biblioteca di S. Domenico,* 89–100; D'Amato, *I Domenicani a Bologna,* I, 378–83.
79. Avellini, "Note," 127n47; Alce and D'Amato, *La biblioteca di S. Domenico,* 107–8; Alce, "La stamperia."
80. Franz Schott, who visited Bologna in 1600, notes in his *Itinerarii Italiae Germaniaeque libri IV* (Cologne: Gualtherus, 1620) that there were two public libraries in Bologna, one at San Salvatore and another one ("maggiore, ma non migliore") at San Domenico; see Sorbelli, *Bologna negli scrittori stranieri,* I, 113.
81. Fanti, "Le chiese di Bologna," 3.
82. De Franceschi, "Le biblioteche a Bologna," 333–34.
83. See Trombelli, *Memorie istoriche concernenti le due canoniche,* 101, 265–66.
84. Laurent, *Fabio Vigili,* 162–72; Degni, "I manoscritti greci," 197–98. See also Sorbelli, *La Biblioteca Capitolare,* 4–7; De Franceschi, "Le biblioteche a Bologna," 333–39.
85. Laurent, *Fabio Vigili,* xxxiv–xxxvii, 266–347; Degni, "I manoscritti greci," 198–200.
86. Conrad Gesner, *Bibliotheca universalis* (Tiguri: Apud Christophorum Froschouerum, 1545), f. 6v, cited in Tavoni, "Il patrimonio bibliografico a stampa," 83n2. Bologna's libraries are hardly mentioned, however, by John Caius in his account of his travels in Italy in 1543 to find Greek books for a new edition of Galen; see his *De libris propriis,* 194–98.
87. For works by and on Plato, see Laurent, *Fabio Vigili,* 309–11, items 202–209. For works related to Aristotle, see 311–18, items 210–263; also 306, items 170–172 and 176.
88. For grammar and rhetoric: Laurent, *Fabio Vigili,* 320–21, items 288–300. For classical and humanist authors, 323–30, 344, and passim.
89. Laurent, *Fabio Vigili,* 331–32, items 410–418 (astronomy); 335–36, items 431–440 (medicine).
90. du Rieu, "Katalog der Handschriften"; Sorbelli, *La Biblioteca Capitolare,* 4–7.

91. Jean Mabillon, *Museum Italicum* (Paris: Martin, 1687), I, 195ff., in Sorbelli, *Bologna negli scrittori stranieri,* I, esp. 215–25. The manuscript of Lactantius in question (BUB, ms. 701) in fact dates to the second half of the fifth century according to *Codices latini antiquiores,* ed. Lowe, III, no. 280.
92. Tavoni, "Il patrimonio bibliografico a stampa"; Bacchi and Miani, "Vicende del patrimonio librario bolognese."
93. Sorbelli, *La Biblioteca Capitolare,* 7–12; De Franceschi, "Le biblioteche a Bologna," 339–43.
94. Laurent, *Fabio Vigili,* 236–65. The inventory was first provided in Frati, "Inventario della biblioteca francescana di Bologna."
95. Sorbelli, *La Biblioteca Capitolare,* 7–8; see in particular the extract of his testament, reported there (p. 8), in which he states: "Item reliquit, voluit et mandavit quod omnes libri scientie medicine ipsius testatoris in cartis edinis seu membranis scripti et tam testuales quam commentales ponantur et catenantur in armario seu librario conventus ecclesie sancti Francisci . . . pro utilitate et comodo pauperum studentium dicti ordinis in dicto conventu Bononie."
96. Laurent, *Fabio Vigili,* 259–63, items 499–572.
97. Laurent, *Fabio Vigili,* 108–21.
98. If Vigili's information is correct, there were eighteen desks (*scanni*) on the right-hand side and thirteen on the left. Thus the six *scanni* reserved for books on arts and medicine represented around a fifth of the total. This confirms that the library was focused on other subjects.
99. *La Biblioteca del Convento di San Francesco;* Fanti, *Bologna: Biblioteca di San Francesco.* The manuscripts include three works on physics (mss. 44, 101, 144) from the seventeenth and eighteenth centuries, in all likelihood from a conventual context. Rita De Tata kindly informs me that over forty manuscripts belonging to San Francesco were destined to the BUB (ASB, Assunteria d'Istituto, Diversorum, b. 23), and that some thirty of these are currently identifiable.
100. *La Biblioteca del Convento di San Francesco* and *Chartularium Studii Bononiensis S. Francisci.*
101. Alce and D'Amato, *La biblioteca di S. Domenico in Bologna,* 101–3.
102. Alce and D'Amato, *La biblioteca di S. Domenico in Bologna,* 102.
103. See Sorbelli, *La Biblioteca Capitolare,* 56–57 and passim.
104. See the documentation for the Collegio Montalto in ASB, Demaniale, 72/7293, ff. 103v (2 October 1614) and 126r (20 July 1621); for the initial setup of the Collegio Panolini, including the library, see ASB, Archivio dello Studio, b. 160.
105. Laurent, *Fabio Vigili,* 175–79. Although some of these books were sold before 1372, others continue to appear in the 1453 inventory as well as the

sixteenth-century one of Fabio Vigili; see García y García and Piana, "Los manuscritos," 82.

106. For the 1453 inventory as a whole, see Piana, *Ricerche,* 53–55; for a revised edition of the last section, see García and Piana, "Los manuscritos," 83–87. On the classical manuscripts, see Gil Fernandez, *De codicibus albornotianis.* The current manuscript holdings are described in Maffei et al., *I codici del Collegio di Spagna.*

107. Laurent, *Fabio Vigili,* 1–10. See Petrella, "Nella cella di fra Leandro," 106. Other useful details can be gleaned from the eighteenth-century Miscellanea Tioli (BUB, ms. 2948, vols. XI [498ff] and XII [225–61]) and from AAV, Miscellanea, Arm. II, no. 33, which at f. 453 has five folios of an *Index manuscriptorum qui reperiuntur in Bibliotheca Bononien. Collegi Hispanorum.*

108. Laurent, *Fabio Vigili,* 180–202. Some comments in Sorbelli, *La Biblioteca Capitolare,* 16–21.

109. See the statutes in *Chartularium Studii Bononiensis,* II, 289–313. Also Vasina, "Lo 'Studio' nei rapporti," 57–59; Piana, *Nuovi documenti,* 166–67.

110. Laurent, *Fabio Vigili,* 180–202.

111. Galeazzi, "Il Collegio Gregoriano," 255, 257.

112. *Acta Nationis Germanicae,* 356, 365, 394, 400, 405 (inventories compiled in 1335, 1344, 1379, 1396, and 1516, respectively).

113. Malagola, "I libri della Nazione Tedesca," with info. on 312–13 on the inventory of books from 1641; Frati, "La biblioteca della Nazione Alemanna."

114. Frati, "La biblioteca della Nazione Alemanna," 198, refers to a "miscellanea manoscritta n. 278 (n. 3), già appartenuta ad Ubaldo Zanetti, un *Inventario delli libri che presentemente si ritrovano nella Biblioteca dell'inclita Nazione Alemanna, da consegnarsi a Carlo Pasini bibliotecario destinato alla custodia di questa Biblioteca.*"

115. Frati, "La biblioteca della Nazione Alemanna," 197. See also the situation in Padua described in Rossetti, "Le biblioteche delle 'Nationes' nello Studio di Padova."

116. Frati, Vatielli, and Galli, "Biblioteche della Provincia di Bologna," 25–26.

117. In the case of the Collegio Gregoriano, Sorbelli (*La Biblioteca Capitolare,* 21) wonders whether the "libri extra librariam" were on loan to students in their rooms—or possibly to others outside the Collegio. The first of these possibilities seems more likely.

118. Poliziano was clearly able to see the collection of the Collegio di Spagna's library, for he registered several of its items in his notes (Laurent, *Fabio Vigili,* 1–10). He also recorded books at least from the libraries of San Francesco (e.g., 115, items 64 and 66–67) and the cathedral (Pesenti, "Diario odeporico-bibliografico inedito del Poliziano," 234; repr. in Poliziano, *Opera omnia,* III, 160). Oddly, the documents transcribed by Pesenti do

not refer to the books in San Domenico and elsewhere, but the manuscript is very hard to decipher and still awaits a full edition, as promised by Manlio Pastore Stocchi.

119. For the later period, there are, of course, numerous witnesses of printed books owned by students and graduates; for a recent study, centered on *studia* outside of Bologna, see Graheli, "Italian Books and French Medical Libraries."

120. Greci, "Libri e prestiti di libri," 243–45. To my knowledge, instances of professors or cultural figures renting books out, as opposed to lending them, are not well attested (but see the case of Giovanni Gaspare da Sala, who registered loans—or, more likely, rentals—to his students; idem, "Libri e prestiti di libri," 246). The matter deserves further study.

121. Zanazzo, "Una famiglia di medici," 172, cited in Pezzarossa, "'Canon est litterarum,'" 30n24.

122. At his death in 1467, Marcanova had a collection of 521 books, which he was wont to lend out (like others, he kept a separate register of these loans). On his collection, see Sighinolfi, "La biblioteca"; Vitali, "L'umanista padovano Giovanni Marcanova"; Pesenti, "Gli inventari," 258; Pezzarossa, "'Vita mihi ducitur inter paginas,'" 118–19. For Garzoni, see Manfrè I and II; cf. De Tata, "'Per Instituti aedes migraverit,'" 339–40n25, and De Franceschi, "Le biblioteche a Bologna," 309–13. For Beroaldo, see Pezzarossa, "'Vita mihi ducitur inter paginas,'" 123–30; idem, "'Canon est litterarum'"; De Franceschi, "Le biblioteche a Bologna," 313–17.

123. See at least Walsby, "Book Lists and Their Meaning"; Pesenti, "Gli inventari"; Cerotti, "Scheletri di biblioteche, fisionomia di lettori"; Barbieri, "Elenchi librari."

124. See Pezzarossa, "'Canon est litterarum'"; idem, "'Vita mihi ducitur inter paginas.'"

125. Frati, "I manoscritti posseduti da Carlo Ghisilieri," provided only a (partial and somewhat faulty) transcription, without commenting on the works themselves. I am preparing a study and revised edition of Ghisilieri's list. G. Tamba, "Ghisilieri, Carlo," *DBI,* LIV (2000), 23–25, places Ghisilieri's death in 1463.

126. Lines, "Teachers," 289–90, no. 46; Avellini, "Promozione libraria," 95–100.

127. ASB, Demaniale, S. Michele in Bosco, 158/2330, f. 100r; the two entries, not dated, come right after the note of a loan to Bornio dated 29 September; Lines, "Leon Battista Alberti e lo Studio," 386n36.

128. See Sabbadini, "Giovanni Toscanella," especially the letter to Iohannes de Anania (a professor of canon law teaching in Bologna during these years) quoted on 122–23.

129. ASB, Demaniale, S. Michele in Bosco, 158/2330, ff. 11r and 100r; Lines, "Leon Battista Alberti e lo Studio," 386n36.

130. Lines, *Aristotle's* Ethics, 408, no. 50.
131. For the translations of Bruni (1370–1444) and Argyropoulos (c. 1415–1487), see Lines, *Aristotle's* Ethics, 483–84, 487–89. For the standard translations and coverage in moral philosophy teaching in fifteenth-century Italy, see 100–108.
132. The list is in BUB, ms. 921, f. 197v (transcribed in Manfrè II, 54).
133. Bernardo Garzoni ("Bernardus de Venetiis") received his degree in Bologna in 1420 and taught medicine there at least from 1425 to 1449 before moving to Rome, where he died in 1456 (Lines, *Aristotle's* Ethics, 406, no. 44, and the literature cited there).
134. For the teaching of Nicolò Fava Sr. (testified 1406–1439), see Lines, "Teachers," 287–88, no. 36; idem, *Aristotle's* Ethics, 400, no. 19.
135. Johannes borrowed "primum canonem Avicenne"; he is listed on the rolls as teaching surgery and medicine in Bologna in 1438–1445, 1447–1449, and 1451–1475 (Cristiani, 23, no. 153). The identity of Daniel de Neapoli is not known to me; he does not appear on the rolls.
136. For Baviero Bonitti da Imola's teaching career, see Lines, "Teachers," 292, no. 59.
137. Dallari, IV, 61.
138. Manfrè I and II, plus summary in De Franceschi, "Le biblioteche a Bologna nel Quattrocento," 309–13.
139. For astronomy, see BUB, ms. 132 (Manfrè II, 18–19). For logic and metaphysics, see BUB, ms. 159 (Manfrè II, 19–20). For ethics, see John Buridan's *Questions on the Ethics* in BUB, ms. 366 (Manfrè II, 22–23).
140. For Giovanni's Cicero manuscript, see BUB, ms. 466 (Manfrè II, 25). Giovanni gifted BUB, ms. 752, a manuscript with historical materials on Bologna, to San Giacomo Maggiore in 1494 (Manfrè II, 47). See also BUB, ms. 1610, a commentary of Guarino Veronese on Virgil (Manfrè II, 59–60). On both of these and the problems they pose, see Manfrè I, 270–71.
141. For instance, BUB, ms. 731-I, contains Avicenna's *Canon*. The flyleaf reads "1466 adì primo de novembre ego Johannes Garzonus die, mense et anno supradicto incepi legere primam quarti Avicenne" (Manfrè II, 30); also BUB, ms. 747, lectures of Giovanni Garzoni in 1471 (Manfrè II, 42).
142. BUB, ms. 920 (Manfrè II, 53); see §4.1.
143. On Leandro Alberti, see Petrella, "Nella cella di fra Leandro"; on Cornelio Lambertini, see Calore, "Una fornita biblioteca," 93–110.
144. For Aldrovandi's teaching, see Lines, "Teachers," no. 170. For his museum and library, see Bacchi, "Ulisse Aldrovandi e i suoi libri"; Duroselle-Melish and Lines, "The Library of Ulisse Aldrovandi"; Scappini, Torricelli, and Tugnoli Pattaro, *Lo Studio Aldrovandi*. For his contacts with printers and publishers, which enabled the library to grow, see Ventura Folli, "La natura 'scritta,'" 495–506; Bacchi, "Ulisse Aldrovandi e i suoi libri," 295–99;

Duroselle-Melish, "A Local-Transnational Business"; De Tata, "Il commercio librario a Bologna."

145. Savelli, "Biblioteche professionali e censura ecclesiastica."

146. Cf. John Dee, who had a likewise difficult-to-navigate library. See *John Dee's Library Catalogue.* I am grateful to Sara Miglietti for suggesting Dee as a useful comparison.

147. Duroselle-Melish, "A Local-Transnational Business," 33–34; Duroselle-Melish and Lines, "The Library of Ulisse Aldrovandi," 151–52; also see Fantuzzi, "La biblioteca arcivescovile"; Prodi, *Il cardinale Gabriele Paleotti,* II, 264–68; Montecchi, "La biblioteca arcivescovile."

148. Prodi, *Il cardinale Gabriele Paleotti,* II, 245–64. The fullest study is McCuaig, *Carlo Sigonio.*

149. BUB, ms. Aldrov. 136, vol. VI, ff. 19r–33r: *Catalogus librorum ex bibliotheca Ca[roli] Sigonii;* the list is datable to between 1571 and 1578.

150. Simeoni, "Documenti," 207–26. Note that the inventory of the books he kept in his villa in Modena has not survived (200). Simeoni goes on to transcribe the inventory of Sigonio's other goods, including items of clothing and furniture (226–30). For Sigonio's last will and testament, see Franciosi, *Scritti varii,* 80–92.

151. Cf. the number 682 given in Simeoni, "Documenti," 199; this may have been computed with reference to the multivolume works.

152. These elements are similar to those present in the probate inventory (c. 1602) of Cornelio Lambertini's library, which included a comparable number of books; see Calore, "Una fornita biblioteca." Calore is mistaken, however, in emphasizing (108) the uniqueness of the inventory in question.

153. See the descriptions of these works in EDIT16 (CNCE 32273, 32246, and 47820).

154. See Sigonio's letter to his former student Camillo Coccapani, professor in Ferrara, on 15 May 1582, in Franciosi, *Scritti varii,* 75–76.

155. Tiraboschi, V, 97–119; Pirri, "Gregorio XIII e l'eredità della biblioteca"; McCuaig, *Carlo Sigonio,* 93–95.

156. For a partial analysis of the books listed in the probate inventory, see Simeoni, "Documenti," 199–202.

157. Simeoni, "Documenti," 193.

158. Bacchi, "Ulisse Aldrovandi e i suoi libri," 343; Dall'Olio, "L'attività dell'Inquisizione di Bologna," 1121; Lines, "La biblioteca di Ulisse Aldrovandi in Palazzo Pubblico."

159. De Tata, "'Per Instituti aedes migraverit,'" 328–45.

160. De Tata, "'Per Instituti aedes migraverit,'" description by Giuseppe Simonio Assemani (1720) in BUB, ms. 2951. Now see Machaeva, *Catalogo dei manoscritti islamici.*

161. De Tata, "'Per Instituti aedes migraverit,'" 346–70; further details of these changes, which eventually gave rise to the present Biblioteca Universitaria, in Frati, "La Biblioteca dell'Istituto delle Scienze"; Miani and Bacchi, "I fondi manoscritti e le raccolte di incunaboli e cinquecentine"; Bacchi and Miani, "Vicende del patrimonio librario bolognese."
162. De Tata, "'Per Instituti aedes migraverit,'" 365–66; Bacchi and Miani, "Vicende del patrimonio librario bolognese"; Miani, "Provenienza: B. XIV. I manoscritti di Papa Lambertini."
163. For the opening times of the Istituto's library, see Montefani Caprara's letters to Flaminio Scarselli (BUB, ms. 72, vol. VII). For a printed set of the library's regulations, see Biblioteca della Pontificia Università di Bologna, *Regolamento interno della Biblioteca* ([Bologna]: Tipografia Arcivescovile, [1829]). I am grateful to Rita De Tata for this information. Some scholars have argued that there was no public library in Bologna until the establishment of the Biblioteca dell'Archiginnasio in the nineteenth century. See Colombo, "La biblioteca negata"; Tavoni, "Il patrimonio bibliografico," 78–79.
164. For some pointers to the extensive literature on university libraries elsewhere in Europe, see at least *Les Livres des maîtres de Sorbonne.*
165. Pesenti, *La Biblioteca universitaria di Padova;* De Rosa, *Una biblioteca universitaria del secondo '600;* Grendler, *Universities,* 505–6.
166. See de Ridder-Symoens, "Management and Resources."
167. For some examples, see *Catholic Church and Modern Science,* I.3, 2603–4; also Marcus, *Forbidden Knowledge,* 25–26, 41–43, 45–46.
168. On the Index, the standard work is *Index des livres interdits.* Useful bibliography in (among others) *Church, Censorship and Culture in Early Modern Italy;* Wolf, *Index: Der Vatikan und die verbotenen Bücher;* Frajese, *Nascita dell'Indice;* Lombardo, "An Inevitable Trouble"; E. Rebellato, "Congregazione dell'Indice," *DSI,* I, 386–89; J. M. De Bujanda, "Indici dei libri proibiti, Cinquecento," *DSI,* II, 775–78; idem, "Indici dei libri proibiti, Roma," *DSI,* II, 780–84.
169. For a succinct outline of some of the positions, see Marcus, *Forbidden Knowledge,* 4–7.
170. Dejob, *De l'influence du Concile de Trente;* Grendler, *The Roman Inquisition and the Venetian Press.* For what follows, also see Chapter 8.
171. Occasional information on the Inquisition and the *studium* is found in Dall'Olio, "L'attività dell'Inquisizione di Bologna"; idem, *Eretici e inquisitori;* A. Borromeo, "Congregazione del Santo Ufficio," *DSI,* I, 389–91; A. Prosperi, "Inquisizione romana," *DSI,* I, 815–27; and esp. S. Ferretto, "Università, Italia," *DSI,* III, 1610–12. Now see also De Tata, *Il commercio librario,* 146–47, 150–52.
172. Prodi, *Il cardinale Gabriele Paleotti,* I, 125–26; II, 236–37; Marcus, *Forbidden Knowledge,* 37–39. For the broader Italian practices in the area of securing

reading licenses, see Marcus, *Forbidden Knowledge,* 131–66; eadem, "Bibliography and Book Bureaucracy."

173. Fragnito, "'In questo vasto mare'"; eadem, "The Central and Peripheral Organization of Censorship"; eadem, *Proibito capire,* 191–231.
174. Prodi, *Il cardinale Gabriele Paleotti,* II, 236–43.
175. Dall'Olio, "L'attività dell'Inquisizione di Bologna," 1119–20.
176. Zaccagnini, *Lo Studio,* 162n1; Teach Gnudi and Pierce Webster, *Gaspare Tagliacozzi,* 185–86. More generally, on the activity of the Index with regard to Fuchs, see *Catholic Church and Modern Science,* I.2, 1622–72.
177. Marcus, *Forbidden Knowledge,* 59–75.
178. See Camillo Paleotti's (unsent) draft of a letter to the printer Paulus Manutius, in Prodi, *Il cardinale Gabriele Paleotti,* II, 245.
179. Cicognani, "Lo Studio di Bologna," 197–204; Rotondò, "Nuovi documenti," 168–69. More recently, see Savelli, "La biblioteca disciplinata," 873, 917–18, 922–23, 943–44; Marcus, *Forbidden Knowledge,* ad indicem. For Cardano's teaching, see §7.1.2.
180. On Aldrovandi and the Index, see Bacchi, "Ulisse Aldrovandi e i suoi libri," 333–49; specifically on the licenses he received, with particular emphasis on Zwinger, see 346–49.
181. Bacchi, "Ulisse Aldrovandi e i suoi libri," 340–41.
182. Bacchi, "Ulisse Aldrovandi e i suoi libri," 337–39.
183. *Catholic Church and Modern Science,* I.3, 2634.
184. Dall'Olio, "L'attività dell'Inquisizione di Bologna," 1121.
185. *Catholic Church and Modern Science,* I.1, 440–585.
186. D'Amato, *I Domenicani a Bologna,* I, 611, relying on the diary of Giacomo Rinieri, now available as *Cronaca, 1535–1549,* ed. Armando Antonelli and Riccardo Pedrini (Bologna: Costa, 1998).
187. Dall'Olio, *Eretici e inquisitori,* 125–28.
188. Rotondò, "Per la storia dell'eresia," 141–43; D'Amato, *I Domenicani a Bologna,* I, 614–16; Battistella, "Processi d'eresia nel Collegio di Spagna," 167–70.
189. Rotondò, "Per la storia dell'eresia," passim and 144–47.
190. Dall'Olio, *Eretici e inquisitori,* 109; see also Rotondò, "Per la storia dell'eresia a Bologna," 140–41 and, for further information on Accolti's time as a student in Bologna, Ristori, "Benedetto Accolti," 231–36.
191. I cannot comment here on the broader issue of justice and punishment, on which see Blanshei and Cucini, "Criminal Justice and Conflict Resolution," with rich bibliography.
192. Carcereri, "Cristoforo Dossena."
193. Dall'Olio, *Eretici e inquisitori,* 244–45.
194. Dall'Olio, *Eretici e inquisitori,* 281–85.
195. Some early examples (kindly communicated to me by Rita De Tata) in AAB, Bibl. A 25 / 29 are: *Bando che non si possino vendere, comprare, imprestare,*

tenere, & leggere libri prohibiti di sorte alcuna: Et l'ordine che hanno da tenere, & osservare, gli stampatori, librari, & altre persone, sopra ciò (Bologna: Giovanni Rossi, 1566, dated 19 April); *Ordini da osservarsi da librari, & stampatori, & altri circa i libri, & cose stampate per commandamento di Monsignor Illustrissimo Paleotti Vescovo di Bologna, & del Reverendo Padre Inquisitore di detta Città* (Bologna: per Alessandro Benaccio, 1573). See also Battistella, *Il S. Officio e la riforma religiosa,* 189–91 (with text of 1603 prohibition).

196. *Catholic Church and Modern Science,* I.1, 734–41.
197. Dall'Olio, "L'attività dell'Inquisizione di Bologna," 1126; Battistella, *Il S. Officio e la riforma religiosa in Bologna,* 158–61.
198. Parmeggiani, "Mendicant Orders and the Repression of Heresy."
199. For the importance of the *Apostolici regiminis* and the "Pomponazzi affair," see §8.2.
200. D'Amato, *I Domenicani a Bologna,* I, 468–69; and esp. *L'Italia dell'inquisitore.*
201. D'Amato, *I Domenicani a Bologna,* II, 733.
202. Dall'Olio, "L'attività dell'Inquisizione di Bologna," 1141–42.
203. Dall'Olio, "L'attività dell'Inquisizione di Bologna 1148–51.
204. For a view from the University of Pisa, see Prosperi, "Anime in trappola."

5. THE RISE OF THE HUMANITIES

1. Siraisi, *Taddeo Alderotti.*
2. Lines, "Natural Philosophy and Mathematics," 193, table III; idem, "Natural Philosophy in Renaissance Italy."
3. See the edition with English translation in *Angelo Poliziano's* Lamia*: Text, Translation, and Introductory Studies,* ed. Christopher S. Celenza (Leiden: Brill, 2010), 183–203, esp. §71; my comments in "Defining Philosophy," 289–93; and Godman, "The Angel from Heaven."
4. See, among others, Campana, "The Origin of the Word 'Humanist'"; Grendler, "Five Italian Occurrences of *Umanista.*"
5. Kristeller, "Humanism and Scholasticism"; idem, *Renaissance Thought and Its Sources.* A germane (and rather different) vision in Garin, *Medioevo e Rinascimento,* and idem, *L'Umanesimo italiano.* Witt, *"In the Footsteps of the Ancients,"* underlines the transformations of humanism over time.
6. For Greek, see Botley, *Learning Greek;* Ciccolella, *Donati Graeci.* Studies of how Hebrew and Arabic were learned in Italy are few; now see *Il Rinascimento parla ebraico.* For a broader view, see at least Grafton and Weinberg, *"I Have Always Loved the Holy Tongue,"* chap. 2 and bibliography.
7. See *Rethinking Virtue, Reforming Society.*
8. Among several excellent studies, see Grafton, *Defenders of the Text,* and the collection *The Classical Tradition.*
9. Schmitt, *Aristotle and the Renaissance;* Kraye, "Philologists and Philosophers."

10. Grafton and Jardine, *From Humanism to the Humanities;* Black, *Humanism and Education;* cf. Grendler, *Schooling.*
11. Kristeller, "Die italienische Universitäten"; Garin, "La concezione dell'università"; Grendler, *Universities,* 199–248; Lines, "Humanism and the Italian Universities."
12. Avellini, "Università e umanesimo." Calcaterra provides a brief but acute survey of some interpretations of humanism and observes that "il concetto letterario di humanitas non nacque affatto fuori dell'università, ma entro l'università stessa" (*Alma mater studiorum,* 141–47; quotation at 144).
13. Calcaterra, *Alma mater studiorum,* 66–86, 136–38; Grendler, *Universities,* 199–203.
14. Overviews in Calcaterra, *Alma mater studiorum,* 141–59; Raimondi, *Codro e l'umanesimo a Bologna;* idem, "Quattrocento bolognese: università e umanesimo"; idem, "Da Bologna a Venezia"; Anselmi, *Le frontiere degli umanisti;* Bacchelli, "L'insegnamento di umanità a Bologna"; Grendler, *Universities,* 209–10, 216–19, 224, 229–31, 241, 242–43. Less informative (and lacking references) is Kristeller, "The University of Bologna and the Renaissance." For sketches of and bibliography on Bolognese teachers of humanities between 1400 and 1550, see Chines; and eadem, *La parola degli antichi.*
15. Inter alia, see Malagola, *Antonio Urceo,* 35–38, 46–48, 60–62. Tortelli was in Bologna from 1441 to at least 1444; see Regoliosi, *Nel cantiere del Valla,* 12–14; eadem, "Nuove ricerche," 164–65; Perotti taught rhetoric in 1451–1453 (Dallari, I, 31, 34; Chines, no. 195); see also Lollini, "Bessarione e Niccolò Perotti a Bologna."
16. On the elementary teaching received by schoolchildren more generally, see Grendler, *Schooling;* cf. Black, *Humanism and Education.*
17. For Bologna, the first record I know of is the teaching of Giovanni Lamola in 1440–1441 (appointed to *Rhetorica, Poesia et Studia humanitatis;* Dallari, I, 15); from 1515 to 1532 there was a teaching of *litterae humanitatis diebus festivis* (Dallari, passim).
18. For the different kinds of lectures, see §2.2.1.
19. See the discussion of these chairs in Chapter 2. Useful comments in Costa, "La prima cattedra d'umanità."
20. Dallari, IV, 49.
21. Some appointments are to *philosophia graeca et latina* with Constantinus de Cancellariis (1504–1505; Dallari, I, 188) and Clarus Franciscus de Genulis (1505–1506; Dallari, I, 191); *philosophia graeca diebus festivis* with Nicolò Leoniceno (1508–1509; Dallari, I, 202); and *medicina graeca et latina* with Clarus Franciscus de Genulis (1506–1507; Dallari, I, 195).
22. See the roll for 1499–1500 (Dallari, I, 173–75). I exclude here and in what follows the *lecturae universitatis* offered by students and school-level teaching of grammar (often designated *grammatica pro quarteriis*), writing, arithmetic, and geometry.

23. Dallari, III, 342.
24. Simeoni, *Storia della Università,* 42–46; Calcaterra, *Alma mater studiorum,* 214–18. For Lipsius's negotiations with various Italian universities, see Papy, *"Italiam Vestram Amo supra Omnes Terras!"*
25. The rolls do not start specifying the actual temporal sequence of teachings until 1583–1584 (Dallari, II, 213–16), making it hard to judge which subjects were placed in direct competition with the humanities. Even then, humanities teachers are usually instructed to teach *ad beneplacitum,* and few lectures survive (see also Grendler, *Universities,* 236–37), so reconstructing a professor's program of teaching often depends on indirect sources such as letters, lesson plans, prolusions, or fortuitous indications in manuscript or printed lectures.
26. Two Bolognese prolusions by Lapo are published in Müllner, *Reden und Briefe,* 130–39 (for a course on rhetoric, but actually in praise of all the liberal arts) and 139–42 (on moral philosophy, delivered in 1436). On his stay, plagued by illness and cut short by an invitation to Rome, see Celenza, *Renaissance Humanism and the Papal Curia,* 7. For Battista Guarino, see Chines, no. 109; Gino Pistilli, "Guarini, Battista," *DBI,* LX (2003), 339–45. For Dal Pozzo, see Chines, no. 211; Rosario Contarino, "Dal Pozzo, Francesco, detto il Puteolano," *DBI,* XXXII (1986), 213–16. Gasparino Barzizza may have taught in 1426–1428 (Grendler, *Universities,* 208), but no payments are recorded for him. I have not found traces of the teaching of Guarino Veronese, who supposedly taught in Bologna in 1426–1427 (Malagola, *Antonio Urceo,* 49–52).
27. For Beroaldo, in addition to Grendler, *Universities,* 218–19 (note 85 for previous studies), now see Bacchelli, "L'insegnamento di umanità a Bologna," 160–67; and esp. Severi, *Filippo Beroaldo il Vecchio,* and idem, *Leggere i moderni con gli antichi*, 153–225. Also Malagola, *Antonio Urceo,* 222–23 and Appendix XVII.
28. Dallari, I, 90, 93; he is also listed on the roll for 1474–1475 (Dallari, I, 96) but not in the payments.
29. He appears on the rolls for 1479–1480 for *Rhetorica et poesia de sero* (Dallari, I, 110), but not in that year's payments.
30. ASB, Quartironi, b. 34, a. 1504; Alessandro Achillini (philosophy) and Leonello da Faenza (medicine) were paid the same amount. All others were usually paid at most half of that.
31. Beroaldo had 1,200 copies printed of his commentary on Apuleius, *Asinus aureus* (Bologna: Benedetto Faelli, 1500); see Bacchi, "Tipografi e Università," esp. 101–2.
32. For a listing and editions, see Chines, no. 36; Severi, *Filippo Beroaldo,* 39–53. For Beroaldo's commentary technique, see Casella, "Il metodo dei commentatori umanistici"; Sandy, "Lex commentandi."
33. The last of these orations was probably delivered in 1500, when Beroaldo's commentary on Apuleius appeared; the others date to 1480–1490;

their exact dates are uncertain, apart from Propertius (probably 1487) and the *Tusculan Disputations* and Horace (probably 1490); see Severi, *Filippo Beroaldo,* 59–62. The first edition of the *Orationes et poemata* (Bologna: Plato de Benedictis, 1491) does not include the prolusion to Apuleius, for which see *Orationes multifariae* (Bologna: Benedictus Hectoris, 1500). See also Chines, 12–13, for an overview of the editions of Beroaldo's orations.

34. For all of these, further details in Severi, *Filippo Beroaldo,* 211–20.
35. Poliziano's stop in Bologna—on a journey between Florence and Venice accompanied by Giovanni Pico della Mirandola taken in June and July 1491—included a visit to Beroaldo's classroom, in what must have been an instance of private teaching, given that it took place on a Thursday: "Die 9 Junii Bononie hora 9 1491 die Jovis audivi die quarto Beroaldum legentem epistolam Horatianam ibi 'Non sane credere Mena'"; see Delcorno Branca, "Filologia e cultura volgare," 130.
36. Mariotti, "Lezioni di Beroaldo il Vecchio," 582; Severi, *Filippo Beroaldo,* 219–20.
37. See D'Amico, "The Progress of Renaissance Latin Prose," 360–69.
38. For a fuller picture, see Reeve, "Classical Scholarship"; Fantazzi, "Revival of Classical Texts," with bibliography.
39. For the debate and what follows, see D'Amico, "The Progress of Renaissance Latin Prose"; Fantazzi, "Imitation, Emulation"; Turnberg, "Neo-Latin Prose Style"; Dellaneva, "Following Their Own Genius"; Cotugno, *La scienza della parola,* 30n28.
40. D'Amico, "The Progress of Renaissance Latin Prose," 362; Raimondi, *Codro e l'Umanesimo,* 90–92; Krautter, *Philologische Methode,* 72–125.
41. D'Amico, "The Progress of Renaissance Latin Prose," 362–63, 377–82; Raimondi, *Codro e l'Umanesimo,* 93–102; idem, "Il primo commento umanistico a Lucrezio." On the Lucretius commentary, see also (with full bibliography) Palmer, *Reading Lucretius,* esp. 155–61; Nicoli, "Il giudizio su Epicuro"; eadem, "Atoms, Elements, Seeds." For Pio's life and works, see Daniele Conti, "Pio, Giovanni Battista," *DBI,* LXXXIV (2015), 87–91.
42. Hardin, "Encountering Plautus," esp. 796–99; Ventura, "Il 'Comicus' per i grammatici." For Bocchi's place within contemporary stylistic debates, useful comments in Watson, *Achille Bocchi,* 9–12.
43. Raimondi, *Codro e l'Umanesimo,* 231–47. For a broad characterization of Bologna's peculiar brand of humanism (in which esotericism, encyclopedism, philosophy, and ironic wit played a large role), see Raimondi, "Quattrocento bolognese"; Anselmi, Avellini, and Raimondi, "Il Rinascimento padano."

44. See *The Letters of Giovanni Garzoni: Bolognese Humanist and Physician (1419–1505),* ed. L. R. Lind (Atlanta, GA: Scholars Press, 1992), letter 486 and xvi–xviii, xxiv–xxv. Raimondi, "Quattrocento bolognese," 45–48, dismisses him as a rigid follower of Cicero. Cf. Avellini, "Per uno studio del problema dell'eloquenza." Roberta Ridolfi, "Garzoni, Giovanni," *DBI,* LII (1999), 438–40, is unaware of Lind's work and largely repeats Fantuzzi, IV, 78–100, and IX, 115–28. For Garzoni's studies with Valla, see Mantovani, "Giovanni Garzoni," 64–66. On his books, see Manfrè I and II.
45. There was a gap of three years (1520–1523) during which Amaseo taught Greek in Padua. From 1538 Amaseo held the first of Bologna's "cattedre eminenti" in humanities (Costa, "La prima cattedra d'umanità," 27–28). Amaseo taught in Rome from 1544 to 1550 and became secretary of Latin letters to Pope Julius III in the last two years of his life. On Amaseo, see Liruti, *Notizie,* II, 349–84; Rino Avesani, "Amaseo, Romolo Quirino," *DBI,* II (1960), 660–66; Chines, no. 4; Roberto Norbedo, "Amaseo Romolo Quirino," *Dizionario biografico dei friulani* (http://www.dizionariobiograficodeifriulani.it/amaseo-romolo-quirino/, accessed 9 May 2020); Zaccagnini, *Storia dello Studio,* 281–84; Calcaterra, *Alma mater studiorum,* 195–97; Costa, "La prima cattedra d'umanità," 27–30. For evidence of Amaseo's teaching, see his *Orationum volumen* (Bologna: apud J. Rubrium, 1564, 1580), in particular his *De ratione et ordine studiorum.*
46. Details in Watson, *Achille Bocchi,* 8, 159n41.
47. On the academy's purpose and Amaseo's involvement in the academy and relations with Bocchi, helpful comments in Watson, *Achille Bocchi,* esp. 21–22, 59–63, 153.
48. Calcaterra, *Alma mater studiorum,* 194–203, esp. 202.
49. The initiative was first noted by Costa, "Contributo," 24–25.
50. See Fantuzzi, VIII, 26.
51. The identity of Colombini is not known to me: he is not listed among the Riformatori dello Studio or the professors in these years.
52. In Lisini, "Due lettere inedite," 16: "E mancò poco, agli anni passati, che non venissi a stare anch'io a Bologna, havendomi proposto il S. Dott. Colombini che avea intentione da cotesta S. di erigere in cotesto Studio la cattedra di lingua toscana con provvisione di 400 ducati; ma per non essere io sbrigato e poi per la sua precocie morte non se n'è fatto altro. Se a V.S. paresse, come da sé, rinovellar la pratica, me ne riporto a Lei, e le bacio per fine caramente le mani."
53. ASB, Assunteria di Studio, b. 91 (folder "Proposta di istituzione di una cattedra di lingua toscana nello Studio"): "dalla quale si potessero apparare le regole e i precetti dello scrivere, che sono incogniti alla maggior parte degli huomini et a quelli particolarmente che ne fanno maggior

professione." For the full document, see Costa, "Contributo," 24–25. Note that, contrary to Costa's claim, the proposal in this document came from the Riformatori, not the Assunti.

54. Costa, "Contributo," 24.
55. The Riformatori advise "molto più sarebbe conveniente, che la lingua nostra presente et materna, nella quale di già sono ridotte quasi tutte le scienze, si coltivasse et imparasse, di maniera che potesse scriversi et parlarsi senza errori, di mille scrittori in questo idioma quattro non si ritrovano, che rettamente e senza bisogno d'amenda scritta l'habbiano" (Costa, "Contributo," 24–25).
56. Rossi, "La prima cattedra," 15–16. The teaching of *lingua toscana* in Siena lasted until 1743, when it was joined to humanities.
57. Brugi, "Un parere di Scipione Maffei," 585; see also del Negro, "'Pura favella latina.'"
58. del Negro, "'Pura favella latina,'" 128–29.
59. The fundamental study remains Rossi, *La prima cattedra;* see also *Lettere di Diomede Borghesi,* ed. Campori (Bologna: Gaetano Romagnoli, 1868; repr., Bologna: Commissione per i testi di lingua, 1968); Cappagli, "Diomede Borghesi e Celso Cittadini"; and esp. Maraschio and Poggi Salani, "L'insegnamento di lingua."
60. See, among others, Waquet, *Latin,* 154, 156–57; Grendler, *Universities,* 151–52.
61. See *Il volgare come lingua di cultura.* For the use of the vernacular in Renaissance philosophical discussions, see at least *"Aristotele fatto volgare"* and *Vernacular Aristotelianism in Italy.*
62. For this section, see the exhaustive survey by Pezzarossa, "La storiografia a Bologna."
63. Fantuzzi, IV, 78–100; for his saints' lives, see Frazier, *Possible Lives,* 169–219, 395–414. For a modern edition of his history of Bologna: Garzoni, *Historiae Bononienses,* ed. Alessandra Mantovani (Bologna: Bononia University Press, 2010).
64. Mantovani, "Giovanni Garzoni," 75–79.
65. Grendler, *Universities,* 217–18; see also Raimondi, *Codro,* 54–58; Chines, no. 211.
66. Grendler, *Universities,* 219.
67. Pezzarossa, "La storiografia a Bologna," 224–26, 236–43; Fasoli, "Appunti sulla 'Historia Bononiensis'"; McCuaig, *Sigonio,* chaps. 2–3.
68. Antonio Rotondò, "Bocchi, Achille," *DBI,* XI (1969), 67–70; Chines, "Filologia e arcana sapienza."
69. Sigonio's prolusion on the *Poetics* delivered in Bologna in 1570—unedited and never studied—is in Milan, BAmbr. D 221 inf., ff. 46r–56r (see Kristeller, *Iter,* I, 284b). His only published course prolusion for Bologna

(November 1563) is in his *Opera omnia,* ed. Ludovico Muratori (Milan: in aedibus Palatinis, 1732–1737), VI, 545–52, and provides no valuable details on his teaching. See also Zaccagnini, *Storia dello Studio,* 288–95; Calcaterra, *Alma mater studiorum,* 203–7, 214–15; Biondi, "Insegnare a Bologna." It is worth noting that Sigonio's translation of Aristotle's *Rhetoric* appeared in Bologna in 1565 (Cranz, *A Bibliography,* 108.488; cf. Lohr, II, 421), possibly in part as an outgrowth of his teaching there.

70. Costa, "La prima cattedra," 34–47; Vincenzo Lavenia, "Sigonio, Carlo," *DBI,* XCII (2018), online.

71. Costa, "La prima cattedra," 58–60; Robertus Titius, *In celeberrimo Bononiensi gymnasio humaniorum leterarum . . . Ad Caesaris commentarios De bello gallico. Praelectiones quatuor* (Bologna: apud haeredes Ioannis Rossij, 1598).

72. Lodovico Scapinelli, "Oratio et dissertationes XV in T. Livium," in *Opere del dottore Lodovico Scapinelli patrizio modenese soprannominati Il cieco,* ed. Pompilio Pozzetti, 2 vols. (Parma: dalla reale tipografia, 1801), II, 5–22; on Scapinelli, see the introduction by Pozzetti (i, esp. xxxv–lx), which partly corrects Tiraboschi, V, 49–63; Calcaterra, *Alma mater studiorum,* 215.

73. ASB, Annue Lezioni, b. 60, ff. 443r–446v.

74. For Italy, see most recently Bovier, "Commenter les Histoires et les Annales de Tacite." I am grateful to Ingrid De Smet for this reference.

75. See Clizia Carminati, "Malvezzi, Virgilio," *DBI,* LXVIII (2007), 336–42; Virgilio Malvezzi, *Opere,* ed. Edoardo Ripari (Bologna: Persiani, 2013). I am grateful to Andrea Severi for pointing me to this author.

76. Wilson, *From Byzantium to Italy,* 3–7; for Boccaccio's role in establishing this chair, see most recently Santagata, *Boccaccio,* 206–11. The only detailed survey known to me of the teaching of Greek in Bologna is Malagola, *Antonio Urceo,* 18–136, which is by now sorely out of date.

77. Malagola, *Antonio Urceo,* 39–41; Dallari, IV, 49 (where he is called "Iohannes Hisparus"). The payments indicate that, at L. 110, Aurispa's salary was higher than that of any teachers of grammar, rhetoric, or philosophy that year; see ASB, Tesoreria, b. 82, ff. 300r, 309v. Grendler, *Universities,* 209, notes that Aurispa was "less a scholar than a dealer in Greek manuscripts."

78. For Theodorus, see Malagola, *Antonio Urceo,* 39; Dallari, IV, 51, 53; Grendler, *Universities,* 209–10. Theodorus's salary for the two years was only L. 20 and L. 35, respectively; see ASB, Tesoreria, b. 82 (1424–1428), ff. 47v–358r, 392r–405v; also Zaoli, "Di alcuni *rotuli,*" 228–29. Guarino Veronese seems to have been in Bologna c. 1426–1427; although Malagola (*Antonio Urceo,* 49–52) states that he taught Greek, he is not recorded in the *studium*'s payments (Dallari, IV, 53). Barzizza ("Guasparino de Pergamo") appears on the rolls for 1426–1428 as teaching rhetoric and poetry (Dallari, IV, 53, 55; Grendler, *Universities,* 208) and may not have taken

up the appointment—no payments to him are indicated in the commune's accounts.

79. See most recently De Keyser, *Francesco Filelfo, Man of Letters.* I wish to thank Jeroen De Keyser for checking the details below on Filelfo.

80. Paolo Viti, "Filelfo, Francesco," *DBI,* XLVII (1997), 613–26; Wilson, *From Byzantium to Italy,* 55–61.

81. For the details of Filelfo's lectureship (not recorded in the payments for 1428–1429), see Dallari, IV, 56; Chines, 51–55; Lines, *Aristotle's* Ethics, 404; Filelfo's letter (23 February 1428) to Giovanni Aurispa, in Filelfo, *Collected Letters,* I, 73–74; cf. Malagola, *Antonio Urceo,* 53–58. Filelfo should not be confused with the lowly teacher of grammar Franciscus de Tolentino.

82. Wilson, *From Byzantium to Italy,* 57, 59; Resta, "Filelfo tra Bisanzio e Roma," 14.

83. Letter (7 July 1428) to Ambrogio Traversari, in Filelfo, *Collected Letters,* I, 82.

84. See Chapter 2; and Malagola, *Statuta universitatis scolarium* (1405), rub. 38. Unfortunately, Filelfo's surviving inaugural lectures are vague and seldom specify a precise teaching text: one of these (Müllner, *Reden und Briefe,* 155–58, without indication of date or place), possibly delivered in March 1428, may refer to a Greek literary text. Another one (151–54), dated December 1428, generically praises rhetoric as a subject of study. On Filelfo's Bolognese orations, see Gualdo Rosa, "Una prolusione inedita di Francesco Filelfo," 276–77.

85. The enquirer was Nicolò Fava, a Bolognese professor. See Filelfo, *Collected Letters,* I, 77–78 (letter to Fava, 14 May 1429), 90–91 (letter to Fava, 5 August 1428); Lines, *Aristotle's* Ethics, 296–97.

86. Filelfo was actually in the city only from January to June 1439. He did not take up an appointment in 1471, listed in the rolls (Dallari, I, 87): see Viti, "Filelfo, Francesco"; cf. Malagola, *Antonio Urceo,* 58, 430–31.

87. Gualdo Rosa, "Una prolusione inedita del Filelfo," 280–87, esp. 286n32, 287n34.

88. Calcaterra, *Alma mater studiorum,* 151–52; Malagola, *Antonio Urceo,* 39–41.

89. For Alberti, see Lines, "Leon Battista Alberti e lo Studio di Bologna."

90. The Bolognese Lianori (c. 1425–1477) was probably part of the circle around the humanist Tortelli, who sojourned in Bologna to study theology (1441–1445) and heavily influenced figures such as the Servite Filippo Fabri, as well as the teacher of rhetoric Niccolò Volpe and his students. He taught Greek letters (and, in his first year, moral philosophy) at the University of Bologna from 1455 to 1458 and was highly paid. To my knowledge, no testimonies to Lianori's teaching survive, but he was known for his facility in writing in Greek and for a rich collection of Greek manuscripts (which, however, he may have acquired after leaving Bologna for

Rome and elsewhere, in the service of Pope Pius II). See Chines, no. 142; Lines, *Aristotle's* Ethics, 408, no. 52; Franco Bacchelli, "Lianori, Lianoro," *DBI,* LXV (2005), 9–12; Martínez Manzano, "Autógrafos griegos de Lianoro Lianori"; Marsico, "Il Tacito di Lianoro Lianori." The fundamental study remains Frati, "Lianoro de' Lianori."

91. For the information below, see Emilio Bigi, "Andronico Callisto," in *DBI,* III (1961), 162–63; Malagola, *Antonio Urceo,* 37–38, 41–42; Cammelli, "Andronico Callisto"; Lines, *Aristotle's* Ethics, 410, no. 61. For the subjects of his Greek lectures, see Botley, "Greek Literature in Exile"; idem, *Learning Greek,* 81–82, 101, 103, 108–10. Most recently, Monfasani, "Andronicus Callistus on the Science of Physics."
92. On Bessarion's stay in Bologna (1450–1455), which deserves a closer study, see Nasalli Rocca, "Il Cardinal Bessarione"; Lollini, "Bessarione e Niccolò Perotti a Bologna"; Severi, "Perotti e Morandi nella disputa Valla-Bracciolini."
93. Botley, "Greek Literature in Exile," 183.
94. The fundamental works on Codro are Bartolomeo Bianchini, *Codri vita a Bartholomeo Blanchino Bononiensi condita ad Minum Roscium Senatorem Bononiensem* (six folios, usually bound together with the editions of Codro's *Opera* printed in 1502 and later; see Urceo, *Orationes, seu sermones*); Malagola, *Antonio Urceo;* Raimondi, *Codro;* Gualdo Rosa, "Cortesi Urceo"; Bacchelli, "L'insegnamento di umanità," 155–60; and, most recently, Ventura, *Codro.*
95. For his prolusions, see Codro, *Sermones,* with text and facing Italian translation.
96. For the chronological order of the prolusions, see Bacchelli, "L'insegnamento di umanità," 174n16. Also Raimondi, *Codro,* 129–31; Gualdo Rosa, "Cortesi Urceo."
97. Raimondi, *Codro,* 254–55.
98. See Raimondi, *Codro,* 153–54, with reference to *Sermo* IX.
99. See Ventura, *Codro,* 216–18, which also discusses a copy of this volume (now BCAB 16.M.I.16) possibly owned by Codro.
100. For a discussion of what constituted the various areas of logic, see Ebbesen, "What Counted as Logic in the Thirteenth Century?"; on the teaching of logic in Bologna, see Maierù, *University Training,* 93–116.
101. For Codro's reputation as a writer of Latin verse, see Gualdo Rosa, "Cortesi Urceo."
102. His private teaching was directed at least to the youngster Camillo Paleotti (son of the renowned jurist Vincenzo and father of Gabriele, who served as bishop and then archbishop of Bologna), who after Codro's death taught rhetoric and poetry in the *studium* (1503–13; Dallari, passim); see Ventura, *Codro,* 37–38, 172–74, 199 (for other disciples, 69). Codro's public activity is testified by the rolls.

103. Ventura, *Codro,* chap. 3. For Isocrates, see BUB, ms. 12, b. 1, item 2; for Porphyry and Aristotle, see BUB, ms. 12, b. 1, item 7.
104. See Raimondi, *Codro,* 172–76 (who assumes that the translations are by Codro); but see Ventura, *Codro,* 34, 191–98, for an explanation of contrasting opinions.
105. The text (scribed by Pirro Vizzani and preserved in Florence, BNC, II VII 125) is studied and edited by López Zamora, "Antonius Urceus"; see also Ventura, *Codro,* 200–201. On earlier translations, teaching, and editions of Hesiod, see Botley, *Learning Greek,* 100–102. The translation dates to a period before 1495 and can possibly be assigned to 1487–1488.
106. See Ciccolella, *Donati Graeci,* 130–33, for Battista Guarino's teaching of Greek.
107. Botley, *Learning Greek,* 96.
108. In addition to translation from Latin to Italian, pupils had to translate from Italian to Latin; see the exercises of Gabriele Paleotti on Cicero's letters in Bologna, Archivio Isolani, F. 74.207 (CN 101) (Prodi, *Il cardinale Gabriele Paleotti,* I, 53).
109. Botley, *Learning Greek,* 82.
110. Raimondi, *Codro,* 130; Codro, *Sermones,* I, 52–59, 319. For Codro's fascination with Homer, see esp. Raimondi, *Codro,* 187–201.
111. Codro, *Sermones,* II, 108–112 (*Sermo* VII).
112. "Statui ergo linguam graecam latine interpretari" (Codro, *Sermones,* II, 114).
113. For Theocritus, see the first lines of *Sermo* VIII (II, 140). For Euripides, see *Sermo* I.
114. Codro, *Sermones,* II, 137–51.
115. ASB, Studio Alidosi, b. 44; see Ventura, *Codro,* 199–200.
116. For Greek lexica in the period, see esp. Botley, *Learning Greek,* 55–70.
117. Ciccolella, *Donati Graeci,* 118–24, 131; Botley, *Learning Greek,* 7–12, 14–31, and Appendix 1 (120–123, where Lascaris's 1480 edition is item 5).
118. See Appendix 1 in Botley, *Learning Greek;* Malagola, *Antonio Urceo,* 85–87; Balsamo, "Università e editoria," 125–26.
119. See Chapter 4. As an example of how things could go wrong when a printer attempted to print a Greek text without the proper investment, see the story behind the first printing of Galen's *Methodus medendi* in Venice in 1500, as told in Geanakoplos, *Byzantium and the Renaissance,* 204–10; and Nutton, "Hellenism Postponed," 162.
120. See ASB, Studio Alidosi, b. 44, unnumbered fascicles, to be described in a separate publication.
121. Ciccolella, *Donati Graeci,* 124–29.
122. Botley, *Learning Greek,* 65–66, and Appendix 2, no. 6.
123. For Bolognese familiarity with Crastoni, see Giovanni Battista Spagnoli Mantovano's dedication of one of his *sylvae* to him (Bologna: per Bene-

dictum Hectoris, 1502): *Ad Io. Crestonum carmelitam, qui composuit lexicon, id est, vocabularium graecum.* I am grateful to Andrea Severi for this reference.

124. For the evidence that Copernicus studied with Codro, see Malagola, *Antonio Urceo,* 335–39, and Ventura, *Codro,* 75–76; for Crastoni's lexicon, see Botley, *Learning Greek,* 64–65; the 1499 edition is listed in Appendix 2, no. 8. Copernicus's richly annotated copy is held in Uppsala's University Library.

125. Cited and translated in Botley, *Learning Greek,* 66. The interest is confirmed by Codro's biographer, Bianchini: "Vocabulario graeco plura de suo addidit, multa emendavit: nonnulla entiamnum quae in ruinis latinae linguae delituerant, pertinaci studio, atqui ingenii bonitate, in lucem eruit." I am grateful to Giacomo Ventura for this reference.

126. Ciccolella, *Donati Graeci,* 129–30; Botley, *Learning Greek,* 77–78. Ventura, *Codro,* 214–16, questions, however, whether mss. BAV, Ottob. gr. 166, and Florence, BLaur, Plut. 31, 20, should be attributed to Codro.

127. With Giuliano Grecolino (t. 1500–1506, 1511–1512), on whom see Malagola, *Antonio Urceo,* 93–94, 103–4; Dallari, I, passim; Paolo Bombace (t. 1506–1510), see Dallari, I, passim; and Achille Bocchi (t. 1507–1512), see Malagola, *Antonio Urceo,* 94–96; Dallari, I, passim.

128. Pietro, also called Petrus de Aegina, graecus, is listed on the rolls until 1527, but his presence may well have been irregular, because in 1525 the Senate commented that the chair of Greek had been unoccupied for several years (Malagola, *Antonio Urceo,* 96–98; Dallari, passim; Chines, no. 268).

129. Some information comes from a German student of Pietro da Egina, Johannes Lange, *Epistolae medicinales* (Frankfurt: apud Heredes Andreae Wecheli, 1589), 523, where he states that Pietro taught Aristophanes's comedies. It is unclear whether this was in the context of public or private teaching, but Lange names the (later) Pope Leo as his study companion in Greek. If this information is trustworthy, it must refer to the year 1511, when Giovanni de' Medici (Leo X, r. 1513–1521) was papal legate in Bologna and would hardly have been sitting with other students.

130. For Strozzi, see Malagola, *Antonio Urceo,* 100; Chines, no. 243. For Pompilio, see Liruti, *Notizie,* II, 371–73; Malagola, *Antonio Urceo,* 100–102; Rino Avesani, "Amaseo, Pompilio," *DBI,* II (1960), 658–60; Chines, no. 3; Lorenzo di Lenardo, "Amaseo Pompilio," *Dizionario biografico dei friulani* (http://www.dizionariobiograficodeifriulani.it/amaseo-pompilio/, accessed 9 May 2020). The Englishman John Caius, who had a considerable interest in Greek (and especially medical) manuscripts, mentions that he observed the lectures of Pompilio Amaseo and Achille Bocchi in Bologna, apparently because of their use of the old pronunciation of Greek (*De libris propriis,* 199; *Autobibliography,* 79).

131. *Pompilii Amasei de Bonononiensium scholarum exaedificatione oratio* (Bologna: Giovanni Rossi, 1563); the oration is clearly in honor of the newly built Archiginnasio building.
132. On Bombace, see Fantuzzi, II, 276–81; Malagola, *Antonio Urceo,* 94; Dallari, I, passim; Elpidio Mioni, "Bombace, Paolo," *DBI,* XI (1969), 373–76; Chines, no. 45; Martin Lowry, "Paolo Bombace," in *Contemporaries of Erasmus,* I, 163–65; Manoussakas, *Gli umanisti greci.*
133. Bombace and Erasmus became fast friends and engaged in a lengthy correspondence.
134. For Forteguerri's pace of teaching, see Botley, *Learning Greek,* 83–84.
135. On Robortello, see esp. Liruti, *Notizie,* II, 413–83; Weinberg, *A History of Literary Criticism,* I, 388–404; Lohr, II, 388; Sergio Cappello, "Robortello Francesco" in *Nuovo Liruti: Dizionario biografico dei friulani,* II, *L'età veneta,* ed. C. Scalon et al. (Udine, 2009), 2151–57 (http://www.dizionariobiografico deifriulani.it/robortello-francesco/, accessed 10 May 2020), and the bibliography there; Matteo Venier, "Robortello, Francesco," *DBI,* LXXXVII (2016), 827–31; most recently, Sgarbi, *Francesco Robortello.*
136. Francesco Robortello, *In librum Aristotelis De arte poetica explicationes* (Florence: L. Torrentino, 1548); idem, *De historica facultate, disputatio . . . De rhetorica facultate . . . Annotationum in varia tam Graecorum quam Latinorum loca libri duo . . .* (Florence: L. Torrentino, 1548).
137. Moral philosophy teaching in Italian universities was almost always based on the *Nicomachean Ethics;* see Lines, *Aristotle's* Ethics, chap. 2.
138. Dallari, II, passim; Liruti, *Notizie,* II, 362; Tiraboschi, IV, 127–28.
139. The Bolognese records do not list Robortello among the degree recipients for arts (see Bronzino); it is therefore likely that he received his degree at another university that charged less, or that he requested it from one of the counts palatine. This makes it hard to determine when he left Bologna.
140. On mid-sixteenth-century works on the *Poetics,* see at least Weinberg, *A History of Literary Criticism,* I, 349–423; Javitch, "The Assimilation of Aristotle's *Poetics*"; and the revisionist collection *The Reception of Aristotle's* Poetics.
141. For Averroes, see Hardison Jr., "The Place of Averroes' Commentary on the *Poetics.*" For Poliziano, see Godman, "Poliziano's Poetics and Literary History," 169–77. For the importance of the *Poetics* for Valla, see Magnani, "Aristotelianism and Metricology."
142. Lardet, "Georges de Trébizonde"; *La Rhétorique d'Aristote.*
143. On the *Poetics,* see Cotugno, "Le *Annotationi* di Piccolomini e la *Poetica* di Castelvetro." On the *Rhetoric,* see Mack, *History of Renaissance Rhetoric,* 24–26, 169–76 (see 175n51 for the *Poetics*); Green, "The Reception of Aristot-

le's *Rhetoric*." The fundamental reference point remains Weinberg, *A History of Literary Criticism*.

144. While in Bologna (1541–1542), Benedetto Varchi owned notes from Maggi's lectures on the *Poetics* and was being asked to share them with friends; see Lines, "Philosophy Teaching and Filiations of Learning."
145. Maggi lectured on the *Poetics* at the University of Ferrara, where he started teaching in 1543; lectures from 1546–1547 survive in manuscript; see Elisabetta Selmi, "Maggi, Vincenzo," *DBI,* LXVII (2006), 365–69; his commentary appeared in print in 1550.
146. BAV, Vat. lat. 6528, ff. 156r–191v; see Sgarbi, "Francesco Robortello on Topics"; idem, "Francesco Robortello's Rhetoric"; idem, *Francesco Robortello,* 34. Cf. Costa, "La prima cattedra d'umanità," 32–34.
147. Franciscus Robortellus, *De artificio dicendi* (Bologna: Alessandro Benacci, 1560, 1567).
148. Fantuzzi, VII, 180–82; Dallari, passim.
149. Dallari, II, 178.
150. Sebastiano Regoli, *In primum Aeneidos Virgilii librum ex Aristotelis De arte poetica et Rhetorica praeceptis explicationes* (Bologna: Giovanni Rossi, 1563), followed up by idem, *In librum primum Aeneidos . . . pars altera* (Bologna: Alessandro Benacci, 1565). Regoli also published *In Ciceronis orationem in C. Verrem primam explicationes* (Bologna: Giovanni Rossi [1564?]). In what follows, page references to the 1563 work are given in the text.
151. Regoli was thus looking to the *Poetics* as a prescriptive text, as others had done in the years before him. See Javitch, "The Emergence of Poetic Genre Theory."
152. For examples, see Kallendorf, *In Praise of Aeneas.*
153. "Cum finis hominis sit foelicitas, quae est actio cum virtute, ut ait Aristoteles libro primo Rhetoricorum et Ethicorum, poeta effingens Aeneam suum omnia ad virtutis normam gerentem, eum ad summam foelicitatem perducit, quod est optimi poetae officium et finis. Poetica enim, ut Rhetorica, inservit politicae, quae ut regina caeteris artibus imperat, cuius finis est efficere beatos, nec id assequi potest nisi ante bon[o]s reddiderit" (Regoli, *In primum Aeneidos Virgilii librum,* 10). This view of politics as the most important of the arts is one famously posited by Aristotle in the *Nicomachean Ethics* (I.2, 1094a26–1094b11).
154. For how widespread or not Regoli's approach was, see Kallendorf, *The Protean Virgil,* 112–14. For my account of Regoli and the reception of the *Poetics,* I am indebted to Bryan Brazeau.
155. See Lines, "Philosophy Teaching and Filiations of Learning"; and §8.2.1.
156. Ulisse Aldrovandi, *Delle statue antiche, che per tutta Roma, in diversi luoghi, et case si veggono,* in *Le antichità della città di Roma* (Venice: Giordano Zileti,

1556), 115–315. Aldrovandi's own copy of the volume, with his reading marks (BUB, A.IV.Q.II.30) is available in digital reproduction at https://amshistorica.unibo.it/130 (accessed 1 July 2021).

157. Various studies have also linked humanism with science and natural philosophy more directly; for both influences and tensions, especially good studies in English are *Natural Particulars;* Grafton with Shelford and Siraisi, *New Worlds, Ancient Texts;* and *Historia: Empiricism and Erudition.*

158. Lines, *Aristotle's* Ethics, 280–81.

159. Daniela Mugnai Carrara has argued for an earlier influence, with Nicolò Leoniceno, while Vivian Nutton has preferred a date around 1530; see Mugnai Carrara, "Curricula e contenuti dell'insegnamento"; Nutton, "Hellenism Postponed"; idem, "Greek Science in the Sixteenth-Century Renaissance." More generally: *The Medical Renaissance of the Sixteenth Century; Humanismus und Medizin;* and *Revisiting Medical Humanism.*

160. Siraisi, "Medicine, Physiology, and Anatomy," 222.

161. The volumes contain: the lectures on *Canon* IV, 1 on fevers (vol. 1, 1466–1467); two sets of lectures on *De urina* and *De pulsu,* respectively (vol. 2, 1473). For a description of vol. 3 (1484), see Kibre, "Giovanni Garzoni," but note that her description does not match the sequence of the volumes; see also Manfrè II; Cristiani, no. 140.

162. The fundamental work is Siraisi, *Avicenna,* which does not, however, discuss Garzoni.

163. Grendler, *Universities,* 337–39. Not all humanists, however, were enthused about anatomy; see, in particular, Henricus Cornelius Agrippa of Nettesheim as discussed in Siraisi, "Medicine, Physiology and Anatomy," 222–27.

164. For Leoniceno, see Mugnai Carrara, *La biblioteca di Nicolò Leoniceno;* Nutton, *Renaissance Medicine.*

165. Useful considerations in Nutton, "Hellenism Postponed."

166. ASB, Annue Lezioni, b. 60, f. 577r–579v.

167. Bianchi, *Studi sull'aristotelismo,* 180–83; Lines, "I classici," 83. The topic is surprisingly under-researched, and conclusions can therefore be only tentative.

168. Lines, *Aristotle's* Ethics, 333–34.

169. Osler, "Humanists and Jurists"; the situation was similar in other universities, such as Pavia: see Azzolini et al., "La Facoltà di Arti e Medicina," 521–46.

170. Malagola, *Antonio Urceo,* 301–4. See Jean de Pins, *Letters and Fragments,* ed. Jan Pendergrass (Geneva: Droz, 2007), ad indicem.

171. Jean de Pins, *Divae Catherinae Senensis simul et clarissimi Philippi Beroaldi Bononiensis vita* (Bologna: Benedetto Ettore, 1505); Urceus (Codro), *Orationes seu sermones.*

172. See esp. Caprioli, *Indagini sul Bolognini;* Dionisotti, "Filologia umanistica e testi giuridici"; Grendler, *Universities,* 436–43.

173. Delcorno Branca, "Filologia e cultura volgare," 127–29, with bibliography.
174. Grendler, *Universities,* 439–41; Belloni, "L'insegnamento giuridico."
175. Grendler, *Universities,* 441.
176. Grendler, *Universities,* 451–52.
177. Grendler, *Universities,* 455–56.
178. Vernazza, "La crisi barocca," Belloni, "L'insegnamento giuridico," and Grendler, *Universities,* 453–56, see little room in Bologna for humanistic jurisprudence; while the first two base themselves on a survey of the textbooks used, Grendler's analysis relies more on institutional factors.
179. See Costa, "La prima cattedra," 60–61.
180. L. F. Marsili, *Parallelo* (1709), ed. Bortolotti, 416–17.
181. See Compère, "L'insegnamento della retorica e della lingua greca"; from rather different perspectives, both Garin, "La concezione dell'università," and Kristeller, "Die italienische Universitäten der Renaissance," provide further insights.
182. See the telling subtitle of Kristeller's book *Renaissance Thought: The Classic, Scholastic, and Humanist Strains.*

6. SPECIALIZATION AND SCIENTIFIC INNOVATION

1. For the sources and their coverage, see "Sources and Methodology" in the Introduction.
2. Lines, *Aristotle's* Ethics, 416, 294–300.
3. Dallari, II, 224; Lines, "Reorganizing the Curriculum," 21, 23–24, 31, for the *logico perpetuo.* For comments and bibliography on Baldi, see Lines, *Aristotle's* Ethics, 308–10, 527–28; Busacchi, "Il nuovo spirito di ricerca," 419–20.
4. The monument to Galesi, inscribed in 1592, states: "TE DVCE QUIS DVBITET LOGICES EXOLVERE NEXVS" (*Imago Universitatis,* I, no. 1049). Other professors, such as Claudio Betti, were also widely praised for their teaching of logic.
5. Lines, "Natural Philosophy and Mathematics," 136–40. For comparisons with Florence-Pisa and Padua, see Lines, "University Natural Philosophy" (but disregard table 2-A, where, due to a printing error, subjects are not indicated correctly).
6. Lines, "Teachers," nos. 144 (Boccadiferro), 161 (Mainetti), 166 (Betti), 170 (Aldrovandi), 174 (Cartari), 181 (Pendasio), 192 (Zoppi).
7. Details in Lines, "Natural Philosophy and Mathematics," 144, table V; also Table 2.2 above. For the various kinds of lectures, see §2.2.1.
8. See the discussion at the start of Chapter 2 and passim, particularly with regard to Ulisse Aldrovandi's comments.
9. See Pomponazzi, *Expositio,* vii–xviii. For the contract allowing Pomponazzi freedom to teach what he wished, see Martin, *Subverting Aristotle,* 66 (depending on Podestà, "Di alcuni documenti inediti," 176).

10. Lines, "Philosophy Teaching and Filiations of Learning," table 1.
11. Lines, "Natural Philosophy in Renaissance Italy," 271–72.
12. Aldrovandi played a major role in the annual production of the theriac, a medical compound that was thought to ward off diseases, including the plague. For his involvement, and the more general controversies linked to the composition of the theriac, see Olmi, "Farmacopea antica e medicina moderna."
13. Olmi, *Ulisse Aldrovandi;* Tugnoli Pattaro, *Metodo e sistema delle scienze;* Findlen, *Possessing Nature,* chap. 1. On Aldrovandi's library, see §4.2.2.
14. Luca Ghini had introduced this subject in the 1530s; on Ghini's example, see Sabbatani, "La cattedra dei semplici"; a useful (if rapid) overview in Olmi, "Le scienze naturali," 142, with comments on Aldrovandi at 142–46.
15. BUB, ms. Aldrov. 77, 3 vols.; see Riddle, "Dioscorides," 99.
16. BUB, ms. Aldrov. 21, vol. III, ff. 58–62, 507–16, 522–28 (all undated).
17. Olmi, "Le scienze naturali," 146–48. Calcaterra, *Alma mater studiorum,* 228, and Vernazza, "La crisi barocca," 146, prefer to focus on the brothers Bartolomeo and Giacinto Ambrosini as seventeenth-century representatives of Aldrovandi's legacy, but give no sense of the international context, for which see especially Ogilvie, *The Science of Describing,* and Findlen, "An Artificial Nature." On botany specifically, see Morton, *History of Botanical Science,* esp. chap. 5.
18. Baldini, "La teoria della spiegazione scientifica," 203–6; also Alessandro Ottaviani, "Trionfetti, Lelio," *DBI,* XCVI (2019), online, but note that his listing of Trionfetti's manuscript lectures at the BUB has confused Frati's progressive entry numbers with the shelfmarks. The correct shelfmarks are: BUB, ms. 1432 (4 vols., *Lectiones sive ostensiones botanicae, quas habuit in Horto medico publico Bononiae . . . ,* 1675–1721); ms. 1433 (*Praelusiones botanicae, quas habuit in Horto medico publico . . .*); ms. 1434 (*Exercitationes habitae in Instituto scientiarum Bononiae circa historiam naturalem cursu annorum quinque*); ms. 1435 (*Historia fossilium*); and ms. 1436 (*Specimen . . . historiae naturalis fungorum*). Trionfetti was praised for his teaching of botany by L. F. Marsili in his *Parallelo,* ed. Bortolotti, 414.
19. Masetti Zannini, "Docenti del clero," 187–88, 192 (see also Chapter 8).
20. The early teaching rolls usually refer to the subject as *astrologia,* but this designation is also used in free alternation with *astronomia*—for instance, for the teaching of Giovanni Fondi (listed, with minor breaks, 1428–1473; see Bònoli / Piliarvu, 104–6). The corresponding *lectura universitatis* is called *astrologia* in 1438–1439, but *astronomia* in 1439–1440 (Dallari, I, 12 and 13) and several following years. For the relationships of Renaissance astrology with contiguous fields, see most recently *A Companion to Astrology in the Renaissance,* which includes a large bibliography. Especially

helpful as a general treatment of astrology between 1400 and 1700 is Tessicini, "Astronomia e cosmologia" (with bibliography). Complementary observations in Rutkin, *Sapientia Astrologica,* with full bibliography and particular cautions on the commonly made distinction between "natural' and "judicial" astrology (361 and passim).

21. For this and other genres of astrological literature, see Casali, *Le spie del cielo.* On the practice of producing prognostications, see Tur, "Hora introitus solis in Arietem" (this and other references kindly supplied by Darrel Rutkin). Specifically on Bologna, see Rutkin, *Sapientia Astrologica,* 397–407 and passim; and (less reliably) Palermo, "Dal judiciolo al iudicium."
22. On Cardano's astrological views and practice, see Ernst, "'Veritatis amor dulcissimus'"; Grafton and Siraisi, "Between the Election and My Hopes." For his medical teaching in Bologna, see §7.1.2.
23. For its place in the fifteenth and sixteenth centuries, see Pepe, "Astronomia e matematica," and Biagioli, "The Social Status of Italian Mathematicians." For the medieval background, see Rutkin, *Sapientia Astrologica.* Pistacchio, "L'insegnamento dell'astrologia," is disappointingly generic. The perspective in Thorndike, *History,* V, 234–51, is now very dated, although it still contains interesting details.
24. Dallari, I, 81 and passim.
25. Thorndike, *History,* V, 61, 124, 213–14, 241–44.
26. The *cattedre eminenti* were four special chairs reserved for non-Bolognese academic stars (see §1.2). For Ferrari, see Dallari, II, 162; he was paid L. 400 (in contrast with L. 125 for Bolognetto): see ASB, Quartironi, b. 37, ff. 9–12. Ferrari was listed on the roll for 1565–1566 (Dallari, II, 165), but died in October and did not take up his appointment (Bortolotti, *La storia della matematica,* 79–80). Cf. Bònoli / Piliarvu, 127, 137, and Grendler, *Universities,* 421, both of whom date the change to 1569 with Francesco Burdini instead. For the establishment of regular chairs in mathematics and astronomy in seventeenth-century England, see Feingold, *The Mathematicians' Apprenticeship,* 31–34; Pepe, "James Gregory e i matematici inglesi in Italia."
27. These are the works listed in the rolls, but the rolls sometimes list just the first or the major work that a professor was to teach in a certain year. The order was slightly different in Pisa's 1543 statutes, which specified the sequence *De sphaera,* Euclid, and "certain works of Ptolemy" (which could vary from the *Almagest* or the *Geography* to the *Tetrabiblos*); see Rutkin, "The Use and Abuse of Ptolemy's Tetrabiblos," 141–42.
28. For broader considerations, see Moyer, "The Astronomers' Game."
29. On this work, see most recently Lines, "When Is a Translation Not a Translation?"

30. On Manfredi, see Bònoli / Piliarvu, 111–12; the quotation is given on 111: "Quamvis medicina de se scientia sit perfecta, medicus tamen in opere suo sine astrologia non est perfectus." For a recent treatment of Manfredi, see Duranti, *Mai sotto Saturno.*
31. After 1504, Domenico is no longer listed in the rolls, although his name does appear in the payments for 1504–1505 (L. 300); see ASB, Quartironi, b. 34.
32. See *I pronostici di Domenico Maria da Novara.*
33. Information on Domenico da Novara in Bònoli / Piliarvu, 118–21; see also Tiraboschi, VI, 588–90; Bortolotti, *La storia della matematica,* 20–21; Thorndike, *History,* IV, 480, and V, 234–36; Tabarroni, "Copernico e gli Aristotelici bolognesi"; Westman, *The Copernican Question,* chap. 2; Goddu, *Copernicus and the Aristotelian Tradition,* 187–93 (14–24 for Copernicus's decision to study in Bologna).
34. Though one should be aware that, in several places in Europe, it was carefully taught and studied; see Gingerich, *The Book Nobody Read.*
35. Bònoli / Piliarvu, 127–28.
36. On Danti, see Bònoli / Piliarvu, 137–41, with bibliography; also Masetti Zannini, "Docenti del clero," 177–79; Fiorani, *The Marvel of Maps,* passim.
37. On Cataldi, see Bònoli / Piliarvu, 141–43, with bibliography; Augusto De Ferrari, "Cataldi, Pietro Antonio," *DSI,* III, 125–29; Grendler, *Universities,* 421–22; Baiada / Cavazza, 153. Especially detailed on the development of algebra in Bologna is Bortolotti, *La storia della matematica,* 35–80 (see 87–93 on Cataldi's innovations, such as in the area of infinite number series).
38. On Magini, see Bònoli / Piliarvu, 143–47, with bibliography; Clarke, "Giovanni Antonio Magini (1555–1617)"; Ugo Baldini, "Magini, Giovanni Antonio," *DBI,* LXVII (2006), 413–18. Bortolotti, *La storia della matematica,* 139, sees him as "l'ultimo dei veri scienziati, che si siano dedicati, con intima convinzione, alla Astrologia." Magini's teaching is testified only lightly; according to Baldini there are, however, notes on Book III of Euclid's *Elements* in Milan, BAmbros. A.71.P inf., ff. 97–106.
39. Because the University of Bologna reserved his place at his home institution, Cassini continued to be listed in the rolls. On him, see Bònoli / Piliarvu, 162–67, with bibliography, now complemented by Bònoli, "Cassini e la tradizione astronomica," and Bernardi, *Giovanni Domenico Cassini.* Cassini's Bolognese lectures seem not to have survived apart from those of 1666, on which see Deias, "Un manoscritto inedito." For further comments, Busacchi, "Il nuovo spirito di ricerca," 425–32.
40. Given the prohibition (1616) of espousing Copernicus's teachings and the subsequent condemnation of Galileo (1633), such an endorsement would in any case have been unlikely.
41. Bònoli / Piliarvu, 162–67.

42. On these institutions, see §3.2.
43. On Manfredi, see Bònoli / Piliarvu, 176–79, with bibliography, to which add Ugo Baldini, "Manfredi, Eustachio," *DBI,* LXVIII (2007), 668–76, with important information on his lectures. For these, see also BUB, ms. 9H, item 25.
44. Baldini, "The Roman Inquisition's Condemnation of Astrology." Now see also Marcus, *Forbidden Knowledge,* passim.
45. For instance, it is nearly impossible to separate production from the increasing survival of manuscript and printed works after the fifteenth century and more general patterns such as university professors' readier embrace of print. A closer examination of the incentives for professors to print their works would also be relevant. Ideally one should also distinguish professors with a degree in arts alone from those with a degree in arts and medicine, and those who wrote their works while in Bologna from those who did so while teaching elsewhere.
46. Out of 128 individuals who taught natural philosophy in Bologna in the fourteenth and fifteenth centuries, those known to have written on the subject amount to some sixteen (12.5 percent); seventy professors are listed for the sixteenth century, of whom eighteen (25.7 percent) authored works of natural philosophy. See Lines, "Teachers."
47. See Lines, "Teachers," nos. 144 (Boccadiferro), 166 (Betti), 170 (Aldrovandi), 174 (Cartari), 179 (Galesi), and 181 (Pendasio).
48. Among others, see Lohr, II; Schmitt, *Aristotle and the Renaissance;* Bianchi, "Una caduta senza declino?"; *"Aristotele fatto volgare";* Martin, *Subverting Aristotle;* Del Soldato, *Early Modern Aristotle.*
49. See Bònoli / Piliarvu, 91–123, 125–47.
50. Bònoli / Piliarvu, 129–30 (Vitali), 131–33 (Gaurico). Gaurico, one of the most famous astrologers of his time, did not stay on in Bologna after 1506–1507 because he had apparently offended the lord Giovanni II Bentivoglio by predicting his imminent fall from power.
51. See, for instance, Reif, "The Textbook Tradition"; Schmitt, "The Rise of the Philosophical Textbook"; Grafton, "Textbooks and the Disciplines" (and, more generally, the other essays in *Scholarly Knowledge*).
52. Frans Titelmans, *Compendium naturalis philosophiae* (Antwerp: Simon Cock, 1530). See Lines, "Teaching Physics." Schmitt, "The Rise of the Philosophical Textbook," 794–95 and 803, emphasizes instead the importance of Paris.
53. It received thirty-six editions until 1596 and was reprinted as late as 1658. Even more successful was Titelmans's *Compendium dialecticae ad libros logicorum Aristotelis* (first published in 1533; forty-four editions up to 1621). See Lines, "Teaching Physics," 184.
54. Lines, "Teaching Physics," 195–96. For Aldrovandi's list of authorities, see §6.2.3. There is also evidence that Titelmans's compendium was taught

by a certain J. Rosa in 1593 (see Dublin, Marsh's Library, Z.2.2.5, item 2; Lohr, II, 390, 458; Kristeller, *Iter,* III, 191).

55. Schmitt, "The Rise of the Philosophical Textbook," 796–803.
56. See esp. Baldini, *"Legem impone subactis."*
57. On the reorganization involved in this work and the controversy it represented between Piccolomini and Jacopo Zabarella, see Lines, *Aristotle's* Ethics, 254–65.
58. Piccolomini's *Libri ad scientiam de natura attinentes* was republished, with a few changes, in following years: 1597, 1600, and (as *Naturae totius universi scientia perfecta atque philosophica quinque partibus ordine exactissimo absoluta* . . .) 1628; cf. Lohr, II, 341. On this work now see Claessens, "Francesco Piccolomini on Prime Matter and Extension."
59. See in particular Alessandro Piccolomini, *La prima parte della filosofia naturale* (Rome: Vincenzo Valgrisi, 1551); idem, *La seconda parte della filosofia naturale* (Venice: Vincenzo Valgrisi, 1554), republished in his *Della filosofia naturale* (Venice: Giorgio Cavalli, 1565); Scipion Dupleix, *Cours de philosophie* (Paris: Claude Sonnius, 1626), gathering together his previous works (published separately) on logic, physics, ethics, and metaphysics. On these works, see esp. Caroti, "L' 'Aristotele italiano' di Alessandro Piccolomini"; Giacomotto-Charra, *La Philosophie naturelle en langue française.*
60. Lohr, II; Risse, *Bibliographia philosophica vetus.*
61. Bronzino, 153; Vernazza, "La crisi barocca," 128–29. Apparently Sassi wrote *In Avicennam De indicationum morbi diebus* (Bologna: Giovanni Battista Ferroni, 1664), in 4°, according to the section *Seicentine bolognesi* of the BCAB website.
62. ASB, Annue Lezioni, b. 60, ff. 524r–525v (a. 1655), 542r–543r (a. 1657), 528r–529r (a. 1660).
63. On the Dominican writer Javelli (†1538, possibly in Bologna), a fairly prolific commentator of Aristotle, see Lohr, II, 202–4.
64. ASB, Annue Lezioni, b. 60, ff. 554r–557r (a. 1662–1663), 558r–563r (a. 1668–1669).
65. See ASB, Assunteria di Studio, b. 13, ff. 49v–50v (discussions on the reform of the *studium,* 14 July 1660): "Quarto. Che i dottori Artisti siano obligati a leggere testualmente Aristotele, non per *questiones.*" It is not clear that this proposal passed (see note on f. 53r, 22 August 1660: "Essendosi veduto che non sono stati approvati né il primo né il secondo de' capi della relazione sopra la riforma dello Studio che furono posti a partito, e sospeso di portare gl'altri"), but it reappears among another set of proposals of c. 23 August 1660 in ASB, Assunteria di Studio, b. 2, folder "1660 Senato Consulto."
66. ASB, Annue Lezioni, b. 61, ff. 574r–575v. See Vernazza, "La crisi barocca," 130; Mazzetti, 31.

67. Here the broader context may be the discussion by Domenico Guglielmini about the eternity of the heavenly bodies, something Guglielmini denied in his *De cometarum natura et ortu epistolica dissertatio* (Bologna: typis haeredis Dominici Barberii, 1681), which embraces a Cartesian point of view.
68. Bresadola, "Medicina e filosofia naturale," 394, 396. See esp., on this figure (who also taught medicine and anatomy), Mazzetti, 135; Martinotti, "L'insegnamento dell'anatomia," 134–38.
69. ASB, Annue Lezioni, b. 62, ff. 160r–161r.
70. See the three volumes of BUB, ms. 489 (Frati, *Indice,* no. 295).
71. On the Jesuit Pereira (c. 1535–1610), who taught humanities, philosophy, and theology in the Roman College and produced numerous works on Aristotle, see at least Lohr, II, 313–20.
72. On the influence of Galileo, see Betti, "Il copernicanesimo nello Studio di Bologna"; more recently, Cavazza, "Bologna e Galileo," and Bònoli, "Cassini e la tradizione astronomica" (also other essays in *Galileo e la scuola galileiana*). For that of Copernicus, see Grant, *In Defense of the Earth's Centrality and Immobility;* Russell, "Catholic Astronomers and the Copernican System." For the Index and the works of Copernicus, see *Catholic Church and Modern Science,* I.2, 1473–81.
73. For the following, the indispensable source is Bortolotti, *La storia della matematica;* see also Baiada/Cavazza.
74. For Mengoli's life and a recent survey of the scholarship, see Marta Cavazza, "Mengoli, Pietro," in *DBI,* LXXIII (2009), 486–89. Also eadem, "La cometa," 457–59; Baiada/Cavazza, 159; Bortolotti, *La storia della matematica,* 98–101, 137–38, and passim, for his innovations in mathematics and geometry.
75. For Gambarini, see the manuscript HRC Ranuzzi, Ph 12622; and Lines, "Aristotelismo a Bologna."
76. For Moletti, see Laird, "Nature, Mechanics, and Voluntary Movement."
77. Camarota, "La scienza nelle università."
78. On Mengoli's originality, see Pepe, "Note sulla diffusione della *Géométrie* di Descartes." Bortolotti, *La storia della matematica,* 137, claims that he kept his distance from the innovations of Evangelista Torricelli and that his works are hard to interpret: "fu sua cura costante il rivestire di classico paludamento le notevoli scoperte da lui fatte."
79. ASB, Annue Lezioni, b. 60, ff. 353r–354v and unnumbered. On the plan for 1656–1657, see Vernazza, "La crisi barocca," 140–41.
80. On the contents of mechanics, see Drake and Drabkin, *Mechanics in Sixteenth-Century Italy;* the review of that work in Schmitt, "A Fresh Look at Mechanics"; idem, "Galileo and the Seventeenth-Century Text-Book Tradition"; Rose and Drake, "The Pseudo-Aristotelian 'Questions of

Mechanics' in Renaissance Culture"; and Bertoloni Meli, *Thinking with Objects.*

81. ASB, Annue Lezioni, b. 60, ff. 353r–354v. Baliani (1582–1666) was a well-known mathematician and physicist who entertained a long correspondence with Galileo, among other things on astronomical matters. See most recently Capecchi, "Experiments."
82. ASB, Annue Lezioni, b. 60, unnumbered page.
83. ASB, Annue Lezioni, b. 60, unnumbered page: "Studiose auditor. / Annis praecedentibus proposuimus methodum; hoc anno, rei partem damus, alias partes, vita comite, deinceps daturi. Nullos in praesenti novos terminos adstruimus, neque eos quos antea; latius enim patet oratio, licet conceptus retinere sit necessarium."
84. See Bertoloni Meli, *Thinking with Objects,* 163: "By the 1660s, however, the scene had changed, and some of Galileo's results on falling bodies and parabolic trajectories, for example, were tentatively accepted or at least no longer regarded as a matter of serious controversy."
85. Krisciunas and Bistué, "Notes on the Transmission of Ptolemy's *Almagest,*" esp. 496.
86. ASB, Annue Lezioni, b. 61, ff. 56r–57r. See Vernazza, "La crisi barocca," 142; Dallari, III, passim; Mazzetti, 236, gives the year of his death as 1749.
87. BUB, ms. 111 (five folders).
88. For some examples of *tractatus,* see at least the lectures of Francesco Natali (HRC Ranuzzi, Ph 12763, vol. 2), Ioannes Hieronymus Sbaralea (BUB, ms. 1329), and Jacobus de Sandris (BUB, ms. 1077).
89. For his appointment, see Dallari, II, 141; the document (headed "Auctores quibus utor ad commentandum physicam Aristotelis") is in BUB, ms. Aldrovandi 60, f. xx(r–v). Aldrovandi's commentary remained in manuscript and has so far been overlooked by modern scholars, along with the rest of his production on Aristotle (no entry in Lohr, II). Lecturers elsewhere also prepared a list of their sources, as Sir Henry Savile did in connection with his lectures at Oxford on astronomy and mathematics in the 1570s; see Feingold, *The Mathematicians' Apprenticeship,* 47.
90. This may be a reference to the relevant work in the two-volume Greek edition of Aristotle (Basel: Joannes Bebelius, 1531) owned by Aldrovandi; see Lines, "A Library for Teaching and Study," 321, item 2. But it may also correspond to the separate Greek edition of the *Physics* published by Christian Wechel in 1532 (Lines, "A Library for Teaching and Study," 350, item 83). For his lectures, Aldrovandi would almost certainly have used a Latin text with Averroes's commentary. For a list of printed Averroes commentaries on Aristotle, see Hasse, *Success and Suppression,* 347–54. For those owned by Aldrovandi, see BUB, ms. Aldrov. 147, f. 60r–v; see Lines, "A Li-

brary for Teaching and Study," 352, item 87 (*Physics* with Averroes's digressions, edited by Marco Antonio Zimara, 1540).

91. ASB, Annue Lezioni, b. 60, ff. 470r–471r. Claudius was the son of George Scharpe, a Scotch medic teaching at Montpellier who was recruited for theoretical medicine *supraordinaria* in 1634–1637. See Mazzetti, 286–87 (who gives Claudius's likely year of death as 1648). An alternate candidate to George was Descartes; see Manning, "Descartes."
92. ASB, Annue Lezioni, b. 60, f. 471r: "Praecipui authores qui utemur ut plurimi erunt Averroes, D. Thomas, Scotus, Zabarella."
93. ASB, Annue Lezioni, b. 60, f. 478r.
94. ASB, Annue Lezioni, b. 60, f. 474r; cf. Vernazza, "La crisi barocca," 129, which mistakenly refers to "Erasmus." On evolving interpretations of this book, see Martin, "Francisco Vallés."
95. Martin, *Renaissance Meteorology,* 99–104.
96. ASB, Annue Lezioni, b. 60, f. 621r–v. On Arnoaldi, see Ascanelli, *I fascicoli personali,* 30; Vernazza, "La crisi barocca," 124–25; Mazzetti, 30.
97. ASB, Annue Lezioni, b. 60, ff. 622r–625r (undated). I have used Piccolomini, *Naturae totius universi scientia perfecta,* which contains a section *De philosophorum placitis* on 80–132. The work was earlier known as *Libri ad scientiam de natura attinentes.*
98. On the two figures and their influence outside of Padua, see *La presenza dell'aristotelismo padovano.*
99. On this little-known figure, who among other things wrote a life of Luigi Ferdinando Marsili, see *Anatomie accademiche,* II, 218n51.
100. ASB, Annue Lezioni, b. 62, ff. 274r–277v; Vernazza, "La crisi barocca," 135–36.
101. On the influence of Newtonian light theory in Bologna, including on Francesco Algarotti, see Casini, "The Reception of Newton's *Opticks,*" 220–22; idem, *Newton e la coscienza europea;* Cavazza, *Settecento inquieto,* 237–56. On the French physicist Mariotte (1620–1684), whose interests include optics, see Costabel, *Mariotte savant et philosophe.*
102. ASB, Annue Lezioni, b. 62, ff. 276v–277r.
103. Dallari, passim; Mazzetti, 295, no. 2921; Cavazza, *Settecento inquieto,* 66–70; eadem, "L'Istituto delle Scienze e il sistema accademico bolognese," 322, 323 (and *Storia di Bologna,* III.2, ad indicem).
104. Talbot, "A Successor of Corelli."
105. See the entry by Enrico Giusti (dated 2013) at http://www.treccani.it/enciclopedia/bonaventura-cavalieri_%28Il-Contributo-italiano-alla-storia-del-Pensiero:-Scienze%29/; Bottazzini, "La rivoluzione galileiana a Bologna"; Baldini, "La scuola galileiana," 394–99; Masetti Zannini, "Docenti del clero," 179–80; Bònoli / Piliarvu, 154–58. On his lecture outlines, Baiada / Cavazza, 155; Vernazza, "La crisi barocca," 138–39. In what

follows, I have not attempted to analyze the rich holdings (mainly anonymous) of notebooks and other materials in BCAB, Archivio Gozzadini, b. 27–28, and several BUB manuscripts (e.g., ms. 3647, caps. II and ms. 1072, vol. VII) relating to mathematics, geometry, and astronomy in the seventeenth and eighteenth centuries.

106. ASB, Annue Lezioni, b. 61, unnumbered folios.

107. ASB, Annue Lezioni, b. 61, unnumbered folios: "In omnibus praedictis infrascripti authores videri poterunt [?], nempe pro Ptolemaica sententia eiusdem *Almagestum,* et *Epitome* Regiomontani, cum *Theoricis* Peuerbachii. Pro Copernicana, tantum per hypotesim permissa, eiusdem *Opus de revolutionibus orbium* correctum, *Epitome astronomiae Copernicanae* Kepleri, obtenta a superioribus facultate, sicut et eiusdem *Commentaria de stella Martii, Tabulae Rodulphinae* et *Theoricae* Magini deservient. Pro sententia vero Tychonis et recentiorum, adeat studiosus eiusdem *Progymnasmata,* Longomontani *Astronomiam Danicam* et Lansbergii *Theoricas ac Tabulas,* qui quidem authores ut classici prae caeteris astronomiae cultoribus sunt perlegendi." The timing of this and other mentions of Brahe is interesting; according to Brockliss, "before 1640 no professor [in Paris] had even mentioned the existence of the Tychonic *via media*" (Brockliss, "Copernicus in the University," 193).

108. Bònoli / Piliarvu, 159–62; also Bortolotti, *Storia della matematica,* 143; Vernazza, "La crisi barocca," 137–38; Roberto Marchi, "Montalbani, Ovidio," *DBI,* LXXV (2011), 759–61.

109. On the Accademia dei Vespertini, see Battistini, "Le accademie," 200–201; Betti, "Tra Università e accademie." On the Accademia dei Gelati and the Accademia degli Indomiti, see Battistini, "Le accademie," 191, 193.

110. ASB, Annue Lezioni, b. 60, f. 347r.

111. Ovidio Montalbani, *Cometoscopia ovvero Specolatione intorno alle comete* (Bologna: Giovanni Battista Ferroni, 1646). See Cavazza, "La cometa," esp. 437–39 (for Montalbani), and 441–50, 459–64 (for Montanari).

112. Patergnani, "Ercole Corazzi," 275–78, with bibliography on this new chair (275n3). On Corazzi, see also Masetti Zannini, "Docenti del clero," 173–74, 180.

113. See Patergnani, "Ercole Corazzi" (list of his Bolognese manuscripts at 290–94). Corazzi continued to appear on the Bolognese rolls until 1726–1727, given that his appointment in Turin was a secondment. In the Istituto delle Scienze he taught military architecture; see Simoni, "Scuola d'artiglieria," 134. Corazzi's counsel should be compared with that of Rondelli, who in 1717 provided advice for Turin in his *Informatione intorno alla cattedra di filosofia e di matematica per il nuovo Studio di Torino,* Modena, Biblioteca Estense, Raccolta Rondelli, Filza II, Int. 10, ff. 2r–4r (Maffioli, "Guglielmini," 114–15).

114. For *Logistica* was a kind of mathematics in early modern philosophy. I am grateful to Craig Martin for clarifying this point for me.
115. ASB, Annue Lezioni, b. 61, ff. 234r–235v; see Vernazza, "La crisi barocca," 142–43. Transcriptions of this plan and of the one for 1713-1714 are in Giuntini, "Gabriele Manfredi," 259–60.
116. BUB, ms. 1939, f. 42r (Ercole Corazzi, undated prolusion, ff. 40r–43r): "Ego tamen sic existimo hanc ipsam, de qua tantopere dolent, memoriae tenuitatem, adiumento esse vel maximo ad colendum ingenium, et ad eam sibi pariendam facultatem, qua res praeclarissimas ipsi per se inveniant, inventasque ab alii magna sapientia discutiant. Ergo non recte sibi consulunt, qui veterum geometrarum lucubrationes memoriae mandant et alienis, ut ita dicam, divitiis delectantur."
117. BUB, ms. 1939, ff. 42v–43r: "Mens enim nostra, cum nullis obruatur figuris aut lineis, quas veteri usus geometria omittere nullo modo potest, uno ferme conatu ea percipit omnia quae per improbos alioquin labores numquam assequaeretur. Hinc Analytica studia a rebus sensibilibus multo magis mentem avolvunt, quam Geometrica, viamque latiorem sternunt ad abstracta penetranda.... Non desunt in Archimede et in Apollonio [*deleted:* et in Megarensi] propositiones quarum solutio ex magnorum voluminum lectione dependet... //cumque per Analysim omnia veterum mathematicorum opera paucis diebus complecti atque explicare abbunde possimus, in his tamen velimus aetatem integram immorari?" There is some irony in this disassociation from Archimedes, given that Corazzi dedicated considerable attention to his propositions (see Patergnani, "Ercole Corazzi," 272–74). On the usefulness of algebra vs. Euclidean geometry, see already L. F. Marsili, *Parallelo,* ed. Bortolotti, 415.
118. See the prolusion of May 1723 delivered in Turin (BUB, ms. 1939, ff. 77r–80r), studied in Spallanzani, "La Vecchia Filosofia."
119. For Plato, the allusion is clear already in the first lecture in Corazzi's plan from the year 1717–1718: "In Algebra et Analysi locum habere illam aeternarum cogitationum ἀνάμνησιν sive recordationem, qua dirigitur animus ad recolendas formas menti impressas" (ASB, Annue Lezioni, b. 61, f. 234r).
120. For a summary comparison with developments in moral philosophy, see Lines, "I classici," 82–88.
121. Cf. Simeoni, *Storia della Università,* 110: "Ma il progresso sostanziale dell'insegnamento della Medicina... si può arguire dal suo liberarsi dal legame con la logica e la filosofia e soprattutto dallo sviluppo preso dalle discipline ausiliarie."
122. Martin, "With Aristotelians like These," 139–46. The issue of the relationship between physics and metaphysics in Italy is complex; for the sixteenth

century, see at least Poppi, *Introduzione all'aristotelismo padovano,* 13–44; Kessler, "Metaphysics or Empirical Science?" Little work has been done on the seventeenth century.

123. Busacchi, "Il nuovo spirito di ricerca," esp. 417.

124. Mugnai Carrara, "Curricula e contenuti dell'insegnamento," 213–20; Grmek, "L'Enseignement médico-biologique"; see also Chapter 7.

125. For Montanari's life (1633–1687) and teaching in Bologna (1665–1679), see Rosino, "Geminiano Montanari"; Bònoli / Piliarvu, 169–72; Ivano Dal Prete, "Montanari, Geminiano," *DBI,* LXXV (2011), 816–23. For Malpighi, see §7.3.1.

126. See esp. Maffioli, "Guglielmini, Rondelli," 83–104, which outlines the discussions leading to the establishment of this chair (agreed by the Senate in 1694). For a brief outline, see Baiada / Cavazza, 154. On Guglielmini, see also Bònoli / Piliarvu, 172–74; Anna Rita Capoccia, "Guglielmini, Domenico," *DBI,* LX (2003), 738–42; Bertoloni Meli, *Thinking with Objects,* 181–86; and esp. Maffioli, *Out of Galileo,* 163–326. No course outlines for Guglielmini's teaching seem to survive. The "science of waters," or hydraulics, was a much-discussed issue in the seventeenth century, going back at least to Galileo's teacher Ostilio Ricci (see Bertoloni Meli, *Thinking with Objects,* 80–86); this study was of particular relevance for Bologna in light of ongoing discussions about diverting the river Reno into the Po.

127. Some comments on the limited development of Italian science due to the late reception of analytic geometry are in Baldini, "La scuola galileiana," 442–48; idem, "L'attività scientifica," 492–99 (for Bologna, esp. 493–95).

128. On Bacon's considerable influence in Bologna during this period, see Cavazza, *Settecento inquieto,* 203–5 and passim. I am grateful to Craig Martin for suggesting the possible link between Guglielmini and Bacon. Guglielmini's work is *De salibus dissertatio epistolaris physico-medico-mechanica* (Venice: Alvise Pavini, 1705).

129. Guglielmini, *Della natura de' fiumi, trattato fisico-matematico: In cui si manifestano le principali proprietà de' fiumi, se n'indicano molte sin'hora non conosciute, e si dimostrano d'una maniera facile le cause delle medesime* (Bologna: eredi di Antonio Pisarri a spese di Ludovico Maria Ruinetti libraro al Mercurio, 1697).

130. On Borelli, and particularly his activity within the Accademia del Cimento, see Boschiero, "Giovanni Alfonso Borelli."

131. On the Jesuits and their contribution to scientific debate in seventeenth-century Bologna, see Cavazza, "La scienza, lo Studio, i gesuiti a Bologna"; more broadly, Baldini, "La scuola scientifica emiliana," and Baroncini, "L'insegnamento della filosofia naturale nei collegi."

132. Document edited in Bortolotti, "La fondazione dell'Istituto," 406–19.

133. Baiada / Cavazza, 154.

134. Gomez Lopez, *Le passioni degli atomi.*

135. Cavazza, *Settecento inquieto,* passim.
136. Bortolotti, *La storia della matematica,* 11–12, provides the example of Bonaventura Cavalieri, who (though he had no faith in judicial astrology) had to learn how to cast horoscopes and even published a work on the subject, *Nuova prattica astrologica di fare le direttioni secondo la via rationale, e conforme ancora al fondamento di Kepplero per via di logaritmi* (Bologna: [Domenico Maria] Ferroni, 1639).
137. McConnell, "L. F. Marsigli's Visit to London in 1721," 198–200.
138. See *Anatomie accademiche.*
139. See Cavazza, "Early Work on Electricity and Medicine"; for the literature on Bassi until 2014, see eadem, *Laura Bassi,* 278–85.
140. On the usefulness and flexibility of the *quaestio* format, see at least Grabmann, *Die Geschichte der scholastischen Methode,* passim. For its manifestation in the culture of university disputations, see Lawn, *Rise and Decline;* Novikoff, "Toward a Cultural History of Scholastic Disputation"; Bianchi, "Le università," 50–51; Weijers, *In Search of the Truth.*
141. For criticisms of the universities, see Lupi, *Gli* studia *del papa,* 25–28, 209–15.
142. Lawn, *Rise and Decline,* 2.
143. Lawn, *Rise and Decline,* 144.
144. There is a similar unclarity in the broader chronological survey of Weijers, *In Search of the Truth.* For Italy, see also Grendler, *Universities,* 152–57.
145. For similar features of the *quaestio* in thirteenth- and fourteenth-century Europe in philosophy and theology, leading also to the production of *summae,* see Bianchi, "Le università," 48–55. For the situation in Oxford, where Aristotle was honored only in part despite the statutes (which underlined his authority), see Feingold, *The Mathematicians' Apprenticeship,* and the summary in idem, "Aristotle and the English Universities."
146. For other ways of incorporating Plato, see Grendler, *Universities,* 297–309; but several aspects of early modern philosophy were Platonizing, as attested by—among others—Gravina's inaugural oration in Rome in 1700 (Lupi, *Gli* studia *del papa,* 217).
147. Lawn, *Rise and Decline,* 143. See also Reif, "The Textbook Tradition."
148. Cf. *Artisten und Philosophen,* Part III; Ben-David, *The Scientist's Role in Society,* 54. Now see also Füssel, "Lehre ohne Forschung?," 77–85.
149. Among others, Vernazza, "La crisi barocca," tends to assume that one can chart intellectual innovations on the basis of changes in textbooks used, although at times he draws back from this approach.
150. Vernazza, "La crisi barocca" 149–50.
151. Bianchi, "Le università," 34–36.
152. See the studies of Brendan Dooley, including "La scienza in aula" and "Science Teaching as a Career."

7. FROM THEORY TO PRACTICE

1. Francis Petrarch, "On His Own Ignorance and That of Many Others," in *The Renaissance Philosophy of Man,* ed. Ernst Cassirer, Paul Oskar Kristeller, and John Herman Randall Jr. (Chicago: University of Chicago Press, 1948), 47–139 (quotation at 103).
2. Henricus Cornelius Agrippa, *De incertitudine et vanitate scientiarum declamatio invectiva* (Cologne: Dietrich Baum, 1584). See Siraisi, "Medicine, Physiology, and Anatomy," esp. 222–27.
3. For an overview of some positions, see Porter, "The Scientific Revolution and Universities," 531–35; Feingold, *The Mathematicians' Apprenticeship,* 1–7 and passim. It is safe to say that few aspects of Renaissance thought have been so willfully misunderstood as the scholastic method.
4. Siraisi, *Avicenna,* 98–103.
5. Siraisi, *Medieval and Early Renaissance Medicine,* 79–82.
6. On the distinctions between *theorica* and *practica,* very helpful are Siraisi, *Taddeo Alderotti,* 117–46; Agrimi and Crisciani, *Edocere medicos,* 21–47; Jacquart, "Theory, Everyday Practice." For the inheritance of this distinction from antiquity, see Cunningham, "The Theory / Practice Division of Medicine."
7. See Nutton, *Renaissance Medicine.*
8. ASB, Riformatori dello Studio, b. 21, ff. 2r–4v (*Universae lectiones hic describuntur quas legunt annuatim Artistae in almo nostro Bononiensi Gymnasio [1585–1586]*); Dallari, II, 241. For "ordinary" and other designations, see §2.2.1.
9. The first evidence for these chairs from the rolls comes in 1583 (Dallari, II, 214–16): *theorica* has one supraordinary chair, while *practica* has two (and later, three) such chair-holders. But already in 1563–1564, when he is lecturing on Hippocrates's *Epidemics,* Cardano describes himself as a "supraordinary" lecturer (Siraisi, *The Clock and the Mirror,* 329, entry for BAV, Vat. lat. 5848; cf. Dallari, II, 159, where he is simply listed "Ad lecturam Theoricae medicinae"). Siraisi mistakenly conflates "extraordinary" with "supraordinary" lectures in "L'insegnamento della medicina ippocratica," 154n5, 156 ("Le lezioni sugli altri libri ippocratici devono essere state 'straordinarie,' vale a dire ad arbitrio dell'insegnante").
10. Dallari, II, 215.
11. Siraisi, "Renaissance Readers," 214–15. For the early modern period, most scholarly studies have focused on Padua rather than Bologna.
12. Dallari, IV, 64–65; payments from ASB, Tesoreria, b. 95 (liber ordinarius rationum comunis Bononiae, a. 1431–1434), ff. 392v–396v.
13. On Monti, see Cristiani, no. 234; Lohr, II, 274.
14. Dallari, III, 5–8.
15. On the points above, Siraisi, "Renaissance Readers," 205–7, 214–15; cf. Bernabeo, "La scuola di medicina," 187.

16. See Pesenti, "Arti e medicina"; Crisciani, "Curricula e contenuti dell'insegnamento"; Siraisi, *Taddeo Alderotti,* 96–117.
17. Kibre, *Hippocrates latinus;* revisions and additions in Kristeller, "Bartholomaeus, Musandinus and Maurus of Salerno."
18. For lectures on Galen, see the discussion throughout this section. On Avicenna, *Canon,* I, the only Bolognese lectures known to me are those of Giovanni Costeo (*Disquisitiones physiologicae . . .*, 1589; Siraisi, *Avicenna,* 328–33 and passim; eadem, "Renaissance Readers," 221–23) and Cardano's prolusion of 1563 (see below; cf. Siraisi, *Avicenna,* 257n112). Manuscript lectures for Nicolò Betti Florentiola (t. 1647–1660) also survive, but to my knowledge have not been studied: see BUB, ms. 1077, vol. 1, item 2, containing *Lectiones matutinae super Quartam fen primi libri principis nostri Avicennae habitae anno Domini 1654* (ff. 63r–90r) and his *Lectiones matutinae de morbis particularibus internis efficientibus corporibus ipsis naturalibus habitae anno 1658 et 1659 in celeberrimo studio Bononiensi* (ff. 91r–107r). Both lecture series are incomplete. See Frati, *Indice,* no. 581; Frati, *Inventario,* IV, f. 454r–v. For Betti we also have his lecture outlines for 1654 in ASB, Annue Lezioni, b. 60, ff. 508r–509v (cf. Piccinno, *Fonti,* 30, item 21). As detailed at the end of this section, several manuscripts of other lectures for seventeenth- and eighteenth-century Bologna still require investigation, including for teachers such as Giacomo Sandri.
19. These texts and the definitions they provided are discussed in Ottosson, *Scholastic Medicine and Philosophy;* Siraisi, "Medicine, Physiology, and Anatomy," 219n18.
20. On the reception of Hippocrates, good starting points are Nutton, "Ippocrate nel Rinascimento"; Rütten, "Hippocrates and the Construction of 'Progress'"; idem, "Commenti ippocratici"; Siraisi, "L'insegnamento della medicina ippocratica"; Monfort, *Janus Cornarius et la redécouverte d'Hippocrate.*
21. For the following, see esp. Costa, "Gerolamo Cardano"; Simili, "Gerolamo Cardano lettore e medico"; Siraisi, "L'insegnamento della medicina ippocratica." For Cardano, in addition to Giuliano Gliozzi, "Cardano, Gerolamo," *DBI,* XIX (1976), 758–63, and Grafton, *Cardano's Cosmos,* now see Guido Giglioni, "Girolamo [Geronimo] Cardano," in *The Stanford Encyclopedia of Philosophy Online* (Summer 2019 edition), ed. Edward N. Zalta, https://plato.stanford.edu/archives/sum2019/entries/cardano/.
22. The appointment of Cardano was thrust onto Bologna by the pontiff, despite the Bolognese authorities' considerable reluctance—indeed, opposition; see Simili, "Gerolamo Cardano . . . Nota 2."
23. See the heading of that year's lectures in BAV, Vat. lat. 5848, f. 1r: "Hieronymi Cardani Mediolanensis civisque Bononiensis professoris supra ordinarii medicinae in expositione primorum librorum Epidemiorum

praefatio anni MCDLXIII" (quoted in Siraisi, *The Clock and the Mirror,* 285n29).

24. See Ulisse Aldrovandi, *Informatione del Rotulo del Studio di Bologna de' Philosophi et Medici all'Illustrissimo Cardinale Paleotto,* dated 26 September 1573, where he states that the *theorico sopraordinario* taught at the fourth morning hour and includes under that rubric Corti, Vittori, Cardano, but also Antonio Fracanzani, whom the rolls mention for 1562–1564 (Dallari, II, 156 and 159) as a teacher of *practica post tertiam:* "Viene per la quarta Hora et ultima il Theorico Sopraordinario, nella qual hora leggeva il Curtio, il Vittorio, il Fracanzano et ultimamente il Cardano, quali erano uomini celeberrimi" (BCAB, ms. B.3803, f. 4r). On Aldrovandi's document, see Lines, "Reorganizing the Curriculum," 11–13.
25. See Siraisi, *The Clock and the Mirror,* 122–23, and 126–31 on the reasons behind these specific texts. See also Pigeaud, "L'Hippocratisme de Cardan"; Martin, "Printed Medical Commentaries and Authenticity" (for Cardano, 21, 23–25).
26. Siraisi, "L'insegnamento della medicina ippocratica," 165–69; eadem, *The Clock and the Mirror,* 120–21, 132–33. See Cardano's statement "Galenus . . . homo fuit, et multis modis decipi potuit" (*Aph.* 1.17, *Opera* VIII, 251, cited in Siraisi, *The Clock and the Mirror,* 296n117). It is worth noting that this statement follows closely that of Pomponazzi on Aristotle in his *In septimum Physicorum:* "Aristoteles etiam fuit homo et decipi potuit" (Nardi, *Saggi sull'aristotelismo padovano,* 263n98), which in turn probably depended on an earlier *topos.* On the issue of authority in Renaissance medicine, see at least Toellner, "Zum Begriff der Autorität."
27. Hence the appropriateness of Siraisi's chapter title "The New Hippocrates" in *The Clock and the Mirror,* 119–45. See also Hirai, *Medical Humanism,* 110–14.
28. Siraisi, "Cardano, Hippocrates and Criticism of Galen"; eadem, *The Clock and the Mirror,* 132–34.
29. Siraisi, *The Clock and the Mirror,* 122–23; the work is in his *Opera omnia,* VIII, 213–580.
30. Siraisi, *The Clock and the Mirror,* 132.
31. For Cardano's view of the function of philology, see Siraisi, "L'insegnamento della medicina ippocratica," 163–65. The point can be usefully related to Cardano's insistence on *prudentia,* on which see Grafton, "Cardano's *Proxeneta*"; Giglioni, "Girolamo Cardano: University Student and Professor."
32. Cardano, *In Hippocratis Aphorismos,* in *Opera omnia,* VIII, 217b: "oportebit medicam artem per Aphorismos traditam discere, ut ea possimus commode et tempestive uti."
33. See, for example, his discussion of aphorism I, 12, in *Opera omnia,* VIII, 232b–238b.

34. The letter to Cesi is in Cardano, *Opera omnia,* IX, 453–54; the Bolognese prolusion is on 458–61.
35. Cardano, *Opera omnia,* IX, 473: "Et circa hoc sciendum quod sunt sex habitus valde similes. Primus est intellectus principiorum, qui non est scientia sed est nobilior illa, sed non est scientia, quia non est cum ratione seu discursu. Secundus est habitus qui deducitur ex principiis, et hic vocatur scientia. Tertius est habitus qui deducitur ratione ex sensibilibus tanquam principiis, et hic est habitus scientiae (non tamen scientia vera), in quo genere est medicina. Quartus est habitus deductus ex scientia per rationem, et hic vocatur scientia practica quia tendit in opus." Cited more fully in Siraisi, *Avicenna,* 232n24.
36. Siraisi, *Avicenna,* 232.
37. Siraisi, *Avicenna,* passim.
38. Both sets of lectures (never printed) are in London, Wellcome Library, ms 216: *In quartum acutorum Hippocratis* (ff. 1r–65v; unnumbered lectures dated 21 May to 12 July 1539) and *In artem medicinalem Galeni* (ff. 66r–281r, sixty-nine lectures dated 4 November 1539 to 15 April 1540; these lecture notes are incomplete, as indicated by the heading [only] for the lecture of 16 April, after lecture sixty-nine). On the Galen lectures, see Nutton, "'Qui magni Galeni doctrinam in re medica primus revocavit'"; Siraisi, *Avicenna,* 188–92 and passim. I am much indebted to Vivian Nutton for my understanding of Corti.
39. London, Wellcome Library, ms 216, f. 73v: "Item medicus semper debet speculari sicut omnis alia ars factiva. Si modi faciendi sunt per se noti, non indigent arte et cum hoc speculatione. Omnis ergo ars docens modum faciendi non notum, necesse est concludat ex epeculativis. Et in hoc proportionalis est omnibus aliis factivis artibus medicina."
40. Matteo Corti, *In Mundini Anatomen explicatio* (Pavia: Francesco Moscherini and Giovanni Battista Negri, 1550).
41. For his career and relevant bibliography, see Lines, "Teachers," no. 130. On his Galen commentary *Theoricae latitudinum medicinae liber,* see one of the very few discussions of Vittori: Maclean, "Diagrams in the Defence of Galen," 146–48. Some repertories give "Vettori" as the preferred version of his name; see https://data.cerl.org/thesaurus/cnp01875341 (accessed 14 August 2020).
42. Lohr, II, 481–82. Some evidence suggests that Vittori was a firm Aristotelian and defended him against the accusations of Pomponazzi; see Nardi, *Saggi sull'aristotelismo padovano,* 263n98.
43. In the first category, there are works by Vittori such as *Medicinalia consilia ad varia morborum genera . . .* (Venice: Vincenzo Valgrisi, 1551) and *Practicae magnae . . . de morbis curandis, ad tyrones, tomi duo* (Venice: Vincenzo Valgrisi, 1562). In the second category are Vittori's *Opus theorice latitudinum medicine*

ad libros Tegni Galleni [Bologna: Benedetto Ettore, 1516], not in EDIT16 but cited by Cristiani, no. 348, and included in the 1551 edition of the *Prognostic* commentary below (the work is referred to various times in Maclean, *Logic,* passim); idem, *In Hippocratis Prognostica commentariis* (Florence: Lorenzo Torrentino, 1551).

44. Vittori, *Commentaria in Hippocratis Aphorismos,* 1–9.
45. Vittori, *Commentaria,* 7–8: "Quo fit, ut ars medicinae sit longa, quoniam iudicium ex experientia est fallax et periculosum."
46. Dallari, ad indicem. Zecchi graduated in arts and medicine on 17 December 1558 (Bronzino, 56). For biographical data, see the sources cited in the CERL Thesaurus (http://thesaurus.cerl.org/record/cnp01352683).
47. N. F. J. Eloy, *Dictionnaire historique de la médicine ancienne et moderne* (Paris: H. Hoyois, 1778), IV, 614.
48. See Dallari, II, 221, where Zecchi is listed at "Ioannes Cecchius" and is the first listed of five teachers of the subject during the second morning hour. The professor of *theorica supraordinaria* during that year was Francesco Ceccarelli. Zecchi's lectures on Hippocrates are in his *In primam divi Hippocratis Aphorismorum sectionem dilucidissimae lectiones* (1586, indicated hereafter as *Aph. lectiones*).
49. For the dedicatee, see www.idref.fr/077136519 (accessed 15 August 2020). Zecchi sought his patronage in vain; King Stephanus died just a few months after the book's appearance. On Mercuri, see Lisa Roscioni, "Mercurio, Scipione," *DBI,* LXXIII (2009), 626–29, who, however, does not note his responsibility for the scholia of Zecchi's work. Mercuri graduated in arts and medicine on 12 December 1584 (Bronzino, 92) and held a *lectura universitatis* in medicine in 1584–1585 (Dallari, II, 218).
50. This had become a matter of increasing interest, particularly thanks to the studies of Girolamo Mercuriale, such as his *Censura et dispositio operum Hippocratis* (Venice: L. Giunti, 1583). At the time of Zecchi's publication, Mercuriale was still a professor of medicine in Padua; he would arrive in Bologna in 1587 and stay until 1592. During that period, he published the Greek text of Hippocrates along with a Latin translation: *Hippocratis Coi Opera quae extant Graece et Latine veterum codicum collatione restituta* (Venice: L. Giunti, 1588). See Giuseppe Ongaro, "Mercuriale, Girolamo," *DBI,* LXXIII (2009), 620–25.
51. Zecchi, *Aph. lectiones,* 3. Possibly an aspect either of Zecchi's prudentialism or of the contemporary religious turn (see Chapter 8).
52. Zecchi, *Aph. lectiones,* 5. Mercuri is less coy about naming and criticizing Cardano, who by this point has been dead for ten years (12).
53. Zecchi, *Aph. lectiones,* 4: "Propositum Hippocratis in hoc opere est, universa medicinae praecepta scribere, quae gaudeant tribus hisce conditionibus. Prima, ut sint recondita, non omnibus nota; quo fit, ut in hoc

opere non tractet de dissectione anathomica, quae est necessaria, quoniam tunc pueris haec nota erat. Secunda conditio, quod praecepta sint spectantia ad ipsam medicinae partem activam, non autem ad theoricam; ob hanc causam non de elementis, non de temperamentis, non de humoribus, non de spiritibus, neque de facultatibus pertractavit, sed solum ea contemplatus est, quae ad activae medicinae partem spectant. Tertia conditio, ut isthaec praecepta paucissimis verbis explicari possent; ob id de simplicibus et compositis medicamentis in hoc opere sermo non habetur, quoniam haec non possunt compendio et paucissimis verbis perstringi."

54. Siraisi, "Renaissance Readers," 218; eadem, *Avicenna,* 98–103, 229–31. On earlier and contemporary discussions of medicine as art or science, see Maclean, *Logic,* 70–76, and bibliography cited there; Siraisi, "Medicine, Physiology, and Anatomy," 221, 222–27.
55. Siraisi, *Avicenna,* 101–2.
56. Zecchi, *Aph. lectiones,* 10: "*Ars longa.* Ars est habitus cum recta ratione factivus ex Aristotele sexto Ethicorum capitulo quinto; quae quidem ars longa est et quod attinet ad inventionem et ad disciplinam. Ex quo loco duo colligimus, medicinam apud Hippocratem esse artem, non scientiam; colligimus etiam, medicum non posse instituere praesidia opportuna." Cf. Maclean, *Logic,* 74–75, who emphasizes Duncan Liddel's view (1628) of medicine as *poiētikē.*
57. Zecchi, *Aph. lectiones,* 18–21, quotation at 18: "Medicina tota factiva debet dici, nulla ex parte scientia."
58. Zecchi, *Aph. lectiones,* 20: "quoniam eam a naturali philosophia separavit Aristoteles vulgata illa propositione 'Ubi desinit philosophus, ibi incipit medicus.'" For a study and hefty bibliography of the history of this expression (which derived from the Aristotelian tradition in *De sensu et sensato,* 436a20–22, and *De iuventute et senectute,* 480b28, and enjoyed a considerable *fortuna* in the Renaissance, also in an almost identical variant employed by Da Monte), see most recently Bianchi, "'Ubi desinit physicus, ibi medicus incipit.'" The pioneering study is Schmitt, "Aristotle among the Physicians." Also see Siraisi, "Renaissance Readers."
59. Zecchi, *Aph. lectiones,* 20: "Ubi notare oportet, philosophum separare medicinam a philosophia, non penes res consideratas, cum eadem et a philosopho et a medico considerentur, sed penes considerandi modum: nam contemplatur philosophus veritatis tantum gratia; medicus autem, ut suas contemplationes ad opus, nimirum ad sanitatem, redigere possit."
60. Zecchi, *Aph. lectiones,* 21: "Concludatur igitur medicinam artem esse et non scientiam. Hinc colligitur, quod non potest proprie dividi in theoricam et practicam, quoniam practicum et theoricum sunt differentiae scientiae tamquam generis; at semoto genere, amoventur et differentiae. Cum

itaque medicina scientia dici non possit, nec in theoricam nec in practicam dividi poterit."

61. Siraisi, "Renaissance Readers," 221–23; eadem, *Avicenna,* 230–31. See Giovanni Costeo, *Disquisitionum physiologicarum . . . in primam primi Canonis Avicennae sectionem libri sex* (Bologna: Giovanni Rossi, 1589).
62. Oddo Oddi, *In primam Aphorismorum Hippocratis sectionem elaboratissima et lucidatissima expositio . . . ,* ed. Marco Oddi (Padua: Cristoforo Griffio, 1564), followed a few years later by idem, *In primam et secundam Aphorismorum Hippocratis sectionem* (Venice: Paolo e Antonio Meietti, 1572; repr., Padua: Paolo Meietti, 1588, 1589); idem, *In primam totam Fen primi libri Canonis Avicennae . . .* (Venice: Paolo e Antonio Meietti, 1575). Also Bernardino Paterno, *Explanationes in primam Fen prima Canonis Avicennae habita Patavii, dum primum theoricae ordinariae locum teneret* (Venice: Francesco De Franceschi senese, 1596).
63. On the relevance of Aristotelian philosophy to Renaissance medicine, see Schmitt, "Aristotle among the Physicians."
64. On Oddi and Paterno, see Siraisi, *Avicenna,* 232–35 and passim.
65. On Santorio, see Siraisi, *Avicenna,* 235–38 and passim; Jan Purnis, "Sanctorius," in *ERP* (2016). His *Commentaria in primam sectionem aphorismorum Hippocratis* (Venice: Marco Antonio Brogolli, 1629) is not mentioned in M. D. Grmek, "Santorio, Santorio," *DSB,* XII, 101–4.
66. Zecchi, *Aph. lectiones,* 24.
67. ASB, Annue Lezioni, b. 60, f. 510r (outline of lectures for 1642 on the *Aphorisms;* Piccinno, *Fonti,* 29, item 21). The list of Ercole Betti's authorities includes personalities such as Fonseca and Capodivacca in addition to Zecchi and Mercuriale. Mercuriale's engagement with Hippocrates is well known: see Jouanna, "Mercuriale, commentateur et éditeur d'Hippocrate." Mercuriale taught in Bologna from 1587 to 1592, but the only lectures to have survived from that period are *De vino et acqua,* published as part of his *Praelectiones Pisanae in epidemicas Hippocratis historias, non minus ad theoricam atque practicam medicinam* (Venice: Bernardo Giunta, 1597). In Pisa he lectured at least on Hippocrates's *Epidemics.*
68. See Zecchi's *Consultationes medicinales* (first volume printed in Rome: Guglielmo Facciotti, 1599; repr., Venice, 1617).
69. Daniel Sennert, *Institutionum medicinae libri V* (Wittenberg: Schurer, 1611). See Siraisi, *Avicenna,* 101n77; and esp. King, *The Road to Medical Enlightenment,* 16, 181–83.
70. George Scharpe, *Institutionum medicarum pars prima, a Claudio authoris filio philosopho, medico, et Bononiae professore in lucem edita: Illustrissimo Bononiensi Senatui dicata* (Bologna: Giacomo Monti, 1638), esp. 8–10.
71. These elements had previously been applied to *practica* alone: see Scharpe, *Institutionum medicarum pars prima,* 10.

72. For Giraldo's degree, see Bronzino, 209 (24 July 1687 in arts and medicine); for his *Theses,* see ASB, Riformatori dello Studio, b. 61 (Tesi e conclusioni dei lettori), item 7 (and Salterini, 163): "I. Medicina quamvis possit multifariam dividi, brevis tamen divisio est, qua in conservativam et curativam partitur" (3); "VII. . . . Hippocratis doctrinam de conferentia subsequente evacuationem, in qua talia purgantur, qualia purgari oportet, non ita veram esse arbitramus, quin aliquae etiam excretiones ad quas sequitur morbi levamen interdum noxia sint censendae" (5). Giraldo is listed on the rolls from 1698 to 1732 (Dallari, passim).
73. On Guglielmini, see §6.2.4.
74. Domenico Guglielmini, *Commentaria in primam Aphorismorum Hippocratis sectionem . . . ,* ed. Josephus Ferdinandus Gulielminus (Bologna: Thomas Colli ex typographia S. Thomae Aquinatis, 1748), esp. 34–36.
75. Domenico Guglielmini, "Pro theoria medica adversus empiricam sectam praelectio habita Patavii die 2 Maii 1702," in *Opera omnia mathematica, hydraulica, medica et physica,* 2 vols. (Geneva: Cramer, Perachon & Socii, 1719), II, 65 (57–72): "asserendum videtur, medentium opus nil aliud esse quam perpetuum, sed vere et solide, philosophari, et praxim exercere nil aliud quam theoricam medicinae partem in usum et aegrorum beneficium convertere." The Empiricist sect in medicine dated from ancient times and emphasized cures and experience in medicine rather than an examination of causes; it also tended to downplay the importance of anatomy (Nutton, *Ancient Medicine,* 150–52). It gained a strong following in sixteenth-century Italy among both learned and more popular physicians such as the Bolognese Leonardo Fioravanti (on whom see Eamon, "'With the Rules of Life and an Enema'"). For further details, see §8.2.1.
76. See ASB, Annue Lezioni, b. 62, ff. 131r–136v, esp. f. 131r–v (Piccinno, *Fonti,* 62, item 123). The literature on Oretti is limited; he obtained his degree in arts and medicine in 1694 (Bronzino, 212, and *Tributo di lodi poetiche dedicate al merito singolare del signore Francesco Antonio Oretti nobile di Bologna, che prende la laurea dottorale in filosofia e medicina* [Bologna: eredi del Sarti, 1694]) and in 1737 was made professor emeritus, though he continued to appear in the rolls until his death in 1746 (Mazzetti, 227, no. 2276). For the role of the sciences in medicine (particularly in Padua), see *Scientiae in the History of Medicine.*
77. Nutton, "Medieval Western Europe," 160–64; Siraisi, *Medieval and Early Renaissance Medicine,* 153–86.
78. See Malagola, *Statuta universitatis scolarium* (1405), 246–47, rub. 35. As seen in Chapter 2, the textbooks specified included the work of Bruno da Longoburgo as well as selections from the works of Galen, Rasis, and Avicenna; see also Siraisi, *Medieval and Early Renaissance Medicine,* 178.

79. An examination is already suggested in the statutes of the College of Arts and Medicine of 1378 (Malagola, *Statuti Collegio* [1378], 442–43, rub. 29) and continues through at least 1410 (Malagola, *Statuti Collegio* [1410], 516–17, rub. 24): the candidate is to be given two passages (*puncta*) in the morning to be examined in the evening, extracted from Avicenna, *Canon,* IV.3, and Bruno, *Chirurgia* (teaching of Avicenna, *Canon,* IV.3–6, confirmed in rolls for 1466–1467; Forni, *Chirurgia,* 55). The statutes do not, however, specify a degree in the subject, and Forni, *Chirurgia,* 54, insists that there was only a *licentia* conferred by passing the exam and a *privilegium* given by the college of doctors. Pomata, *Contracting a Cure,* 62, suggests (on the basis of the 1507 statutes of the College of Medicine) that surgeons could receive the doctoral degree, but she does not specify whether that was in medicine or surgery. I have not found awards of doctorates in surgery specifically in Bronzino. For the learned character of surgery, see esp. *Renaissance Surgery* (I owe this reference to Caroline Petit).
80. Aranzi's proposal was approved by the Cardinale Legate Alessandro Sforza (26 September 1570) and the Assunti di Studio (27 September 1570); see Martinotti, "L'insegnamento dell'anatomia," 80–91; Forni, *Chirurgia,* 75–76. Nutton ("Humanist Surgery," 81) notes that anatomy started to achieve independence and separate status from surgery in Padua around the middle of the sixteenth century (with Vesalius, Faloppia, Fabricius).
81. Pazzini, "Modernità e tradizione," 397–400.
82. Martinotti, "L'insegnamento dell'anatomia," 50–51.
83. Martinotti, "L'insegnamento dell'anatomia," 53–56.
84. On these (sometimes excessive) numbers, see Martinotti, "L'insegnamento dell'anatomia," 90–91, 93–95, 139–41.
85. Dallari, passim.
86. Bernabeo, "La Scuola di Medicina," 190; see esp. Martinotti, "L'insegnamento dell'anatomia," 88–90, 95–97, 122–26, 129–44. Brief comments in Teach Gnudi and Pierce Webster, *Gaspare Tagliacozzi,* 101–2.
87. Previous public dissections took place in specially mounted theaters, which then needed to be dismantled. The practice was widespread throughout Italy; see Klestinec, *Theaters of Anatomy;* Mattone and Olivari, "Le istituzioni del sapere universitario." On the new anatomical theater, see Giovanna Ferrari, "Public Anatomy Lessons"; cf. Robison, *Healers in the Making,* 103–8.
88. *Il teatro anatomico.*
89. ASB, Riformatori dello Studio, b. 20, f. 3v.
90. A helpful survey of several textbooks in surgery is Siraisi, *Medieval and Early Renaissance Medicine,* 162–74.
91. Siraisi, *Medieval and Early Renaissance Medicine,* 71.
92. Siraisi, *Taddeo Alderotti,* 55–58, 109–10.

93. Berengario, *Commentaria . . . super anatomia Mundini* (hereafter, abbreviated to *Commentaria*). On Berengario, the fundamental studies are Putti, *Berengario da Carpi,* with notes on the editions of Berengario's works at 131–62; and French, "Berengario da Carpi"; cf. Forni, *Chirurgia,* 62–67. Most recently, see the exhibition catalogue *Berengario da Carpi.*
94. Particularly important for Berengario's contribution to practice is his *Tractatus de fractura calvae sive cranei* (first ed., Bologna: Girolamo Benedetti, 1518), discussed and translated into Italian in Putti, *Berengario da Carpi,* 241–345. For the illustrations in Berengario, see Putti, *Berengario da Carpi,* 165–99; French, "Berengario da Carpi," 61–62.
95. Martinotti, "L'insegnamento dell'anatomia," 62–63, 66–69, 73–75; Wear, "Medicine in Early Modern Europe," 268–70.
96. Berengario, *Commentaria,* f. 443r, discusses Berengario's observations on the brain and the contrary opinions of others and concludes: "Multi tamen aliter sentiunt, sed sensus in hoc est iudex." See French, "Berengario da Carpi," 53, for other examples.
97. Berengario, *Commentaria,* f. 5r–v: "Cuius utilitas in multis cognoscitur"; "Ego enim pluries cognovi"; "album mixtum rubedini cognovi"; "Qui color non cognoscitur in mortuis"; "hoc etiam cognosci potest"; "sicut experti . . . [gemmas] cognoscunt."
98. Berengario, *Commentaria,* f. 5v: "cognoscuntur aegritudines ab operatione laesa et operationes laesae cognoscuntur habendo cognitionem operationum membrorum, et talis cognitio non habetur nisi per bonam anatomiam. Igitur anatomia est necessaria, et non solum in cognoscendis aegritudinibus, verum etiam in curandis et etiam in praeservandis et conservandis corporibus in sanitate, et sine tali cognitione plerumque erratur. . . . Et iuvat non solum anatomia in cura perficienda, verum etiam ad prognosticum."
99. Berengario, *Commentaria,* f. 6r: "Alio modo capitur anatomia pro scientia, et hoc dupliciter. Primo modo capitur pro scientia qua cognoscuntur membra tam simplicia quam compositae et eorum operationes, compositiones, colligantiae, situs et huiusmodi. . . . Alio modo capitur anatomia pro scientia cognitionis membrorum, ubi etiam traditur modus operandi cum manu actu et demonstrandi ipsa membra."
100. Berengario, *Commentaria,* f. 6v: "sed pro quanto ego video Avicennam de ea loqui, ubi theoricae loquitur, ideo dico eam esse partem medicinae theoricae. Et haec sufficiant de diffinitionis anatomiae. Utrum autem anatomia ut superius diffinita magis dicatur ars quam scientia, non est presentis negotii." On anatomy and theoretical medicine, cf. French, "Berengario da Carpi," 60.
101. Berengario, *Commentaria,* f. 6v: "Quartum autem videndum est, quid requiratur ad hoc, quod aliquis sit bonus anatomes sive anatomicus. Dico

quod primo et ante omnia oportere quod sit instructus in scientia medicinae et cum sibi annexo et delectetur legere ac pluries legere quae Aristoteles et Galenus et Avicenna et alii de animalibus dixerint, tam de vivis quam de mortuis, et quid dixerint iuniores."

102. French concedes that "it would be quite wrong to think that Berengario's practical instincts led him out of scholastic anatomy and into a new methodology based on sense perception" ("Berengario da Carpi," 52), but later emphasizes the importance for him of *anatomia sensibilis.*

103. Berengario, *Commentaria . . . super anatomia Mundini,* f. 459r: "quod hoc non videatur ad sensum, ego dubito quod Galenus magis sit imaginatus quod Rhete mirabile sit in loco antedicto . . . totaliter est concludendum Galenum errasse . . . credo quod alii omnes post Galenum ponant rhete mirabile per opinionem ipsius . . . haec tamen dixi cum reverentia." For other examples, French, "Berengario da Carpi," 56. The *rete mirabile* was (in Galenic thought) "a vascular network at the base of the brain" and gave rise to "a 'psychic *pneuma*' that circulated in the ventricles of the brain and throughout the nervous system" (Nutton, *Ancient Medicine,* 240). See also Siraisi, *Avicenna,* 338–39.

104. French, "Berengario da Carpi," 57.

105. Iacopo Berengario, *Isagogae breves perlucidae ac uberrimae in anatomiam humani corporis a communi medicorum academia usitatam,* 2nd ed. (Bologna: Benedetto Faelli, 1523); see Martinotti, "L'insegnamento," 58–59; Putti, *Berengario da Carpi,* 150–54.

106. Siraisi, *Medieval and Early Renaissance Medicine,* 87.

107. Baldassarri, "Seeking Intellectual Evidence," 50–59.

108. Nutton, "Humanist Surgery," esp. 78–80. On translations of Galen in the period, the fundamental study remains Durling, "A Chronological Census," supplemented various times, including in (and as explained by) Fortuna and Raia, "Corrigenda and Addenda." Now see the helpful website galenolatino.com. On the *fortuna* of the *Introduction,* see Petit, "The Fate of a Greek Medical Handbook."

109. Nutton, "Humanist Surgery," 84–85.

110. Nutton, "Humanist Surgery," 82–87. See Ambroise Paré, *Illustrations de la manière de traicter les playes faictes tant par hacquebutes que par flèches* (Paris: V. Gaulterot, 1545); Jacques Dalechamps, *Chirurgie françoise* (Lyon: Guillaume Rouillé, 1570).

111. I am grateful to Sara Miglietti for this observation.

112. See Guido Guidi (Vidius), *Chirurgia e graeco in latinum conversa* (Paris: Petrus Galterius, 1544), discussed in Nutton, "Humanist Surgery," 87–88.

113. G. C. Aranzi, *In Hippocratis librum de vulneribus capitis commentarius brevis, ex J. Caes. Arantii . . . lectionibus collectus, per Claudium Porralium* (Lyon: L. Cloquemin, 1579; repr., Munich: G. K. Saur, 1989–1990). See Forni, *La chirurgia,* 86–88; Nutton, "Humanist Surgery," 88–90.

114. Nutton, "Humanist Surgery," 89.
115. EDIT16 lists Venetian editions of 1586 and 1587 (both by Iacobus Brechtanus) and 1595 (by Bartholomeus Carampelius).
116. Pierce Webster and Teach Gnudi, "Documenti inediti." Fuller information (with supplementary and different documentation) in Teach Gnudi and Pierce Webster, *Gaspare Tagliacozzi.* Now see also Paolo Savoia, "Tagliacozzi, Gaspare," *DBI,* XCIV (2019), online.
117. On Tagliacozzi's education and student days, see Teach Gnudi and Pierce Webster, *Gaspare Tagliacozzi,* 27–88 (to be treated with caution in its more speculative parts, such as on the importance of Girolamo Cardano's teaching for Tagliacozzi). On plastic surgery in Italy, the classic study is Corradi, "Dell'antica autoplastica italiana." Now see Ortiz Monasterio, *Dolor y bellezza;* Gadebusch Bondio, *Medizinische Ästhetik;* Santoni-Rugiu and Sykes, *History of Plastic Surgery,* 167–212; Savoia, *Cosmesi e chirurgia.* Also helpful is Monga, "Odeporica e medicina," which comments on earlier achievements in the field by the Vianeo family in Tropea (Calabria).
118. Pierce Webster and Teach Gnudi, "Documenti inediti," 90, doc. XXXI.
119. Teach Gnudi and Pierce Webster, *Gaspare Tagliacozzi,* 65, 149–52, 156–63, and passim.
120. Pierce Webster and Teach Gnudi, "Documenti inediti," 27–28; Teach Gnudi and Pierce Webster, *Gaspare Tagliacozzi,* 146–48.
121. For a detailed summary, see Teach Gnudi and Pierce Webster, *Gaspare Tagliacozzi,* 197–216.
122. From the translation by Virginia Burrell in Teach Gnudi and Pierce Webster, *Gaspare Tagliacozzi,* 453; see Tagliacozzi, *De curtorum chirurgia,* ded. letter (no pag.): "Itaque in id, qua potui, cura et diligentia incubui, cum meae professionis esset, ut aliquid etiam in hoc genere praestari et ad commodum publicum in lucem prodire possit. In quo id me effecisse credo, ut ego non solum aliis medendo profuerim, sed hanc partem ad veram artis normam tandem reduxerim, quo et scriptis tradi et iuxta eius leges unusquisque vel mediocriter exercitatus, tuto et feliciter operari valeat."
123. Tagliacozzi, *De curtorum chirurgia:* "Quare dignum ratus, ut quis suam hac etiam in parte impenderet operam, et praecipue cum audissem esse quosdam in Calabria qui, usu potius anormi et fortuito quam ratione confirmato, hanc artem, si tamen ars dicenda est, tractaverint."
124. Tagliacozzi, *De curtorum chirurgia,* 1–2: "Nam si ipsam medicinam artem caeterarum omnium praestantissimam vocare, et iure quidem merito, non dedignamur, tam ob subiecti nobilitatem, quam ob finis quem in operando spectet, praestantiam (taceo varietatem rerum) atque ideo dignissimam, ut in illius signa unusquisque conveniat, idem et huic arti nostrae, non iniqui iudices possumus concedere, quae tantae matris filia, ex ipsis medicinae visceribus progenita, ratione enutrita, experientia

confirmata, operum eius aemula tandem in solem prodit et hominum oculis sese conspiciendam subiicit."

125. For references to Zecchi, see Teach Gnudi and Pierce Webster, *Gaspare Tagliacozzi,* ad indicem; but the authors do not clarify what the relationship between the two medical doctors may have been.
126. See the account of these various developments in Wear, "Medicine in Early Modern Europe"; Porter, "The Eighteenth Century." The works of Paracelsus (Theophrast von Hohenheim, 1493 / 1494–1541) were not prohibited until 1580; see *Catholic Church and Modern Science,* I.3, 2166–96. It is clear, however, that they were known to the medical doctor Fabrizio Bartoletti (t. 1613–1626); see Grendler, *The University of Mantua,* chap. 5.
127. For the following, I have relied on the outlines in Bertoloni Meli, *Mechanism, Experiment, Disease,* 307–30; Cavazza, "The Uselessness of Anatomy"; eadem, *Settecento inquieto,* 185–200; Pistacchio, "Il contrasto tra Malpighi e Sbaraglia"; Bresadola, "Medicina e filosofia naturale," 376–96. For biographical details, see also Cesare Preti, "Malpighi, Marcello," *DBI,* LXVIII (2007), 271–76; Marco Bresadola, "Sbaraglia, Giovanni Girolamo," *DBI,* XCI (2019), 169–71. Good work is being done by Luca Tonetti and others on previously unstudied manuscripts and notes by Malpighi in the BUB.
128. The work is misleadingly signed off "Scribebam raptim Gottingae idibus Septembris 1687"; repr. in Malpighi, *Opera posthuma,* 258–67.
129. Malpighi, *Opera posthuma,* 264.
130. Malpighi, "Responsio ad epistolam cui titulus est, *De recentiorum medicorum studio dissertatio epistolaris ad amicum,*" in idem, *Opera posthuma,* 276–387; Bresadola, "Medicina e filosofia naturale," 388–91.
131. Bertoloni Meli, *Mechanism, Experiment, Disease,* 321.
132. For this paragraph, see Bertoloni Meli, *Mechanism, Experiment, Disease,* 331–44.
133. Modern edition in *Consulti di Marcello Malpighi (1675–1694),* ed. G. Plessi and R. A. Bernabeo, 3 vols. (Bologna: Istituto per la Storia dell'Università, 1988–1992).
134. Gentilcore, "The Organisation of Medical Practice."
135. Forni, *Chirurgia,* 113; Cavazza, *Settecento inquieto,* 59, 74, 75; Mazzetti, 280, no. 2784; Fantuzzi, VII, 306.
136. For Sandri's lectures, see the (somewhat disordered) contents of BUB, ms. 1077.
137. ASB, Annue Lezioni, b. 61, ff. 7r–16r (Piccinno, *Fonti,* 35, item 2).
138. Life and bibliography in Giuseppe Gullino and Cesare Preti, "Marsili, Luigi Ferdinando," *DBI,* LXX (2008), 771–81. Also see the discussion of the Istituto delle Scienze in §3.2.
139. L. F. Marsili, *Parallelo,* ed. Bortolotti, 410–13 (medicine), 415 (mathematics); see also Cavazza, *Settecento inquieto,* 207–9.

140. L. F. Marsili, *Parallelo,* ed. Bortolotti, 415: "deve servire più d'ogni altra ai nostri figli."
141. L. F. Marsili, *Parallelo,* ed. Bortolotti, 410–11: "L'anatomia insegna la struttura organica, e questa dai nostri antichi padri nell'Università fu instituita con quel metodo di sofistici argomenti, più per far spiccare l'esperienza di argomentare, che la dottrina dimostrativa per erudire gli scolari. Questa maniera deve avere la sua conservazione per un puro decoro delle cattedre, senza però che le Signorie Vostre Illustrissime negligano di sentire il mio riverente consiglio."
142. "Le Costituzioni dell'Istituto delle Scienze," in Bertolotti, "La fondazione dell'Istituto," 423–35, cap. V (428–30); esp.: "Avranno i professori particolare avvertenza di non fare negli esercizi alcuno studio o discorso scientifico, che convenisse alla forma d'una lezione, o che si potesse chiamare una lezione propria delle cattedre del Pubblico Studio, dovendo gli esercizi versare principalmente nella pratica delle osservazioni, operazioni, esperimenti, ed altre cose di simile natura. S'imputerà a gran colpa la trascuraggine di questo articolo" (429, art. 3). On the original relationship between the two, also Cavazza, "L'Istituto delle Scienze e il sistema accademico bolognese," 329–31.
143. Gullino and Preti, "Marsili, Luigi Ferdinando."
144. Maffioli, "Guglielmini, Rondelli," 113; Mazzetti, 270, no. 2692, indicates that he was made emeritus (but remained on the rolls) until his death in 1738–1739.
145. Maffioli, "Guglielmini, Rondelli," esp. 81–93.
146. Or, more fully, "Ostensione delle operazioni chirurgiche nei cadaveri," according to the instruction of Benedict XIV on 23 August 1742, in *Lettere, brevi, chirografi, bolle, ed apostoliche determinazioni prese dalla Santità di Nostro Signore Papa Benedetto XIV,* 3 vols. (Bologna: Longhi, 1749–1756), I, 258.
147. See Veggetti, "Pier Paolo Molinelli," 121–23. On Molinelli, see also Forni, *Chirurgia,* 132–36; Pantaleoni and Bernabeo, "Pier Paolo Molinelli"; Mazzetti, 213, no. 2134; Fantuzzi, *Notizie,* VI, 37.
148. Brockliss, "Copernicus in the University," 190.
149. A. F. Marsili, *Memorie per riparare i pregiudizi.*
150. Brambilla, "La medicina nel Settecento."
151. Pozzi, *Orationes duae,* esp. 33–35.
152. *Scientiae in the History of Medicine.*

8. THE RELIGIOUS TURN

1. See Zarri, "Chiesa, religione, società"; Mazzone, "Vita religiosa e vita civile"; Giacomelli, "Le Bolle pontificie."
2. For excellent work on these topics, see the note above and Marcus, *Forbidden Knowledge;* Turrini and Valenti, "L'educazione religiosa"; Dall'Olio,

"L'attività dell'Inquisizione di Bologna"; and, more broadly, *Catholic Church and Modern Science,* I.1, 1–413 (with numerous documents). I offer some limited comments in §4.3.

3. Zarri, "Chiesa, religione, società," 948–76; eadem, "The Church, Civic Religion, and Civic Identity," 373–77. For the religious climate of the second half of the seventeenth century, see Antonio di Paolo Masini, *Bologna perlustrata,* 3 vols. (Bologna: Vittorio Benacci, 1666 [1650]; repr., Bologna: Forni, 1986). For confraternities, see esp. Fanti, *Confraternite e città;* Terpstra, *Lay Confraternities;* and idem, "Confraternities and Civil Society."
4. Zarri, "Chiesa, religione, società," 983.
5. Prodi, *Il cardinale Gabriele Paleotti,* II, 75–136. On music, see Elvidio Surian, "Bologna," in Grove Music Online, with a rich bibliography, at https://doi.org/10.1093/gmo/9781561592630.article.03453 (I wish to thank Eugenio Refini for this reference and access to this entry); on Bolognese painting, the classic essay (with particular attention to Guido Reni and devotional images) is Fumaroli, "Le Golgotha bolonais."
6. See Dooley, "Social Control."
7. For Bologna (as for other early modern universities, both north and south of the Alps), the religious piety of students and professors has attracted little scholarly attention except for cases of deviance or heterodoxy. For some stimulating observations, see Füssel, "Zwischen Beten und Fluchen."
8. As observed by von Greyerz, *Religion and Culture,* 11–12, "the social elite of the sixteenth and seventeenth centuries participated actively in the popular culture of its day."
9. For the teaching of theology in Padua, see Poppi, *Ricerche sulla teologia e la scienza;* Gaetano, "Renaissance Thomism"; Grendler, *Universities,* 367–68. For the situation in Pavia, Bernuzzi, "L'insegnamento della Teologia."
10. Ehrle, *Statuti:* the privilege for the faculty dates from 1362; the first statutes are from 1364.
11. So far I am aware of only four such instances: Jacobus de Thedrisiis, O.F.M., and Guido de Guetiis, O.P., in 1387–1388 (Dallari, IV, 16); Michael (Aiguani) de Bononia, O.Carm., who taught "Psalterium sacre theologie" in 1394–1395 (ASB, Condotta, bollette, b. 61, f. 114r); and Christophorus de Bononia, O.E.S.A., who taught *sacra scriptura* "in cathedrali ecclesia Sancti Petri certis diebus et horis" for a salary of L. 25 in 1411–1412 (ASB, Tesoreria, b. 48, f. 153r, dated 30 July 1412; cf. Dallari, IV, 32–33). In what follows I use "theology" as a shorthand also for allied subjects such as sacred scriptures and metaphysics.
12. Dallari, I, 11–12; II, 119–20, 461–62; III, 66–69. I exclude teachings such as arithmetic, grammar *pro quarteriis,* and *lecturae universitatis,* as well as the *anatomici emeriti* listed in 1749.

13. Theology did not have its own teaching roll: its teachings were simply added to those of arts and medicine, as also happened in the case of Padua and other Italian universities.
14. A long list is given in Masetti Zannini, "Docenti del clero," esp. 175–88.
15. For more extensive bibliography in relationship to some of the following points, see Lines, "Reorganizing the Curriculum," 2–3. The seminal reference point is Turrini, "L'insegnamento della teologia," which considers the teaching of theology throughout Bologna and not just in the *studium* (for which see esp. 448–51, 457–64).
16. Dallari, II, 167; Turrini, "L'insegnamento della teologia," 457–58; cf. Vernazza, "La crisi barocca," 132–33, 173; and Simeoni, *Storia della Università,* 119–23.
17. Dallari, II, 271. On dogmatic theology and its first (and very influential) teacher, the Dominican friar Vincenzo Ludovico Gotti—who taught from 1719 to 1743—see Turrini, "L'insegnamento della teologia," 460–63, which emphasizes its progressive aspects but also suggests that there were hesitations about introducing it.
18. Turrini, "L'insegnamento della teologia," 458–60, 462, and passim. Hebrew was taught in the university from 1464 to 1490 by the *converso* Vincentius de Bononia (Dallari, I, passim). For the difficulties in restarting this teaching under Archbishop Paleotti, see Prodi, *Il cardinale Gabriele Paleotti,* II, 225–26. The introduction of Hebrew, Arabic, and Chaldean was required "as soon as possible" ("quanto prima") by the legate Sacchetti's 1639 *Ordinationi,* but evidently had no effect.
19. For cases of conscience, see Dallari, II, 414. This teaching, which was popular and had been assigned to numerous (up to four) instructors, came to cease after 1736; see Turrini, "L'insegnamento della teologia," 458 and passim; eadem, "Le letture di casi di coscienza." The subject was first taught to the clergy in Bologna's cathedral, a development encouraged by Bishop Giovanni Campeggi (1553–1563); see Turrini, *La coscienza e le leggi.* For moral theology, Dallari, II, 172; Turrini, "L'insegnamento della teologia," 458. For church history, canons, and church councils, Dallari, III.1, 269, 271; Turrini, "L'insegnamento della teologia," 462.
20. Turrini, "Le letture di casi di coscienza," 228–29.
21. Metaphysics had two lecturers (one a Franciscan, the other a Servite) until 1566, when it was assigned to just one (usually a Franciscan). On the way in which the religious orders came to provide lecturers in specific subjects to the *studium,* see Turrini, "L'insegnamento della teologia," 448–51. Unlike Turrini, however, I believe that metaphysics needs to be considered as part of the teachings allied with theology. Grendler, *Universities,* chap. 10, correctly brackets metaphysics with theology (see 366–72 for comments on the subject's teaching in Padua).

22. *Universae lectiones hic describuntur quas legunt annuatim Artistae in almo nostro Bononiensi Gymnasio [1585–1586],* in ASB, Riformatori dello Studio, b. 21, ff. 2r–4v. The rolls do not start specifying the contents of the teaching of metaphysics until 1591.
23. Lines, "Reorganizing the Curriculum," 11–13. This was still the view in the early eighteenth century according to Bartolomeo Aldrovandi's *Quo ordine studiis incumbendum sit,* where metaphysics is placed immediately after logic. See this chapter's Conclusion.
24. See quotation in Turrini, "L'insegnamento della teologia," 449. The request resulted in a compromise: lecturers from the Celestines and the Dominicans were added in 1649 (Dallari, II, 461 and passim), at least for a time.
25. Sacchetti, *Ordinationi,* points 29 and 46.
26. ASB, Annue Lezioni, b. 60, f. 428r–v: "Textum Aristotelis interpretabor iuxta expositionem Divi Thomae. Quaestiones resolvam ex principiis et doctrina eiusdem. Pro interpretatione igitur textus discipuli perpetuo adhereant comento S. Thomae. Pro prima quaestione videant Suarez et alios apud ipsum citatos, imprimis vero S. Thomam. Pro reliquis omnibus quaestionibus videant Flandram et alios quos idem auctor citat, imprimis vero S. Thomam." See also Vernazza, "La crisi barocca," 125.
27. On contemporary discussions about what metaphysics considered, see *I dibattiti sull'oggetto della metafisica.*
28. ASB, Annue Lezioni, b. 61, f. 74r–v.
29. ASB, Annue Lezioni, b. 61, f. 427.
30. *The Council of Trent: The Canons and Decrees of the Sacred and Oecumenical Council of Trent,* ed. and trans. J. Waterworth (London: Dolman, 1848), 24–27 (Session V, Decree of Reformation, chap. 1); cf. *Conciliorum Oecumenicorum Decreta,* 668–69.
31. *The Council of Trent,* 255–56 (Session XXV, Decree on Reformation, chap. 2); *Conciliorum Oecumenicorum Decreta,* 785.
32. For general comments and some historiographical context, see von Greyerz, *Religion and Culture,* esp. 44–49, 52–55.
33. Hersche, *Italien im Barockzeitalter,* 183–96.
34. For more details on what follows, see Lines, "Papal Power"; idem, "Reorganizing the Curriculum."
35. Letters from the cardinal nephew Filippo Boncompagni to the Bolognese archbishop and the Senate make explicit reference to the desire to implement the council's decrees; see Lines, "Papal Power," 664n4; ASB, Senato, Bolle e Brevi (copie manoscritte e a stampa), b. 14, f. 125r–v, respectively. See §1.3.3.
36. Prodi, *Il cardinale Gabriele Paleotti,* I, 208; idem, *Il sacramento del potere,* 313ff; Dall'Olio, *Eretici e inquisitori,* 400n24.

37. Gaspare Tagliacozzi took an oath of adherence to the Catholic faith, supported by two witnesses attesting that he was a "true and Catholic Christian," on 11 Sept. 1570, the day before his doctoral exam in medicine (Pierce Webster and Teach Gnudi, "Documenti inediti," 23–24, 92–93). For further archival sources, see Dall'Olio, *Eretici e inquisitori,* 400n24 (note that private tutors were subject to this oath as well). On how this oath compares to similar requirements in Protestant German-speaking lands, see Prodi, "Il giuramento universitario"; Roggero, "Professori e studenti," 1050–57; Grendler, *Universities,* 194–95.
38. Grendler, *Universities,* 183–86, 191–94, 484–86, 506–7; Kristeller, "Learned Women," 202–4, in the context of Elena Cornaro's degree in Padua (1678).
39. See the essays and bibliographical pointers in *Lauree.*
40. A point emphasized by Turrini, "L'insegnamento della teologia," 447–49.
41. On threats from these, see esp. Prodi, *Il cardinale Gabriele Paleotti,* II, 225–26, 243; Dall'Olio, *Eretici e inquisitori,* 294–305. For a recent sketch, Paolo Prodi, "Paleotti, Gabriele," *DBI,* LXXX (2014), 431–34.
42. Prodi, *Il cardinale Gabriele Paleotti,* II, 138–45; Turrini, "Le letture di casi di coscienza." This teaching had actually been instituted a few years earlier, under Bishop Giovanni Campeggi; see Zarri, "Chiesa, religione, società," 952. On the seminary students, who were taught by the Jesuits in combined classes but who tended to drag down the general level, see Grendler, *The Jesuits and Italian Universities,* 283–84.
43. Prodi, *Il cardinale Gabriele Paleotti,* II, 225–26. As late as 1820, the professor of Greek and Oriental languages, Giuseppe Mezzofanti, had to defend the usefulness of learning Greek; see Masetti Zannini, "Docenti del clero," 174.
44. Turrini, "L'insegnamento della teologia," 448n42.
45. See Lines, "Reorganizing the Curriculum," 18; the *Memoria,* in ASB, Assunteria di Studio, b. 1 (9 December 1585), states: "Intendendosi che dagli Illustri Signori Quaranta si è al presente per fare provisione a diverse cose dello studio, è parso bene a Mons. Ill.mo et Rev.mo Cardinale Paleotti Arcivescovo per debito dell'ufficio suo, di ricordare l'infrascritte cose. Primamente che saria bisogno d'uno che insegnasse la lingua Hebraica, com'è stato constituito nel Concilio Viennense. . . . Et parimente un professore di lingua Greca necessaria alla cognitione della scrittura sacra. . . . Il Concilio Tridentino sess. 5, c. 1 ordina 'Quod in gymnasiis publicis habeatur lectio sacrae scripturae caeterorum omnium maxime necessaria et honorifica.' Però essendo questa la lettura che sola et principalmente preme al Sacro Concilio, si ricorda che non deve essere inferiore in modo alcuno di stipendio all'altre di Theologia."
46. Prodi, *Il cardinale Gabriele Paleotti,* II, 224; Lines, "Reorganizing the Curriculum," 17–18, 36–41; see §1.1.1.

47. Lines, "Gabriele Paleotti."
48. For a testimony of the perceived lack of religious devotion in Bologna in the early 1570s, particularly among students, see Dall'Olio, *Eretici e inquisitori,* 398–99.
49. Prodi, *Il cardinale Gabriele Paleotti,* II, 214–68; Dall'Olio, *Eretici e inquisitori,* 401–3.
50. Contained in *Archiepiscopale Bononiense sive de Bononiensis Ecclesiae administratione, auctore Gabriele Paleoto S.R.E. Cardinali* (Rome: Giulio Burchioni and Giovanni Angelo Ruffinelli, 1594), pars V. Carlo Sigonio is named there as the statutes' author.
51. On this association (which took its name from the Catholic view that Mary had not died, but had been assumed to heaven), see Fabrini, *Le congregazioni dei Gesuiti,* 17–20; Prodi, *Il cardinale Gabriele Paleotti,* II, 215–20, 439; Brizzi, *Formazione,* 76, 94–95; Grendler, *The Jesuits and Italian Universities,* 285–86; and esp. Turrini, "'Me et totam congregationem defende.'"
52. Grendler, *The Jesuits and Italian Universities,* 291–97.
53. Turrini, "L'insegnamento della teologia."
54. For these institutions, see Prodi, *Il cardinale Gabriele Paleotti,* II, 143; Turrini, "L'insegnamento della teologia," 449.
55. On the problem of the unicity of the intellect and how it was treated in the sixteenth century, see Hasse, *Success and Suppression,* 214–29, 243–46, 491n114.
56. Craig Martin, "Averroism, Renaissance," in *ERP* (2018); Leen Spruit, "Pietro Pomponazzi," in *The Stanford Encyclopedia of Philosophy* (online); Nardi, "Intorno alla 'quaestio' magliabechiana," 332–39; Des Chene, *Life's Form,* chap. 4.
57. Bianchi, *Il vescovo e i filosofi.*
58. Bianchi, *Pour une histoire,* 87–108; see esp. quotations at 99n1 and 102n1.
59. A case in point is Alessandro Achillini; see Nardi, "I *Quolibeta de intelligentiis* di Alessandro Achillini."
60. G. D. Mansi et al., *Sacrorum conciliorum nova et amplissima collectio,* XXXII (Paris: H. Welter, 1902), 842–43, quoted in Kraye, "The Immortality of the Soul," 64n1. For a discussion of the difficulties of interpreting this bull, see Bianchi, *Pour une histoire,* 119–24.
61. For a concise and helpful description of these positions, see Spruit, "The Pomponazzi Affair," 227–28.
62. Kraye, "The Immortality of the Soul," 54–57. For the bibliography on Barozzi's decree, see Bianchi, *Pour une histoire,* 119n1; Hasse, *Success and Suppression,* 485n39. Here and in what follows I use labels such as "Alexandrist" and "Averroist" as a shorthand for approaches that make heavy (but not necessarily exclusive) use of the positions of either Alexander of Aphrodisias or of Averroes, often in rough agreement with one of the two. One

should keep in mind, however, that Renaissance interpreters rarely followed one single commentator; rather, they usually used such sources in combination.

63. Mansi et al., *Sacrorum conciliorum,* col. 842 (also edited in Di Napoli, *L'immortalità dell'anima,* 221); the full text of this point reads: "Insuper omnibus et singulis philosophis in universitatibus studiorum generalium et alibi publice legentibus districte praecipiendo mandamus, ut cum philosophorum principia aut conclusiones, in quibus a recta fide deviare noscuntur, auditoribus suis legerint seu explanaverint, quale hoc est de animae mortalitate aut unitate et mundi aeternitate ac alia huiusmodi, teneantur eisdem veritatem religionis christianae omni conatu manifestam facere et persuadendo pro posse docere ac omni studio huiusmodi philosophorum argumenta, cum omnia solubilia existant, pro viribus excludere atque resolvere."
64. Here I cannot address the complex issue of the so-called double-truth, on which see Bianchi, *Pour une histoire;* idem, "From Pope Urban VIII to Bishop Étienne Tempier."
65. Bianchi, *Pour une histoire,* 128–30, 147–48; Kraye, "The Immortality of the Soul," 62; Beretta, "Orthodoxie philosophique," 14; Monfasani, "Aristotelians, Platonists, and the Missing Ockhamists," 259–60 and passim.
66. See ASB, Assunteria di Studio, b. 2, unnumbered folder ("1657, Bolla di Clemente VII confermante le Costituzioni di Innocenzo XI contro le spoposizioni di Giansenio").
67. See, for the eighteenth century, Cavarzere, "The Workings of a Papal Institution" (general treatment); Bortolotti, *La storia della matematica,* 145–46, 156–58 (the latter on the difficulties of Francesco Maria Zanotti in Bologna).
68. For a helpful overview, see Bianchi, *Pour une histoire,* 119–30.
69. The literature on Pomponazzi's treatise is immense; for it and the immediate aftermath, see at least Di Napoli, *L'immortalità dell'anima nel Rinascimento,* 227–338; Kessler, "The Intellective Soul," 500–507; Kraye, "The Immortality of the Soul," 62–64; Spruit, "The Pomponazzi Affair," 231–40; and MacLean, "Heterodoxy in Natural Philosophy and Medicine."
70. Representative positions are Grendler, "Intellectual Freedom in Italian Universities," and Bianchi, *Pour une histoire,* 130–56, respectively. For a further perspective, see Cappiello, "I filosofi e la *lex*." For the longer view, see Bianchi, "From Pope Urban VIII to Bishop Étienne Tempier."
71. The bibliography on Boccadiferro is remarkably thin. What follows summarizes a much more detailed treatment (with fuller references) in my "Philosophy Teaching and Filiations of Learning." Some basic biographical and bibliographical information in Fantuzzi, II, 212–17; Lohr, II, 57–65; Leen Spruit, "Boccadiferro, Ludovico," in *ERP* (2017).

72. Cappiello, "I filosofi e la *lex*."
73. Bianchi, *Pour une histoire,* 134–41. On these institutions, see the information in *DSI,* passim.
74. I have used BUB, ms. 1958, ff. 9r–183v, a fair copy of student notes, though other manuscripts too require study. There is also a set of printed lectures, but these appeared posthumously and differ in many ways from the manuscript tradition and are less useful for investigating the issues explored here; see Boccadiferro, *Lectiones super III libros De anima Aristotelis* (Venice: Giovanni Battista Somasco e fratelli, 1566). For some of the points below, a fundamental article is Nardi, "Intorno alla 'quaestio' magliabechiana."
75. BUB, ms. 1958, f. 43v: "et in hoc bene dixit Averroes et fuit totus peripatethicus, et ista mihi videtur vera Aristotelis sententia, licet—uti dixi—Aristoteles erraverit secundum veritatem; secundum tamen peripatheticos ita est et sic apud peripatheticos oportet nos solvere quaestionem de praedestinatione et alia multa quae accidunt Theologis quae aliquando sunt insolubilia."
76. BUB, ms. 1958, ff. 99v–100r.
77. BUB, ms. 1958, ff. 100v–101r.
78. BUB, ms. 1958, ff. 116v–117r.
79. BUB, ms. 1958, f. 123r: "omnia ista sunt falsa et deberent potius isti fateri Aristotelem errasse et non cognovisse ista quam ita extorquere verba Aristotelis. Et Aristotelis habuit alium modum dicendi et opinandi de hac . . . quam sit veritas. Errat ergo Aristoteles? Errat, et quid tum? Est ne miraculum Aristotelem errasse? Erravit enim in hoc et alia."
80. BUB, ms. 1958, f. 131v: "Quid scivit Aristoteles de veritate? Haec est veritas, et erravit Aristoteles, quia . . . in sacris litteris, missus est Angelus Gabriel. Ignoravit enim Aristoteles istam veritatem et sic ista est veritas tenenda. Habemus ergo quod secundum veritatem debemus tenere animam rationalem multiplicatam numero et creatam a Deo eterna autem a parte post; oppinio autem Aristotelis est in oppositum, quod scilicet anima rationalis sit una numero, eterna a parte ante et a parte post. Haec est oppinio peripathetica et Aristotelis, veritas tamen in oppositum et hactenus ista."
81. See Bianchi, "'Aristotele fu un uomo e potè errare.'"
82. Lines, "Teachers," 313, no. 166. For Betti's teaching of moral philosophy, see Lines, *Aristotle's* Ethics, 310–24.
83. Betti's lectures are in BUB, mss. 288 (11 vols.), 289 (13 vols.); and BCAB, mss. B.3422–3434 (13 vols.); cf. Lohr, II, 42–43. For Betti's lectures and writings on *De anima,* see BUB, ms. 288, vols. II, III, VIII, X; ms. 289, vols. III, IX; BCAB, mss. B.3426, B.3428, B.3432, B.3433 (cf. Lohr, II, 42–43).
84. I have used BCAB, ms. B.3426 (98 folios, autograph manuscript, undated); quotation at f. 81r (Book III, *textus* 33).

85. Here I cannot address the question of whether the *Micrologia* represents Betti's definitive approach to theologically sensitive issues. Some biographers point to a (presumably lost) treatise on the soul in which he supposedly spoke, not as a Christian but as a philosopher, and claimed that the soul, once separated from the body, is deprived of fundamental faculties. Apparently this work did not pass muster with the local inquisitor and thus never appeared in print. See Giorgio Stabile, "Betti, Claudio, detto Betto giovane," *DBI,* IX (1967), 713–14 (whose speculations on the possible date of the treatise rest, however, on a faulty chronology). The matter deserves further critical attention.
86. Brief details in Augusto de Ferrari, "Cartari, Gian Lodovico," *DBI,* XX (1977), 788–89; Lohr, II, 80.
87. Cartari, *De immortalitate atque pluralitate animae,* ff. 3v–4r: "Ita quid id philosophorum Principi falso tribui graviter ferens, hoc commentariolo eum animam rationalem immortalem asseruisse ostendere contendi, eorum rationes refutans atque evertens, qui aliter opinati fuerint."
88. For a valuable sampling of some such initiatives, see *Christian Readings of Aristotle.*
89. For instance, Alessandro Achillini's commentary on the *Physics* begins "Deus illuminatio mea sit," whereas at the start of the *De elementis* one reads, "Luminum clarissima lux, qua omnes aliae veritates illustrantur, me per umbras materiae tutum ab errore per Filium hominis ducas in te ipsum" (see Nardi, "Appunti sull'averroista bolognese Alessandro Achillini," 278–79).
90. Cartari, *De immortalitate atque pluralitate animae,* f. 124r: "Et haec ad laudem Dei omnipotentis ac eius Filii Iesu Christi determinata sint. In quibus si quid esset dictum quod veritati Catholicae repugnaret, id asserendo aliorum dicta intelligatur et non quod ita sentiam, quia in iis et omnibus aliis determinationi Sacrosanctae Romanae Ecclesiae semper me subiicio et stare intendo, sicque Deus me adiuvet."
91. Cartari's theses of 18 March 1557 have survived (ASB, Riformatori dello Studio, b. 59, item 2), but, as is often the case, they are not very informative.
92. For documents related to Balducci's investigations, see *Catholic Church and Modern Science,* ad indicem.
93. For an overview of the activities of the Inquisition in Bologna (which may have become established already in the thirteenth century), see dall'Olio, "Bologna," in *DSI,* I, 211–13; and especially, for these years, idem, *Eretici e inquisitori,* 255–417 (rapid summary in idem, "L'attività dell'Inquisizione di Bologna," 1111–13). In 1567–1568 a professor of law (Aldobrandino Fondazza) was removed from the teaching roll and tried in Rome because he was suspected of heresy; upon his return to Bologna,

he was not readmitted to teaching: although he had not been found guilty and therefore had not recanted, he was perhaps still considered suspect (cf. Dall'Olio, *Eretici e inquisitori,* 382–84).

94. Cardano's *De varietate rerum* was later placed on the Index. For other works by Cardano that were either censored or prohibited, see Marcus, *Forbidden Knowledge,* passim; and esp. *Catholic Church and Modern Science,* I.2, 1033–1472.

95. On Grisostomo, see Baldini and Spruit, "Cardano e Aldrovandi," 156–60.

96. On Aldrovandi, useful insights and new documents in Baldini and Spruit, "Cardano e Aldrovandi," and *Catholic Church and Modern Science,* I.1, 727–43; also Beretta, "Orthodoxie philosophique," 18–19; and, most recently, Regier, "Reading Cardano with the Roman Inquisition." See also §4.3.

97. Bianchi, *Pour une histoire,* 146–47; Beretta, "'Omnibus Christianae, Catholicaeque philosophiae amantibus: D. D.,'" 317–21.

98. Mazzetti, 221, no. 2211.

99. For Natali's public lectures, see ASB, Annue Lezioni, b. 60, ff. 326r–338r, covering various years between 1642 and 1649 (cf. Vernazza, "La crisi barocca," 127). For his private lectures, see HRC Ranuzzi, Ph12763, 5 vols., containing his 1651 lectures on *De generatione et corruptione* (vol. 1), his 1649–1650 lectures on the *Physics* (vol. 2), his 1650–1651 lectures on *De coelo et mundo* (vol. 3), his 1652 lectures on *De anima* (vol. 4), and his 1641 lectures on logic (vol. 5). The note-takers were Silvio Antonio and Angelo Ranuzzi, whose father, Marco Antonio, was a fairly prominent local nobleman. Silvio Antonio apparently died early in life. See Francesca Boris, "Ranuzzi, Angelo," *DBI,* LXXXVI (2016), 460–62; *Ranuzzi,* 111ff.

100. HRC Ranuzzi, Ph12763, vol. 4: *In libros Aristotelis de Anima explicatos usque ad Tex. 65 inclusive libri secundi ex privatis Perill. et Excell. D. Doctoris Francisci Natalis lectionibus scriptis a Silvio Antonio Ranutio cum indice materiarum et quaestionum A.D. 1652 Bononiae.*

101. These points are covered especially in his question *Utrum haec consideratio spectet ad philosophiam naturalem* (HRC Ranuzzi, Ph12763, vol. 4, ff. 14r–17v) at the end of Book I.

102. HRC Ranuzzi, Ph12763, vol. 3, ff. 91v–92r: "Quantum autem ad ordinem orbium Antiquorum aliqui ut Arixtarcus . . . atque Ptolomeus, et postea Copernicus et ultimo Galileus sic statuebant ordinem universi: solem in medio mundi immobilem ponebant, circa quem orbem Mercurii, deinde orbem Veneris collocabant, circa hunc orbem terrae una cum elementis, et circa terram lunae orbem, circa omnia haec orbem Martis, deinde caelum Iovis et postea sphaeram Saturni et ultimo firmamentum. Verum haec opinio ultimo damnata est ab Ecclesia tanquam fidei nostrae opposita, et alias etiam ab astrologis fuit improbata, et nostrum non est eam examinare."

103. At least some Jesuits of the time, such as Niccolò Cabeo, may have encouraged such an approach; see Martin, *Renaissance Meteorology,* 119–21.
104. For the decree of the Congregation of the Index, see *The Galileo Affair: A Documentary* History, ed. and trans. Maurice A. Finocchiaro (Berkeley: University of California Press, 1989), 148–50. The publications of Eustachio Manfredi show that Copernicanism was still not allowed to be taught except as a hypothesis in 1729, when his *De annuis inerrantium stellarum aberrationibus* (Bologna: typis Constantii Pisarri S. Inquisitionis impressoris) had difficulties receiving the *imprimatur* because of its presentation of the rotation of the earth. See Baldini, "Manfredi, Eustachio." For a recent outline and the context of Galileo's condemnation, see Marcus, *Forbidden Knowledge,* 226–36.
105. Bianchi, "Agostino Oreggi," 578–80; idem, "From Urban VIII to Bishop Étienne Tempier."
106. Exceptions include Fortunio Liceti (t. 1637–1645), whose outline of lectures on *De anima* for 1642, though terse, does promise to focus on Book III and the "main questions usually raised on this third book by the classic commentators (*a classicis interpretibus*)," though it does not specify which ones exactly these are; see ASB, Annue Lezioni, b. 60, f. 390r (Vernazza, "La crisi barocca," 126). Also see Carlo Sassi's lectures on the soul in 1666–1667, where he does address points such as the unicity of the intellect in ASB, Annue Lezioni, b. 60, ff. 568r–569v (Vernazza, "La crisi barocca," 128–29). Even Sassi, however, is inconsistent: his 1657–1658 lectures on the soul (ASB, Annue Lezioni, b. 60, ff. 542r–543v) seem to avoid controversial issues when dealing with *De anima,* Book III, and rely heavily on theologically impeccable commentators such as Thomas, Toletus, and Javelli.
107. ASB, Annue Lezioni, b. 61, f. 158v: "Tandem si tempus et lectionum ordo permitent, ab animalibus cunctis, animi solius hominis descriptionem progredietur; utpote mixti illius, cui soli simplex haec facultas vegetandi, sentiendi et intelligendi convenit. In homine vero (seclusa anima rationali, de qua seorsim in metaphysica sermo habebitur) organicum primo corporis structuram compendiose exponet." For a similar approach, with emphasis on physiology, see the lecture plan on *De anima* by Pier Francesco Peggi for 1717–1718 (ASB, Annue Lezioni, b. 61, f. 252r–v; Vernazza, "La crisi barocca," 133–34), which concludes: "Universae autem animasticae physiologiae exponendae ea erit ratio, ut Aristotelis dogmata unacum modernorum sententiis coniungantur; quo scilicet in hac parte philosophiae naturalis praecipua nullum eorum quae aut veteris aur recentioris sunt scholae, studiosis auditoribus subtrahatur."
108. Baldini, "L'attività scientifica," 524–25; Cavazza, "Riforma dell'Università," 247: "Fu infatti lo sforzo di mostrare la compatibilità, basata

sull'autonomia reciproca, del campo della natura e dell'esperienza e di quello della rivelazione e della fede, oggetto rispettivamente della filosofia—cioè la scienza della natura—e della teologia, che portò a privilegiare spesso una concezione accentuatamente sperimentalistica, utilitaristica, metafisicamente neutrale della nuova scienza, a curvare insomma in senso baconiano la lezione galileiana."

109. See https://catalogo.beniculturali.it/detail/HistoricOrArtisticProperty/0800024727 (accessed 15 December 2021).

110. See Alessandro Ottaviani, "Trionfetti, Lelio," *DBI,* XCVI (2019), online; cf. Dallari, III, passim; Vernazza, "La crisi barocca," 145, for his supposed conservatism. Also §6.1.1.

111. BCAB, ms. B.1449, containing his *Sex ultimi ex octo Physicorum libri . . . explicati* (187 pp.), as well as *De coelo et mundo compendiosa explicatio* (170 pp.).

112. Baldini, "La teoria della spiegazione scientifica," 206.

113. BUB, ms. 489, 3 vols. (c. 1732); these lectures are not part of Collina's published *corpus* in his *Opere,* 5 vols. (Bologna: Costantino Pisarri, 1744–1745) and are not mentioned in Madga Vigilante, "Collina, Bonifacio," *DBI,* XXVII (1982), 58–60.

114. BUB, ms. 1066, vol. III (64 folios), containing Pietro Mengoli, *Arithmeticae realis lectiones secundae.* See esp. Baroncini, "Introduzione ad una teologia matematica."

115. BUB, ms. 1066, vol. III, f. 2r: "Horum itaque omnium dispositionem contemplor a Deo processisse per ministerium Angelorum in numero, pondere et mensura, ut dicitur in libro Sapientiae cap. 11 vers. 21."

116. The most detailed examination is Baroncini, "Introduzione ad una teologia matematica."

117. Baroncini, "La filosofia naturale nello Studio bolognese."

118. I owe consideration of this possibility to Sara Miglietti. On this current, see esp. Blair, "Mosaic Physics"; Harrison, "Physico-Theology"; *Physico-Theology;* Dooley, "Antonio Vallisneri."

119. For the gap between Giulio Valeriani Bonomi and Claudio Betti, see Lines, *Aristotle's* Ethics, 416–17.

120. For a detailed sketch of moral philosophy in Bologna, see Lines, *Aristotle's* Ethics, 289–324.

121. ASB, Annue Lezioni, b. 60, f. 396r–v.

122. See also Vernazza, "La crisi barocca," 125. On the attention to various sources for moral philosophy and which of them received most in the Renaissance, see Lines and Kraye, "Sources for Ethics in the Renaissance." On the reception of Stoicism and Epicureanism specifically, see Kraye, "Moral Philosophy," 360–86. On the potential connections between moral philosophy and Christianity, see Bianchi, "Renaissance Readings of the *Nicomachean Ethics.*"

123. Dallari, III, ad indicem. This member of the Aldrovandi family has received very little attention, but the rich documentation would support a detailed investigation. See Vernazza, "La crisi barocca," 130–32.
124. BUB, ms. 111, b. 5, unnumbered pages for 1709–1710; cf. also ASB, Annue Lezioni, b. 61, f. 449, with Aldrovandi's lectures on the same subject, but for 1714–1715 (see ASB, Annue Lezioni, b. 62, f. 37, for the same subject in 1729–1730).
125. Bernabeo, "La Scuola di Medicina," 190.
126. The following is based on Cavazza, *Settecento inquieto,* 51–56, 79–118; eadem, "Riforma dell'università"; eadem, "Marsili, Antonio Felice," *DBI,* LXX (2008), 751–55; Dallari, III, passim. On seventeenth-century atomism, see Baldini, "Il corpuscolarismo italiano del Seicento."
127. See the theses of Marsili containing some of these perspectives: *Concordia Democriti et Aristotelis ex ipsis doctrinis Peripatus iterato firmius stabilita* (Bologna: Giacomo Monti, 1669).
128. Augusto de Ferrari, "Ciampoli, Giovanni Battista," *DBI,* XXV (1981), 147–52.
129. See A. F. Marsili, *Memorie per riparare i pregiudizi.*
130. Helpful comments in Giacomelli, "Le Bolle pontificie," 319–22, presenting Archdeacon Marsili as a conservative representative of the Catholic Reformation.
131. L. F. Marsili, *Parallelo.* See §7.3.2.
132. L. F. Marsili, *Parallelo,* 409–10, 416–17.
133. *Costituzioni,* in Bortolotti, "La fondazione dell'Istituto," 426–27: "Art. 1. Li professori, e qualunque persona si eserciterà in questo Istituto, dovranno riconoscere per Autore Dio Ottimo Massimo, ed implorare da Lui, a maggior sua gloria, la conservazione e gli avanzamenti, mediante intercessione della Santissima Vergine Maria. Ed acciocchè si provi efficace protettrice di quest'Opera, in tutti gli strumenti e scritture si praticherà l'epoca ab incarnatione; lasciando per altro che, in ciò che riguarda le osservazioni astronomiche, si usi la pratica e lo stile dell'era corrente.

    Art. 2. Saranno pure riconosciuti e venerati per protettori S. Tommaso d'Aquino, S. Carlo Borromeo, e la nostra S. Caterina de' Vigri, e nella Cappella domestica, che si erigerà ne l'Istituto, dovrà solennizzarsi da professori e studenti la Festa della Santissima Annunciazione, con la celebrazione d'una messa, in rendimento di grazia a S.D. de' beni che si ritraggono dall'istituto, e delle sue infinite misericordie, usate specialmente in tal giorno col generale conte Luigi Ferdinando Marsili."
134. Turrini, "L'insegnamento della teologia," 462–63; on Gotti, see Vernazza, "La crisi barocca," 171.

135. Fattori, "I papi bolognesi e la città," 1290–95, for his interest in local libraries and the Istituto delle Scienze; Giacomelli, "La storia di Bologna dal 1650 al 1796," esp. 109–10.
136. Fattori, "I papi bolognesi e la città," 1308n75.
137. Fattori, "Lambertini a Bologna."
138. Schmitt, "Science in the Italian Universities"; idem, "Philosophy and Science in Sixteenth-Century Italian Universities."
139. A well-known representative of this position is Dejob, *De l'influence du Concile de Trente.* Much of the work written by Catholics subsequently has been dedicated to contesting this view.
140. Cavazza, "Riforma dell'università," 246–47; Baldini, "L'attività scientifica," 513–26.
141. Baldini, "La scuola galileiana."
142. Bianchi, *Pour une histoire.*
143. Grendler, *The Jesuits and Italian Universities,* 297, 424–25; Fabrini, *Lo Studio pubblico di Bologna ed i gesuiti,* 63–64; cf. Turrini, "Le letture di casi di coscienza"; Simeoni, *Storia della Università,* 90–92. Turrini, "L'insegnamenteo della teologia," rightly notes that, in Bologna, the Jesuits were not the only game in town when it came to teaching theology; in addition to various other religious orders, she also points to the influence of the doctors of the Collegio di Spagna, who obtained several appointments in the *studium* beginning in the late seventeenth century (456).
144. For the course plans surviving in ASB, Annue Lezioni, b. 61, I have found the following: for 1713–1714, thirteen of forty-seven plans relate to theology; for 1714–1715, the figures are twelve out of forty; for 1717–1718, eight out of thirty-one. See ASB, Annue Lezioni, b. 62 for course plans from 1729 onward.
145. On the honorary lectureship, see Turrini, "L'insegnamento della teologia," 448n144.
146. For a comparative treatment of some issues (which does not, however, consider the Italian situation), see Verger, "L'insegnamento della teologia."
147. On the influence of Paleotti and Marsili, see also Turrini, "L'insegnamento della teologia," 447–48, 463–64.
148. Sacchetti, *Ordinationi.*
149. See esp. Mazzone, "Vita religiosa e vita civile."
150. Turrini, "L'insegnamento della teologia," 448–51.
151. Prodi, *Il cardinale Gabriele Paleotti,* II, 222.
152. ASB, Senato, Partiti, b. 9, 14 December 1574: "Iustis et rationabilibus causis censuit Senatus ab uno tantum lectore lecturam sacrae Theologiae publice in scholis magnis legi debere."
153. Useful comments in Turrini, "L'insegnamento della teologia," 463–64.
154. Among others, Tuttle, *Piazza Maggiore;* idem, *The Neptune Fountain.*

155. Carnevali, "Cheap, Everyday Print," 252–57.
156. Zarri, "The Church, Civic Religion, and Civic Identity," 368–73.
157. Turrini, "'Me et totam congregationem defende.'"
158. Alberigo, "Il Concilio di Trento a Bologna."
159. Vittori, *Commentarii in prognostica Hippocratis,* 13. Vittori also cites Ephesians 2 for the role of works, faith, and grace in salvation.
160. Vittori, *Commentarii in prognostica Hippocratis,* 18.
161. Vittori, *Commentaria in Hippocratis Aphorismos,* 652: "manibus ad coelum elevatis Deo excelso et eius filio unico Iesu Christo Domino nostro gratias ago de misericordia quam mihi fecerunt per eorum gratiam, per quam praesentibus Aphorismorum commentariis, bona mente validoque intellectu finem desideratum imposui hac ora undecima et die tertia mensis Iulii, anno ab ortu domini nostri Iesu Christi quingentesimo supra millesimum et quinquagesimo quinto, quo medicinam theoricam in doctissimo Bononiensi Gymnasio foelicissime edocebam, ad laudem et gloriam Dei omnipotentis mihi in hoc seculo quietam vitam largientis, et in alio sempiternam. Et per gratiam Christi Domini nostri, qui ab omnibus periculis corporis et animae me defendat et protegat. Et ad honorem beatae Virginis Mariae protectricis nostrae, cuius praeces sumat ille qui pro nobis natus est, ut per eas ducat nos in rectam viam salutis aeternae. Amen."
162. Pozzi, *Orationes duae:* "ostendebat . . . quam magnum extitisset in condendis corporibus Dei opus et sapientia, tuendisque amor et providentia." See 11–12 and passim for the work's religious flavor.
163. It is unclear whether Italian professors based their approach—as was typical in Protestant countries—on an intensive use of the Scriptures. Examples of such an orientation in Italy (but largely from outside the classroom context) are provided in Barnett, *After the Flood,* 20–49 (on Camilla Erculiani in Padua); Berns, *The Bible and Natural Philosophy.*
164. For his degree, see Bronzino, 217; for his teaching, Dallari, III, passim. Aldrovandi reputedly prepared Laura Danielli Landi (daughter of the professor Stefano Danielli) for her semiofficial philosophical conclusions; see Orlandi, *Notizie degli scrittori bolognesi,* 249; Cavazza, "Between Modesty and Spectacle," 437n13.
165. BUB, ms. 111. For a brief description, see Frati, *Indice,* no. 144, 161–62.
166. For a few details on these teachers, see Mazzetti, 95, no. 860, and 273, no. 2726, respectively.
167. The material on the soul does include a third section, *De anima rationali seu mente* (BUB, ms. 111, b. 3, item 6), but this will require a separate study along with the following item, a *Tractatus de anima, seu de corpore animato,* to see whether any discussion of the immortality of the soul is included.
168. This evidence may seem to be contradicted by the anonymous document from 1716 quoted in Turrini, "L'insegnamento della teologia," 461–62;

however, the author of this memorandum, who was clearly opposed to the introduction of dogmatic theology, may have exaggerated the differences between seculars and the religious in the *studium*.

169. BUB, ms. 111, b. 1, item 9, three pages.
170. Cf. Dall'Olio, *Eretici e inquisitori,* 434–36.
171. See Dall'Olio, *Eretici e inquisitori,* 435–37.
172. On the Venetian College and its role in circumventing the *professio fidei* requirement in Padua, see Grendler, *Universities,* 506–8 (for the background, 191–93), and esp. Rossetti, "I collegi per i dottorati 'auctoritate veneta'"; del Negro, "L'età moderna," 51–54. The Collegio veneto artista started in 1616 (Zen Benetti, "Il Seicento," 14–15, 46). On Siena, see Grendler, *Universities,* 193–94.
173. Hammerstein, "Relations with Authority," 148: "Theology, which was never as important in Italian universities, continued to play an insignificant role." See also Chapter 2.
174. Grendler, *Universities,* chap. 10, covers theology up to around 1600.
175. Schmidt-Biggemann, "New Structures of Knowledge."
176. In Padua, Bishop Gregorio Barbarigo (1664–1697), chancellor of the university, championed a firmly Catholic approach and became involved in the selection of professors (usually reserved to the Senate); see Zen Benetti, "Gregorio Barbarigo." On Salamanca, see Vázquez Janeiro, "La Teología en el siglo XV"; Barriento García, "La Teología, siglos XVI–XVII."
177. Grendler, *Universities,* 186–95.
178. See de Ridder-Symoens, "Mobility" (though degrees of tolerance probably varied depending on who was in authority).

EPILOGUE

1. For a stimulating example, see Bruning, *Innovation in Forschung und Lehre.*
2. For what follows, I have greatly benefited from Grendler, *Universities,* chaps. 1–4, and Lupi, *Gli* studia *del papa.*
3. Lines, "Papal Power."
4. Lines, "Papal Power," 677; see also de Ridder-Symoens, "L'Évolution quantitative et qualitative."
5. For law, see Guerrini, *Collegi dottorali;* for medicine, see specifically the *memoriale* of Bologna's College of Medicine dated 1724 in BUB, ms. 1052, ff. 74r–78r.
6. See del Negro, "L'età moderna," 41. In Padua, the Jesuits failed to establish a permanent foothold in the city: they were expelled in 1606, though they returned in 1657. See, most recently, Grendler, *The Jesuits and Italian Universities,* 115–53.

7. On the relationship between the two, see *Rapporti tra le Università di Padova e Bologna.*
8. Although there were also points of considerable difference, such as the longevity of student privileges: in Padua, students were still approving the teaching rolls in the sixteenth century and lost the last vestiges of such power only in 1560; but, as in Bologna, the office of student rector went unfilled from the start of the seventeenth century, and in 1738 the Venetian government even dissolved the student *universitates* (del Negro, "L'età moderna," 39–41, 44, 68). Another difference was the nature of the relationship between government and university (48–51, 68, and passim).
9. "Quanto allo esempio, [Sua Beneditione] disse che il dover voleva che Padova et gli altri studii pigliassero esempio da Bologna, et non Bologna da loro"; in ASB, Ambasciata, b. 6 (letter from the ambassador to the Senate, 28 September 1583), in Lines, "Reorganizing the Curriculum," 24 and n114.
10. ASB, Assunteria di Studio, b. 13, ff. 56r–57v, 60v–61r (letters between Bologna and its ambassador in Rome, October 1660, requesting the constitutions of the Sapienza in Rome).
11. On the problems of student violence and competition, *L'Università di Padova nei secoli,* 25–28 (*relazione* of Angelo Correr, 8 March 1611), 33, 37–38 (Progetto di riforma dello Studio del professor Ingolfo de Conti, 1614), and 73 (Memoirs of John Evelyn, 1645 and 1646). On difficulties attracting students, Zen Benetti, "Il Seicento," 9–10, 31–32, 34–36 (Progetto di riforma dello Studio del professor Ingolfo de Conti, 1614). On the number of professors, 15–16.
12. Zen Benetti, "Il Seicento," 11–12, 16. For the decreasing length of the course of studies, see also del Negro, "L'età moderna," 63–65. On the teaching posts reserved for Paduan citizens already in the second half of the fifteenth century, see esp. del Negro, "L'età moderna," 36–39, and, for later developments, 45, 65–67 (for the period from 1700 to 1750, del Negro notes that the number of non-Venetian professors fell from 29 percent to 13 percent).
13. Zen Benetti, "Il Seicento," 11–13; del Negro, "L'età moderna," 60–62.
14. See *Rapporti tra le Università di Padova e Bologna.* Some work has been done on other exchanges and rivalries; see, for instance, Denley, "Academic Rivalry and Interchange," and *Les Échanges entre les universités européennes.*
15. Moyer, *The Intellectual World,* 19; De Tata, *Il commercio librario,* 110, 177–80, and ad indicem.
16. See del Negro, "Il Settecento," 199–201 (Pivati, *Riflessioni sopra lo stato presente dello Studio di Padova*).
17. See del Negro, "L'età moderna," 68–70. For various aspects of the reforms taking place in Padua in the eighteenth century, see del Negro, "I 'Pensieri di

Simone Stratico'"; idem, "Bernardo Nani, Lorenzo Morosini e la riforma universitaria del 1761"; idem, "Istituzioni, spazi e progetti culturali nella Padova del secondo Settecento"; Soppelsa, "Itinerari epistemici e riforme istituzionali." The discussions concerning the reforms in Padua are documented in del Negro, "Il Settecento," 209–303.

18. Dooley, "Science Teaching as a Career in Padua," 135–36. The proposal was not accepted, although a modest set of instruments was bought. A laboratory was established in 1738.
19. See del Negro, "Il Settecento," 255–59 (here, 256; *Piano per gli artisti,* possibly by Leopoldo Marc'Antonio Caldani, 1768).
20. See Cavazza, "Fisica generale e fisica sperimentale."
21. For general reflections on recent historiography on Italian universities and future areas of research, see also Brizzi, "La storia delle università in Italia"; Roggero, "Le università in epoca moderna."
22. A notable exception is the documentation on the Natio Germanica (see *Annales, 1595–1619* and *Annales, 1640–1674,* in addition to *La matricola*) and various colleges (e.g., Piana, *Nuovi documenti,* and *Annali del Collegio Ungaro Illirico*).
23. For more detailed comments on the documentation, see the Introduction and Lines, "The University and the City," 458–62.
24. As noted by Frova, "Antiche e moderne edizioni di statuti," 149–50, a critical understanding of the reliability of statutes does not mean that they should not be edited and studied.

BIBLIOGRAPHY

Note: The listing below provides full references for all printed primary sources not mentioned incidentally. Unless they are mentioned more than once, entries in biographical dictionaries and encyclopedias are fully referenced in the relevant endnote.

ARCHIVAL SOURCES

Bologna, Archivio Arcivescovile
  Miscellanee Vecchie

Bologna, Archivio di Stato
  Archivio dello Studio
  Archivio Demaniale
  Assunteria d'Istituto, Diversorum
  Assunteria di Studio
  Comune-Governo, Riformatori dello Stato di Libertà: Libri mandatorum
  Comune-Governo, Riformatori dello Stato di Libertà: Libri partitorum
  Condotta, bollette
  Gabella Grossa, Instrumenti
  Gabella Grossa, Relazioni
  Riformatori dello Studio
  Senato: Ambasciata Bolognese a Roma
  Senato: Bolle e Brevi
  Senato: Lettere del Senato
  Senato: Partiti
  Senato: Provvisioni
  Studio Alidosi
  Tesoreria e Controllatore di Tesoreria
  Ufficio per la condotta degli stipendiari, libri delle bollette

Vatican City, Archivio Apostolico Vaticano (formerly Archivio Segreto Vaticano)
  Congregazione del Concilio: Libri Litter.
  Congregazione del Concilio: Positiones Sess.
  Fondo Confalonieri

Miscellanea, Arm.
Segreteria di Stato, Legazione di Bologna

MANUSCRIPT SOURCES (AN ASTERISK DENOTES ITEMS NOT SEEN PERSONALLY)

Austin, Texas, Harry Ransom Center, Ranuzzi Manuscripts (HRC Ranuzzi)

Ph 12622	Baldassare Gambarini, lectures on philosophy, 1556–1565
Ph 12670	Letters, members of the Accademia degli Oziosi, XVII c.
Ph 12763, 5 vols.	Francesco Natali and Pietro Mengoli, Aristotle lectures, 1641–1652
Ph 12853	Miscellaneous writings and documents (also letters of Camillo Vizzani), XVII c.
Ph 12882	Miscellaneous Bolognese documents, XVII c.

Bologna, Biblioteca Comunale dell'Archiginnasio (BCAB)

*A.127	Works of Aristotle, XIII / XIV c.
B.506	Decisions of the Senate of Bologna
B.1449	Lelio Trionfetti, lectures on *Physics* and *De coelo et mundo,* 1675
B.1946–1968	Catalog of library of San Domenico before its dispersal
B.2037	Catalog of the Gelati's library
B.3182	Diversorum et brevium, 1575–1656
B.3422–3434, 13 vols.	Claudio Betti, lectures on Aristotle's philosophy, XVI c.
B.3803	Ulisse Aldrovandi, *Informatione del Rotulo,* 26 September 1573
*Gozzadini 18–22	Schoolbooks, XVII / XVIII c. of Ulisse Giuseppe di Marcantonio Gozzadini and others
*Gozzadini 261	*Leges legalis Academiae,* 1692

Bologna, Biblioteca Universitaria (BUB)[†]

9H, item 25	Eustachio Manfredi, explanations of geometry, XVIII c.

† N.B.: Manuscript signatures are not identical with the progressive numbers in Frati, *Indice.*

12/b. 1/item 2	Isocrates, *Ad Demonicum,* late XV c.
12/b. 1/item 7	Porphyry, *Isagoge* and Aristotle, *Praedicamenta,* late XV c.
*72, vol. VII	Miscellaneous ms including letters of Montefani Caprara, XVIII c.
111	Autograph items by Bartolomeo Aldrovandi, XVII/XVIII c.
*132	Astronomy ms owned by Garzoni family
*159	Logic and metaphysics ms owned by Garzoni family
288, 11 vols.	Claudio Betti, lectures on Aristotle's philosophy, XVI c.
289, 13 vols.	Claudio Betti, lectures on Aristotle's philosophy, XVI c.
*366	Buridan *Ethics* ms owned by Garzoni family
*466	Cicero ms owned and lent out by Giovanni Garzoni, XV c.
473	Cicero's *Tusculan Disputations,* owned by Bernardo Garzoni, 1436
489, 3 vols.	Bonifacio Collina, lectures on logic, metaphysics, and physics, XVIII c.
731, 3 vols.	Giovanni Garzoni, medical lectures, XV c.
747	Giovanni Garzoni, medical lectures, 1471
*752	Historical materials, ms donated by Giovanni Garzoni to San Giacomo Maggiore, 1494
769	Chronicle by Nicolò Seccadenari, coverage up to 1598
770	Antonio Francesco Ghiselli, *Memorie antiche manoscritte*
896	Pirro Legnani Ferri, *Diario delle cose accadute in Bologna,* written 1756
920	Miscellaneous logic textbook, 1417 and later?
*921	Autograph manuscript of Bernardo Garzoni, XV c.
1052	Statutes of the Colleges of Philosophy and Medicine, 1507 and later
1066, 3 vols.	Pietro Mengoli, *Arithmeticae realis lectiones secundae,* 1682
1072, vol. VII	Anonymous treatises and questions of geometry, astronomy, XVI/XVII c.

1077, 7 vols.	Medical lectures of Giacomo Sandri, Nicolò Betti Florentiola, and others (?), late XVII c. / XVIII c.
1107	Annals of Bologna by G. F. Negri, XVII c.
1329	Giovanni Girolamo Sbaraglia, logic lectures, XVII c.
1394	Collection of statutes, arts and medicine
1432, 4 vols.	Lelio Trionfetti, lectures in Bologna's botanical garden, 1675–1721
*1433	Lelio Trionfetti, prolusions to lectures in botanical garden, as above
*1434	Lelio Trionfetti, *exercitationes* held in the Istituto delle Scienze, XVIII c.
*1435–1436	Lelio Trionfetti, works on natural history, XVIII c.
*1610	Guarino Veronese on Virgil, XV c.
1939	Ercole Corazzi (and others?), prolusions, XVIII c.
1958	Ludovico Boccadiferro, lectures on *De anima,* III, 1535–1536
2137, 5 vols.	Valerio Ranieri, chronicle of Bologna
2320	Misc. manuscript, XVI / XVII c.
2388	Works associated with Claudio Betti and the Accademia dei Velati, 1557 or later
2948, 36 vols.	Miscellanea Tioli, digests of documents in Vatican library / archive, XVIII c.
*2951	Description of L.F. Marsili books by G. S. Assemani, 1720
3647, caps. II, no. 21	Anonymous mathematics lectures, XVII c. (first half)
4679	Misc. manuscript, XVI / XVII c.
Aldrov. 21, vol. III	Ulisse Aldrovandi, miscellaneous writings, XVI c.
Aldrov. 44	Ulisse Aldrovandi, miscellaneous writings, XVI c.
Aldrov. 60	Ulisse Aldrovandi, lectures on Aristotle's *Physics,* 1557
Aldrov. 77, 3 vols.	Ulisse Aldrovandi, writings and lectures (also on Dioscorides), XVI c.
Aldrov. 136, vol. VI	Ulisse Aldrovandi, miscellaneous writings, XVI c.
Aldrov. 147	Ulisse Aldrovandi, library catalog, XVI c. ex.

Florence, Biblioteca Nazionale Centrale

Corte d'Appello, ms. 3 — Payments, *studium* of Florence-Pisa

Kraców, Biblioteka Jagiellońska

*2169 — Baldassare Gambarini, lectures of natural philosophy, XVI c.

Modena, Biblioteca Estense

*Fondo Campori, ms. 460 — Legists, matriculation list 1553–1613

*V 8 19 (lat. 300) — Student notes on Bartolomeo Del Regno's teaching, 1403

Vatican City, Apostolic Library (BAV)

*Ottob. gr. 166 — Greek ms possibly connected to Codro

PRINTED PRIMARY SOURCES†

Acta nationis Germanicae Universitatis Bononiensis ex archetypis Tabularii Malvezziani, iussu Instituti germanici Savignyani, edited by Ernst Friedländer and Carlo Malagola (Bologna-Berlin: Georg Reimer, 1887; repr., Bologna: Sala Bolognese, 1988).

Annales, 1595–1619, edited by Silvia Neri and Carla Penuti (Bologna: CLUEB, 2002; Natio germanica Bononiae, 2).

Annales, 1640–1674, edited by Silvia Neri and Carla Penuti (Bologna: CLUEB, 2008; Natio germanica Bononiae, 3).

Annali del Collegio Ungaro Illirico di Bologna (1553–1764), edited by Maria Luisa Accorsi and Gian Paolo Brizzi (Bologna: CLUEB, 1988).

Aristotle, *The Complete Works of Aristotle: The Revised Oxford Translation,* edited by Jonathan Barnes, 2 vols. (Princeton, NJ: Princeton University Press, 1984).

*Bandini, Ottavio, *Reformationi dello Studio stabilite dall'Illustrissimo et Reverendissimo Mons. Ottavio Bandini Vicelegato et dal molto illustre Signor Reggimento* (broadsheet, n.p., n.d., but 1593).

Berengario da Carpi, Jacobo, *Commentaria cum amplissimis additionibus super anatomia Mundini una cum textu eiusdem in pristinum et verum nitorem redacto* (Bologna: Girolamo Benedetti, 1521).

† NB: items marked with an asterisk are planned for inclusion in Lines, *Selected Documents.*

Bianchini, Bartolomeo, *Codri vita a Bartholomeo Blanchino Bononiensi condita ad Minum Roscium Senatorem Bononiensem* (6 folios, usually bound together with the editions of Codro's *Opera* printed in 1502).

Borghesi, Diomede, *Lettere di Diomede Borghesi,* edited by Giuseppe Campori (Bologna: G. Romagnoli, 1868).

Caius, John, *De libris propriis* in untitled edition of multiple works by Caius, edited by S. Jebb (London: Impensis Car. Davis, 1729); English translation in *An Autobibliography by John Caius,* edited by Vivian Nutton (London: Routledge, 2018).

Cardano, Girolamo, *Opera omnia,* 10 vols. (Lyon: Aumptibus Ioannis Antonii Huguetan et Marci Antonii Ravaud, 1663; repr., Stuttgart-Bad Cannstatt: Frommann, 1966).

Cartari, Giovanni Ludovico, *De immortalitate atque pluralitate animae secundum Aristotelem* (Bologna: Fausto Bonardo, 1587).

*Casoni, Lorenzo, *Ordinazioni rinovate e rispettivamente riformate dall'eminentissimo e reverendissimo Sig. Cardinale Lorenzo Casoni, Legato a Latere della Città di Bologna, per conservare la dignità e riputazione dello Studio di Bologna* (Bologna: dalli successori del Benacci, per la Stamperia Camerale, 1713).

Catholic Church and Modern Science: Documents from the Archives of the Roman Congregations of the Holy Office and the Index, vol. I: *Sixteenth-Century Documents,* edited by Ugo Baldini and Leen Spruit (Rome: Libreria Editrice Vaticana, 2009).

Chartularium Studii Bononiensis: Documenti per la storia dell'Università di Bologna dalle origini fino al secolo xv, 15 vols. (Bologna: Istituto per la Storia dell'Università di Bologna, 1909–1988).

Chartularium Studii Bononiensis S. Francisci (saec. 13–16), edited by Celestino Piana (Florence: Collegio San Bonaventura, 1970).

Conciliorum Oecumenicorum Decreta, edited by Giuseppe Alberigo et al. (Bologna: Edizioni Dehoniane, 1991).

Documenti per la storia dell'Università di Pavia nella seconda metà del '400, vol. III, edited by Simona Iaria (Milan: Cisalpino, 2010).

Ehrle, Francesco, *I più antichi Statuti della Facoltà teologica di Bologna* (Bologna: Istituto per la storia dell'Università di Bologna, 1932).

Filelfo, Francesco, *Collected Letters: Epistularum libri XLVIII,* critical edition by Jeroen De Keyser, 4 vols. (Alessandria: Edizioni dell'Orso, 2015).

*Gaetani, Enrico, *Ordinationi fatte et stabilite dall'illustrissimo et reverendissimo Monsignor il Cardinale Caietano Legato et molto Ill. <s>ig. Quaranta* (Bologna: Alessandro Benacci, 1586).

*Giustiniani, Benedetto, *Philosophiae ac Medicinae scholarium bononiensis gymnasii statuta sub felicissimis auspiciis illustrissimi ac reverendissimi cardinali Ius-*

tiniani Bononiae de Latere legati, instaurata 1609 (Bononiae: Vittorio Benacci, 1612).

Kress, Georg Freiherr van, "Briefe eines Nürnberger Studenten [= Christoph Kress] aus Leipzig und Bologna (1556–1560)," *Mitteilungen des Vereins für Geschichte der Stadt Nürnberg* 11 (1895): 97–172.

*Landriani, Marsilio, *Ordinationi fatte et stabilite per conservare le dignità et reputatione del studio di Bologna* (Bologna: Vittorio Benacci, 1602).

Il "Liber secretus iuris caesarei" dell'Università di Bologna [1378–1450], edited by Albano Sorbelli, 2 vols. (Bologna: Istituto per la Storia dell'Università di Bologna, 1938–1942).

Il "Liber secretus iuris caesarei" dell'Università di Bologna. 1451–1500, edited by Celestino Piana (Milan: A. Giuffrè, 1984).

Malpighi, Marcello, *Opera posthuma* (Amsterdam: Apud Georgium Gallet, 1700).

*Marsili, Antonio Felice, *Memorie per riparare i pregiudizi dell'Università dello Studio di Bologna, e ridurlo ad una facile e perfetta riforma* (Bologna: Per gli eredi di Antonio Pissarri, 1689), edited in Bortolotti, "La fondazione dell'Istituto," 386–403.

*Marsili, Luigi Ferdinando, *Parallelo dello stato moderno della Università di Bologna con l'altre di là de' Monti,* edited in Bortolotti, "La fondazione dell'Istituto," 405–19.

La matricola / Die Matrikel, 1573–1602, 1707–1727, edited by M. Luisa Accorsi with the collaboration of Claudia Zonta (Bologna: CLUEB, 1999; Natio germanica Bononiae, 1).

Müllner, Karl, *Reden und Briefe italienischer Humanisten* (Vienna: A. Hölder, 1899).

Piana, Celestino, *Nuovi documenti sull'Università di Bologna e sul Collegio di Spagna* (Bologna: Publicaciones del Real colegio de Espana, 1976).

Piccolomini, Francesco, *Naturae totius universi scientia perfecta atque philosophica quinque partibus ordine exactissimo absoluta* (Frankfurt: n.p., 1628).

Poliziano, Angelo, *Opera omnia,* 3 vols. (Turin: Bottega d'Erasmo, 1970–1971).

Pozzi, Giuseppe, *Orationes duae quibus accedit epistolare anatomicum commentariolum* (Bologna: Lelio Volpe, 1732).

*Sacchetti, Giulio, *Ordinationi fatte e stabilite per conservare la dignità e riputatione dello Studio di Bologna publicate in Bologna alli 12 di luglio 1641* (Bologna: Per l'Herede del Benacci Stampatore Camerale, 1641).

Sacco, Filippo Carlo, *Statuta civilia et criminalia civitatis Bononiae,* 2 vols. (Bologna: Costantino Pisarri, 1735–1737).

Statuta Nationis Germanicae Universitatis Bononiae, 1292–1750, edited by Paolo Colliva (Bologna: Associazione Italo-Tedesca di Bologna, 1975; repr., Minerva, 1995).

Tagliacozzi, Gaspare, *De curtorum chirurgia per insitionem* (Venice: Gaspare Bindoni il Giovane, 1597).

Trombetti Budriesi, Anna Laura, *Gli statuti del collegio dei dottori, giudici e avvocati di Bologna (1393–1467) e la loro matricola (fino al 1776)* (Bologna: Deputazione di storia patria, 1990).

Urceo, Antonio Cortesi (Codro), *Orationes seu sermones ut ipse appellabat: Epistolae. Silvae. Satyrae. Eglogae. Epigrammata* (Bologna: Giovanni Antonio Benedetti, 1502).

——, *Sermones,* edited and translated by Loredana Chines, Andrea Severi, and Giacomo Ventura, 3 vols. (Rome: Carocci, 2013–2021).

Vittori, Benedetto, *Commentaria in Hippocratis Aphorismos* (Venice: Vincenzo Valgrisi, 1556).

——, *Commentarii in prognostica Hippocratis* (Florence: Lorenzo Torrentino, 1551).

Zecchi, Giovanni, *Ioannis Zecchi Bononiensis, philosophi ac medici praestantissimi, et in florentissimo Bononiensi gymnasio primi theorici ordinarii eruditissimi In primam divi Hippocratis Aphorismorum sectionem dilucidissimae lectiones. Quibus accedunt tractatus quatuor insignes, admirabili quadam methodo digesti, De purgatione videlicet, De sanguinis missione, De criticis diebus ac De morbo Galico (!), a Scipione ex Mercuriis Romano philosopho ac medico summa diligentia ab ore autoris excepti. Eiusdem Scipionis Mercurii Romani Scholia in singulas lectiones* (Bologna: Giovanni Rossi, 1586).

CRITICAL LITERATURE

Ady, Cecilia M., *The Bentivoglio of Bologna: A Study in Despotism* (London: Oxford University Press, 1937).

Agrimi, Jole, and Chiara Crisciani, *Edocere medicos: Medicina scolastica nei secoli XIII–XV* (Naples: Guerini e Associati, 1988).

Alberigo, Giuseppe, "Il Concilio di Trento a Bologna (1547–1548)," in *Storia di Bologna,* ed. Zangheri, III.2, 1177–1212.

Alce, Venturino, "La stamperia bolognese di San Tommaso d'Aquino," *Culta Bononia* 6 (1974): 30–60.

Alce, Venturino, and Alfonso D'Amato, *La biblioteca di S. Domenico in Bologna* (Florence: Olschki, 1961).

Aldrovandi, L., "Commentario alle lettere di uno studente tedesco da Bologna (Cristoforo Kress, 1559–60)," *AMDSR,* s. III, 14 (1896), 14–41.

Alma mater librorum: Nove secoli di editoria bolognese per l'Università (Bologna: CLUEB, il Mulino, Nuovo Alfa, Zanichelli, 1988).

Almum Studium Papiense: Storia dell'Università di Pavia, edited by Dario Mantovani, 2 vols. (4 tomes) ([Milan:] Cisalpino, 2012–2017).

Anatomie accademiche, edited by Walter Tega, 3 vols. (Bologna: il Mulino, 1986–1993).

Andreoni, Annalisa, *La via della dottrina: Le lezioni accademiche di Benedetto Varchi* (Pisa: ETS, 2012).

Angelini, Annarita, "Introduzione," in *Anatomie accademiche,* III, 13–309.

——, *Simboli e questioni: L'eterodossia culturale di Achille Bocchi e dell'Hermathena* (Bologna: Pendragon, 2003).

Angelozzi, Giancarlo, "'Insegnarli la vita christiana insieme con bone lettere': Il convitto gesuitico e la formazione delle classi dirigenti," in *Studenti e università degli studenti,* 261–82.

Angelozzi, Giancarlo, and Cesarina Casanova, *La nobiltà disciplinata: Violenza nobiliare, procedure di giustizia e scienza cavalleresca a Bologna nel XVII secolo* (Bologna: CLUEB, 2003).

Anselmi, Gian Mario, *Le frontiere degli umanisti* (Bologna: CLUEB, 1988).

Anselmi, Gian Mario, Luisa Avellini, and Ezio Raimondi, "Il Rinascimento padano," in *Letteratura italiana: Storia e geografia,* edited by A. Asor Rosa, II.1 (Turin: Einaudi, 1988), 521–91.

L'Archiginnasio: Il palazzo, l'università, la biblioteca, edited by Giancarlo Roversi, 2 vols. (Bologna: Credito romagnolo, 1987).

"Aristotele fatto volgare": Tradizione aristotelica e cultura volgare nel Rinascimento, edited by David A. Lines and Eugenio Refini (Pisa: ETS, 2014 [but 2015]).

Arnzen, Rüdiger, "Vergessene Pflichtlektüre: Al-Qabisis astrologische Lehrschrift im Europäischen Mittelalter," *Zeitschrift für Geschichte der Arabisch-Islamischen Wissenschaften* 13 (1999): 93–128.

Artisten und Philosophen: Wissenschafts- und Wirkungsgeschichte einer Fakultät vom 13. bis zum 19. Jahrhundert, edited by Rainer Christoph Schwinges (Basel: Schwabe, 1999).

Ascanelli, Pietro, *I fascicoli personali dei lettori artisti della Assunteria di studio all'Archivio di Stato di Bologna (Archivio dell'Università): Studio documentario e bio-bibliografico* (Forlì, Valbonesi, 1968).

Ateneo e Chiesa di Bologna. Convegno di studi, Bologna, 13–15 aprile 1989 (Bologna: Istituto per la Storia della Chiesa, 1992).

Atlante della letteratura italiana, edited by Sergio Luzzatto and Gabriele Pedullà, vol. II: *Dalla controriforma alla Restaurazione,* edited by Erminia Irace (Turin: Einaudi, 2011).

Atlante storico delle città italiane—Emilia-Romagna, II.3: *Bologna: Da una crisi all'altra (secoli XIV–XVII),* edited by Rolando Dondarini and Carlo De Angelis (Bologna: Grafis Edizioni, 1997).

Avellini, Luisa, "In margine a: *Alma mater librorum:* Nove secoli di editoria bolognese per l'Università," *Schede umanistiche* 3 (1989): 63–77.

——, "Note sui domenicani. I libri e l'umanesimo a Bologna," in *Filologia umanistica: Per Gianvito Resta,* edited by Vincenzo Fera and Giacomo Ferraù, 3 vols. (Padua: Antenore, 1997), I, 107–27.

——, "Per uno studio del problema dell'eloquenza nell'opera di Giovanni Garzoni," *SMSUB,* n.s., 3 (1983): 83–104.

——, "Promozione libraria nel Quattrocento bolognese," in *Sul libro bolognese del Rinascimento,* edited by Luigi Balsamo and Leonardo Quaquarelli (Bologna: CLUEB, 1994), 77–127.

——, "Università e umanesimo," in *Le università dell'Europa,* VI, 19–43.

Azzolini, Monica, Mariarosa Cortesi, Chiara Crisciani, Marilyn Nicoud, and Paolo Rosso, "La Facoltà di Arti e Medicina," in *Almum Studium Papiense,* I.1, 515–70.

Bacchelli, Franco, "L'insegnamento di umanità a Bologna tra il Quattrocento e il Cinquecento," in *Storia di Bologna,* ed. Zangheri, III.2, 149–78.

——, "La legazione bolognese del Cardinal Bessarione (1450–1455)," in *Bessarione e l'Umanesimo: Catalogo della mostra di Venezia,* edited by G. Fiaccadori, M. Zorzi, and G. Publiese Carratelli (Naples: Vivarium 1994), 137–47.

Bacchi, Maria Cristina, "Tipografi e Università nel Quattrocento," in *Alma mater librorum,* 91–113.

——, "Ulisse Aldrovandi e i suoi libri," *L'Archiginnasio: Bollettino della Biblioteca Comunale di Bologna* 100 (2005): 255–366.

Bacchi, Maria Cristina, and Laura Miani, "Vicende del patrimonio librario bolognese: Manoscritti e incunaboli della Biblioteca Universitaria di Bologna—I libri prelevati dall'Istituto delle Scienze e dal Convento di SS. Salvatore nel 1796," in *Pio VI Braschi e Pio VII Chiaramonti: Due pontefici cesenati nel bicentenario della Campagna d'Italia—Atti del convegno internazionale, maggio 1997* (Bologna: CLUEB, 1998), 369–475.

Bakker, Paul J. J. M., "Les 'Palestrae' de Jean de Spello: Exercices scolaires d'un maître en médecine à Perouse au XIVe siècle," *Early Science and Medicine* 3 (1998): 289–322.

Baldassarri, Fabrizio "Seeking Intellectual Evidence in the Sciences," in *Evidence in the Age of the New Sciences,* edited by James A. T. Lancaster and Richard Raiswell (Cham: Springer, 2018), 47–75.

Baldelli, Franca, "Lo Studio bolognese tra Sei e Settecento," in *Scienza e letteratura,* 255–69.

——, "Tentativi di regolamentazione e riforme dello Studio bolognese nel '700," *Il Carrobbio* 10 (1984): 9–26.

Baldini, Ugo, "L'attività scientifica nel primo Settecento," in *Storia d'Italia. Annali 3: Scienza e tecnica nella cultura e nella società dal Rinascimento a oggi,* edited by G. Micheli (Turin: Einaudi, 1980), 467–529.

——, "Il corpuscolarismo italiano del Seicento: Problemi di metodo e prospettive di ricerca," in *Ricerche sull'atomismo del Seicento: Atti del Convegno di studio di Santa Margherita Ligure (14–16 ottobre 1976)* (Florence: La nuova Italia, 1977), 1–76.

——, *"Legem impone subactis": Studi su filosofia e scienza dei Gesuiti in Italia, 1540–1632* (Rome: Bulzoni, 1992).

——, "The Roman Inquisition's Condemnation of Astrology: Antecedents, Reasons and Consequences," in *Church, Censorship and Culture in Early Modern Italy,* 79–110.

——, "La scuola galileiana," in *Storia d'Italia. Annali 3. Scienza e tecnica nella cultura e nella società dal Rinascimento a oggi,* edited by Gianni Micheli (Turin: Einaudi, 1980), 383–468.

——, "La scuola scientifica emiliana della Compagnia di Gesù, 1600–1660: Linee di una ricostruzione archivistica," in *Università e cultura a Bologna e Ferrara* (Florence: Olschki, 1989), 109–78.

——, "La teoria della spiegazione scientifica a Bologna e Padova (1680–1730): Influenze e differenze," in *Rapporti tra le università di Padova e Bologna,* 191–254.

Baldini, Ugo, and Leen Spruit, "Cardano e Aldrovandi nelle lettere del Sant'Uffizio romano all'inquisitore di Bologna (1571–1573)," *Bruniana & Campanelliana* 6 (2000): 145–63.

Balsamo, Luigi, "Editoria a Bologna nei secoli XV–XVIII," in *Alma mater librorum,* 74–76.

——, "Imprese tipografiche in Emilia nel '400: Aspetti economici," in idem, *Produzione e circolazione libraria,* 11–43.

——, "Il libro per l'università nell'età moderna," in *Le università dell'Europa,* VI, 45–65.

—— "Primordi della stampa tipografica a Modena: 1473 anziché 1475," in idem, *Produzione e circolazione libraria,* 89–99.

——, *Produzione e circolazione libraria in Emilia (XV–XVIII sec.)* (Parma: Casanova, 1983).

——, "Università e editoria nel Quattrocento e Cinquecento," in *L'università a Bologna,* II, 123–32.

Balugani, Marta, "Università e stampa a Bologna a metà del Cinquecento: Opere a stampa dei docenti del decennio 1550–1560" (Università degli Studi di Bologna, tesi di laurea, a.a. 1991–1992, relatore Paolo Prodi).

Barbieri, Edoardo, "Elenchi librari e storia delle biblioteche nella prima Età moderna: Alcune osservazioni," in *Margarita amicorum: Studi di cultura europea per Agostino Sottili,* 2 vols., edited by Fabio Forner, Carla Maria Monti, and Paul Gerhard Schmidt (Milan: V&P, 2005), I, 81–102.

Barnett, Lydia, *After the Flood: Imagining the Global Environment in Early Modern Europe* (Baltimore: Johns Hopkins University Press, 2019).

Baroncini, Gabriele, "La filosofia naturale nello Studio bolognese (1650–1750): Preliminari di una ricerca," in *Scienza e letteratura,* 271–92.

——, "L'insegnamento della filosofia naturale nei collegi italiani dei Gesuiti (1610–1670): un esempio di nuovo aristotelismo," in *La "Ratio studiorum":*

Modelli culturali e pratiche educative dei Gesuiti in Italia tra Cinque e Seicento, edited by Gian Paolo Brizzi (Rome: Bulzoni, 1981), 163–215.

——, "Introduzione ad una teologia matematica del tardo seicento: L'*Arithmetica Realis* (1675) di Pietro Mengoli," *SMSUB,* n.s., 3 (1983): 315–92.

Barriento García, José, "La Teología, siglos XVI–XVII," in *Historia de la Universidad de Salamanca,* III.1, 203–50.

Barsanti, Paolo, *Il pubblico insegnamento in Lucca dal sec. XIV alla fine del secolo XVIII* (Lucca: n.p., 1905).

Battistella, Antonio, "Processi d'eresia nel Collegio di Spagna (1553–1554): Episodio della storia della Riforma in Bologna," *AMDSR,* s. III, 19 (1901): 138–83. Also published separately by N. Zanichelli.

——, *Il S. Officio e la riforma religiosa in Bologna* (Bologna: Nicola Zanichelli, 1905).

Battistini, Andrea, "Le accademie nel XVI e nel XVII secolo," in *Storia di Bologna,* ed. Zangheri, III.2, 179–208.

——, "La cultura scientifica nel collegio bolognese," in *Dall'isola alla città,* 157–69.

Bellomo, Manlio, *Saggio sull'università nell'età del diritto comune* (Catania: Giannotta, 1979; repr., Rome: Il cigno Galileo Galilei, 1992, 1996, 2004).

Belloni, Annalisa, "L'insegnamento giuridico in Italia e in Francia nei primi decenni del Cinquecento e l'emigrazione di Andrea Alciato," in *Università in Europa: Le istituzioni universitarie dal Medio Evo ai nostri giorni: Strutture, organizzazione, funzionamento—Atti del Convegno Internazionale di Studi, Milazzo 28 settembre–2 ottobre 1993,* edited by Andrea Romano (Soveria Manelli: Rubettino, 1995), 137–58.

Ben-David, Joseph, *The Scientist's Role in Society: A Comparative Study* (Englewood Cliffs, NJ: Prentice-Hall, 1971).

Berardo Pio, "Lo Studium e il papato tra XIV e XV secolo," in *Politica e "Studium": Nuove prospettive e ricerche—Atti del Convegno, Bologna 18 ottobre 2003* (Bologna: Istituto per la Storia dell'Università di Bologna, 2005), 157–82.

Berengario da Carpi: Il medico del Rinascimento, edited by Manuela Rossi and Tania Previdi ([Carpi]: APM, 2018).

Beretta, Francesco, "'Omnibus Christianae, Catholicaeque philosophiae amantibus: D. D.': Le *Tractatus syllepticus* de Melchior Inchofer, censeur de Galilée," *Freiburger Zeitschrift für Philosophie und Theologie* 48 (2001): 301–28.

——, "Orthodoxie philosophique et Inquisition romaine aux 16e–17e siècles: Un essai d'interpretation," *Historia Philosophica* 3 (2005): 67–96.

Bergamini, Maria Grazia, "Dai Gelati alla Renia (1670–1698): Appunti per una storia delle accademie letterarie bolognesi," in *La Colonia Renia: Profilo documentario e critico dell'Arcadia bolognese,* vol. II: *Momenti e problemi,* edited by Mario Saccenti (Modena: Mucchi, 1988), 5–52.

Bernabeo, Raffaele A., "La scuola di medicina fra XVI e XX secolo," in *L'Università a Bologna,* II, 185–94.

Bernardi, Gabriella, *Giovanni Domenico Cassini: A Modern Astronomer in the 17th Century* (Berlin: Springer, 2017).

Berns, Andrew D., *The Bible and Natural Philosophy in Renaissance Italy: Jewish and Christian Physicians in Search of Truth* (Cambridge: Cambridge University Press, 2014).

Bernuzzi, Marco, "L'insegnamento della Teologia: Discipline e strumenti," in *Almum Studium Papiense,* I.2, 1151–86.

Bertoloni Meli, Domenico, *Mechanism, Experiment, Disease: Marcello Malpighi and Seventeenth-Century Anatomy* (Baltimore: Johns Hopkins University Press, 2011).

——, *Thinking with Objects: The Transformation of Mechanics in the Seventeenth Century* (Baltimore: Johns Hopkins University Press, 2006).

Betti, Gian Luigi, "Il copernicanesimo nello Studio di Bologna," in *La diffusione del copernicanesimo in Italia (1543–1610),* edited by Massimo Bucciantini and Maurizio Torrini (Florence: Olschki, 1977), 67–81.

——, "Tra Università e accademie: Note sulla cultura bolognese del primo Seicento," *Strenna storica bolognese* 37 (1987): 83–98.

Biagioli, Mario, "The Social Status of Italian Mathematicians, 1450–1600," *History of Science* 27.1 (1989): 41–95.

Bianchi, Luca, "Agostino Oreggi, qualificatore del *Dialogo,* e i limiti della conoscenza scientifica," in *"Largo campo di filosofare": Eurosymposium Galileo 2001,* edited by José Montesinos and Carlos Solís Santos (La Orotava: Funación Canaria Horotava de Historia de la Ciencia, 2001), 575–84.

——, "'Aristotele fu un uomo e potè errare': Sulle origini medievali della critica al 'principio di autorità,'" in idem, *Studi sull'aristotelismo,* 101–24.

——, "Una caduta senza declino? Considerazioni sulla crisi dell'aristotelismo fra Rinascimento ed età moderna," in idem, *Studi sull'aristotelismo,* 133–83.

——, *Censure et liberté intellectuelle à l'Université de Paris* (Paris: Les Belles Lettres, 1999).

——, "I contenuti dell'insegnamento: Arti liberali e filosofia nei secoli XIII–XVI," in *Storia delle università in Italia,* II, 117–41.

——, "Fra Ermolao Barbaro e Ludovico Boccadiferro: Qualche considerazione sulle trasformazioni della 'fisica medievale' nel Rinascimento italiano," *Medioevo: Rivista di storia della filosofia medievale* 29 (2004): 341–78.

——, "From Pope Urban VIII to Bishop Étienne Tempier: The Strange History of the 'Doctrine of the Double Truth,'" *Freiburger Zeitschrift für Philosophie und Theologie* 64.1 (2017): 9–26.

——, *Pour une histoire de la "double vérité"* (Paris: Vrin, 2008).

——, "Renaissance Readings of the *Nicomachean Ethics,*" in *Rethinking Virtue, Reforming Society,* 131–67.

——, *Studi sull'aristotelismo del Rinascimento* (Padua: Il Poligrafo, 2003).

——, "'Ubi desinit physicus, ibi medicus incipit,'" in *Summa doctrina et certa experientia: Studi su filosofia e medicina per Chiara Crisciani,* edited by Gabriella Zuccolin (Florence: SISMEL-Edizioni del Galluzzo, 2017), 5–28.

——, "Le università e il 'decollo scientifico' dell'Occidente," in *La filosofia nelle università secoli XIII–XIV,* edited by Luca Bianchi (Scandicci [Firenze]: La nuova Italia, 1997), 25–62.

——, *Il vescovo e i filosofi: La condanna parigina del 1277 e l'evoluzione dell'aristotelismo scolastico* (Bergamo: Lubrina, 1990).

La Biblioteca del Convento di San Francesco di Bologna: Incunaboli e Cinquecentine. Catalogo, edited by Gino Zanotti, with entries by Zita Zanardi (Bologna: Forni, 2007).

Bingen, Nicole, "Les Étudiants de langue française dans les universités italiennes à la Renaissance: Mise à jour du recensement et analyse des données," in *Les échanges entre les universités,* 25–43.

——, "Studenti francofoni nelle università italiane del Rinascimento: Censimento e analisi dei dati," *ASUI* 8 (2004): 283–97.

Biondi, Albano, "Insegnare a Bologna: Le esperienze di un grande maestro—Carlo Sigonio," in *L'Università a Bologna,* I, 87–95.

Black, Robert, *Education and Society in Florentine Tuscany: Teachers, Pupils and Schools, c. 1250–1500* (Leiden: Brill, 2007-).

——, *Humanism and Education in Medieval and Renaissance Society: Tradition and Innovation in Latin Schools from the Twelfth to the Fifteenth Century* (Cambridge: Cambridge University Press, 2001).

Blair, Ann, "Mosaic Physics and the Search for a Pious Natural Philosophy in the Late Renaissance," *Isis* 91.1 (March 2000): 32–58.

——, "Student Manuscripts and the Textbook," in *Scholarly Knowledge,* 39–73.

Blanshei, Sarah Rubin, "Introduction: History and Historiography of Bologna," in *A Companion to Medieval and Renaissance Bologna,* 1–25.

Blanshei, Sarah Rubin, and Sara Cucini, "Criminal Justice and Conflict Resolution," in *A Companion to Medieval and Renaissance Bologna,* 335–60.

Boehm, Laetitia, "*Cancellarius Universitatis:* Die Universität zwischen Korporation und Staatsanstalt," in eadem, *Geschichtsdenken, Bildungsgeschichte, Wissensorganisation: Ausgewählte Aufsätze von Laetitia Boehm anläßlich ihres 65. Geburtstages* (Berlin: Duncker & Humblot, 1996), 605–713.

Boffito, Giuseppe, and Francesco Fracassetti, *Il collegio San Luigi dei Padri Barnabiti in Bologna, 1773–1873–1923* (Florence: Tip. Giuntina, 1925).

Bologna: Cultural Crossroads from the Medieval to the Baroque: Recent Anglo-American Scholarship, edited by Gian Mario Anselmi, Angela De Benedictis, and Nicholas Terpstra (Bologna: Bononia University Press, 2013).

Bologna trema (1943–1944): Fotoconfronti di Bernardino Salvati e Paolo Veggetti—Con un racconto di Giovanni Greco e Davide Monda (Bologna: Pendragon, 2003).

Bonifati, Giovanni, *Dal libro manoscritto al libro stampato: Sistemi di mercato a Bologna e a Firenze agli albori del capitalismo* (Turin: Rosenberg & Sellier, 2008).

Bònoli, Fabrizio, "Cassini e la tradizione astronomica galileiana a Bologna," in *Galileo e la scuola galileiana,* 171–88.

Bononia manifesta: Catalogo dei bandi, editti, costituzioni e provvedimenti diversi, Stampati nel XVI secolo per Bologna e il suo territorio, edited by Zita Zanardi (Florence: Olschki, 1996).

Bononia manifesta: Supplemento al Catalogo dei bandi, editti, costituzioni e provvedimenti diversi, stampati nel XVI secolo per Bologna e il suo territorio, edited by Zita Zanardi (Florence: Olschki, 2014).

Bortolotti, Ettore, "La fondazione dell'Istituto e la riforma dello 'studio' di Bologna," in *Memorie intorno a Luigi Ferdinando Marsili, pubblicate nel secondo centenario della morte* (Bologna: Nicola Zanichelli, 1930), 383–471.

——, *La storia della matematica nell'Università di Bologna* (Bologna: Zanichelli, 1947).

Boschiero, Luciano, "Giovanni Alfonso Borelli (1608-1679)," in idem, *Experiment and Natural Philosophy in Seventeenth-Century Tuscany: The History of the Accademia del Cimento* (Dordrecht: Springer, 2007), 59–91.

Botley, Paul, "Greek Literature in Exile: The Books of Andronicus Callistus, 1475-1476," *Dumbarton Oaks Papers* 72 (2019): 181–96.

——, *Learning Greek in Western Europe, 1396–1529: Grammars, Lexica, and Classroom Texts* (Philadelphia: American Philosophical Society, 2010).

Bottazzini, Umberto, "La rivoluzione galileiana a Bologna: Bonaventura Cavalieri," in *Storia illustrata di Bologna,* VI, 141–60.

Bovier, Kevin, "Commenter les *Histoires* et les *Annales* de Tacite à la Renaissance: De Philippe Béroalde le Jeune à Giovanni Ferrerio (ca. 1515-1570)" (PhD dissertation, University of Geneva, 2020).

Brambilla, Elena, "*Bricolage* didattico: L'uso della dettatura nelle Università e i repertori di luoghi comuni scritti dagli scolari," in *Dalla pecia all'e-book,* 205–15.

——, "Collegi dei dottori universitari e collegi professionali," in *Storia delle università in Italia,* II, 303–45.

——, "La medicina nel Settecento: Dal monopolio dogmatico alla professione scientifica," in *Storia d'Italia,* Annali 7, *Malattia e medicina,* edited by F. Della Peruta (Turin: Einaudi, 1984), 3–147.

——, "*Verba* e *res:* Arti della memoria e logica nella tradizione scolastico-universitaria," in eadem, *Genealogie del sapere: Università, professioni giuridiche e nobiltà togata in Italia, 13°–17° secolo—Con un saggio sull'arte della memoria* (Milan: UNICOPLI, 2005), 159-218.

Bresadola, Marco, "Medicina e filosofia naturale: L'indagine sul vivente a Bologna tra Seicento e Settecento," in *Storia di Bologna,* ed. Zangheri, III.2, 375–436.

Brill's Encyclopaedia of the Neo-Latin World, edited by Philip Ford, Jan Bloemendal, and Charles Fantazzi (Leiden: Brill, 2014).

Brizzi, Gian Paolo, "ASFE: Una banca dati per lo studio della mobilità universitaria e per un *onomasticon* dei laureati in Italia nell'età moderna," *ASUI* 8 (2004): 449–55.

——, "Aspetti della presenza della Nazione germanica a Bologna nella seconda metà del XVI secolo," in *La matricola,* 31–38 (German translation, 39–47).

——, "I collegi per borsisti e lo Studio Bolognese: Caratteri ed evoluzione di un'istituzione educativo-assistenziale fra XIII e XVIII secolo," *SMSUB,* n.s., 4 (1984): 9–186.

——, "I collegi religiosi: La Compagnia di Gesù," in *I secoli moderni: Le istituzioni e il pensiero,* edited by Luigi Balsamo et al. (Cinisello Balsamo: Silvana Editoriale, 1987), 111–25.

——, "Da *domus pauperum scholarium* a collegio d'educazione: Università e collegi in Europa (secoli XII–XVIII)," in *Disciplina dell'anima, disciplina del corpo e disciplina della società tra Medioevo ed età moderna,* edited by Paolo Prodi (Bologna: il Mulino, 1994), 809–40.

——, "Una fonte per la storia studentesca: I 'libri amicorum,'" in *Studenti, università, città nella storia padovana: Atti del Convegno, Padova 6–8 febbraio 1998,* edited by Francesco Piovan and Luciana Sitran Rea (Triest: LINT, 2001), 389–402.

——, *La formazione della classe dirigente nel Sei–Settecento* (Bologna: il Mulino, 1976; repr. Bologna: il Mulino, 2015).

——, "Il governo dello Studio e l'organizzazione della didattica nell'età moderna," in *Storia illustrata di Bologna,* VI, 101–20.

——, "L'identità dello studente fra Medioevo ed età moderna," in *Identità collettive fra Medioevo ed età moderna,* edited by Paolo Prodi and Wolfgang Reinhard (Bologna: CLUEB, 2002), 313–32.

——, "Istruzione e istituzioni educative a Bologna nell'età moderna," in *Storia della Chiesa di Bologna,* edited by Paolo Prodi and Lorenzo Paolini, 2 vols. (Bergamo: Bolis, 1997), II, 285–305.

——, "The Jesuits and Universities in Italy," in *European Universities in the Age of Reformation and Counter Reformation,* 187–97.

——, "Maestri e studenti a Bologna nell'età moderna," in *Storia illustrata di Bologna,* VI, 121–40.

——, "Matricole ed effettivi: Aspetti della presenza studentesca a Bologna fra Cinque e Seicento," in *Studenti e università degli studenti,* 225–59.

——, "Modi e forme della presenza studentesca a Bologna in età moderna," in *L'Università a Bologna,* II, 59–74.

——, "Per una geografia umana delle università italiane: Studenti e laureati in età moderna," in *Lauree,* 113–42.

——, "La pratica del viaggio d'istruzione in Italia nel Sei–Settecento," *Annali dell'Istituto storico italo-germanico in Trento* 2 (1976): 203–91.

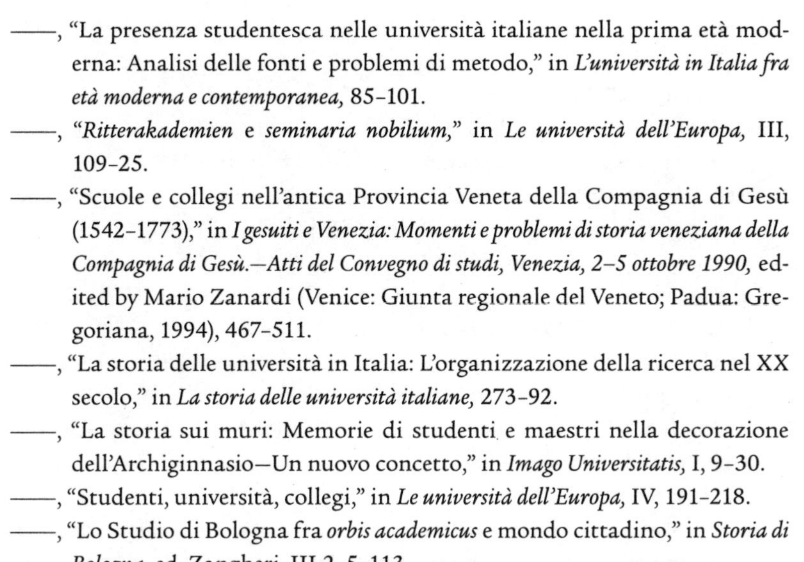

——, "La presenza studentesca nelle università italiane nella prima età moderna: Analisi delle fonti e problemi di metodo," in *L'università in Italia fra età moderna e contemporanea,* 85–101.

——, "*Ritterakademien* e *seminaria nobilium,*" in *Le università dell'Europa,* III, 109–25.

——, "Scuole e collegi nell'antica Provincia Veneta della Compagnia di Gesù (1542–1773)," in *I gesuiti e Venezia: Momenti e problemi di storia veneziana della Compagnia di Gesù.—Atti del Convegno di studi, Venezia, 2–5 ottobre 1990,* edited by Mario Zanardi (Venice: Giunta regionale del Veneto; Padua: Gregoriana, 1994), 467–511.

——, "La storia delle università in Italia: L'organizzazione della ricerca nel XX secolo," in *La storia delle università italiane,* 273–92.

——, "La storia sui muri: Memorie di studenti e maestri nella decorazione dell'Archiginnasio—Un nuovo concetto," in *Imago Universitatis,* I, 9–30.

——, "Studenti, università, collegi," in *Le università dell'Europa,* IV, 191–218.

——, "Lo Studio di Bologna fra *orbis academicus* e mondo cittadino," in *Storia di Bologna,* ed. Zangheri, III.2, 5–113.

——, "Town and Gown? Bologna 1560: La città di fronte a una rivolta degli studenti," in *Amicitiae pignus: Studi storici per Piero del Negro,* edited by Ugo Baldini and Gian Paolo Brizzi (Milan: Edizioni Unicopli, 2013), 87–104.

——, "Università e collegi," in *Storia delle università in Italia,* II, 347–87.

Brockliss, L. W. B., "Copernicus in the University: The French Experience," in *New Perspectives on Renaissance Thought,* 190–213.

——, "Curricula," in *A History of the University in Europe,* II, 563–620.

——, *French Higher Education in the Seventeenth and Eighteenth Centuries: A Cultural History* (Oxford: Clarendon Press, 1987).

——, *The University of Oxford: A History* (Oxford: Oxford University Press, 2016).

Brugi, Biagio, "Il catalogo dei libri degli stationarii negli statuti della università bolognese dei giuristi," *SMSUB* 5 (1920): 3–44.

——, "Un parere di Scipione Maffei intorno allo Studio di Padova sui principî del Settecento: Edizione dal testo originale con introduzione e note del prof. Biagio Brugi, M.E.," *Atti del Reale Istituto Veneto di scienze, lettere ed arti* 69.2 (1909–1910): 575–91.

Bruning, Jens, *Innovation in Forschung und Lehre: Die Philosophische Fakultät der Universität Helmstedt in der Frühaufklärung, 1680–1740* (Wiesbaden: Harrassowitz, 2012).

Bühler, Curt F., *The Fifteenth-Century Book: The Scribes, the Printers, the Decorators* (Philadelphia: University of Pennsylvania Press, 1960).

——, *The University and the Press in Fifteenth-Century Bologna* (Notre Dame, IN: Mediaeval Institute, University of Notre Dame, 1958).

Busacchi, Vincenzo, "Il nuovo spirito di ricerca e lo sperimentalismo nell'opera poco nota di medici e non medici nel '600 a Bologna," *SMSUB,* n.s., 1 (1956): 417–33.

Buzzetti, Dino, "La Faculté des arts dans les universités de l'Europe méridionale," in *L'enseignement des disciplines à la Faculté des arts,* 457–66.

Buzzetti, Dino, Roberto Lambertini, and Andrea Tabarroni, "Tradizione testuale e insegnamento nell'Università di medicina e arti di Bologna dei secoli XIV e XV," *ASUI* 1 (1997): 77–95.

Cagni, Giuseppe, "Il pontificio collegio 'Montalto' in Bologna (1585–1797)," *Barnabiti studi* 5 (1988): 1–188.

Calcaterra, Carlo, *Alma mater studiorum: L'università di Bologna nella storia della cultura e della civiltà* (Bologna: Zanichelli, 1948).

Calore, Marina, "Una fornita biblioteca di fine '500: Predilezioni librarie di Cornelio Lambertini conte del Poggio e senatore di Bologna," *Strenna storica bolognese* 61 (2011): 93–110.

Camarota, Michele, "La scienza nelle università," in *Il contributo italiano alla storia del pensiero—Scienze* (2013; consulted online at treccani.it on 24 January 2021).

The Cambridge History of Later Medieval Philosophy: From the Rediscovery of Aristotle to the Disintegration of Scholasticism, 1100–1600, edited by Norman Kretzmann, Anthony Kenny, Jan Pinborg, and Eleonore Stump (Cambridge: Cambridge University Press, 1982).

The Cambridge History of Renaissance Philosophy, edited by Charles B. Schmitt, Quentin Skinner, Eckhard Kessler, and Jill Kraye (Cambridge: Cambridge University Press, 1988).

Cammelli, G., "Andronico Callisto," *La Rinascita* 5 (1942): 180–88, 200.

Campana, Augusto, "The Origin of the Word 'Humanist,'" *Journal of the Warburg and Courtauld Institutes* 1 (1946): 60–73.

Capaccioni, Andrea, "Biblioteche e università dal medioevo al Settecento," in *Maestri, insegnamenti e libri a Perugia,* 207–20.

Capecchi, Danilo, "Experiments, Mathematics and Principles of Natural Philosophy in the Epistemology of Giovanni Battista Baliani," *Advances in Historical Studies* 6 (2017): 78–94.

Cappagli, Alessandra, "Diomede Borghesi e Celso Cittadini lettori di toscana favella," in *Tra Rinascimento e strutture attuali: Saggi di linguistica italiana. Atti del 1° Convegno della Società Internazionale di Linguistica e Filologia Italiana (Siena, 28–31 marzo 1989),* edited by L. Giannelli et al., 2 vols. (Turin: Rosenberg and Sellier, 1991), I, 23–35.

Cappiello, Annalisa, "I filosofi e la *lex:* Pietro Pomponazzi, Ludovico Boccadiferro e le misure censorie del 1513," *Rinascimento,* n.s. 58 (2018): 87–104.

Caprioli, Severino, *Indagini sul Bolognini: Giurisprudenza e filologia nel Quattrocento italiano* (Milan: Giuffrè, 1969).

Carcereri, L., "Cristoforo Dossena Francesco Linguardo e un Giordano librai processati per eresia a Bologna," *L'Archiginnasio* 5 (1910): 177–92.

Carlsmith, Christopher, "'Cacciò fuori un grande bastone bianco': Conflict between the Collegio Ancarano and the Seminarians in Early Modern Bologna," in *The Culture of Violence in Late Medieval and Early Modern Italy,* edited by Fabrizio Riccciardelli and Samuel Cohn Jr. (Florence: Le Lettere, 2012), 191–216.

——, "Collegiate Conflict: Two Brawls in Bologna between the Collegio di Spagna and the Collegio Montalto, 1672–1673," in *Le università e la violenza studentesca,* 47–63.

——, "Quarrels under the Portico: Student Violence in Modern Italian Universities," in *Student Revolt, City, and Society in Europe: From the Middle Ages to the Present,* edited by Pieter Dhondt and Elizabethanne Boran (New York: Routledge, 2018), 39–53.

——, "*Siam Ungari!* Honour, Nationalism, and Student Conflict in Seventeenth-Century Bologna," *History of Universities* 26.2 (2012): 113–49.

——, "Student Colleges in Early Modern Bologna," in *Bologna: Cultural Crossroads,* 71–81.

——, "Student Conflict in the *Brevis Relatio* of the Hungarian-Illyrian College, 1675," in *Renaissance Studies in Honor of Joseph Connors,* edited by L. Waldman and M. Israels, 3 vols. (Florence: Olschki, 2013), 325–36.

Carnevali, Rebecca, "Cheap, Everyday Print: Jobbing Printing and Its Users in Post-Tridentine Bologna" (unpublished PhD dissertation, University of Warwick, 2019).

Caroti, Stefano, "L' 'Aristotele italiano' di Alessandro Piccolomini: Un progetto sistematico di filosofia naturale in volgare a metà '500," in *Il volgare come lingua di cultura,* 361–401.

——, *L'astrologia in Italia: Profezie, oroscopi e segreti celesti, dagli zodiaci romani alla tradizione islamica, dalle corti rinascimentali alle scuole moderne—Storia, documenti, personaggi* (Rome: Newton Compton, 1983).

Carroll, Stuart, "Revenge and Reconciliation in Early Modern Italy," *Past & Present* 233.1 (November 2016): 101–42.

Casali, Elide, *Le spie del cielo: Oroscopi, lunari e almanacchi nell'Italia moderna* (Turin: Einaudi, 2003).

Casella, Maria Teresa, "Il metodo dei commentatori umanistici esemplato su Beroaldo," *Studi medievali,* s. III, 16.2 (1975): 627–701.

Casey, John Patrick, "Boethius' Works on Logic in the Middle Ages," in *A Companion to Boethius in the Middle Ages* (Leiden: Brill, 2012), 193–220.

Casini, Paolo, *Newton e la coscienza europea* (Bologna: il Mulino, 1983).

——, "The Reception of Newton's *Opticks* in Italy," in *Renaissance and Revolution,* 215–27.

La Cattedrale di San Pietro in Bologna, edited by Roberto Terra (Cinisello Balsamo, Milano: Silvana Editoriale, 1997).

Cavarzere, Marco, "The Workings of a Papal Institution: Roman Censorship and Italian Authors in the Seventeenth Century," in *Pratiken der frühen Neuzeit: Akteure, Handlungen, Artefakten,* edited by Arndt Brendfecke (Cologne/Vienna: Weimar/Böhlau, 2000), 371–85.

Cavazza, Francesco, *Le scuole dell'antico Studio bolognese* (Milan: Ulrico Hoepli, 1896).

Cavazza, Marta, "Between Modesty and Spectacle: Women and Science in Eighteenth Century Italy," in *Italy's Eighteenth Century: Gender and Culture in the Age of the Grand Tour,* edited by Paula Findlen, Catherine Sama, and Wendy Wassyng Roworth (Stanford: Stanford University Press, 2009), 275–302.

——, "Bologna e Galileo: Da Cesare Marsili agli Inquieti," in *Galileo e la scuola galileiana,* 155–70.

——, "La cometa del 1680–81: Astrologi e astronomi a confronto," *SMSUB,* n.s., 3 (1983): 409–66.

——, "'Dottrici' e lettrici dell'Università di Bologna nel Settecento," *ASUI* 1 (1997): 109–25.

——, "Early Work on Electricity and Medicine in the Bologna Academy of Sciences: Laura Bassi and Giuseppe Veratti," in *Electricity and Life: Episodes in the History of Hybrid Objects,* edited by Giuliano Pancaldi (Bologna: CIS, Università di Bologna, 2011), 7–33.

——, "Fisica generale e fisica sperimentale nelle istituzioni scientifiche emiliane del Settecento," *Studi settecenteschi* 18 (1998): 321–42.

——, "Innovazione e compromesso: L'Istituto delle Scienze e il sistema accademico bolognese del Settecento," in *Storia di Bologna,* ed. Zangheri, III.2, 317–74.

——, "L'insegnamento delle scienze sperimentali nell'Istituto delle Scienze di Bologna," in *Le università e le scienze: Prospettive storiche e attuali,* Relazioni presentate al convegno internazionale, Bologna, 18 settembre 1991, edited by Giuliano Pancaldi (Bologna: CIS, 1993), 155–68 (English translation, 169–79).

——, "L'Istituto delle Scienze: Il contesto cittadino—La costruzione di una nuova 'Casa di Salomone,'" in *L'Università a Bologna,* II, 165–74.

——, "L'Istituto delle Scienze e il sistema accademico bolognese," in *Storia di Bologna,* ed. Zangheri, III.2, 317–74.

——, *Laura Bassi: Donne, genere e scienza nell'Italia del Settecento* (Milan: Editrice Bibliografica, 2020).

——, "Riforma dell'università e nuove accademie nella politica culturale dell'Arcidiacono Marsili," in *Università, Accademie e Società scientifiche in Italia e in Germania dal Cinquecento al Settecento,* edited by Laetitia Boehm and Ezio Raimondi (Bologna: il Mulino, 1982), 248–82.

——, "La scienza, lo Studio, i gesuiti a Bologna nella metà del Seicento," *Giornale di astronomia* 32.1 (2006): 11–19.

——, *Settecento inquieto: Alle origini dell'Istituto delle Scienze di Bologna* (Bologna: il Mulino, 1990).

——, "The Uselessness of Anatomy: Mini and Sbaraglia versus Malpighi," in *Marcello Malpighi,* 129–45.

Ceccarelli, Francesco, "*Scholarum Exaedificatio:* La costruzione del palazzo dell'Archiginnasio e la piazza delle scuole di Bologna," in *L'università e la città: Il ruolo di Padova e degli altri atenei italiani nello sviluppo urbano—Atti del convegno di studi, Padova, 4–6 dicembre 2003,* edited by Giuliana Mazzi (Bologna: CLUEB, 2006), 47–65.

Ceccarelli, Francesco, and Daniele Pascale Guidotti Magnani, *Il portico bolognese: Storia, architettura, città* (Bologna: Bononia University Press, 2021).

Celenza, Christopher S., *Renaissance Humanism and the Papal Curia: Lapo da Castiglionchio the Younger's* De curiae commodis (Ann Arbor: University of Michigan Press, 1999).

Cencetti, Giorgio, "Alcuni documenti sul commercio libraio bolognese al principio del secolo XVI," in idem, *Lo Studio di Bologna,* 237–44.

——, *Gli archivi dello Studio bolognese* (Bologna: Zanichelli, 1938).

——, "La laurea nelle università medioevali," in idem, *Lo Studio di Bologna,* 77–93.

——, *Lo Studio di Bologna: Aspetti momenti e problemi (1935–1970),* edited by R. Ferrara, G. Orlandelli, and A. Vasina (Bologna: CLUEB, 1989).

——, "Sulle origini dello Studio di Bologna," in idem, *Lo Studio di Bologna,* 17–27.

Cerotti, L., "Scheletri di biblioteche, fisionomia di lettori: Gli 'inventari di biblioteca' come materiali per una anatomia ricostruttiva della cultura libraria di antico regime," in *Libri, biblioteche e cultura nell'Italia del Cinque e Seicento,* edited by Edoardo Barbieri and Danilo Zardin (Milan: Vita e pensiero, 2002), 373–432.

Chambers, David S., "*Studium Urbis* and *gabella studii:* The University of Rome in the Fifteenth Century," in *Cultural Aspects of the Italian Renaissance,* edited by C. H. Clough (Manchester: Manchester University Press, 1976), 68–110.

Chandelier, Joel, *Avicenne et la médecine en Italie: Le Canon dans les universités* (Paris: Champion, 2017).

Chimienti, Michele, *Monete della zecca di Bologna* (Bologna: Edizioni Format.bo, 2009).

Chines, Loredana, "Filologia e arcana sapienza: L'umanista Achille Bocchi commentatore ed esegeta," *Studi e problemi di critica testuale* 60 (2000): 71–80.

——, "Il lettore elegante di Achille Bocchi," in *Le virtuose adunanze,* 227–35.

——, *La parola degli antichi: Umanesimo emiliano tra scuola e poesia* (Rome: Carocci, 1998).

Christian Readings of Aristotle from the Middle Ages to the Renaissance, edited by Luca Bianchi (Turnhout: Brepols, 2011).

Church, Censorship and Culture in Early Modern Italy, edited by Gigliola Fragnito (Cambridge: Cambridge University Press, 2001).

Ciccolella, Federica, *Donati Graeci: Learning Greek in the Renaissance* (Leiden: Brill, 2008).

Cicognani, Paola, "Lo Studio di Bologna nella seconda metà del '500 (dal carteggio degli ambasciatori bolognesi a Roma)" (tesi di laurea, Facoltà di Magistero, Università di Bologna, relatore Paolo Prodi, a.a. 1963-1964).

Claessens, G., "Francesco Piccolomini on Prime Matter and Extension," *Vivarium* 50.2 (2012): 225-44.

Clarke, Angus G., "Giovanni Antonio Magini (1555-1617) and Late Renaissance Astrology" (unpublished PhD thesis, Warburg Institute, University of London, 1985).

The Classical Tradition, edited by Anthony Grafton, Glenn W. Most, and Salvatore Settis (Cambridge, MA: Belknap Press of Harvard University Press, 2010).

I classici e l'Università umanistica: Atti del Convegno di Pavia, 22–24 novembre 2001, edited by Luciano Gargan and Maria Pia Mussini Sacchi (Messina: Centro Interdipartimentale di Studi Umanistici, 2006).

Cobban, Alan B., "Medieval Student Power," *Past and Present* 53.1 (1971): 28-66.

——, *The Medieval Universities: Their Development and Organization* (London: Methuen, 1975).

Cochrane, Eric, *Florence in the Forgotten Centuries, 1527–1800* (Chicago: University of Chicago Press, 1973).

Codices latini antiquiores: A Palaeographical Guide to Latin Manuscripts prior to the Ninth Century, edited by E. A. Lowe, 11 vols. (Oxford: Clarendon Press, 1934-1971).

Codina Mir, Gabriel, *Aux sources de la pédagogie des Jésuites: Le "modus parisiensis"* (Rome: Institutum Historicum Societatis Iesu, 1968).

——, "The 'Modus Parisiensis,'" in *The Jesuit* Ratio Studiorum, 28-49.

Cogo, G., "Francesco Buzzacarini poeta latino del sec. XV," *Il propugnatore,* n.s., 5 (1892): 446-63.

I collegi universitari in Europa tra il XIV e il XVIII secolo: Atti del Convegno di Studi della Commissione internazionale per la storia delle Università (Siena-Bologna, 16-19 maggio 1988), edited by Domenico Maffei and Hilde de Ridder-Symoens (Milan: Giuffrè, 1991).

Colliva, Paolo, "Bologna dal XIV al XVIII secolo: 'Governo misto' o signoria senatoria?," in *Storia dell'Emilia Romagna,* edited by Aldo Berselli, 2 vols. (Bologna: University Press, 1975-1977), II, 13-34.

——, "'Nationes' ed 'Universitates' nella vita e nello Studio di Bologna: La Nazione germanica ed i suoi statuti," in idem, *Scritti minori,* edited by Giovanna Morelli and Nicoletta Sarti (Milan: Giuffrè, 1996), 543-76.

Colombo, Enzo, "La biblioteca negata: Marco Antonio Collina Sbaraglia e i suoi tentativi di fondare una 'pubblica libreria' a Bologna nei primi decenni del '700," *Il Carrobbio* 9 (1983): 108–29.

La Colonia Renia: Profilo documentario e critico dell'Arcadia bolognese—Documenti bio-bibliografici, 2 vols, edited by Mario Saccenti (Modena: Mucchi, 1988).

A Companion to Astrology in the Renaissance, edited by Brendan Dooley (Leiden: Brill, 2014).

A Companion to Medieval and Renaissance Bologna, edited by Sarah Rubin Blanshei (Leiden: Brill, 2018).

Compère, Marie Madeleine, "L'insegnamento della retorica e della lingua greca," in *Le università dell'Europa,* VI, 109–25.

Conrad, Lawrence I., Michael Neve, Vivian Nutton, Roy Porter, and Andrew Wear, *The Western Medical Tradition, 800 BC to AD 1800* (Cambridge: Cambridge University Press, 1995).

Conte, Emanuele, *Accademie studentesche a Roma nel Cinquecento: De modis docendi et discendi iure* (Rome: Edizioni dell'Ateneo, 1985).

Contemporaries of Erasmus: A Biographical Register of the Renaissance and Reformation, edited by Peter G. Bietenholz and Thomas B. Deutscher, 3 vols. (Toronto: University of Toronto Press, 1985–1987).

Corradi, Alfonso, "Dell'antica autoplastica italiana," *Memorie del Reale Istituto Lombardo di Scienze e Lettere: Classe di scienze matematiche e naturali,* s. III, 13 (1877): 225–73.

Cortese, Ennio, "L'Università di Bologna e il Collegio di Spagna nel Cinquecento: Uno scontro tra i rettori Cesare Rivera e Diego Gasque," in *Studi in memoria di Giuliana d'Amelio,* 2 vols. (Milan: Giuffré, 1978), I, 219–72.

Costa, Emilio, "Contributo alla storia dello Studio bolognese durante il secolo XVII," *SMSUB* 3 (1912): 1–88.

——, "La fondazione dell'Istituto delle Scienze ed una riforma dello Studio bolognese proposta da Luigi Ferdinando Marsili," *SMSUB* 5 (1920): 45–66.

——, "Gerolamo Cardano allo Studio di Bologna," *Archivio storico italiano,* s. V, 35 (1905): 425–36.

——, "La prima cattedra d'umanità nello Studio bolognese durante il secolo XVI," *SMSUB* 1 (1909): 23–63.

——, *Ulisse Aldrovandi e lo Studio bolognese nella seconda metà del secolo XVI* (Bologna: Stabilimento poligrafico emiliano, 1907).

Costabel, Pierre, *Mariotte savant et philosophe (†1684): Analyse d'une renommée* (Paris: J. Vrin, 1986).

Cotugno, Alessio, "Le *Annotationi* di Piccolomini e la *Poetica* di Castelvetro a confronto: Tecnica argomentativa, vocabolario critico, dispositivi esegetici," in *Forms of Conflict and Rivalries in Renaissance Europe,* edited by David A. Lines, Marc Laureys, and Jill Kraye (Göttingen: V&R, 2015), 161–205.

——, *La scienza della parola: Retorica e linguistica di Sperone Speroni* (Bologna: il Mulino, 2018).

Cranz, F. Edward, *A Bibliography of Aristotle Editions, 1501–1600,* 2nd ed., with addenda and revisions by Charles B. Schmitt (Baden-Baden: Koerner, 1984).

Crisciani, Chiara, "Curricula e contenuti dell'insegnamento: La medicina dalle origini al secolo XV," in *Storia delle università in Italia,* II, 183–203.

Crisciani, Chiara, Roberto Lambertini, and Andrea Tabarroni, "Due manoscritti con questioni mediche: Note e schede (prima metà del secolo XIV)," in *Frontières des savoirs en Italie à l'époque des premières universités (XIIIe–XVe s.),* edited by Joël Chandelier and Aurélien Robert (Rome: École Française de Rome, 2015), 387–431.

Cultura universitaria e pubblici poteri a Bologna dal XII al XV secolo, edited by Ovidio Capitani (Bologna: Istituto per la Storia di Bologna, 1990).

Cunningham, Andrew, "The Theory / Practice Division of Medicine: Two Late-Alexandrian Legacies," in *History of Traditional Medicine,* edited by T. Ogawa (Osaka: Taniguchi Foundation, 1986), 303–24.

d'Amato, Alfonso, *La Chiesa e l'Università di Bologna* (Bologna: L. Parma, 1998).

——, *I domenicani a Bologna,* 2 vols. (Bologna: ESD, 1988).

D'Amico, John, "The Progress of Renaissance Latin Prose: The Case of Apuleianism," *Renaissance Quarterly* 37.3 (Autumn 1984): 351–92.

Dai collegi medievali alle residenze universitarie: Aspetti religiosi, politici, culturali, edited by Gian Paolo Brizzi and Antonello Mattone (Bologna: CLUEB, 2010).

Dall'isola alla città: I Gesuiti a Bologna, edited by Gian Paolo Brizzi and Anna Maria Matteucci (Bologna: Nuova Alfa, 1988).

Dall'Olio, Guido, "L'attività dell'Inquisizione di Bologna dal XVI al XVIII secolo," in *Storia di Bologna,* ed. Zangheri, III.2, 1097–1176.

——, *Eretici e inquisitori nella Bologna del Cinquecento* (Bologna: Istituto per la Storia di Bologna, 1999).

Dalla lectura all'e-learning, edited by Andrea Romano (Bologna: CLUEB, 2015).

Dalla pecia all'e-book, libri per l'Università: Stampa, editoria, circolazione e lettura: Atti del Convegno internazionale di studi, 21–25 ottobre 2008, edited by Gian Paolo Brizzi and Maria Gioia Tavoni (Bologna: CLUEB, 2009).

Daltri, Andrea, "La decorazione parietale dell'Archiginnasio: Una forma di autorappresentazione studentesca," *ASUI* 7 (2003): 287–306.

——, "*Memorie* e consigliature nella decorazione parietale dell'Archiginnasio," in *Imago Universitatis,* I, 31–50.

Database of Italian Academies, https://www.bl.uk/catalogues/ItalianAcademies/About.aspx.

De Angelis, Carlo, "Istituzioni e città sino alla fine del Seicento," in *Atlante storico delle città italiane: Bologna,* III, 57–116.

De Benedictis, Angela, "La fine dell'autonomia studentesca tra autorità e disciplinamento," in *Studenti e università degli studenti,* 193–223.

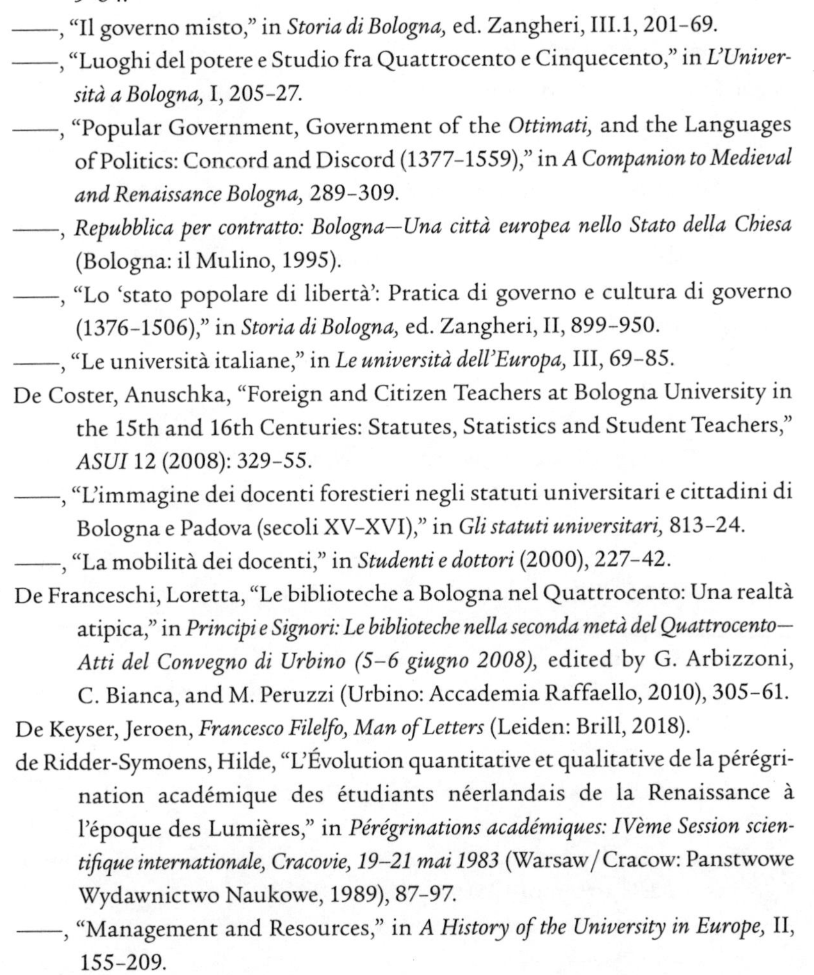

——, "Governo cittadino e riforme a Bologna nel Settecento," in *Famiglie senatorie e istituzioni cittadine a Bologna nel Settecento, Atti del I° colloquio, Bologna, 2–3 febbraio 1980* (Bologna: Istituto per la Storia di Bologna, 1980), 9–54.

——, "Il governo misto," in *Storia di Bologna,* ed. Zangheri, III.1, 201–69.

——, "Luoghi del potere e Studio fra Quattrocento e Cinquecento," in *L'Università a Bologna,* I, 205–27.

——, "Popular Government, Government of the *Ottimati,* and the Languages of Politics: Concord and Discord (1377–1559)," in *A Companion to Medieval and Renaissance Bologna,* 289–309.

——, *Repubblica per contratto: Bologna—Una città europea nello Stato della Chiesa* (Bologna: il Mulino, 1995).

——, "Lo 'stato popolare di libertà': Pratica di governo e cultura di governo (1376–1506)," in *Storia di Bologna,* ed. Zangheri, II, 899–950.

——, "Le università italiane," in *Le università dell'Europa,* III, 69–85.

De Coster, Anuschka, "Foreign and Citizen Teachers at Bologna University in the 15th and 16th Centuries: Statutes, Statistics and Student Teachers," *ASUI* 12 (2008): 329–55.

——, "L'immagine dei docenti forestieri negli statuti universitari e cittadini di Bologna e Padova (secoli XV–XVI)," in *Gli statuti universitari,* 813–24.

——, "La mobilità dei docenti," in *Studenti e dottori* (2000), 227–42.

De Franceschi, Loretta, "Le biblioteche a Bologna nel Quattrocento: Una realtà atipica," in *Principi e Signori: Le biblioteche nella seconda metà del Quattrocento—Atti del Convegno di Urbino (5–6 giugno 2008),* edited by G. Arbizzoni, C. Bianca, and M. Peruzzi (Urbino: Accademia Raffaello, 2010), 305–61.

De Keyser, Jeroen, *Francesco Filelfo, Man of Letters* (Leiden: Brill, 2018).

de Ridder-Symoens, Hilde, "L'Évolution quantitative et qualitative de la pérégrination académique des étudiants néerlandais de la Renaissance à l'époque des Lumières," in *Pérégrinations académiques: IVème Session scientifique internationale, Cracovie, 19–21 mai 1983* (Warsaw / Cracow: Panstwowe Wydawnictwo Naukowe, 1989), 87–97.

——, "Management and Resources," in *A History of the University in Europe,* II, 155–209.

——, "Mobility," in *A History of the University in Europe,* II, 419–31.

de Rijk, L. M., *Die mittelalterlichen Traktate De modo opponendi et respondendi: Einleitung und Ausgabe der einschlägigen Texte* (Münster: Aschenderoff, 1980).

De Rosa, Stefano, *Una biblioteca universitaria del secondo '600: La Libraria di Sapienza dello studio pisano (1666–1700)* (Florence: Olschki, 1983).

De Tata, Rita, "Il commercio librario a Bologna tra '500 e '600: I librai di Ulisse Aldrovandi," *Bibliothecae* 6.1 (2017): 39–91.

——, *Il commercio librario a Bologna tra XV e XVI secolo* (Milan: FrancoAngeli, 2021).

——, "'Per Instituti aedes migraverit': La collocazione dei manoscritti della Biblioteca Universitaria di Bologna dalle origini ai nostri giorni," *L'Archiginnasio* 88 (1993): 323–418.

De Vergottini, Giovanni, "Lo Studio di Bologna, l'Impero e il Papato," *SMUB,* n.s., 1 (1956): 19–95; repr. in idem, *Scritti di storia del diritto italiano,* edited by Guido Rossi, 2 vols. (Milan: A. Giuffrè, 1977), II, 695–792.

Degni, Paola, "I manoscritti greci della biblioteca del monastero del SS. Salvatore di Bologna attraverso gli inventari. Prime considerazioni," *Estudios bizantinos* 3 (2015): 189–206.

Deias, Dalia, "Un manoscritto inedito di Gian Domenico Cassini: Le *Leçons d'astronomie* tenute a Bologna nel 1666" (unpublished dissertation, Corso di Laurea Magistrale in Astrofisica e Cosmologia, University of Bologna, a.a. 2010–2011, relatore Fabrizio Bònoli).

Dejob, Charles, *De l'influence du Concile de Trente sur la littérature et le beaux-arts chez les peuple catholiques* (Paris: E. Thorin, 1884; repr., Geneva: Slatkine Reprints, 1969).

del Negro, Piero, "Bernardo Nani, Lorenzo Morosini e la riforma universitaria del 1761," *Quaderni per la storia dell'Università di Padova* 19 (1986): 87–141.

——, "L'età moderna," in *L'Università di Padova: Otto secoli di storia,* edited by Piero del Negro (Padua: Signum Padova, 2001), 35–71.

——, "Istituzioni, spazi e progetti culturali nella Padova del secondo Settecento," in *Cultura, intellettuali e circolazione delle idee nel '700,* edited by Renato Pasta (Milan: Franco Angeli, 1990), 163–80.

—— "'Leggere a mente senza portare scritti o carta d'alcuna sorte': Le peculiarità della didattica padovana in età moderna," *ASUI* 19.1 (2015): 77–101.

——, "I 'Pensieri di Simone Stratico sull'Università di Padova' (1760)," *Quaderni per la storia dell'Università di Padova* 17 (1984): 191–229.

——, "'Pura favella latina,' 'latino ordinario,' 'buono e pulito italiano' e 'italiano anzi padovano': I 'vari linguaggi' della didattica universitaria nella Padova del Settecento," *ASUI* 3 (1999): 121–41.

——, "Il Settecento fino alla caduta della Repubblica," in *L'Università di Padova nei secoli,* 149–340.

Del Soldato, Eva, *Early Modern Aristotle: On the Making and Unmaking of Authority* (Philadelphia: University of Pennsylvania Press, 2020).

——, *Simone Porzio: Un aristotelico tra natura e grazia* (Rome: Edizioni di Storia e Letteratura, 2010).

Delcorno Branca, Daniela, "Filologia e cultura volgare nell'umanesimo bolognese," in *Lorenzo Valla e l'umanesimo bolognese,* 117–51.

Dellaneva, JoAnn, "Following Their Own Genius: Debates on Ciceronianism in 16th-Century Italy," in *Brill's Companion to the Reception of Cicero,* edited by William H. F. Altman (Leiden: Brill, 2015), 357–76.

Denifle, Heinrich, *Die Entstehung der Universitäten des Mittelalters bis 1400* (Berlin: Weidmann, 1885; facsimile repr., Graz: Akademische Druck- u. Verlagsanstalt, 1956).

Denley, Peter, "Academic Rivalry and Interchange: The Universities of Siena and Florence," in *Florence and Italy: Renaissance Studies in Honour of Nicolai Rubinstein,* edited by Peter Denley and Caroline Elam (London: Committee for Medieval Studies, Westfield College, 1988), 193–208.

—— "The Collegiate Movement in Italian Universities in the Late Middle Ages," *History of Universities* 10 (1991): 29–91.

——, *Commune and Studio in Late Medieval and Renaissance Siena* (Bologna: CLUEB, 2006).

——, "Teologia, poteri, ordini, università nel tardo Medioevo: Aspetti istituzionali," *Memorie domenicane* 45 (2014): 11–27.

Des Chene, Dennis, *Life's Form: Late Aristotelian Conceptions of the Soul* (Ithaca, NY: Cornell University Press, 2000).

Destrez, Jean, *La Pecia dans les manuscrits universitaires du XIIIe et du XIVe siècles* (Paris: J. Vautrain, 1935).

Di Napoli, Giovanni, *L'immortalità dell'anima nel Rinascimento* (Turin: Società Editrice Internazionale, 1963).

di Simone, Maria Rosa, "Admission," in *A History of the University in Europe,* II, 285–325.

——, "Per una storia delle Università europee: Consistenze, e composizione del corpo studentesco dal Cinquecento al Settecento," *Clio* 12 (1986): 349–88.

I dibattiti sull'oggetto della metafisica dal tardo medioevo alla prima età moderna, special issue of *Medioevo: Rivista di storia della filosofia medievale* 34 (2009), edited by Marco Forlivesi and Gregorio Piaia.

Dionisotti, Carlo, "Filologia umanistica e testi giuridici fra Quattro e Cinquecento," in *La critica del testo: Atti del secondo Congresso internazionale della Società italiana di Storia del Diritto* (Florence: Olschki, 1971), 189–204.

Diplomi di laurea conservati nell'Archivio storico dell'Università di Bologna, edited by Ilaria Maggiulli (Rimini: Panozzo, 2016).

Dod, Bernard, "Aristoteles Latinus," in *The Cambridge History of Later Medieval Philosophy,* 45–79.

Dolcini, Carlo, "Pepe, Irnerio, Graziano: Alle origini dello 'Studium' di Bologna," in *L'Università a Bologna,* I, 17–27.

——, "Lo Studium fino al XIII secolo," in *Storia di Bologna,* ed. Zangheri, II, 477–98.

Donattini, "Il mondo portato a Bologna," in *Storia di Bologna,* ed. Zangheri, III.2, 537–682.

Dondarini, Rolando, "La crisi del XIV secolo," in *Storia di Bologna,* ed. Zangheri, II, 867–97.

——, "Provvedimenti e aspetti normativi nella costituzione dello studio bolognese," in *Gli statuti universitari,* 61–79.

——, "Il tramonto del Comune e la signoria bentivolesca," in *Atlante storico delle città italiane. Bologna,* III, 33–56.

Dooley, Brendan, "Antonio Vallisneri between Faith and Flood," in *Physico-Theology,* 194–206.

——, "Science Teaching as a Career in Padua in the Early Eighteenth Century: The Case of Giovanni Poleni," *History of Universities* 4 (1984): 115–51.

——, "La scienza in aula nella rivoluzione scientifica: Dallo Sbaraglia al Vallisneri," *Quaderni per la storia dello Studio di Padova* 21 (1988): 23–44.

——, "Social Control and the Italian Universities: From Renaissance to Illuminismo," *Journal of Modern History* 61 (1989): 205–39.

Dragoni, Giorgio, "Marsigli, Benedict XIV and the Bolognese Institute of the Sciences," in *Renaissance and Revolution,* 229–37.

Drake, Stillman, and I. E. Drabkin, *Mechanics in Sixteenth-Century Italy* (Madison: University of Wisconsin Press, 1969).

du Rieu, W. N., "Katalog der Handschriften in der Bibliothek der regulierten Chorherren zu S. Salvatore in Bologna," *Handelingen van de Maatschappij der Nederlansche Letterkunde* (1864), repr. in *Intelligenz-Blatt zum Serapeum,* 27.14 (31 July 1866), 105–9; 27.15 (15 August 1866), 113–17; 27.16 (31 August 1866), 121–26.

Duranti, Tommaso, "Il collegio dei dottori di medicina di Bologna: Università, professioni e ruolo sociale in un organismo oligarchico della fine del medioevo," *ASUI* 21.2 (2017): 151–77.

——, "*Libertas,* Oligarchy, Papacy: Government in the Quattrocento," in *A Companion to Medieval and Renaissance Bologna,* 260–88.

——, *Mai sotto Saturno: Girolamo Manfredi, medico e astrologo* (Bologna: CLUEB, 2008).

——, "La scuola medica e l'insegnamento della medicina a Bologna nel XIV secolo," in *L'università in tempo di crisi,* 81–94.

Durling, Richard J., "A Chronological Census of Printed Editions and Translations of Galen," *Journal of the Warburg and Courtauld Institutes* 24 (1961): 230–305.

Duroselle-Melish, Caroline, "A Local-Transnational Business: The Book Trade in Late Renaissance Bologna," in *Bologna: Cultural Crossroads,* 27–42.

Duroselle-Melish, Caroline, and David A. Lines, "The Library of Ulisse Aldrovandi (†1605): Acquiring and Organizing Books in Sixteenth-Century Bologna," *The Library: The Transactions of the Bibliographical Society,* s. VII, 16.2 (June 2015): 133–61.

Eamon, William, "'With the Rules of Life and an Enema': Leonardo Fioravanti's Medical Primitivism," in *Renaissance and Revolution,* 29–44.

Early Modern Universities: Networks of Higher Learning, edited by Anja-Silvia Goeing, Glyn Parry, and Mordechai Feingold (Leiden: Brill, 2021).

Ebbesen, Sten, "The Aristotelian Commentator," in *The Cambridge Companion to Boethius,* edited by John Marenbon (Cambridge: Cambridge University Press, 2009), 34–55.

——, "What Counted as Logic in the Thirteenth Century?," in *Methods and Methodologies: Aristotelian Logic East and West, 500–1500,* edited by Margaret Cameron and John Marenbon (Leiden: Brill, 2011), 93–107.

Les Échanges entre les universités européennes à la Renaissance: Colloque international organisé par la Société Française d'Étude du XVIe siècle et l'Association Renaissance–Humanisme–Réforme. Valence, 15–18 mai 2002, edited by Michel Bideaux and Marie-Madeleine Fragonard (Geneva: Droz, 2003).

El aprendizaje de la medicina en el mundo medieval: Las fronteras de la eseñanza universitaria, edited by Cornelius O'Boyle et al., special issue of *Dynamis* 20 (2000).

L'Enseignement des disciplines à la Faculté des arts, Paris et Oxford, XIIIe–XVe siècles: Actes du colloque international, edited by Olga Weijers (Turnhout: Brepols, 1997).

Ernst, Germana, "'Veritatis amor dulcissimus': Aspects of Cardano's Astrology," in *Secrets of Nature,* 39–68.

European Universities in the Age of Reformation and Counter Reformation, edited by Helga Robinson-Hammerstein (Dublin: Four Courts Press, 1998).

Fabrini, Natale, *Le congregazioni dei Gesuiti a Bologna* (Rome: Stella mattutina, 1946).

——, *Lo studio pubblico di Bologna ed i Gesuiti* (Bologna: L. Parma, 1941).

Fantazzi, Charles, "Imitation, Emulation, Ciceronianism, Anti-Ciceronianism," in *Brill's Encyclopaedia of the Neo-Latin World* (consulted online on 15 May 2020).

——, "Revival of Classical Texts," in *Brill's Encyclopaedia of the Neo-Latin World* (consulted online on 15 May 2020).

Fanti, Mario, *Bologna: Biblioteca di San Francesco dei Frati Minori Conventuali* (Florence: Olschki, 1990; Inventari dei manoscritti delle biblioteche d'Italia, vol. CVI).

——, "Bologna nell'età moderna (1506–1796)," in *Storia di Bologna,* ed. Ferri and Roversi, 185–255.

——, "Le chiese di Bologna," in *Storia illustrata di Bologna,* III, 1–20.

——, *Confraternite e città a Bologna nel medioevo e nell'età moderna* (Rome: Herder, 2001).

——, "Inventario dei manoscritti della Biblioteca di S. Francesco in Bologna," *L'Archiginnasio* 53–54 (1958–1959): 285–321.

——, "Prima dell'Archiginnasio: Dalla curia Bulgari alle scuole di S. Petronio," in *L'Archiginnasio: Il palazzo, l'università, la biblioteca,* I, 17–64.

——, "Tentativi di riforma del Collegio di Spagna nella seconda metà del Cinquecento," in *El cardenal Albornoz y el Colegio de España,* edited by

Evelio Verdera y Tuells, 6 vols. (Bologna: Real Colegio de España, 1972-1979), II, 465-521.

Fantini, Rodolfo, *L'istruzione popolare a Bologna fino al 1860* (Bologna: Zanichelli, 1971).

Fantuzzi, Luciana, "La biblioteca arcivescovile di Bologna" (unpublished tesi di laurea, Facoltà di Lettere, Università di Bologna, relatore Prof. Albano Sorbelli, a.a. 1939-1940).

Fasoli, Gina, "Appunti sulla 'Historia Bononiensis' ed altre opere di Carlo Sigonio (1522-1584)," in eadem, *Scritti di storia medievale,* 683-710.

——, "Bologna nell'età medievale (1115-1506)," in *Storia di Bologna,* ed. Ferri and Roversi, 127-84.

——, "La composizione del falso diploma Teodosiano," in eadem, *Scritti di storia medievale,* 584-608.

——, "Il falso privilegio di Teodosio II per lo Studio di Bologna," in *Fälschungen im Mittelalter: Internationaler Kongreß der Monumenta Germaniae Historica, München 16-19 September 1986,* 6 vols. (Hannover: Hahnsche Buchhandlung, 1988; Monumenta Germaniae Historica. Schriften, 33), 627-41.

——, *Per la storia dell'Università di Bologna nel Medio Evo* (Bologna: Patron, 1970).

——, *Scritti di storia medievale,* edited by F. Bocchi, A. Carile, and A. I. Pini (Bologna: La fotocromo emiliana, 1974).

Fasoli, Gina, and G. B. Pighi, "Il privilegio teodosiano: Edizione critica e commento a cura di G. Fasoli e G. B. Pighi," *SMSUB,* n.s., 2 (1961): 55-94.

Fattori, Maria Teresa, "Lambertini a Bologna, 1731-1740," *Storia della Chiesa in Italia* 61.2 (2007): 417-61.

——, "I papi bolognesi e la città," in *Storia di Bologna,* ed. Zangheri, III.2, 1267-1308.

Fava, Domenico, "Un grande libraio-editore di Bologna del Quattrocento: Sigismondo dei Libri," *Gutenberg Jahrbuch* (1941): 80-97.

Favaro, Antonio, "Lo Studio di Padova e la Compagnia di Gesù sul finire del secolo decimosesto: Narrazione documentata," *Atti del r. Istituto veneto di scienze, lettere e arti,* s. V, 4 (1877-1878): 401-535.

Federici Vescovini, Graziella, "Astronomia e medicina all'Università di Bologna nel secolo XIV e agli inizi del XV," in *Seventh Centenary of the Teaching of Astronomy in Bologna 1297-1997,* edited by Pierluigi Battistini et al. (Bologna: CLUEB, 2001), 122-50.

——, "I programmi degli insegnamenti del collegio di medicina, filosofia e astrologia, dello statuto dell'Università di Bologna del 1405," in *Roma, magistra mundi: Itineraria culturae medievalis—Mélanges offerts au Père L. E. Boyle à l'occasion de son 75ᵉ anniversaire,* edited by Jacqueline Hamesse, 3 vols. (Louvain-la-Neuve: Fédération Internationale des Instituts d'Études Médiévales, 1998), I, 193-223.

Feingold, Mordechai, "Aristotle and the English Universities in the Seventeenth Century: A Re-evaluation," in *European Universities,* 135–48.

——, *The Mathematicians' Apprenticeship: Science, Universities and Society in England, 1560–1640* (Cambridge: Cambridge University Press, 1984).

Ferraresi, Alessandra, "Il *curriculum* delle Arti," in *Almum Studium Papiense,* I.2, 1067–1110.

Ferrari, Giovanna, "Public Anatomy Lessons and the Carnival: The Anatomy Theatre of Bologna," *Past & Present* 117.1 (November 1987): 50–106.

Ferrari, Mirella, "Libri e studenti nelle università medievali," *Vita e pensiero* (2000): 493–500.

Ferrari, Saverio, "I fondi librari delle corporazioni religiose confluiti in età napoleonica," in *Biblioteca Comunale dell'Archiginnasio Bologna,* edited by Pierangelo Bellettini (Florence: Nardini, 2001), 51–65.

Findlen, Paula, "Always among Men: Laura Bassi at the Bologna Academy of the Sciences (1732–78)," in *Laura Bassi: Emblema e primato nella scienza del Settecento,* edited by Luisa Cifarelli and Raffaella Simili (Bologna: SISS, 2012), 189–206.

——, "An Artificial Nature: Anatomy Theaters, Botanical Gardens, and Natural History Collections," in *The Cambridge History of Early Modern Science,* edited by Katharine Park and Lorraine J. Daston (Cambridge: Cambridge University Press, 2005), 272–89.

——, "The Formation of a Scientific Community: Natural History in Sixteenth-Century Italy," in *Natural Particulars: Renaissance Natural Philosophy and the Disciplines,* edited by Anthony Grafton and Nancy Siraisi (Cambridge, MA: MIT Press, 1999), 360–400.

——, *Possessing Nature: Museums, Collecting, and Scientific Culture in Early Modern Italy* (Berkeley: University of California Press, 1994).

——, "Science as a Career in Enlightenment Italy: The Strategies of Laura Bassi," *Isis* 84.3 (September 1993): 441–69.

——, "The Scientist and the Saint: Laura Bassi's Enlightened Catholicism," in *Women, Enlightenment and Catholicism: A Transnational Biographical History,* edited by Ulrich L. Lehner (Abingdon: Routledge, 2017), 114–31.

——, "Translating the New Science: Women and the Circulation of Knowledge," *Configurations* 3 (1995): 167–206.

Fiorani, Francesca, *The Marvel of Maps: Art, Cartography and Politics in Renaissance Italy* (New Haven, CT: Yale University Press, 2005).

Focà, Alfredo, *Maestro Bruno da Longobucco* (Reggio Calabria: Laruffo Editore, 2004).

Forlivesi, Marco, *La filosofia universitaria tra XV e XVII secolo* (Padua: CLEUP, 2013).

Forni, Giuseppe Gherardo, *L'insegnamento della Chirurgia nello Studio di Bologna dalle origini a tutto il secolo XIX* (Bologna: Cappelli, 1948).

Fortuna, Stefania, and Annamaria Raia, "Corrigenda and Addenda to Diels' *Galenica* by Richard J. Durling: III. Manuscripts and Editions," *Traditio* 61 (2006): 1–30.

Foschi, Paola, "La fabbrica dell'Archiginnasio," in *L'Archiginnasio: Il palazzo, l'università, la biblioteca,* I, 88–98.

Fosi, Irene, *Papal Justice: Subjects and Courts in the Papal State, 1500–1750,* trans. T. V. Cohen (Washington, DC: Catholic University of America Press, 2011).

Fragnito, Gigliola, "The Central and Peripheral Organization of Censorship," in *Church, Censorship and Culture in Early Modern Italy,* 13–49.

——, "'In questo vasto mare de libri prohibiti et sospesi tra tanti scogli di varietà et controversie': La censura ecclesiastica tra la fine del Cinquecento e i primi del Seicento," in *Censura ecclesiastica e cultura politica in Italia tra Cinquecento e Seicento.* VI giornata Luigi Firpo. Atti del Convegno 5 marzo 1999, edited by Cristina Stango (Florence: Olschki, 2001), 1–35.

——, *Proibito capire: La Chiesa e il volgare nella prima età moderna* (Bologna: il Mulino, 2005).

Frajese, Vittorio, *Nascita dell'Indice: La censura ecclesiastica dal Rinascimento alla Controriforma* (Brescia: Morcelliana, 2006).

Francesco Filelfo, Man of Letters, edited by Jeroen De Keyser (Leiden: Brill, 2019).

Franciosi, Giovanni, *Scritti varii* (Florence: Le Monnier, 1878).

Frati, Lodovico, "La biblioteca del convento dei Domenicani in Bologna," *L'Archiginnasio* 5 (1910): 217–33.

——, "La biblioteca della Nazione Alemanna in Bologna," *L'Archiginnasio* 4 (1909): 196–98.

——, "La biblioteca dell'Istituto delle Scienze di Bologna dalle origini alla morte di Ludovico Montefani Caprara," *Rivista delle biblioteche* 3.25-26-27 (1890): 1–19.

——, *Catalogo dei manoscritti di Ulisse Aldrovandi* (Bologna: Nicola Zanichelli, 1907).

——, "Inventario della biblioteca francescana di Bologna," *Miscellanea francescana di storia, lettere ed arti* 5 (1890): 210–20.

——, "Lianoro de' Lianori ellenista bolognese," *SMSUB* 10 (1930): 165–77.

——, "Ludovico Bolognini," *SMSUB* 1 (1907): 117–41.

——, "I manoscritti posseduti da Carlo Ghisilieri," *Rivista delle biblioteche e degli archivi* 10 (1899): 31–34.

Frati, Lodovico, Francesco Vatielli, and Romeo Galli, "Biblioteche della Provincia di Bologna (Bologna, Imola)," in *Tesori delle biblioteche d'Italia—Emilia e Romagna,* edited by Domenico Fava (Milan: Hoepli, 1932), 1–38.

Frazier, Alison Knowles, *Possible Lives: Authors and Saints in Renaissance Italy* (New York: Columbia University Press, 2005).

Freedman, Joseph S., *Philosophy and the Arts in Central Europe, 1500–1700: Teaching and Texts at Schools and Universities* (Aldershot: Variorum, 1999).

French, Roger K., "Astrology in Medical Practice," in *Practical Medicine from Salerno to the Black Death,* edited by Luis Garcia-Ballester et al. (Cambridge:

Cambridge University Press, 1994), 30–59; now in idem, *Ancients and Moderns in the Medical Sciences: From Hippocrates to Harvey* (Aldershot: Ashgate, 2000).

—— "Berengario da Carpi and the Use of Commentary in Anatomical Tradition," in *The Medical Renaissance of the Sixteenth Century,* 42–74.

Frijhoff, Willem, "Graduation and Careers," in *A History of the University in Europe,* II, 355–415.

——, *Modifications des fonctions sociales de l'université: L'université et les professions du XV au XIX siècle* (Bologna: Bologna University Press, 1995).

Frova, Carla, "Antiche e moderne edizioni di statuti universitari italiani," in *Gli statuti universitari,* 145–53.

——, "The Financing of the University of Rome (15th–16th Centuries)," *CIAN-Revista de historia de las universidades* 24.1 (2021): 4–33.

——, "Possedere libri," in *Maestri, insegnamenti e libri a Perugia,* 191–206.

——, *Scritti sullo Studium Perusinum,* edited by Erika Bellini with Maria Alessandra Panzanelli Fratoni (Perugia: Deputazione di storia patria per l'Umbria, 2011).

Fumaroli, Marc, "Le Golgotha bolonais," in idem, *L'école du silence: Le sentiment des images au XVIIe siècle* (Paris: Flammarion, 1994), 183–322.

Füssel, Marian, "Lehre ohne Forschung? Zu den Praktiken des Wissens and der Universität der Frühen Neuzeit," in *Akademische Wissenskulturen: Praktiken des Lehrens und Forschens vom Mittelalter bis zur Moderne,* edited by Martin Kintzinger and Sita Steckel with Julia Crispin (Basel: Schwabe, 2015), 59–87.

——, "Zwischen Beten und Fluchen: Zur Religiosität der Studenten in der Frühen Neuzeit," in *Universität, Religion und Kirchen,* 455–78.

Gadebusch Bondio, Mariacarla, *Medizinische Ästhetik: Kosmetik und plastische Chirurgie zwischen Antike und früher Neuzeit* (Munich: Fink, 2005).

Gaetano, Matthew T., "Renaissance Thomism at the University of Padua, 1465–1583" (unpublished PhD dissertation, University of Pennsylvania, 2013).

Galeazzi, Giorgio, "Il Collegio Gregoriano a Bologna (1371–1474)," *Strenna storica bolognese* 55 (2005): 251–67.

Galileo e la scuola galileiana nelle università del Seicento, edited by Luigi Pepe (Bologna: CLUEB, 2011).

Gallo, Franco A., "La musica in alcune prolusioni universitarie bolognesi del XV secolo," *Sapere e/è potere,* II, 205–15.

García y García, Antonio, and Celestino Piana, "Los manuscritos filosófico-teológicos, históricos y cientificos del Real Colegio de Espanã de Bolonia," *Salmanticensis* 14 (1967): 81–169.

Gardi, Andrea, *Il cardinale Enrico Caetani e la legazione di Bologna* (Rome: Fondazione Camillo Caetani, 1985).

——, "Il cardinale legato come rettore provinciale: Enrico Caetani a Bologna (1586–1587)," *Società e storia* 8 (1985): 1–36.

——, "Lineamenti della storia politica di Bologna: Da Giulio II a Innocenzo X," in *Storia di Bologna,* ed. Zangheri, III.1, 3–59.

——, "Making of an Oligarchy: The Ruling Classes of Bologna," in *A Companion to Medieval and Renaissance Bologna,* 310–34.

——, "Riflessioni sopra i primi Gelati," in *Un tremore di foglie: Scritti e studi in ricordo di Anna Panicali,* edited by Andrea Csillaghy et al., 2 vols. (Udine: Forum, 2011), II, 423–34.

——, *Lo Stato in provincia: L'amministrazione della Legazione di Bologna durante il regno di Sisto V (1585–1590)* (Bologna: Istituto per la Storia di Bologna, 1994).

Gareffi, Andrea, "L'Hermathena di Federico Zuccari, di Lelio Guidiccioni e Achille Bocchi," in *La parola e l'immagine: Studi in onore di Gianni Venturi* (Florence: Olschki, 2011), I, 341–60.

Gargan, Luciano, "Biblioteche pubbliche in Italia nel secolo XV," in *Niccolò V nel sesto centenario della nascita: Atti del Convegno internazionale di studi, Sarzana, 8–10 ottobre 1998,* edited by Franco Bonatti and Antonio Manfredi (Città del Vaticano: Biblioteca apostolica Vaticana, 2000), 9–20.

——, "La lettura dei classici a Bologna, Padova e Pavia fra Tre e Quattrocento," in *I classici e l'Università umanistica,* 459–85.

Garin, Eugenio, "La concezione dell'università in Italia nell'età del Rinascimento," in *Les Universités européennes du XIVe au XVIIIe siècle: Aspects et problèmes—Actes du Colloque international à l'occasion du VIe centenaire de l'Université Jagellone de Cracovie (6–8 mai 1964)* (Geneva: Droz, 1967), 84–93.

——, *Medioevo e Rinascimento: Studi e ricerche* (Rome: Laterza, 1987).

——, *L'Umanesimo italiano: Filosofia e vita civile nel Rinascimento* (Bari: Laterza, 1952).

Gascoigne, John, "L'università e i *philosophes,*" in *Le università dell'Europa,* VI, 91–105.

Gatti, Elena, *Francesco Platone de' Benedetti: Il principe dei tipografi bolognesi fra corte e* Studium *(1482–1496)* (Udine: FORUM, 2018).

Gavinelli, Simona, "Manoscritti a Pavia tra *Studium* e biblioteca del castello," in *Almum Studium Papiense,* I.1, 713–30.

Geanakoplos, Deno John, *Byzantium and the Renaissance: Greek Scholars in Venice—Studies in the Dissemination of Greek Learning from Byantium to Western Europe* (Hamden, CT: Archon Books, 1973).

Gentilcore, David, "The Organisation of Medical Practice in Malpighi's Italy," in *Marcello Malpighi,* 75–110.

Gesuiti e università in Europa (secoli XVI–XVIII): Atti del Convegno di studi, Parma, 13–15 dicembre 2001, edited by Gian Paolo Brizzi and Roberto Greci (Bologna: CLUEB, 2002).

Giacomelli, Alfeo, "Le Bolle pontificie relative all'Università di Bologna dal 1450 al 1800 con particolare riferimento a Benedetto XIV," in *Ateneo e Chiesa di Bologna,* 265–352.

——, *Carlo Grassi e le riforme bolognesi del settecento,* 2 vols. (Bologna: Atesa, 1979).

——, "La storia di Bologna dal 1650 al 1796: Un racconto e una cronologia," in *Storia di Bologna,* ed. Zangheri, III.1, 61–197.

Giacomotto-Charra, Violaine, *La Philosophie naturelle en langue française: Des premiers texts à l'oeuvre de Scipion Dupleix* (Geneva: Droz, 2020).

Gieysztor, Aleksander, "Management and Resources," in *A History of the University in Europe,* I, 108–43.

Giglioni, Guido, "Girolamo Cardano: University Student and Professor," *Renaissance Studies* 27.4 (2013): 517–32.

Gil Fernandez, Juan, *De codicibus albornotianis ad graecas latinasque litteras pertinentibus commentarius* (Bologna: Istituto di Filologia Classica, 1964).

Gingerich, Owen, *The Book Nobody Read: Chasing the Revolutions of Nicolaus Copernicus* (New York: Walker & Co., 2004).

Giuntini, Sandra, "Gabriele Manfredi e l'insegnamento della matematica a Bologna nel XVIII secolo," *Bollettino di storia delle scienze matematiche* 29.2 (2009): 207–82.

Giusberti, Fabio, and Francesca Roversi Monaco, "Economy and Demography," in *A Companion to Medieval and Renaissance Bologna,* 154–84.

Goddu, André, *Copernicus and the Aristotelian Tradition: Education, Reading and Philosophy in Copernicus's Path to Heliocentrism* (Leiden: Brill, 2010).

Godman, Peter, "The Angel from Heaven," in *From Poliziano to Machiavelli: Florentine Humanism in the High Renaissance,* edited by Peter Godman (Princeton, NJ: Princeton University Press, 1998), 80–133.

——, "Poliziano's Poetics and Literary History," *Interpres* 13 (1993): 110–209.

Gomez Lopez, Susanna, *Le passioni degli atomi: Montanari e Rossetti—Una polemica tra galileiani* (Florence: Olschki, 1997).

Gordini, Gian Domenico, "La Facoltà teologica dello studio bolognese," in *Ateneo e Chiesa di Bologna,* 13–35.

Grabmann, Martin, *Die Geschichte der scholastischen Methode: Nach den gedruckten und ungedruckten Quellen dargestellt,* 2 vols. (Berlin: Akademie, 1986).

Grafton, Anthony, *Cardano's Cosmos: The Worlds and Works of a Renaissance Astrologer* (Cambridge, MA: Harvard University Press, 1999).

——, "Cardano's *Proxeneta:* Prudence for Professors," *Bruniana et Campanelliana* 7 (2001): 363–80.

——, *Defenders of the Text: The Traditions of Scholarship in an Age of Science, 1450–1800* (Cambridge, MA: Harvard University Press, 1991).

——, "Textbooks and the Disciplines," in *Scholarly Knowledge,* 11–36.

Grafton, Anthony, and Lisa Jardine, *From Humanism to the Humanities: Education and the Liberal Arts in Fifteenth- and Sixteenth-Century Europe* (London: Duckworth, 1986).

Grafton, Anthony, with April Shelford and Nancy Siraisi, *New Worlds, Ancient Texts: The Power of Tradition and the Shock of Discovery* (Cambridge, MA: Belknap Press of Harvard University Press, 1992).

Grafton, Anthony, and Nancy Siraisi, "Between the Election and My Hopes: Girolamo Cardano and Medical Astrology," in *Secrets of Nature,* 69–131.

Grafton, Anthony, and Joanna Weinberg, with Alastair Hamilton, *"I Have Always Loved the Holy Tongue": Isaac Casaubon, the Jews, and a Forgotten Chapter in Renaissance Scholarship* (Cambridge, MA: Belknap Press of Harvard University Press, 2011).

Graheli, Shanti, "Italian Books and French Medical Libraries in the Renaissance," in *Books in Motion in Early Modern Europe: Beyond Production, Circulation and Consumption,* edited by Daniel Bellingradt, Paul Nelles, and Jeroen Salman (Cham: Palgrave Macmillan, 2017), 243–66.

Grandi, Renzo, *I monumenti dei dottori e la scultura a Bologna (1267–1348)* (Bologna: Istituto per la Storia di Bologna, 1982).

Grant, Edward, *In Defense of the Earth's Centrality and Immobility: Scholastic Reaction to Copernicanism in the Seventeenth Century* (Philadelphia: American Philosophical Society, 1984).

Greci, Roberto, "Bologna nel Duecento," in *Storia di Bologna,* ed. Zangheri, II, 499–579.

——, "Libri e prestiti di libri in alcune biblioteche private bolognesi del secolo XV," *La bibliofilia* 85 (1983): 341–54, repr. in *Libri manoscritti e a stampa da Pomposa all'Umanesimo,* edited by Luigi Balsamo (Florence: Olschki, 1985), 241–55.

Green, Lawrence D., "The Reception of Aristotle's *Rhetoric* in the Renaissance," in *Peripatetic Rhetoric after Aristotle: Rugers University Studies in Classical Humanities* (Oxford / New Brunswick, NJ: Transaction Publishers, 1994), 320–48.

Grendler, Paul F., "Fencing, Playing Ball, and Dancing in Italian Renaissance Universities," in *Sport and Culture in Early Modern Europe / Le Sport dans la civilisation de l'Europe pré-moderne,* edited by John McClelland and Brian Merrilees (Toronto: Centre for Reformation and Renaissance Studies, 2009), 295–318.

——, "Five Italian Occurrences of *Umanista,* 1540–1574," *Renaissance Quarterly* 20.3 (1967): 317–25.

——, "Intellectual Freedom in Italian Universities: The Controversy over the Immortality of the Soul," in *Le contrôle des idées à la Renaissance,* edited by J. M. de Bujanda (Geneva: Droz, 1996), 31–48.

——, *The Jesuits and Italian Universities, 1548–1773* (Washington, DC: Catholic University of America Press, 2017).

——, *The Roman Inquisition and the Venetian Press, 1540–1605* (Princeton, NJ: Princeton University Press, 1977).

——, *Schooling in Renaissance Italy: Literacy and Learning, 1300–1600* (Baltimore: Johns Hopkins University Press, 1989).

——, "I tentativi dei gesuiti d'entrare nelle università italiane tra '500 e '600," in *Gesuiti e università in Europa (secoli XVI–XVIII): Atti del Convegno di studi,*

Parma, 13–15 dicembre 2001, edited by Gian Paolo Brizzi and Roberto Greci (Bologna: CLUEB, 2002), 37–51.

——, *The Universities of the Italian Renaissance* (Baltimore: Johns Hopkins University Press, 2002).

——, *The University of Mantua, the Gonzaga, and the Jesuits, 1584–1630* (Baltimore: Johns Hopkins University Press, 2009).

Grmek, M. D., "L'Enseignement médico-biologique à Bologne de Mondino à Malpighi," in *Universitates e Università: Atti del Convegno, Bologna, 16–21 novembre 1987* (Bologna: Bologna University Press, 1995), 285–94.

Gualandi, Michelangelo, *Il processo fatto in Bologna l'anno 1564 a Torquato Tasso* (Bologna: n.p., 1862).

Gualdo Rosa, Lucia, "Cortesi Urceo, Antonio, detto Codro," *DBI,* XXIX (1983), 773–78.

——, "Una prolusione inedita di Francesco Filelfo del 1429, rielaborata dal figlio Gian Mario nel 1467," in *Francesco Filelfo nel quinto centenario della morte: Atti del XVII convegno di studi maceratesi (Tolentino, 27–30 settembre 1981)* (Padua: Antenore, 1986), 275–323.

Guerrini, Maria Teresa, "L'Accademia degli Impazienti: Un esperimento nella Bologna di fine Seicento," *ASUI* 18 (2014): 327–39.

——, "A proposito di ASFE: Fonti complementari per lo studio della presenza studentesca a Bologna in età moderna," in *Università e formazione dei ceti dirigenti,* 299–305.

——, *Collegi dottorali in conflitto: I togati bolognesi e la Costituzione di Benedetto XIV, 1744* (Bologna: CLUEB, 2012).

——, "La pratica del viaggio di istruzione verso i principali centri universitari italiani nel Cinquecento," *Storicamente* 2.11 (2006), online at doi: 10.1473 / stor385.

——, *"Qui voluerit in iure promoveri . . .": I dottori in diritto nello Studio di Bologna (1501–1796)* (Bologna: CLUEB, 2005).

——, "Tra docenza pubblica e insegnamento privato: I lettori dello Studio di Bologna in epoca moderna," in *Dalla lectura all'e-learning,* 183–94.

——, "Université et académies à Bologne: Quelques réflexions sur une relation pluriséculaire," *Diciottesimo secolo* 3 (2018): 1–22.

Guidicini, Giuseppe, *Cose notabili della città di Bologna, ossia Storia cronologica de' suoi stabili sacri, pubblici e privati,* 5 vols. (Bologna: Tipografica Militare, già delle Scienze, 1873; repr., Bologna: Forni, 1972).

——, *I riformatori dello stato di libertà della città di Bologna dal 1394 al 1797,* 3 vols. (Bologna: Regia Tipografia, 1876–1877).

Gurreri, Clizia, "'Haec est ultima voluntas': B4333 un inedito bolognese—Per una prima lettura del testamento di Melchiorre Zoppio tra gli Accademici Gelati il Caliginoso," in *Letteratura e arti dal Barocco al postmoderno* (2012), 60–80 (http://sinestesieonline.it/wp-content/uploads/2018/03/Numero02-Anno01-Settembre2012.pdf, accessed 11 September 2018).

——, "'Nec longum tempus': L'Accademia dei Gelati tra XVI e XVII secolo (1588–1614)," in *The Italian Academies, 1525–1700,* 186–96.

Hamesse, Jacqueline, "Reportatio et transmission de textes," in *The Editing of Theological and Philosophical Texts from the Middle Ages,* edited by Monika Asztalos (Stockholm: Almquist and Wiksell International, 1986), 11–34.

——, "La Technique de la réportation," in *L'Enseignement des disciplines,* 405–21.

Hammerstein, Notker, "Relations with Authority," in *A History of the University in Europe,* II, 114–53.

Hardin, Richard F., "Encountering Plautus in the Renaissance: A Humanist Debate on Comedy," *Renaissance Quarterly* 60.3 (Fall 2007): 789–818.

Hardison, O. B., Jr., "The Place of Averroes' Commentary on the *Poetics* in the History of Medieval Criticism," in *Medieval and Renaissance Studies: Proceedings of the Southeastern Institute of Medieval and Renaissance Studies, Summer 1968,* edited by John Lievsay (Durham, NC: Duke University Press, 1970), 57–81.

Harrison, Peter, "Physico-Theology and the Mixed Sciences: The Role of Theology in Early Modern Natural Philosophy," in *The Science of Nature in the Seventeenth Century,* edited by Peter R. Anstey and John A. Schuster (Dordrecht: Springer, 2005), 165–83.

Hasse, Dag Niklaus, *Success and Suppression: Arabic Sciences and Philosophy in the Renaissance* (Cambridge, MA: Harvard University Press, 2016).

Hengst, Karl, *Jesuiten an Universitäten und Jesuitenuniversitäten* (Paderborn: n.p., 1981).

Hersche, Peter, *Italien im Barockzeitalter 1600–1750: Eine Sozial- und Kulturgeschichte* (Vienna: Böhlau, 1999).

——, "Die Marginalisierung der Universität im katholischen Europa des Barockzeitalters: Das Beispiel Italien," in *Universität, Religion und Kirchen,* edited by Rainer Christoph Schwinges (Basel: Schwabe, 2011), 267–76.

Hessel, Alfred, *Storia della città di Bologna: 1116–1280,* edited by Gina Fasoli (Bologna: Alfa, 1975).

Hirai, Hiro, *Medical Humanism and Natural Philosophy: Renaissance Debates on Matter, Life, and the Soul* (Leiden: Brill, 2011).

Hirsch, Rudolf, *Printing, Selling and Reading, 1450–1550,* 2nd ed. (Wiesbaden: Otto Harrassowitz, 1974).

Historia: Empiricism and Erudition in Early Modern Europe, edited by Gianna Pomata and Nancy G. Siraisi (Cambridge, MA: MIT Press, 2014).

Historia de la Universidad de Salamanca, 4 vols. (Salamanca: Ediciones Universidad de Salamanca, 2002–2009).

A History of the University in Europe, gen. ed. Walter Rüegg, 4 vols. (Cambridge: Cambridge University Press, 1991–2010).

The History of the University of Oxford, edited by T. H. Aston, 8 vols. (Oxford: Oxford University Press, 1984–2000).

Humanismus und Medizin, edited by Rudolf Schmitz and Gundolf Keil (Weinheim: Acta Humaniora, 1984).

Hyde, John, "Commune, University, and Society in Early Medieval Bologna," in *Universities in Politics: Case Studies from the Late Middle Ages and Early Modern Period,* edited by John W. Baldwin and Richard A. Goldthwaite (Baltimore: Johns Hopkins University Press, 1972), 17–46.

Imago Universitatis: Celebrazioni e autorappresentazioni di maestri e studenti nella decorazione parietale dell'Archiginnasio, edited by Gian Paolo Brizzi with Andrea Daltri, 2 vols. (Bologna: Bononia University Press, 2011–2012).

Index des livres interdits, edited by Jesùs Martìnez de Bujanda, 11 vols. (Sherbrooke: Centre d'études de la Renaissance, Éditions de l'Université de Sherbrooke, 1985–2002).

L'insegnamento della logica a Bologna nel XIV secolo, edited by Dino Buzzetti, Maurizio Ferriani, and Andrea Tabarroni, special issue of *SMSUB,* n.s., 8 (1992).

L'Italia dell'inquisitore: Storia e geografia dell'Italia del Cinquecento nella Descrittione di Leandro Alberti. Atti del Convegno internazionale di studi, Bologna, 27–29 maggio 2004, edited by Massimo Donattini (Bologna: Bononia University Press, 2007).

The Italian Academies, 1525–1700: Networks of Culture, Innovation and Dissent, edited by Jane D. Everson, Denis V. Reidy, and Lisa Sampson (Oxford: Legenda, 2016).

Italian Academies of the Sixteenth Century, edited by David S. Chambers and François Quiviger (London: Warburg Institute, 1995).

Jacquart, Danielle, "Principales étapes dans la transmission des textes de médecine (XIe et XIVe siècle)," in *Rencontres de cultures dans la philosophie médiévale: Traductions et traducteurs de l'Antiquité tardive au XIVe siècle,* edited by Jacqueline Hamesse and Marta Fattori (Louvain-la Neuve: Publications de l'Institut d'études médiévales, 1990), 251–71.

——, "La Question disputée dans les Facultés de médecine," in *Les Questions disputées et les questions quodlibétiques dans les Facultés de théologie, de droit et de médecine,* edited by Bernardo C. Bazàn et al. (Turnhout: Brepols, 1985), 279–315.

——, "Theory, Everyday Practice, and Three Fifteenth-Century Physicians," *Osiris* 6 (1990): 140–60.

Javitch, Daniel, "The Assimilation of Aristotle's *Poetics* in Sixteenth Century Italy," in *The Cambridge History of Literary Criticism,* vol. III: *The Renaissance,* edited by Glyn Norton (Cambridge: Cambridge University Press, 1999), 53–65.

——, "The Emergence of Poetic Genre Theory in the Sixteenth Century," *Modern Language Quarterly* 59.2 (1988): 139–69.

The Jesuit Ratio Studiorum: *400th Anniversary Perspectives,* edited by Vincent J. Duminucco (New York: Fordham University Press, 2000).

Les Jésuites à la Renaissance: Système éducatif et production du savoir, edited by Luce Giard (Paris: Presses universitaires de France, 1995).

John Dee's Library Catalogue, edited by Julian Roberts and Andrew G. Watson (London: Bibliographical Society, 1990).

Jouanna, Jacques, "Mercuriale, commentateur et éditeur d'Hippocrate," in *Girolamo Mercuriale: Medicina e cultura nell'Europa del Cinquecento,* edited by Alessandro Arcangeli and Vivian Nutton (Florence: Olschki, 2008), 269–300.

Kagan, Richard L., "Le università in Italia," *Società e storia* 7 (1985): 275–317.

——, "Universities in Italy 1500–1700," in *Les universités européennes,* vol. I: *Histoire sociale des populations étudiantes,* 153–86.

Kallendorf, Craig, *In Praise of Aeneas: Virgil and Epideictic Rhetoric in the Early Italian Renaissance* (Hanover, NH: University Press of New England, 1989).

——, *The Protean Virgil: Material Form and the Reception of the Classics* (Oxford: Oxford University Press, 2015).

Kessler, Eckhard, "The Intellective Soul," in *The Cambridge History of Renaissance Philosophy,* 485–534.

——, "Metaphysics or Empirical Science? The Two Faces of Aristotelian Natural Philosophy in the Sixteenth Century," in *Renaissance Readings of the Corpus Aristotelicum,* edited by Marianne Pade (Copenhagen: Museum Tusculanum, 2001), 79–101.

Kibre, Pearl, "Giovanni Garzoni of Bologna (1419–1505), Professor of Medicine and Defender of Astrology," *Isis* 58.4 (1967): 504–15.

——, *Hippocrates Latinus: Repertorium of Hippocratic Writings in the Latin Middle Ages* (New York: Fordham University Press, 1985).

——, *Scholarly Privileges in the Middle Ages: The Rights, Privileges, and Immunities of Scholars and Universities at Bologna, Padua, Paris, and Oxford* (London: Mediaeval Academy of America, 1961).

King, Lester S., *The Road to Medical Enlightenment, 1650–1695* (London: Macdonald, 1970).

Klestinec, Cynthia, *Theaters of Anatomy: Students, Teachers, and Traditions of Dissection in Renaissance Venice* (Baltimore: Johns Hopkins University Press, 2011).

Koeppler, H., "Frederick Barbarossa and the Schools of Bologna: Some Remarks on the 'Authentica Habita,'" *English Historical Review* 54 (1939): 577–607.

Krautter, Konrad, *Philologische Methode und humanistische Existenz: Filippo Beroaldo und sein Kommentar zum Goldenen Esel des Apuleius* (Munich: Wilhelm Fink, 1971).

Kraye, Jill, "The Immortality of the Soul in the Renaissance: Between Natural Philosophy and Theology," *Signatures* 1 (2000): 51–68 (available online at http://www.chiuni.ac.uk/info/documents/signature_pdfs/Signatures_Vol1.pdf).

——, "Moral Philosophy," in *The Cambridge History of Renaissance Philosophy,* 303–86.

——, "Philologists and Philosophers," in *The Cambridge Companion to Renaissance Humanism,* edited by Jill Kraye (Cambridge: Cambridge University Press, 1996), 142–60.

Krisciunas, Kevin, and Belén Bistué, "Notes on the Transmission of Ptolemy's *Almagest:* The Era of Copernicus," *Journal of Astronomical History and Heritage* 22.3 (2019): 492–502.

Kristeller, Paul O., "Bartholomaeus, Musandinus and Maurus of Salerno and Other Early Commentators of the *Articella,* with a Tentative List of Texts and Manuscripts," *Italia medioevale e umanistica* 19 (1976): 57–87.

——, "The Curriculum of the Italian Universities from the Middle Ages to the Renaissance," in idem, *Studies,* IV, 75–96.

——, "Humanism and Scholasticism," in idem, *Studies,* I, 553–93.

——, "Die italienische Universitäten der Renaissance," in idem, *Studies,* IV, 97–113.

——, *Iter Italicum: A Finding List of Uncatalogued or Incompletely Catalogued Manuscripts of the Renaissance in Italian and Other Libraries,* 7 vols. (Leiden: Brill, 1963–1997).

——, "Learned Women of Early Modern Italy: Humanists and University Scholars," in idem, *Studies,* II, 185–205.

——, *Renaissance Thought: The Classic, Scholastic, and Humanist Strains* (New York: Harper and Row, 1961).

——, *Renaissance Thought and Its Sources,* edited by Michael Mooney (New York: Columbia University Press, 1979).

——, *Studies in Renaissance Thought and Letters,* 4 vols. (Rome: Edizioni di Storia e Letteratura, 1956–1996).

——, "The University of Bologna and the Renaissance," *SMSUB,* n.s., 1 (1956): 313–23.

Laird, W. Roy, "Nature, Mechanics, and Voluntary Movement in Giuseppe Moletti's Lectures on the *Mechanical Problems,*" in *Mechanics and Natural Philosophy before the Scientific Revolution,* edited by Walter Roy Laird and Sophie Roux (Dordrecht: Springer, 2008), 173–83.

Lambertini, Roberto, "Intersezioni: Ancora su *Studia* mendicanti e facoltà di teologia a Bologna," in *L'università in tempo di crisi,* 113–21.

Lardet, Pierre, "Georges de Trébizonde, traducteur et scholiaste de la Rhetorique d'Aristote," in *Les Traducteurs au travail: Leurs manuscripts et leurs méthodes. Actes du Colloque international organisé par le "Ettore Majorana Centre for Scientific Culture" (Erice, 30 septembre–6 octobre 1999),* edited by Jacqueline Hamesse (Brepols: Turnhout, 2001), 311–48.

Lauree: Università e gradi accademici in Italia nel medioevo e nella prima età moderna, edited by Anna Esposito and Umberto Longo (Bologna: CLUEB, 2013).

Laurent, M.-H., O.P., *Fabio Vigili et les bibliothèques de Bologne au début du XVI*[e] *siècle d'après le ms. Barb. Lat. 3185* (Vatican City: Biblioteca Apostolica Vaticana, 1943).

Lawn, Brian, *The Rise and Decline of the Scholastic Quaestio Disputata: With Special Emphasis on Its Use in the Teaching of Medicine and Science* (Leiden: Brill, 1993).

Leibetseder, Mathis, *Die Kavalierstour: Adelige Erziehungsreisen im 17. und 18. Jahrhundert* (Cologne: Böhlau Verlag, 2004).

Libri in collegio: Jean Jacobs e il Collegio dei Fiamminghi in Bologna tra passato e presente, Bologna–Bruxelles 1995 (Bologna: Università degli Studi, 1995).

Lines, David A., "Aristotelismo a Bologna fra Università e Accademia: Baldassar Gambarini e l'Accademia degli Oziosi," in *Rinascimento veneto e Rinascimento europeo / European and Venetian Renaissance,* edited by Romana Bassi (Pisa: ETS, 2019 [but 2020]), 35–46.

——, *Aristotle's* Ethics *in the Italian Renaissance (ca. 1300–1650): The Universities and the Problem of Moral Education* (Leiden: Brill, 2002).

——, "La biblioteca di Ulisse Aldrovandi in Palazzo Pubblico: Un inventario seicentesco," in *Biblioteche filosofiche private: Strumenti e prospettive di ricerca,* edited by Renzo Ragghianti and Alessandro Savorelli (Pisa: Edizioni della Normale, 2014), 113–32.

——, "I classici nell'università umanistica: La scuola filosofica," in *I classici e l'Università umanistica,* 71–88.

——, "Defining Philosophy in Fifteenth-Century Humanism: Four Case Studies," in *Et Amicorum: Essays on Renaissance Humanism and Philosophy in Honour of Jill Kraye,* edited by Anthony Ossa-Richardson and Margaret Meserve (Leiden: Brill, 2018), 281–97.

——, "Gabriele Paleotti and the University of Bologna: Documents from Bologna's Archivio Arcivescovile," in *Bologna: Cultural Crossroads,* 57–69.

——, "Humanism and the Italian Universities," in *Humanism and Creativity in the Italian Renaissance: Essays in Honor of Ronald G. Witt,* edited by Chrisopher S. Celenza and Kenneth Gouwens (Leiden: Brill, 2006), 323–42.

——, "Leon Battista Alberti e lo Studio di Bologna negli anni Venti," in *La vita e il mondo di Leon Battista Alberti, Atti dei convegni internazionali del Comitato Nazionale VI centenario della nascita di Leon Battista Alberti (Genova, 19–21 Febbraio 2004),* edited by M. Aguzzoli et al., 2 vols. (Florence: Olschki, 2008), II, 377–95.

——, "A Library for Teaching and Study: Ulisse Aldrovandi's Aristotelian Texts," in *Les Labyrinthes de l'esprit: Collections et bibliothèques à la Renaissance / Renaissance Libraries and Collections,* edited by Rosanna Gorris Camos and Alexandre Vanautgaerden (Geneva: Droz, 2015), 303–79.

——, "Managing Academic Insubordination at the University of Bologna," in *Management and Resolution of Conflict and Rivalries in Renaissance Europe,* ed-

ited by Jill Kraye, David A. Lines, and Marc Laureys (Göttingen: V&R, forthcoming).

——, "Moral Philosophy in the Universities of Medieval and Renaissance Europe," *History of Universities* 20.1 (2005): 38–80.

——, "Natural Philosophy and Mathematics in Sixteenth-Century Bologna," *Science and Education* 15 (2006): 131–50.

——, "Natural Philosophy in Renaissance Italy: The University of Bologna and the Beginnings of Specialization," in *Science and Universities,* 267–323.

——, "A Papal Legate's *Relatione* and the Bolognese *Studio* around 1611," in *Università e formazione dei ceti dirigenti,* 237–45.

——, "Papal Power and University Control in Early Modern Italy: Bologna and Gregory XIII," *Sixteenth Century Journal* 44.3 (Fall 2013): 663–82.

——, "Philosophy Teaching and Filiations of Learning in Sixteenth-Century Bologna: Ludovico Boccadiferro's Early *De Anima* Lectures," in *Filosofia e medicina in Italia fra medioevo e prima età moderna,* edited by Luca Bianchi and Luigi Campi (Turnhout: Brepols, in press).

——, "Reorganizing the Curriculum: Teaching and Learning in the University of Bologna, c. 1560–c. 1590," *History of Universities* 26.2 (2012): 1–59.

——, *Selected Documents for the University of Bologna,* 2 vols. (Turnhout: Brepols, forthcoming).

——, "Structures and Networks of Learning in Early Modern Bologna," in *Early Modern Universities,* 43–62.

——, "Teaching Physics in Louvain and Bologna: Frans Titelmans and Ulisse Aldrovandi," in *Scholarly Knowledge,* 183–203.

——, "The University and the City: Cultural Interactions," in *A Companion to Medieval and Renaissance Bologna,* 436–73.

——, "University Natural Philosophy in Renaissance Italy: The Decline of Aristotelianism?," in *The Dynamics of Aristotelian Natural Philosophy,* edited by Cees Leijenhorst, Christoph Lüthy, and Jan M.M.H. Thijssen (Leiden: Brill, 2002), 323–42.

——, "The University of the Artists in Bologna, 1586–1713," in *Galileo e la scuola galileiana,* 141–53.

——, "When Is a Translation Not a Translation? Girolamo Manfredi's *De homine* (1474)," in *"In Other Words": Translating Philosophy in the Fifteenth and Sixteenth Centuries,* edited by David A. Lines and Anna Laura Puliafito, special issue of *Rivista di storia della filosofia* 74.2 (2019): 287–307.

Lines, David A., and Jill Kraye, "Sources for Ethics in the Renaissance: The Expanding Canon," in *Rethinking Virtue, Reforming Society,* 29–56.

Linguaggi, metodi, strumenti dell'insegnamento universitario in Europa (secc. XIII–XXI), special issue of *ASUI* 19.1 (2015).

Liruti, Gian Giuseppe, *Notizie delle vite ed opere scritte da letterati del Friuli,* 4 vols. (Venice: Modesto Fenzo, 1760–1830; repr., Bologna: Forni, 1971).

Lisini, Alessandro, "Due lettere inedite di Celso Cittadini," *Miscellanea storica senese* 5 (1898): 14–17.

Les Livres des maîtres de Sorbonne: Histoire et rayonnement du collège et de ses bibliothèques du XIIIe siècle à la Renaissance, edited by Claire Angotti, Gilbert Fournier, and Donatella Nebbiai (Paris: Publications de la Sorbonne, 2017).

Lollini, Fabrizio, "Bessarione e Niccolò Perotti a Bologna: Due episodi poco noti," *Schede umanistiche* 4 (1990): 55–61.

Lombardo, Simone, "An Inevitable Trouble: Italian Historiography of the Last Decade about Censorship in Early Modern Age (XVI–XVII centuries)—Some Notes," *Bibliothecae* 7.1 (2018): 188–234.

López Zamora, Jesilis, "Antonius Urceus, *Hesiodi Opera et dies* (Florencia, BNCF, Ms. Naz. II.VII.125) edición crítica," *Humanistica Lovaniensia* 65 (2016): 95–130.

Lorenzo Valla e l'umanesimo bolognese: Atti del Convegno internazionale Comitato Nazionale VI centenario della nascita di Lorenzo Valla, Bologna, 25–26 gennaio 2008, edited by Gian Mario Anselmi and Marta Guerra (Bologna: Bononia University Press, 2009).

Loschiavo, Luigi, "I canonici regolari di S. Agostino e l'Università," in *Ateneo e Chiesa di Bologna,* 55–88.

Lucchesi, Carlo, "L'antica libreria dei Padri Domenicani di Bologna alla luce del suo inventario," *AMDSR* 5 (1939–1940): 205–50.

Lucioli, Francesco, "Intorno all'Accademia del Viridario," in *Le virtuose adunanze,* 237–48.

Luoghi e metodi dell'insegnamento nell'Italia medioevale (secoli XII–XIV): Atti del Convegno Internazionale di Studi, Lecce–Otranto, 6–8 ottobre 1986, edited by Luciano Gargan and Oronzo Limone (Galatina: Congedo, 1989).

Lupi, Regina, *Gli* studia *del papa: Nuova cultura e tentativi di riforma tra Sei e Settecento* (Florence: Centro Editoriale Toscano, 2006).

Machaeva, Orazgozel, *Catalogo dei manoscritti islamici conservati nella Biblioteca Universitaria di Bologna,* vol. I (Bologna: Persiani, 2017).

Mack, Peter, *A History of Renaissance Rhetoric, 1380–1620* (Oxford: Oxford University Press, 2011).

Maclean, Ian, "Diagrams in the Defence of Galen: Medical Uses of Tables, Squares, Dichotomies, Wheels, and Latitudes, 1480–1574," in *Transmitting Knowledge: Words, Images and Instruments in Early Modern Europe,* edited by Sachiko Kusukawa and Ian Maclean (Oxford: Oxford University Press, 2006), 135–64.

——, *Episodes in the Life of the Early Modern Learned Book* (Leiden: Brill, 2021).

——, "Heterodoxy in Natural Philosophy and Medicine: Pietro Pomponazzi, Guglielmo Gratarolo, Girolamo Cardano," in *Heterodoxy in Early Modern Science and Religion,* edited by John Brooke and Ian MacLean (Oxford: Oxford University Press, 2005), 1–29.

——, *Logic, Signs and Nature in the Renaissance* (Cambridge: Cambridge University Press, 2002).

Maestri, insegnamenti e libri a Perugia: Contributi per la storia dell'Università, 1308–2008, edited by Carla Frova, Ferdinando Treggiari, and Maria Alessandra Panzanelli Fratoni (Milan: Skira, 2009).

Maffei, Domenico, "Un trattato di Bonaccorso degli Elisei e i più antichi statuti dello Studio di Bologna nel manoscritto 22 della Robbins Collection," *Bulletin of Medieval Canon Law* 5 (1975): 73–101.

Maffei, Domenico, et al., *I codici del Collegio di Spagna di Bologna* (Milan: Giuffrè, 1992).

Maffioli, Cesare S., "Guglielmini, Rondelli e la nuova cattedra d'idrometria," *SMSUB,* n.s., 6 (1987): 81–124.

——, *Out of Galileo: The Science of Waters, 1628–1718* (Rotterdam: Erasmus Publishing, 1994).

Maggiulli, Ilaria, "'Li scolari per il più vivono, et vestono à guisa di soldati, con grande licenza . . .': 1564, un episodio di violenza studentesca a Bologna," *ASUI* 18 (2014): 313–26.

——, "'Tu ne menti per la gola': Scontri tra scolari dello Studio bolognese nella seconda metà del XVI secolo," in *Le università e la violenza studentesca,* 27–46.

Magnani, Nicola, "Aristotelianism and Metricology in Giorgio Valla's *De poetica,*" *Studi e problemi di critica testuale* 100 (2020): 173–97.

Maïer, Anneliese, *Die Vorläufer Galileis im 14. Jahrhundert: Studien zur Naturphilosophie der Spätscholastik* (Rome: Edizioni di Storia e Letteratura, 1949).

Maierù, Alfonso "Gli atti scolastici nelle università italiane," in *Luoghi e metodi dell'insegnamento,* 247–88.

——, "L'insegnamento della logica a Bologna nel secolo XIV e il manoscritto antoniano 391," in *Rapporti tra le Università di Padova e Bologna,* 1–24.

——, *University Training in Medieval Europe,* translated and edited by D. N. Pryds (Leiden: Brill, 1994).

Malagola, Carlo, *Della vita e delle opere di Antonio Urceo detto Codro: Studi e ricerche* (Bologna: Fava e Garagnani, 1878).

——, "I libri della Nazione Tedesca presso lo Studio bolognese," in idem, *Monografie storiche,* 303–64.

——, *Monografie storiche sullo Studio bolognese* (Bologna: Nicola Zanichelli, 1888; repr., Bologna: Forni, 1979, and New Delhi: Isha Books, 2013).

——, *I rettori: Dall'antico studio alla moderna università,* revised and augmented by Gian Paolo Brizzi (Bologna: n.p., 1988).

——, "I rettori nell'antico Studio e nella moderna Università di Bologna," in idem, *Monografie storiche,* 1–127.

Manning, Gideon, "Descartes and the Bologna Affair," *British Journal for the History of Science* 47.1 (March 2014): 1–13.

Mantovani, Alessandra, "Giovanni Garzoni: Uno scolaro del Valla alla corte dei Bentivoglio," in *Lorenzo Valla e l'umanesimo bolognese,* 59–83.

Mantovani, Dario, "Il Collegio dei dottori in Arti e Medicina in Pavia in età spagnola: Notizie dal manoscritto ritrovato," in *Almum Studium Papiense,* I.2, 895–910.

——, "Tracce del perduto statuto dell'*Universitas artistarum et medicorum Studii Papiensis,*" in *Almum Studium Papiense,* I.1, 309–20.

Manuels, programmes de cours et techniques d'enseignement dans les universités médiévales: Actes du Colloque international de Louvain-la-Neuve (9–11 septembre 1993), edited by Jacqueline Hamesse (Louvain: Institut d'études médiévales, 1994).

Mara DeSilva, Jennifer, "Ecclesiastical Dynasticism in Early Modern Bologna: The Canonical Chapters of San Pietro and San Petronio," in *Bologna: Cultural Crossroads,* 173–91.

Maraschio, Nicoletta, and Teresa Poggi Salani, "L'insegnamento di lingua di Diomede Borghesi e Celso Cittadini: Idea di norma e idea di storia," *Studi linguistici italiani* 17 (1991): 204–32.

Marcello Malpighi: Anatomist and Physician, edited by Domenico Bertoloni Meli (Florence: Olschki, 1997).

Marchesini, Daniele, "Lo studente di collegio a Bologna: Aspetti della vita quotidiana," in *Studenti e università degli studenti,* 283–317.

Marcus, Hannah, "Bibliography and Book Bureaucracy: Reading Licenses and the Circulation of Prohibited Books in Counter-Reformation Italy," *Papers of the Bibliographical Society of America* 110 (2016): 433–57.

——, *Forbidden Knowledge: Medicine, Science, and Censorship in Early Modern Italy* (Chicago: University of Chicago Press, 2020).

Mariotti, Italo, "Lezioni di Beroaldo il Vecchio sulla *Tebaide,*" in *Tradizione classica e letteratura umanistica: Per Alessandro Perosa,* edited by Roberto Cardini et al. (Rome: Bulzoni, 1985), II, 577–93; repr. in idem, *Scritti minori,* edited by Marco Scaffai (Bologna: Patron, 2006), 405–19.

Marsico, Clementina, "Il Tacito di Lianoro Lianori (London, British Library, Add. 8904)," *Italia medievale e umanistica* 55 (2014): 303–20.

Martellozzo Forin, Elda, "Conti palatini e lauree conferite per privilegio: L'esempio padovano del sec. XV," *ASUI* 3 (1999): 79–119.

Martin, Craig, "Francisco Vallés and the Renaissance Reinterpretation of Aristotle's 'Meteorologica' IV as a Medical Text," *Early Science and Medicine* 7.1 (2002): 1–30.

——, "Printed Medical Commentaries and Authenticity: The Case of *De alimento,*" *Journal of the Washington Academy of Sciences* 90.4 (Winter 2004): 17–28.

——, *Renaissance Meteorology: Pomponazzi to Descartes* (Baltimore: Johns Hopkins University Press, 2011).

——, *Subverting Aristotle: Religion, History, and Philosophy in Early Modern Science* (Baltimore: Johns Hopkins University Press, 2014).

———, "With Aristotelians like These, Who Needs Anti-Aristotelians? Chymical Corpuscular Matter Theory in Niccolò Cabeo's Meteorology," *Early Science and Medicine*11.2 (2006): 135–61.

Martínez Manzano, Teresa, "Autógrafos griegos de Lianoro Lianori," *Scriptorium* 58.1 (January 2004): 10–25.

Martinotti, G., "L'insegnamento dell'anatomia in Bologna prima del secolo XIX,' *SMSUB* 2 (1911): 1–146.

Masetti Zannini, Gian Lodovico, "Docenti del clero secolare e regolare nelle facoltà scientifiche dell'Università di Bologna," in *Ateneo e Chiesa di Bologna,* 171–96.

———, "Scolari e dottori del Cinquecento a Bologna (note e documenti)," *Strenna storica bolognese* 30 (1980): 215–34.

Matsen, Herbert S., "Selected Extant Latin Documents Pertaining to the 'Studio' of Bologna around 1500," in *Acta Conventus Neo-latini Bononiensis: Proceedings of the Fourth International Congress of Neo-Latin Studies, Bologna, 26 August to 1 September 1979,* edited by R. J. Schoek (Binghamton, NY: Center for Medieval and Early Renaissance Studies, 1985), 292–302.

Mattone, Antonello, and Tiziana Olivari, "Dal manoscritto alla stampa: Il libro universitario italiano nel XV secolo," in *Manoscritti, editoria e biblioteche dal Medioevo all'età contemporanea: Studi offerti a Domenico Maffei per il suo ottantesimo compleanno,* edited by Mario Ascheri-Gaetano Colli, 3 vols. (Rome: Roma nel Rinascimento, 2006), II, 679–730.

———, "Le istituzioni del sapere universitario: Teatri anatomici e orti botanici nell'età moderna," in *Storia delle università in Italia,* II, 437–95.

———, "Il libro universitario e le biblioteche degli studi nel medioevo e nell'età moderna," in *Storia delle università in Italia,* II, 389–435.

Mazzanti, Giuseppe, "Lo Studium nel XIV secolo," in *Storia di Bologna,* ed. Zangheri, II, 951–75.

Mazzarello, Paolo, and Valentina Cani, "Insegnare la Medicina," in *Almum Studium Papiense,* I.2, 1111–38.

Mazzetti, Stefano, *Memorie storiche sopra l'Università e l'Istituto delle Scienze di Bologna e sopra gli stabilimenti e i corpi scientifici alla medesima addetti* (Bologna: Tipi di S. Tommaso d'Aquino, 1840).

Mazzone, Umberto, "'Evellant vicia . . . aedificent virtutes': Il cardinal legato come elemento di disciplinamento nello Stato della Chiesa," in *Disciplina dell'anima, disciplina del corpo e disciplina della società tra Medioevo ed età moderna,* edited by Paolo Prodi with Carla Penuti (Bologna: il Mulino, 1994), 691–731.

———, "Vita religiosa e vita civile tra centro e periferia: Persone e istituzioni," in *Storia di Bologna,* ed. Zangheri, III.2, 1005–95.

Mazzotti, Massimo, "Maria Gaetana Agnesi: Mathematics and the Making of the Catholic Enlightenment," *Isis* 92.4 (December 2001): 657–63.

McConnell, Anita, "L. F. Marsigli's Visit to London in 1721, and His Report on the Royal Society," *Notes and Records of the Royal Society of London* 47.2 (1993): 179–204.

McCuaig, William, *Carlo Sigonio: The Changing World of the Late Renaissance* (Princeton, NJ: Princeton University Press, 1989).

McKitterick, David, *Print, Manuscript and the Search for Order, 1450–1830* (Cambridge: Cambridge University Press, 2006).

McVaugh, Michael R., *The Rational Surgery of the Middle Ages* (Florence: SISMEL, 2006).

The Medical Renaissance of the Sixteenth Century, edited by A. Wear, R. K. French, and I. M. Lonies (Cambridge: Cambridge University Press, 1985).

Miani, Laura, "Provenienza: B. XIV. I manoscritti di Papa Lambertini alla Biblioteca Universitaria di Bologna," in *Storia, medicina e diritto nei trattati di Prospero Lambertini Benedetto XIV,* edited by Maria Teresa Fattori (Rome: Edizioni di Storia e Letteratura, 2013), 3–45.

Miani, Laura, and Maria Cristina Bacchi, "I fondi manoscritti e le raccolte di incunaboli e cinquecentine della Biblioteca Universitaria come fonti per la storia della cultura rinascimentale," *Schede umanistiche* 3 (1989): 5–45.

Mischiati, Oscar, "Un'inedita testimonianza su Bartolomeo Ramis de Pareia," *Fontes artis musicae* 13 (1966): 84–86.

Monfasani, John, "Andronicus Callistus on the Science of Physics," in *Edizioni, traduzioni e tradizioni filosofiche (secoli XII–XVI): Studi per Pietro B. Rossi,* edited by Luca Bianchi, Onorato Grassi, and Cecilia Panti, 2 vols. (Rome: Aracne, 2018), 413–28.

——, "Aristotelians, Platonists, and the Missing Ockhamists: Philosophical Liberty in Pre-Reformation Italy," *Renaissance Quarterly* 46 (1993): 247–76.

——, "The Rise and Fall of Renaissance Italy," *Aevum* 89.3 (2015): 465–81.

Monfort, Marie-Laure, *Janus Cornarius et la redécouverte d'Hippocrate à la Renaissance* (Turnhout: Brepols, 2018).

Monga, Luigi, "Odeporica e medicina: I viaggiatori del Cinquecento e la rinoplastica," *Italica* 69 (1992): 378–93.

Montecchi, Giorgio, "La biblioteca arcivescovile di Bologna dal cardinale Paleotti a papa Lambertini," in *Produzione e circolazione libraria a Bologna nel Settecento,* 369–82.

Monti, Aldino, "Il 'lungo' Quattrocento bolognese: Agricoltura, sviluppo, istituzioni," in *Storia di Bologna,* ed. Zangheri, II, 1043–88.

Morelli, Giovanna, "I collegi di diritto nello Studio di Bologna fra XIV e XVII secolo: Considerazioni preliminari," *Il Carrobbio* 8 (1982): 249–58.

——, *Copisti a Bologna, 1265–1270* (Turnhout: Brepols, 2006).

——, "'De studio scolarium civitatis Bononie manutenendo': Gli Statuti del Comune (1335–1454) per la tutela dello Studio e delle Università degli scolari,' *L'Archiginnasio* 76 (1981): 79–165.

——, "L'editoria medievale bolognese," in *Alma mater librorum,* 50–73.

Morton, Alan G., *History of Botanical Science: An Account of the Development of Botany from Ancient Times to the Present Day* (London: Academic Press, 1981).

Moyer, Ann, "The Astronomers' Game: Astrology and University Culture in the Fifteenth and Sixteenth Centuries," *Early Science and Medicine* 4 (1999): 228–50.

——, *The Intellectual World of Sixteenth-Century Florence: Humanists and Culture in the Age of Cosimo I* (Cambridge: Cambridge University Press, 2020).

Mugnai Carrara, Daniela, *La biblioteca di Nicolò Leoniceno: Tra Aristotele e Galeno—Cultura e libri di un medico umanista* (Florence: Olschki, 1991).

——, "Curricula e contenuti dell'insegnamento: La medicina dal XVI secolo a 1800," in *Storia delle università in Italia,* II, 205–27.

Mulchahey, M. Michèle, "The Dominicans' Studium at Bologna and Its Relationship with the University in the Thirteenth Century," in *Praedicatores/Doctores,* 17–30.

——, *"First the Bow Is Bent in Study": Dominican Education before 1350* (Toronto: Pontifical Institute of Mediaeval Studies, 1998).

Muñoz Garcia, Angel, "Albert of Saxony, Bibliography," *Bulletin de philosophie médiévale* 32 (1990): 161–90.

Murano, Giovanna, "I libri di uno Studium generale: L'antica libraria del Convento di San Domenico di Bologna," *ASUI* 13 (2009): 287–304.

——, "Opere di Galeno nella facoltà di medicina di Bologna," *Italia medioevale e umanistica* 45 (2004): 137–66.

Nardi, Bruno, "Appunti sull'averroista Alessandro Achillini," in idem, *Studi su Pietro Pomponazzi,* 225–79.

——, "Intorno alla 'quaestio' magliabechiana 'An anima rationalis sit forma substantialis' attribuita al Pomponazzi," in idem, *Studi su Pietro Pomponazzi,* 320–70.

——, "I *Quolibeta de intelligentiis* di Alessandro Achillini," in idem, *Saggi sull'aristotelismo padovano dal secolo XIV al XVI,* 179–223.

——, *Saggi sull'aristotelismo padovano dal secolo XIV al XVI* (Florence: G. C. Sansoni, 1958).

——, *Studi su Pietro Pomponazzi* (Florence: Felice Le Monnier, 1965).

Nardi, Paolo, "La *migratio* delle scuole universitarie da Bologna a Siena: Il problema della continuità istituzionale," in *L'università in tempo di crisi,* 123–33.

——, "Relations with Authority," in *A History of the University in Europe,* I, 77–107.

Nasalli Rocca di Corneliano, Emilio, "Il Cardinal Bessarione legato pontificio in Bologna (1450–1455): Saggio sulla costituzione dello Stato pontificio e sulla legislazione e la vita giuridica del '400," *AMDSR,* s. IV, 20 (1930): 17–80.

Natural Particulars: Nature and the Disciplines in Renaissance Europe, edited by Anthony Grafton and Nancy G. Siraisi (Cambridge, MA: MIT Press, 1999).

Navarro Brotóns, Víctor, *Disciplinas, saberes y prácticas: Filosofía natural, matemáticas y astronomía en la sociedad española de la época moderna* (Valencia: Universitat de València, 2014).

Negruzzo, Simona, "I Collegi di educazione," in *Almum Studium Papiense,* I.2, 961–76.

——, "La *Facultas Theologiae,*" in *Almum Studium Papiense,* I.1, 609–30.

New Perspectives on Renaissance Thought: Essays in the History of Science, Education and Philosophy in Memory of Charles B. Schmitt, edited by John Henry and Sarah Hutton (London: Duckworth, 1990).

Nicoli, Elena, "Atoms, Elements, Seeds: A Renaissance Interpreter of Lucretius' Atomism," in *Lucretius: Poet and Philosopher: Background and Fortunes of* De rerum natura, edited by Philip R. Hardie, Valentina Prosperi, and Diego Zucca (Berlin: De Gruyter, 2020), 235–50.

——, "Il giudizio su Epicuro nel commento di Giovan Battista Pio a Lucrezio," in *Il culto di Epicuro: Testi, iconografia e paesaggio,* edited by Marco Beretta, Francesco Citti, and Alessandro Iannucci (Florence: Olschki, 2014), 227–54.

Notizie e insegne delle Accademie di Bologna, da un manoscritto del secolo XVIII, edited by Mario Fanti (Bologna: Rotary Club di Bologna Est, 1983).

Novikoff, Alex J., "Toward a Cultural History of Scholastic Disputation," *American Historical Review* 117.2 (April 2012): 331–64.

Nuovo, Angela, *The Book Trade in the Italian Renaissance* (Leiden: Brill, 2013).

Nuovo, Angela, and Francesco Ammannati, "Investigating Book Prices in Early Modern Europe: Questions and Sources," *JLIS.it* 8.3 (2017): 1–25.

Nutton, Vivian, *Ancient Medicine,* 2nd ed. (Milton Park, UK: Routledge, 2013).

——, "Fracastoro's Theory of Contagion: The Seed That Fell among the Thorns?," in *Renaissance Medical Learning: Evolution of a Tradition, Osiris,* s. II, 6 (1990): 196–234.

——, "Greek Science in the Sixteenth-Century Renaissance," in *Renaissance and Revolution,* 15–28.

——, "Hellenism Postponed: Some Aspects of Renaissance Medicine, 1490–1530," *Sudhoffs Archiv* 81.2 (1997): 158–70.

——, "Humanist Surgery," in *The Medical Renaissance of the Sixteenth Century,* 75–99.

——, "Ippocrate nel Rinascimento," in *Interpretare e curare: Medicina e salute nel Rinascimento,* edited by Maria Conforti, Andrea Carlino, and Antonio Clericuzio (Rome: Carrocci, 2014), 21–42.

——, "Medieval Western Europe, 1000–1500," in Conrad et al., *The Western Medical Tradition,* 139–205.

——, "'Qui magni Galeni doctrinam in re medica primus revocavit': Matteo Corti und der Galenismus im medizinischen Unterricht der Renaissance," in *Der Humanismus und die oberen Fakultäten,* edited by G. Keil (Weinheim: VDA, 1987), 173–84.

——, *Renaissance Medicine: A Short History of European Medicine in the Sixteenth Century* (London: Routledge, 2022).

Ogilvie, Brian W., *The Science of Describing: Natural History in Renaissance Europe* (Chicago: University of Chicago Press, 2006).

Olmi, Giuseppe, "Farmacopea antica e medicina moderna: La disputa sulla teriaca nel Cinquecento bolognese," *Physis* 19 (1977): 197–246.

——. "Le scienze naturali nella prima età moderna," in *L'Università a Bologna,* II, 141–52.

——, *Ulisse Aldrovandi: Scienza e natura nel secondo Cinquecento* (Trento: Libera Università degli Studi, 1976).

Orlandelli, Gianfranco, "Il codice scolastico bolognese," in *L'università a Bologna,* I, 113–31.

——, "I testi manoscritti," in *Alma mater librorum,* 15–23.

Orlandi, Pellegrino Antonio, *Notizie degli scrittori bolognesi e dell'opere loro stampate e manoscritte* (Bologna: Constantino Pisarri, 1714).

Ortiz Monasterio, Fernando, *Dolor y bellezza: Gaspare Tagliacozzi cirujano del Renacimiento* (n.p.: Landucci, 2000).

Osler, Douglas J., "Humanists and Jurists at Bologna: Filippo Beroaldo and His School," in *Bologna: Cultural Crossroads,* 3–11.

Osservanza francescana e Università di Bologna: Cultura laica e religiosa tra Umanesimo e Rinascimento—Studi in occasione delle celebrazioni per i 760 anni del Convento dell'Osservanza e nono centenario dell'Università di Bologna, 21–22 maggio 1988 (Bologna: Banca del Monte di Bologna e Ravenna, 1988).

Otterspeer, Willem, *Groepsportret met Dame,* 2 vols. (Amsterdam: Bert Bakker, 2000–2002).

——, "The University of Leiden: An Eclectic Institution," in *Science and Universities,* 324–33.

Ottosson, Per-Gunnar, *Scholastic Medicine and Philosophy: A Study of Commentaries on Galen's* Tegni (Naples: Bibliopolis, 1984).

Padovani, Andrea, "Lo Studium nel XV secolo," in *Storia di Bologna,* ed. Zangheri, II, 1017–41.

Palermo, Paola, "Dal judiciolo al iudicium: La produzione divinatoria nello Studio di Bologna (1470–1560)," *Teca* 8.8 (2015): 9–42.

Palmer, Ada, *Reading Lucretius in the Renaissance* (Cambridge, MA: Harvard University Press, 2014).

Pantaleoni, M., and R. Bernabeo, "Pier Paolo Molinelli e l'istituzione della cattedra di medicina operatoria in Bologna," in *Atti della 5ª biennale della Marca e dello Studio Firmano . . . 1963* (Fermo: n.p., 1963), 369–85.

Paolini, Lorenzo, "L'Arcidiacono della Chiesa bolognese e i collegi dei dottori dello Studio," in *Domus Episcopi: Il palazzo arcivescovile di Bologna,* edited by Roberto Terra (San Giorgio di Piano: Minerva, 2002), 254–66.

——, "La chiesa di Bologna e lo Studio nella prima metà del Duecento," in *L'origine dell'Ordine dei Predicatori e l'Università di Bologna,* edited by Giovanni Bertuzzi (Bologna: Edizioni Studio Domenicano, 2006), 23–42.

——, "La Chiesa e la città (secoli XI–XIII)," in *Storia di Bologna,* II, 653–759.

——, "L'evoluzione di una funzione ecclesiastica: L'arcidiacono e lo Studio a Bologna nel XIII secolo," *Studi medievali,* s. III, 29.1 (1988): 129–72.

——, "La figura dell'Arcidiacono nei rapporti fra lo Studio e la Città," in *Cultura universitaria e pubblici poteri a Bologna dal XII al XV secolo: Atti del I° convegno (Bologna, 20–21 maggio 1988),* edited by Ovidio Capitani (Bologna: Istituto per la Storia di Bologna, 1990), 31–71.

Papy, Jan, "*Italiam Vestram Amo supra Omnes Terras!* Lipsius' Attitude towards Italy and Italian Humanism of the Late Sixteenth Century," *Humanistica Lovaniensia* 47 (1998): 245–77.

Paquet, Jacques, *Les Matricules universitaires* (Turnhout: Brepols, 1992).

Park, Katharine, *Doctors and Medicine in Early Renaissance Florence* (Princeton, NJ: Princeton University Press, 1985).

Parmeggiani, Riccardo, "L'arcidiacono bolognese tra Chiesa, città e *studium,*" in *L'università in tempo di crisi,* 95–111.

——, "Mendicant Orders and the Repression of Heresy," in *A Companion to Medieval and Renaissance Bologna,* 411–35.

Pascoe, Louis B., "Response to Gabriel Codina, S.J.," in *The Jesuit* Ratio Studiorum, 50–55.

Patergnani, Elisa, "Ercole Corazzi tra le Università di Padova, Bologna e Torino," *Bollettino delle scienze matematiche* 37.2 (December 2017): 267–97.

Patetta, Federico, et al., *L'Università di Torino nei secoli XVI e XVII* (Turin: Giappichelli, 1972).

Pazzini, Adalberto, "Modernità e tradizione nella storia della facoltà medica di Bologna," *SMSUB,* n.s., 1 (1956): 391–415.

La pedagogia della Compagnia di Gesù: Atti del Convegno Internazionale, Messina 14–16 novembre 1991, edited by F. Guerello and P. Schiavone (Messina: ESUR Ignatianum, 1992).

Pedersen, Olaf, "The Origins of the 'Theorica Planetarum,'" *Journal for the History of Astronomy* 12 (1981): 113–23.

——, "Tradition and Innovation," in *A History of the University in Europe,* II, 451–88.

Pegoretti, Anna, "Filosofanti," *Le Tre Corone: Rivista internazionale di studi su Dante, Petrarca, Boccaccio* 2 (2015): 11–70.

Pellegrini, Letizia, "La biblioteca e i codici di San Domenico (secc. XIII–XV)," in *Praedicatores / Doctores,* 143–59.

Pepe, Luigi, "Astronomia e matematica nelle università italiane del Quattrocento," in *Luca Pacioli e la matematica nel Rinascimento,* edited by Enrico Giusti (Città di Castello: Petruzzi, 1998), 29–49.

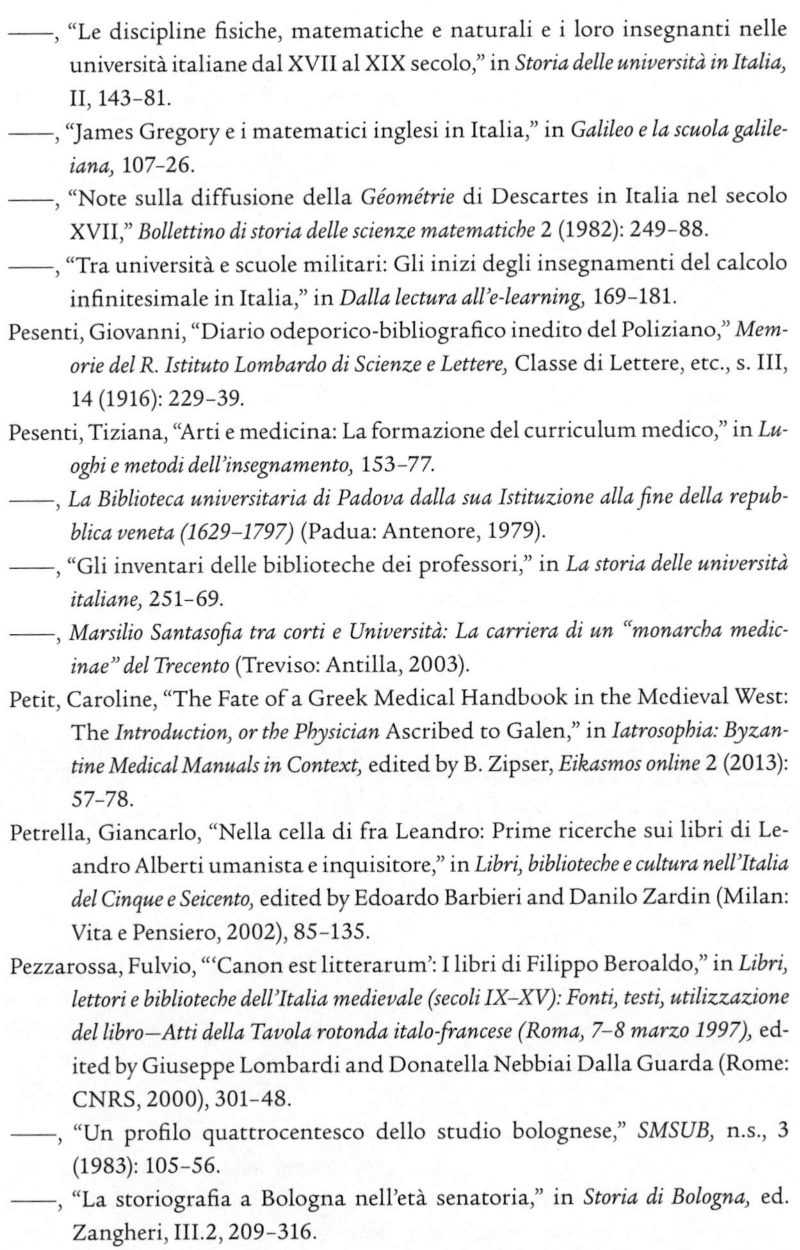

——, "Le discipline fisiche, matematiche e naturali e i loro insegnanti nelle università italiane dal XVII al XIX secolo," in *Storia delle università in Italia,* II, 143–81.

——, "James Gregory e i matematici inglesi in Italia," in *Galileo e la scuola galileiana,* 107–26.

——, "Note sulla diffusione della *Géométrie* di Descartes in Italia nel secolo XVII," *Bollettino di storia delle scienze matematiche* 2 (1982): 249–88.

——, "Tra università e scuole militari: Gli inizi degli insegnamenti del calcolo infinitesimale in Italia," in *Dalla lectura all'e-learning,* 169–181.

Pesenti, Giovanni, "Diario odeporico-bibliografico inedito del Poliziano," *Memorie del R. Istituto Lombardo di Scienze e Lettere,* Classe di Lettere, etc., s. III, 14 (1916): 229–39.

Pesenti, Tiziana, "Arti e medicina: La formazione del curriculum medico," in *Luoghi e metodi dell'insegnamento,* 153–77.

——, *La Biblioteca universitaria di Padova dalla sua Istituzione alla fine della repubblica veneta (1629–1797)* (Padua: Antenore, 1979).

——, "Gli inventari delle biblioteche dei professori," in *La storia delle università italiane,* 251–69.

——, *Marsilio Santasofia tra corti e Università: La carriera di un "monarcha medicinae" del Trecento* (Treviso: Antilla, 2003).

Petit, Caroline, "The Fate of a Greek Medical Handbook in the Medieval West: The *Introduction, or the Physician* Ascribed to Galen," in *Iatrosophia: Byzantine Medical Manuals in Context,* edited by B. Zipser, *Eikasmos online* 2 (2013): 57–78.

Petrella, Giancarlo, "Nella cella di fra Leandro: Prime ricerche sui libri di Leandro Alberti umanista e inquisitore," in *Libri, biblioteche e cultura nell'Italia del Cinque e Seicento,* edited by Edoardo Barbieri and Danilo Zardin (Milan: Vita e Pensiero, 2002), 85–135.

Pezzarossa, Fulvio, "'Canon est litterarum': I libri di Filippo Beroaldo," in *Libri, lettori e biblioteche dell'Italia medievale (secoli IX–XV): Fonti, testi, utilizzazione del libro—Atti della Tavola rotonda italo-francese (Roma, 7–8 marzo 1997),* edited by Giuseppe Lombardi and Donatella Nebbiai Dalla Guarda (Rome: CNRS, 2000), 301–48.

——, "Un profilo quattrocentesco dello studio bolognese," *SMSUB,* n.s., 3 (1983): 105–56.

——, "La storiografia a Bologna nell'età senatoria," in *Storia di Bologna,* ed. Zangheri, III.2, 209–316.

——, "'Vita mihi ducitur inter paginas': La biblioteca di Filippo Beroaldo il Vecchio," *Schede umanistiche,* n.s., 11 (1997): 109–30.

Physico-Theology: Religion and Science in Europe, 1650–1750, edited by Ann Blair and Kaspar von Greyerz (Baltimore: Johns Hopkins University Press, 2020).

Piana, Celestino, "La facoltà teologica dell'Università di Bologna nel 1444–1458," *Archivum historicum franciscanum* 53 (1960): 361–441.

——, "La facoltà teologica di Bologna nella prima metà del Cinquecento," *Archivum historicum franciscanum* 62 (1969): 196–266.

——, *Nuove ricerche su le Università di Bologna e di Parma* (Florence: Quaracchi, 1966).

——, *Ricerche su le Università di Bologna e di Parma nel secolo XV* (Florence: Quaracchi, 1964).

Piccinno, Lucia, *Fonti per l'insegnamento della medicina nello Studio bolognese: I programmi delle lezioni (secoli 17.–18.)* (Bologna: CLUEB, 2006).

Pierce Webster, Jerome, and Martha Teach Gnudi, "Documenti inediti intorno alla vita di Gaspare Tagliacozzi," *SMSUB* 13 (1935): 3–149.

Pigeaud, Jérôme, "L'Hippocratisme de Cardan: Étude sur le commentaire d'AEL par Cardan," *Res publica litterarum* 8 (1975): 219–29.

Pini, Antonio Ivan, "Federico II, lo Studio di Bologna e il 'Falso Teodosiano,'" in idem, *Studio, università e città,* 66–84.

——, "Le *nationes* studentesche nel modello universitario bolognese del medioevo," in idem, *Studio, università e città,* 210–18.

——, "Per una storia sociale dell'università: I bidelli bolognesi nel XIII secolo," in idem, *Studio, università e città,* 288–323.

——, *Studio, università e città nel medioevo bolognese* (Bologna: CLUEB, 2005).

Pirri, Pietro, "Gregorio XIII e l'eredità della biblioteca di Carlo Sigonio," in *Studi di storia dell'arte, bibliologia ed erudizione in onore di Alfredo Petrucci,* edited by Francesco Barberi et al. (Milan: C. Bestetti, 1969), 89–96.

Pissavino, Paolo C., "Università e Accademie," in *Almum Studium Papiense,* I.2, 1223–58.

Pistacchio, Bonifacio, "Il contrasto tra Malpighi e Sbaraglia, esemplare del difficile rapporto tra ricerca di base e medicina pratica," *SMSUB,* n.s., 9 (1995): 85–93.

——, "L'insegnamento dell'astrologia nell'Università di Bologna," *Strenna storica bolognese* 42 (1992): 317–28.

Podestà, Bartolomeo, "Di alcuni documenti inediti riguardanti il Pomponazzi, lettore nello Studio bolognese," *AMDSR* 6 (1867): 133–80.

Poli, Liliana, "Contributi sopra Sigismondo de' Libri," *La bibliofilia* 51 (1949): 9–27.

Pomata, Gianna, *Contracting a Cure: Patients, Healers, and the Law in Early Modern Bologna* (Baltimore: Johns Hopkins University Press, 1998).

Poppi, Antonino, *Introduzione all'aristotelismo padovano,* 2nd ed. (Padua: Antenore, 1991).

——, *Ricerche sulla teologia e la scienza nella Scuola padovana del Cinque e Seicento* (Soveria Mannelli: Scuola Rubbettino, 2001).

Porter, Roy, "The Eighteenth Century," in Conrad et al., *The Western Medical Tradition,* 371–475.

——, "The Scientific Revolution and Universities," in *A History of the University in Europe,* II, 530–62.

Poulle, Emmanuel, *Les Tables Alphonsines avec les Canons de Jean de Saxe* (Paris: Éditions du CNRS, 1984).

Praedicatores / Doctores: Lo studium generale *dei frati Predicatori nella cultura bolognese tra il '200 e il '300,* edited by Roberto Lambertini, special issue of *Memorie domenicane,* n.s., 39 (2008).

La presenza dell'aristotelismo padovano nella filosofia della prima modernità, edited by Gregorio Piaia (Rome: Antenore, 2002).

Prodi, Paolo, *Il cardinale Gabriele Paleotti (1522–1597),* 2 vols. (Rome: Edizioni di Storia e Letteratura, 1959-1967).

——, "Il giuramento universitario tra corporazione, ideologia e confessione religiosa," in *Sapere e / è potere,* III, 23–35.

——, *Il sacramento del potere: Il giuramento politico nella storia costituzionale dell'Occidente* (Bologna: il Mulino, 1992).

Produzione e circolazione libraria a Bologna nel Settecento: Avvio di un'indagine, edited by Luigi Balsamo (Bologna: Istituto per la Storia di Bologna, 1987).

I pronostici di Domenico Maria da Novara, edited by Fabrizio Bònoli, Giuseppe Bezza, Salvo De Meis, and Cinzia Colavita (Florence: Olschki, 2012).

Prosperi, Adriano, "Anime in trappola: Confessione e censura ecclesiastica all'Università di Pisa tra '500 e '600," *Belfagor* 54 (1999): 257–87.

Puccetti, S., "Achille Bocchi: La vita, l'Accademia Bocchiana, il carteggio" (unpublished tesi di laurea, 2 vols., Università di Firenze, a.a. 1989–1990, relatore Antonio Rotondò).

Putti, Vittorio, *Berengario da Carpi: Saggio biografico e bibliografico seguito dalla traduzione del "De fractura calvae sive cranei"* (Bologna: Cappelli, 1937).

Quaglioni, Diego, "Dal manoscritto alla stampa: Agli inizi della tipografia giuridica bolognese," in *Juristische Buchproduktion im Mittelalter,* edited by Vincenzo Colli (Frankfurt am Main: V. Klostermann, 2002), 599–617.

Quaquarelli, Leonardo, *Il Quattrocento dei copisti: Bologna: Seconda edizione riveduta e corretta con aggiunta di specimina di scritture* (Bologna: I libri di Emil, 2014).

——, "Umanesimo e lettura dei classici alla scuola bolognese di Niccolò Volpe," *Schede umanistiche* 1 (1999): 98–120.

Quondam, Amadeo, "L'Accademia," in *Letteratura italiana,* general editor Alberto Asor Rosa, vol. I: *Il letterato e le istituzioni* (Turin: Einaudi, 1982), 823–98.

——, "Il metronomo classicista," in *I Gesuiti e la Ratio studiorum,* edited by Manfred Hinz, Roberto Righi, and Danilo Zardin (Rome: Bulzoni, 2004), 379–507.

Raimondi, Ezio, *Codro e l'Umanesimo a Bologna* (Bologna: Cesare Zuffi, 1950; repr., Bologna: il Mulino, 1987).

——, "Da Bologna a Venezia," in idem, *Politica e commedia,* 59–100.

——, "Il primo commento umanistico a Lucrezio," in idem, *Politica e commedia,* 101–40.

——, *Politica e commedia: Dal Beroaldo al Machiavelli* (Bologna: il Mulino, 1972).

——, "Quattrocento bolognese: Università e umanesimo," in idem, *Politica e commedia,* 15–58.

——, "Umanesimo e università nel Quattrocento Bolognese," *SMSUB,* n.s., 1 (1956): 325–56.

Ranuzzi: Storia, genealogia e iconografia, edited by Giuliano Malvezzi Campeggi (Bologna: Costa, 2000).

Rapporti tra le Università di Padova e Bologna: Ricerche di filosofia, medicina e scienza—Omaggio dell'Università di Padova all'Alma mater bolognese nel suo nono centenario, edited by Lucia Rossetti (Triest: LINT, 1988).

Rashdall, Hastings, *The Universities of Europe in the Middle Ages,* 3 vols., new ed. by F. M. Powicke and A. B. Emden (Oxford: Clarendon Press / Oxford University Press, 1936; repr., Oxford: Clarendon Press, 1987).

The Reception of Aristotle's Poetics *in the Italian Renaissance and Beyond: New Directions in Criticism,* edited by Bryan Brazeau (London: Bloomsbury, 2020).

Reeve, Michael, "Classical Scholarship," in *The Cambridge Companion to Renaissance Humanism,* edited by Jill Kraye (Cambridge: Cambridge University Press, 1996), 20–46.

Regier, Jonathan, "Reading Cardano with the Roman Inquisition: Astrology, Celestial Physics, and the Force of Heresy," *Isis* 110.4 (2019): 661–79.

Regoliosi, Mariangela, *Nel cantiere del Valla: Elaborazione e montaggio delle* Elegantiae (Rome: Bulzoni, 1993).

——. "Nuove ricerche intorno a Giovanni Tortelli: II," *Italia medioevale e umanistica* 12 (1969): 129–92.

Reif, Patricia, "The Textbook Tradition in Natural Philosophy, 1600–1650," *Journal of the History of Ideas* 30 (1969): 17–32.

Renaissance and Renewal in the Twelfth Century, edited by Robert L. Benson and Giles Constable, with Carol D. Lanham (Oxford: Clarendon Press, 1982).

Renaissance and Revolution: Humanists, Scholars, Craftsmen and Natural Philosophers in Early Modern Europe, edited by J. V. Field and Frank A. J. L. James (Cambridge: Cambridge University Press, 1993; repr., Cambridge: Cambridge University Press, 1997).

Renaissance Surgery: Between Learning and Craft, edited by Cynthia Klestinec and Domenico Bertoloni Meli, special issue of *Journal of the History of Medicine and Allied Sciences* 77.11 (2017).

Resta, Gianvito, "Filelfo tra Bisanzio e Roma," in *Francesco Filelfo nel quinto centenario della morte: Atti del XVII Convegno di studi maceratesi (Tolentino, 27–30 settembre 1981)* (Padua: Antenore, 1986), 1–60.

Rethinking Virtue, Reforming Society: New Directions in Renaissance Ethics, c. 1350–1650, edited by David A. Lines and Sabrina Ebbersmeyer (Turnhout: Brepols, 2013).

Revisiting Medical Humanism in Renaissance Europe, edited by Caroline Petit, special issue of *Arts et savoirs,* 15 (2021), https://journals.openedition.org/aes/3542.

La Rhétorique d'Aristote: Traditions et commentaires, de l'Antiquité au XVIIe *siècle—Actes du colloque (Aix-en-Provence, 9–12 julliet 1995),* edited by I. Rosier and F. Desbordes (Paris: Vrin, 1998).

Rhodes, Dennis E., "Due questioni di bibliografia bolognese del Cinquecento," *L'Archiginnasio* 81 (1986): 321–24.

Ricci, Corrado, *Monumenti sepolcrali di lettori dello Studio bolognese* (Bologna: Fava e Garagnani, 1888).

Richardson, Brian, *Manuscript Culture in Renaissance Italy* (New York: Cambridge University Press, 2009).

Riddle, John M., "Dioscorides," in *Catalogus Translationum et Commentariorum,* edited by Paul O. Kristeller et al. (Washington, DC: Catholic University of America / Toronto: Pontifical Institute of Mediaeval Studies, 1960–), IV, 1–143.

Il Rinascimento parla ebraico, edited by Giulio Busi and Silvana Greco (Cinisello Balsamo: Silvana Editoriale, 2019).

Risse, Wilhelm, *Bibliographia philosophica vetus: Repertorium generale systematicum operum philosophicorum usque ad annum MDCCC typis impressorum,* 9 vols. (Hildesheim: G. Olms Verlag, 1998).

Ristori, Renzo, "Benedetto Accolti: A proposito di un riformato toscano del Cinquecento," *Rinascimento,* n.s., 2 (1962): 225–312.

Robertson, Ian, *Tyranny under the Mantle of St Peter: Pope Paul II and Bologna* (Turnhout: Brepols, 2002).

Robison, Kira, *Healers in the Making: Students, Physicians, and Medical Education in Medieval Bologna* (Leiden: Brill, 2021).

Roest, Bernd, *A History of Franciscan Education (c. 1210–1517)* (Leiden: Brill, 2000).

Roggero, Marina, "I collegi universitari in età moderna," in *L'università in Italia fra età moderna e contemporanea,* 111–33.

——, "Professori e studenti nelle università tra crisi e riforme," in *Storia d'Italia, Annali* 4 (Turin: Einaudi, 1981), 1039–81.

——, "Le università in epoca moderna: Ricerche e prospettive," in *La storia delle università italiane,* 311–34.

Rolet, Anne, *Dans le cercle d'Achille Bocchi: Culture emblématique et practiques académiques à Bologna au XVI*[e] *siècle* (Tours: Presses universitaires François Rabelais, 2019).

Romano, Antonella, *La Contre-Réforme mathématique: Constitution et diffusion d'une culture mathématique jésuite à la Renaissance (1540–1640)* (Rome: École Française de Rome, 1999).

Roncuzzi Roversi Monaco, Valeria, *L'Archiginnasio: Guida al Palazzo e alla Biblioteca* (Bologna: Nuova Alfa Éditoriale, 1988).

Rose, Paul Lawrence, and Stillman Drake, "The Pseudo-Aristotelian 'Questions of Mechanics' in Renaissance Culture," *Studies in the Renaissance* 18 (1971): 65–104.

Rosino, Leonida, "Geminiano Montanari astronomo della seconda metà del Seicento a Bologna e Padova," in *Rapporti tra le università di Padova e Bologna,* 173–89.

Rossetti, Lucia, "Le biblioteche delle 'Nationes' nello Studio di Padova," *Quaderni per la storia dell'Università di Padova* 2 (1969): 53–67.

——, "I collegi per i dottorati 'auctoritate veneta,'" in *Viridarium floridum: Studi di storia veneta offerti dagli allievi a Paolo Sambin,* edited by Maria Chiara Billanovich, Giorgio Cracco, and Antonio Rigon (Padua: Antenore, 1984), 365–86.

Rossi, Guido, "'Universitas scholarium' e comune (sec. XII–XIV)," *SMUB,* n.s., 1 (1956): 173–266.

Rossi, Pietro, *La prima cattedra di "lingua toscana" (dai ruoli dello Studio senese, 1588–1743)* (Turin: Bocca, 1910).

Rossi Monti, Martino, "Paulus Scalichius: His Thought, Sources, and Fortune," *Prilozi za istraživanje hrvatske filozofske baštine* 45.2 (90) (2019): 339–82.

Rotondò, Antonio, "Nuovi documenti per la storia dell' 'Indice dei libri proibiti' (1572–1638)," *Rinascimento,* n.s., 3 (1963): 145–211.

——, "Per la storia dell'eresia a Bologna nel secolo XVI," *Rinascimento,* n.s., 2 (1962): 107–54.

Russell, John L., S.J., "Catholic Astronomers and the Copernican System after the Condemnation of Galileo," *Annals of Science* 46.4 (1989): 365–86.

Rutkin, H. Darrel, *Sapientia Astrologica: Astrology, Magic and Natural Knowledge, ca. 1250–1800,* vol. I (Cham: Springer, 2019).

——, "The Use and Abuse of Ptolemy's Tetrabiblos in Renaissance and Early Modern Europe: Two Case Studies (Giovanni Pico della Mirandola and Filippo Fantoni)," in *Ptolemy in Perspective: Use and Criticism of His Work from Antiquity to the Nineteenth Century,* edited by Alexander Jones (Dordrecht: Springer, 2010), 135–49.

Rütten, Thomas, "Commenti ippocratici in età moderna," *Medicina nei secoli arte e scienza* 17.2 (2005): 443–68.

——, "Hippocrates and the Construction of 'Progress' in Sixteenth- and Seventeenth-Century Medicine," in *Reinventing Hippocrates,* edited by David Cantor (Aldershot: Ashgate, 2002), 37–58.

Sabbadini, Remigio, "Giovanni Toscanella," *Giornale linguistico* 17 (1891): 119–37.

——, *Il metodo degli umanisti* (Florence: F. Le Monnier, 1922; repr., Rome: Edizioni di Storia e Letteratura, 2018).

Sabbatani, Luigi, "La cattedra dei semplici fondata a Bologna da Luca Ghini," *SMSUB* 9 (1926): 13–53.

Sandy, Gerald, "Lex commentandi: Philippe Béroalde et le commentaire humaniste," *Bibliothèque d'Humanisme et Renaissance* 69.2 (2007): 399–423.

Santagata, Marco, *Boccaccio: Fragilità di un genio* (Milan: Mondadori, 2019).

Santoni-Rugiu, Paolo, and Philip J. Sykes, *A History of Plastic Surgery* (Berlin: Springer, 2007).

Sapere e / è potere: Discipline, dispute e professioni nell'università medievale e moderna: Il caso bolognese a confronto—Atti del quarto convegno, Bologna, 13–15 aprile 1989, edited by Luisa Avellini, Angela De Benedictis, and Andrea Crisciani, 3 vols. (Bologna: Istituto per la Storia di Bologna, 1990 [but 1991]).

Sarti, Nicoletta, "Le edizioni degli statuti dello *Studium* bolognese: Stato dell'opera," in *Gli statuti universitari,* 155–70.

Savelli, Rodolfo, "La biblioteca disciplinata: Una 'libraria' cinquecentesca tra censura e dissimulazione," in *Tra diritto e storia: Studi in onore di Luigi Berlinguer promossi dalle Università di Siena e di Sassari* (Soveria Mannelli: Rubettino, 2008), 865–944.

——, "Biblioteche professionali e censura ecclesiastica (XVI–XVII sec.)," in *Le Livre scientifique aux débuts de l'époque moderne: Entrepôts et trafics annonaires en Méditerranée,* special issue of *Mélanges de l'École Française de Rome: Italie et Méditerranée* 120.2 (2008): 453–72.

Savoia, Paolo, *Cosmesi e chirurgia: Bellezza, dolore e medicina nell'Italia moderna* (Milan: Editrice bibliografica, 2017).

Scaglione, Aldo, *The Liberal Arts and the Jesuit College System* (Amsterdam: John Benjamins, 1986).

Scappini, Cristiana, Maria Pia Torricelli, and Sandra Tugnoli Pattaro, *Lo Studio Aldrovandi in Palazzo Pubblico, 1617–1742* (Bologna: CLUEB, 1993).

Schmidt-Biggemann, Wilhelm, "New Structures of Knowledge," in *A History of the University in Europe,* II, 489–530.

Schmitt, Charles B., "Aristotelianism in the Veneto and the Origins of Modern Science: Some Considerations on the Problem of Continuity," in idem, *The Aristotelian Tradition,* item 1.

——, *The Aristotelian Tradition and Renaissance Universities* (London: Variorum, 1984).

——, "Aristotle among the Physicians," in *The Medical Renaissance of the Sixteenth Century,* 1–15.

——, *Aristotle and the Renaissance* (Cambridge, MA: Harvard University Press, 1983).

——, "A Fresh Look at Mechanics in Sixteenth-Century Italy," in idem, *Studies in Renaissance Philosophy and Science* (London: Variorum, 1981), item XII.

——, "Galileo and the Seventeenth-Century Text-book Tradition," in *Novità celesti e crisi del sapere: Atti del convegno internazionale di studi galileiani,* edited by Paolo Galluzzi (Florence: Giunti Barbèra, 1984), 217–28.

——, "Philosophy and Science in Sixteenth-Century Italian Universities," in idem, *The Aristotelian Tradition,* item XV.

——, "The Rise of the Philosophical Textbook," in *The Cambridge History of Renaissance Philosophy,* 792–804.

——, "Science in the Italian Universities in the Sixteenth and Early Seventeenth Centuries," in idem, *The Aristotelian Tradition,* item XIV.

Scholarly Knowledge: Textbooks in Early Modern Europe, edited by Emidio Campi et al. (Geneva: Droz, 2008).

Schütze, Sebastian, *Kardinal Maffeo Barberini, später Papst Urban VIII., und die Entstehung des römischen Hochbarock* (Munich: Hirmer, 2007).

Science and Universities of Early Modern Europe: Teaching, Specialization, Professionalization, edited by David A. Lines, special issue of *Early Science and Medicine* 6.4 (2001).

Scientiae in the History of Medicine, edited by Fabrizio Baldassarri and Fabio Zampieri, special issue of *Storia della medicina* 4 (2021).

Scienza e letteratura nella cultura italiana del Settecento, edited by Renzo Cremante and Walter Tega (Bologna: il Mulino, 1984).

Scribal Culture in Italy, 1450–1700, edited by Filippo de Vivo and Brian Richardson, special issue of *Italian Studies* 66.2 (2011).

Secrets of Nature: Astrology and Alchemy in Early Modern Europe, edited by William R. Newman and Anthony Grafton (Cambridge, MA: MIT Press, 2001).

Serrai, Alfredo, "Biblioteche private in Italia: Guida storico-bibliografica," in *Manoscritti, editoria e biblioteche dal Medioevo all'età contemporanea: Studi offerti a Domenico Maffei per il suo ottantesimo compleanno,* edited by Mario Ascheri and Gaetano Colli (Rome: Roma nel Rinascimento, 2006), III, 23–46.

Severi, Andrea, *Filippo Beroaldo il Vecchio, un maestro per l'Europa: Da commentatore di classici a classico moderno (1481–1550)* (Bologna: il Mulino, 2015).

——, *Leggere i moderni con gli antichi e gli antichi coi moderni: Petrarca, Valla e Beroaldo* (Bologna: Pàtron, 2017).

——, "Perotti e Morandi nella disputa Valla-Bracciolini: Umanesimo bolognese tra nuove e vecchie tendenze," in *Lorenzo Valla e l'umanesimo bolognese,* 93–114.

Sgarbi, Marco, *Francesco Robortello (1516–1567): Architectural Genius of the Humanities* (New York: Routledge, 2020).

——, "Francesco Robortello on Topics," *Viator* 47 (2016): 365–88.

——, "Francesco Robortello's Rhetoric: On the Orator and His Arguments," *Rhetorica* 34 (2016): 243–67.

Sighinolfi, Lino, "La biblioteca di Giovanni Marcanova," in *Collectanea variae doctrinae Leoni S. Olschki bibliopolae florentino sexagenario* (Munich: Rosenthal, 1921), 187–222.

——, "Francesco Puteolano e le origini della stampa, in Bologna e in Parma," *La bibliofilia* 15 (1913–1914), 263–66, 331–44, 383–92, 451–67.

Simeoni, Luigi, "Documenti sulla vita e la biblioteca di Carlo Sigonio," *SMSUB* 11 (1933): 185–262.

——, *Storia della Università di Bologna,* vol. II: *L'età moderna (1500–1888)* (Bologna: Zanichelli, 1940; repr., Bologna: Forni, 1988).

Simili, Alessandro, "Gerolamo Cardano lettore e medico a Bologna: Nota 2—Il soggiorno e gli insegnamenti," *L'Archiginnasio* 61 (1966): 384–507.

——, *I lettori di medicina e chirurgia dello Studio di Bologna dal 1460 al 1500 (profili bio-bibliografici)* (Bologna: La Grafica Emiliana, 1941).

Simoni, Fulvio, "Scuola d'artiglieria, laboratorio scientifico, museo delle meraviglie: Apparenza e sostanza dell'architettura militare nell'Istituto delle Scienze di Bologna," in *La scienza delle armi: Luigi Ferdinando Marsili, 1658–1730* (Bologna: Pendragon, 2012), 125–41.

Siraisi, Nancy G., *Arts and Sciences at Padua: The* Studium *of Padua before 1350* (Toronto: Pontifical Institute of Mediaeval Studies, 1973).

——, *Avicenna in Renaissance Italy: The Canon and Medical Teaching in Italian Universities after 1500* (Princeton, NJ: Princeton University Press, 1987).

——, "Cardano, Hippocrates and Criticism of Galen," in *Girolamo Cardano: Philosoph, Naturforscher, Arzt,* edited by Eckhard Kessler (Wiesbaden: Harrassowitz, 1994), 131–55.

——, *The Clock and the Mirror: Girolamo Cardano and Renaissance Medicine* (Princeton, NJ: Princeton University Press, 1997).

——, "The Faculty of Medicine," in *A History of the University in Europe,* I, 360–87.

——, "L'insegnamento della medicina ippocratica di Girolamo Cardano a Bologna," in *Sapere e/è potere,* II, 153–71.

——, "Medicine, Physiology, and Anatomy in Early Sixteenth-Century Critiques of the Arts and Sciences," in *New Perspectives on Renaissance Thought,* 214–29.

——, *Medieval and Early Renaissance Medicine: An Introduction to Knowledge and Practice* (Chicago: University of Chicago Press, 1990).

——, "Renaissance Readers and Avicenna's Organization of Medical Knowledge," in eadem, *Medicine and the Italian Universities, 1250–1600* (Leiden: Brill, 2001), 203–25.

——, *Taddeo Alderotti and His Pupils: Two Generations of Italian Medical Learning* (Princeton, NJ: Princeton University Press, 1981).

Soetermeer, Frank, *Utrumque jus in peciis: Aspetti della produzione libraria a Bologna fra Due e Trecento* (Milan: Giuffrè, 1997).

Soppelsa, Maria Luisa, "Itinerari epistemici e riforme istituzionali nello Studio di Padova tra Sei e Settecento," in *Aristotelismo e scienza moderna: Atti del 25° anno accademico del Centro per la storia della tradizione aristotelica nel Veneto,* edited by Luigi Olivieri (Padua: Antenore, 1983), II, 961–92.

Sorbelli, Albano, *La Biblioteca Capitolare della Cattedrale di Bologna* (Bologna: Nicola Zanichelli, 1904).

——, *Bologna negli scrittori stranieri,* 4 vols. (Bologna: Nicola Zanichelli, 1927–1933).

——, "Carlo Sigonio e la Società tipografica bolognese," *La bibliofilia* 23 (1921): 95–105.

——, *Corpus chartarum Italiae ad rem typographicam pertinentium ab arte inventa ad ann. MDL,* vol. I: *Bologna,* edited by Maria Gioia Tavoni (Rome: Istituto Poligrafico e Zecca dello Stato-Libreria dello Stato, 2004).

——, *L'esame nell'università durante il medioevo* (Bologna: Istituto per la storia dell'Università di Bologna, 1942).

——, "La libreria di uno stampatore bibliofilo del Quattrocento," in *Studi e ricerche sulla storia della stampa del Quattrocento* (Milan: Hoepli, 1942), 259–336.

——, "Il magazzino librario e la privata biblioteca di un grande tipografo del secolo XV (Plato Benedetti)," *Gutenberg-Jahrbuch* (1935): 93–99.

——, *Storia della stampa in Bologna* (Bologna: N. Zanichelli 1929; repr., Bologna: Forni, 2003).

——, *Storia della Università di Bologna,* vol. I: *Il Medioevo (secoli XI–XV)* (Bologna: N. Zanichelli, 1940; repr., Bologna: Forni, 1987).

Sottili, Agostino, "Le istituzioni universitarie," in *I classici e l'Università umanistica,* 3–70.

——, "Eine Postille zum artistischen Curriculum," in *Artisten und Philosophen,* 405–59.

Southern, Richard, *The Making of the Middle Ages* (New Haven, CT: Yale University Press, 1953).

Spadafora, Mirella, *"Felicem peragrat Italiam": Viaggio di istruzione in Italia di Veit Künigl giovane barone del Tirolo del Sud (1607–1609; 1609–1611)—Libro delle spese di viaggio* (Bologna: CLUEB, 2012).

——, "*Instruction:* Istruzioni per un precettore in viaggio in Italia con i suoi pupilli nella seconda metà del Cinquecento," *ASUI* 11 (2007): 311–25.

Spallanzani, Maria Franca, "La Vecchia Filosofia, la Nuova Filosofia e i professori di matematica: Un'orazione di Ercole Corazzi," *Giornale critico della filosofia italiana,* s. VI, 13 (1993): 120–41.

Spruit, Leen, "The Pomponazzi Affair: The Controversy over the Immortality of the Soul," in *Routledge Companion to Sixteenth-Century Philosophy,* edited by H. Lagerlund and B. Hill (New York: Routledge, 2017), 231–40.

Stallybrass, Peter, "Printing and the Manuscript Revolution," in *Explorations in Communication and History,* edited by Barbie Zelizer (London: Routledge, 2008), 111–18.

Gli statuti universitari: Tradizione dei testi e valenze politiche—Atti del Convegno internazionale di studi, Messina–Milazzo, 13–18 aprile 2004, edited by Andrea Romano (Bologna: CLUEB, 2007).

Steffen, Walter, *Die studentische Autonomie im mittelalterlichen Bologna: Eine Untersuchung über die Stellung der Studenten und ihrer Universitas gegenüber Professoren und Stadtregierung im 13. / 14. Jahrhundert* (Bern: Peter Lang, 1981).

Stelzer, W., "Zum Scholarenprivileg Friedrich Barbarossas, *Autentica Habita,*" *Deutsches Archiv für Erforschung des Mittelalters* 34 (1978): 123–65.

Stone, Lawrence, "The Educational Revolution in England, 1560–1640," *Past and Present* 28 (1964): 41–80.

Storia della Compagnia di Gesù in Italia, edited by Pietro Tacchi Venturi and Mario Scaduto, 5 vols. to date (Rome: Società Dante Alighieri, 1910–).

Storia delle università in Italia, edited by Gian Paolo Brizzi, Piero del Negro, and Andrea Romano, 3 vols. (Messina: Sicania, 2007).

La storia delle università italiane: Analisi, fonti, indirizzi di ricerca—Atti del Convegno di Padova, 27–29 ottobre 1994, edited by Luciana Sitran Rea (Triest: LINT, 1996).

Storia di Bologna, edited by Antonio Ferri and Giancarlo Roversi (Bologna: Bononia University Press, 2005).

Storia di Bologna, edited by Renato Zangheri, 4 vols. (Bologna: Bononia University Press, 2005–2013).

Storia illustrata di Bologna, edited by Walter Tega, 8 vols. (San Marino: AIEP / Milan: Nuova editoriale AIEP, 1987–1991).

Studenti e dottori nelle università italiane (origini–XX secolo), edited by Gian Paolo Brizzi (Bologna: CLUEB, 2000).

Studenti e università degli studenti dal XII al XIX secolo, edited by Gian Paolo Brizzi and Antonio Ivan Pini, special issue of *SMSUB,* n.s., 7 (1988).

Studieren im Rom der Renaissance, edited by Michael Matheus and Rainer Christoph Schwinges (Zurich: vdf, 2020 in open access).

Tabarroni, Giorgio, "Copernico e gli Aristotelici bolognesi," in *L'Università a Bologna,* I, 173–203.

Talbot, Michael, "A Successor of Corelli: Antonio Montanari and His Sonatas," *Recercare* 17 (2005): 211–51.

Tavoni, Maria Gioia, "Il patrimonio bibliografico a stampa della biblioteca del SS. Salvatore," in *Giovanni Grisostomo Trombelli (1697–1784) e i Canonici Regolari del SS. Salvatore,* edited by Maria Gioia Tavoni and Gabriella Zarri (Modena: Mucchi Editore, 1991), 71–87.

——, "Stampa e fortuna delle opere di Ulisse Aldrovandi," *AMDSR,* n.s., 42 (1992): 207–24.

——, "Tipografi e produzione libraria," in *Produzione e circolazione libraria a Bologna nel Settecento,* 91–242.

Teach Gnudi, Martha, and Jerome Pierce Webster, *The Life and Times of Gaspare Tagliacozzi, Surgeon of Bologna, 1545–1599, with a Documented Study of the Scientific and Cultural Life of Bologna in the Sixteenth Century* (New York: H. Reichner, 1950).

Il teatro anatomico: Storia e restauri, edited by Camillo Semenzato, with the collaboration of Vittorio Dal Plaz and Maurizio Ripa Bonati (Padua: Università degli Studi di Padova, 1994).

Tega, Walter, "L'Istituto delle Scienze: L'orizzonte europeo—Diario scientifico degli accademici bolognesi," in *L'Università a Bologna,* II, 175–84.

Terpstra, Nicholas, "Confraternities and Civil Society," in *A Companion to Medieval and Renaissance Bologna,* 386–410.

——, *Cultures of Charity: Women, Politics, and the Reform of Poor Relief in Renaissance Italy* (Cambridge, MA: Harvard University Press, 2013).

——, *Lay Confraternities and Civic Religion in Renaissance Bologna* (Cambridge: Cambridge University Press, 1995).

Tervoort, Ad, *The Iter Italicum and the Northern Netherlands: Dutch Students at Italian Universities and Their Role in the Netherlands' Society (1462–1575)* (Leiden: Brill, 2005).

Tessicini, Dario, "Astronomia e cosmologia," in *Il contributo italiano alla storia del pensiero—Scienze* (2013), online at https://www.treccani.it/enciclopedia/astronomia-e-cosmologia_%28Il-Contributo-italiano-alla-storia-del-Pensiero:-Scienze%29/ (accessed 3 January 2021).

Testa, Simone, *Italian Academies and Their Networks, 1525–1700: From Local to Global* (Houndmills, UK: Palgrave Macmillan, 2015).

Thorndike, Lynn, *A History of Magic and Experimental Science,* 8 vols. (New York: Macmillan and Columbia University Press, 1923–1958).

Tinti, Paolo, "Le tesi a stampa nei collegi gesuitici d'età moderna (sec. XVII–XVIII)," in *Dalla lectura all'e-learning,* 263–76.

Toellner, Richard, "Zum Begriff der Autorität in der Medizin der Renaissance," in *Humanismus und Medizin,* 159–80.

Torrão, João Manuel Nunes, "D. Jerónimo Osório e o Tratado 'De Gloria'" (PhD dissertation, University of Coimbra, 1991).

Trombelli, Giovanni Crisostomo, *Memorie istoriche concernenti le due canoniche di S. Maria di Reno, e di S. Salvatore insieme unite* (Bologna: Girolamo Corciolani ed eredi Colli a S. Tommaso d'Aquino, 1752).

Trombetti Budriesi, Anna Laura, "Bologna 1334–1376," in *Storia di Bologna,* ed. Zangheri, II, 761–866.

——, "L'esame di laurea presso lo Studio bolognese: Laureati in diritto civile nel secolo XV," in *Studenti e università degli studenti,* 137–91.

Tugnoli Aprile, Alessandra, *I libri di famiglia dei da Sala* (Spoleto: Centro italiano di studi sull'Alto medioevo, 1997).

Tugnoli Pattaro, Sandra, *Metodo e sistema delle scienze nel pensiero di Ulisse Aldrovandi* (Bologna: CLUEB, 1981).

Tur, Alexandre, "Hora introitus solis in Arietem: Les Prédictions astrologiques annuelles latines dans l'Europe du XVe siècle" (unpublished PhD dissertation, University of Orléans, 2018).

Turnberg, Terence, "Neo-Latin Prose Style (from Petrarch to c. 1650)," in *Brill's Encyclopaedia of the Neo-Latin World* (consulted online on 15 May 2020).

Turrini, Miriam, *La coscienza e le leggi: Morale e diritto nei testi per la confessione nella prima età moderna* (Bologna: il Mulino, 1991).

——, "L'insegnamento della teologia," in *Storia di Bologna,* ed. Zangheri, III.2, 437–94.

——, "Le letture di casi di coscienza e di teologia morale nello studio bolognese del Sei-Settecento: La definizione di una disciplina e la formazione del clero," in *Sapere e/è potere,* III, 223–36.

——, "'Me et totam congregationem defende': Identità personale e collettiva nella Congregazione dell'Assunta di Bologna," in *Problemi di identità tra Medioevo ed Età Moderna: Seminari e bibliografia,* edited by Paolo Prodi and Valerio Marchetti (Bologna: CLUEB, 2001), 155–77.

Turrini, Miriam, and Annamaria Valenti, "L'educazione religiosa," in *Il catechismo e la grammatica,* vol. I: *Istruzione e controllo sociale nell'area emiliana e romagnola nel '700,* edited by Gian Paolo Brizzi (Bologna: il Mulino, 1985), 347–423.

Tuttle, Richard J., *The Neptune Fountain in Bologna: Bronze, Marble, and Water in the Making of a Papal City* (Turnhout: Harvey Miller, 2015).

——, "Il palazzo dell'Archiginnasio in una relazione inedita di Pier Donato Cesi," in *L'Archiginnasio: Il palazzo, l'università, la biblioteca,* I, 65–85.

——, *Piazza Maggiore: Studi su Bologna nel Cinquecento* (Venice: Marsilio, 2001).

Über Mobilität von Studierenden und Gelehrten zwischen dem Reich und Italien (1400–1600), edited by Suse Andreson and Rainer Christoph Schwinges (Zurich: vdf, 2011).

L'Università a Bologna, 2 vols., vol. I: *Personaggi, momenti e luoghi dalle origini al XVI secolo,* edited by Ovidio Capitani; vol. II: *Maestri, studenti e luoghi dal XVI al XX secolo,* edited by Gian Paolo Brizzi, Lino Marini, Paolo Pombeni (Bologna: Cassa di Risparmio di Bologna, 1987–1988).

Le università dell'Europa, edited by Gian Paolo Brizzi and Jacques Verger, 6 vols. (Cinisello Balsamo: Silvana Editoriale, 1990–1995).

L'Università di Padova nei secoli (1601–1805), edited by Piero del Negro and Francesco Piovan (Treviso: Antilia, 2002).

Università e formazione dei ceti dirigenti: Per Gian Paolo Brizzi, pellegrino dei saperi, edited by Giancarlo Angelozzi, Maria Teresa Guerrini, and Giuseppe Olmi (Bologna: Bononia University Press, 2015).

Le università e la violenza studentesca, edited by Christopher Carlsmith, special issue, *ASUI* 20.1 (2016).

L'università in Italia fra età moderna e contemporanea: Aspetti e momenti, edited by Gian Paolo Brizzi and Angelo Varni (Bologna: CLUEB, 1991).

L'università in tempo di crisi: Revisioni e novità dei saperi e delle istituzioni nel Trecento, da Bologna all'Europa, edited by Berardo Pio and Riccardo Parmeggiani (Bologna: CLUEB, 2016).

Die universitären Kollegien im Europa des Mittelalters und der Renaissance, edited by Andreas Sohn and Jacques Verger (Bochum: Winkler, 2011).

Universität, Religion und Kirchen, edited by Rainer Christoph Schwinges (Basel: Schwabe Verlag, 2011).

Les Universités européennes du XVIe au XVIIIe siècle, edited by Dominique Julia, Jacques Revel, and Roger Chartier, 2 vols. (Paris: Éditions de l'École des hautes études en sciences sociales, 1986–1989).

Vasina, Augusto, "Bologna nello Stato della Chiesa. Autorità papale, clero locale, Comune e Studio fra XIII e XV secolo," in *Cultura universitaria e pubblici poteri a Bologna dal XII al XV secolo. Atti del secondo convegno. Bologna 20-21 maggio 1988,* edited by Ovidio Capitani (Bologna: Istituto per la Storia di Bologna, 1990), 125–50.

——, "Dal Comune verso la Signoria (1274–1334)," in *Storia di Bologna,* ed. Zangheri, II, 581–651.

——, "Lo 'Studio' nei rapporti colle realtà cittadine e il mondo esterno nei secoli XII–XIV," in *L'Università a Bologna,* I, 29–59.

Vázquez Janeiro, Isaac, "La Teología en el siglo XV," in *Historia de la Universidad de Salamanca,* III.1, 171–201.

Veggetti, Emilio, "Pier Paolo Molinelli e la prima cattedra italiana di medicina operatoria," *SMSUB* 9 (1926): 110–43.

Venditti, Gianni, with Beatrice Quaglieri, *Archivio Boncompagni Ludovisi: Inventario,* 5 vols. (Vatican City: Archivio Segreto Vaticano, 2008).

Ventura, Giacomo, *Codro tra Bologna e l'Europa* (Bologna: Pàtron, 2019).

——, "Il 'Comicus' per i grammatici: Plauto tra filologia e imitazione nella Bologna del primo Cinquecento," in *Atti congresso Adi 2017: Le forme del comico* (Florence: Società Editrice Fiorentina, 2019), 166–75.

Ventura Folli, Irene, "La natura 'scritta': La 'libraria' di Ulisse Aldrovandi (1522–1605)," in *Bibliothecae selectae da Cusano a Leopardi,* edited by Eugenio Canone (Florence: Leo S. Olschki, 1993), 495–506.

Verardi Ventura, S., "L'ordinamento bolognese dei secoli XVI–XVII," *L'Archiginnasio* 74 (1979): 181–425.

Verger, Jacques, "L'insegnamento della teologia nell'età delle riforme e dei lumi," in *Le università dell'Europa,* VI, 127–45.

——, "Patterns," in *A History of the University in Europe,* I, 35–74.

Vernacular Aristotelianism in Italy from the Fourteenth to the Seventeenth Century, edited by Luca Bianchi, Simon Gilson, and Jill Kraye (London: Warburg Institute, 2016).

Vernazza, Guido, "La crisi barocca nei programmi didattici dello Studio bolognese," *SMSUB,* n.s., 2 (1961): 95–177.

Violence and Justice in Bologna: 1250–1700, edited by Sarah Rubin Blanshei (Lanham, MD: Lexington Books, 2018).

Le virtuose adunanze: La cultura accademica tra 16° e 18° secolo, edited by Clizia Gurreri and Ilaria Bianchi (Avellino: Sinestesie, 2015).

Vitali, Maria Cristina, "Contributi di Giovanni Marcanova all'aristotelismo veneto," in *Aristotelismo veneto e scienza moderna: Atti del 25° anno accademico del Centro per la Storia della Tradizione Aristotelica nel Veneto,* edited by Luigi Olivieri, 2 vols. (Padua: Antenore, 1983), II, 1035–46.

——, "L'umanista padovano Giovanni Marcanova (1410/1418-1467) e la sua biblioteca," *Ateneo Veneto* 21 (1983): 127–61.

Il volgare come lingua di cultura dal Trecento al Cinquecento: Atti del Convegno Internazionale, Mantova, 18–20 ottobre 2001, edited by A. Calzona et al. (Florence: Olschki, 2003).

von Greyerz, Kaspar, *Religion and Culture in Early Modern Europe, 1500–1800* (Oxford: Oxford University Press, 2008).

von Pastor, Ludwig, *The History of the Popes from the Close of the Middle Ages,* 40 vols. (St. Louis: Herder, 1923-1969).

Walsby, Malcolm, "Book Lists and Their Meanings," in *Documenting the Early Book World: Inventories and Catalogues in Manuscript and Print,* edited by Malcolm Walsby and Natasha Constantinidou (Leiden: Brill, 2013), 1–24.

Waquet, Françoise, *Latin, or, the Empire of a Sign: From the Sixteenth to the Twentieth Century* (New York: Verso, 2001).

Watson, Elizabeth See, *Achille Bocchi and the Emblem Book as Symbolic Form* (Cambridge: Cambridge University Press, 1993).

Wear, Andrew, "Medicine in Early Modern Europe, 1500–1700," in Conrad et al., *The Western Medical Tradition,* 215–361.

Weijers, Olga, *La "disputatio" dans les Facultés des arts au moyen âge* (Turnhout: Brepols, 2002).

——, *In Search of the Truth: A History of Disputation Techniques from Antiquity to Early Modern Times* (Turnhout: Brepols, 2013).

——, *Queritur utrum: Recherches sur la "disputatio" dans les universités médiévales* (Turnhout: Brepols, 2009).

——, *Terminologie des universités au XIIIe siècle* (Rome: Edizioni dell'Ateneo, 1987).

Weinberg, Bernard, *A History of Literary Criticism,* 2 vols. (Chicago: University of Chicago Press, 1961).

Wells, Maria Xenia Zevelechi, *The Ranuzzi Manuscripts* (Austin: Humanities Research Center, University of Texas, 1980).

Westman, Robert S., *The Copernican Question: Prognostication, Skepticism, and Celestial Order* (Berkeley: University of California Press, 2001).

Wilson, Nigel G., *From Byzantium to Italy: Greek Studies in the Italian Renaissance,* 2nd ed. (London: Bloomsbury, 2016).

Witt, Ronald G., *"In the Footsteps of the Ancients": The Origins of Humanism from Lovato to Bruni* (Leiden: Brill, 2000).

Wolf, Hubert, *Index: Der Vatikan und die verbotenen Bücher* (Munich: Beck, 2006).

Woolfson, Jonathan, *Padua and the Tudors: English Students in Italy, 1485–1603* (Toronto: University of Toronto Press, 1998).

Zaccagnini, Guido, "Le scuole e la libreria del convento di San Domenico in Bologna dalle origini al secolo XVI," *AMDSR,* s. IV, 17 (1927): 228–327.

——, *Storia dello Studio di Bologna durante il Rinascimento* (Geneva: Olschki, 1930).

Zanazzo, M., "Una famiglia di medici a Padova nel XV secolo: I Noale—Gli inizi, i progressi economici, sociali, culturali," *Quaderni per la storia dell'Università di Padova* 26 (1993–1994): 149–98.

Zanella, Gabriele, "Bibliografia per la storia dell'Università di Bologna dalle origini al 1945, aggiornata al 1983," *SMSUB,* n.s., 5 (1985): 5–261.

Zannini, Andrea, "I maestri: Carriere, metodi didattici, posizione sociale, rapporti con le professioni," in *Storia delle università in Italia,* II, 37–63.

——, "Stipendi e status sociale dei docenti universitari," *ASUI* 3 (1999): 9–39.

Zanobi, Bandino Giacomo, *Le ben regolate città: Modelli politici nel governo delle periferie pontificie in età moderna* (Rome: Bulzoni, 1994).

Zaoli, Giuseppe, "Di alcuni *rotuli* dello Studio della prima metà del secolo XV," *SMSUB* 4 (1920): 191–249.

——, "Lo Studio bolognese e papa Martino V (anni 1416–20)," *SMSUB* 3 (1912): 107–88.

Zarri, Gabriella, "Chiesa, religione, società (secoli XV–XVIII)," in *Storia di Bologna,* ed. Zangheri, III.2, 885–1003.

——, "The Church, Civic Religion, and Civic Identity," in *A Companion to Medieval and Renaissance Bologna,* 361–85.

Zen Benetti, Francesca, "Gregorio Barbarigo: Da studente a cancelliere dell'Università di Padova," in *Gregorio Barbarigo patrizio veneto, vescovo e cardinale nella tarda controriforma (1625–1697): Atti del convegno di studi, Padova 7–10 novembre 1996,* edited by Liliana Billanovich and Pierantonio Gios (Padua: Istituto per la storia ecclesiastica padovana, 1999), 295–314.

——, "Il Seicento," in *L'Università di Padova nei secoli,* 7–148.

Zuffo, Cristina, "La stampa in Bologna nell'età della controriforma" (unpublished tesi di laurea, Università di Bologna, relatore Prof. Paolo Prodi, a.a. 1968–1969).

ACKNOWLEDGMENTS

This study builds on my 2002 book on the teaching of moral philosophy at various Italian universities (including Bologna) and develops arguments presented in a series of publications since then dealing with Bologna's institutional context more specifically. It has therefore been in gestation for much longer than I would have liked, but this prolonged period has also allowed me to draw on the expertise of many more scholars and on some significant developments in the field from the last few years. It is a pleasure to acknowledge the many debts that I have accumulated along the way and to be able to recognize properly those who have supported me.

Research for this book began in earnest in 2005–2006 with a fellowship at Villa I Tatti (The Harvard Center for Italian Renaissance Studies), where the project especially benefited from conversations with Monica Azzolini, Alison Frazier, Marc Laureys, Lodi Nauta, Darrel Rutkin, and Nick Terpstra. It has been furthered by several subsequent grants and fellowships. I am grateful for financial assistance from the University of Miami, Florida (where I once taught), the British Academy (Small Grants scheme), and the Wellcome Trust. A two-month fellowship at Bologna's Institute for Advanced Studies in 2016 provided the necessary space to conduct concentrated archival and library research.

Two conferences in particular helped my research gel around specific subtopics of the book. In 2011 Gian Mario Anselmi, Angela De Benedictis, and Nick Terpstra organized a meeting in Bologna centered around recent Anglo-American scholarship. It was a pleasure to meet many scholars working on Bologna and to compare our research findings and approaches in an international setting, both at the conference itself and in the subsequent publication. A conference organized by Luca Bianchi and Gigi Campi in Milan in 2019 was more specifically focused on arts and medicine in the Italian universities and helped me sharpen my thoughts about the relationship of philosophy and religion in Bologna, a major theme in this book. It has also been heartening to see the activity of research and publication across Italy on the culture of the early modern universities, much of it promoted by the Centro interuniversitario per la storia delle università italiane (CISUI), whose activities I have often (and gratefully) been a part of.

Compared to other collections in Italy, those in Bologna are still used rather less frequently and intensively (although that has been changing rapidly in recent years). I am thankful to the various archivists, particularly at the Archivio di Stato, who facilitated my search for materials, as well as those at the Archivio Arcivescovile. In addition to the Biblioteca Comunale dell'Archiginnasio, I made particular use of the rich collections of lectures held by the rare books department of the Biblioteca Universitaria. Maria Cristina Bacchi, Rita De Tata, Laura Miani, and others over the years expedited my research there in every way possible, and the staff under the new regime has also been extremely kind and ready to help. Thanks are due as well to the staff of the two other main collections of primary materials relevant to my research: the Archivio Segreto Vaticano (now the Achivio Apostolico Vaticano) and the Harry Ransom Center in Austin, Texas, whose Ranuzzi Manuscripts are a veritable (and unexplored) gold mine.

I have also received a great deal of assistance from libraries in the United Kingdom. Warwick Library staff (especially Kate Courage) responded efficiently and with good humor to a veritable flood of requests (particularly during the pandemic) for articles, books, and other publications. The Warburg Institute Library held many materials that were hard or impossible to consult elsewhere in the country and is always a welcome second home.

Numerous colleagues in Bologna have been supportive conversation partners over the years. In particular, I wish to thank (both for their research insights and for their kindness) Gian Paolo Brizzi, Rita De Tata, Andrea Gardi, and Maria Teresa Guerrini. Other colleagues with whom I have had fruitful contact include Annarita Angelini, Gian Mario Anselmi, Monica Azzolini, Marco Beretta, Fabrizio Bònoli, Mauro Carboni, Francesco Ceccarelli, Laura Chines, Angela De Benedictis, Tommaso Duranti, Laura Mantovani, Lara Michelacci, Leonardo Quaquarelli, Andrea Severi, Andrea Tabarroni, and Giacomo Ventura.

Outside of Bologna, I have benefited from the insights of many friends and colleagues. Particular thanks go to Nancy Siraisi for her model of exemplary scholarship and close reading of university lectures, as well as her patience in dealing with questions I had at an early research stage. Conversations with Luca Boschetto, Gian Mario Cao, Simon Gilson, and Jill Kraye greatly contributed to giving this book its current shape. For my thoughts on Aldrovandi's books, I am particularly indebted to Caroline Duroselle-Melish and Ian Maclean.

At the University of Warwick, I have benefited from the collegiality and support of my department of Italian Studies and of the larger academic community working on Renaissance and early modern topics (and even on Bologna) in the Centre for the Study of the Renaissance. Among them, the research interests of Paul Botley, Jonathan Davies, Ingrid De Smet, Lorenzo Pericolo, and Caroline Petit have been especially relevant and helpful. Also important have been the continued conversations with former students such as Rebecca Carnevali and Gloria Moorman. I am thankful for an environment in which I can easily test my ideas against those of others.

Numerous scholars sent me offprints, books, and other materials that were hard to obtain during periods of library closures. Here I would like to thank David Gentilcore, Vivian Nutton, Caroline Petit, and Thomas Rütten for their publications on medicine; Luca Bianchi and Andrea Tabarroni for philosophy; Marc Laureys, Andrea Severi, and Giacomo Ventura for rhetoric; and Darrel Rutkin and Dario Tessicini for astronomy.

This book has been much improved by the observations and criticisms of those who have generously commented on various parts of it. In particular, I wish to thank Paul Botley, Bryan Brazeau, Gian Paolo Brizzi, Rebecca Carnevali, Alessio Cotugno, Chiara Crisciani, Ingrid De Smet, Rita De Tata, Matthew Gaetano, Andrea Gardi, Maria Teresa Guerrini, Ian Maclean, Craig Martin, Vivian Nutton, Caroline Petit, Darrel Rutkin, Andrea Severi, Dario Tessicini, Miriam Turrini, Giacomo Venturi, and Eleanore Webb. Nick Terpstra and the two anonymous reviewers for Harvard University Press provided a number of highly valuable suggestions and corrections. Above all I am thankful to Sara Miglietti, for her generosity in making available to me numerous publications at the Warburg Institute and especially for her detailed and critical comments on the whole manuscript. One could not ask for a more rigorous and helpful reader. All remaining faults are, of course, my own.

I am also thankful to the audiences in numerous settings on which I tried out my developing ideas for this book, including those at numerous meetings of the Renaissance Society of America and at invited lectures for the Universities of Austin (Texas), Bologna, Harvard, Innsbruck, Johns Hopkins, Lausanne, Munich, Oxford, Reading, University College London, Venice, and Vercelli. The enthusiasm of the participants in the Kenilworth Community Course encouraged me to persevere with the book.

The professionalism and efficiency with which Harvard University Press worked with me in getting this book ready for publication have been exemplary. I was fortunate to have a highly skilled editor in Emily Silk and strongly benefited from the careful copyediting of Wendy Nelson and John Donohue. The series editor, Nick Terpstra, provided much-needed encouragement and numerous constructive criticisms and suggestions, leading to considerable improvements in the book's final shape. I am extremely happy that the book is appearing in the present series.

I would not have been able to bring this study to completion without the enormous support of my wife, Grace, who has done far more than her share of child-minding and household chores for many years and has been patient with me and this project well beyond what was reasonable. In many ways it reflects our joint love for Bologna, and it is thus fitting for the book to be dedicated to her.

INDEX

Notes: Page numbers in *italics* indicate figures and tables. Unless otherwise indicated, institutions, offices, places, and curriculum-related features in the index refer to the Bolognese context.